American Films Abroad

American Films Abroad

Hollywood's Domination of the World's Movie Screens from the 1890s to the Present

by

Kerry Segrave

McFarland & Company, Inc., Publishers
Jefferson, North Carolina, and London

British Library Cataloguing-in-Publication data are available

Library of Congress Cataloguing-in-Publication Data

Segrave, Kerry, 1944–
    American films abroad : Hollywood's domination of the world's
movie screens from the 1890s to the present / by Kerry Segrave.
        p.   cm.
    Includes bibliographical references and index.
    ISBN 0-7864-0346-2 (library binding : 50# alkaline paper) ♾
    1. Motion pictures, American—Marketing.   2. Motion picture
industry—United States—History.   I. Title.
PN1993.5.U6S368   1997
384'.83—dc21   97-20549
                                                                CIP

Manufactured in the United States of America

*McFarland & Company, Inc., Publishers
    Box 611, Jefferson, North Carolina 28640*

Contents

Preface

This book traces the history of American films abroad from the late 1890s to 1995, concentrating on how the U.S. industry came to control the world's film screens and how it maintained that domination. Emphasis is on the cartel formed by the eight major Hollywood studios—its leadership, its philosophy, its block booking practices, its control over both the exhibition and distribution sectors and its relationship with the government departments of State and Commerce. While the cartel has long proclaimed that the industry functions without government subsidy, it has received massive indirect government aid in various ways. This book tells how other nations have tried to fight U.S. film domination over the years and how the cartel has responded.

With the growth in the number of television stations and the appearance of home video, worldwide film revenue for Hollywood has soared from $2.5 billion in 1980 ($2 billion of that from theatrical release) to an estimated $15 billion in 1992 ($3.44 billion from theatrical release). This increase has led the cartel to fight even harder to control the market, complaining of discrimination and lack of access for Hollywood product in nations where it has long controlled eighty percent or more of the screen time.

Research for this book was conducted at the University of Victoria library. Among the materials consulted were newspaper indexes, periodical indexes covering general interest magazines and books on film history for various countries. Additionally, the back files of *Variety* magazine were searched and provided extensive information.

1. In the Beginning Was Europe, Especially France: 1895–1919

From the film industry's beginning with the Edison peepshow in America in 1894 and the Lumière's unveiling in a Paris cafe in December 1895, until the time of World War I, international film exhibition was not dominated by American product. Motion pictures came and went from country to country with few or no restrictions. Although no one country dominated screens to the extent the U.S. would in later years, France led the way with producer/distributor Pathé Frères being the leading French firm. As one historian observed, "The French movie industry had been the world's biggest supplier up to 1914, its leading firms, Gaumont and Pathé, dominating international distribution networks."[1]

Prior to the war, the film scene in India was reported to be extremely international with France, led by Pathé, being the leading source but also screening film from Italian, British, German, Danish and American firms. While U.S. product had made an appearance in South Africa by around 1910, one newspaper commented indirectly on market penetration when it observed that acting in American films was more restrained "than in the case of numberless French films which flood the market." Names of U.S. producers such as Vitagraph, Edison, American Biograph and others were advertised widely, instead of the names of the players, as was the worldwide custom of the time.[2]

In the last few years of the 1890s Brazilian Paschoal Segreto and his brother Alfonso opened the first permanent cinema in Rio de Janeiro. Soon they had several venues and were showing films imported from both Europe and the U.S. Alfonso made frequent trips to both areas to bring back the latest product. Around 1911 independent distributors appeared in Rio acting as local middlemen by importing films, then contracting with exhibitors to screen them.[3]

First to exploit U.S. pictures in the West Indies and South America was famed silent film director Edwin S. Porter. He traveled the region with an Edison projector from the fall of 1896 until the summer of 1897 as a traveling road show. Maracaibo, Venezuela, businessman Luis Mendez visited the U.S. in 1896 buying the rights to screen Edison product in Venezuela and Colombia. One South American publication noted, "Until 1914 the European film, chiefly by Pathé, Gaumont, Eclipse, and Art, ruled this market." Latin American film historian Gaizka Usabel stated that from the beginning of the 1900s Pathé had dominated the Latin American market with its branches in Buenos Aires, Rio, Havana and Mexico City.[4]

Illustrating the international scope of the Australian film scene was the screening of an Indian film there in 1900 and a Japanese picture in 1906. Although it was an open, multinational market with films from around the globe being screened, Australian writers Ina Bertrand and William Routt observed that French product dominated the market with French and Italian chase comedies (which predated Mack Sennett's Keystone Kops) being particularly popular. Pathé established its first Australian branch in Melbourne in 1909.[5]

A Sydney correspondent for the trade publication *Variety* noted in 1909 that the U.S. film *The Guerrilla* was then playing. He went on to declare that "American films have a fidelity that is commendable, while the French films are too stereotyped to arouse enthusiasm." It was more wishful thinking than reality at that time. Another Australian film writer was Diane Collins, who stated in the 1980s that before World War I films came from many nations but "the very large number of European films is one of the sharpest contrasts with today. French films were particularly numerous." Pathé's logo appeared on the screen more than that of any other producer.[6]

Even in Canada there was tough sledding for the American films with the French producers having a strong presence. *Variety* speculated it was "because of the French names and origin of the Pathé films that Canadians take so kindly to them. Canada is full of French people and French descendants, and they like to look at the people and places which the Pathés use." According to that logic, Americans should have flocked to see British movies.[7]

Canada had no native film industry to speak of, causing some public agitation prior to and during World War I for native-made pictures. In the federal election of 1911, when the Liberal government's policy of open trade with the U.S. became a national issue, Canadians expressed a desire for native films related to their own lives and culture. During the war, Canadians felt American pictures insulted them with too much U.S. flag waving and patriotism. Editorials in leading Canadian newspapers demanded domestic films supporting the war effort and extolling the bravery of Canadian forces. *Moving Picture World* was an American trade journal upset by that campaign, writing that "Canadian imperialists are complaining about having to witness too many deeds of Yankee valor in moving pictures."[8]

Recognizing the potential of the Canadian market, American Consul General in Winnipeg John Edward Jones wrote in 1909, "In this country where all forms of entertainment are scarce, moving pictures are welcomed, and there is no reason why the manufacturers of the United States should not control the business."[9]

Pathé opened a New York office in 1904. By 1908 it had become the largest single source of motion pictures in the U.S. market. In 1909 Pathé opened an office in Manila. Five years later the company had 41 offices around the world, besides the Paris home office, from Kiev to Budapest to Calcutta to Barcelona to New York to London to Melbourne. One of the keys to Pathé's success was that it produced and distributed its films from its own offices set up in each country or area as soon as the market became big enough. U.S. producers faced a sharply expanding domestic market which kept them busy trying to keep up with that expansion as well as doing battle with each other to claim a dominant place within the American industry. Not being able to fully satisfy home demand—one of the reasons foreign makers such as Pathé could enter the U.S. market—lessened the need or incentive for U.S. producers to intensely pursue foreign markets. Sales to foreign areas by the U.S. producers were usually done through agents in those nations until after the industry first attempted to organize in 1908. The first American producer to establish a foreign branch office appears to have been Vitagraph, which set up shop in both London and Paris in 1906.[10]

Of the films released in 1912 in Romania, 70.7 percent were French, 16.4 percent American and 10.1 percent Italian. There, like everywhere at the time, competition and recognition was brand vs. brand such as Pathé versus Vitagraph or the French producer Gaumont against American Biograph. The selling of a picture based on "star" content was still in a rudimentary stage of development.[11]

Looking at the Central and South American market, film historian Kristin Thompson remarked, "It is apparent how inexpertly organized the prewar American export business was. Central and South America present some striking examples of how American methods failed to adapt to local conditions." A cinema owner in Durango, Mexico, in 1912 tried to import all his films from the U.S. but the length of time and uncertainty of regular shipment made the venture a money loser. He added, "The explanatory matter was printed in the English language, an innovation which proved anything but popular." Many complaints arose due to the English-only intertitles in the films. Only midway through the war did the Americans begin to translate the title cards into local tongues. Intertitles began to be used in most silent films from around 1905-1906 onward. Prior to that, they were uncommon. As pictures became longer with more complicated plot lines, intertitle cards were more and more necessary. However, often the intertitle consisted of only a word or two such as "Remorse," "Guilt," "Elation" or "Comes the Dawn" to indicate mood or time change.[12]

Inexpert organization may have been less important than Hollywood's condescending attitude towards the Central American audience, which extended beyond failing to provide translations. According to *Literary Digest*, those Central American spectators yelled, jumped up and down, talked to the screen "and in their childish delight over scene and incident they can successfully lose all sense of its unreality." French and Italian producers had the strongest presence in the Latin American market prior to the war with the U.S. studios having no substantial place.[13]

In the Orient in the 1912-1913 period, Pathé was described as having "a virtual monopoly" although that market was small with just three cinemas in Singapore and six more in the rest of the Malay Peninsula. American Biograph did get a few films into the area but they were distributed by Pathé. The entire Far East area was regarded by American producers as a "junk market." One area dominated by the U.S. was the Philippines, then a formal American colony, where in 1911 most product screened was American. One exhibitor there complained that 90 percent of U.S. films he received were worn to the point of almost being unscreenable, with splices, torn sprockets and missing ends and titles. Even prints such as those could be hard to obtain because, said the exhibitor, "Every exchange and factory of repute in the United States had been so rushed with business that the former could not consider the question of rentals abroad until their own circuits had been supplied."[14]

Before World War I, American films had a dominant position only in Germany and Britain, among the important markets. Around 1913, 31 percent of films released in Germany were American made, 27 percent Italian, 12 percent German and 10 percent British. All the major U.S. producers had representation in Britain by around 1911, some with branches but mostly through agents. U.S. screen presence amounted to 50 to 60 percent of the British releases in the 1910 to 1914 period. Distribution in America was mostly through standing orders and exclusive contracts which tied cinemas to whichever film service they chose. This practice soon came to be called block booking. Under that practice, an exhibitor agreed to take all the product from a particular producer or group. Standing orders meant each producer sold about the same number of prints per film, giving it a financial base. It made it harder for foreign firms to distribute in the U.S. market as exhibitors were booked up. Trade journals abroad were calling America a "closed market" for their pictures. Compared to that method, the British market was much more open and competitive. Producers sold to distributors (called renters in the U.K.) who in turn rented them to as many houses as they could. With no exclusive contracts a film might be rented to a number of exhibitors in the same districts. Due to this open market system, almost twice as many titles came into the market as were needed.

About 350 films were offered each week in Britain in 1914 but none could be sold before a trade showing to renters and exhibitors. Perhaps 150 of those pictures would actually be sold and released. At that time about 200 films came onto the market each week in America. Of that number, approximately 160 were actually released with 130 of those sold by standing orders before they were even shot. Illustrating the degree of competition in the prewar U.S. markets was the fact that domestic films comprised two-thirds of U.S. releases yet Pathé was the single largest source of releases although it likely had less than ten percent of the total market.[15]

With the exception of Germany and Britain, a large portion of Europe was served almost exclusively by French, Italian and British firms. David Horsley, a partner in a large U.S. studio, toured Europe in 1913 to assess the film situation. On his return he stated that on the Continent "very few American films are shown in the theaters." Unlike Pathé, which recognized the advantage of establishing branches wherever possible, U.S. producers largely did not then follow the example. Far East showmen George and Leon Mooser had offices in a couple of China's largest cities in 1913 where they were starting to distribute product of a few U.S. studios.[16]

Ben Brodsky owned around eighty houses in China, each of which had standing room for 5,000 to 10,000 people. Seats were not provided as the patron "would never know enough to go home." American pictures were not too popular at Brodsky's cinemas because the audience did not understand them, despite the fact that at least some of them had inserted Chinese characters.[17]

One attempt to emulate Pathé's style came in Britain—a country with a substantial U.S. presence and screen penetration. By 1912-1913 members of the U.S. cartel were engaged in an attempt to organize the film rental business in Britain, to bring it into their own hands. It was reported the Americans had formed an "arrangement among themselves" to oppose moves in that market by Pathé to strengthen its position. Yet most U.S. studios were represented by an agent, not a direct presence. *Variety* explained the British distribution system meant a good film sold while sales were much less likely for bad films, unlike in the U.S. with its standing order system which made it "pretty soft" for U.S. producers. "The English system also opens the way for the keenest competition. Only merit is rewarded."[18]

Hollywood had no foreign problem to speak of before World War I because it had no foreign trade to speak of. The cartel showed only minor interest in launching any kind of organized assault on other countries. Outside the cartel, only Universal had a few distribution outlets abroad. Said one historian, "None of the other companies undertook to compete with the lusty motion picture industries in Italy, Germany, France and England, for the industries in those countries were then as well developed as our own. In fact, they were in some cases far more mature."[19]

What kept the American producers from a more vigorous move to foreign markets was that expanding domestic market, fueled by the growth in the number of nickelodeons followed by an increase in large-capacity, plush movie palaces. The U.S. producers also did not follow the lead of Pathé in establishing branch offices, being content to mostly deal through agents. Much of the failure could be attributed to the lack of organization and internal competition within the domestic market. Before the U.S. was ready to take on the world, it was necessary for the domestic industry to become "rationalized" in capitalist fashion. That is, a cohesive cartel would have to form up to first dominate and effectively control the domestic arena. The period of the late 1800s to the early 1900s was a time of cartel formation in many industries. Public fears and agitation led in 1890 to the passage of the Sherman Antitrust Act, which was supposed to limit such activity. Mostly, though, it was a public relations gesture designed more to quiet critics than block cartel formation. That Sherman act would be used against the film industry in 1913 and then again in the late 1940s. It had no effect in preventing the cartel formed in the film industry in the 1920s nor did it have any effect on the industry in the 1940s save to break a production/distribution/exhibition cartel into a production/ distribution cartel and a separate exhibition cartel. Both domestic and international market control by the major U.S. producers was unaffected.

First attempts to form a U.S. cartel took place early in 1908 with the Edison company, Vitagraph and others combining into the Film Service Association (FSA). As of March of that year, FSA members stopped handling foreign pictures except those of Pathé and of Meliès, another large French concern. Vitagraph's William Rock declared the move helped the industry as it "shut out the importation of foreign stuff that was not suitable or good enough for the American market." Of course, it was a move to limit competition in the U.S. However, a second would-be cartel, the Biograph Association of Licensees, led by the producer American Biograph, continued to compete viciously with the Edison-led FSA. Later in 1908 those two groups merged to form the Motion Picture Patents Company (MPPC—commonly referred to simply as "The Trust"). Pathé was a member of that group and was licensed to import and make films without limit. Only one other importer, George Kleine, had a license from the MPPC. That firm could only bring in 3,000 feet of film per week—the equivalent of three one-reel pictures with a running time of about ten minutes each. As one observer stated, "The MPPC's provisions restricted imports."[20]

Within a year or so, the Trust gave birth to a separate company called General Film which acted as its distribution arm. Soon it came to dominate the domestic market selling films made by MPPC members although it never established a presence in foreign nations. (Perhaps it was fully occupied domestically trying to supply and tie up exhibitors with standing orders to keep out non–Trust members.) Most of the industry figures who would go on to lead the studios which formed the lasting Hollywood cartel were not members of the MPPC.

The Trust lacked any sort of vision for the industry with members refusing to give actors screen credit, reasoning (correctly) that such a move would lead to rapidly escalating salaries. It was naive to think the public would show no interest in who was on the screen, always content to attend a film solely on the basis it was made by, say, Vitagraph. People began to write to producers wanting to know who was that little blond girl, for example. One such player was Biograph's Florence Lawrence, known publicly only as The Biograph Girl. In 1910 Carl Laemmle lured her to his IMP (Independent Motion Pictures) studio with the promise of a higher salary and, more importantly, screen credit. It was the birth of the star system although Lawrence herself faded into obscurity in just a few years. Laemmle leaked a fabricated story to the press that Lawrence had been killed by a streetcar. After the resultant publicity began to fade, he denounced IMP's enemies for circulating lies. Thus, the publicity system focusing on stars developed. IMP was not a member of the Trust. One distributor not beaten by General Film was William Fox, who launched an antitrust suit against the MPPC in 1913. Fox was also outside the Trust.[21]

Theda Bara was another star who was relentlessly hyped during the height of her career. She was a Fox superstar from 1915 to 1920. Most of the stories released about the "Vamp" were totally false, but exotic and interesting. Star publicity even then went around the globe. By 1917 Hollywood stars such as Mary Pickford, Charles Chaplin, Douglas Fairbanks, Norma Talmadge, Mabel Normand, Roscoe "Fatty" Arbuckle and many others were firmly established in, for example, South Africa.[22]

W. W. Hodkinson was an executive with General Film who left the firm in 1912 to form the distributor Paramount Pictures to handle non-Trust product. He was disgruntled with General's policy of being content to distribute cheaply produced films to exhibitors with the rental being a flat rate. Hodkinson saw a future wherein films would become increasingly expensive and lavishly made while all distribution fees would be a percentage of the box office take with a minimum guarantee to insure that most, if not all, of the risk fell on the exhibitor. These men would all be major figures in the final cartel. They, and others, battled the MPPC, causing it to be essentially ineffective from about 1913, although it would not formally vanish until 1917 when courts ordered it to cease its unlawful activities. Of its members, only Vitagraph would still be around after World War I. The most important development within the domestic industry to this point was the development and then predominance of the system of block booking. It would come to assist the Americans greatly in gaining and keeping control of foreign markets.[23]

Hodkinson was also a firm believer in building large, plush cinemas. Nickelodeons and early theaters were often literally just rented storefronts with a hundred or so chairs set out on the floor and anything on the back wall—even a sheet or just a new coat of paint—that would hold an image. It was too easy for someone to open one of those places. Building big, expensive houses would limit entry to the exhibition market.

Production of pictures also made free entry far too easy for the liking of the cartel-to-be units. With most films being short—ten to twenty minutes—too many people with access to a camera could become producer/distributors without much time, money or trouble. The tendency to longer feature films of first 40 or 45 minutes, then up to 60-70 minutes, and so on, would limit entry to the field as would higher and higher salaries paid to actors within the star system. In addition, the cost of the publicity machine attendant to the star system drove costs up even more. Soon only the rich would have entry into any phase of filmmaking. Bigger theaters led to a need for more films; which led to higher salaries; which led to a need for more publicity; which led to higher costs; which led to a need for bigger houses to recover those costs. With a large, affluent population, the American market was able to stand the costs—as other markets could not—and return them with profits to the producers. Nevertheless, those higher costs focused the industry as never before on finding new markets—foreign markets. The great film units which would comprise the Hollywood cartel began to form up around 1914; the process continued into the mid–1920s. The business-friendly federal administrations of the era favored such combining, as they would in the Reagan/Bush 1980s.

A second attempt at organizing happened when a majority of producers, distributors plus a scattering of exhibitors formed the National Association of the Motion Picture Industry (NAMPI) in 1916. Mainly it formed to present a united front against growing protest from the public demanding censorship of pictures due to a perceived excessive preoccupation with celluloid sex, alcohol consumption and gambling. NAMPI spent much of its time battling against censorship at various state capitals. Attempting to meet reform group demands in 1919, NAMPI voted to censor its producer members' films. Two years after that, the organization adopted a set of 13 standards relating to the screen depiction of sex, gambling, drinking and so on. However, NAMPI was not a strong organization. With much internal dissension, members distrusted each other too much to cooperate. As a result, NAMPI's resolutions were never taken seriously by the members. For that matter, it was not clear the group meant them to be anything other than a public relations gesture. Reform group pressure increased over the so-called sex pictures as well as real-life sex scandals involving Hollywood players and the huge salaries paid to actors. The cry for government intervention grew louder. Quietly NAMPI disbanded in 1921 to be replaced at the start of the next year by the Motion Picture Producers and Distributors Association (MPPDA). Limited to the powerful producer/distributors—exhibitors not involved in at least one of those functions were excluded—it contained all the giant companies then forming. One of NAMPI's weaknesses was the fact it had no single, dominant leader. That flaw was corrected with the appointment of a man outside the industry who had high government connections. He was Will H. Hays, the so-called "czar" of the film industry. This cartel would last.[24]

Government involvement in the industry began in the fiscal year 1912-1913 when the U.S. Commerce Department first began keeping records on the export of film, as it did for most commodities. In 1916, after NAMPI had formed, the U.S. State Department sent instructions to U.S. consuls that they should report from their areas on the market for American pictures. Some of the information requested included the number of cinemas in the area, their size, admission prices, who distributed films, rental rates, etc. It marked the beginning of a close relationship between the industry cartel and the federal government, particularly the Commerce and State Departments. As time passed, more and more help was extended by the government. A wealth of information was assembled and made freely available to the industry. The cost of the federal government was paid by all U.S. citizens while the benefits were accrued to a wealthy few in the industry. It was the socialism function of North American capitalism—socialize the costs, privatize the profits.[25]

The companies that came to dominate the U.S. industry numbered eight; the Big Five were Metro-Goldwyn-Mayer, Paramount Pictures, 20th Century–Fox Film Corporation (hereafter referred to as Fox), RKO Radio Pictures Inc. and Warner Bros. Inc. All were vertically integrated production/distribution/exhibition entities. None of the Little Three, Universal Pictures, United Artists and Columbia Pictures, were involved in exhibition, at least in the early stages of the cartel. While they didn't all form under those names, when the MPPDA organized most existed in their earlier units.

Nickelodeon pioneer Marcus Loew, after several years of expansion, formed the exhibition concern Loew's Consolidated Enterprises in 1910, incorporated as Loew's Inc. in 1919. The producer Metro Pictures Corporation was acquired in 1920. Four years later Loew's took over the producing Goldwyn Company, itself begun in 1917. Thus the entity became Metro-Goldwyn (Samuel Goldwyn left to continue as an independent producer in a new concern). Soon thereafter, in 1924, MG acquired the producing assets of Louis B. Mayer Pictures and the firm was renamed Metro-Goldwyn-Mayer (MGM). To simplify the corporate structure, the entire production and distribution organization was vested in Loew's Inc. in 1936-37 with MGM being used as a trade name.

Adolph Zukor also started with nickelodeons and penny arcades, moving into production in 1912 by forming Engadine Corporation which quickly was renamed Famous Players. Hodkinson's Paramount Pictures distributed Zukor product as well as that of producer Jesse L. Lasky Feature Play Company. Zukor engineered a merger resulting in the formation of the Famous Players-Lasky Corporation in 1916. In the following year it merged with a dozen other firms, including Paramount, being renamed Paramount Famous Lasky Corporation in 1927. A few years later the name was changed to Paramount Publix Corporation When that entity was adjudicated bankrupt, it was reorganized in 1935 as Paramount Pictures Inc.

Another nickelodeon pioneer was William Fox, who entered the business at the turn of the century. Later he formed a distribution concern. In 1915 Fox Film Corporation was organized to combine production, distribution and exhibition under one name. Due to internal conflicts, Fox was ousted from his own company in the early 1930s. In 1935 Fox merged with Darryl F. Zanuck's and Joseph Schenck's major producing concern 20th Century Pictures to form 20th Century–Fox. RKO began life in 1921 when it started as a joint enterprise of the Radio Corporation of America (RCA—controlled by Rockefeller money) and the Keith-Orpheum cinema circuit (originally separate vaudeville circuits). Financial troubles hit the firm in the late 1940s with RKO ceasing production in the 1950s.

Harry M. Warner opened a nickelodeon around 1904, moving into distribution in 1913 with his brothers Sam, Albert and Jack. That entity incorporated as Warner Bros. in 1923. One year later they acquired their first cinema. Warner then acquired Vitagraph in 1925, the 250-cinema chain Stanley Corporation of America in 1928 and the major producer First National Pictures, also in 1928. Carl Laemmle started as an exhibitor in 1906, then soon after formed his own production concern, IMP. In 1912 Laemmle amalgamated his own companies along with several others, including the producer Bison, as Universal Pictures. Four of Hollywood's biggest names of the era, Charlie Chaplin, Mary Pickford, Douglas Fairbanks and director D. W. Griffith, joined forces in 1919 to form the producer/distributor entity United Artists (UA). Columbia was formed in 1920 by the brothers Harry and Jack Cohn together with Joe Brandt, all of whom had previously worked together at Universal. Initially the producing concern was named CBC Film Sales Company, rechristened Columbia in 1924.[26]

These eight units, the majors, would dominate the U.S. and foreign markets up to the present, with some minor changes. It was difficult for an independent American producer to crack the domestic market, and even harder to obtain screen time in another country. Walt Disney set up his namesake animation company in Hollywood in 1923. Until after World War II Disney produced only short subjects (save for a few full-length animation features). From 1929 to 1931 Disney product was distributed by Columbia. Unsatisfied with low advances and Columbia's practice of block booking his work with cartoons made by others that he considered inferior, Disney turned to UA in 1932 as a distributor. Five years later he switched to RKO. With RKO's financial problems, Disney broke with it in the early 1950s to form his own distribution arm—Buena Vista. Although Disney had been a member of the MPPDA in the 1930s and 1940s, it was not then a major. To become a major, membership was necessary in that group but not sufficient by itself. In its first few decades, MPPDA membership usually numbered 20 some firms; some were small concerns with direct filmmaking connections while some were only peripherally connected, such as Western Electric (a major supplier of hardware for cinema conversion to sound) which was a member in the 1920s and 1930s. Regardless of membership numbers in the MPPDA, the Big Eight ruled the film industry both at home and abroad. After cartel formation, those eight grew bigger and stronger until the demise of RKO and the move by Disney into feature production. Other cartel changes followed in the modern era.[27]

Thus the period from approximately 1914 to 1922 marked the "rationalization" of the U.S. film industry into a functioning, formidable cartel. Elements necessary for domination were being implemented: actor salaries soared due to the star system, pictures got longer and more expensive to make, cinemas became more elaborate and more expensive to build and block booking was established and imposed around the globe, closing down much of the market to those outside the cartel. The expensive Hollywood publicity machine was up and running. All of these items severely limited entry into the market for newcomers, particularly those with limited finances. Less affluent nations than America were hard pressed to compete as costs escalated.

Despite rising costs, actually because of rising costs since cartels were formed precisely to squeeze monopoly-sized profits out of the system, the industry was incredibly lucrative. Negative costs for a film in 1909 averaged $1,000, in 1915 it was $25,000, in 1920 the average cost was $150,000 for a film. The negative cost included all costs involved in producing the final negative—not included were such expenses as the cost of striking positive prints, advertising and distribution. On a typical 1915 film the producer/distributor share of the box office receipts averaged $100,000. Subtracting distribution fees of $35,000, print costs and advertising of $10,000 and the negative cost of $25,000 left the producer with a profit of $30,000. Turning out 52 such movies a year yielded annual profits of $1.5 million.[28]

Setting up distribution offices abroad gave a company greater control over the situation as well as eliminating the necessity of sharing profits with local distributors. Universal opened branches in Japan, India and Singapore in 1916, Java in 1917; by 1918 it had 20 foreign branches. Prior to late 1915, Fox had no foreign offices or agents at all. That ended with the opening of branches in Montreal, Argentina and Brazil in 1915, multiple offices in Britain and Australia in 1916, branches in Norway, Sweden, Spain, Portugal, Uruguay and Paraguay in 1917 and an office in France in 1918. For a time Paramount stayed with the system of using native agents. From 1916 to 1918 it established them throughout the world; thereafter it set up its own branches. First National announced in 1917 that Australia's biggest film distributor, Australian Films Ltd. with its 70 cinema chain, had "joined" the First National exhibition circuit.[29]

In 1914, after the war broke out, Universal sent a film scout to Latin America to check out the scene. It was the first major to show interest in that area. By 1916 Fox and Universal had each established branches in Brazil, Chile and Argentina. Those two producers and Famous Players also had established subsidiaries in Mexico prior to the end of the war.[30]

When World War I began in August 1914, the U.S. industry received the final impetus and advantage necessary to take control of the world film market. Just a month after hostilities began, a trade journal enthused "Within the next year or so the demand for American films in Europe will be large enough to justify a greater 'invasion' than Europe has ever known before." Also pointed out was that "there is no doubt that more distributing stations on the continent will be needed in the future." *Variety* exclaimed in October 1914 that because of the war the future of the U.S. film industry looked bright "with the practical elimination of the foreign feature as a competitor and a menace to the American feature film industry." Two months later, British importer of pictures Roy E. Aitken explained the conflict "should work direct advantage to the American manufacturer, and if the war continues should also create a new market for American films in South America, which has been supplied largely by European manufacturers." Some people saw a war; others saw an opportunity.[31]

Domination of the world's screens did not come automatically to the U.S. units at the start of hostilities. A backlog of product of perhaps six months or so was maintained by most producers. However, new production was drastically reduced throughout Europe. Shipping problems from Europe to other areas played havoc with what little product remained. Yet exhibitors around the world needed product to fill their screens. Although American movies had not been too prevalent in Australia before the war, by the early 1920s they controlled 95 percent of the market. Referring to the period 1913 to 1916, one modern-era Australian writer commented cynically, "As everyone knew even then, only the Americans had the secret of making films which 'appealed to the masses.'" That idea that U.S. movies were popular solely because they were the best, that only Americans knew how to make good films, would become a mantra chanted by the majors to explain their dominance and to deflect criticism in nations determined to reduce that share. People around the globe did indeed love to go to the movies, but U.S. interests were disingenuous in making the unsupported assertion that only U.S. films would draw in the masses. In fact, the masses usually were limited to a choice between an American film or none at all. Much later boycotts of certain nations by the majors would show that people continued to attend films, even when no U.S. features were to be found.[32]

By 1916 or so, the U.S. had come to a dominant position in South and Central America, formerly a market dominated by the Europeans. Films from Europe still arrived but only in a trickle. One estimate put the number of U.S. movies used in Latin America at just 15 percent in 1915. Colombia was then still showing mostly French and Italian pictures in spite of efforts by some American producers to crack the market. When a U.S. film industry executive investigated in person, he determined that U.S. product sent there was typically secondhand or inferior prints which fared poorly in comparison with

European features; that those films which bothered at all to translate intertitles used bad Spanish. He complained to his New York home office, "Stop using Colombia and the rest of South America for a 'waste basket' in which to dump the plays the American public refuses to see." Reportedly when some Colombia houses ran out of European fare they offered live entertainment in combination with the reduced number of films, or closed down completely, rather than turn to American product.[33]

Italian producers were upset enough about the loss of their formerly strong South American markets that in 1919 they sent a delegation there to investigate the reasons for the decline in their exports to the region.[34]

Brazil was an example of the remarkable turnaround in market share. In 1913 that country imported 18.7 metric tons of film with 8.5 tons coming from France, 8.2 tons from Italy, 0.6 tons from the U.S., 0.3 tons from Germany, 0.2 tons from Britain, 0.9 tons from all others. Just seven years later, in 1920, Brazil imported 27.5 metric tons of film, 18.5 tons from the U.S., 2.6 tons from Germany, 2.8 tons from Italy, 1.6 tons from France, 0.5 tons from Britain, 1.5 tons from all others. In 1929 Brazil imported 37.9 metric tons with the U.S. supplying 33.6 tons, France 2.3 tons, Germany 1.5 tons, Britain 0.4 tons, everybody else—including Italy—0.1 tons.[35]

Japan had two types of cinemas. One catered to the laboring class, showing mostly Japanese movies, while those houses patronized by the "better class of Japanese" screened a combination of native and foreign films or the latter completely. Order of preference in 1916 for foreign films was French, Italian, British and American. One reason for the low showing by the U.S. was that, reported *Variety*, "European films are cheaper." Another area where U.S. films were not in favor, added the publication, was Brazil, where exhibitors complained they had to nonetheless accept U.S. product because of the severe shortage of European films.[36]

Complaints about the high cost and low quality of the U.S. films were common enough that in September 1916, 12 foreign film executives representing almost as many countries (including Australia, India, South Africa, Japan, China, France and Britain) met in New York City to address the problem. They wanted to try and pick one person from among them who would then select for export to their home countries U.S. movies that would please foreign exhibitors as to price and star. Those film buyers were annoyed with rental rates charged by the majors, often based on "stars" in a film who were little known outside the U.S. It was a fledgling group which never got off the ground.[37]

Domination of the British market strengthened in 1915 when its open market for films was forever shattered. U.S. producer Essanay's London office announced that henceforth it would rent product directly to exhibitors on an exclusive basis. With Chaplin under contract to them at the time, Essanay used his star power to force exhibitors to take three reels of its films every week in order to get the Chaplin releases. Thus fewer cinemas got to screen Chaplin in first run, plus they had to take unwanted product. Gone were the days when exhibitors got to preview pictures, bidding only on those they wished to screen. Block booking had arrived in Britain. Cinema owners complained loudly. Newspapers such as the *Daily Mail* and the *Evening News* came out in support of the exhibitors. None of it had an effect. General opposition to the arrival of U.S. films en mass increased as well. While the newspapers condemned block booking, they also attacked all U.S. movies on the grounds they were backed by German capital. All the "proof" they could muster on that score was the German-sounding names such as Adolph Zukor and Carl Laemmle.[38]

A perceived growth in juvenile delinquency in Britain was laid by many at the feet of U.S. pictures. Sheffield, England, U.S. Consul J. M. Savage concurred with the idea, seeing the films as a cause rather than, say, parental absence and war disruptions. In a letter to the Department of Commerce, Savage stated that the objectionable films "would disappear if the film producing business were more largely in the hands of British manufacturers."[39]

Frustration was expressed by the British film industry in 1915 over the increasingly closed nature of the U.S. market to foreigners. The managing director of one of Britain's largest cinema chains complained that while England was an open market, the U.S. was not. He remarked, "We cannot secure a footing in the United States. We have given the matter careful study and can only conclude it is not the desire of the American to encourage foreign features. In our opinion they figure every penny contributed toward the support of foreign productions helps to build up opposition."[40]

Even as he spoke, that open British market was being shut by the Americans. Within a few years of Essanay's imposition of block booking, the practice was used by most of the majors. Exhibitors were contractually tied up for one to two years in advance for films which had not been previewed, or made, or even thought up. Said film historian Kristin Thompson, "Britain went from being one of the most flexible, open markets in the world to one of the most rigid, closed ones." Open play dates at cinemas were eliminated. Trade journal *Bioscope* noted the effects of the U.S. system on British production when it wrote that the British filmmaker's "market is so restricted by circumstances that he simply cannot afford to spend so much money on his pictures as his American rival. In consequence, it is inevitable that through no fault of his own his work must often be inferior to American work upon which money has been lavished by manufacturers possessing practically limitless sources of profit." America's share of the British film market in 1916 to 1917 was 75 to 90 percent. Before the war, French films occupied 80 percent of the French market; by early 1917 that was down to 37 percent with the U.S. supplying 30.4 percent, Italy 20.7 percent and Britain 11.8 percent.[41]

With the entry of America into World War I in April 1917, a partnership developed between government and the film industry. Quickly the U.S. Congress created the Committee on Public Information (known as the Creel Committee after chairman George Creel) to spread "the Gospel of Americanism." In this attempt to sell America abroad, the government employed films, books, English language classes and advertisements. It was a massive effort to promote American culture and values abroad. At the request of the Secretary of the Treasury that year, NAMPI president William A. Brady called a meeting of important film figures, getting them involved in domestic concerns such as the Liberty Loan Drive. President Woodrow Wilson asked Brady to set up methods of distributing U.S. and Allied nations' movies in France, Italy and Russia. NAMPI's War Cooperation Committee then set up a special group, the American Cinema Commission, to distribute films in Europe. That commission decided which films would go abroad, working in conjunction with the Division of Films, by then established as part of the Creel Committee. Upon the formation of the Division of Films, Wilson remarked, "The film has come to rank as the very highest medium for the dissemination of public intelligence, and since it speaks a universal language, it lends itself importantly to the presentation of America's plans and purposes."[42]

In mid–1918, a representative of the Division of Films said, "It may be true to say that the government has gone into partnership with the moving picture industry to the end that the unique and tremendous power of the moving picture as an instrument of propaganda may be utilized to the fullest possible extent for the nation's needs." By leading the way for U.S. pictures, the Division helped establish American films more firmly in some areas. All of the films going abroad—some were non-fiction in the areas of health, education and so forth—had to have a War Trade Board license. Creel obtained a War Trade Board ruling that every application to export films had to be endorsed by the Creel Committee. Also aiding the industry was Creel's promise to expedite film shipments by dealing with red tape and securing shipping space. In return, Hollywood agreed to three conditions: all export shipments were to contain 20 percent educational material; no U.S. movies would be rented to an exhibitor who refused to screen Creel-sponsored product; no U.S. films were to be rented to a cinema which screened German films.[43]

Representatives of the Division of Films visited various nations in late 1917 and 1918 establishing distribution channels. One such agent was Guy Croswell Smith, who in 1918 went to Scandinavia where about 50 percent of product screened was German. Smith was able to reduce the German share down to around 3 percent just after the war, with product from the Allies (mostly U.S.) making up about 90 percent of the market. According to Creel's official report, all the footage exported to Holland "was sold, not given, to the Dutch exhibitors for the total sum of $57,340.80, with a very considerable profit to the American producers, for whose future benefit, moreover, an American market was thus established." Division of Films head Charles Hart visited Switzerland, where he surveyed the Swiss distributors wishing to acquire the commercial U.S. films. Closing a deal with one of them, he remarked, "Financial arrangements of this sale were such that we were able to satisfy the producers." Thus the Creel group acted as a selling agent for Hollywood. The Division of Films ceased operating in February 1919. Hart summed up one of his group's most significant contributions to the U.S. film industry as being "the elimination of the German films" from the markets.[44]

Late in the war, American product was used in Russian prison camps to "disseminate American propaganda" among the 1.5 million German and Austrian prisoners of war. The Creel Committee then maintained a dozen or so cinemas, one in every Russian and Siberian prison camp. Sparking that project was the idea that when the prisoners returned home to Germany, they would take with them "a knowledge of what America was fighting for, and force democracy to surface in Germany." George Creel declared the movies were "being used to reveal the real America and not the America so consistently pictured by the German press."[45]

According to Samuel Goldwyn, not long after the U.S. entered World War I he and other producers were summoned to the White House by President Wilson, who asked them to urgently rush as many of their films as possible to France to give heart to the French people, to let them know the nature of their new ally.[46]

There were a few disadvantages for the industry attributable to the war. Film was added to the Export Conservation list in July 1918. It was also subject to shipping restrictions as troops and war material got priority. Exports to South America were embargoed totally in July and August. These various disruptions, along with the general war situation, did depress U.S. exports slightly for a brief period. Restrictions were all removed by December 1918, allowing unrestrained export of movies once again.[47]

Exports of American exposed film (positives and negatives) totaled 32,192,018 linear feet in fiscal 1913 (July 1, 1912–June 30, 1913). That was the first year the Commerce Department compiled such statistics. By fiscal 1917, exports had increased to 158,751,786 feet, dropping slightly to 146,342,191 feet the following year. Important markets were France, Canada, Brazil, Italy and Australia. Biggest customer was Europe with Britain, France and Italy taking around 47 percent of the export total in 1917. While Italy took just 397,680 feet in the first eleven months of 1915, that nation took over eleven million feet in comparable periods in each of 1916 and 1917. Italian film personnel complained the rental prices of American films were too great.[48]

At the close of 1918, *Variety* reiterated that America's greatest cinema rivals prior to the war were France and Italy but then production "went to zero in both." Without mentioning anything about the supposed superior quality of U.S. movies, the trade publication concluded, "It is a significant fact that the really golden age of American films dates from 1914—the year the war started.... Our late entrance into the war and our remoteness have enabled us to maintain this advantage."[49]

Despite this seemingly rosy future, there were some worries, mostly centering around currency devaluation in many European lands in the wake of the war. Those devaluations against the dollar lowered receipts to the majors. From 1919 to the early 1920s, most currencies devalued against the U.S. dollar; the price in pounds for a British buyer of American goods rose 64 percent between 1916 and 1920. In 1928 the French franc was worth just 20 percent of its prewar value. Returning from a 1919 European trip, U.S. film executive David Howells reported, "The American film is beginning to lose ground, not because of any deterioration in quality, but because of the ruinous rate of exchange and the exorbitant demands of the American producers." Howells counseled exporters to lower prices. However, producers were loath to do so as they had become used to receiving 35–40 percent of a film's total revenue from foreign outlets. *Motion Picture World* explained why prices could not be lowered: "The foreign market, by enlarging the scope of the manufacturer, makes it possible for American pictures to be produced on a scale that warrants investments above $50,000." Failure to stabilize the foreign market, or its loans, would mean "the American producer cannot continue the sumptuous production of pictures the American public has learned to expect." Any lowering of prices abroad could lead to production cutbacks or a reduction in profit.[50]

Carl Laemmle joined the discussion with a letter published in *Bioscope* in which he illogically explained the situation. Pointing out the steep rise in film production costs in the previous few years, Laemmle said, "Hitherto, the foreign markets have had an easy time of it. They have not had to share their proportionate burden of the cost of production. The new conditions and the new costs, however, have forced an entire change in this respect. Pictures now cost so much that the markets of the whole world must assume their just share of the burden." It was an argument not only against lower prices for foreign nations, but perhaps an increase. It was precisely because American film production costs then depended on world revenues that skyrocketing salaries could be paid to actors, and for screen rights.[51]

Variety spread the gloom around by complaining about the devalued European currencies with articles headlined "Foreign Sales Outlook Poor" and "Foreign Market Dead." However, American films had over 80 percent of the Brazilian market by the early 1920s while by 1918 in South Africa, European movies were almost all gone with the result that "American films soon dominated the South African cinema and audiences were forced to endure not only shoddy methods but an unscrupulous choice of theme." With the tremendous demand for movies resulting from war conditions, the inevitable result was shoddy production with "American firms being the worst culprits and permitting releases which offended the most accommodating public and caused the most docile critics to protest."[52]

Currency worries proved to be a minor, and brief, annoyance which soon was forgotten with a quickly stabilized world. As the 1920s began, American movies clearly and totally dominated the world film market. There was nobody close enough to even be in the running for number two. All the former serious rivals had been decimated by the war. Such nations did not return to normal the day after hostilities ceased. Many more years were needed to reconstruct their societies; filmmaking was rarely a top priority. Prewar leader Pathé found itself unable to recapture much of its own home market. Mistakenly it decided to concentrate on the U.S. market where it had enjoyed considerable prewar success. However, the U.S. cartel had since formed and block booked the land, resulting in a much more controlled, concentrated market. America was closed. Pathé withered away with its remains swallowed up by RKO in the early 1930s.

What kind of movies were being exported? The U.S. magazine *Current Opinion* showcased the views of French movie critic Gabriele Buffet in 1917. She was described as "brilliant." Buffet attacked European films nation by nation as so much trash while praising American product as bold and new with the plots being advanced by a "succession of facts of direct significance. Fisticuffs, kisses, falls, chases."[53]

America's film invasion did not pass unnoticed in the countries involved in 1918 and 1919. Protests were mounted. Some countries levied import duties during the 1910s on film imports but they did so on a wide variety of commodities. Movies were never singled out for special treatment or sanctions by a nation. Such taxation was for fairly minor amounts with Hollywood paying little or no attention to it.

Early in 1919, reported *Variety*, U.S. producers were "said to have made ready for an invasion of the German and Austrian territory with film barred from the enemy zone during the war." Several million feet of films were stacked up on the Danish and Scandinavian coasts ready to be shipped in after the final peace documents were signed. Later that year the German government embargoed all American film to protect the German movie industry as well as to conserve currency. However, a number of films were smuggled in, distributed and exhibited. Austria imposed no controls but the value of its money was so low that Americans were not trying to place films there.[54]

Still smarting over U.S. war films which extolled American forces to the exclusion of their own, some Canadians made noises in 1919 to have more British product and less U.S. movies screened. However, Britain wasn't producing many movies itself just then. Canadian domestic production was effectively zero. Whenever one of the U.S. majors opened a Canadian branch it was U.S. citizens who got the jobs, another sore point in Canada. Other concerns included "the fact that there is so much money leaving the country in the shape of profits to the American concerns" and that Canadian youth "rather than drinking in Canadian and British ideals is imbibing American ideals; in fact, the influx is looked upon in the nature of a sort of unconscious but insidious propaganda."[55]

Britain had its own problems with the American invasion. Formed in 1918 with the purpose of promoting and encouraging the exhibition of British movies throughout the Empire, the British Screen Club focused on Australia since "the foreign films there are a danger to the continuity of British thought and ideals."[56]

Controversy heated up in 1919 after Famous Players–Lasky (Paramount) announced plans to invade Britain with a chain of their own cinemas. Condemning the plans as an "invasion of the mother country by foreigners," British cinema owners held a protest meeting. Another annoyance was that Famous had been imposing block booking on venues for several years. With the movie backlog from the war, Famous had altered the practice from imposing blocks of eight movies to 21 then up to 50 and finally up to blocks of 104 films. Exhibitors accepted the practice because they needed product for their screens and to get the most popular features. The result was that most theaters were booked up for 12 months in advance.[57]

At a summer meeting of the Cinematograph Exhibitors' Association, held in Glasgow in 1919, group vice-president R. C. Buchanan and others called for government action against the "American invasion." Buchanan moved a resolution pledging all exhibitors to refuse to book any product or enter into any contracts with Famous unless his group was satisfied the American firm was not involved in any way in building or acquiring cinemas. That resolution was passed unanimously. As well, Buchanan denounced "the infamous system of block booking by which exhibitors must contract to take 104 pictures a year." Labor leader J. A. Seddon told the exhibitors, "There is going to be a great scramble for the trade of the world, and we cannot see the peaceful penetration and capture of such a powerful means of popular education as the picture houses." One month later a second meeting was held involving others in the film industry, such as producers and native distributors. Unanimously they decided to support the earlier resolution. Other resolutions adopted called for government support for the film industry and for capital to refrain from investing in cinemas under foreign control. Noting Britain then had less than 4,000 theaters, Buchanan said they sent back to the U.S. in total from £3,000 to £15,000 for each American film screened while in the U.S. with some 20,000 cinemas, the average return on the small number of British films screened there was £800. America's movie market was essentially closed to British movies, he concluded. Twenty million people went to the movies each week in Britain. Hoping to bring the situation to the attention of those people, Buchanan's group declared it would circulate pamphlets while theaters themselves would be visited by hundreds of speakers from the industry.[58]

When the *New York Times* editorialized on the issue that summer, it noted that 90 percent of movies screened in Britain were American while the proportion of British films exhibited in the U.S. was "perhaps one percent." It was not a balance of trade issue, thought the newspaper, but rather that "moving pictures are propaganda. What advertises America advertises the goods we have to sell.... The moving picture carries the flag and the band wagon is manned by commercial drummers."[59]

Small movements against the invasion of U.S. movies were beginning to make themselves heard in 1918-1919. They would grow increasingly louder. However, as 1920 dawned the American product was in control of the world's film screens. The eagle soared alone.

2. Consolidating Control: 1920s

One of the first orders of business for the major studios in the 1920s was the formal creation of a cartel. The industry had matured enough to be in the final stages of rationalization, allowing it to exist in a harmonious fashion. Only with a stable, effective cartel could the U.S. majors hope to maintain and expand their worldwide film domination, partly handed to them by the war. Earlier attempts at cartel formation had failed due to a lack of internal cohesion, too much ease of entry into the ranks of the independent producers and a domestic market expanding too rapidly to be effectively controlled. Industrial changes such as a star-driven system which escalated production costs and a move to large, expensive-to-build venues ended such problems. The new cartel extensively used block booking worldwide to drive out interlopers. Earlier cartels were hampered because they had no publicly known, politically well-connected leader to speak with one voice for the industry. Appointing such a figure to head the cartel allowed it to be perceived domestically as addressing the growing public complaints against perceived immoral films.

A search for such a leader began in 1921 with Will H. Hays accepting the industry's offer. Thus, early in 1922, the Motion Picture Producers and Distributors of America (MPPDA) was formed with Hays as president of the group. It contained 23 members, with exhibitors excluded altogether. Power within the group rested with the eight majors, or the component parts still yet to be merged. Politically active all his life, Hays began as a Republican precinct committeeman in his native Sullivan County, Indiana. Rising within the party, he became chairman of the Republican National Committee from where he directed the 1920 presidential election victory of Warren Harding. As his reward Harding named Hays to his cabinet in the office of Postmaster General. It was that post Hays vacated to head the MPPDA. From its formation, the MPPDA had a Foreign Relations Committee which later came to be called the International Department. That committee was headed by Frederick L. Herron from 1922 to 1941. Its function was to maintain contacts with the branches of its member companies in foreign nations, officials in those nations who dealt with film imports and "with our diplomatic agents and with the State Department in Washington." One of Herron's duties, wrote Hays' biographer, was to try "by persuasive argument to get American and foreign diplomatic officials to intervene when the clash of international interests became too violent." Hays made his first trip to Europe in 1923. Speaking of the role of motion pictures as a goodwill ambassador, he said of the U.S. industry, "It assumed responsibilities that have made it almost an adjunct of our State Department."[1]

Hays once announced that what the U.S. needed was "more business in government and less government in business" yet it never stopped him from demanding government help for his industry. In a 1980s book on Ronald Reagan and entertainment conglomerate MCA, author Dan Moldea wrote that Hays had been "deeply involved in the Teapot Dome scandal, having taken a $260,000 bribe on behalf of the Republican Party." That incident involved the secret transfer of lucrative oil leases from the government to private concerns—for a price. Dragging on for years in the 1920s, the Dome scandal ended with one Cabinet member receiving a jail sentence. Moldea also noted that "Hays routinely hired gangsters to bust unions and break heads to avert strikes against the film industry."[2]

One of the first items addressed by the MPPDA was the public perception of films and the industry itself as being generally immoral and the purveyor of unacceptable imagery. All MPPDA members appointed representatives to a Public Relations Committee. Each studio's agent was charged with looking over all scripts to supposedly request elimination of scenes that might be objectionable both domestically and in foreign parts. He was also expected to visit sets to make sure the director did not deviate from the approved script. It was little more than a public relations gesture. Not surprisingly, public pressure continued. Censorship bills aimed at motion pictures were introduced in 32 state legislatures in 1922. As part of its foundation documents, the MPPDA promised, somewhat vaguely, to behave itself. With public pressure mounting, the group adopted a more definite "formula" to guide its members in what not to put on film. A more formal set of guidelines was adopted by the MPPDA in 1927 containing the now-famous "Don'ts and Be Carefuls"—11 Don'ts and 26 Be Carefuls. Mostly it was little more than rhetoric with cartel members ignoring the guidelines; compliance was voluntary with no sanctions against rule breakers. Citizens continued to complain. In 1930 the cartel formalized its guidelines still further into the Production Code. Still there was heavy pressure from the public, particularly religious groups. Particularly vociferous in their film criticism was the nationwide group the Legion of Decency, set up in April 1934, by a committee of Catholic bishops. Just three months later the MPPDA responded by changing the studio relations committee into a Production Code Administration, headed by Joseph Breen. Thus, that year, the MPPDA finished the "voluntary imposition" of the Code and its administration on its members.

As part of that Code, a script was vetted at every step from outline to treatment to shooting script. The finished film was also inspected. An acceptable motion picture got a seal of approval from the MPPDA. Without one, there was little likelihood of getting it exhibited. That Code is with us today although in a different form—as a letter grading system such as G or R which replaced the Code in the late 1960s. The industry adopted these measures fearing that if it did not do something, the government might step in and impose even harsher regulations.[3]

Appointing a man like Hays gave the industry close links to the government. It was, and is, a policy often followed by industries. The interlock between the government and the film industry became almost seamless. At times it would be hard to tell where one stopped and the other started. Bringing in an outsider like Hays allowed the film industry to present an image that a moral, upright, high-ranking man had been brought to Hollywood to clean up the place, to set it on an ethical path. Hays was regularly referred to as the "czar" of the industry. Undoubtedly it was good public relations. Baseball had hired its own "czar" in the aftermath of gambling scandals. However, Hays had no power or control except that which the studios gave him. He was the man who would make public pronouncements for the industry as a whole but all Hays was to the industry was a lackey—albeit a very well paid one. If the media presented him differently, if the public bought that image, Hollywood did not object. It became common for the MPPDA to be called simply "the Hays Office" with the Production Code called "the Hays Code." So close was the government/industry relationship that Hays' reception in Europe and his access to government leaders struck him as though, he said, he was a "quasi-government representative."[4]

A few years later, journalist Roger Shaw commented on the Hays Office, "At the very summit of American Moviedom stands a super-structure erected by the producers themselves ... this super-alliance of the whole industry makes for greater efficiency and progress."[5]

So successful was the MPPDA that equivalents were formed in other countries. Between 1921 and 1924, Hollywood's avoidance of tax in Australia and its control of the local film industry brought it under a series of parliamentary attacks. That led to the 1924 formation of the Motion Picture Distributors' Association (MPDA)—modeled directly on the MPPDA. As its president the group appointed Sir Victor Wilson, a Knight of the British Empire and a minister in S. M. Bruce's federal government. Of the seven companies which formed the MPDA, six were American with only one, Australasian Films, being Australian. Upon formation, the MPDA announced it was created to "protect the motion picture industry from the vicious attacks upon it by individuals who managed to secure considerable attention from the daily press which in turn stimulated parliamentary debate." Over the years much of the group's success in warding off hostile legislation was attributed to the connections of

Wilson. As Australian historian John Tulloch noted, the real functions of the MPDA were to extend and protect American dominance of the economic system of the Australian film industry by upholding the open market, low import taxes, block booking, harmony between exhibitor and distributors and minimal taxation of exported profits.[6]

Canada had an unofficial lobby group in operation from about 1922. Two years later the Motion Picture Distributors and Exhibitors of Canada (MPDE) was officially formed with the purpose of lobbying against any restrictions on the import of American films, at any level of Canadian government. Headed by John Alexander Cooper, it became known as the "Cooper Organization." The group began its life with a loan of $2,500 from the Hays Office. Most of its operating funds came from U.S. distributors. Of its total revenue of $27,236 in 1929, $21,841 was supplied by American firms—80 percent. Film historian Manjunath Pendakur wrote, "The Hays Office controlled the Cooper Organization and directed its policies and activities from New York ... An examination of its membership reveals that it was made up primarily of New York distributors who represented U.S. producers."[7]

During a 1930 federal government investigation of the Canadian film situation, Cooper admitted all the exhibitor members of his group were Famous Players employees and that their inclusion as members was just window dressing. The MPDE had the name "Exhibitors" in its title to make it appear to be a broader based group when it lobbied the federal government in Ottawa. Cooper explained to the commission that he arranged with Paramount that "we should have 20 of their men as members nominally in order that when I went to Ottawa ... I would be able to say that I represented some of the theater interests." That commission concluded that the MPDE was related to the MPPDA; that it was "financed by U.S. producers"; that it was a "mere offshoot of the corresponding organization in the United States, presided over by Mr. Will Hays ... and which in fact dictates its policies and controls its activities."[8]

Hollywood's star system meant more expensive films. That increased budget called for a more expensive publicity and advertising blitz on behalf of the films. Typical of foreign efforts was that which took place in Australia in the 1920s. When *The Vanishing Race* screened in Sydney, ten reportedly authentic members of the Hopi and Navajo tribes were specially imported to build teepees, put on war paint and generally whoop it up in a live stage prologue before each screening of the film. It did a huge business.[9]

Publicity managers in Hollywood who invented the personalities and love lives of actors became just as important in foreign countries. Australian director Ken Hall started out as a film publicity flak. He came to believe it was "plain hogwash" that people would turn out to see a picture because it was good. It had to be "sold to the public." Advertising and publicity were integral to the industry by the 1920s and partly explain how Hollywood maintained its dominance. In 1925 an Australian film trade journal proclaimed "the public does not ... know what it wants until it sees it. And then it has to be thoroughly sold on the belief that it actually does want it." Pressbooks and other promotional material were sent to Australia from the U.S. with instructions on how to exploit each movie. Local publicity people performed a sort of cultural translation. Besides newspaper ads, posters were widely used to promote movies with as many as 100,000 printed to hype a big film. When *The Ten Commandments* was released, a standard advertising kit for use in towns of just 3,000 population included 3,000 small booklets (distributed by the cinema), 200 posters and 300 other assorted items.[10]

Major campaigns were conducted by the U.S. distributors or by the large Australian exhibition chains (usually in conjunction with distributors) to coincide with a movie's first-run, big-city release. It was hoped that enough interest would be generated to carry the film through its second, third and fourth runs in smaller and smaller centers. For *The Ten Commandments* Paramount organized 11 road shows which toured Australia with a packaged publicity campaign. In return for booking the roadshow, an exhibitor received an agent who spent two weeks in town doing all the promotion and who then produced before each screening the "Grand Atmospheric Egyptian Prologue" using local people in a live pageant depicting events in the life of the Pharaoh. American distributors forced exhibitors to accept contracts containing clauses guaranteeing publicity campaigns for their films which were to be in U.S. style and on a U.S. scale. Owners of independent and suburban cinemas often complained about those demands, sometimes refusing to buy the advertising accessories which distributors supplied with every film. Those independent owners were already victimized because once they had signed, said Australian film writer Diane Collins, "worn and damaged films arrived, contracted films often failed to materialize (except at special prices) and in small towns exorbitant rentals were extracted through threats to sell to rival picture shows."[11]

Part of the publicity for *Ben Hur* included a man in Roman costume who drove a chariot from Sydney to Melbourne. A 30-foot brontosaurus roamed the streets of Perth to announce *The Lost World*. When *The Iron Horse* arrived, six "Indians" on ponies raced through the streets of Australian cities. Cinema lobbies were regularly transformed into pirate ships, or Indian Camps, or tropical islands. In conjunction with the 1925 release of *Peter Pan* the Australian public could buy *Peter Pan* cigarettes, books, toy planes, photos, caps, statuettes and pendants. Most of these extravagant publicity campaigns died out worldwide in the 1920s and early 1930s as a result of financial pressure from the Depression and the uncertain returns from such campaigns. Publicity would concentrate more and more on magazine and newspaper coverage with much material generated from real, but mostly imaginary, Hollywood events and lifestyles. Much of it passed as news or unbiased observations although more likely than not it came from the pen of a Hollywood-paid flack.[12]

During the 1920s in Australia, the U.S. majors put as much pressure on their employees as they did on the public. Fox's Sydney convention in 1920 brought together representatives from all over the country; they were subjected to eight days of company rhetoric. It was modeled after ones held in America—some Australians also attended those affairs. In a cable sent to the 1926 Paramount convention held in Atlantic City, the Australian Paramount employees chanted, "Our lives, our energies and our unswerving devotion to the Foreign Legion of Paramount. Our regret is that we have but one life to dedicate! ... We believe more than words can tell in the greatness of our organization, the vision of our leaders, and the unassailable excellence of our product." Employees of all the majors were swamped with memos, house organs and other assorted inspirational material. All promoted the central values of U.S. capitalism—individualism, success as the result of hard work along with personal merit and social and geographic mobility unhindered by any type of class restrictions. During sales campaigns, Paramount literally collected pledges of support from its staff. These were duly published in house organs. Each branch had a sales quota it was expected to meet; salesmen had personal quotas within each branch. Successful branches and salesmen received rewards of cash or "suitably inscribed" gold watches. The least successful branch received its own trophy—the "Tombstone"—intended to inspire better future performance.[13]

During the 1927-1928 hearings held by the Indian Cinematograph Committee into the nation's film situation, the committee noted that newspapers included "critiques" of foreign films more often than of Indian movies. By way of explanation, a Bombay editor explained those critiques came from the foreign producers, ready to go straight to the printer. When asked what would happen if he criticized a movie honestly, he said, "Our trade is so closely interwoven with the interests of the producers and exhibitors that we cannot possibly think of doing so." A Calcutta journalist told a similar tale to the commission.[14]

Control of the exhibition segment was crucial to the stability of the cartel and its dominance, both domestically and worldwide. The greater the exhibition base, the greater the amount of money which would flow back to the producers to support those escalating film budgets. One method of control was achieved through block booking. Another method was through theater building and theater buying. Domestically Paramount began such a program in 1919, had 300 cinemas by 1921 and close to 1,000 10 years later. Fox and Warner bought venues by the hundreds while Universal was a little more modest. MGM began its life as a large theater chain. Warner started to acquire cinemas in September 1924, using the standard major's tactic of building or acquiring large, plush venues in the downtowns of large cities. That studio turned to theater acquisition after making vociferous charges of gross monopolizing of the industry by the Big Three of the day—MGM, First National and Famous Players–Lasky. Warner complained it was hard to get screen time for its product. If it was difficult for Warner—then, of course, a full fledged Hollywood major—to get screen time, imagine the difficulties faced by an independent producer from another nation trying to place a film in the U.S. A few years later, Warner got its revenge when it acquired First National. By then it owned hundreds of cinemas domestically.[15]

Lack of theaters was a problem in some parts of the world. Writing in *Scientific American* in 1921, O. R. Geyer applauded the huge increase in U.S. film exports in just three years but also observed that most of that business went to Western Europe and South America with the rest of the world largely untouched. "In order to attain the highest possible development in these countries," he wrote, "many thousands of theaters must be built, and hundreds of millions of dollars will be required to finance these operations. This capital will come from the leading bankers of America and Europe." Geyer felt there would be no trouble in obtaining such a vast sum of money because "capitalists have heard of the vast profits to be obtained from the production and distribution of high grade pictures."[16]

The majors used the same methods to control the foreign exhibition area as they did at home. Paramount moved into chain ownership of cinemas in Canada in 1920 through Famous Players Canadian Corporation (FPCC). Within a few years, FPCC owned over 200 theaters in Canada. By 1925, 95 percent of all movies screened in Canada were American; a second source put the figure at 98.7 percent. Trying to explain the lack of British or Continental European product was not easy for the exhibitors. "To save their faces, the American owners of Canadian theaters circulate the old story that British films are much inferior to American films and that their audiences will not tolerate them," reported one observer. In acquiring cinemas the majors were always selective, going after large capacity, elegant venues in big city cores. That was where the first-run films played; it was there the big money was made. Economic control in the industry was partly achieved by controlling that first-run market. That control rested on newer, bigger and more comfortable cinemas, which is what the majors acquired. Life got more difficult for the smaller, independent exhibitors. During the mid–1920s in the prime Canadian city of Toronto, FPCC owned or controlled 37 of 92 cinemas (40 percent) but owned 45,763 of the 70,743 total seats in the city (64 percent). When FPCC bought a theater it invariably made an offer too low to be acceptable to the owner. The expected refusal would be followed by pressure tactics such as FPCC using its influence to make bookings for the target difficult to obtain, assisting competitors, cutting admission prices at competing theaters and so forth.[17]

During 1926 Marcus Loew took over management of Gaumont's string of cinemas in France through the formation of GMG (Gaumont-Metro-Goldwyn). He then introduced U.S. exhibition methods in those venues. A few months later the French government responded by awarding Loew the medal of the Légion d'Honneur.[18]

Variety reported that several U.S. majors were then buying or leasing theaters in Europe in anticipation of growing "government interference" against the screening of their movies. Foreign governments were against that move, feeling it would be more difficult to control the screening of U.S. films if the theaters were owned by Americans.[19]

By 1924 Paramount had 100 offices in operation throughout the world. Five years later, 125 branches distributed Paramount movies in 70 countries. By then Paramount also owned theaters in London, Paris, Tokyo, Havana, Barcelona, Stockholm and Mexico City.[20]

Commerce Department executive C. J. North reported that one unnamed producer which had five foreign branches in 1913 had 106 by 1926, two others had nearly 70 each and another (which had not existed in 1920) had 42 offices overseas.[21]

Occasionally there were setbacks to the majors' rule. In South Africa the African Films Trust had been formed, consisting of seven independent distributors. The biggest exhibitor led a second entity, the African Theaters Ltd. Late in 1925 MGM announced in the South African Press that it would open its own distribution branch there within 60 days. It did not, finally entering into an agreement with African Films to distribute MGM product. The following year United Artists sent agents to scout the country with a view to establishing a chain of theaters. Motivation for that possibility was the fact that African Films insisted on buying UA product (and all others) on a flat rate basis, refusing to pay the percentage rental which UA imposed most everywhere else. Faced with the threat of UA–owned cinemas, African Theaters engaged in a publicity war with UA, whose agents were renting town halls to show films. One newspaper, the *Natal Mercury*, supported African Theaters by denouncing the arrival of UA as an unjustified incursion and a menace to local interests. Near the end of that year, 1926, UA promptly withdrew from the market, both as an exhibitor and direct distributor, giving as a reason "the limited population of South Africa and the few towns of any importance." Actually, UA had been quietly negotiating with African Films, finally reaching agreement for them to distribute UA films. While the South African industry withstood that onslaught—largely because it was well-organized—most nations were unable to do so. The majors would soon return to South Africa, with much greater success.[22]

Block and blind booking of movies continued to be used by the majors to control world markets. Blind booking was the practice of forcing an exhibitor to take an existing film without the benefit of a preview screening while block booking compelled a cinema to take an as yet unmade series of films for a designated period of time. In India during the 1920s, U.S. movies usually appeared 18 months after their American release. Almost never were exhibitors allowed to see them in advance. Distributors argued it was not blind booking since the exhibitors were told the titles and were able to get information from the trade papers.[23]

Every distributor in Canada engaged in block and blind booking except UA, which had a policy of not selling blocks of pictures. That tactic was forced on the independent cinemas but not the chains. The power of the Famous Players cinema chain allowed it to select the films it wanted for any available time not taken by output of its Paramount parent. Before each season began, distributors would present Famous with a list of proposed releases, giving Famous first chance to book. Famous was thus able to choose all the potential box office hits. While Famous had enough power to refuse certain offerings, the independent theaters did not. Frederick Guest owned four independent houses in Hamilton, Ontario. Testifying at an inquiry he remarked, "Block booking means death, in the end, for independent exhibitors. As things are now, we have no chance with Famous Players when we are compelled to line up all the product of all these companies ... when I sign for pictures I have got to take the whole year's product of say Warners, and second run ... or none." When asked at the inquiry why the independent exhibitors had to buy blocks of movies and why they could not select the films they wanted to screen, Canada RKO distributing company manager, Percy Taylor, answered, "Who will pay for the production of the other pictures?" Block booking was economically sound for producer/distributors as it saved marketing costs for each film separately as well as creating a minimum assured market—no matter what the quality of the movie. It reduced competition. All available screen time was monopolized by distributors who sold in blocks. Canadian historian Manjunath Pendakur commented, "It was difficult or almost impossible for an independently produced film to get playing time."[24]

Early in the 1920s the London *Times* attacked the practice on several occasions, urging a revision in the block booking system because "many of the picture theatres find themselves with their programmes booked for a year ahead, if not longer." A few years later, in 1926, Marcus Loew addressed a gathering of exhibitors in Bristol, England. One cinema owner complained about block booking, "What we are up against is the fact that our theaters are booked up 18 months ahead with American films. We must change that." In a rare moment of candor, Loew responded by agreeing that if British producers were to make any headway, block booking "would have to be abolished."[25]

New Zealand High Commissioner in London James Parr, a former minister of education in New Zealand, noted that in his country 95 percent of films screened were American and just 2 percent were from Britain. Regarding American film domination in both Australia and New Zealand, Parr complained the U.S. had a "stranglehold of the industry owing to the block booking system."[26]

Some countries complained that American films were too costly to rent; others argued they were too cheaply priced. While American films dominated Chilean screens, U.S. Commercial Attaché at Santiago Rollo S. Smith worried they would lose their hold if they didn't lower their price to compete with European product. Good European films cost Chilean importers $400 to $500 while American movies of the same grade cost $700 to $800, going as high as $2,000 for blockbusters. Smith noted that local production of movies was zero in Chile. One handicap for local would-be producers was the high cost of raw film stock, obtainable in the early 1920s primarily only from the U.S.[27]

By the mid–1920s about 85 percent of movies screened in Buenos Aires, Argentina were American. Only a decade earlier, French and Italian product had ruled those screens. One observer felt that U.S. dominance would decline in the near future due to a declining Argentine currency "and the high prices demanded by American producers." Argentina also had virtually no local production.[28]

On the other hand, the complaint in India was that U.S. movies were offered at lower prices than films from any other nation, including India. To recoup its cost, an Indian producer usually had to receive about RS 20,000 from a distributor. However, an importer of a U.S. picture could usually purchase Indian distribution rights for a fraction of that amount. In 1927 an importer of some Columbia movies paid as little as RS 2,000 per film for distribution rights in India, Ceylon and Burma. India then had a relatively small but active local film industry. During 1926–1927, 85 percent of movies released in India were foreign (mostly American). Although local Indian releases amounted to just 15 percent, it was not as insubstantial as it appeared. Local producers held a much lower market share in many, much-richer nations.[29]

John Tulloch wrote that Australian exhibitors in the 1920s were able to get films "at costs far below equivalent Australian-produced material." Those Australian cinema owners "wanted" Hollywood films not simply because they were "best" but because "they were cheapest, and because their system of distribution through block booking assured continuity of supply for a year or two ahead." By buying into block booking, exhibitors in Australia, and all other nations, effectively helped to pre-fund those U.S. films. At the same time they deprived their nation's own producers of financing both directly (by not making investments at home) and indirectly (by denying screening to home product as screens had been monopolized by block booking). Australia had no local production to speak of in the 1920s.[30]

Different versions of the cost of American films were not as contradictory as they seemed. While motion pictures are a commodity similar in many ways to automobiles or sweaters or cameras, they differ in one important respect: Films can be priced at almost any level and still turn a profit. Some fine independent features are turned out today for less than $100,000 in the U.S.; many turkeys produced by Hollywood majors cost $40 million or more.

Consider a widget manufacturer selling his product in the U.S. for $7 and making $1 profit per sale. If he perceived an unmet need for widgets in say, Haiti, entered that market to find his perception correct but learned the Haitians could only pay 50¢ for a widget, that manufacturer would quickly withdraw from that market. Yet film is able to exist and thrive under those conditions. A Hollywood release will cost the spectator $7 or so in a first-run American house. It can make a profit solely on its North American release. That same film can be screened in Haiti for 50¢ a head. It can make a profit there under those conditions; it is even possible that the rate of profit will be higher in Haiti than in the U.S. Thus Hollywood set prices in countries on the basis of what was needed to control the market. Prices were high in Argentina and Chile because there was no competition from a local industry. European films were cheaper but the American system of block booking, as well as publicity blitzes plus the star cult, held them at bay. While such countries often wished to have a lesser U.S. screen presence, they did not favor any other specific country. Prices were perceived as cheap in India and Australia because India did have a small but vital local industry. Cheaply priced U.S. movies were useful in undermining that. Australia had no local industry but due to its ties to Britain, it (and other nations such as Canada and South Africa) regarded British films as virtually home product. In those years when Australia and Canada agitated against U.S. films, they called not for Australian and Canadian product but for British films to occupy the screens. Thus U.S. product had a lower price in Australia since British product was available to be quickly inserted as home product.

American arrogance and lack of concern for moviegoers could be seen in the fact that many of the films went into foreign lands with no subtitles in the local language. In the late 1920s some of the movies going into India did have local subtitles; however, with the high level of illiteracy, many cinemas employed official readers or demonstrators for those in attendance who could not read. That type of situation was used as a rationale by an unidentified U.S. film executive to justify no translations in the region. He remarked in 1923 that subtitles were unnecessary in Japan because every cinema screening foreign movies employed a lecturer who took the place of the titles. Universal and Famous both owned theaters in Japan. U.S. Consul Stuart J. Fuller, stationed in Tientsin, China, suggested that interest in American films could be greatly increased "by inserting well-worded Chinese texts in addition to those in English." Most U.S. majors were then screening movies in China with the popularity of the stars being about the same in China as in the U.S., reported Fuller.[31]

It was in the 1920s that Hollywood was first accused of double-shooting films—a tame version for the U.S. and a raunchier version for foreign nations. The added "sexual" scenes, thought *Variety*, "couldn't be shown here without causing a popular riot." Those foreign versions gave the impression "America is manufacturing pretty raw stuff just to get the business," worried the trade paper, reflecting that "pressure could be brought to bear effectively to prevent anything being sent abroad calculated to discredit American business in general." Such reports were frequent enough that an investigation was conducted by Francis Holley of the federal Bureau of Commercial Economics. Holley concluded that any such product came from "adventurers" in the trade and not from any of the majors.[32]

Similar reports surfaced later that decade in 1926 when *Variety* reported on the practice again. This time the paper said the practice took place because other nations, particularly Latin countries and France, wanted more risqué films. Hollywood even had a name for the practice, calling the procedure "adding ginger scenes." *Variety* was quick to note that independent producers sexed up their product more than the producers affiliated with the Hays organization. A few months later an article in *Harper's* acknowledged the practice of double shooting had been a fact but that it had stopped completely by then, for unknown reasons. During the 1920s many foreign lands established a bewildering variety of censorship machinery. One of the motivations was certainly Hollywood's films.[33]

As mentioned previously, Germany instituted an embargo on the import of U.S. films in 1919. However, smuggling was apparently rampant for late in 1920 the German government, at the request of native producers, directed police officials to prevent the further exhibition of American movies which continued to be smuggled across the border. German producers pointed out that the home country had been flooded by Americans with their movies (the majority of them being several years old) "which they sold so cheaply that theatrical proprietors were able to exhibit them at only a fraction of the cost of German films." It was the backlog of U.S. movies which had built up during the war years, unscreened in Germany, that Americans were pouring into the country.[34]

On January 1, 1921, Germany put into effect the first quota on film imports. Under its terms Germany allowed in a certain amount of film each year equal to 15 percent of the negative footage produced in Germany in 1919. In practice the amount of film imported was allowed to exceed that amount, to suit the needs of the market. This move by Germany was the first time a country had taken specific sanctions against movies. Any moves in the past had been limited to taxes or duties imposed on a variety of items, sometimes including films. While discussion of all sanctions throughout this book might make it appear the restrictions were only applied against U.S. product, those restrictions, unless otherwise noted, were always nondiscriminatory in that they applied to all foreign movies. (In every case, though, it was only the American films which caused a problem. Clearly, all such laws and regulations were indeed targeted at U.S. product.)[35]

Before the National Association of the Motion Picture Industry (NAMPI) disappeared in 1921 to have some of its members reincarnate as the MPPDA, it took a stand on the German problem. NAMPI filed a brief with the House Committee on Ways and Means to "place in the hands of the president the power to issue a proclamation or set in motion any other machinery that would result in retaliatory measures in this country similar in form, scope and operation to that militating against us." Prompting the brief was the fact that U.S. movies were limited in "at least one European country"—unnamed but obviously Germany. Worried about the infamous domino effect, NAMPI's brief argued that several other European nations sought to boycott U.S. pictures on the "unjust" contention they carried American propaganda. "Why this 'Americanizing influence' should be particularly feared and shunned as a vicious one by any nation is quite mysterious," said NAMPI. Also, pouted NAMPI, Germany was free of restrictions to "dump" their films in America.[36]

Within America a movement quickly formed in 1921 to oppose German films here. Founded in Los Angeles, the group included members of the American Legion, the Screen Writers' Association, the Directors' Association and the Hollywood Board of Trade. They fired off a resolution to President Harding, among others, protesting the German move. Legion members were the group's driving force with members of the Hollywood Post claiming responsibility for forcing the early closing of the German film *The Cabinet of Dr. Caligari* in Los Angeles as a result of boycott activities. That group hoped it would become a national organization functioning as a check system on all foreign movies. It did not.[37]

Germany tinkered with its quota law trying (unsuccessfully) to impose a one-for-one contingent plan whereby one U.S. film would be allowed into Germany for each home-produced product. However, by 1924 Germany was producing about 100 films per year while imports (almost all American) numbered 200 to 300. U.S. Commercial Attaché C. E. Herring in Berlin remarked that the German market could take no more than 400 movies yearly but that 600 "high class" American films were available every year. *Variety* observed that in late 1924 Berlin was "flooded" with U.S. pictures, that American films "smother German-made." Film producers in Germany increased their agitation to save home production by advocating limiting the import of foreign films to a small number—to establish such a law and actually enforce it. At the same time, the majority of attendees at a meeting of the League of German Cinema Owners endorsed a resolution that the government not permit the import of any foreign films in 1925. The resolution was promulgated due to "the threatened inundation of Germany by American films."[38]

In response to all the German agitation, Hays met with members of the foreign sales departments of the majors in the U.S., because Germans "were finding it impossible to get distribution of their product in this country." No outcome from that meeting was reported. Even then some German exhibitors were reportedly against any quota, fearing a drying-up of American product would slash their attendance and drive them to a financial loss (or even to bankruptcy). This type of division within a nation's film industry segments— some favoring U.S. movies, some against—would occur time after time. It made it difficult for a country to establish and enforce sanctions. When a government turned to its film industry for suggestions on legislation, it got conflicting and contradictory recommendations. In trying to draft laws to satisfy both segments, nations often adopted weak measures which had little chance of success. Resulting from American control of distribution and from block booking, that internal dissension always worked to the advantage of U.S. film domination.[39]

Discussing that situation in a general way, the European head of a U.S. major pointed out that any threat to remove or limit American movies "naturally enlists the theater owner on our side. What political power he may have is therefore drafted for us."[40]

As of January 1, 1925, Germany changed its regulation officially to one whereby one import license would be granted to each distributor for each German film it had handled in the previous year. Theoretically, foreign movies could never be more than 50 percent of the market on average. In practice the law came up short but was nonetheless successful to a degree. Of the movies passing through the office of the censor in Germany in 1925, 40.9 percent were German, 41.7 percent were American with all others totaling 17.4 percent. For 1929 those figures were, respectively, 45.1 percent, 33.3 percent and 21.6 percent. It was a system that discouraged direct distribution in Germany by the majors, who mostly turned to using local agents.[41]

Analyzing the mood in Germany to support the film quota *Literary Digest* commented, "German producers have been favored by a growing dislike on the part of the public for American films.... One hears criticisms of American productions from all quarters." One producer complained, "American film comes out of a factory like so many yards of cotton." Canvassing others such as actors, trade organization officials and film newspaper editors, the periodical concluded all were agreed that the public was sick of U.S. product. Surprising to the magazine was the industry unity in all areas of German film in opposing U.S. film domination.[42]

American majors did not sit idly by after the imposition of the German one-for-one contingent plan. Journalist Lincoln Eyre remarked in late 1925 in the *New York Times* that it was possible the German film industry would be controlled by American interests in a few months. That is, unless Hollywood's majors "can achieve their aims peacefully, a war of price cutting and financial strategy is at hand that might relegate Germany to the position of England in the world of film production and leave the United States absolute dictator of movies in the European continent." Fox was making six films in Germany—allowing it to import six U.S. movies.[43]

Diplomatic representations were made in Berlin on behalf of the majors arguing for the abolition of the contingent system. If any sanction had to be imposed, Hollywood preferred a tariff. Wealthy as Hollywood was, a tariff was barely noticeable. For less wealthy nations, however, tariffs could be a real barrier. With only tariffs applied there was no limit on the number of pictures allowed imported, something Hollywood strived for. In refusing to alter the contingent system, Germans argued they were protecting an infant industry. For the *New York Times* that argument was merely a facade with the real objection to American films being "on the ground of business rivalry; and to this the reply is that the film should be put on a tariff basis, like any other commodity."[44]

A bigger move by the majors came in 1925 when Universal attempted to buy into the German conglomerate UFA, a producer/distributor/exhibitor which owned around 150 cinemas in Germany. UFA was then cash strapped. In exchange for a loan of $3.6 million, Universal was to receive guaranteed distribution in Germany. However, Paramount and MGM wanted the deal for themselves. They pressured Universal/UFA by threatening to build a chain of theaters in Germany screening their best films at bargain prices. When the smoke cleared, Universal agreed to step aside in return for UFA agreeing to distribute a few of their movies in Germany and a few other domestic perks given Universal by Paramount and MGM. Those two majors lent UFA $4 million in exchange for the distribution of their films on its screens. Noted the *New York Times*, "Famous Players and Metro-Goldwyn, of course, will provide the bulk of the productions to be shown in UFA houses, which incidentally, offer by far the greatest exhibition facilities in this country." A joint company set up by the three guaranteed the U.S. majors of 20 films each distributed by UFA every year. It gave them two-thirds of the total screening time on UFA's circuit. In return, Paramount and MGM agreed to release in the U.S. ten German movies per year, on condition they were "suitable for American taste." During the battle over UFA, the most telling point used by Paramount/MGM to drive out Universal, reported the *Times*, "was the threat to build as many theaters in Germany as UFA now owns and to show in them at cut-rate prices their finest American pictures." Such an eventuality might have caused UFA's collapse. As it was, UFA continued to founder in the German economic chaos of the 1920s–1930s with the joint venture dissolved in 1931, resulting in both MGM and Paramount setting up their own German distribution in 1931. (Universal had done the same when it severed its UFA affiliation in 1928.) Ultimately the almost-broke UFA was taken over by rightwing German elements who steered it into a leading position in the coming Nazi regime.[45]

During 1923 in Germany a total of 253 German films and 164 foreign ones were exhibited. Three years later, under the contingency rule, 186 German and 304 foreign movies were shown. Because of the one-for-one rule, that meant 118 films produced in Germany were never exhibited—they were made just to obtain an import license. They were quota quickies made for only

$3,000 to $4,000 each. Profits from the screenings of U.S. films covered the costs of those local films. One estimate was that German theaters could absorb at most 261 native pictures, which would cost about $12 million in total. An equivalent number of American movies, average cost of $200,000, would total $52.2 million in production costs. German cinemas could rent those $52 million worth of films for one quarter (or less) of the $12 million home product— an amount most of which German producers had to recoup in Germany.[46]

Cinema owners in Germany formally split into two groups in 1926. At an annual convention that year, owners passed a resolution asking the government to impose a one-for-two contingent plan whereby one foreign movie would be admitted for every two local productions. That proposal was rejected by the government. According to Acting Commercial Attaché Douglas Miller at Berlin, the situation was not as dangerous as the convention made it appear since a minority of theater owners had broken away to form a separate group— one favorably disposed to U.S. movies.[47]

Any hope the Paramount/MGM/UFA pact would lead to more screenings of German movies in America proved groundless. In 1925, 250 U.S. pictures were imported into Germany while only five German films came to the U.S. Two years later, one source reported that since the quota was imposed, Germany's "business with America, which was negligible, has not progressed in the slightest, in spite of various high-sounding contracts made with leading American producing firms."[48]

One of the major influences in getting the government to reject the one-for-two contingent proposal was UFA, which vigorously lobbied the government to reject it. Unexpectedly the German government abolished the contingent system at the end of 1927, replacing it with a method of import control setting out specifically the number of foreign films to be admitted. It amounted to a reduction which Hollywood fretted "will have to be practically in its entirety absorbed by the American producers." For the fiscal year July 1, 1929, to June 30, 1930, Germany issued a total of 210 import permits—160 to qualified film renters (defined as independent German companies who had sold German movies abroad with those films having received adequate foreign public exposure) and fifty permits to be issued at the discretion of the government's film commissioner.[49]

Hollywood responded with a shudder. Hays and the majors lobbied the U.S. government, complaining the move was a death knell for them. They demanded the Commerce Department take up the matter and hopefully rule the action as discriminatory, in violation of international law. As far as *Variety* was concerned, the commercial significance in the German action was "to cut down the most effective propaganda for American goods." If the majors could not obtain satisfactory changes in Germany, they stated, they intended to work with American bankers who made loans to Germany and who held the nation's financial obligations.[50]

When *Variety* reassessed the situation early in 1929 it noted "consterna-tion" was still rife in Hollywood. Around that time an international confer-ence on Germany, held in Geneva, forced the nation to remove all import and export regulations, subject to reciprocity. The only exception allowed was for motion pictures which the conference defined as a cultural medium—an idea *Variety* found to be "strange and unusual." With the German quota to be vari-able, set year to year, it appeared that just enough import licenses would be granted to fill the screen time after all German movies had been slotted. The real reason for the quota, thought *Variety* was not to force American films out but to force the U.S. to buy their product. Oddly, it argued there was no need for tight film controls because "Germans will always prefer German-produced films. That has been demonstrated at every box office. The home product reflects the native customs, habits and preferences which have been deeply ingrained." Conventional wisdom was, and remains, that everybody in the world loves U.S. films more than any others, including their own nation's.[51]

France began to seriously consider imposing sanctions in 1927. Films from that country had been unable to crack the U.S. market while their own market struggled under the weight of the U.S. product. As far as the French were concerned, the American market was a closed and discriminatory one. It was an argument unacceptable to the *New York Times* which explained that French films failed in the U.S. because they failed to "take into consideration American psychology and taste and lack the brisk continuity necessary for sus-tained interest." In 1927, just 5 percent of movies screened in France were French-made. Eighty percent of the films screened were American; a total of 368 U.S. films were released there that year. In contrast, only eight French movies were bought for the U.S.—not necessarily released.[52]

Even before any regulations were formulated, theater owners announced at an association meeting that they would close their cinemas in the face of any decree forcing them to show some specified amount of French product on their screens. They were worried because, noted the press, "Many theaters are bound up in block booking contracts with American companies." Regulations were sud-denly imposed on March 1, 1928. For each French film a U.S. concern pur-chased for distribution, and actually released for screening in America, it would be allowed to release four U.S. movies in France. Explaining the reasons for the regulation Minister of Public Instruction Edouard Herriot told his Congress, "This industry, which is in place of third importance in the commercial world, has almost completely disappeared here. In the United States it is to be the most important business next to steel. In France many foreign film producers have become the owners of the theaters where their pictures are shown. All of those who have the best interest of France at heart would be moved if I were to show them a list of Paris and provincial theaters which are now under for-eign control. And this number is steadily growing—bought with the spectators' money." Herriot described France as being "colonized" by "hostile propaganda."[53]

Immediately the cartel made loud noises that under such regulations it might not be profitable to continue to operate in France. More worried was *Variety*, which foresaw the total absence of American movies in France due to the decree. These pronouncements were less than subtle hints of a boycott. Particularly galling to the Americans was the proviso that French films had to be purchased for distribution and screened. Often the majors would purchase foreign movies to satisfy a particular nation's laws but never intended to—and didn't—release them for showing in America. They were put on shelves to gather dust with the cost of purchasing rights simply being considered part of the cost of getting U.S. movies into that nation. *Variety* concluded, "American producers are bound to suffer severe losses if authorities at Washington do not act."[54]

Hays quickly dispatched MPPDA employee Harold L. Smith to France to undo the regulation. Hays also got the U.S. Ambassador to France Myron T. Herrick, whom Hays knew "intimately," to work on the problem. Herrick made a strong appeal to Edouard Herriot. Soon after that, Frederick Herron, the MPPDA's foreign department chief, and Hays arrived in Paris to pressure the French. Speaking about protectionist measures in France, Germany and Britain, Herron warned that in an all-out international film war the continental industry would land "on the rocks" as the U.S. majors had "a lot of trump cards up their sleeves." Conceding that few French movies were released in the U.S. Herron argued it was because the French (and everybody else) didn't study the American market. "If Europe asks for American opinion on their stories and their pictures while in the making stage, we will certainly grant it. Up to the present Europe has gone ahead without seeking our advice." On the home front, French cinema owners lobbied against the measures.[55]

Early in April the French government's Cinema Commission temporarily suspended the regulation—which had never actually been put into effect. Forced exhibition, and purchase, of French pictures was the wall here. Said one U.S. insider, "Free the market of all restrictions forcing us to buy French films and we will cooperate in the fullest way in any reasonable arrangements for the sale of French pictures in the United States. Force us to buy French products whether suitable to our needs or not and we will very likely quit the French market." France was then producing around 100 films per year. Most of those did not even get exhibited in France due to U.S. control and domination.[56]

Unbelievably, when *Variety* examined the issue, it wrote that the U.S. producers could not afford to spend $1 million in France for French product "since American film distribution in France, on the total, registers a loss rather than a profit on the year." Why then did they distribute there? Because, according to *Variety*, "France has been used by American producers and distributors as the show window for American pictures." Popularity in France made it easier to sell U.S. films in Europe. The ungrateful French might find the U.S.

majors decamping to another European center to be blessed as a show window, perhaps Vienna or Brussels. Also threatened was that U.S. producers might strip all things French out of American movies—just what they were or how often they appeared went unstated. Such a move, warned *Variety*, would cost France $250 million in lost tourist trade drawn yearly from America.[57]

Through April, France held firm on the regulation, although it was still suspended. Hays wanted it dropped altogether, announcing his group could live with a tariff. Unofficially the U.S. Embassy in France told Herriot that a careful investigation of the measure would be deemed advisable. Reportedly Washington prepared an attack to retaliate "against those foreign governments which are making it difficult for American pictures abroad," because "if France gets away with it, every other foreign nation will attempt like restrictions." Options included tariffs on all French imports to the U.S. and calling in French debt held by Americans. Hays warned the French of a complete boycott of their film market by the majors if the measure was put into effect.[58]

Early in May the beleaguered French capitulated. During the final 11-hour bargaining session, French negotiators faced Hays, other MPPDA people, Herrick, Commercial Attaché at Paris William A. MacLean, Motion Picture Trade Commissioner in Europe for the Department of Commerce George C. Canty and representatives of the U.S. majors. French cinema owners had also continued their pressure. France implemented a revised measure which allowed the U.S. to import 50 percent of the number of films arriving in 1927, with no restrictions at all. Beyond that number, U.S. interests were granted seven import licenses for every film they produced in France, or seven licenses for each purchase of a French film—with no obligation to distribute or exhibit them anywhere outside of France. Or, they could buy import licenses from French producers who also received seven import licenses for each production. Upon his departure from Paris, Hays assured the French industry that the Americans would give a "sympathetic hearing" to all French pictures offered for sale in the U.S. but that the deciding factor would be "merit." Rejoicing in the deal, the *New York Times* enthused, "The American victory in France will, it is believed, discourage further attempts along the line of enforced exports and serve to maintain foreign film regulations within the bounds of reason." The removal of enforced purchase and exhibition of films was a major victory for the Americans. Equally enthusiastic was the magazine *The Independent* which concluded that Hays "has made a good bargain."[59]

Writing to President Herbert Hoover about what had happened in France Hays stated, "I went immediately to France, and with the assistance of the Department of Commerce, the Department of State and the American Embassy there got [the regulation] changed, as you know. They abandoned the principle of enforced exports and we agreed to the regulation that for every seven films which we imported we would buy one French film to be distributed by us in France or any place or not distributed at all."[60]

Since that law was good for one year only, negotiations started up again early in 1929. During 1928, 341 U.S. films were imported into France with 123 entering free of restrictions while the other 218 were licensed under the seven-to-one quota; that is to say, 31 French pictures were either bought, distributed or made to obtain the necessary permits.[61]

French industry people pressed the government to adopt more stringent regulations, arguing the current ones were almost useless. Leading French producer Jean Sapene stated that unless American film distributors bought foreign pictures and exhibited them in the U.S., the entire European industry would band together to exclude U.S. movies. All European producers believed the U.S. industry had a tacit understanding to keep foreign movies out of the home market, making counter measures necessary. Sapene explained that in the 1928 negotiations in France, Hays promised Sapene that he would look into the possibilities of distributing French films in the U.S. However, he did nothing. Although Sapene repeatedly queried Hays on that topic, those communications were ignored.[62]

Exhibitors remained opposed to more stringent rules with 2,000 house owners and managers signing a petition to that effect. A second source reported exhibitors were absent or less vocal in defense of U.S. product during the 1929 talks. Native producers complained that American distributors cut the prices of their movies to such a low rate that France needed quota laws in order to sell their product at a profit. The remainder of the French industry was solidly united in endorsing their proposal of a three-to-one quota rule. Most French newspapers supported the producers against the U.S., criticizing Americans for their boycott threats and for State Department intervention.[63]

The first response by the U.S. majors in 1929 was their refusal to sign any new contracts with exhibitors for the coming season. This was a boycott of sorts; however, there were sufficient U.S. pictures already in France and passed by the censor to last for at least six months. The State Department delivered a formal note to the French foreign office protesting any more stringent rules. Speaking of the European situation in general, and exaggerating enormously, the *New York Times* fretted, "The representation of the American film industry has been reduced each year until at the present moment it is doing less business on this side of the Atlantic than at any period since the war."[64]

During negotiations, the U.S. pushed for an open market, a proposal to which the French were described as being "violently opposed." As in 1928, Hays then argued for a tariff on each foreign film entering the country with some portion of those receipts being doled out to native producers. French negotiators held out for a three-to-one quota, compromising to propose 30 percent of the number of films admitted the previous year be allowed in free of restrictions before the quota kicked in—as compared to the old rule's 50 percent freely admitted. Hollywood argued a principle was at stake, not just in France but throughout Europe, with Hollywood not wanting France to prevail lest other nations follow the example. During the 1929 fight, as the *New York Times* reported, "The industry is receiving the active backing of the State Department.... The Americans refuse to submit further to anything which gives the impression of paying for the privilege of doing business." Under pressure, France proposed a four-to-one quota. Immediately Hollywood rejected that, claiming it was no better than three-to-one and that it was impossible to operate under such a quota. Calling the present French market conditions unstable, Hollywood hinted they planned to invest large new sums of money in French houses in the future, if the market was stable. At the request of Hollywood, the State Department informed the French government the four-to-one quota was unacceptable.[65]

Negotiations remained stalemated for months. In June, 1929, in the U.S. Congress Senator Shortridge of California attacked the French over the four-to-one proposal, urging the U.S. to retaliate against French exports to America if such a measure was adopted by the French. On the other side of the Atlantic, French congressman Gerard told his fellow legislators that something should be done to stop the onslaught of U.S. movies. Sapene commented, "The truth is that the Americans are trying to enslave Europe to their ideas through propaganda by means of the cinema which brings American propaganda before the whole world. It is the best and least costly means of favoring development of their influence." Stepping up the pressure, State instructed the U.S. Ambassador to France to inform the French government that if the proposed four-to-one quota was enacted, Hollywood could withdraw from France completely. When Secretary of State Henry L. Stimson announced he was not an active participant in negotiations but just acted as an intermediary, *Variety* reported film men were left "gasping" because "it left Americans completely at the mercy of the French."[66]

Hollywood played more hardball in mid–June when the majors discharged around 1,000 of their French employees. One day later those people held a mass meeting to protest French proposals. Was it orchestrated by the majors? Frederick Herron reiterated that Hollywood would withdraw from France if the four-to-one quota were imposed: "We will only go back there on the condition that there is no quota on films. We are willing to pay a legitimate fee and will reenter paying a border tax, but nothing else.... It is frankly a case of a very few in France against the nation. The exhibitors there voted against the proposed quota law." Several months later the French backed down by offering to continue the status quo for another year. When Hollywood refused that, the *New York Times* remarked, "It must be said that unbiased observers are inclined to feel that the American position is too dogmatic."[67]

Late in September, 1929, an agreement was reached to continue the status quo of a seven-to-one quota with the 50 percent free admission maintained on a year to year basis for an indefinite period of time, until the two sides worked out a definite accord upon a principle other than the quota system.

One extra concession was wrung from the French. As before when a native producer made a film he got seven import licenses which he could sell to anybody, including U.S. majors. In the 1929 agreement the French agreed to insure that native producers selling those licenses would not be allowed to ask "prohibitive" amounts for them. The government would control the cost of each import license at around $160 to $200 each. In other words, there would be no free competition.[68]

During those 1929 negotiations the Hays organization insisted discussions had to be the responsibility of the State Department as France only gave credence to high foreign officials. Whether reluctantly or not, State accepted and played that role with Hollywood personnel attending the talks as technical advisors.[69]

The Paris paper *Le Matin* editorialized on June 7, 1929, "Americans are trying to subject Europe to their ideas and they think, correctly, that motion picture propaganda which enables putting American propaganda before the eyes of every public, is the best and least costly way of favoring the development of their influence…. It has been said in the U.S. that since American films have been sent out en masse throughout the world, American export business has increased to extraordinary proportions and that the sale of all American products had followed the conquest of the screens…. If protective measures are not maintained, the Americans will saddle themselves completely on us, will own our theaters, will own the film factories … foreign seizure of an industry vital to France." In the few years previous to that editorial such majors as Fox, Famous, Universal and First National had indeed acquired key cinemas. Those houses were fixed up, regardless of expense, in order (observed the *New York Times*) to make "the contrast in comfort and attention afforded to patrons by French and American theaters too obvious to be ignored."[70]

Summarizing the dispute, writer Reginald Kauffman told readers of the *North American Review* in 1930 that the quota system was used by "powerful European forces" with the "aggressors' motive" being to invade the U.S. Spinning blatant untruths, Kauffman continued that Hollywood wanted success everywhere no matter what "so they bought every Gaelic film that they thought might earn its way. Unfortunately, in nine out of ten they thought wrong." That was why they then bought no French product, he concluded. Mentioning the refusal of the majors to enter into new contracts with the French from the spring of 1929 onward, Kauffman gave the impression that exhibitors then had to stop showing U.S. films, resulting in "howls" from theater owners and audiences with the French holding out until September when "they capitulated." One month later that article was condensed in the *Review of Reviews*, concentrating on the howl from the audience and the U.S. "shutdown" of business. Because of the backlog of product in France, the exhibition of U.S. movies was not disrupted or altered in any way during the 1929 period when Hollywood refused to sign deals for new product. An agreement was reached before that backlog was exhausted. No report on the impasse ever mentioned the audience as being involved publicly in the fight, either for or against U.S. movies.[71]

Agitation in Britain for some type of control of U.S. movies was underway at least as early as 1923. Producers were then lobbying their government. That year in the House of Commons, MP Arthur Holbrook urged the adoption of a 33 percent import tax on American films as the native industry was being destroyed. Agreeing it "was being killed by American importation," the U.K. government nonetheless declined to adopt the tax, believing it would be ineffective. The government declared it was still talking to producers. Approximately 85 to 90 percent of movies screened in Britain at the time were American; in the U.S. about one-half to 1 percent of movies exhibited were British. Said one British producer, "The war enabled the Americans to develop the foreign field so that they can dump their products here at a price so low the British cannot meet it." Another producer remarked, "The American home markets more than reimburse their manufacturers for their outlay, so that every penny paid by British theaters for leading American films is clear profit for the Yankees, yet they pay no British income tax."[72]

Variety observed that U.S. film dominance in Britain, and its financial returns from that position, "is so far in excess of those made by England that comparisons can barely be made." Noting the agitation, the journal thought any plans to limit U.S. movies would hit a snag when exhibitors realized where their biggest grosses came from and stepped forward to fight any regulations. Acknowledged by *Variety* was the fact that British producers were fighting for protection "so that American distributors could not practically give away their product in England to force out English-produced pictures."[73]

A British writer observed that the U.S. could only prosper in the film industry if the American public had spending money. Some of that money came from trade done with Europe in all sorts of goods since "a whole lot of your export trade in general is caused by the screen. Folks here want lots of things they see for the first time in the movies." Thus was created "consciousness" of the many things America could supply to Europe. However, the overwhelming predominance of U.S. movies had to be maintained to keep that consciousness active. This writer lamented that what the British lacked was salesmanship: "America has sold us a lot of good pictures and a mighty heap of bad ones. We have sold her an occasional good one, but none of the bad ones."[74]

Lord Newton rose in the British House of Lords in 1925 to condemn the U.S. monopolizing of the screens. Noting that 90 percent of movies screened in the Empire were U.S.–made, Newton complained it showed "the British exhibitor sides with the Hollywood invader against the British producer.... If we are condemned to witness perpetual rubbish, for heaven's sake let it be English rubbish in preference to American." Explaining further he added,

"Americans realized almost simultaneously with the cinema the heaven-sent method of advertising themselves, their country, methods, wares, ideas and even language, and they seized on it as a method of persuading the whole world that America was really the only country that counted." Finishing up, Newton thundered a warning that Britons "shall be slaves to the American film magnate." Responding for the government, Viscount Peel said it was difficult to see how anything short of prohibiting U.S. films could secure space for British producers. He worried "there would be great opposition from the exhibiting side of the film industry" to such a proposal.[75]

In response to Lord Newton, the *New York Times* editorialized that British exhibitors did indeed side with "the Hollywood invader against the British producer." If American films were popular, wrote the editor, "It is the fault of the British scenario writers." A year later the same paper editorialized about the British efforts to establish a quota, describing them as "pathetic or amusing." Rather than impose quotas, the editor sneered the British should "make better films than the Americans do."[76]

An editorial in the *Times* (London) came out in favor of some kind of government support for the home industry. In the editor's mind the notion had grown up that British films "are not good films" precisely because they were so rarely screened. A lack of money was the only problem plaguing the industry, thought the newspaper. The disappearance of British films from the home country and from around the world was a severe problem since all over the Empire, "the cinema makes the United States' point of view so familiar that the British point of view is unable to obtain expression. Within the immeasurable reach of this mighty weapon our commerce, our history, our politics, our national ideals and achievements lie at the mercy of our friendly rivals; and thus the decrepitude of our film industry brings directly a loss of money and indirectly a still more serious loss of opportunity and of influence in every field."[77]

One item the exhibitors did oppose was block booking. In a report prepared by the Cinematograph Exhibitors' Association (CEA) on the practice, they discovered that 100 percent of exhibitors were booked ahead for six months, 50 percent for at least one year and 25 percent for 18 months. Distributors encouraged block booking because of "the certainty of getting rid of his 'dud' films by throwing in a few 'winners' at first, by way of encouragement." With pressure on it to respond, the British government wanted the industry to agree on a protective measure. Distributors, producers and the General Council of the CEA ratified the quota idea but it was then rejected by a plebiscite of the exhibitors. On a plebiscite about block booking, the CEA membership overwhelmingly voted in favor of abolishing the practice. In an effort to not antagonize the exhibitors, Hollywood made repeated statements in Britain that they had no intention of buying theaters in Britain.[78]

Increasingly frustrated by the internal dissension, the president of the

British Board of Trade (roughly equivalent to the U.S. Commerce Department) told the industry at the end of 1925 to come up with a plan to save itself or the government would impose one of its own. Although the original plan generated by the industry calling for the compulsory showing of British films died under the weight of vehement exhibitor opposition, CEA President T. Ormiston still favored it, explaining, "If we do nothing in this matter there is a possibility that in about two years' time we will be absolutely in the grip of an American monopoly and what hope would we have in 1928 if American film producers told us the price of film hiring was to be double what it was in 1926."[79]

Finally in spring, 1927, a quota bill was introduced in Parliament. It would begin in 1928 with distributors being required to lease 7½ percent British product while exhibitors would be required to screen 7½ percent British product. Those percentages would increase to 25 percent by 1935 and stay there indefinitely. At the time only 12 British movies were being made, or in sight. From August 1, 1925, to July 31, 1926, 761 movies were screened in Britain; 664 were U.S.–made and 28 were British. Exhibitors opposed the bill. Referring to Hollywood's Washington connections, *Variety* remarked. "With such a powerful group of allies the picture industry will undoubtedly be assisted materially in finding a legislative or some other form of reprisal" in case the bill passed.[80]

A report from the U.K. said American movies were becoming vastly unpopular due to "aggressive selling methods, housing the exhibitors, complete disregard for the prejudices and tastes of other nationalities, far too much blah about America's desire to take foreign movies, strong-arm methods in the British Dominions and the boycotting by the American distributors who control the field in the Colonies." Films were distributed by the Americans with a take-it-or-leave-it attitude "secure in the belief that you control the market. You did." Daily newspapers took almost daily slams at U.S. movies (not the "highbrow" papers but the popular dailies such as the *Daily Mail* and the *Express*). For the British reported it was the same old story: If pictures were made at a cost the home market could stand, then production had to be starved; if they were made to U.S. standards their costs could not be recouped in the home market. It was a vicious circle.[81]

A writer in the *London Daily Express* declared in 1927 that in England "the bulk of picturegoers are Americanized to an extent that makes them regard the British film as a foreign film. They talk America, think America, dream America; we have several million people, mostly women who, to all intents and purposes, are temporary American citizens."[82]

During debate on the bill, Board of Trade President Philip Cunliffe-Lister noted the American monopoly of Canada's industry, saying, "The effect of the constant exhibition of foreign films on the sentiment, habits and thought of the people is obvious. The pictures show the foreign flag, styles, standards, habits, advertisements, etc." Some candor came from Clarence J. North, who was in charge of motion pictures within the Commerce Department's Bureau of Foreign and Domestic Commerce. North wrote, of the MPPDA, "There is no question but that the American companies and the Hays organization as well have never made even the faintest gesture towards compromise or have they indicated any particular willingness to show British films in this country.... I believe that if they had been willing to do so, they would never have had this quota row."[83]

A compromise resulted in the passage of the Cinematograph Act which took effect at the start of 1928 by banning blind booking and block booking (although small blocks could be booked for a limited period, the practice was essentially dead). Later in the year, exhibitors were required to screen 5 percent British product while distributors had to acquire 7½ percent British product. Those percentages were to rise over time until they reached 20 percent for both groups in 1938, at which time the act would expire. U.S. reporter Frank Tilley hoped the Hollywood majors would not be too hard on the British films they had to distribute, as far as rental terms went because, "The American distributor has the whip hand and can dictate terms.... why not play ball and keep it sweet. U.S. films make enough velvet out of it to be able to afford to do it. They make enough by ducking Profits Tax to be able to afford a British film a break once in a while."[84]

Before the quota was imposed, Britain produced 26 films in 1926. In the first year of the quota, that number jumped to 128 features. While the Home Secretary attributed the increase to the quota, many of those films were produced cheaply and quickly—quota quickies—simply to comply with the law. U.K. film executive A. C. Bromhead complained that America was the one country "where it was very difficult to secure reciprocity." Hays biographer Raymond Moley said of the British quota law, "No American company could even remotely hope to fulfill this quota with quality films. As a result, to comply with the law, the American subsidiaries were compelled in the main to fill their quota with hastily made pictures of little or no entertainment value— the notorious 'quota quickies.'" As the majors tried to negotiate an elimination or reduction in the quota, they pledged, if a reduction took place, to produce quality films.[85]

Other European nations tried various methods to exert control over American films. In Poland in 1926, municipal authorities exercised their authority over box office prices by imposing an admission tax varying from 50 to 100 percent on foreign movies and ten to 50 percent on domestic product. Almost immediately Polish exhibitors staged a protest strike, closing all of Warsaw's cinemas. Poland's interior minister asked the owners to reopen immediately with a 75 percent tax in place temporarily until a committee could be struck to lower the tax to something on the order of 40 to 60 percent. Owners rejected the proposal. That shutting-down was said to be costing U.S.

producers $10,000 per week. Commented *Variety*, "That any government could presume to tax admission 75 percent is enough in itself to drive exhibitors to any extremity. It might also stand as a reason why there is foreign 'dumping' of American pictures." Working with and through the U.S. Foreign Office, Hollywood brought pressure to bear in particular against the Polish minister of foreign affairs and interior minister, both said to be sympathetic to U.S. film interests. That strike ended in September, 1926, with the taxes withdrawn. Warsaw municipal authorities were outraged over the foreign interference. Poland then attempted to introduce a ten-to-one contingent plan — ten movies could be imported for each native production. Pressure from Hollywood reduced it first to twenty-to-one, then caused it to disappear altogether.[86]

Hungary introduced regulations in 1926 requiring importers to pay a duty of 3,000 crowns per meter of exposed film and to sponsor one Hungarian film for every 30 sent into Hungary. Responding to that measure, Hollywood announced a boycott on the shipment of movies to Hungary. They closed their Budapest offices, dismissing over 100 employees. Hollywood argued the Hungarian market was not large enough to support paying the tax while the market abroad for Hungarian films they would have to sponsor was negligible. Hays traveled to Budapest to protest against the regulation. Hungary soon dropped it. Instead, foreign films were required to pay a tax of $80 each and the money went to a fund to subsidize domestic production. Some time later it was pronounced to have worked "so far without results." Three years later in 1929, Hungary introduced a more modest measure. For every 20 movies imported into Hungary a distributor had to purchase one contingent license. Each locally made film received one license. A film was defined as having a minimum length of 1,500 feet (running time of about 15 minutes) and costing a minimum of $12,000.[87]

Austria was made viable as a market for the majors by the Allies who helped that nation stabilize its currency situation in 1923. Ninety percent of films screened then were German-produced. After stabilization there were eight U.S. films screened to every one German movie. U.S. screen dominance became so pervasive so quickly, Austria felt compelled to respond.[88]

Beginning in September, 1925, Austria imposed a twenty-to-one quota plan. For each locally produced product, the producer received twenty import permits, which could be sold on the open market. Generally those permits sold for $120 to $150 each. As of January, 1927, Austrian officials modified the plan to a ten-to-one ratio. Unhappy with that, MPPDA European representative Edward G. Lowry was dispatched to Vienna where he negotiated with Minister of Commerce Schuerff. It was decided that the ratio would be allowed to fluctuate unofficially with the needs of the home market—estimated to be then about 400. America supplied 75 percent of them. That is, unofficially America would be allowed to import to meet the market's needs regardless of local production amounts. Lowry announced he was pleased by the friendly attitude he found in Vienna and there was "no disagreement" between the sides. The full impact of that deal was observable by the middle of 1927 when Austria had produced just one film—four others were underway. Austrian officials were then threatening to halve imports altogether. U.S. government officials pressed the Austrians to end the contingent system even though it was effectively dead. Austria refused. Hollywood grumbled that the Austrians were trying to force them to produce films in that country. The status quo continued.[89]

Czechoslovakia proposed to put a quota in place in 1928 requiring the purchase of one native movie for every 25 foreign ones screened. Worried such measures would spread all over Europe, Hollywood industry officials asserted, "America's only salvation is to call a halt to this high-handed business method and refuse to sell pictures under these conditions." They felt American films were so superior that public demand in Europe would force the dropping of restrictions.[90]

Italy imposed a quota in 1927 although it only applied to first-run houses of which there were just 50 out of 3,000. The actual quota was unspecified, left to the discretion of the minister of national economy who could vary it depending on the amount of home production. In those houses affected, no less than 10 percent of the screen time (except for the period July 1 to September 30 when people went outdoors instead of to the movies) was to be devoted to showing Italian films. Given the minor impact of the measure, Hollywood was not worried, seeing the bill not as a threat but as a "gracious move to a few members of the Fascist party who want to seem to do something for their friends."[91]

As of January, 1929, things got tougher for U.S. interests when M. Bisi, head of Italy's semiofficial picture company Enti, announced that all American movies would be barred unless the producers agreed to turn them all over to Enti for selection. Bisi would then select the best ones with distribution by Enti. Exhibitors would be charged 20 percent of their gross with half of that amount going to U.S. producers, the other half to Enti. Unselected films by Bisi would be returned to the U.S. companies to distribute themselves.[92]

With the motion picture industry reported to rank number six among U.S. industries and with the level of agitation in Europe against Hollywood films as high as it was, the U.S. government stationed a special Trade Commissioner in Europe specifically to keep his eye on the situation. It was his duty to monitor changes in film regulations and to gather information on conditions that could affect the industry. Based in Paris, George R. Canty worked under Commerce Secretary Herbert Hoover, who appointed him to the post in 1926.[93]

Canty thought attempts to legislate out American films would be self-defeating as it would involve a loss of money. Using Darwinian language Canty remarked, "Europe is gradually facing the survival of the fittest in filmdom." However, the public was not enthusiastic. On his return to America after six months in Europe, Famous Players executive Herman Wobber said, "There is great opposition to American-made films all over Europe, an opposition which reflects in a sense the general resentment against this nation. They resent the greater production which gives them 75 percent of their motion pictures from America.[94]

Imposition of quotas in various nations upset *Variety* to such an extent the periodical even portrayed the U.S. as a helpless victim. "There is only one trouble, the American distributors are trying to fight the battle of restrictions in the open, using fair methods, while the European resorts to trickery." Unless U.S. distributors got together and showed 100 percent cooperation in the European market, *Variety* fretted, "their profits will be cut in half within the next year" with a continued reduction thereafter "until films from the States will not exist" in Europe. Claiming most European film companies were interconnected, *Variety* then wrote of the French law, "Had the Americans been of one accord they could have turned this proposition over to the Hays organization." It was time for America to see that Europe was united and "the only way to fight it is by concerted action." A more reasoned editorial appeared in the *New York Times* where the idea of restrictions was found to be "not surprising" considering the U.S. control of the world's screens was "almost absolute." Another complaint described as "intelligible" was that many Europeans complained about the effect of Hollywood Americanizing the world.[95]

While the concept of a united film Europe might have aided the area in resisting the U.S. invasion, it existed only in the mind of *Variety*. There was talk in 1920 of a possible film alliance between Germany and Italy's major producers and again in 1926 over a proposal for an alliance between France and Germany. Nothing came from such rumors.[96]

At a 1927 film trade dinner, Will Hays deplored the trade barriers then erected or threatened. Claiming competition was not between countries "but between good pictures and better pictures," Hays condemned artificial trade barriers as destructive elements that "cannot operate to the advantage of those industries they would protect nor to those they would retard." Hays and Hollywood hoped that a League of Nations World Economic Conference held in 1927–1928 in Geneva would do away with quotas. However, during those talks, France, Germany and Italy explicitly insisted on the right to regulate imported films, blocking American attempts to impose "free trade." Commerce Department official C. J. North understood the situation, commenting that "such European countries as feel that they want to have film restriction are going to have it irrespective of the Geneva or any other conference."[97]

Throughout the 1920s, one of the major markets for U.S. motion pictures was Australia, the number one importer in 1922 and 1926–1929. In the other years it was number two or three. Most of the majors had branches there distributing directly. Film historian Diane Collins commented that the huge advertising budgets commanded by the majors meant that local film trade magazines "soon parroted viewpoints congenial to American interests." John Tulloch also observed that the Australian trade press could be relied on by Hollywood to make its case; the trades could manipulate fears of local exhibitors that any local production enforced by regulation would drive audiences away. During that period the majors owned very few Australian houses. De facto control was exerted through block and blind booking. Two large native chains developed, Union Theaters and Hoyts. Under Hollywood pressure they built the large palatial venues favored by the majors. Hollywood did not need to buy in.[98]

U.S. distributors refused to deal with any small exhibitors who themselves tried to set up booking cooperatives. Small exhibitor hostility resulting from such treatment at the hands of Hollywood could have perhaps opened up a space for the screening of native features. It did not happen because of booking control, local trade press hostility as well as the effects of heavy advertising outlays which enclosed the exhibitors within the hegemonic big-star, big-film syndrome. With the Hollywood economy based on the standardized product sold cheaply to huge world audience, there was never any attempt to diversify the product for differentiated audiences. "The task of the American publicity machine," wrote Tulloch, "was to homogenize audiences and sell them the same product." Hollywood representative Bernon T. Woodle visited Australia in 1924 ostensibly to find out how American films could be made more acceptable to Australian audiences. More a gesture of show than substance, Woodle heard repeated complaints that the "scream of the eagle" was "unduly loud." In addition, citizens expressed boredom with specific American institutions on film such as football. As the complaints over U.S. domination of Australian screens grew during the 1920s, the local trade press did its job by trying to downplay the amount of money flowing out of the country to Hollywood. Instead the press eulogized Hollywood for its "millions of dollars" spent on "behalf" of Australians' entertainment in return for a "trickle of profits."[99]

To try and stem the U.S. tide, the government of Australia imposed a 50 percent increase in duty on movies produced in nations other than Britain. Importers paid two cents per foot on British-produced product and three cents on other countries' features. On a program running 90 minutes, the duty would be about $180 on a British film, $270 on a U.S. picture. A general meeting of importers and exhibitors held a protest meeting, then unsuccessfully lobbied the government against the increased duty. Paramount, Fox and Universal led that movement.[100]

A few years later, *The Bulletin* of Sydney argued motion pictures should be taxed on their real worth taking into account the total cost of production, number of prints in existence and the high salaries paid to actors, not some small arbitrary value placed on it. As an analogy the magazine noted there was one pound of tobacco imported there for every one foot of film imported. Both came from the U.S. yet the tobacco was taxed 14 to 15 times as much as the film. Considering the number of locals employed in distributing and exhibiting U.S. product, *The Bulletin* argued, "If Australia made its own pictures occupation more useful would be found for at least three times that number, for an established film industry is a great employer of labor."[101]

Protests continued with the *Sunday Times* newspaper declaring in 1926 that millions of pounds were being sent out of the country tax-free by the majors while their movies were "disrupting the empire, belittling the Englishman and undermining the morals of young folk." In response the New South Wales government threatened to place a 25 percent tax on the proceeds of film rentals.[102]

Growing agitation over the film domination by the U.S. led Australia to hold a Royal Commission inquiry into the film industry. Hearings took place over eight months with Hollywood's control of Australia's screens at around 90 percent at the time. One method of control surfaced during the hearings when several American agents admitted having bought rights to British films but then deliberately kept them off the market in favor of their own films. When the inquiry concluded, the commission did endorse the idea of a quota but suggested it be set at only 5 percent and apply to all "British" product rather than exclusively Australian. As functionally useless as the recommendation was, it was ignored by the government.[103]

According to details from the Australian Commonwealth Film Commission, the percentage of U.S. films in Australia in 1926 was 93.5 percent, 86.8 percent in 1927. Annual movie attendance was 110 million admissions who paid a gross of $27.5 million at the box office of which $3.75 million left Australia as dollars in New York (assuming a distributor/exhibitor split of 40/60 on 90 percent U.S. penetration, the majors would have grossed around $10 million from the box office). Duty remained at three cents per foot, yielding $153,580 in total duties on U.S. film imports. Agitation against American domination was then led by former theater owner Hugh D. MacIntosh, who alleged that U.S. distributors were evading the payment of income tax to the tune of over $2.5 million a year by charging their movies to their Australian branches at prices which left little or no apparent profit for the Australian subsidiaries of the U.S. corporations. It was an early example of transfer pricing whereby subsidiaries of companies in different jurisdictions artificially manipulated prices charged/paid to each other for goods or services to evade taxes. MacIntosh had a forum for his complaints as he owned a chain of newspapers. *Variety* claimed there was no foundation to his charges, dismissing him as a malcontent because Paramount would not place ads in his papers. The publication did not challenge the federal data.[104]

Australia Commonwealth Minister of Trade and Customs H. S. Gullet attacked the majors in 1929, accusing them of opposing an entertainment tax as well as attempting to evade custom duties on the import of motion picture equipment in past years. "American picture interests must be taught that they are not a law unto themselves. Australia has never had a form of entertainment requiring so much constant and vigorous control as the cinema," he said.[105]

Much of the criticism directed at Hollywood product in the 1920s was race based—with most of that coming from supersensitive whites in the colonies. Those critics must have looked long and hard to see what they feared, for Hollywood did little enough to promote racial equality in its films. Australia's *Bulletin* magazine complained in 1923 that American movies "clothed miscegenation with the false glamour of romance—and this in a country where the preservation of race purity is the all-in-all." After touring the Federated Malay States and Singapore, Britain's Sir Hesketh Bell complained that Hollywood made movies that spread Communist propaganda as well as undermined the prestige of white people and colonial rule. Such critics led to the establishment of a censorship board in that nation.[106]

In a resolution sent to the Board of Trade, the Federation of British Industries urged more British films on screens because "many American films exhibited in British overseas dominions, such as India, impair British prestige among the natives by exhibiting the worst sides of life as supposedly lived by white men and women." Even though the characters on screen were not British, the Federation believed the prestige of the entire white race was lowered in the eyes of natives. A former British film censor in Bengal agreed, adding, "Such stuff is deplorable enough in European countries, but is absolutely fatal in the East and tends to undermine the prestige that Sahib and Memsahib have enjoyed for generations." Bengal, India, film censors were also appalled by the amount of on-screen drinking; "The American producer, in an effort to make his point, invariably shows white men and women in exaggerated states of drunkenness. Such scenes shown to an illiterate Indian audience can have no other effect than to lower the prestige of the white women and the white race in general." Burma's director of public instruction, J. M. Symms, declared U.S. pictures to be "inartistic and vulgar, harmful to the white woman's reputation."[107]

Famed literary figure Aldous Huxley complained that U.S. films in the Far East depicted a "world of crooks and half-wits, morons and sharpers." He added, "White men complain that the attitudes of members of the colored races is not so respectful as it was. Can one be astonished?" After Orientals viewed these films, Huxley wondered why they did not rise up and rebel against white rulers. To his question Huxley responded, "But fortunately for us, the Oriental is patient and long-suffering.... The colored people think a great deal less of us than they did, even though they may be too cautious to act on their opinions." Agreeing that other factors such as wars and native education were involved, Huxley concluded, "But the share of Hollywood in lowering the white man's prestige is by no means inconsiderable. A people whose own propagandists proclaim it to be mentally and morally deficient, cannot expect to be looked up to."[108]

Criticism of U.S. product ranged over other issues besides racism. In 1921 the *Bulletin* declared that behind much of the industrial unrest then occurring in Australia was the image of affluence daily seen in U.S. movies. A few years later, the West Australian branch of the National Council of Women told a League of Nations committee that the wealthy environments in some films made poorer children discontented, accentuating the "bitter class conflict."[109]

On occasion, complaints came from within America. The *Literary Digest* groused that much of Latin America, the Far East and other parts of Asia were used as a dumping ground for low quality American films. However, the people in those nations were to blame because "they have little artistic sense. They demand sensationalism, the crude and prurient." According to this article, a woman in Java gave up a projected visit to the U.S. because the films taught her that "bandits, holdups, murders and risks" made up the daily fare in America.[110]

New Zealand High Commissioner in London James Parr described U.S. movies as "cheap, trashy and harmful," having a very poor effect on youth. He wanted to see "a ruthless campaign against the pernicious and un–British propaganda" coming from the screen. Much of Europe was reportedly angry due to the perception that their nationals were stereotyped and/or cast as villains. Europeans were protesting the U.S. practice of "making all the cads and fools and scoundrels of the screen of European nationality."[111]

Europeans also complained about the general patriotism and American flag-waving found on-screen. One U.S. representative in Europe wrote home to his studio to ask Hollywood to go easy on the propaganda, saying, "We would certainly kick if 90 percent of our films were British or Italian or French and had to see a lot of flag-waving by foreigners. The Europeans have a legitimate kick. There is no question about it, we've got the world market now, but it will go against us some day if we continue to display our patriotism to European audiences.... Let us keep the patriotic scenes for home-consumption and clip them out when the films come abroad." Some Britons complained that an insidious anti-alcohol (dry) propaganda campaign was underway with the "dry forces in America ... slipping over some quiet but effective propaganda." Prohibition was then in effect in the U.S.[112]

Britain's powerful film critic G. A. Atkinson lashed out at U.S. movies as a "torrent of sophisticated barbarism" that weakened marriage ideals, scoffed at parenthood, despised decency and worshipped no God except money. Englishman Lord Lee of Fareham went so far as to label American films a "positive menace to the world." They gushed over with "cheap sentiment, loaded down with vice, lust, greed, infidelity, murder, depravity, nationalism, non–American villains, overly pretentious and endlessly commercial."[113]

Norwegian Tancred Ibsen, grandson of the famed dramatist, complained that American films "are constructed mechanically, strictly as a business proposition, with happy endings, to provide profitable entertainment." Deploring the absence of thought in those films, he declared that "in spite of the fact that even the best material is often used it is cooked to pieces and remains just so much worthless broth, the real nutritive value being thrown away."[114]

India's British-owned press attacked America's films so persistently that First National took ads in the *Times of India* to try and counter the criticism. An editorial in that paper exclaimed that Hollywood pictures were "false prophets, and false prophets are dangerous though despicable. The question remains as to how they can be silenced, or perhaps hidden is more accurate." It was an American monopoly that was "disseminating the gospel according to Los Angeles." In response to all the criticism in India, the nation's government struck a committee composed equally of Britons and Indians to tour the country to inquire into the effects of films. They determined films were not harmful.[115]

Speaking to a crowd of 1,500 school children in London in 1929, Boy Scouts founder Lord Baden-Powell admitted he went to motion pictures regularly but that he could not stand "those rotten American films, with their silly plots."[116]

By 1922 American product controlled about 95 percent of the South American market. While Hollywood prevailed on the screens, its publicity machine prevailed off the screen. Photos of Hollywood stars appeared in Sunday papers. Syndicated gossip columns on life in Hollywood were published in all cities of Latin America. Throughout that period, wrote historian Gaizel Usabel, "Hollywood treated Latin America as a poor market. American film producers sent prints that, after being used in the U.S. theaters, had scratches, missing frames, if not complete scenes."[117]

Speaking at a 1927 dinner of the Associated Motion Picture Advertisers, Chilean Ambassador to the U.S. Miguel Cruchaga Tocornal criticized American movies by saying, "Imagination in the production of moving pictures has clothed the men from other American countries with a mental and material garb which only belong in the property room of a wandering musical comedy." In particular he criticized the myth of Spanish-American men serenading their women under balconies, portraying all those who hailed from south of the Rio Grande as villains, and depicting an Argentinean in the dress of a bullfighter although that sport was then banned there. When Hays addressed the dinner group he cited the film as the universal language: "More and more will it be directed to increasing intercourse between nations, with consequent mutual respect that intercourse engenders, until a genuine internationalism is conceived, an internationalism founded upon a real and a generous regard for each other and for each other's rights." Addressing the matter of imparting morals and decency, Commerce Secretary Herbert Hoover told the crowd, "I trust in the good faith of this great body of men who dominate the industry in the United States to carry out this profound obligation—that is, that every picture shown to our people and every picture shown to the South American peoples which build for that respect and confidence which is the real guarantee of peace and progress."[118]

In other ways the majors treated Latin America with contempt. United Artists opened its Havana, Cuba, branch in 1920 or 1921. In 1922 branch manager Harry Weiner wrote to his head office asking for financial information on his branch to be prepared when government inspectors came to investigate. Cuba had a law requiring companies to pay a 4 percent federal tax on profits. That law also stipulated that all offices were to keep books and show "profits and losses." UA Havana books were kept at the American head office. Weiner noted that the U.S. had never paid one cent to anybody nor paid a $650 annual municipal license. Near the end of 1927 Otto B. Mantell was appointed UA Mexican manager. After reviewing the tax situation, Mantell found that most U.S. producers were not paying taxes because they showed losses on their books. Not unaware of the situation, the Mexican government created a new 8 percent tax on royalties or rental receipts sent out of the country "in order to get some revenues out of motion picture distributors." According to Mantell, UA was the only company paying the 8 percent tax. Since 1924 Universal had not paid any taxes by "debiting themselves on their books ... purely fictitious figures ... [showing] a loss of about 100,000 p. per year."[119]

Writing in the *Bulletin of the Pan American Union*, Muriel Baily remarked that a common criticism of U.S. pictures in Latin America was that of poor translations, decreasing the ability of spectators to comprehend the story. Perhaps in response to some of the critics, ambassadors and ministers from 18 Central and South American embassies got a transcontinental trip from Washington to Los Angeles, courtesy of the film industry. Will Hays arranged the trip as part of the Monroe Centennial Exposition in Los Angeles in 1923. The purpose of the trip was to give the Latin Americans a greater insight into the film industry.[120]

Department of Commerce Commercial Attaché C. A. McQueen, who was based in Santiago, Chile, boasted in 1923 that the U.S. film "exploitation" in Latin America had reached "a high degree of perfection." He did think that some means of bringing those films to the poorer classes, who could not afford to pay prevailing admission rates, was needed.[121]

Just before World War I, Brazil received 90 percent of its film imports from France and Italy. By the beginning of the 1920s, America furnished 78 percent of the movies screened in Rio de Janeiro with 10 percent from Germany, 6 percent from France. After a trip to Brazil, Commerce Department Assistant Trade Commissioner Bernard H. Noll remarked that sometimes representatives of U.S. producers placed American films on the market at prices higher than the exhibitor felt he could pay. Noll thought Brazil's uneducated class liked Western and adventure films the best while the educated people preferred society dramas, detective and mystery movies.[122]

Attempting to assist the native industry, Brazilian authorities instituted a tax on imported raw film stock which was much lower than the tax imposed on exposed film. However, importers began claiming that most of their film was raw stock in order to take advantage of the lower tax rate. In response the government adopted a single tax rate on film stock between the two old rates. That amounted to an unfair burden on native producers who had to pay the same tax rate on raw stock as importers paid on exposed film. All raw stock then had to be imported as no company produced it locally. That struggle in Brazil over tax rates lasted for years with no resolution.[123]

Argentina enjoyed a boom in its native industry from 1915 to 1921 when 100 features were produced. That country also achieved a presence in other Latin American nations during that time. Around 1920 the U.S. majors launched a major marketing offensive in Argentina. One of the first changes was the establishment of direct distribution subsidiaries, cutting out those Argentinean distributors who had previously handled the product. As the 1920s progressed, native production fell while U.S. imports rose. Soon Argentina was the second largest importer of American films (after Australia, before Brazil). By the end of the decade, when the national industry had become nearly paralyzed, national films accounted for only 10 percent of the domestic box office. Foreign markets for Argentine pictures had by then been totally lost.[124]

Mexico responded to the U.S. onslaught in the 1920s by banning their films on a regular basis. Apparently these bans were lifted as quickly as they were applied. Bans were imposed, for example, in 1922, 1924 and 1927. Sometimes those stops were placed on a few films, sometimes on the product on a single producer, sometimes on a group of studios. Always the bans had to do with Mexican authorities believing the films showed Mexico and Mexicans in an unfavorable light. Reporting on the Mexican troubles, *Variety* stated that U.S. producers had long wanted to withdraw from Mexico "since the rentals are comparatively negligible." What held them back was the fear that a Mexican alliance with other governments could lead to an attempt to have all U.S. product banned in all Latin American nations if the U.S. producers refused product to Mexico.[125]

India saw the number of its theaters increase from 150 in 1923 to 265 in 1927. That led to a sharply increased demand for films with exhibitors often faced with nightmare uncertainties about film supply causing them to sometimes take "foreign films they did not want." In 1926–1927, 15 percent of features released in India were Indian while 85 percent were foreign, mostly American. The *Times of India* editorialized, "No language is too strong to condemn the films with which America is plaguing India." Hindu members of the Indian Legislature demanded the government do something to prevent the continuance of "this evil stream of misrepresentation." However, they were told it was not possible. Criticism was vocal enough for the government, through the Indian Cinematograph Committee, to hold hearings on the situation. What emerged from those 1927–1928 hearings was a growing preference for Indian films, although some exhibitors who wanted them could not afford them. That committee offered various suggestions to aid the local industry but were a divided group in many ways. Indian members of the committee recommended a quota plan; British members rejected it. Due perhaps to such dissension, the government adopted no recommendations at all; no subsidies or quotas were enacted to aid native producers. Despite the U.S. dominance in India, *Variety* worried the native industry showed great promise. Although Indian features had not then made it into first-run houses, those Indian films had "driven from the field the American serial picture formerly shown at the theaters now exhibiting Indian-made pictures."[126]

Canadian writer Michael Spencer observed that in the 1920s Canada's film efforts were already "in the hands of the American majors who made sure that the box office returns made no contribution to another national film industry." Paramount's Famous Players theater chain was then on its way to becoming the largest theater chain in Canada.[127]

At their 1926 convention, Canada's Independent Order of Daughters of the British Empire slammed American films for their "subtle influence on the minds of the young." That group urged the federal government to extend a tariff preference to films produced in the British Isles as well as arguing that every exhibitor be forced to screen a quota of British films.[128]

A Canadian trade paper commented, "The American film industry has become vastly unpopular ... it has aroused unfavorable criticism in its development through poor pictures, poor business tactics and worse publicity ... it has been most undiplomatic and shortsighted in its handling of the foreign film situation."[129]

Around that same time, Canadian Arthur David Kean (producer of the film *Policing the Plains*) complained that distribution firms refused to see his film and that he could induce no house to screen it, even for free. Famous Players refused him trans–Canada bookings—no other company in Canada was then capable of arranging bookings right across the country. Also alleged by Kean was that Famous was freezing British films out of Canada on instructions from the New York head office. Famous denied that charge.[130]

In the province of British Columbia the legislature dealt with a film quota measure in 1929, as part of a larger bill. When that measure became publicly known, Cooper's organization, the MPDE, received a telegram from W. R. Marshall, vice-president of the Film Board of Trade in Vancouver. "Exhibitors lining up to oppose this measure and it is vital that distributors unite to kill the bill," said Marshall. "Heavy lobbying will be necessary to attain results and start should be made Monday.... Adequate financial appropriations from your office urgently required and suggest same be wired." Immediately $5,000 was dispatched by the MPDE. Within four days the quota feature was eliminated from the bill before it was introduced in the legislature. That the MPDE quickly sent money to the Film Board of Trade in Vancouver was not surprising since the Cooper group had set up film boards of trade in each Canadian city. Those boards existed in key U.S. cities at that time as well.[131]

Federal government ambivalence went a long way to explain government inaction with regard to assisting native producers. Canadian government Motion Picture Bureau director Ray Peck defined the creating of a picture industry in purely branch plant terms. He observed in 1927, "I do not entirely agree with the thought ... that the experiment of allowing American producers to get a footing in Canada would be a dangerous one. We invite Americans to come over to Canada to make automobiles and a thousand and one other things, and why not invite them to come over and make pictures, but make them the way the British markets demand."[132]

The idea that films screened in other countries led to sales of other goods from the film exporting nation developed at least as early as late in World War I. *Collier's* observed, about trade to be won in Europe once the war ended, "Well, consider what the American moving picture is doing in other countries. It is familiarizing South America and Africa, Asia and Europe with American habits and customs. It is educating them up to the American standard of living. It is showing them American clothes and furniture, automobiles and houses. And it is subtly but surely creating a desire for these American-made articles." Even the "educational" pictures sent abroad by the Creel Commission were often little more than ads for the products of the firm donating the film footage. For example, an educational film on agriculture might prominently feature equipment of a particular U.S. agricultural machinery manufacturer. In charge of that committee's work in Spain was Frank J. Marion, who reported, "Trade follows the film. The projection of industrial pictures, backed by distribution of the product advertised, will create an immediate outlet for goods of American manufacture." That awareness of the indirect commercial benefits was one reason for quota legislation in Europe in the 1920s, according to Department of Commerce official C. J. North. "The film is a silent salesman of great effectiveness, and by that method much trade is being diverted to America," said North. "Moreover, through American motion pictures, the ideals, culture, customs and tradition of the United States are gradually undermining those of other countries. The film industry of these other countries must be built up as a barrier against this subtle Americanization process."[133]

Will Hays and other MPPDA staffers successfully convinced business and government officials that trade followed the film. It gave Hollywood added leverage in getting the federal government to assist it in its battles against foreign restrictions. One MPPDA representative remarked in a speech that motion pictures "are advertising American goods to the world ... our films are doing more to sell American goods than 100,000 traveling salesmen could do." Hays and others often cited a Department of Commerce estimate that for every foot of film sent abroad, one dollar's worth of other goods was exported.[134]

Department of Commerce Assistant Trade Commissioner Bernard H. Noll reported in 1921 that Brazilians "follow closely American fashion and copy American styles of clothing, architecture, automobiles and interior decorations which are shown in films sent to Brazil from the United States."[135]

By 1924 the Commerce Department considered the film industry to be the fourth or fifth most important American industry. *Variety* reported the export of pictures "is looked upon by many experts as a barometer of business conditions throughout the foreign nations."[136]

Writing in the *Saturday Evening Post* in 1925, Edward Lowry said that what concerned those abroad was "that the pictures have become a factor in international trade. They are making the United States the best-known and most widely advertised country to the very remotest habitations of man on the globe." From Spain, the Near East, Chile, Argentina and Brazil came demands for U.S. office furniture, shoes, hardware, clothing and types of California bungalows. When Britain's Prince of Wales said in 1923 that trade followed the film, it provoked a good deal of nervousness in Europe. London's *Morning Post* remarked, "If the United States abolished its diplomatic and consular services, kept its ships in harbor and its tourists at home, and retired from the world's markets, its citizens, its problems, its town and countryside, its roads, motor cars, counting houses and saloons would still be familiar in the uttermost corners of the world.... The film is to America what the flag was once to Britain. By its means Uncle Sam may hope some day, if he be not checked in time, to Americanize the world."[137]

U.S. Commercial Attaché in Berlin Douglas Miller reported to Commerce Secretary Herbert Hoover, "No one has yet been able to estimate the large amount of advertising for American goods that has come through the motion pictures and the stage." British shoe manufacturers were said to have complained because they had to retool to produce American-style shoes then wanted in the Near East—from the influence of films. In Brazil a car featured in one American picture was suddenly in great demand. Citizens in an unnamed European country were reportedly demanding clothing like that seen in U.S. movies.[138]

In an unnamed European nation, a U.S. film representative took a journalist to a restaurant which then had nine U.S. cash registers. After seeing them in a film, the restaurant owner asked the exhibitor for information about them. That exhibitor took him to the movie representative who provided him with the business machine company's address.[139]

Noting that 85 percent of all films shown in the eastern and western hemispheres were American, Lowry boasted, "It is perhaps as nearly a world monopoly as can be devised." Lowry felt the appeal to foreign trade from film was incidental and unexpected. American producers, he felt, "have never thought of themselves or of their product as part of an art, trade, craft or profession. To themselves, they have always been an industry, and it is as an industry exporting a manufactured product that apparently cannot be made elsewhere with equal success that they now disturb the foreigners whose quest is international trade." In Lowry's view the incontestable fact of U.S. world film dominance was something for which Hollywood could take no credit: "Lady luck dealt our producers a hand of all aces." With the U.S. having 40 percent of the world's theaters and with domestic attendance of 50 million per week, U.S. producers could turn out $1 million super-features and recoup the costs at home. No other nation could do that. Lowry concluded that American product displayed prosperity, happiness, "a higher standard of living in clothing, houses, interiors, motor cars—all the material appurtenances of good living. It has awakened desires in them for some of the things we possess. That is what has made the movie a factor in trade and in our international relationship. That is why trade begins to follow the film."[140]

A few months later, journalist Charles Merz exclaimed that "certainly no nation ever possessed so effective an instrument for overseas development. The moving picture has achieved, unwittingly, what different powers in different times have built navies, levied taxes, intrigued, coerced and slaughtered in order to achieve. Not unnaturally, the conquest has left certain traces of resentment." Merz added, "The American movie is in the spearhead of a new trade offensive, sinister if you happen to be on the wrong end of it." He reported that U.S. autos were ordered abroad after screen stars were seen driving in them, China wanted sewing machines, wealthy Peruvians desired player pianos; Grand Rapids, Michigan, received orders from Japan for mission armchairs seen and admired in U.S. films.[141]

Nathan Golden, the assistant chief of the Motion Picture Section in Commerce's Bureau of Foreign and Domestic Commerce, summarized the situation in 1928 in the *Congressional Digest* by pointing out that American movies had become very strong, indirect salesmen of American goods. The U.S. businessman "has begun to realize that the many lines of American products from gowns to automobiles which form the setting of nearly every movie scene are daily being brought to the attention of the millions of every land where American films are shown, and they realize further that admiration is often the prelude to purchase." At a recent convention of bathroom fitting manufacturers it was noted, remarked Golden, that the bathtub "which heretofore had been considered in some quarters a menace is fast becoming a solace." In a pamphlet, the American Chamber of Commerce in Brazil said, "There are many American products which arouse buying interest when presented in the cinemas of Brazil. One of the most striking examples is the spread of the American style of bungalow architecture. The requests received from Brazilians for photographs of houses used in street scenes has been too numerous to allow any doubt about a direct connection between the movement in Brazil and American pictures." Swimming pools were more numerous in Latin America because "they have formed a pleasant background for so many pictures." British shoe manufacturers protested they were being forced to install new machinery to make shoes such as those worn by Hollywood stars. After a film screened in Rio de Janeiro featuring a famous star driving a certain auto in a climactic chase, sales of that auto increased 35 percent. Golden concluded that no American visitor in Europe could fail to notice the change in style for men's clothing, belts, collars, and silk hosiery toward the American style: "The films have undoubtedly contributed a great deal in this direction."[142]

The idea that films screened abroad led to greater sales of various American products created enough of a furor overseas that Hays and other members of his organization abruptly stopped publicly trumpeting that fact. Upon returning from Europe in 1926, Universal's publicity director said, "Mr. Hays must convince our friends that we are not trying to sell BVDs to Polynesians nor make foreigners like our cigarettes." Merz noted in *Harper's Monthly Magazine* in 1926 that Hays no longer spoke openly of the film/trade link, regarding it as an indiscretion which could only lead to more foreign agitation against U.S. film dominance. Privately, of course, he continued to hold that view. An example of Hays' new public approach could be seen in a speech he delivered in France in 1928 touting the usefulness of films in promoting international goodwill, understanding, peace and so on. Films caused people to get to know one another and when they knew one another well, said Hays, "They found difficulty in hating." One French critic accused Hays of confusing harmony with Americanization by assuming that "the only way to assure peace is to Americanize the thoughts, the language and the souls of foreigners." Of course, Hays was only engaging in rhetoric; it was a safer way to tout U.S. films than to link them openly with trading advantages. An editorial in the *New York Times* also downplayed the film/trade link. Discussing European restrictions, the article said some Europeans "have gone so far to contend that their national business suffers through the creation of an appetite for articles of American manufacture, as shown in the films." Actually, it was the Americans who first loudly pointed out the link; then it became a target for foreign critics.[143]

Formal government involvement in the film industry began around 1912 with much government-sponsored market research done by the Department of Commerce. It amounted to a substantial subsidy for a business engaged in foreign commerce. By 1923 this collection of economic intelligence on motion pictures by the government had been underway for over a decade. Julius Klein was the head of the Commerce Department's Bureau of Foreign and Domestic Commerce. Within that bureau, films were monitored under the Specialties

Division, which added personnel who concentrated on films. In a 1923 letter Klein said, "We are becoming more and more interested in this matter of the trade promoting possibilities of American films." He also suggested "our plans for the new fiscal year contemplate some special efforts toward making the pictures even more effective media in behalf of our trade in foreign countries.... I feel ... that the commercial influence of our dramatic pictures is only beginning to be understood." Klein called on Hays "to command our organization whenever we may be in a position to serve you." A November, 1924, Commerce Department circular sent to all commercial attachés and trade commissioners abroad said, regarding the MPPDA and the film industry, "We are particularly anxious that our services to this industry should be effective and that we should make a special point of keeping it posted on all development affecting it throughout the world."[144]

An example of these mid–1920s reports came from Spanish-U.S. Vice-Consul J. F. Harrington in a cable to Commerce. He noted that Malaga, Spain, had four houses seating 2,800 in total with admission prices running from three cents to ten cents. Ninety percent of movies screened were American. From Naples, Italy, Consul Julian C. Dorp reported audiences liked lots of action, crime stories and Westerns with lots of riding and shooting, all ending with virtue triumphant. "It is not a critical audience, nor one inclined to be captious about details which would disturb a more sophisticated public," he added. The consul in Java thought film producers missed an opportunity to boost "Made in America" as nothing on the films showed the country of origin. Algeria's U.S. consul reported the Arab was quickly coming to admire U.S. films while his former liking for Italian movies was "failing." He added that "superior" American product had recently allowed exhibitors to double and triple admission prices with no loss of attendance. One criticism was that endings did not agree with French ideas so producers should supply two or more possible endings, allowing the Algerian exhibitor to pick the one he found most appealing. Reports such as these were transmitted to the Commerce Department by several hundred representatives of the U.S. government scattered across the globe.[145]

In response to foreign restrictions, Hays began to vigorously lobby Commerce around 1924 to create a special Motion Picture Section within the Bureau of Foreign and Domestic Commerce. Film's position then within the Specialties Division was a step up from the 1910s when motion pictures came within the Miscellaneous Division. Early in 1925 a bill before the House Appropriations Committee contained a budget of $15,000 for such a section. Hays had spoken to Director Klein of the bureau on the need for more funding to better gather information on foreign quotas and other legislation on behalf of Hollywood. That 1925 effort failed although Clarence J. North of the Specialties Division was placed in overall charge of motion picture work. He was to draw up plans "for closer cooperation with the motion picture industry and the maximum of service to it."[146]

When a similar bill came up the following year, Washington MPPDA representatives testified that agitation or legislation against U.S. movies was going on in 16 foreign nations, emphasizing how important foreign markets were. Also testifying before the Appropriations Committee was Klein. In answer to the question that export of U.S. films produced $9 million for Hollywood, Klein said he thought that was only 10 percent of the total revenues Hollywood received from abroad. Observing that many of the studios received 25 percent of their business from abroad, Klein pointed out that for other commodities such as autos, tires, shoes and cotton goods the foreign share amounted to 7 to 10 percent. Said Klein, "The motion picture concerns have a big stake in the foreign field, more so than many important industries already covered by existing commodity divisions." Arguing that films abroad influenced the entire export trade of America, leading to more export sales of all U.S. goods, Klein gave as evidence the situation in South America prior to the war when all styles of clothing were patterned after London and Paris. On a recent visit there, Klein found all ready-to-wear clothing was exactly the same as that found in America. Inquiring into this situation, Klein said he was told it was all due to the influence of "pictures of American styles upon the natives."[147]

Representatives of MPPDA testified that if the foreign income were cut off or seriously curtailed, "the American industry, as a whole, would face bankruptcy." Claiming the foreign market would soon rival in size the domestic market, the MPPDA pointed out their films created a demand for a variety of American products "and have been an important aid to the American manufacturer. Foreign film producers, with limited returns from their limited number of theaters, have been forced to keep costs below $50,000 for each picture. The United States, on the other hand, can give an American producer a profit on a picture costing $50,000 through domestic showings alone.... The aid which the Department of Commerce can give will be of great importance in determining whether American motion pictures will continue to secure nearly 30 percent of their revenues from abroad, or whether this will be cut down with consequent dislocation of the trade at home."[148]

That year, 1926, Congress approved the $15,000 establishing the Motion Picture Section. C. J. North was its head, with Nathan D. Golden his assistant; a special Trade Commissioner, George R. Canty, was appointed in Europe. Information was funneled to this section from 60 Commerce foreign offices and from 300 consular offices. The section produced articles on film for various commerce department publications, gathered almost every conceivable statistic on the industry abroad (such as details on legislation, methods of distribution abroad, average rental fees, admission prices, number of cinemas, seating capacity and progress of wiring as sound arrived). All this information was furnished on request to the industry. Section staff members contributed articles to the popular press proselytizing for U.S. film exports. The Commerce Department made its overseas facilities available for traveling film people. Historian Kristin Thompson commented, "As a result, members of the trade had access to a remarkable amount of material on foreign markets."[149]

Golden commented that European workers everywhere were striving to better their conditions "because American films have shown how their colleagues in this country are treated and the luxuries they enjoy." He urged business and other industries to support Hollywood in its fights against restrictions because if Hollywood failed, "other industries may find a dropping off in their financial returns from foreign markets."[150]

Early in 1926, Hays asked State to file protests with nations pressing "harmful legislation against one of America's greatest industries." Named as particular trouble spots were England, France, Czechoslovakia, Austria, Hungary, Australia and Holland. The State Department obligingly sent a circular to all embassies and consulates asking for film reports from their areas. "You are authorized ... to take ... appropriate steps ... to protect the interests in question," said the circular. In a complaint about foreign restrictions sent to Commerce by the Hays Organization, it called them "the expression of a commercial conspiracy against America, engineered by a small group of people who saw a business opportunity in exploiting the political prejudices of the non-motion picture section of the public." No acknowledgment was made by the MPPDA that culture might be an issue. In a reply from North to Herron the former wrote, "I honestly do think that the cultural argument is one which can honestly be advanced in good faith and which must be legitimately met.... (I am not overlooking the fact either in the case of England that the fact that she was losing trade through the influence of American films had a considerable amount to do with her adoption of legislation.)"[151]

When Fred Eastman attacked U.S. films in the press for their low moral tone, he was particularly appalled by the Motion Picture Section because (while it did so much work for Hollywood) the section had no control over the content of the movies. "Why not a bureau to spread smallpox?" he wondered cynically.[152]

In 1929 it was announced that the section was upgraded another step to become the Motion Picture Division. North and Golden remained as director and assistant chief. Commerce official O. P. Hopkins remarked that besides revenues from the direct sales of movies abroad, such films "in giving to other nations illustrations of the comforts and conveniences of American life, contribute materially to the sale of American merchandise abroad."[153]

When that division was established, North specifically asked the MPPDA's Herron to consult on the membership of an advisory committee to act as a general guide for the work of the new division.[154]

Government support to Hollywood was always a more important factor than commonly acknowledged. European states may have imposed quotas or set tariffs but they never provided the kind of precise feedback on trade matters as afforded by Klein's Bureau of Foreign and Domestic Trade. Moreover, federal governments of the 1920s generally encouraged "self regulation" which forestalled extraneous state regulations. Although monopoly practices were technically restricted domestically, they were encouraged for use abroad. One observer noted of Hays that "although a private sector plenipotentiary, he was empowered by the U.S. government to threaten boycotts in the event of obstacles to American entry."[155]

When America exported a total of 32 million feet in 1913, Europe took 17 million feet, Latin America 1.5 million feet and the Far East (mainly Australia and New Zealand) took 4.5 million feet. All of the European footage except for 300,000 was taken by Britain. By 1917 export footage reached 158 million feet, rising to 175 million feet in 1920. For the years 1921–1925 export footage (in millions of feet) was 141, 134, 148, 178 and 236.[156]

According to some sources, by 1922 American film control of foreign markets was 95 percent in South America, 90 percent in Australia, 85 percent in Continental Europe, 85 percent in Britain, but just 8 percent in the Far East.[157]

A breakdown for 1925 found that U.S. films generated 35 percent of their foreign revenue from Britain and held 95 percent of the screen time. For Germany those figures were, respectively, 10 percent, 60 percent; in Australia/New Zealand 8 percent, 95 percent; in Scandinavia 6 percent, 85 percent; for Argentina 5 percent, 90 percent; Canada 5 percent, 95 percent; France 3 percent, 70 percent; Japan 3 percent, 30 percent.[158]

C. J. North gave a detailed breakdown of U.S. domination for 1925. Of the 86 million feet exported to Europe that year, Britain took 36 million, France 14 million and Germany 6.5 million. Germany had taken only 25,000 feet in 1913 while France took 275,000 feet that year, moving to 4 million in 1923, 8 million the following year. North noted there was much agitation in all three nations to stem the inflow. Of Britain he commented, "It seems almost inevitable that some sort of legislation ... will be passed sooner or later" against U.S. movies. Italy took just 8,000 feet in 1913 but imported almost 3 million feet in 1925. North noted that while Italy was one of the world's largest producers of motion pictures before the war, by 1925 production had fallen away to "almost nothing." Spain took 4 million feet, having 95 percent screen occupation by U.S. product. Holland and Belgium screened 80 to 90 percent U.S. pictures while American film occupation was over 50 percent in Lithuania, Latvia, Estonia and Poland; it was about 70 percent in Austria, Czechoslovakia and Hungary. U.S. domination was also strong in Bulgaria, Romania, Greece, Turkey and Yugoslavia; however, observed North, lack of houses "and the low scale of living in these countries keeps royalties to a minimum."[159]

Almost all the movies screened in Venezuela, Colombia, the Guineas, Peru, Bolivia, Ecuador, Paraguay and Uruguay were American. Argentina screened 90 percent U.S., took 275,000 feet in 1913 and 20.5 million in 1925.

Brazil exhibited 90 percent-plus American, took 200,000 feet in 1913 and 10.7 million in 1925. In Cuba over 90 percent of the films screened were U.S.–made with the Cubans moving from taking 12,000 feet in 1913 to 6 million in 1925. Mexico was dominated to the same extent, taking 7.5 million feet in 1925. While all the Central American nations exhibited U.S. product 80 to 90 percent of the time, North remarked that "the purchasing power of the inhabitants is small and in consequence the rentals are very low." Australia took 2 million feet in 1913, 23 million in 1925 with 95 percent American screen content. Japan took less than 500,000 feet in 1913, 9 million in 1925. However, Japan was the only important market where U.S. films were not a majority— 30 percent U.S., 70 percent native-made. China took 3 million feet in 1925 but, said North, "As in the case of Japan her people vastly prefer Chinese pictures to those from other sources." India also took 3 million feet that year but it was another nation "where poverty greatly hampers the spread of American motion pictures." Added North, "Signs are not lacking that the people of India prefer to patronize their own pictures if these are at all capably produced." Canada took 10 million feet in 1913, 23 million in 1925. "If Canada were considered as part of the foreign field it would rank third…. However, conditions in Canada are so like those in the United States and access is so easy that it is regarded by the industry as part of the domestic market," commented North. To this day Canada is still treated as part of the U.S. by Hollywood in that when it releases figures for the top grossing films of the previous weekend, Canadian numbers are included in those "domestic" figures.[160]

North commented in 1926 that U.S. films constituted about 90 percent of all film screenings in the world (outside the U.S.), running from about 95 percent in the Anglo-Saxon nations of Britain, Canada, Australia, New Zealand and South Africa down to around 70 percent in Central European countries. Japan remained a notable laggard, still screening less than 50 percent U.S. films. Japan had developed a strong local industry, thought North, "by methods particularly adapted to Oriental ideas of entertainment." In 1925 America released 578 features (minimum running time of 45 minutes) compared to Germany 120, Britain 50, France 40. The rest of the world produced about 300. "This total foreign product offers little competition with ours in neutral markets or even in their own," said North. British houses screened 4 percent British, 94 percent U.S. while France screened 80 percent American, 15 percent French.[161]

Exports for fiscal 1926 dropped slightly to 224 million feet (216 million of those were positives). Top markets were Australia (25 million feet), Canada (22.5 million), Argentina (20.5 million), Britain (15.6 million) and France (14 million); the next five markets were Brazil, Mexico, Japan, Straits Settlements and Germany.[162]

For 1927 America exported 232 million feet of film with Europe producing 70 percent of Hollywood's foreign revenue. Journalist Robert Shaw called it not an invasion but "it is a real foreign invitation, and that invitation has been accepted. Through this medium American ideas are spreading everywhere, exerting without a question a unifying influence." The five main markets in 1918 were, in order, Britain, France, Canada, Italy and Australia. In 1927 they were, Australia, Argentina, Brazil, England and Canada. "As well as almost completely monopolizing our home market, which seems to prefer its own American-made films to anything that can be produced abroad," said Shaw, U.S. films held 85 percent of the rest of the world's screen time.[163]

Hollywood produced some 555 features in 1928, 335 from the eight majors with Europe producing 500 features (100–120 in Britain, 200–250 in Germany, 100 from France, 75 from the rest of Europe). Of those European features only some 300 ever made it to a screen, even in their home country. The rest were shelved, often made only to satisfy a quota requirement.[164]

Agitation and legislation in the three major European nations did erode U.S. domination somewhat. By 1928 the American share was 39.4 percent in Germany, 71.7 percent in Britain and 53.6 percent in France.[165]

Trade in film was completely lopsided in favor of the U.S. For the years 1918 to 1925, America exported a total of 1,245,496,233 feet of exposed film. Over the same period the U.S. imported 53,559,559 feet, a ratio of 25 to 1. While the U.S. exported 224 million feet in 1926, imports totaled 4.4 million feet. Back in 1913 America imported almost 16 million feet of exposed film (against exports of 32 million feet that year). It was all downhill after that. With U.S. control of distribution and exhibition, almost all of the exported films were ultimately screened. However, precisely for the same reason many of the imports to the U.S. never made it to a screen. Of the 125 foreign films arriving in the U.S. in 1922, just six were sold and exhibited. A few years later, C. J. North noted that most foreign movies arriving in America were never exhibited before paying customers; "a few foreign pictures—perhaps a dozen—are shown in the United States each year."[166]

One source outlined that Hollywood occasionally brought the Canadian and U.S. rights to a British film, to satisfy the Canadian demand for such product, "but they do not show the British films in America." In another account, U.K. film writer William Seabury stated foreign movies were denied access to America "for the sufficient reason that this market can now be profitably reached only through one or more of a group of not more than ten national American distributors of pictures, each of which is busily engaged in marketing its own brand of pictures through its own sales or rental organizations and through theaters owned, controlled or operated by one or more of this group."[167]

Variety estimated that during the period 1925 to 1927 Hollywood producers cleared $75 million per year from foreign sales while the U.S. likely paid out very little to foreign producers given the small number of films actually screened in America. As a comparison, American publishers paid foreign writers $1.5 million in royalties in 1925 while foreign publishers paid American writers the same amount. *Variety* did add that the $75 million figure was conservative. Famous Players reported their foreign business exceeded $1 million per month. North estimated the foreign take at $50–$75 million for 1925. Whatever the amount, it constituted approximately 30 percent of the industry's world gross "which is a far greater average than for almost any other American product entering into foreign trade. The vital necessity to the motion picture of maintaining this source of revenue unimpaired can easily be realized." Seventy percent of that foreign revenue came from Europe, 14 percent from Latin America, 14 percent from the Far East and 2 percent from Africa.[168]

Usually the reason given for Hollywood's dominance was that American films were the best and that was why they held screen control. For reasons never explained, no other country was capable of producing good films. Also for reasons never explained, people in virtually every nation on earth just naturally preferred U.S. product to that of their homeland or any other land. Occasionally more cogent assessments appeared in the press. Journalist Charles Merz observed that America had 20,000 theaters with only five other nations having as much as one-tenth as many. "One result is the ability to spend money on production and to recoup it here at home which—rather than any technical excellence or genius in the matter of acting ... gives the American picture its commanding lead abroad."[169]

Speaking of the publicity machine, one source said the American film "is ballyhooed from the time of the buying of the story, and kept before the eyes of the public through its making and to its conclusion." An often expressed flip side to the idea that U.S. movies were the best was articulated by *Variety* when it said, "It is admitted abroad, on the inside, even by the most enthusiastic patriots, that the European product is far inferior to the American product."[170]

Journalist Victoria de Grazia wrote, "In all cases, European firms were dependent on export markets, whereas in the United States the costs of production were amortized on the vast home market, enabling firms to market their products abroad at very low cost. In Europe, wartime regulations probably hampered rapid adjustment to postwar economic conditions, making it harder to respond to American competition." The Commerce Department observed that the war halted foreign film production, giving a great impetus to American products. As a result, "foreign trade in American films has been built up practically against no opposition." In 1928 Louis B. Mayer argued that with the saturation point almost reached in the U.S. and with the cost of film production steadily increasing, Hollywood, of necessity, must "develop its foreign markets for future existence.... The cost of the finished product is no greater than if it be produced for one particular country or community. It is therefore possible for the picture producers to develop markets that other industries cannot attempt to enter."[171]

Poaching of talent was another reason for Hollywood's domination. *Variety* noted that by reason of superior capital Hollywood "can command talent everywhere. Poland, Berlin, Vienna and Scandinavia send us their loveliest sirens to produce 'American films.'" Samuel Goldwyn, then producing at UA, mentioned poaching indirectly during an attack on film quotas when he said that no one cared that *Passion*—a German film—was a hit in America. "It was highly praised and the consequence was that Ernst Lubitsch, the director, and Pola Negri, one of the principals, were brought to Hollywood. Subsequently Emil Jannings came over, too." Surveying Hollywood talent in 1928, it was found that 12 of its directors, 8 scenario writers, 33 actors, 15 actresses and 6 of its leading executives hailed from the U.K. That same year an unfounded rumor circulated that European nations were planning to recall all of their Hollywood-based actors, writers and directors to their birth countries to strengthen Europe's film industry. Mary Pickford, who emigrated from Canada to become "America's Sweetheart," was described in the 1920s by the State Department as the ablest "ambassador" in acquiring goodwill ever sent abroad by the U.S.[172]

Saturday Evening Post writer Courtney Cooper pointed out that in Europe, "the minute a good star or a good director is developed, across the sea that star or director goes, to the golden harvest of Hollywood. There's a very good reason for it"—money, of course.[173]

North argued there were two reasons for U.S. control. The lesser of the two was that "the real strides in the development of motion picture production and distribution began about 1914." For the following seven years or more, America's chief rivals—England, France, Germany and Italy—were either at war or in the throes of reconstruction while at no time in that period did the war disrupt U.S. production. "Hence, when those other countries were able to resume the production of motion pictures, they found themselves entirely outdistanced." The most important reason, thought North, was those 20,000 houses and a nightly attendance of millions, more than all of Europe could muster, five times as many theaters as in Britain, six times as many as in Germany and ten times as many as in France or Italy. It allowed U.S. producers to spend much more money on a film, build more expensive sets and generate more spectacular mob scenes. "They have been able to secure, irrespective of country, the services of those people—whether stars, directors, scenarists, cameramen or technicians—who know how to make the kind of movies that people want to see."[174]

Will Hays' biographer Raymond Moley stated that European producers were prone to blame World War I for their reverses and U.S. success. However, he said, "This is only a partial explanation at best. The real reason is that motion pictures are as indigenous to America as diamonds are to South Africa, and equally difficult to transplant." American movies set the pace and "their superior entertainment quality is recognized throughout the movie-going world." Yet Moley also noted the American advantage of a huge, prosperous domestic market and "relatively low taxation." As European producers tried to rehabilitate their film industries, the effect of the war became fully apparent, acknowledged Moley. "The lack of capital, the heavy taxes, the comparative poverty of the citizenry of most countries and the absence of the movie 'habit' so far as concerned domestic films—these were staggering handicaps to the revival of domestic production."[175]

Just as the Americans bragged about the trade advantages of film exports, so did they brag about their control of the world's screens. Typical was Charles Merz, who wrote in 1926 that there was not a single country in the world "with the exception of a few far-off and privately managed colonies of France, in which American films do not outnumber the sum total of all other films," with the outnumbering going as high as four- or five-to-one. Merz conveniently overlooked Japan but he was generally right. All of this bragging did not sit well in foreign quarters, leading to increased pressure to control the invasion.[176]

North argued in 1926 that the press and media had called attention in "brazen accents" to the manner in which U.S. pictures dominated the film world. Suggesting no overstatements should be made, he said, "While the underlying truth of this statement cannot be questioned, the trombone-like quality of these utterances has only served to rouse antagonism in high quarters in a number of foreign countries and has led to agitation for legislation against American films." That agitation was caused in part, thought North, by the flaunting in boastful terms of our film supremacy before people who would be none too disposed towards the character of our movies even though we never said a word on the subject."[177]

An International Film Congress was held in 1926 in Paris, hosted by the League of Nations. While the ostensible purpose of the congress was intellectual rather than economic, U.S. figures generally stayed away. The Hays Office refused to attend at first claiming too little notice of the meeting had been given. (It was originally scheduled for June 1925, postponed to August, then October, and then put off until September 1926.) Observers worried the congress was an anti–American ploy. Frederick Herron of the MPPDA explained the group's refusal to attend by saying, "We felt that the congress at this time might easily develop into an anti–American affair if we took part in it, and as the foreign situation is none too happy at present we did not want to complicate it."[178]

At another time and speaking more generally Herron tried to counter critics of Hollywood by arguing that U.S. movies were "culturally and ideologically neutral, if not benign."[179]

Hays and the MPPDA tried to keep a low public profile. "The Hays organization is very quiet on the export and import figures, the variance between them being so great that they regard their publication as dangerous propaganda and because they fear the foreign trade might regard their publication as an attempt to 'rub it in,'" reported *Variety*.[180]

Nonetheless, the chauvinism of the U.S. film industry and the trade press worked against Hays overseas. Domestic trade publications which regularly and loudly trumpeted American screen dominance were widely read abroad. A 1927 article noted the consternation that caused for the MPPDA: "Complaints are made by executives in the foreign departments of distributing companies that too much export news is appearing in the trade papers." Hays and Herron were both warning executives in the foreign departments of distributors that the trades provided too much "ammunition" for foreign politicians. Those printed facts and figures of dominance awakened readers, stirring them onward to agitate for protective legislation. Herron also contacted Julius Klein to complain about the release of material in some U.S. newspapers and periodicals which documented the screen control. Herron requested all such material be centralized in Washington and that he be permitted to sanitize it before release. Hays had met with editors of the trades to ask them to ease off. When U.S. consuls in, say, Britain reported a 90 percent U.S. presence, it set off a furor and was a difficult item to deal with, especially when the U.S. complained of "restrictions or an impeded market." Denying he or Hays had warned distributors, Herron said the only suggestion he made to them was to do away with excess flag waving and patriotism and "in ballyhooing themselves as the best producers in the world and in quoting extravagant, and often inflated, salaries and receipts." At every opportunity when he was abroad, Hays and his staff denied the intentional use of American films as ads for other goods as well as downplaying the overwhelming proportion of screen time taken up by U.S. pictures. Since the evidence was so abundantly apparent, the MPPDA was singularly unsuccessful.[181]

Also unhappy with U.S. screen dominance was State Department executive Horace Villard, who wrote in a 1929 memo, "It is debatable whether the present widespread exhibition of American motion pictures is desirable from the viewpoint of the United States." Villard worried over the "cheap emotionalism," immorality and especially the overemphasis on scenes of wealth in U.S. films because the latter gave the impression the U.S. was "the land where every one achieves financial or industrial success. There is the further tendency in the ostentatious depiction of riches and the attributes of wealth to make for unrest and dissatisfaction abroad, which in turn gives impetus to attempted immigration with resulting disillusion and resentment." Presumably that resentment would come from not being allowed to emigrate to America or of being allowed to do so only to find the American dream less than it appeared on the screen.[182]

During the postwar era until the late 1920s, the U.S. firmly established itself as the dominant force in nearly all world markets. However, there were a few exceptions. Germany was more or less holding its own as well as maintaining a small presence abroad. Japan kept the largest part of its home market to itself due largely to several strong, vertically integrated film firms. A few small markets, such as Persia, were impoverished to such an extent that Hollywood was mainly content to ignore them.[183]

America's home market, the world's largest, was protected by the exclusionary distribution networks. Hollywood pressed its advantage over the Europeans in those years; as one historian noted, "Beginning with booking offices, then establishing their own distribution subsidiaries and occasionally investing in first-run theaters as well, they sought to monopolize control of distribution, exhibition and equipment manufacture." Assisting in that control was the MPPDA, which was "brutally single-minded in the face of competition from foreign and small domestic firms."[184]

Everything seemed stable and well under Hollywood's control near the end of the 1920s. Then came sound.

3. The Eagle Screams in English: 1928–1930

The arrival of film industry innovations depended, of course, on the development of an efficient and financially viable technology. But there was more involved than that. Also important was the structure of the industry and whether and when they were prepared to accept the new technology. A satisfied, high-profit industry would resist and forestall the arrival of any new technology. Given an inevitable arrival of the new method, the timing of the arrival depended on the degree and vigor of competition within that industry. Sound films could have arrived much earlier than they did—the first being usually considered the October, 1927, Warner release *The Jazz Singer*. A sound-on-disc system was presented in Sydney, Australia, as early as 1906. Likely that one was not technologically feasible. Reportedly it could not amplify loudly enough. America's Western Electric, working in conjunction with Bell Telephone Laboratories, had been developing sound-on-disc for some time. They effectively demonstrated the first major sound-on-disc system in 1924. Hollywood rejected it for commercial, not technical, reasons. With huge stocks of silent films on hand, and with stars they knew to have poor "talkie" voices on long-term contracts, the majors had no compelling reason to welcome sound films. Business was very good and very profitable with the industry structured as it was. Competing with Western at that time was Fox, which was touting a sound-on-film system. As a journalist wrote in that era, the sound film "invention had been made long ago but it had not been adopted because up to that time there had been a good market for silent films."[1]

Later in the 1920s the film business seemed to have stagnated somewhat. Warner was one of the more disaffected majors, having complained about its own ability to gain screen time—to which they responded by buying up a lot of cinemas. It was left to the malcontent Warner to gamble on breaking ranks and committing itself to sound films. Warner's success with sound caused the other majors to quickly fall into line. Sound-on-disc won the war and was used for all sound films, but only until around 1931, by which time everyone had shifted to the more efficient sound-on-film system. Due to their control of theaters domestically, through ownership and block booking, almost all venues were forced to convert to sound whether they wanted to or not. All the majors stopped producing silents by 1930, which meant that any theater which refused to convert to sound had no new product to screen.[2]

In 1928 *Variety* worried about the market for American sound films in foreign lands, fearing that the market for such films might fall 50 percent outside English-speaking nations. Foreign revenue, then about 30 percent of the total take, was estimated to perhaps fall to as low as 15 percent of the total. One person not worried that year was film mogul Louis B. Mayer, who assumed the popularity of U.S. films would lead to the use of English as a universal language. Critics in foreign countries worried about that very possibility.[3]

Leading daily newspapers in Mexico City, among them *El Universal*, started a campaign against U.S. talkies in 1929 claiming the showing of English-speaking films would damage the Spanish language. Not opposed to sound films in general, the newspapers wanted English dialogue removed and replaced by Spanish dialogue or titles. In response the government of the Federal District prohibited titles printed in foreign languages, making it obligatory to print captions in Spanish only. The MPPDA's Herron called that Mexican legislation a "malicious attack," adding, "I presume the next move will be to issue an order demanding that our representatives in Mexico cease speaking English entirely." A year later the Mexican government doubled the tax levy on English talkies to try and encourage more Spanish talkies in their market.[4]

What Mexico got, said *Time* magazine, was dialogue delivered either with badly written Spanish titles superimposed or with Spanish voices crudely dubbed on the sound track.[5]

Brazil historian Randal Johnson observed that the coming of sound filled some in Brazil with enthusiasm over the thought that, because of language differences, local production would be fostered. Although such hopes sprang up in many lands, they were always dashed as the optimists had underestimated the cost of sound equipment (causing all nations to fall further behind the U.S.) and because they misjudged the willingness of local audiences to continue to attend U.S. screenings. Latin American film historian Gaizka Usabel remarked that the coming of talkies "paralyzed" Latin American film production. A member of the Sao Paulo, Brazil, city council introduced a measure in 1929 providing a fine of $60 for each exhibition of a talking film in any foreign language. He also petitioned the Brazilian federal government to take action to prevent the showing of foreign talkies on the grounds they were unpatriotic and prejudicial to the Portuguese tongue.[6]

Argentina's leading newspaper *La Prensa* launched an editorial attack on the U.S. talkies, pointing out Argentine orchestras provided live musical accompaniment for silent films. With the coming of sound they were all thrown out of work; this happened in many areas of the world, unleashing heavy criticism. Calling on the government to adopt restrictive measures against foreign talkies, the editorial stated those films were "forcing into Argentina a spiritual consciousness of a foreign language, inferior dramatization and unconventional social standards, which must rapidly undermine present Argentine standards. One of the gravest features lies in the familiarization with inferior mental standards and social customs." The next day *La Prensa* editorialized again, claiming that local agents of U.S. producers refused to allow cinemas to show anything except talkies or to have an orchestra in the house under penalty of paying double rental for the film.[7]

The first talkies released in Latin America had the original English dialogue with cut-in titles (intertitles) in Spanish. This silent film method of dealing with text stopped the sound film's action dead, drawing hisses in Argentina. For the next day's screening of one such movie, the producer withdrew the offending titles, added a Spanish prologue to explain what was to happen and then exhibited the film in English; "The public was satisfied," said one account. Wherever the intertitle method was used it was a failure—action was always stopped dead as all the explanatory text was introduced on the screen. Dubbing a film into the foreign language was not effective during the first few years of talkies as mixing was not then in use, making it necessary that all sound had to be recorded simultaneously. It meant that synchronized sound was virtually impossible during those years. So far out of synch were sound and action that audiences were disconcerted.[8]

When Universal released *Broadway* in Buenos Aires they billed it as the first Spanish talkie, mostly though it was just titles in Castilian Spanish with a bit of actual dialogue. What dialogue there was, was roundly booed as its idiom was not understood. The accents and the titles were also booed. Throughout the length of the film the crowd displayed what was described as "unseemly behavior." Particularly shocking to *Variety* was the fact the film premiere was scaled at a high box office price so only "the best people socially attended."[9]

Agitation against U.S. talkies was just as intense in Europe. Belgrade, Yugoslavia, cinema owners told distributors they would refuse to take any further talkies unless they contained plenty of musical numbers and a minimum of dialogue. The reason was that the majority of the audience understood no English—films arrived with no Yugoslav titles or dialogue. Polish cinema owners threatened to boycott U.S. talkies unless rental rates were considerably reduced. With the advent of sound, rental rates increased dramatically, but the cinemas emptied—partly because of language, partly due to the Depression. Prague was the scene of riots and attacks against houses showing German talkies. Several Czech newspapers, including *Ceske Slovo*, alleged the attacks were inspired by importers of American films. A spokesman for the majors denied the charge, counter charging there was "proof" the allegation was used to excite prejudice against U.S. movies among German-speaking Czechs. Those papers said they made their allegations on the basis of information from police headquarters.[10]

Initially Germany received the silent version of U.S. talkies, that is, English dialogue was removed entirely while German intertitles were added. Spectators got to see, but not hear, two actors converse for several minutes followed by lengthy title material in German explaining what had just been said. Such movies were greeted with "boos and hisses." Such was American arrogance that Hollywood maintained its presence in Germany for the first year of talkies there, 1929, by sending in films just as they appeared in the U.S., sometimes without intertitles. *The Singing Fool* played Berlin with no German material of any description. Hollywood was confident it could keep going in Germany for a full year on the novelty of talkies with music, "No matter whether the audience understands the dialogue or not. But that will be the finish," reported *Variety*.[11]

Italy's Benito Mussolini placed a ban on the import of foreign language films as of January 1930. In response the Rome branch lab of the U.S. producers was busy cutting, splicing and suppressing all dialogue, keeping in only sound effects. Several hundred Italian exhibitors then petitioned the Italian government to allow foreign talkies to have up to 25 percent non–Italian language. Those exhibitors had already "consulted" the likes of Fox, Paramount and Metro asking the American firms to give their support to their petition; they were glad to support the idea. Toward the end of 1930 Mussolini relaxed the law by permitting up to 10 percent foreign dialogue in films for a one-year period. It was largely academic as the original total ban had been loosely enforced, if at all. English language songs had always been left untouched in films.[12]

When *Le Chanteur de jazz* (*The Jazz Singer*) screened in Paris in early 1929, the intertitles were in French, with printed translations for the few moments of dialogue projected on an adjacent screen. Usually the French reaction to early U.S. talkies was highly negative. *Variety* noted that every time one was shown it was booed and razzed as soon as English was spoken, "without exception." A suggested course of action was for Hollywood to delete all English dialogue from a film before screening it in France. During the screening of a film called *New Orleans*, the crowd turned so ugly with cries of "enough of English" that police had to be called. Copying Mussolini's edict somewhat, the French announced that films with English dialogue could be shown only in cinemas devoted to English talkies; there was just one such house in all of France. Universal responded by announcing it would release *All Quiet on the Western Front* in France with the dialogue out and only sound effects remaining.[13]

When Spain proposed a law banning foreign language pictures, modeled on Italy's, Spanish Minister of Public Information Duke J. Alba came to

America's defense. Newspapers had argued in favor of such a law with the Americans having "great difficulty to get their side before the public." Alba was a friend of Mary Pickford, Douglas Fairbanks and other globe-trotting stars. So cordial was the minister to U.S. films in Spain that Hollywood dubbed him Duke Jimmy.[14]

A different problem surfaced in Japan where the film censors, who spoke Oxford English, were unfamiliar with American slang. Every time they came across a word they did not understand, they banned it.[15]

Even in English-speaking countries there were problems. The British criticized both the accent and the idiom with some wanting a ban on the product to protect the purity of "English English." Australia worried anew about the "Americanization of Australians." In South Africa, British films had made a small comeback on that nation's screens by the end of the 1920s. However, with the coming of sound those screens were reported by an observer as being "swamped by American competition and by 1931, the South African talkie cinema was almost totally American ... Apart from a few outstanding films, talkies of the time were of very poor quality. Audiences complained bitterly of being not only bored but disgusted. The nasal twang of the voices grated unpleasantly, the language itself was often totally incomprehensible and the plots were of a nature to appeal only to American audiences, being either unintelligible or repellent to the local public."[16]

At the very end of 1929 the *New York Times* reported that most U.S. talkies went abroad as originally created for domestic screening. Claiming such pictures were popular, especially singing and dancing films, in a dozen or more non–English-speaking European nations, the article acknowledged "signs of restlessness" were noticed in audiences "when long periods of English dialogue occur." With a lack of funds seriously limiting production of European talkies, the *Times* was confident America would dominate the sound market as much as it had the silent screen if it was "ready to step in with native language talkies as soon as the novelty of the American talkies wears off." One worry was that European-language films would have to be made in Europe if they were to be acceptable to the masses.[17]

Paramount general manager Sidney Kent said his company had no intention of producing in Europe, that dubbing had produced unsatisfactory results and that foreign-language versions were too expensive to produce in Hollywood. In short, he admitted Paramount did not know how to produce talkies for Europe. What Paramount did generally, through the end of 1929, was to extract dialogue from their action pictures (those had a small amount of talk) and add subtitles. Kent acknowledged that movies which depended on dialogue and not action to tell their story were "unsuitable for offering to the foreign market."[18]

Most of the majors were equally mystified as to how to produce sound films for the non–English-speaking world. Dubbing did not work in 1929 or

1930 due to poor technology. Cutting the text material in on intertitle cards broke down the action if much explanatory text was needed. Musical films were popular since they needed a minimum of writing to keep audiences up to the story, as did action films such as Westerns. Songs in musicals were always left in English with no attempt made to translate them. For the Commerce Department, Canty reported that in Central Europe American movies "that combine song and dance with occasional sequences of the English language have found satisfactory appeal" unlike straight dialogue movies. Poland received talkies with the dialogue passages cut out completely and replaced with intertitles. That was the cheapest way to translate a film and was used for the less lucrative markets. In early 1931 that method was still in use in Egypt, using French intertitles to replace dialogue and having Arabic captions projected on a second screen. Superimposed subtitles were used in a few small markets such as Holland and Sweden. Observers found that method also worked best when there was a minimum of dialogue; otherwise they distracted the audience. Commerce noted that early attempts at dubbing "were all but laughed off the screen" because they sounded crude and were impossible to synchronize. Another method was to make the entire picture over with a new set of actors speaking in a different language. That method was the most expensive and was tried by most studios, but only a few times each. Obviously, that method was self-defeating since it negated the star system publicity machine. For example, using the same sets, the Spanish-speaking designates would come in and film, say, the Katharine Hepburn and Spencer Tracy roles; then the French designates would do the same. Thus the star vehicle would go overseas without the stars. One source put the cost of intertitling a foreign version of a silent film at about $2,500 while the foreign-language version of a talkie cost $30,000 to $50,000.[19]

One example of multiple-language shooting involved Laurel and Hardy, who in 1929 were making mostly shorts (two to three reels, 20 to 30 minutes running time) for the Hal Roach studio with MGM distributing. Roach supplied the comics with four separate supporting casts, filming with those foreign actors in French, Spanish, Italian and German. Laurel and Hardy wrote their lines on a blackboard out of camera range in their own phonetic approximation of the sounds spoken to them by a language coach. After the English version of a scene was shot, the other languages were done one by one. Roach reported, "The prices we got in South American countries and Spain were fantastic. A Laurel and Hardy short in the Argentine will be like a feature picture. They'd run some other picture with it, but the big attraction was the two-reel comedy." Ten shorts and one feature-length vehicle were made that way by the comedy team before the method was abandoned. While the method solidified the appeal of Laurel and Hardy and made good profits, it was dropped as it proved to be a time-consuming and complicated procedure, to say nothing of exhausting the comics.[20]

By the summer of 1930 journalist William Johnston reported there were 10,000 wired houses in North America with about 2,000 wired venues abroad. Wired houses showed almost exclusively U.S. films. Economic factors and national pride were at stake in the agitation against U.S. talkies, thought Johnston. "Take the matter alone of an international business language, with its important bearing on trade. What is the language to be?... Could there be a better advance agent of a language than this new promotive force?... Also concerned, and to a much greater extent in dollars and cents is the export trade of many important manufacturing industries in the United States." Johnston believed Europe was "slow on the trigger" in turning to sound, disregarding the enormous cost involved in the new technique. Half of the foreign wired houses were located in the U.K. Ninety percent of those were equipped with U.S. hardware. It was then believed that films could be made in only five languages (English, French, German, Spanish and Italian). Other language groups were not big enough or not rich enough. With some 31 languages spoken in Europe, speakers of the other 26 tongues "are going to be disturbed at having to hear another language upon their screen."[21]

Despite the hue and cry over American talkies in 1930, the U.S. exported 274 million feet of exposed film, slightly less than the 282 million feet in 1929 but more than the 222 million feet exported in 1928. By mid–1931 Europe (excluding Russia) had some 5,000 wired houses. A different source concluded that "sound has been more of a blessing to Hollywood than a threat."[22]

With the advent of sound, the costs of producing feature films jumped dramatically, doubling and tripling. Cinemas faced expenses in converting to sound, and so did the producers who needed new hardware. They also had to make all their film stages soundproof, or rebuild them completely. In the days of silent films, an airplane flying over a studio shooting an 1800s Western was not a problem. When that film was shot in sound, the airplane noise was indeed a problem. French producers Pathé and Gaumont both entered the sound field but in 1932 Gaumont went bankrupt. Two years later Pathé-Natan (they had earlier merged) capital was almost depleted. "[N]ot only were costs higher, but in addition distribution had become even more concentrated in American hands," observed a historian.[23]

Vienna, Austria, theater owners announced in May, 1930, they would boycott the further purchase of expensive U.S.–made sound apparatus, seeing it all as a plot by Hollywood to force talkies on them, necessitating the purchase of expensive hardware.[24] In Germany the quota system faced the threat of being killed because Germany was producing much less product than in the silent days, rendering the one for one law next to useless.[25]

During the brief period Hollywood remade films in foreign languages, *Variety* estimated the average film cost $250,000. From that was subtracted $115,000 in savable expenditures on the foreign version with the extra cost being 30 percent of the remaining $135,000—about $40,000—for each foreign-language version. Average return for a U.S. silent movie in France was $40,000. With the arrival of sound, enthused *Variety* "indications now are that the $200,000 mark can be easily reached with regular talkies."[26]

One thing the advent of sound did was to speed up industry self-regulation by making it more difficult, time-consuming and costly to modify prints after production was completed. This was one of many reasons Hollywood soon adopted more formally the Production Code which they more or less adhered to. Hollywood was less in the business of entertaining everybody than it was in attempting to offend no one.[27]

Language problems had mostly ceased by 1931 or 1932 when dubbing and subtitling provided the two standard solutions still used to this day. Technological advances had made them acceptable methods. Dubbing cost $20,000 compared to the $40,000 or so involved in shooting in a foreign language. Subtitling was the cheapest method by far, around $5,000. Less lucrative markets usually got a subtitled version while richer areas such as Europe normally received a dubbed version. A second reason for that difference was due to the strenuous hostility toward English on the screen, concentrated in Europe— prompting Italy's law, for example. Subtitling a film for Italy would not remove English from the screen, but dubbing did. Once the changeover to sound began, its timing was controlled and orchestrated around the world by Hollywood, through their control of distribution and exhibition, and their money. Although the Depression was underway, it was not allowed to derail the coming of sound to any extent. With Hollywood producing only talkies, cinemas had to convert and foreign studios had to produce talkies. Sound abroad was introduced from about 1929 to 1932. Although the Depression had some impact on U.S. exports, it did nothing to shake the domination of America, which remained as strong as ever. That period marked the last time there was anything amounting to widespread hope that U.S. domination of the world's screens could be broken. Hopes in so many nations that sound films would aid and foster a native film industry, which would decrease U.S. screen presence, proved baseless.[28]

4. One Film Suits All: 1930s

As the 1930s began, the cartel was in its final form which would dominate the world's screens up to the present. Worries about the coming of sound
had proved groundless, at least for the Hollywood majors who had plenty of
money to make the transition. Their domination, both domestic and foreign,
was unshaken. While the film industry did suffer somewhat economically in
the 1930s, it was due to the Depression and the industry suffered less than
many others. As the cartel solidified in both form and control, it changed both
the software and hardware to favor itself, in ways already mentioned. Each
change made it harder for independents to enter the industry. Those new,
large cinemas played on the fact that filmgoing was attractive to people for
reasons over and above seeing a particular movie, at least to some extent. Owners of large cinemas gravitated naturally to producers who churned out a steady
supply of highly visible product. Hollywood's majors naturally turned to huge
cinemas to screen their high-cost output. Another aspect of software was
altered in the 1930s: the short film died. (Serials continued to be run until
well after World War II.) As the film industry matured, films became longer
in length. Even superstars were forced to yield. During the early 1930s, Laurel
and Hardy sound shorts were tremendously successful with the comics being
known and loved around the globe. Both men felt their best work was done
in shorts, 20- to 30-minute films. Neither wanted to abandon that format for
feature-length films but were forced to do so. Hardy's biographer John McCabe
said the change was necessary because exhibitors were "asking for more and
more full-length films. It was the day of the double-feature and inevitably the
boys would have to accommodate to this need." Yet there is no evidence the
change was exhibitor-driven. From the point of view of the producers it was
a good idea since it was more costly for a newcomer to produce a film of at
least 60 minutes than it was to turn out a 20-minute effort. Competition was
again limited. Domestically the standard film program became two features,
an A and a B. Items such as the Bowery Boys films, the Blondie series and
innumerable Westerns were Bs which mostly ran in the 60–69-minute range
with the A feature in the 90-minute range. In addition, the program usually

contained a cartoon and a newsreel. However, the self-contained short film died in the 1930s. That domestic program remained unchanged until it was reworked in the 1950s due to the effects of television.[1]

Internationally Hollywood exerted the same type of control over program length and format. Mexican houses customarily showed four to five features, plus shorts, per program. In 1935 distributors and exhibitors "agreed" to limit programs to two features plus three shorts. That caused revenue to double for the distributors, not surprisingly, as admission prices were not lowered. Buenos Aires houses offered what was reportedly the longest film program in the world, screening around five features plus several shorts, all for the admission price of 25¢ U.S. The running time for such a program was seven to eight hours. It was the 1940s before all such long programs finally ended, replaced by a more standard U.S. format. Those changes, stated a Latin American film historian, "had been recommended by American distributors and fought by Argentine theater owners for a long time."[2]

By this time Wall Street had a large stake in Hollywood, resulting in the studio system being refined and honed into a conservative straitjacket. Any artistic impulses which emerged were relentlessly sought out and ruthlessly suppressed. What counted in filmmaking then were the aspects of photography, costumes and staging—elements of filmmaking which could be most standardized and controlled. Items such as a director's creativity and control were subordinated to the dictates of the producer's profit fixation. A British writer pointed out the financial interlock between General Electric Company, American Telephone and Telegraph Company, Western Electric Company and the majors, complaining, "If we must resign ourselves to the prospect of the world's film and broadcasting being controlled by a handful of men in the United States, it is at least desirable that the public should know the facts of the case ... because ... the ultimate issue is not merely control of entertainment but also control of propaganda." After the success of the first talkie, *The Jazz Singer*, Western Electric boosted its domestic installation charge for conversion to sound from $5,000 to $25,000 per house.[3]

Rockefeller money had been in Hollywood for some time in RKO; his Chase National Bank was into Fox. By the mid–1930s J. P. Morgan banking money—through AT&T, in turn through Western Electric—was invested in several of the major studios while Wall Street firms Dillon Read & Co. along with Lehman Brothers and Standard Capital were each tied in to one or more of the major studios. A. H. Giannini (later Bank of America) had a stake in a couple of the majors.[4]

A German commentator noted that the alignment of Hollywood with the electrical industry came with the condition that the majors would produce only sound pictures from then onward. That infusion of new capital went partly into production and partly into large advertising budgets needed to stimulate public interest. The German wrote, "American or Americanized talkies were to rule the theaters of Europe. Americans bought or financed European theaters, supported or controlled film companies." In this man's view, individuality represented a danger to the highly concentrated film industry. To neutralize such people, Hollywood's usual response was to make them harmless by buying them out. "The more the industry is concentrated under the sole management of Americans, the easier it will be for people who might raise the standard to be excluded. The purpose of the Americans is not to make as good films as possible. Their chief purpose is the organization itself," he concluded.[5]

Film Historian David Robinson described American films of the 1930s as "characterized by the bland, optimistic, essentially unreal and reactionary virtues its films overtly or more subtly preached." U.S. movies virtually disregarded the international political conflicts of the 1930s. While the Depression itself was not completely ignored, Hollywood responded by energetically asserting faith in the existing economic and social system. A film like *The House of Rothschild* was basically a promotional piece for the banking industry—then badly in need of a public relations boost. Between 1935 and 1938 the American box office was dominated by child star Shirley Temple who personified a banal faith in the future. She was supplanted as number one at the box office by another juvenile, Mickey Rooney, who ruled from 1939 to 1942.[6]

Given the state of Hollywood's worldwide domination, grandiose plans began to run through the minds of bankers and Will Hays. In 1930 Wall Street financial interests and bankers sent representatives abroad to try and create a worldwide alliance. "Internationalization of the film industry on a scale which will take in every important company in the world, besides some indies, all of whom will be shunted into one worldwide faction under American supervision, is the plan now being formulated in Wall Street by bankers," reported *Variety*. Fueling that effort was the worry that America could not produce as many talkies as silents—due to a lack of good ideas and good dialogue writers—while the demand for talkies was skyrocketing. Bankers hoped their plan would insure American control even if Hollywood itself faltered.[7]

At the same time Hays was quietly recruiting foreign film men to become members of the MPPDA. Before being asked to join, a name was discussed in cartel chambers to determine if he was acceptable. Most of those approached were flattered, seeing a chance to crack the U.S. market in which, said *Variety*, the national theater chains "have considered a bare handful of dates for foreign-mades over here." Another reason for Hays' plan was that he thought the MPPDA might have an easier time dealing with foreign governments if it had foreign members. Summarizing the plan, *Variety* wrote, "World dictatorship of films is revealed as the aim of the Hays organization. The network, to include the most aggressive of the foreign industry's representatives, is materializing." Actually, it was not. Nothing came of either Hays' plan or the bankers' vision. No foreigners were enrolled in the MPPDA. Perhaps the continuing U.S.

dominance put to rest any worries which Hays or the bankers had at that time.[8]

Criticism of American films continued from around the world in the 1930s. French missionaries in Africa issued a call to Catholic and Protestant churches to form their own film studio in order to produce moral and religious movies because American films had presented "the white man's crimes and love scenes to the detriment of the morals of the African people."[9]

A writer in a religious periodical stated, "One of the greatest handicaps to mission activities today is the factor of motion pictures. Due to their popularity, Hollywood films had in just a few years in the Far East done more to modify the ideas and conduct of the Orientals than missionaries have done through the past century.... Most missionaries agree that American movies are the great stumbling blocks hindering the advancement of the Kingdom of God.... If the Gospel of Jesus Christ is going to win its place among foreign peoples, especially the Orientals, a reform of motion pictures in the Western world is greatly needed."[10]

One U.S. journalist recapped foreign opposition to Hollywood output for the standard reasons of its portrayal or crime, wealth, false values and so on, arguing that "America must take the responsibility as well as the profits.... The international menace of American films must ultimately be met and overcome at home."[11]

With some U.S. films banned in foreign lands, Lancaster, Pennsylvania, clergyman Dr. Clifford Gray Twombley wondered if it meant "that America, instead of becoming the savior of the world, is becoming the debaucher and corrupter of the world?" Twombley cited as an example that the "infidel" nation of Turkey was aroused enough to ban kids under fifteen from attending the cinema. That fact amazed the *Literary Digest* because "we were wont to look upon Turkey as outside the pale of civilization." Episcopalian churchman Bishop Oldham thundered from his Albany, New York, pulpit one Sunday in an appeal for action against those who were "flooding America and the world with filth fit only for the corruption of morons." Hesketh Bell, former governor of Uganda and Northern Nigeria, was still in a lather because "nothing has done more to destroy the prestige of the white man among the colored races than these deplorable pictures."[12]

China implemented film censorship for the first time near the end of the 1920s when *Ben Hur* was barred on the grounds it glorified "Christian superstition." In the International Settlement area (the part of Shanghai controlled by whites), "The unwritten but tacitly accepted law of Settlement censorship is to prevent the showing of anything liable to jeopardize the status or interests of the white race." Reporter Wilbur Burton declared, "There can be no doubt ... that the cinema portrayal of western life has materially weakened 'white prestige.'"[13]

French author Jaques Deval had four of his novels filmed by Hollywood by the mid–1930s. He hated them all. In *Marie Galante*, the version destined for France had the title character do as she did in the novel while in the U.S. version Hollywood substituted a happy, sappy ending. Even though he watched the film in a French house, Deval complained about "this poor, wishy-washy and silly story, incomprehensible from beginning to end ... And my desolation was no greater than that of the other spectators."[14]

Cuba's government tried to get involved in controlling Hollywood by establishing an office in New York City in 1936 to censor American movies before they arrived in Cuba. No censorship was imposed on the pictures of other nations. Immediately the majors announced a boycott, vowing to ship no more films to Cuba. Officials in Havana received a protest against the action from that city's U.S. Embassy. Within a week or so, Cuba withdrew the censorship plan; the majors then immediately lifted their film boycott.[15]

Ral Garrachaga, Chancellor of the Argentine Consulate in San Francisco, went to Hollywood at the request of his government to urge Hollywood to send better films to his country since the Argentine government considered the product they were receiving contained plots "low in mental capacity, designed for infantile intellects and were poorly directed."[16]

When British censors asked Metro to make a few cuts in *Ah, Wilderness*, Metro refused, threatening to withdraw the film completely from the U.K. Censors then opened negotiations with Metro, resulting in the film being released in England in virtually the same form as it was in America.[17]

Censorship around the world was varied and idiosyncratic. Cruelty to animals was a strict taboo in England, Japan cut all kissing scenes, Sweden made cuts to scenes involving distortion in the portrayal of courts of justice, the Dutch East Indies had a list of some 30 no-nos, Denmark took out a scene from *The Awful Truth* because an actor appeared in his undershorts, Belgium banned kids under 16 from *Dodsworth*, Peru banned *A Tale of Two Cities*, Turkey axed religious scenes from the *Garden of Allah*, Panama banned *Armored Car* due to its gangster theme, South Africa embargoed *Sworn Enemy* for the same reason while Mexico banned *Lawless Rider* because a character depicted as a Mexican was kicked around and laughed at. American slang was often cut because it was not understood or because it had a different meaning abroad; Australia removed the word "bum" from the phrase "a bum leg." Normally the majors received notice of required changes, making them in Hollywood before shipping the movie abroad.[18]

Lashing out at general detractors of U.S. films, Hays called them "the uninformed, the malicious or those who wring a livelihood from derogation."[19]

When *Variety* tried to summarize the situation in 1937, the result was confusion. Noting that censors all over the world were clamping down on American films, the article then turned around to say "squawks are fewer." Most of the majors were said to do their own censoring with experts on each studio lot who knew "each foreign idiosyncrasy, weakness, prejudice, preference and tender spot." Another way of looking at the censorship, thought the newspaper, was that Hollywood's pre-release censorship promoted international good feeling because "precautions now are taken to avoid giving offense." Nonetheless, no matter how much Hollywood might bend to not offend foreigners, *Variety* soothed its readers by declaring Hollywood still produced output distinctly American. "They are still the subtlest and most efficient form of propaganda any nation has ever had at its command. They are still the best machinery for flooding the world with the idea that the American way of living is best, that this Republic with all its shortcomings is a garden spot in a world too full of woe."[20]

Despite the so-called experts on every lot, stereotypes of foreigners continued in American product. Latin America as seen in U.S. films, wrote *Nation* reporter Anthony Bower, "must seem a very odd place indeed—hopelessly addicted to the rumba, inhabited by swarthy gigolos and torrid women who reply to any question put by their virile visiting cousins with shrill cries of "Sí, sí." He suggested Hollywood produce pictures in which Latin Americans were treated as equals and "not as a sub-race with amusing foibles."[21]

One reason those studio experts were ineffectual was that keeping to a minimum material that might prove to be a stumbling block in international distribution was not their main job at all. Rather, noted one source, "In the early 1930s their primary function was handling studio publicity in dealing with representatives of the foreign press in Hollywood."[22]

Often Hollywood removed any specific tags in a film which would have identified the villain clearly as coming from a specific country, such as Mexico. However, the character would still be left dark, swarthy and wearing a sombrero—perhaps igniting protests from a larger number of nations. Historian Ruth Vasey pointed out, "The MPPDA's policy of clouding the origins of screen characters is clearly evident" while another observer exclaimed in 1934 that "the foreign villain—even the naturalized villain—is disappearing from the motion picture." Hollywood even attempted to use the power of creating ethnic villains against those who would deny it what it considered its due on that nation's screens. When Japan threatened to reduce the intake of U.S. movies late in the 1930s, U.S. negotiators warned the Japanese if that happened they might become the villains in American pictures. Explained the U.S. consulate, "Almost every plot must have a villain, and the American producers find it difficult to discover a nationality for such villains, encouraging violent opposition from any country of which the villain happens to be a national—an opposition which sometimes results in the exclusion or boycott of films with consequent financial losses…. Should the producing companies decide that some one country is determined to rule them out entirely so that resentment as to villains from that particular country would not diminish the financial returns of their films, they might consider it an opportunity." When Jack Warner wrote to producer Bryan Foy in 1939 (German and Italian markets were then rapidly closing down) to warn him about the dangers of offending the French, Chinese or Mexicans in his production, Warner added that "if we can't do business in Italy and Germany, that is another story, as they can't very well blackmail us."[23]

Often the foreign audience was blamed for the dross that showed up on its screens. One writer argued that the propaganda value of U.S. films, in tropical nations especially, was directly dependent upon the audience's capacity to follow the show; "This they cannot be induced even to attempt to do unless it contains a maximum of action of the violent variety that they prefer and appreciate. Finally, the worth of this action is entirely lost unless the 'right' and 'wrong' sides are clearly defined throughout by a noticeable difference in garb or some other simple trick." Added was the thought that "actions of criminals and nations that are horrific to us are a positive delight to many millions of people. It is thus useless to attempt to damn the villain by showing him indulging in wholesale butcheries. Such activity is heartily cheered throughout half the world."[24]

Writing in *Reader's Digest* in 1936, Meyer Levin claimed foreigners were responsible for war films. Arguing there was then a terrific sentiment in America against any kind of war, the U.S. nonetheless had to accept war propaganda in her films because her movies were made for the world market and other countries did not want antiwar films. "Americans, paying the heavy share of the moviemaker's income, would accept antiwar films. Foreign countries, paying the lighter share, dictate the policy," Levin concluded. Asking himself whether or not a producer could ignore the foreign market and make a film designed for America, Levin answered, "He probably could. But it wouldn't be as big a profit."[25]

MGM executive David Lewis, who was in charge of Cuba, rationalized the chauvinistic U.S. practice of sometimes sending films abroad *sans* foreign titles or dubbing. Lewis said Cuban audiences liked American films: "They disliked any dubbed sound effects and insist on the original product, with the stars speaking in their own voices. Usually Spanish subtitles are added to the film." Of course, that meant that sometimes no titles were added. When Hays' biographer Raymond Moley looked at the various restrictions imposed on U.S. films from the 1920s to 1938 he concluded, "With a few notable exceptions, the motion pictures made abroad were not comparable in drawing power to American films—subsidies, protection and quota legislation notwithstanding ... the public demand for American films continued to grow." One reason for that popularity growth was due in part to efforts of the Hays office "to convince foreign officials that the international exchange of films involved mutual advantages that go beyond the purely economic factors."[26]

When it came to producing a foreign version of that U.S. film that the entire world loved, what mattered most was cost, not audience needs or comfort. Hollywood's foreign departments were upset in the late 1930s by the amount of verbiage in their studios' output. Aside from the high expenditure involved in dubbing or titling pictures with a lot of dialogue, the executives worried the vast number of titles detracted from attention to the screen, "thereby hurting U.S. features." An average feature film then needed 800 to 1,200 titles with the most verbose pictures reaching as high as 1,500 titles. During the final part of the silent era, features averaged 140 to 170 intertitles, with a maximum up to about 200. If there was a tendency by Hollywood to reduce the number of titles, it was undercut because there were always people in the house who understood English and reacted to the dialogue. If no subtitles were provided, others in the house were annoyed. Grumbled film executives, "This superfluity of titles, caused by wordiness of screen vehicles, costs plenty and detracts from the effectiveness of the feature's pictorial art and plot development." Some foreign department executives lobbied their studios for more Westerns, outdoor epics and spectacles as a way around verbose talkers.[27]

Dubbing was more expensive than subtitling and was used only if a market justified the cost; in all other markets subtitles were used. Hollywood had its own ideas about what foreign audiences wanted, needed, liked, etc. Apparently they were generated in Hollywood by rich, white male executives as no foreign sources were cited. A piece of conventional wisdom had it that Latin America liked every bit of dialogue reproduced in titles while in Sweden and the Netherlands audiences wanted only the most "vital" dialogue. Thus, the same motion picture could have 1,200 titles in Latin America but only 300 in Sweden. This contradicts the idea that the number of titles could not be cut since there were always some audience members who understood English and reacted. One other point about wordy films was particularly cogent. Hollywood worried that so much English dialogue would poison the atmosphere, causing more agitation in the host country to erect barriers to curb the English language on the screen. Due to the chauvinistic delivery of U.S. films abroad with slipshod handling of subtitles and dubbing, foreign audiences may indeed have preferred Westerns, war films, spectacles and so on, simply because it was easier to follow the plot, not because they had some type of disposition to attend "simple" films as Hollywood so often rationalized.[28]

One response to all the foreign criticism was the hope that the entire world would adopt the Hays Code of film production. Under pressure from the Hays Office, the Canadian province of Quebec discarded its own censorship standards in 1931, adopting the Hays Code as its own. Quebec was chosen as the target for pressure by Hollywood because of its then–Roman Catholic Church-driven strict censorship in which a picture was accepted or rejected, with no changes or alterations allowed. Seen as a first victory in establishing American moral standards in films on other areas, the Quebec move caused *Variety* to enthuse, "That all government will eventually recognize in the Code a set of regulations that cannot be duplicated for general fairness, protection of public morals and at the same time preserve the entertaining qualities of showmanship, is the expectancy of leaders of American filmdom." Motion pictures "should possess one moral language and interpretation guide throughout the world." If the Hays Code was abided by throughout the world, "it will exert an influence to the benefit of all nations."[29]

Domestically that Code was often ignored in the early 1930s. The resulting and increasing pressure from lobbyists finally caused the cartel to adopt the Hays Code in 1934 in a more formal way, establishing Joseph Breen to oversee it. From then on the majors had to obtain a seal of approval from the Breen Administration if they wanted to exhibit a film domestically. Movies were often previewed before groups of religious and moral watchdog people in Hollywood—usually women—to insure that nothing controversial slipped past the studio's moral gatekeepers. With the Code more fully in place, Hollywood executives were even more annoyed with foreign criticism of American product on content grounds. In dealing smoke and mirrors to the public, they had convinced themselves they really were pure and wholesome. Hays was more hopeful in 1934 that the remainder of the world would adopt America's Code. It would mean "the world accepting better pictures as acknowledged by existent previewing groups on the Coast. Simplified, it means, if accepted, that Europe will suspend its own box office judgment for the recommendation of American women groups." Needless to say, the idea went nowhere.[30]

Studios continued to blithely ignore the Code in order to shoot double for a separate foreign version. One example was the previously mentioned adaptation of Deval's *Marie Galante*. Another was Mae West's *Belle of the Nineties* which was slated to go overseas as originally shot. It did not pass Hays Code muster, so a cleaned-up version was re-cut for the U.S. theaters. Usually the foreign version differed from the domestic release by being sexier. So prevalent did the practice of double shooting become that Hays stepped in to announce that all films abroad had to be shown in the same version as shown at home. Studios who violated the rule and screened films abroad without the Hays purity seal would be fined $25,000. When *Belle* eventually went abroad, it was the sanitized domestic version that was shipped.[31]

One type of double shooting was with respect to British notions of global white supremacy. Representations that were contrary to British requirements were covered by protection shots—special shots that could be inserted in the relevant prints. Central themes of the films needed to be consonant with an imperialist outlook but it was hardly likely American films deviated from that outlook. Given the state of race relations in America, it is hard to imagine a U.S. film giving offense by presenting blacks as equal beings, and so forth, since depiction of race relations in U.S. films had to first be acceptable within the limits acceptable to the southern U.S. states.[32]

Ownership and control of theaters continued as a major method of Hollywood domination. During 1931 MGM announced it would build a super-cinema in Johannesburg, South Africa, the first of a chain that was to extend throughout all large towns in that nation. MGM was reportedly not satisfied with the terms on which its product was bought for the South African market. After some delay MGM opened the Metro Theater in Johannesburg in November 1932. Holding 3,000 people, the venue was lavishly decorated, had thick carpets, copies of French Impressionist paintings on the walls and sumptuous cosmetic rooms. There was nothing like it anywhere in the city. Metro's "Mighty Wurlitzer" organ was said to have cost £15,000 alone. All of this was at the height of the Depression. Historian Thelma Gutsche wrote that "the cinema ingratiated itself into the affection of the public with as much effect as through the films it showed.... the public no longer had a discriminating interest in films and had become the acquiescent victims of the habit of 'going to the cinema,' regardless of its programs." Fox arrived in South Africa in 1938, causing a large chain of cinemas to be built. None of them were owned by Fox; a few were leased. Mostly Fox just organized local capital. One of the reasons a local might be given bank loans in his country was that he had a block booking agreement with, say, Fox, which guaranteed he would always have product to screen, at predetermined prices. Such people were, naturally, very much beholden to the Americans. From May 1938 to December 1939, Fox caused 40 cinemas to open; most were plush. Fox also concluded a 1938 agreement with UA to distribute the latter's films in those new houses (there was not enough Fox product to go around).[33]

MGM owned houses in such far-flung locales as Mexico City, Durban, Bombay, Brisbane, Sao Paulo, Rio de Janeiro, Montevideo, Santiago and Lima.[34]

Direct ownership of cinemas in Australia was not undertaken by Hollywood through the end of the 1920s. However, before 1930, as Australian film historian John Tulloch observed, "there was pressure from America on Australian companies to provide 'appropriate' cinemas for the Hollywood product"—those being large palatial venues. With block booking and appropriate houses there was little need for the majors to directly control houses. In Australia two large chains developed, Union Theaters and Hoyts, both of whom built appropriate houses. When the Depression arrived, Union was not financially ready to go to sound—RCA and Western Electric marketed their system in Australia. U.S. distributors cut off product and upped the rental rates to Union. During the battle played out over the following few years, Hoyts and Union merged to try and better withstand pressure from the majors, and out of financial need. However, by the time things settled down, Fox had bought a controlling interest in the Hoyt chain while Universal signed a deal with the merged entity—called General Theaters Corporation of Australasia—requiring it to guarantee exhibition of all films distributed by Universal. Within a few years MGM and Paramount followed Fox's lead as each acquired its own chain of first-run venues in Australia.[35]

Distribution control was another method of maintaining domination.

When distributors offered foreign films at attractive rates, exhibitors found it less attractive to screen their own nation's films. This antagonized native producers and distributors. Thus, the distributor drove a wedge between production and exhibition. In a nation like Brazil in the 1930s, money was scarce for many things, including film production. A native industry tried to establish itself by producing a lot of short material for domestic screens. Hollywood countered that by providing Brazilian exhibitors the by-then-standard newsreel which was found on most film programs, for free. Exhibitors had a choice between taking a free U.S. newsreel for the shorts' spot on the program or of paying money to rent a short film made by Brazilians.[36]

Attractive rental rates were not offered in countries which had no native industry nor one trying to emerge. In such instances, rental rates were decidedly unattractive. Danish and Swedish exhibitors held a meeting in 1930 at which they adopted a resolution threatening to take joint action against U.S. pictures if "ruinous" rental rates were not reduced. They claimed those rates had escalated to an "exorbitant" level with the advent of talkies. Since those films were in English and not understood by the vast majority of the audience, the exhibitors argued there was no increase in box office receipts to justify higher rentals (although not stated directly, the implication was that no subtitles were provided either). A year later the municipality of Copenhagen did a study which was said to have found a connection between U.S. distributors and virtually every Copenhagen cinema. During a city council debate on the domination, one councilor remarked, "The theaters are reduced to the position of trust-owned houses for the display of trust products. The trusts have even succeeded in obtaining representation on the committee of the Ministry of Justice for reorganizing the Danish cinema licensing system. Their smartness in business is to be more admired than their films."[37]

Canada held an inquiry into the film industry in 1930 under the Federal Combines Investigation Act, chaired by Peter White. Independent exhibitors had been complaining for years about being squeezed out of the market by U.S. domination. Virtually no Canadian films were being produced. Hearings were held behind closed doors for two months. Prior to UA's Canadian general manager Haskell Masters' appearance as a witness on behalf of the Cooper organization, UA counsel Edward T. Raferty instructed Masters not to take the stand until he received direct instructions from Raferty. At a Hays Office Law Committee meeting hurriedly called in New York, Raferty told them how an RKO branch manager in Canada had been "subjected to a grueling examination" by the inquiry with much of his testimony being "ill advised and badly handled." Raferty hired a Toronto law firm to prepare favorable witnesses and documents to show the independents were not treated unfairly. At the public part of the inquiry, White's general conclusion was that since at least 1926 a combine existed, naming as its members all the U.S. distributors, one Canadian distributor, Famous Players theater chain and the Cooper organization.

Regarding block and blind booking, White concluded those practices "prevail generally" in Canada and "by reason of the consequent overbuying ... and the showing of inferior pictures, the system of distribution by block booking and blind booking is decidedly detrimental to the public." White also found that Famous Players had a monopoly or dominant position in practically all Canadian cities and towns with over 10,000 in population.[38]

One witness was crown counsel R. H. Greer, who argued in favor of establishing a quota for British movies which was indicated since the American producers would prevent "so far as it is possible ... the showing of British pictures in their theaters as a regular part of their show."[39]

That inquiry opened the way for federal prosecution of the cited companies since combines were illegal in Canada. Commenting smugly on that fact was the New York Times which said, "But it is a long way from the opinion of a commissioner to the verdict of a jury." During the two years preceding the inquiry, White determined Canada produced almost no films with screen time being held by U.S. product 92.5 percent of the time. British product had the remaining 7.5 percent. Although a federal law was violated, for unclear reasons the case was tried as a provincial government lawsuit in Ontario. Due to rather vague laws and what one observer called weak prosecution by the state, the defendants were all found not guilty of restraining trade. The Ontario government did not appeal the decision nor did the federal government amend the law to give it more power to deal with monopolistic practices in the industry.[40]

Block booking was also being attacked domestically with bills being introduced into Congress on a regular basis to eliminate the practice in America. One of the first such efforts was a bill introduced by Senator Brookhart (S. 1003) on May 7, 1929. It was designed to make block and blind booking illegal as well as the control of theaters by producers and distributors. Ten years later, Fox president Sidney R. Smith testified before a Senate subcommittee to lobby against an antiblock booking bill then being considered. Perhaps to gain sympathy, Smith discussed Fox's foreign situation, complaining that a $1.25 million business had been "completely wiped out by the civil war" in Spain; that a lucrative business in China, built up after years of effort, had been "largely destroyed by the Japanese invasion"; that a former prosperous business in Japan had "wasted away to practically nothing"; and that Fox had recently been "forced" out of Italy by a state monopoly that proposed to buy Fox pictures "at practically nothing and keep the profit for itself."[41]

Publicity continued to play a large role as a driving force in Hollywood control. During the Depression and beyond, print journalism came to the fore. Before television arrived, over 400 journalists worked out of Hollywood where they both created and fueled the demand. Some, such as Louella Parsons and Hedda Hopper, became celebrities themselves. In Australia during the 1930s and 1940s firms such as Paramount, MGM, RKO and Hoyts Theaters sponsored regular radio programming of music and Hollywood gossip. Wrote historian Diane Collins, "Open an Australian newspaper or magazine in the 1930s and 1940s and there were beauty hints, short stories, fashion photos and studio news—all supplied gratis by companies like MGM." Such material could also be found in the publications of trade unions, charities and churches. An Anglican paper, the *Church Standard*, had photos of Hollywood starlets modeling clothes from their latest movies while the Catholic *Freeman's Journal* published articles on Hollywood's child stars, publicity stunts and happy marriages. Much of that material was channeled into mass circulation women's magazines; one of the most successful in Australia was *Women's Weekly*. In its 1933 premier issue was an article titled "Knit Yourself a Scarf Worn by Jeannette MacDonald."[42]

Combining the publicity and star machine was exemplified by the activities of Mary Pickford and Douglas Fairbanks (then married), who returned to the U.S. in 1930 after their seventh trip abroad as sort of goodwill ambassadors. Everywhere they went from London to Kyoto to Athens to Yugoslavia to Alexandria, they were said to have been moved by huge crowds of fans. Such junkets were paid for by the State Department. Said Pickford, "The cheering crowds of the Far East were shouting not for me but for the American motion picture and the American people and for the world of make-believe. Therefore I hold that, in a large sense, we were ambassadors, not only of the motion picture industry but of our own country." According to Pickford, all countries and all classes loved American movies.[43]

Talent poaching continued in the 1930s. That practice, observed one writer, "not only weakened their competitors, but also recruited the affections and loyalties of foreign populations." Speaking before the House of Representatives Naturalization Committee in 1937, MPPDA lawyer Gabriel L. Hess stated, "Some of the worldwide character and appeal of American motion pictures must be credited to the employment of foreign actors in American studios…. It is reasonable to assume that to a certain extent foreign markets have been created and held by the pride and interest of the people of a country in actors of their nationality who in pictures made in America become outstanding international screen personalities." To the committee Hess cited Greta Garbo, Charles Laughton and Maurice Chevalier. Others who could have been named included Marlene Dietrich, Charles Boyer, Sonja Henie and David Niven. Garbo was never overwhelmingly popular in America, depending on foreign markets to make her films profitable.[44]

Government/film industry relations remained strong and cozy in the 1930s. Julius Klein of the Commerce Department held meetings in Paris in 1930 with American commercial attachés from Germany, Switzerland, Belgium, Holland, Spain, France, Italy and Czechoslovakia to examine the foreign film market and prepare reports and recommendations for the industry, all at no direct cost to Hollywood. From those meetings came a consensus that the Continental market held great promise. U.S. producers were advised to limit languages to English, French and German as there were not enough wired houses in other nations to make enough money from other languages. It was also recommended that those films be produced not in foreign countries but in the U.S. That was due to a Commerce worry that legislation adverse to foreign production might be passed "overnight" in America—unions and others often complained about job losses and so on when Hollywood produced films outside of America. Klein's group concluded that "American interests should have a wider working participation in foreign houses which are properly equipped for talkies, those to be located in key European cities," Noting the higher costs involved in producing talkies had reduced European productions, Klein reported, "Because of this situation competition is weakened and the outcome is inferior quality native production which means poor entertainment."[45]

Some effects from the Depression did cause a scaleback of the Commerce's Motion Picture Division, which was merged back into the Specialties Division in July, 1933, for the purposes of economy. Former unit head C. J. North was dropped with his assistant Nathan D. Golden remaining on in charge of the smaller unit. Golden was based in Washington with George Canty being the unit's Berlin-based European representative. Illustrating the close ties between the cartel and Washington was the 1933 appointment by Will Hays of Fay Allport, a former U.S. commercial attaché in the Berlin embassy and other European cities, as MPPDA European representative, based first in Paris, then in London. Allport stayed in that post until 1957.[46]

Four years later the film unit was again upgraded to the Motion Picture Division, after lobbying by Herron. Commerce Secretary Roper announced its duties would include a more "intensive campaign" of assistance to U.S. films in the sale abroad of motion pictures and film hardware. Golden remained the unit's head. Roper stated that almost 40 percent of Hollywood's revenues came from abroad and "the indirect benefits to this country are of still greater importance." According to Bureau of Foreign and Domestic Commerce director Alexander Dye, "Goods shown in the American movies, such as American household articles, automobiles, industrial machinery, clothing and many other items, owe much of their popularity abroad to the fact that millions see them in our pictures."[47]

Hays regularly called on the government to take general action to favor the film industry. In 1934 he requested that the feds include motion pictures in forthcoming negotiations on tariff matters. During a 1937 lunch meeting with President Franklin Roosevelt at the White House, he told Roosevelt of the various restrictions imposed on American films abroad expressing the hope they would be eased. Hays publicly praised the State Department for its "very fine" attitude towards films and its assistance in many nations to bring down barriers.[48]

Despite all the government efforts to aid Hollywood, the *New York Times* groused in 1935 that it was not enough. Speaking of a specific dispute in which Spain barred Paramount's *The Devil Is a Woman*, and a few other such cases, the newspaper noted Hollywood was united in an effort to "compel Washington to give the picture business the same protection afforded steel, oil and similar industries." Hollywood planned to send an agent to Secretary of State Cordell Hull immediately "with stringent demands that the government take some action against the campaign being waged abroad against American pictures." According to this article, the producers felt "bitter" over supposed neglect by Washington, going so far as to criticize Hays for "a spineless attitude" in not making enough demands on the government. Ignoring all evidence, this *Times* report claimed that "little interest was given to the industry in the past" by the government. If this disinterest continued, warned the article, "within five years—ten at the most—England will dominate the world film market."[49]

The majors continued to complain from time to time that the government was not giving them enough aid. When Metro's film *Rasputin and the Empress* was banned in a few countries in 1934, MGM started an active campaign by Hollywood to get more government protection on film issues throughout the world. Feeling that American embassies and consulates around the world "are not cooperating sufficiently with picture companies or giving them the protection due American companies," MGM's attitude was that as soon as something such as a ban was imposed, U.S. government agents should take immediate and automatic action to reverse the restrictions since that film "being commercial property owned by an American concern, is being unjustly dealt with by a banning." Other producers such as Paramount agreed. When apprised of a restriction, the Hays Office took action, of course, but the majors felt they should not have to go there for help in the first place because "the aid ought to be forthcoming as a matter of course and automatically."[50]

One method used by foreign governments against Hollywood to try and stem the money drain out of their countries was by passing laws limiting the amount of money which could be remitted overseas. In 1930 Australia enacted such a rule, prohibiting foreign film distributors from sending money back to America. Accumulated capital was held in Australian banks to the credit of the distributors. Due to the Depression there was a shortage of local capital. The Australian government hoped Hollywood could be persuaded to invest the money locally. While money could not be exported, it could be invested locally in a variety of ways. Within a year similar laws were passed in Chile, Argentina, Colombia, Peru, Hungary and Germany. Exact dollar amounts embargoed were unknown but reportedly Fox had $1 million tied up in Australia after the law had been in effect for a year or so. Metro had shipped all its money out by exercising an option in Australia of paying the government a 20 percent tax. No such option existed in the other nations. Some distributors found ways around the embargoes—"frozen coin," as *Variety* called it. One company in South America paid cash to a U.S. oil company branch there for its native payroll. In return the oil concern head office in America turned over dollars to the studio in the U.S. Other such deals were individually arranged. Hollywood could not retaliate directly by holding back cash from foreign films screened in the U.S. because, as *Variety* noted, "On film payment alone America owes the rest of the world practically nothing throughout the year, whereas considerable amounts are incoming." Such restrictions were often short-lived with nations imposing the coin freeze quickly lifting them. During the 1930s it was not a major method used to try and contain Hollywood from bleeding too much money out of a country. It would be used to a greater extent at the end of World War II.[51]

Why did the cartel members continue to stay in countries where money was frozen, leaving the future of embargoed money in doubt? *Variety* thought it was because no profitable opportunity should be overlooked and, perhaps more cogently, "They believe the playing of their pictures in these countries means added popularity for American product and keeps the films of that particular nation from cutting into receipts in other foreign markets." In other words, it was important for the cartel to control the screens with their product, keeping native ones off and ultimately keep the native industry from emerging at all, even if the cartel's profits were meager or nonexistent.[52]

As in the 1920s, Europe was more successful in the 1930s in attempting to implement legislation to control Hollywood's domination whereas the financially weaker Latin American area was less successful. Every time a country there made an attempt at control, it was quickly hammered down. Mexico imposed regulations whereby a foreign distributor which released 50 or more films per year in Mexico was required to buy one Mexican picture for American distribution. Urging the MPPDA to intervene, Hollywood complained, "There are no films produced in Mexico of sufficiently good quality to compete in the American market and that this regulation simply means an additional tax on the moving picture industry, since the Mexican films could not be used." The majors also worried that the decree might establish a precedent to be followed by other Latin American nations. That regulation was quickly dropped.[53]

Changing tactics, Mexico then introduced a proposal in 1931 to levy a tax on foreign movies. Immediately the majors announced a boycott moving to ship no new product to Mexico. Internally exhibitors pressed the government to drop the proposal. After a boycott of several months, the Mexican government did abandon the tax idea. Years later, in 1938, unionized Mexican workers in the film industry demanded the government ban all foreign-made films or impose a duty so high it would accomplish the same thing. Government officials argued such a move would throw Mexicans out of work because there was no home product to fill the houses. Film workers wanted the ban to allow the development of home product. Approximately 85 to 90 percent of all motion pictures screened in Mexico then were American-made. In rejecting the demand, legislators told the workers they "must have foreign pictures, especially U.S. productions" due to the dearth of native product. Commenting on that defeat, *Variety* wondered if "it is only a temporary halt to the complete domination previously exercised by the union group." Given the U.S. screen dominance, what sort of dominance did the Mexicans exercise?[54]

Brazil's government imposed a new tax on imported foreign films in 1931. Theater owners protested this move, claiming many of them would be forced to shut down despite the fact those exhibitors had been hard hit "by the increased cost of the rental of American films ... Representatives of the American film interests in Brazil are aiding the exhibitors in their appeal for a reduction in duties." That new tax was dropped.[55]

A more modest attempt was made in 1934 when a new Brazilian decree required that all screenings which included a feature of over 1,000 meters in length, must include a national film with a minimum length of 100 meters (three to four minutes running time). Exhibitors opposed this measure also, arguing for free trade and free enterprise but also asking for a price ceiling on what they would have to pay for exhibiting national films. Theater owners did not mention they received free U.S. newsreels.[56]

Despite the fact that an estimated 80 percent of Brazilians were illiterate and the population had "low spending power," Hollywood estimated that in 1934 the distributors' share of film revenues was $3 to $3.5 million with $2.6 million of that going to America. Admission prices ranged from 29¢ at the best first-run houses down to 6½¢ at subsequent-run venues. Distributors received from 30 to 50 percent of the gross. While dubbing in Portuguese had been tried briefly at the start of the 1930s, it was quickly abandoned as educated Brazilians had a "preference" for English dialogue. Films went there with subtitles which tended to rule out pictures with a lot of dialogue and certain comedy such as the Marx Brothers "whose humor cannot be translated." Fortunately for Hollywood, Brazilians "preferred" musicals and action features. Some 75 percent of features screened in Brazil were American. Eight U.S. producers had offices in Rio de Janeiro with most also having branches in Sao Paulo and other cities. The only other foreign producer with an office in Brazil was Germany's UFA—by then subsidized by the German government.[57]

Argentina's government raised the tax on imported films almost twentyfold in 1931 when the old tax of $2 per kilo was increased to $37.50 per kilo. Native film interests praised the move, noting it would help the home industry, but cautioned that the tax "is only apparently damaging several importers, who will meet the new condition by making prints locally." If a studio sent ten positive prints of a film to a country, it normally struck them at home.

Each print would have been taxed separately. However, if the studio sent a negative print into a country—where ten positives would be struck locally—the Argentine tax would have been levied just once, on the entering negative. Hollywood, of course, preferred to strike prints at home. Nevertheless the majors were outraged. Threatening a boycott, the majors gave Argentina a one-month period to adopt a "reasonable attitude." Prior to the expiry of that period, the majors canceled all newspaper ads for their then-screening product. Papers responded by refusing to make any textual reference to any film, such as local reviews or Hollywood-supplied gossip items. Acting reasonably, Argentina dropped its increased tax before the month was up.[58]

In 1936 about 85 percent of all motion pictures screened in Latin America were U.S.–produced; that figure dropped to around 70 percent in 1939 due to a slight increase from Europe (to end soon with the war) but mostly from an increase in native production. Paramount South American distribution executive John L. Day warned in 1937 that increased native production in Argentina and Brazil was "imperiling the Hollywood product." Some 25 films would be made in those countries in the coming year and they were "popular outside the big cities, where American films still dominate." Complaining about Brazil limiting the showing of many pictures to adults—thus almost wiping out the matinee trade—Day commented, "Appeals to the United States Embassy are frequent, but the State Department has not often been successful in annulling such rulings."[59]

Toward the end of the 1930s when the U.S. government adopted a Good Neighbor Policy designed to expand and consolidate their economic, political and cultural ties with Latin American nations, the *New York Times* reported, "No major industry in the United States has plumped more suddenly and completely" for its objectives than Hollywood. Driving that government policy was a general erosion of the European market with war just around the corner.[60]

If Hollywood's Latin share was declining slightly, it was the result of the product shipped in. Many of the films supposedly made with Latin audiences in mind, infuriated the spectators. *Viva Villa* (MGM, 1934) portrayed the Mexican hero Pancho Villa as a blood-thirsty bandit, while in *Juarez* (Warner Bros., 1939) the Emperor Maximillian became the film's hero rather than the Mexican-Indian president. In addition, critics were irate that Hollywood regarded all nations south of the Rio Grande as basically the same with the same customs, habits and so forth. *Time* magazine observed that "Hollywood could never make the kind of picture that Latinos enjoy most." An example cited was the Argentine film *Petroleo* (Oil) which did big box office business throughout the area. Its villain was a Yankee imperialist who arrived in Argentina to do the natives out of their oil wells. However, he was defeated in his efforts by the locals.[61]

Hollywood insisted that all the majors issue standing orders to their story departments to keep a special watch for material with special appeal to Latin America. This was part of a greater concentration in that area in the late 1930s as war loomed over Europe, threatening to shut that market down. However, one story department executive confided to a reporter that he had no success in finding such Latin material. Perhaps that was because, said *Variety*, "they don't know exactly what they are looking for."[62]

Early in 1939 *New York Times* reporter Robert Sherwood described Argentineans as "naturally" anti–Nazi but also suspicious of U.S. businessmen. When he asked an American Embassy employee in Buenos Aires what the U.S. was doing to counter Nazi propaganda flowing into Argentina, the official pointed to a movie marquee playing a Loretta Young film, explaining, "That's our greatest weapon." According to him, the three Americans who had accomplished wonders by visiting Argentina were President Roosevelt, Secretary of State Cordell Hull and Tyrone Power.[63]

Assessing the South American market in general that same year, *Variety* found a few things to worry about—at a time when U.S. penetration was at least 70 percent. One was the people were too poor to pay out as much money as Hollywood expected. Another was that a greater show of interest by the majors in the region developed a belief in Latin American nations that U.S. distributors relied so heavily on them for revenue that exhibitors might be emboldened to try and extract concessions. At least some exhibitors requested all–Spanish films. Trying to keep certain exhibitors happy led a major or two on occasion to "buying up a lot of inferior Spanish product to augment their English stuff." (Those requests would involve a U.S. distributor buying up the rights to, say, one Mexican film, two Chilean films, one Argentinean effort, and so forth, then releasing them all throughout Latin America.) Despite those requests, most majors refused to even buy cheap Spanish product because "if they're unable to market their regular line of features, it is better to shelve what is left over than to establish a competitive line."[64]

Japan was the only nation in the 1930s that tried to deal with American domination with a cartel of its own. Two huge integrated Japanese-owned film companies, Toho and Shochiku, came to their own agreement to divide up foreign distributors. Thus Paramount, RKO, Warner, Columbia and Universal were, said *Variety*, "the vassals of the Toho chain" while Fox, MGM and United Artists "dance to the tune of Shochiku buyers." Painting the U.S. cartel as virtually impotent, the trade publication wailed, "Because the representatives of the American producers here never seem to be able to get together when their interests are threatened, there is little likelihood that they will be able to do anything to break the present combo against them." MGM tried an end run around the system by attempting to build its own house in downtown Tokyo, only to be denied the necessary police permit. Of course, the majors were making a profit in Japan although it may not have been as high as they would have liked. For the U.S. majors, getting everything they demanded and reaching a compromise were one and the same thing. Rather hysterically, *Variety* titled its report "Japs Ganging up on U.S." None of it would matter in the near future as the Japanese government finally shut the market to U.S. movies due to the coming world war.[65]

Yet just three years before the above report, *Variety* pointed out that in 1933 Japan produced 55 features against 271 imports, of which 247 were American. It was observed that "some of them were pretty bad ... plenty of dogs wished on the public." It was in response to such a situation that Japan responded with a strengthened cartel of its own.[66]

Everywhere, it seemed, viewing American films was a learning experience. Dr. Bernard Dodge, president of Syria's Beirut University, declared, "Hollywood is the intellectual center of the world, in the minds of Syrians and their neighbors in Asia Minor." Those people, he added, "do not wholly trust the European powers, and when seeking to learn more about modern life they turn to America, knowing that we have no 'imperialistic designs in the Near East.'"[67]

A 1934 report by Wilbur Burton about China claimed it was not from missionaries, gunboats or businessmen that the Chinese learned about the West but "it is from the cinema ... particularly the United States" films. With theaters mainly only in the largest cities and expensive admission prices, estimates were that the cinema was available to only about 20 percent of the population By the mid–1930s, nearly all the majors had offices in Shanghai and in other cities. Almost the entire U.S. annual output of some 300 features were screened in China. That country produced just 67 films in 1933, and all but 14 were silent. Old American silents were still being screened in many places while U.S. talkies were regularly exhibited in the interior in unwired venues, effectively rendering them silent movies. Films generally showed up in China three to six months after their U.S. release. During 1934, American films were 78 percent of those screened, Japanese 10 percent, Chinese 8.5 percent, British 2.5 percent, all others 1 percent.[68]

Burton remarked in 1934 that almost all U.S. releases in China had no Chinese subtitles, but that a printed program was handed out to patrons. Annoyed about that fact, the Chinese government, after lobbying by locals, passed a regulation effective July 1, 1933, requiring all talkies to carry Chinese subtitles. Conferring with the government, MPPDA representatives got officials to postpone implementation of the law indefinitely, although it was not removed from the books. Hollywood argued that for the amount of business it did in China it could not afford to add subtitles—at a cost of $500 in a Hollywood lab for the average feature. Had the government not relented, the majors threatened a full boycott. A 1937 report from China observed that U.S. films there carried "no titles." Mid-1930s costs of importing a U.S. movie into China consisted solely of about $800 in customs duties for an average-length feature and $200 to $300 for censorship charges in Shanghai. Burton noted, "The business is very profitable, at least for the Americans."[69]

Australia's state of New South Wales (NSW) held an inquiry into the film industry in 1934. Witnesses testified that U.S. distributors combined to control film prices to exhibitors. Those allegations were denied by the Americans who argued that each distributor fixed his own prices. Union Theaters executive Stuart F. Doyle told how his company had been pressured in 1927 and 1928 to raise extra capital in order to build more plush cinemas for the screening of American product. Union yielded to the pressure, doing as required by the Americans. But from that debt, the Depression, the cost of conversion to sound and from the continued demand by U.S. distributors for rental rates higher than the exhibitor felt it could afford, Union eventually went bankrupt, Doyle explained.[70]

The only significant recommendation from that inquiry was that quota legislation be enacted. In October 1935, NSW put into force a quota for distributors and exhibitors with the former required to "acquire" a minimum of 5 percent of their inventory from U.K. production in the first year rising to 15 percent in the fifteenth year of the quota. Just over a year later only three Australian films had been completed. Citizens were not investing in film production; the state gave no aid. Worded in a fuzzy and vague fashion, the quota act seemed to say that if an insufficient number of pictures were made locally to fill the quota, then foreign distributors had to produce in NSW to make up the difference. U.S. distributors had no intention of producing locally unless forced to by the government—which did nothing. Distributors insisted the word "acquire" did not compel them to produce to meet any shortfall. *Variety* commented that the quota was ignored by everyone.[71]

NSW government officials took a harder public stance early in 1937 by informing the distributors they had to honor the quota's provisions even if it was necessary to undertake production in Australia to meet its terms. First, though, the government announced it would ignore the quota and its violations for 1936. Under the act, distributors had to carry an inventory of 7.5 percent in 1937. RKO foreign head Phil Reisman, who was in Australia on a general visit at the time of the announcement, set off a storm when he declared that RKO would not produce films in Australia no matter what. Financially the market was not worth it, Reisman explained, stressing that all the majors were with him on those points. In fact, the cartel did take a unified stand, threatening a complete walkout from the country if the law was not changed. American distributors at the time usually sent in a negative print—the necessary number of positives being struck in Australia—in order to pay customs on just one print, lowering their expenses. Regarding the financial situation of the Australian film market at the time, the *New York Times* reported that "American exporters of films to Australia are more advantageously placed than almost any other foreign manufacturer." Local producers wanted taxes levied on each copy of the print circulating in Australia.[72]

Despite the government rhetoric, nothing happened with the quota.

Native producers agitated for legislation to enforce the quota. As a compromise NSW dropped the quota percentages to 3 percent for distributors and 2.5 percent for exhibitors. Local producers agreed to the reduction because they believed the government would actually enforce it. Both of them believed the U.S. majors would abide by it. No sooner was the ink dry than the distributors announced they would ignore the quota. Instead they challenged the quota law in court, claiming it was unconstitutional with only the federal government having the power to set a quota. One observer felt a quota would be upheld or installed at some level if for no other reason than as a backlash because politicians were "so aroused by alleged high-handed methods used by certain U.S. distributors" to fight the law. World War II ended that particular wrangle with no final decision. Film historian Ina Bertrand noted the first NSW quota lapsed into ineffectiveness "because of the determined efforts of the foreign importers of films against participating in any manner with Australian producers." As to the 3 percent quota rule, she wrote it was "made with the foreign importers of films apparent agreement, but the moment it became law they instituted what might be termed as a sit-down strike, claiming that the legislation was 'unconstitutional.'" The result was that measures by Parliament and the efforts of local producers were both nullified because they found it impossible "against the constant propaganda issued by the foreign importers to influence public capital into the production of Australian films. Apart from the strong propaganda which has been used so consistently by the foreign importers of films against the possibility of making films in Australia has come the repeated assertions that Australians do not want to see pictures made in their own country." Ironically, the U.S. firms had a supply of cheaply made U.K. product which had been produced or bought to meet the British quota law. While much of that material was unscreenable, some could have been imported to Australia to meet that quota—films produced anywhere in the British Dominions were regarded as home product. Yet the majors did not consider that as a tactic for the cartel was not prepared to withstand any competition if at all possible, no matter how small nor of what quality. For the majors, in the ideal world every screen should show a U.S. film every moment it was in use.[73]

While Canada's federal officials had determined they would introduce no film quota laws, individual provinces did make some efforts of their own. Ontario in 1931, British Columbia in 1932 and Alberta in 1933 each attempted to implement quotas for the exhibition and distribution of British Empire motion pictures. None of the bills were ever implemented with strong lobbying by the MPDE (the Cooper organization) playing a major role in all the demises. Although rejecting the idea of a quota, federal Canadian authorities did propose imposing a 13 percent tax in the 1930s on the gross rentals of foreign films. Intense lobbying followed with that idea being dropped. With war in the offing early in 1939 it was reintroduced as a 5 percent tax. This time the U.S. cartel accepted it with minimal protest.[74]

Canada went so far as to lead a general British Empire fight against the general concept of quotas. At the Imperial Economic Conference held in Canada in 1932 (attended by representatives from Empire nations), delegates refused to recommend quotas for exhibiting U.K. films in the Dominion nations, or raising such quotas where they already existed. Reportedly Canada led that fight. Instead delegates recommended perhaps a small tax might be imposed by nations on foreign (non–U.K.) films entering their nations. Nonetheless, even that was left up to individual nations. Not surprisingly, the Americans were happy, with the *New York Times* declaring the main reason for refusing to endorse quotas was the "superiority" of U.S. pictures. Another factor of importance cited was "that most of the talented British actors had allied themselves with Hollywood, leaving little for the United Kingdom to offer in competition." In other words, they had been poached.[75]

While the majors operated in unison as a cartel, they could not abide it when others did the same. For a number of years in Canada the majors had imposed their Standard Exhibition Contract (used in the U.S.) on Canadian exhibitors. It contained a clause prohibiting exhibitors from uniting together into booking combinations—which would have increased the power of the independents. The majors had long refused to sell anything to exhibitors attempting to combine. Under the contract, house owners who violated the contract in any way were put on a blacklist with distributors instructed not to sell films to them. That Standard Contract was held illegal under the Sherman Anti-Trust Act in 1930 by the U.S. Supreme Court as being in restraint of trade.[76]

Europe was the area with the biggest financial market for American films; it was there that the fiercest battles were fought in the 1930s. In March 1932, Yugoslavia imposed a quota law requiring foreign concerns to either produce there or to buy 70 meters of native product for every 1,000 meters of film imported—rising to 150 meters per 1,000 in January 1934. Of the 250 movies imported annually into Yugoslavia, 170 were American-made. The cartel announced it would withdraw from the nation unless the law was rescinded. U.S. government officials made representation against the measures "which are regarded by American interests as confiscatory." Yugoslavian cinema owners joined in to protest the rules. When the government failed to back down, Paramount and MGM closed their offices in Belgrade in May, dismissing their employees. A full boycott was then in effect with no films from any majors being shipped in.[77]

Toward the end of 1932, unidentified Yugoslavian film executives reportedly asked the cartel to return, promising to try and get the quota rescinded at the next legislative setting. That offer was flatly rejected with the U.S. insisting changes had to occur before they would return. All the while exhibitors continued to oppose the quota. Negotiations for the cartel were carried out by George Canty, Commerce's film executive stationed in Europe for just such occasions. He made several trips to Belgrade "to straighten things out." Around March 1933, the Yugoslav government capitulated by removing the quota completely. By then about 200 U.S. films were piled up and "ready to go."[78]

Czechoslovakia imposed a quota plan in 1933 whereby for every four movies imported, one Czech film had to be produced. Acting in usual fashion, the cartel walked out of the country, imposing a boycott. One year later the Czechs offered a compromise by proposing a seven-to-one quota—rejected by the cartel. Negotiations, done by Canty with apparently no MPPDA agents on the scene, took two years. Canty thought he had a deal at around the 18-month mark when representatives of two of the majors got in touch with the Czech government on their own, indicating they were beginning to weaken. That threw negotiations off course for a time. When Canty finally struck a deal in January 1935, he dutifully cabled the news to the Hays Office in Washington. Under the terms of the pact there were no restrictions at all on the import of U.S. movies except for a "registration fee" on each foreign film imported, an unstated amount which had not then been worked out.[79]

Belgium was almost ready in 1935 to pass a law barring all dubbed films except those dubbed in Belgium. Local actors testified in favor of the proposal while the majors argued they could not make a profit if forced to adhere to such a law. American producers already made one dubbed French version in France (due to that nation's law) and did not want to do another. French-speaking parts of Belgium received that French-dubbed version while the Flemish-speaking areas received only the English-language release. American producers argued it would cost them $10,000 to dub an average film in Belgium, against their average take of $6,500 per film. Belgians declared films could be dubbed there for $2,000. That proposed law was not enacted.[80]

As different European nations imposed various restrictions, some gross overreactions appeared in the domestic press. One unnamed major studio foreign department head said they were seriously thinking of shutting down all of Europe. It was not a case of threatening the area, he explained, "It's a matter of defending property." He added that U.S. producers were spending a good deal of money on the European market but making "very little profit out of the market." *Business Week* reported in 1937 that for the first ten months of that fiscal year 171 million feet of film had been exported, a gain of 9 million feet over the corresponding period in 1936. Then noting the restrictions and closing markets in Europe, the report concluded, "It serves to illustrate what the wave of nationalism has done to this one-time American monopoly." Note the past tense used here. That conclusion was drawn despite the increase in film exports noted in the same short article by that reporter.[81]

Germany altered its contingent laws in 1930, effectively limiting the number of U.S. films allowed to enter to about 90 with most of the dubbing required to be done in Germany. Soon after Hitler took power the Nazis ordered all Jews to be fired from the majors' German branches. Movies were also barred from that nation on a case-by-case basis, one reason being the presence of a Jewish star. While 205 U.S. pictures entered Germany in 1928, the number was 97 in 1930, 59 in 1932 and down to just 30 in 1936 under the various Nazi restrictions. Despite all the problems for the majors, an August 1935 report in the *New York Times* described the importing of American films into Germany as a "remunerative transaction."[82]

Perhaps that explained why the majors remained friendly with the Nazis for so long. Around 1936 MGM chief Louis Mayer met with George Gyssling, Nazi consul-general in Los Angeles, to discuss how best certain films with an anti–German slant might be presented to the Nazi government without giving offense. As late as 1938 MGM maintained its Berlin offices with an Aryan staff, years after Hitler ordered such companies to fire their Jewish employees. According to biographer Charles Higham, Mayer authorized the supply of personal prints of MGM movies to both Hitler and Mussolini with the practice not being discontinued until the outset of war in Europe and then "only because the dictators will fail to return the prints." Many of the films Hitler saw and enjoyed privately were officially banned in Germany by Joseph Goebbels. Despite the constant efforts of Douglas Miller, commercial attaché to the U.S. Berlin embassy, from 1936 it had been almost impossible to make "open market" arrangements for exhibiting U.S. movies in Germany. This resulted in Warner, Universal, RKO and Columbia closing down their German offices. However, MGM, Paramount and Fox all kept their branches open through 1938 or 1939.[83]

When MGM contract actress Myrna Loy visited Amsterdam in June 1939, a studio representative warned her she was far too outspoken in her public criticizing of Hitler and his treatment of the Jews. On her return to Hollywood, Loy received a note from MGM's Arthur Loew advising her not to mix politics with her career as Loew had substantial investments in Germany. Years later Loy wrote in her memoirs, "Oh Lord, this still makes me so mad I could spit. Here I was fighting for the Jews and they're telling me to lay off because there's still money to be made in Germany."[84]

When Hitler's favorite filmmaker, Leni Riefenstahl, visited the U.S. to publicize her film of the 1936 Berlin Olympic Games, she arrived in Hollywood in November 1936, not long after the pogrom known as Kristallnacht. She wanted to meet Mayer at the MGM studio but he declined at the last minute, suggesting instead he meet her at her hotel. Viewing that as a snub, Riefenstahl declined. Will Hays agreed to meet her but canceled at the last minute. All but hard-core Nazi supporters shunned her in America. One who did not was Walt Disney, who gave her a personal three-hour tour of his studio. Reportedly he told her he would love to run her film but since projectionists were strongly unionized it might provoke a strike resulting in his product being boycotted by theater chains. Later Disney claimed he did not know who Riefenstahl was when he gave her the tour.[85]

Mayer hosted a July 1939 luncheon at MGM for 200 film executives, stars and other personnel in honor of Dr. Frank Buchman, founder of the Oxford Group, also known as the Moral Rearmament Movement. That event was attacked by the left as Buchman was considered pro–Nazi with his group said to contain considerable anti–Semitic sentiment. Hays introduced Buchman. Gyssling gave a party in Beverly Hills in April 1940 for Hitler's personal representative, the SS general Charles, Duke of Saxe-Coburg-Gotha. Among the guests were Gary Cooper, Walt Disney, Mr. and Mrs. Randolph Hearst, Will Hays and ambassadors from friendly nations such as Argentina, Italy and Chile.[86]

During Italy's first golden age of film from 1910 to 1920, it was a leading film exporter. From 1925 to 1930 Italy produced only 16 to 17 movies per year. Although it passed a law in 1927 requiring all first-run houses to reserve one day in ten for home product—which would have required domestic production of fifty films per year—by the early 1930s Italian motion picture production was still stagnant at about 17 per year. America was then supplying 60 percent of Italy's film imports, taking 90 percent of the foreign gross. Around 1933 Italian dictator Benito Mussolini started to make noises about clamping down on U.S. film domination. A *New York Times* reporter fretted that if put into effect, "big American companies, owing to the state of isolation in which they have hitherto purposely remained, are in danger of being excluded from the Italian market altogether." Another concern from the reporter was for the exhibitor as audiences would have to dwindle in the face of a loss of U.S. movies since they were "recognized as the best in the world." Restrictions were brought in slowly with a cap placed on the number of foreign movies allowed in as well as an edict that only dubbed foreign product was allowed to be exhibited with the dubbing to be done in Italy.[87]

Relenting a little in 1936 on the no-original-language picture rule, Mussolini allowed one house in Rome to screen foreign pictures in the original language, but only to a select audience. To be admitted, one needed a pass from the government which was given to foreign journalists, diplomats, scientists and so forth, but not to the average Italian. That pass allowed the bearer to buy a ticket at the door. Admission costs were twice the normal rate. Passes were fairly easy to obtain if you had connections or looked like a foreigner. That ban on foreign languages on the screen was originally imposed so Italians would not be corrupted by hearing alien tongues.[88]

Things got worse for the majors later in 1936 when Italy imposed a new law which allowed U.S. firms to take only 25 percent of their revenue out of Italy with the remaining 75 percent frozen where it could be used only in Italy in a manner approved by the Italian government. It meant, for example, the majors could not buy Italian bonds with the frozen coin, then sell them outside the country. Nazi Germany then had similar rules in effect except the frozen money could be spent within the country any way the majors wished.

The law was seen as an attempt by Italy to force the majors to produce pictures in Italy—something the government wanted but the majors had no intention of doing. Acting in concert, the majors announced a boycott of Italy, shipping in no more product. Receipts for the cartel amounted to 40 to 50 million lire annually with the new law limiting export of that capital to about 10 to 12 million lire yearly.[89]

Not surprisingly, those moves by Mussolini brought a quick response from the cartel and the U.S. government, besides the boycott. Secretary of State Hull sent an anguished letter on the subject to William Phillips, his ambassador in Rome. Phillips lodged a formal protest with the Italian government. Hays phoned the State Department demanding action, then traveled to Rome with MPPDA executive Harold Smith and met with Italian Foreign Minister Ciano. By himself Hays met for over an hour with Mussolini, and later met with Pope Pius XI. Also involved was the commercial attaché of the Rome U.S. embassy. Within a month or so an agreement was reached. Hays declined to release the details of the accord, leaving it to State. Phillips declared the majors received "all the demands made by American producers and distributors." More money was allowed to be exported; the frozen portion could be used in Italy any way the Americans wanted and the quota on the admission of U.S. films was raised from 49 to 250. Since the majors had been shipping something less than 250 movies into Italy in pre-quota times, the limit of 250 did not distress them.[90]

Regarding those negotiations, Hays' biographer wrote, "It will readily be seen that the cooperation of the United States government officials stood the industry in good stead ... they were prepared to go out of their way to be helpful." Louis Mayer's biographer described the process by writing, "The State Department was involved to the hilt; then, as always, it was the servant of the film industry."[91]

Hal Roach and Vittorio Mussolini (Benito's son) had formed a company called RAM (Roach and Mussolini) to make five films based on grand opera to be released by MGM. At the time, commented an observer, "it was not uncommon for American business leaders, including the heads of movie studios, to express an unabashed admiration for Mussolini." He was admired for his efficiency, considered a bulwark against Communism and he had not then taken a strong line against Jews. Mussolini made a triumphant visit to Hitler in Berlin in October 1936. Soon thereafter Vittorio arrived in Beverly Hills where he was a Hal Roach house guest. Jewish citizens protested, threatening to boycott RAM and Roach/MGM (MGM distributed all Roach product). Celebrities such as Fredric March and James Cagney agitated for the expulsion of the dictator's son. However, wrote Mayer's biographer, "a handful of right-wing, profascist Hollywood figures received the young Mussolini. These included Walt Disney, Gary Cooper, Winifred Sheehan, Will Hays and William Randolph Hearst." Shortly after Vittorio left town, Mayer canceled the RAM deal.[92]

Late in 1938 the Italian government established a complete monopoly over motion picture distribution. Films were to be distributed solely on a flat rental rate instead of on a percentage basis, under terms dictated by the Italian government. That caused a complete walkout by the majors. Prior to that law the majors had worked their way up to about 75 to 80 percent of Italian screen time. Wrote Hays' biographer, "The American companies, unable to operate under such regimentation, were forced to close up shop in Italy." Initially Italian exhibitors feared they would not be able to compensate for the loss of American movies, that people deprived of Gary Cooper and Clark Gable would desert the theaters and that local production would not take up the slack. However, they were relieved to find that neither was the case. As one historian reported, "Domestic output quickly took up the slack, and after several months of uncertainty audience attendance picked up again, demonstrating that by the late '30s the moviegoing habit had become stronger than allegiance to any single star or style. This habit certainly opened up opportunities for domestic products, especially for all kinds of Hollywood imitations." Attendance in Italy increased from 348 million in 1938 to 477 million in 1942 while domestic motion picture output rose to 83 in 1940 and to 119 in 1942.[93]

The situation in France in mid–1931 was greeted with enthusiasm by Hollywood because for the fiscal year 1932 the government had no restrictions placed on the import of U.S. movies, except for internal censorship which had never been a burden in the past to Hollywood. Also cause for celebration was the fact "the American film industry has won its case purely on the merits of its arguments, no quid pro quo entering into the arrangement." In the negotiations leading to that free entry, "the Will Hays organization and the United States government officials have closely cooperated."[94]

Such joy was short-lived as the French government announced in 1932 that no more than 200 foreign movies would be allowed into the country in the coming fiscal year with 125 of those being direct-shot French-language while the other 75 would be allowed in for local dubbing. The cartel worried that Germany would be emboldened by the French move to take similar action of their own. Acting as cheerleader, *Variety* urged that "showdown time has now been reached. U.S. companies must make immediate arrangements to start activity on this side [Paris] or give up the fight." English-language pictures were allowed but limited to a maximum of five houses in Paris and a total of five more in all the rest of France. U.S. producers complained that the requirement to dub in France was "a heavy blow." With more than a little exaggeration, MPPDA executive Harold Smith complained about the French moves by saying to the press, "No such limitation on international commerce has ever been instituted before.... The American film industry hopes Congress will take into consideration these unfair and unjust limitations on their business in France whenever the matter of regulations of imports of French products into the United States is considered. It is apparent that, unless Congress realizes the unfair handicaps placed upon American business abroad and reacts accordingly, sooner or later American trade abroad will be completely anni-hilated." Both State and Commerce were contacted by the MPPDA and told to "get cracking." French film personnel, except for exhibitors, had been a strong lobbying force in favor of the new rules.[95]

French exhibitors protested every step taken against U.S. movies. That, plus pressure from the U.S. government caused the decree to be largely ignored with over 100 dubbed U.S. films being released in France. Additionally, the limit on English-language houses was not heeded. For fiscal 1934, French officials announced 140 dubbed films would be admitted which, commented *Variety*, was "a considerable victory for American producers ... Not likely that American films will be hurt at all." During the six months prior to that announcement, 65 U.S. movies were dubbed inside France. During fiscal 1933 the majors had released about 150 English-language features in France. All of that may have been applauded by exhibitors but frustrated native producers called for a total ban on American film imports for a set period of time in both 1933 and 1934.[96]

France's official film body, the Chambre Syndicale—not connected with the government but considered influential—also recommended legislation to virtually ban all U.S. films from the market for three months. They also wanted to see the customs duty increased from $300 on an average length feature up to $16,666. That organization contained as members all producers and dis-tributors in France. The four U.S. firms still members (Paramount, Univer-sal, Fox and UA) resigned in the face of the proposal; the other majors had resigned earlier for other reasons.[97]

Nothing came from that proposal. As usual the cartel and the U.S. gov-ernment lobbied strongly against it. That caused an unbylined *Variety* reporter who had apparently paid no attention to film history to write, "For the first time the government intervened on behalf of Hollywood producers and made representations against the suggested restrictive program." That active sup-port was described as marking a change in policy on the part of the State Department, by coming openly to the aid of film exporters.[98]

During the furor over U.S. domination in 1934, much of France sided with the exhibitors including Paris paper makers and ink manufacturers. Actors who dubbed in French studios joined the protest against restrictions on U.S. product. Telegrams from the provinces complained that families would go to the poorhouse if cinemas had to shut due to lack of product. Even many French parliamentary deputies lined up with the exhibitors although it appeared to be an unpatriotic stance. It all caused *Variety* to comment, "The Americans, by lining up the exhibs, got French opinion on their side and are turning out to be better patriots than lots of the French themselves."[99]

This is not to say that the French scene lacked some critics of U.S. pic-tures, besides native producers. The aforementioned author Jaques Deval slammed them in newspapers, arguing that America was "hermetically and disdainfully" closed to French films and therefore France should not submit to "pitiful" American movies. French author and critic Georges Duhamel warned that his country and the whole of Europe would be "Americanized" with "the conscious or unconscious propaganda spread through the exhibition of American films" being a danger to French youth. He believed that industrially the French considered America a nation "which merely looks upon the rest of the world as so much territory for commerce of all kinds, including the commerce of films. It has no consideration for the tastes of other countries, and does not modify its exportation product, excepting when and where it finds itself checked in business." It simply tried to force the goods in. As to the question of foreign films in general, "one is not obliged, in the interests of progress, to accept them." Although the French might admire U.S. films for settings, photography and technique, however, thought Duhamel, rarely did they admire them for their "story quality or intellectual value."[100]

Some parliamentary deputies tried to push a tax bill through their legislature which would have reduced taxes only for those cinemas which presented a minimum number of French films (to be set later). However, because of "active lobbying by the American interests and their French friends," the effort failed. In June 1935, French officials announced no new restrictions, a move called by one source "just about the best break American films have had in France for some years." In fact there were no restrictions at all on the number of imported films except the number of dubbed films that could be shown in France was held to 188 movies, a number "which has shown itself to be ample for American distrib purposes."[101]

Just a few months later the French seemed to have a change of heart. Proposals were made to require exhibitors to screen 30 percent local product. That prompted Hollywood to send a quick SOS to the State Department. France's commerce ministry was seen by the Americans as willing to help U.S. movies while ministries concerned with the arts were the ones infected with "the bug of protecting French culture from invasion." Frederick Herron of the MPPDA went to Paris to personally apply pressure. Hollywood particularly disliked theater quotas. Pressure from Herron and State succeeded in killing the proposal.[102]

When a rumor circulated in 1935 that the French would clamp down on foreign films by creating a national agency that would collect all film rentals from exhibitors due the majors and take a slice off the top to be used to subsidize native production, American muscle swung into action again to insure it did not happen. "The idea of a national agency has been advanced several times before, but American interests, aided by French producers and exhibitors, have always successfully opposed its adoption," reported the *New York Times*.[103]

During another worrisome period in France in 1937, Harold Smith of the Hays organization presented the American position before a French Parliament film commission. Smith contended the French industry benefited to the extent of $10,000 for every American film released in France. Curiously, Smith provided no details as to how that "benefit" was generated.[104]

Early in 1939 French lawmakers tried again to do something when a new bill proposed limiting the length of a film program to 10,500 feet, effectively reducing the standard two-feature bill to one feature (the U.S. then had a virtual monopoly on first features in two-feature programs). Of the 400 films released then yearly in France, 275 were American-made. Because of a general trade agreement between the two nations which did not allow physical restrictions on goods, France was somewhat hamstrung in trying to come up with effective restrictions which did not violate that trade accord. As with previous proposals, the film length idea was quickly quashed. Just before war began officially, the quota on dubbed films remained set at 188 annually—America got 150 of them, plus unlimited import of English-language product.[105]

Britain's quota act, in effect from 1928, remained the subject of controversy throughout the 1930s. One U.S. reporter complained in 1930 that due to the exhibitor quota, the British exhibitor was compelled "to show a heavy percentage of British pictures" and that "the British exhibitor has had to show miles of British film." At that time the quota was around 10 percent; exemptions were also granted to cinemas claiming a lack of British product, almost as a matter of course upon application.[106]

A major criticism of the legislation was that in order to meet the quotas, Hollywood turned out cheap and execrable films in Britain (quota quickies) to meet the requirements. Writing in the *Spectator*, U.K. journalist Basil Wright noted it was vitally necessary to protect and subsidize a national film industry; however, certain U.S. firms solved their quota problem "by forming subsidiary English companies and turning out bad films, hastily made, and costing sometimes no more than five or six thousand pounds. The results, in any but the most unscrupulous view, were disastrous."[107]

An editorial in the *Times* of London observed that U.S. producers made quota quickies, then put them on the shelf or rented them to exhibitors as a means of meeting the latter's quota obligations. In that case the rent charged was nominal; "in fact, the 'quota quickies' have been practically given away to smooth the negotiations for the hire of the foreign films in which the renters are really interested." That kept the British independent product off the screen. Thomas Pryor wrote in the *New York Times* that in order to comply with the quota obligations, Hollywood "shopped around," buying or producing movies costing around $10,000; the majority of these films were stored in vaults and forgotten.[108]

Exhibitors in Britain agitated in 1930–31 over what they regarded as excessively high rental charges levied on them by the cartel. Two hundred cinemas had recently gone bankrupt due to those high charges, they claimed. U.S.

interests then owned about 25 percent of British houses. Additionally, British producers complained cinemas booked "junk" British films from the majors in preference to independent native productions. American spokesmen responded by saying buying junk meant that financially they could just scrape by. Said *Variety*, "If an American firm doesn't get all the cheap quota pictures it needs, it makes 'em itself."[109]

Despite the difficulties, many observers considered the quota act a success. In 1927, 723 U.S. features were distributed in Britain, 40 British; for the years 1928 to 1931 those figures were, respectively 558, 95; 495, 87; 519, 142; 470, 139. Basil Wright, despite his criticisms, concluded, "In general, however, the Act achieved its purpose, and the film industry in England is now of considerable size and importance." Financially though, the U.S. did not suffer. One estimate was that between 1935 and 1939 Hollywood's British revenue totaled some $50 million. After deducting a maximum of $15 million in British expenditures, remittances back to America were $35 to $40 million. With that quota act due to expire in 1938, negotiations got underway in a serious fashion in 1936, when the exhibitor quota was at 20 percent—though exemptions were still next to automatic for houses which sought them.[110]

At the 20 percent quota on both exhibitors and distributors in 1936, and with roughly 500 U.S. films released annually, the market required 125 British films for the quota. Yet only about half of that number were considered bookable with the rest "practically all quota junk ... the bulk comprising a complete waste of celluloid." Cinemas defaulting on the quota—those not formally applying for an exemption—were said to be at an all-time high in 1936 (hundreds of venues). Usually the Board of Trade turned a blind eye to defaulters, rarely proceeding against any of them. Two lobby groups, the Cinematograph Exhibitors Association and the Kinematograph Renters Society (KRS), joined forces to lobby the Board of Trade for a new quota act requiring a maximum of 10 or 15 percent screening of local product. "K.R.S. with its strong American interests had the arguments nicely its own way, without overdoing it." At the same time the Cinematograph group presented a petition to the prime minister and other politicians that "all possible steps should be taken to prevent the acquisition of control of more British cinemas by foreign interests now or in the future." Understandably, K.R.S. did not join in that activity.[111]

In its final report the Board of Trade recommended the new act should incorporate new quotas of 20 percent for distributors and 15 percent for exhibitors at the start of the period, moving up to 50 percent for both groups over a ten-year period. During British film industry infighting—usually producers versus exhibitors—over terms of the new quota act, the *Times* of London noted of the inability to control U.S. domination, "A fundamental factor is the chronic inability of the various interests to combine in the face of economic peril; most of the leaders of the industry in Britain seem bent on making it as difficult as possible for the government to help them." While the *Times* was against the

1928 quota law, it favored government help of some kind for the industry, but it did not know what. Later, an editorial in that paper declared, "The fact must be faced that the American hegemony has been achieved by superior merit." Britain's Trade Union Congress demanded the government get tough. Labor leader Tom O'Brien said, "Film is the ambassador of trade and we cannot allow a trade of this magnitude, of this cultural and educational importance, to come under foreign domination."[112]

During debate on the situation, British Consul in New York, J.E.M. Carvell, noted that Hollywood evaded a substantial amount of British income tax on their profits by reclassifying some earnings as royalties. He also described the K.R.S. as a camouflaged branch of the MPPDA.[113]

Early in 1938 the new film bill became effective with distributors facing a quota of 15 percent that first year moving to 20 percent in the second year (12.5 percent for exhibitors the first year). Britain hoped it had solved the quota quickie problem by introducing a minimum amount of money which had to be spent on a film in order for it to qualify—£15,000, $75,000. Many had agitated for a quality test instead of a quantity one but they were defeated. As Basil Wright noted on the minimum cost of a quota film, on one side were big renters who controlled a large proportion of the cinemas along with the big producers which included most of the U.S. interests. On the other side were the independent producers and small exhibitors who argued that a minimum cost might actually help the big concerns since no provision was made for a quality film made for a lesser sum by independent producers. Wright observed, "The British film industry has hitherto shown a regrettable lack of cooperation, both internally and in its relations with the State."[114]

One of the other provisions allowed the majors to satisfy the quota law by buying American distribution rights to a British film instead of making a movie there. At the last minute the House of Lords rejected harsher measures in the act. When Lord Moyne complained bitterly about reduced quotas, Lord Swinton explained the government was not opposed to additional restrictions out of "excessive tenderness" for exhibitors or distributors but because the British industry would lose a chance to distribute movies in America "if we are unreasonable about this bill."[115]

During those 1937–38 negotiations, *Variety* complained Hollywood was getting "little help" from the State Department in dealing with the prospect of tighter British quotas. Yet Mayer's biographer Charles Higham reported that pressure on London came "from MGM's reliable servant, U.S. Secretary of State Cordell Hull, resulting in a slacking of demands" while Hays' biographer Raymond Moley observed that the Hays Office had the cooperation of two sympathetic U.S. ambassadors, Robert W. Bingham and his successor Joseph P. Kennedy. Moley concluded, "The State Department in Washington continued to render all possible and proper assistance." With the coming of war, the new quota act became largely meaningless.[116]

Yet another source noted that the MPAA lobbied furiously through State to defeat the quotas. Kennedy met with the Board of Trade president to argue on behalf of the cartel. Additionally, "Some accounts contend that the Americans threatened to sink a bilateral trade agreement then underway, extracting concessions in the form of lower quotas."[117]

Despite restrictions aimed at reducing the domination of U.S. films in various nations, the effects were not great. In an analysis of the European market in 1933, *Variety* concluded that contingent laws against film imports in Europe "generally defeat their own purpose." Yet it did admit France's home industry had made some gains while Germany's had not. Over the five-year period from 1928 to 1932 the total number of features released in France had dropped 14 percent; for all nonnative films the drop was 30 percent while native releases increased 39 percent. In Germany the number of films distributed dropped 56 percent. The number of nonnative releases dropped 70 percent while the number of German releases also dropped, but only 37 percent. The number of releases dropped in both nations due to the Depression, more in Germany from the added economic effects of losing World War I and the resultant economic chaos. U.S. films were dominant in all nations except Germany—which was first in its own land—and German-speaking Austria. Generally though, with the exception of Germany, no other nation had an important market abroad. In almost every case the only competition the U.S. got in a nation was from that nation itself. For example, Britain released only three features (out of 302) in Spain in 1932; Italy released only four films (out of 259) in Austria; France released seven (out of 639, including shorts) in England while Germany released 18 in England.[118]

Hollywood's output of film during 1935 cost producers $120 million. Approximately $100 million of that was spent by the eight majors, bringing in about $650 million from the box office; the average movie cost about $285,000. Fox produced about 50 films per year in the 1930s. For 1935 they spent a total of $17 million in negative costs (average of $364,000 per film). Domestic rentals (U.S. and Anglo-Canada) totaled $23 million with foreign rental (all other nations plus Franco-Canada) totaling $11 million. In 1938 Fox's negative costs were $25.8 million ($497,000 per film), bringing in $30.9 million domestically, $14.1 million internationally. Other costs were involved, of course, such as promotion, print striking and distribution. Other profits occurred as well as, for example, when studios owned theaters. Hollywood's accounting was more creative than its films since on each production Fox added an overhead figure of about 35 percent to the negative costs to pay for studio personnel not directly involved in making films—from studio executives to general staff to maintenance personnel. Rather than write off a maintenance person's salary of say, $2,000, it was written off as part of the 35 percent surcharge. Since a $1 million film did not necessarily take three times as much time and effort as a $333,000 movie, those fixed cost figures had a high probability of being written off at a higher amount than the actual cost incurred. Thus the $2,000 maintenance salary could be written off at a much higher level, making profits seem smaller than they really were. As well a studio sometimes charged itself exorbitant sums through individual departments covering everything from music to special effects to sound to costumes.[119]

According to Warner executive Sam Morris, the only countries to receive all Warner product in the late 1930s were Britain and Australia while the rest of the world received about 40 percent of the Warners' regular yearly output. Morris thought that typical of the foreign business done by the majors. It seemed that "the most consistent criterion for the extent of a movie's distribution was its cost. Expensive 'prestige' films had to find global acceptance to make a profit, whereas routine program pictures did not have to be shown everywhere to make their money back, and consequently had to make fewer concessions to foreign sensibilities."[120]

Reporting on the year 1936, the Commerce Department stated that despite all the foreign restrictions the year "brought to American film producers the highest foreign revenue since the introduction of sound." Europe made 721 movies that year (Britain 217, Germany 130, France 125, Russia 92, Spain 32, Sweden 27, Czechoslovakia 26 and Hungary 20). Another nearly 700 were produced in other nations while America produced 500 to 600.[121]

Around that time one estimate was that the domestic market (U.S. and Canada) provided the majors with 60 percent of their revenue, foreign contributed 40 percent. Of the foreign take Britain contributed 45 percent, the rest of Europe 25 percent, Australasia 12 percent, Latin America 11 percent, Far East 5 percent, all others 2 percent. Given that Canada contributed some 5 percent, the real domestic/foreign split was 55/45. Foreign trade was dear to the hearts of producers because, said the *New York Times*, "the revenue derived from it can in most cases be counted as clear profit." Profits were not quite that perfect but they were very high. Australia imported 400 American films in 1937, grossing the majors about $10 million ($25,000 per film). Expenses totaled $5.6 million, leaving a net (dollars remitted) of $4.4 million or as *Variety* described it, a net per film of "only about $10,000."[122]

An earlier report in *Variety* estimated that in the 1930–31 period, foreign gross may have represented as low as 20 to 25 percent of the world total gross, as compared to the silent era when internationally gross receipts represented around 40 percent of the world total.[123]

Exports of U.S. films were 215 million feet (200 million feet were sound positives) in 1937, up from 209 million feet in 1936. Commerce Motion Picture Division head Nathan Golden remarked that American movies played in more than 80 countries averaging over 70 percent of the world's screen time (excluding the U.S.), up to 95 percent in some nations. While worried about the various tariffs, quotas and other restrictions existing in some areas, Golden was optimistic due to "the lack of success on the part of foreign countries trying to artificially stimulate their own production." He believed that foreigners in some countries, desiring good movies, might "revolt against the screen propaganda they are being served and thus force a removal of some of the obstacles keeping American films out of their houses." Citing the British quota, Golden observed that Britain produced 225 features in 1937, of which only a handful received world distribution; "ordinarily they were not of the type enjoyed by the motion picture public of the world. Seemingly, they were not even enjoyed by the British public."[124]

One year later Golden reported worriedly that U.S. dominance of the world's screens was off 5 percent, down to 65 percent in 1938. He advised Hollywood to produce Spanish-language films in Hollywood to target Latin America. Thus producers could keep costs to a minimum and have "Spanish-language films available to carry their American product, which is now being frequently shoved into the background by Spanish-speaking productions from Mexico and the Argentine." Penetration in Peru dropped from 70 percent in 1937 to 49 percent in 1938 mainly because of "augmented numbers of Spanish-dialogue pictures from Mexico, Argentina and Peru itself." Even though none of these movies "approached the quality and standard" of American pictures, said Golden, they did consume playing time which might have been America's.[125]

Variety stated in 1938 that U.S. film producers' revenue was about $1 billion domestically (U.S. and Canada), $800 to $900 million foreign, making the split 55/45 in favor of the domestic take. The importance of the foreign market in relation to the total market, said the paper, "is the reason every move to trim income in this field is closely combated." About 27 percent of the world gross (55 percent of the foreign) came from the British Empire. While business still held up in China and Japan, despite the Sino-Japanese War, the Japanese coin remained frozen.[126]

Hollywood producer Walter Wanger had an article published in the prestigious *Foreign Affairs* journal titled "120,000 American Ambassadors." That number came from the fact that Hollywood turned out about 600 films per year with each of those circulated abroad with 200 prints, hence 120,000. Speaking of government assistance in restriction fights, Wanger commented, "The American government has failed to give support, or at least has given ineffectual support, against foreign discriminations and trade barriers set up especially to restrict or stop the distribution of American films. This is a natural extension into the foreign field of the industry's domestic policy of surrendering to almost any sort of objection, criticism or threat." He felt foreign nations would have probably banned U.S. pictures completely "except for the embarrassing fact that the Hollywood product is better." Grudgingly, he did admit the government had made official representation to foreign governments from time to time. "But they must have been fairly mild, because the foreign market has continued to shrink in spite of them…. It seems to me a reasonable contention that the United States government has given inadequate or at least ineffectual support to the motion picture industry in its fight against the discrimination and trade barriers set up by foreign governments." Regarding censorship efforts both at home and abroad, Wanger thought Hollywood yielded to all such criticism; "As a result, not merely have Americans been forced to see on the screen the least common denominator of what the least broad-minded groups at home will approve, but in recent years what is left after the political panics, power ambitions and internal terrors of a dozen foreign nations have done their work. Foreign nations have been dictating American screen policy and stifling what free speech had been left after the incursions of domestic pressure groups and censors." If that were all true, how could the U.S. product be the best quality, as Wanger contended? Urging the industry to fight back, Wanger suggested that any country which restricted American movies "should be met by the immediate and concerted withdrawal of all American film service. That will hurt the offending nation's business revenue from theaters and government revenue from taxes worse than it will hurt us."[127]

Continuing the fictional theme that somehow Hollywood was at the mercy of foreigners, the *New York Times* reported at the beginning of 1939, as some foreign markets shut down, Hollywood was considering topics which they would not have done in the past so as not to offend a foreign customer. Yet there was a dilemma in that the majors could not do those topics because those nations could open up in the future. Costs for making a film were so high that no studio wanted to risk offending anyone for fear of revenue loss. Films costing in excess of $250,000 were reported to "stand little chance of making money in the American market alone." When the report asked itself the obvious question "Couldn't movies be made under that budget?" the *Times* stated flatly, "It cannot be done." Summing it up was the comment, "Producers have always maintained an international outlook. They have always been sensitive about the subject matter of films."[128]

America's domination in world film continued throughout the 1930s with perhaps a slight drop near the end of that period which came about as nations prepared for war. The chauvinistic disregard for Latin Americans left room and a desire for more indigenous product. However, the U.S. control of distribution, exhibition control through ownership to a slight degree and block booking everywhere and the U.S. publicity machine prevented much of an indigenous emergence. Germany and Italy both squeezed out the majors with both developing strong native industries. Both nations demonstrated that countries could get along without American films dominating their screens. This was also true in Japan. Only Germany managed to carve out a bit of a presence in other nations. Nonetheless, America dominated going into World War II and they dominated coming out of World War II. What little competition was trying to emerge (Germany, Italy, Britain and France) once again found themselves smashed, broke and back almost to square one at war's end. Hollywood had nothing to fear from the war but they did not know that in 1939. They were worried.

5. Another War, Another Opportunity: 1939–1945

America's share of world screen time was hardly challenged by the end of the 1930s. If a little had been lost, it was too early to tell if it represented a normal statistical variation or a permanent trend. However, Japan, Italy and Germany were all in the process of virtually closing down their markets to U.S. films; control of the home market was a first and necessary step before a serious export business could occur. In spite of a lack of U.S. product, they all developed a native industry which drew an audience. Germany was the only one with anything approaching a presence in other nations in the late 1930s. During the U.S. fight with the Czechs in the mid–1930s, a deal had almost been struck whereby the U.S. would accept a 12-to-1 quota (12 American films in for each Czech production) with an alternative of a $6,000 fee per film for admission with an unlimited number allowed in. Germany offered a better deal of a 5-to-1 quota or $8,000 per picture to a limit of 180 per year. Ultimately the U.S. prevailed on even better terms but it indicated what might be expected in the future: competition. In Latin America, little native product came forward but what did was usually well received. Any tendencies emerging by the end of the 1930s which could have threatened U.S. hegemonic control were quickly derailed by the war; U.S. control would be maintained. In the beginning of the conflict, however, Hollywood worried a great deal. Later on, the always helpful State Department, along with the armed forces, would restructure the Axis film industries in a way more favorable to Hollywood.[1]

Just prior to the onset of war there were 58 countries that in one way or another were gunning for Hollywood—10 in the British Commonwealth, 11 in Latin America, 26 in Europe, 6 in the Far East and 5 in the Near East—through such measures as state film monopoly, import restrictions and quotas, limitations on distribution of dubbed films (11 nations required the dubbing to be done within their borders), import licenses, preferential tariffs and so forth. Within America the Justice Department had commenced legal action against the cartel for restraint of trade under the Sherman anti-trust act. It would be over a decade later before that action would be resolved. Currency restrictions of some type were then in place in about 20 countries.[2]

Within days of the declaration of war, Paramount's vice president John W. Hicks lamented, "This is the biggest problem the film industry has ever faced." UA vice president Arthur W. Kelly felt that Britain and France would remain good markets, after a period of adjustment, adding a proviso that the "only upset to such calculations would be complete bombardment of all key cities in Great Britain." Reportedly foreign revenue amounted to 33 percent of the majors' total take late in 1939 with half that total (17 percent) coming from the belligerent nations, chiefly Britain, France and Poland. Italy was then written off while in September 1939 MGM, Fox and Paramount were the only majors maintaining skeleton operations in Germany. Both Germany and later Japan would soon be written off by the majors. Some insiders feared a loss of up to 50 percent in business in the belligerent nations; that was a loss of half of 17 percent which, some worried, would cause Hollywood's revenue to drop 8 to 9 percent in total.[3]

Within a month, panic gave way to cooler heads as *Variety* and unnamed government economists found a brighter side; "Blowoff in Europe may not be such a pain as the film industry now fears." As the nations which provided the U.S. with what little competition it faced were fighting, "the American industry would be able to build up its foreign trade in neutral nations, particularly South America." Film men were then plotting strategy "to make hay to the maximum extent." In particular Germany could devote little time to its Latin American business. Even in the belligerent theater, hope was found because "as the war settles down to routine, the restrictions on theaters are bound to be loosened." Additionally, all those soldiers in the trenches, in camps and civilians in general would be clamoring for diversions. If the war settled in for a "long run" with the U.S. staying out, "the American industry ought to tighten its grab on screen time around the globe." One potential trouble area was that more currency restrictions might be thrown up by nations wanting to keep their money to buy munitions.[4]

Calm gave way to fear again as the Nazi overruns of areas were often computed out to a specific dollar loss for Hollywood. The German absorption of Czechoslovakia was "expected to hamper the American motion picture business," concluded the *New York Times*, who noted the Czechs had generated $3 million annually for Hollywood. "The new situation gives German film companies an opportunity to expand and entrench themselves against any efforts by American distributors to cultivate these markets," fretted the newspaper.[5]

When the Soviet Union overran Finland, it was "an additional blow to the diminished foreign market." *Variety* worried that "it will mean another market handed over to the Red film monopoly, with American product treated the same as in the Soviet Union, which furnishes no revenue to the U.S. distributors excepting on single-product deals about once every seven years." After the Nazis overran Belgium and the Netherlands, the speedy *New York Times* reported one week later that that situation cost Hollywood another $2.5 million yearly.[6]

France fell to Germany much more quickly than anyone had expected. Cartel members brooded it could mean a complete blackout in Europe because that latest Nazi victory was seen "as representing a threat to the highly profitable market in Great Britain." Only an early peace "would help remedy a dismal outlook for overseas distributors"; a Nazi invasion of Britain "would badly damage all business on the British Isles." *Variety* found a ray of hope in that sudden fall of France as it meant less physical destruction of the nation than would have occurred in a protracted battle; "not many theaters have been damaged, and there is hope for normal restoration of business."[7]

As the war spread to the Pacific, the *New York Times* tallied up a loss to Hollywood, just days after Pearl Harbor, of $6 million yearly, detailing it at $1 million from China, $1.25 to $1.5 million from the Dutch East Indies, $1.75 to $2 million from the Philippines, $1.25 million from Singapore and $500,000 from Hawaii. (Japan's market had closed previously.)[8]

If Hollywood needed comfort during its early war fears, it could look north to Canada. In 1940 the U.S. Embassy in Ottawa submitted its annual report on the film situation to State in Washington. U.S. embassies in certain countries were required to do so. That report noted there were no Canadian facilities for feature film production "but such production is economically impossible in the case of feature pictures and there is not a national impulse to produce pictures in Canada, such as is found in some countries." Also pointed out in that report was that "United States influence is predominant among Canadian film distributors. It is similarly predominant among exhibitors who own and operate the theaters." Also sending a dispatch was the U.S. consul at Winnipeg who reported American films were more popular than British movies with people on the Canadian prairie because prairie people "are like Americans in their tastes, ideas and mode of life, and what the Americans like they like."[9]

More fractious in their willingness to accept U.S. movies were the Latin Americans, partly due to the disdain with which Hollywood treated them. Honduras banned all foreign films over two years old because too many extremely old ones were turning up in the theaters. MGM announced it would dub some of its films into Spanish (in New York) for Latin Americans because of a growing demand for such product and so spectators would "not have to squint in following the superimposed titles."[10]

Those pictures may have been old but the majors went to great effort to get them around. Train schedules to the interior of such Central American nations as Honduras, Nicaragua, Guatemala and Costa Rica did not permit frequent enough changes of the program so, in the case of Paramount, "peons are dispatched through the bush to take the features in on their backs. One man can carry a normal picture and a program of shorts."[11]

To woo the Latin Americans, Hollywood made a series of films, mostly musicals, set south of the Rio Grande, with disastrous results. *Down Argentine Way* was hissed off South American screens. Other such films featured Carmen Miranda in ludicrous outfits. Latin beauty was represented by Rita Hayworth in *You Were Never Lovelier* while the Ritz Brothers starred in *Argentine Nights*—a movie that provoked anger in Argentina. Concluded one journalist, "The customs and standards of these people, assorted as they are, seem to take a tremendous mauling when shoved into the American film formulas, for apparently our producers want to shape them to our own image—and that, of course, brings from the Latinos outraged cries of pain."[12]

The Good Neighbor Policy initiated by the U.S. government to improve relations with Latin America was restructured as the Office of the Coordinator of Inter-American Affairs (CIAA) in 1940. Early the following year it formed a Motion Picture Division whose members included Nelson Rockefeller (whose family money remained infused into Hollywood) and John Hay Whitney, then vice-president of the Museum of Modern Art and director of its film library. The CIAA was financed by the federal government with the Motion Picture Division dedicated to encourage Latin American themes in movies and better representation of the southern neighbors. "Brazilian Bombshell" Miranda was one of the examples of that policy put into practice by Hollywood. Another was MGM's *Panama Hattie* (released in 1943, but made in 1941) which was hammered by critics at home, then laughed off Panama City screens for its ludicrous portrayal of Panama. Whitney toured Latin America in 1941. Later that year he and Rockefeller met MPPDA executives in Hollywood where all agreed on the need for producing films "to present the truly American life" to Latin Americans.[13]

Bothering the majors was a reported drop in 1940 of $27 million in revenue from the Latin market. Cartel members preferred to blame the drop on the government. "Failure of private or government loans from the U.S. to go through, which would have brought the Latin-Americas additional dollar credits, contributed to the drag in South American trade."[14]

At the start of 1941 Rockefeller led a committee which did a survey to determine how to cement good will between the two regions. Apparently in response to a questionnaire sent to Latin American editors and public relations experts, the answer came back almost unanimously: "Send us U.S. film stars." It was hoped that such live tours could be arranged soon "at least partially at the expense of the United States government." Cartel members first wanted assurances from those nations as to their stars' physical safety since "Latins are so nuts about Hollywood personalities they actually endanger them."[15]

The Disney studios launched their own good will efforts by hyping

Mickey Mouse, Donald Duck and other cartoon characters more intensely. While some Latin schools taught English via Mickey and Donald, many other schools "wailed that the expense of getting the dolls, books, etc., which tie up with the films, were more than they could reasonably put on the line." Walt Disney was mulling over the idea of introducing there "a hundred other gimmicks using Disney characters."[16]

Regarding the films themselves, the majors professed bafflement because "the super sensitivities of the Latin American people developed after three or four features with Latin American locales threatened to jar the good will drive." As they expressed that bafflement, they continued to ship south such turkeys as *Down Argentine Way*, *The Life of Simon Bolivar*, *They Met in Argentina* and everything with Carmen Miranda.[17]

Hollywood got cold feet on the idea of south of the border tours by its stars when some Latin government officials pointed out that such tours would be seen as junkets, which were out of place in a war situation. "What sort of impression do you think we get when we find that we're to be courted into becoming better neighbors by a mass turnout from Hollywood?" asked an unnamed Argentine official. Douglas Fairbanks, Jr., had made such a good will trip to South America, sent on an official mission by President Roosevelt. Many observers felt it was not appropriate to send someone known as an actor on an official mission.[18]

One of the more inane measures taken by the Rockefeller Committee on Latin American relations (part of the CIAA) was to successfully convince Universal to add a prologue to the South American version of Bud Abbott and Lou Costello's *In the Navy* to explain that the U.S. Navy was not really that screwy. It was a compromise reached after the Rockefeller group questioned whether the film should be released in Latin America at all. It was a decision reflecting more on Rockefeller and his view of the southern neighbors than upon that group.[19]

By late 1941, revenue in South America was up 16 percent on the previous year. Latin America represented about 12 percent of U.S. foreign revenue—then about 33 percent of the total take—meaning the 16 percent represented a raise of 1 percent in the world gross.[20]

When Whitney suggested it might be a good idea to assist in the establishment of native film industries in such nations as Mexico and Chile, the majors were apoplectic. They feared the precedent as well as the threat to their own business not only in South America but in other countries. Quite seriously they worried that if Mexico were helped today, it would be Cuba next, then, who knows, maybe Australia and New Zealand. The CIAA had somewhat innocently broached that topic as the U.S. was interested in countering any Nazi influence in South America. Cartel members "always" frowned on the encouragement of native production "and with good reason. Steady flow of native-made product ultimately cuts into the available playing time of

American product," explained *Variety*. Since American movies were the best in the world, why would that be a problem? For the same reasons foreign managers of the majors "generally have fought making deals to handle native product, since such pictures naturally would be competing with Hollywood-made product ... The more outside production that comes in, the less playing time is made available for U.S. screen fare." Regarding the Whitney suggestion, *Variety* said, "This is not understood by the rank and file in these foreign lands. They figure the best good will from the U.S. film industry comes from more and better American pictures." No actual rank and file South Americans were consulted in reaching that very self-serving dismissal of the proposal.[21]

After a seven-year legal battle, the Argentine appellate court threw out charges in 1942 that U.S. movie distributors were in violation of anti-trust laws. Originally convicted by a lower court, they were ordered to pay a $2,000 fine or serve a two-year jail sentence. It all started when an independent cinema owner sued the Argentina Film Distribution Association (it had ten members, the eight majors plus two small, local native firms) charging it refused to supply him with films, fixed ticket prices and imposed fines on exhibitors who broke any of the rules, contentions the lower court agreed with. The higher court dismissed the case on the technicality that the guilty verdict was rendered after the association against which the charges were made had been dissolved. (Of course, that was the reason it was disbanded.) All eight majors continued to operate and distribute as usual.[22]

Mexico's box office generated about $20.6 million for producer/distributors in 1943; about half of that amount went to Hollywood, "which yielded the United States companies about $5,000,000," said the *New York Times*.[23]

If Hollywood was unwilling to aid a native industry, it was more than ready to crush any that might emerge on their own. Argentina's native film industry had made a slow comeback, moving from 28 features made in 1937 to 49 in 1940 to 57 in 1942. (Mexico's production was 27 in 1940, 49 in 1942.) It had carved out a small presence in other South American nations. Politically the country maintained a position of neutrality in the war until 1944. Supposedly because fascism had to be opposed and stopped, Brazil broke its pledge of neutrality under intense pressure from the U.S. Argentina was the only nation in the hemisphere to have trade and diplomatic relations with the Axis powers. Just as important to the U.S. as the "correctness" of not being neutral was the idea of variance from American hegemonic control. An independent policy by any hemispheric nation in any important area was an intolerable affront threatening that control. Unable to get its way initially, the U.S. attacked the Argentine film industry.[24]

During 1941 the three largest majors operating in Argentina had combined revenues of about $300,000 while the two largest native producers took in about $80,000. That sent Paramount's Buenos Aires chief to Nelson Rockefeller's CIAA where he complained that the success of Argentinean movies was threatening U.S. film revenue in South America. In 1942 the CIAA recommended an embargo on the supply of raw film stock to Argentina (South America obtained the vast majority of its raw stock from the U.S.—European suppliers were mostly shut down due to the war). The CIAA also spearheaded an influx of U.S. capital investment into the Mexican film industries and approved large increases in Mexico's allotment of raw stock (there were then shortages in the U.S.). A total embargo was imposed on Argentina's supply for a year or so, doing great damage to the industry, creating a black market, etc., ostensibly because, due to its neutrality, the nation could become a center of Spanish-language pro–Axis propaganda. Although Argentina yielded to the pressure and became officially pro–Allied in 1944, a partial embargo on raw stock continued, even after 1945.[25]

When the CIAA, the State Department and war agencies set quotas for raw film for 1943, the percentages were kept secret. Mexico, Brazil and Chile were favored. Argentina received only one-sixth of its request while no limit was placed on the amount to Mexico. During 1943 Mexico had received 11.4 million feet and was offered more in 1944; Argentina received 3.6 million feet and a warning it might get less in 1944. That year Mexico made 78 movies, Argentina 24; in 1945 it was 79 to 22 in favor of Mexico; as late as 1948 it was Mexico 81, Argentina 41. As Argentina film historian Domingo di Nubila stated, "The Argentine cinema was already ousted from Latin America.... Now, the Argentine cinema was virtually confined to its domestic area." U.S. distributors helped Mexican movies invade Argentinean houses and become popular. One problem had been replaced by another potential problem of similar size. However, the U.S. majors would see to Mexico later. In the meantime it would act as a check on the Argentineans as well as catering to whatever desire might have existed in South America for more indigenous product.[26]

A total of 460 films were released in Brazil in 1941 of which 383 (83 percent) were U.S., 4 Brazilian; of the 347 movies released there in 1945, 310 were American-made (90 percent) while Brazilian productions numbered 6. Publicity efforts pushed the influence of U.S. movies everywhere. In 1941 it was reported that *Gone with the Wind* had a song during a carnival. *Life* magazine, and many others, were popular and were "eagerly pored over by the Brazilian subscriber and all his friends whether they can read English or not." Women who could read virtually no English were said to have bought *Vogue*, carefully studying it for trends in fashion, home furnishings and so on, with the result that "gradually the Brazilian woman makes her living room, her dining table look more North American." Brazilians liked everything American from Ford cars to Donald Duck. There was even an unverified rumor that spinach consumption had increased considerably because of Popeye. Brazilians attended "every" Hollywood film. While Brazilians used to turn to Paris for their clothes and culture, that had all changed recently "and it is almost certainly due to the movies, that younger people have craved American clothes, books and travel."[27]

When Brazilian painter Candido Portinari visited the U.S. he wanted to see all the various places which he had come to know through the movies, wrote journalist Florence Horn. Using more than a little exaggeration, Horn explained, "To him the North American cowboy and New York City were far more real than Brazil's own gauchos and the city of Rio de Janeiro. Our civil war was more vivid than any period of Brazilian history." Admitting that some Hollywood product shipped south had been less than sensitive, Horn argued producers were no longer making such mistakes and anyway, even before producers took the trouble to be accurate, Hollywood did much more good than harm in Brazil. "The movies have done a magnificent job of unconscious propaganda in Brazil ... For the movies have made the United States part of the very mental fiber of every Brazilian except those who live in the remotest jungles and isolated river hamlets."[28]

Within a couple of months of the onset of war, Hollywood's worry about more currency restrictions started to come true when Britain threatened to freeze coin. American ambassador to Britain Joseph Kennedy pressed the government not do to so and to drop the quota act in light of the war. Such efforts were unsuccessful with the British government putting on a freeze in late 1939 on 50 percent of the majors' revenue. The frozen money could be used within Britain in a variety of supervised ways, such as to produce movies, but not to buy theaters. Britain imposed the freeze to conserve currency in order to buy arms—from U.S. manufacturers. Australia also imposed a 50 percent freeze on the majors' revenues.[29]

Americans did not take that blow without protest. During the summer of 1941 President Roosevelt's official envoy Harry L. Hopkins was dispatched to London where he met with government officials to try and free up American money. Using some bizarre arguments, he explained to London that the majors had prepared statistics "to prove that, were it not for their revenue from England and Empire possessions in former years, America's film industry might be insolvent." When that did not work, Hopkins pointed to the production of anti–Nazi movies produced by Hollywood. Next he applied muscle by referring to the financial aid given the U.K. through American Lend-Lease aid—a subsidy program that aided Allies with their war effort. Estimates were that $30 to $40 million were soon frozen in Britain. A few months after Hopkins' visit, Britain released about $8 million of the frozen currency.[30]

Independently the majors lobbied the British to suspend the quota system. Hollywood deserved a break, it argued, because of Lend-Lease aid as well as the fact that America had kept up a steady shipment of movies into Britain despite higher distribution costs and "damages caused by the war."[31]

Also busy was Will Hays, lobbying Washington to help him unfreeze cartel money. Hays' argument to Washington was that the majors badly needed the cash flow. That was an idea the British film people, and some American insiders, openly scoffed at. After a meeting with President Roosevelt, Hays explained he had visited the chief executive to find out whether the cartel was meeting its war obligations. "The motion picture industry believes it is doing all it can for this country and the United Nations, the Allies but I wanted to be sure. So I came in to check up with the president," Hays told the press.[32]

In early 1943 the two governments finally announced all U.S. film coin was unfrozen. Gross rentals to the U.S. then amounted to $80 to $85 million annually from which had to be deducted distribution and overhead expenses in Britain—about 25 percent. Thus $62 million was remitted annually from Britain—dollars in New York.[33]

Even before the war ended, prominent Britishers began to complain loudly about U.S. film domination. Parliamentarians denounced the situation. One British publication pointed out that while some Hollywood majors owned cinemas in London, they did not own British chains except for an interest in Associated British Cinemas held by Warner and a shareholding in Gaumont—British-held by MGM and Fox. Not pointed out was that Britain had only three chains, which did the bulk of the business; Hollywood had a strong say in two of them. *Spectator* writer J. L. Hodson argued that no English observer could be satisfied with the imbalance between U.S. films shown in Britain and of British movies screened in America. In discussing the issue in America, all agreed that British films were essentially non-existent in America. One Hollywood writer told him he thought the cartel was trying to smash the British film industry while a studio executive commented the producers "don't want to buy English pictures made in England, and seldom do."[34]

All those complaints regarding Hollywood's screen domination did not sit well with *Variety*, who editorialized about Britain, "She was wailing about it in '20, hollering about it in '30, and still howling in '40—war and all. Today it has taken on the tone of a whine…. This is an old song she keeps warbling and it doesn't impress." The reason British movies got little distribution in the U.S. was simple: "they're not good enough." *Variety* declared it had no patience for any more such complaints since the answer was so obvious—make better pictures "but stop complaining," thundered the editor.[35]

Very late in 1944, Board of Trade Parliamentary Secretary Captain Waterhouse announced in the House of Commons that the import of American movies into Britain had increased steadily since war began and were then "on such a scale that they must be a matter of concern to the British Board of Trade." For 1939 the U.S. majors had grossed $39 million from Britain, $43 million in 1940, $48 million in 1941, $70 million in 1942 and $88 million in 1943.[36]

Australia received most of its films from the U.S., a bit from Britain and almost nothing from everywhere else. Thus the cartel felt they had a chance to move to a near 100 percent penetration with the war on. Percentages of imports into Australia in 1940 were U.S. 85.2 percent, U.K. 13.1 percent, all others 1.7 percent; in 1941 those numbers were respectively, 89.6 percent, 10.2

percent, 0.2 percent; in 1942, 90.5 percent, 8.7 percent, 0.8 percent; in 1943 89.2 percent, 8.0 percent, 2.8 percent; in 1944, 87.5 percent, 9.4 percent, 3.1 percent; and in 1945, 88.4 percent, 7.7 percent, 3.9 percent. While the U.S. percentage did creep up while British numbers dipped, it seemed the Australian imports from the rest of the world held U.S. penetration to around 88 to 90 percent. Keeping a close eye on everything was Australia's Motion Picture Distributors Association, a lobby group. All of its members were representatives of American firms.[37]

Doing the same job in another nation was the Shanghai-based China Film Board of Trade, another lobby group. It had a total of eight members, all representing U.S. firms. Ninety-five percent of the film business in Shanghai was done by the cartel.[38]

At the time of the Pearl Harbor attack, Japan had been closed to Hollywood for a few years with very little new product going in, and its revenues from the past all frozen. Nonetheless Hollywood was being paid over those years a bit at a time from a San Francisco bank account set up by Japan. Payments were made right up to Pearl Harbor with most of the frozen coin by then having been paid over.[39]

Occupied France excluded all American movies when it was taken by Germany. In the summer of 1942, Vichy France announced it was imposing a full embargo on U.S. films. By then not much new product was entering anyway. Many distributors were playing oldies over and over. At that date, *Variety* reported, most of Europe was closed with the only Continental countries getting shipments being Turkey, Sweden, Switzerland, Finland, Spain and Portugal.[40]

Contradicting the above report, at least for Spain, was an account in the *New York Times* wherein Fox assistant European manager Robert Kreier said that Spanish cinemas were operating with ten-year-old American product as only five new U.S. films had been sent in over the previous five years. Despite those old reruns, Kreier noted that "revenue has steadily maintained prewar dimensions." Due to wear and tear over time, some of those films had shrunk from eight reels down to five. Initially Fox had made duplicates but stopped as raw film stock became harder to obtain. Film damage notwithstanding, he claimed no complaints had been received from cinema operators or spectators, "so grateful are the people just to have the chance of seeing American films."[41]

According to UA European sales manager Lacy W. Kastner, American films were favored even in Nazi-dominated areas where old prints left behind were played to tatters, sometimes reduced to half of their original running time as worn sections were clipped out. He pointed out, "But the Spaniards don't seem to mind." Kastner worked out of Lisbon from where he said he shipped prints to practically all European nations except Germany and Italy.[42]

When Italian Popular Culture Under-Secretary Gastano Polverelli announced in a 1941 speech a ban forbidding the acquisition of new U.S. films, he merely formalized the fact since virtually none had entered over the previous few years. However, the *New York Times* commented, "The fact remains that American films are unquestionably the most popular with Italian fans and they will not feel so happy about it." An odd statement in view of the fact no Hollywood product had screened for years and attendance at mostly Italian-made movies was up over that of the U.S.–dominated 1930s.[43]

Not long after America entered World War II, the U.S. Treasury Department invoked the 1917 Trading with the Enemy Act under which all films leaving the country were subject to full wartime censorship, as well all incoming movies. Soon the Office of War Information's (OWI) Bureau of Motion Pictures opened its Hollywood office to act as a liaison and advise the majors on film content as it related to the government's war information program, both domestically and internationally. Toward the end of 1942 bureau head Lowell Mellet requested studio executives to submit all screen treatments and finished scenarios of all pictures to the OWI before filming began. OWI claimed the plan was just an extension of current practice and in no way constituted blanket censorship, pointing out its powers were advisory only.[44]

When the OWI suggested in 1943 that it handle physical distribution of American films at war's end in areas then held by the Nazis, the majors strongly resisted. Noting they were ready to cooperate with the OWI in getting approved and "worthy" films in as soon as the nations were liberated, the majors wanted to distribute themselves. With an outside agency handling the task, the cartel worried it would have no control over rental rates, length of the run, etc., with the result that later when they did distribute themselves in those areas, "they would be confronted by exhibitor opposition to any sort of terms, play dates, etc."[45]

Although the OWI had only advisory powers over Hollywood, its suggestions were often heeded. Right after the war, when Italy complained about certain prewar Hollywood product showing scenes of copious food, the OWI campaigned to Hollywood to eliminate feasting scenes and overdisplay of food in films that would be sent to food-scarce Europe. Reportedly several movies did have such scenes removed before going abroad. Additionally the OWI asked studios filming product set in Latin America not to show barefoot peasants or any signs of poverty in the backgrounds.[46]

Even American soldiers abroad were a little leery of Hollywood film content. In the armed forces daily newspaper in the European theater, *The Stars and Stripes*, was a 1943 editorial stating there was too much "flag waving" in American films, a level found to be "sickening." If the Hays Office paid more attention to "good taste" in films for foreign consumption, the editor thought it might eliminate the distrust of Americans generated by the bad movies.[47]

Famed author Pearl Buck was also anxious over Hollywood film content. In her capacity as president of the East and West Association, she took a wartime 1942 poll, writing to several hundred motion picture critics on American newspapers and magazines asking them to send her the names of films which could be represented to audiences in the Near and Far East "as being really representative of life in America." A total of 219 individual pictures were named but the top ten were well set apart and ahead of numbers 11 and higher. Two-thirds of those polled voted for one or another of the Andy Hardy series. The top ten were (in order) the Andy Hardy series, *Mr. Deeds Goes to Town, Sergeant York, Boy's Town, One Foot in Heaven, Our Town, Abe Lincoln in Illinois, Mr. Smith Goes to Washington, Blossoms in the Dust* and *Joe Smith, American*. Notable by their absence were films such as *The Grapes of Wrath, I Am a Fugitive from a Chain Gang*, and *Dead End* which to some extent explored issues such as social injustice, racial hatred and prison and tenement abuse.[48]

One of the few media accounts of Hollywood movies in Africa during the war years was filed by Paul Lee in the *New York Times* in 1943. Supposedly he was there in person to witness all he described. In West Africa where a laborer earned about one shilling a day, hundreds of them spent half that sum to go to an open-air cinema to watch a two- to three-year-old American movie, to "gape with open mouths at drawing-room comedy. The smart dialogue doesn't mean much to them, but those I watched were left in speechless awe by the costumes and settings. They never saw anything like it, but it convinces them that America is some country."[49]

During the war, State took over some of the responsibilities for motion pictures which had until then fallen under the scope of Commerce. In July 1939, by presidential order, the State Department absorbed into its various consulates the foreign trade representatives of the Department of Commerce. When State reorganized in January 1944, George Canty was made motion picture specialist in the Telecommunications Division. The chief of that division, Francis de Wolf commented, "American motion pictures as ambassadors of good will—at no cost to the American taxpayer—interpret the American way of life to all the nations of the world ... which may be invaluable from the political, cultural and commercial point of view. On the other hand, the wrong kind of picture may have the opposite effect. Finally—and this is an important consideration—American motion pictures act as salesmen for American products, salesmen that are readily welcomed by their public. For all these reasons, the Department of State and its representatives in foreign countries desire to cooperate fully in the protection of American motion pictures abroad, especially in the difficult postwar era." In return, State expected Hollywood to cooperate fully with the government to insure that films going abroad "will reflect credit on the good name and reputation of this country and its institutions."[50]

When Hays sent a memorandum to State in 1943, he argued for State's assistance in maintaining foreign markets for the cartel. He noted that 40 percent of its product was exported, that its commercial success stemmed from artistic worth, it earned its dominant spot on merit, its films fostered goodwill,

U.S. movies were the product of a large domestic industry whose spending linked it with other industries and that foreign receipts financed the extra quality of the films that the domestic market enjoyed. Hays added that the fate of American movies abroad was a proper concern of the government because of "the right of our government to delivery of our message on the American way of life."[51]

When State circulated a February 1944 memo to American diplomatic offices titled "American Motion Pictures in the Postwar World," it asked for intelligence reports and comments on general and specific types of movies to be shown and which had been shown. "American motion pictures act as salesmen for American products, salesmen that are readily welcomed by their public.... You should fully understand the value of the American motion picture to the national welfare and the importance that the government attaches to the unrestricted distribution of American motion pictures abroad, especially in the postwar period. The Department desires to cooperate fully in the protection of the American motion picture industry abroad," said the memo. The long-range view of State was "to remove existing obstacles to the distribution of American films wherever possible and to prevent any extension of such barriers in the future."[52]

As part of that State memo, the agency conducted a worldwide survey of barriers restricting distribution of American movies on a country-by-country basis "with a view to forcing down the wall." Fueling that desire was the conviction that trade followed the film. Of equal or greater importance was the "value of the screen as an international builder of public opinion."[53]

Nathan Golden remained in Commerce as the chief of its motion picture unit. He argued that U.S. dominance on world screens should "be energetically maintained" after the war because it "is of very real and great importance to our national welfare. The film as a silent salesman for other American products abroad is economically significant, and, as an exponent of the democratic way of life, it has a constructive and invigorating influence on the thought of other countries." His department was then conducting a comprehensive survey of the world's film markets, including such limited ones as the Belgian Congo and the Fiji Islands.[54]

Commenting on all that activity by the government to assist Hollywood, a reporter in 1945 continued the fiction often evident in the media that it rarely happened. That journalist called the activity a "sudden awakening" by Washington as to the power of films to sell American ideas and goods in other lands, and "a belated one."[55]

As the Allies prepared to invade French North Africa in late 1942 and oust the Axis powers, Hollywood stood ready to move instantly into the market in such cities as Algiers and Casablanca. Hays told the studio foreign managers that he had been informed the U.S. government was particularly anxious U.S. movies obtain widespread distribution in Africa, believing that such screen fare was vital to the African campaign.[56]

When U.S. forces stormed into North Africa, American films were right behind them, "winning over to our side" the populace of Algiers and Casablanca. Thus, reported Thomas Pryor in the *New York Times*, the "American motion picture became an implement of offensive warfare in helping to counteract Nazi ideology." Distribution of movies sent there was handled by the regular agents of the cartel members but with a great deal of assistance and oversight from the OWI through its Overseas Motion Picture Bureau (OMPB). Hollywood screenwriter Robert Riskin—who often teamed with director Frank Capra—headed the OMPB, which was responsible for the administration of the government's cultural and informational motion picture program in all areas outside of Canada and South America. Those areas were the responsibility of Nelson Rockefeller's CIAA. Mainly, those programs had to do with the dissemination of nonfiction films such as documentaries plus, of course, "advice to the cartel" concerning Hollywood movies. However, with the launch of the African campaign it became apparent that Riskin's sphere of influence also extended to the selection of regular commercial features for export. As a propaganda tool, and as the Allies moved the Axis out of other lands, it was envisioned "this new war role of the motion picture will become increasingly important."[57]

In preparation of that invasion, the OMPB asked studio executives to submit a list of films that were, or could easily be, equipped with French subtitles. From that list the agency selected the movies it deemed most suitable, transporting them to North Africa with other war priority shipments. Upon arrival those films were turned over to the cartel members' local agents for theater booking in the regular manner. Hollywood executives were elated about those markets being opened up again but expressed resentment and displeasure privately over the censorship and the selection process. Riskin refused to comment except to remark that the OMPB assisted the majors in "an advisory capacity." Among the first batch of films approved to follow U.S. troops into Algiers, and be screened immediately, were *Foreign Correspondent, Bambi, Flight Command, Joe Smith, American* and *The Long Voyage Home.* In the summer of 1943 the OMPB relinquished its "advice"-giving in North Africa, leaving that market to Hollywood to deal with in its usual way.[58]

In discussing how best to reach audiences in newly liberated areas in a comprehensive and timely fashion, UA foreign manager Walter Gould declared, "If American pictures are to follow quickly on the heels of U.S. troops into foreign lands, the films should be made more readily understood there." Gould suggested that for a small additional cost foreign narration could be added to outline the plot and explain screen actions. If used, he felt the cost "would be repaid 20 times in added rentals" because when foreign audiences were obliged "to struggle" with subtitles while trying to follow screen action, "interest is cut 50 percent." The film *The Moon and Sixpence* had been done that way in Spanish and Portuguese with narration to set the story at the outset and further elaboration where needed, at a cost of $2,500 per language. Finally Gould argued that Hollywood had mistaken "passive acceptance" of American movies for complete endorsement. Both State and the CIAA asked for a print to study the method although the idea was never adopted.[59]

During the summer of 1943 the U.S. government had dubbed Hollywood movies into Italian, in 16mm format, prior to the invasion of Sicily. Those prints followed the Army into the area and were immediately screened for the citizens. It was all financed by the OWI, which spent a reported $10 million buying and dubbing 40 Hollywood features. Viewing the effort as a success, the OWI went on to repeat the process in the Balkans, Greece and Yugoslavia after their liberations.[60]

Within 24 hours of the fall of the Italian mainland (beginning in the south) to the Allies, the OWI and OMPB had their film plan in operation. Forty movies selected by the OWI as "best projecting the American scene" and subtitled in Italian were on their way in within those 24 hours. Nine copies of each were shipped, a total of 360 prints. This time the cartel members played no part in distribution with OWI's Laudy Lawrence—MGM's former European manager for many years—running the show. Lawrence negotiated percentage rental deals with cinema owners. In many cases, houses were damaged from the war, short of technical equipment and so on. Lawrence and the OWI remedied that situation by having engineers and technicians from both RCA and Western Electric follow the troops in even more quickly than the movies. They supplied spare parts and did whatever was needed to allow damaged cinemas to open. Meanwhile, in London, OWI's DeLacey Kastner—formerly with Columbia—sat waiting with the same 40 films ready to follow Allied troops into other European nations. Describing those movies, *Variety* said that "all are in the high-budget class, containing entertainment and a hint of the power of the United States, with the propaganda understandable but not too obvious. There will be no crime, horror or western films."[61]

U.S. films playing in Italian houses were still handled solely by the OWI in August 1944 and would be until such time as the Army deemed it permissible for business to be conducted as usual. Working with the Allied Military Government and the Army's Psychological Warfare Branch, the OWI put over 650 Italian theaters back into operation. In the days immediately after the fall of Italy, cinemas operated sporadically due to an irregular power supply. To remedy that, the OWI arranged to have power pumped into the houses from mobile generators. Explaining that films immediately following Allied troops were being used as a psychological warfare weapon, Robert Riskin said, "Thus Hollywood's entertainment films serve as magnets to attract the crowds, which then also see specially prepared Allied documentary subjects and newsreels."[62]

In a spring 1945 report, the OWI was irritated to note that the new Italian government had yet to abolish laws "discriminating against American movies," chief of which was the state monopoly on the importation and distribution of films. That was hardly discriminatory as it applied to all movie imports. Hollywood was upset because it could not extract monopoly profits from Italy with its usual ease.[63]

France and Belgium were treated to the same 40 films upon their liberation. They had, of course, been dubbed in Hollywood. Although the French government never authorized the admission of those films, no initial objection was raised. Around the spring of 1945, French authorities notified the majors (who had then taken over distribution from the OWI) that those films had entered France illegally and that further importation was forbidden. Also noted was the 1930s pact which stipulated that if dubbed foreign movies were to screen in France, the dubbing had to be done there. Hollywood questioned whether the agreement still had any validity in view of all that had happened.[64]

Samuel Goldwyn reported that Hollywood sent teams of trained film men with the forward troops to exhibit U.S. films on the screens of liberated cities as fast as possible. One such team was with the First U.S. Army when it entered Cherbourg, France, under General J. Lawton Collins. "Within hours cinemas of that city were rolling ... Hollywood films were exportable as part of the 'Arsenal of Democracy' and were administered by the Psychological Warfare Division of the Army itself as weapons of war," recalled the producer.[65]

Nathan Golden was excited over the OWI program, exclaiming, "Our American films have followed the troops into North Africa, Sicily and Italy and are doing a tremendous business in the theaters in those regions which have been recaptured. As new territory is conquered by our Allied troops, the market potentialities for our films will increase." Hollywood executives salivated over the prospect that the European market which yielded $30 million before 1939 might now be worth $60 to $75 million (excluding the U.K.). One reporter, noting the amount of money transferred to the majors by the OWI, cautioned, "It has been pointed out that the film industry received $50,000,000 of government money from the OWI for 'carefully selected' films to be distributed in liberated countries, and that it would be unfortunate if a taste of government money, acquired in war time, became habit-forming."[66]

Not repeating the mistake in Italy of waiting for the new government to abolish state-controlled cinema rules, the Allies swept away such protectionist measures almost immediately in Germany after it fell to the Allies. Under the Nazis, the major firm from the pre–Nazi era, UFA, was folded into one even larger state-controlled film monopoly company, UFI. After the Allies entered Germany, UFI was divided up by occupation zones pending its complete dismantling. U.S. interests also insisted on a free-trade policy, supposedly to lay the foundation for a de–Nazified and competitive German cinema, which effectively guaranteed the German industry would be severely hobbled.[67]

Gloomy economic forecasts from Hollywood reached their peak in the mid–1940 to mid–1941 period. At one point *Variety* estimated that the cartel's world take was off a full 20 percent since foreign revenue—40 percent of the world total—was off 50 percent. However, much of that "loss" was admittedly due to the British coin freeze. That money was not really gone. Anyway, it would soon be all paid over. Number one worry then for the studio foreign departments was that an "initial bombing of an open town in England is likely to bring total shuttering of British cinemas—possibly for the duration of the war," and that "German plane raids over France are not making for the best box office."[68]

So depressed were the majors that *Variety* reported: "The long threatened plan of American film companies to draw in their horns on elaborate foreign distribution setups is nearing actuality. It's part of the prolonged consideration of the proposition that foreign business should be subordinated to domestic." Under this plan the majors would remain in New York selling foreign rights to distributors from foreign lands, who themselves maintained New York offices. Thus the money would be paid up front straight into a U.S. bank, leaving the majors with no frozen coin, no quotas or other restrictions to deal with. Consideration of the plan was necessary because "the nationalistic spirit and urge to soak the U.S. film business has caused the bulk of woes in foreign distribution during recent years." Needless to say, no more was heard about that plan.[69]

Perhaps it was quickly forgotten when the majors concentrated on the money actually coming in and also forgot about their worst case scenario— something like every cinema in Europe closed for the duration. For 1942, Hollywood grossed $252 million domestically and $138 to $158 million internationally for a world take of $390 to $410 million. The U.K. generated 22 percent of the world take, Canada 3.3 percent ($13 million), Latin America 4.7 percent ($18.8 million). The remainder of the world still receiving U.S. films contributed 6.2 percent ($25 million).[70]

War time rentals from the British market were reported at around $92 million annually in 1944 with Hollywood clearing 70 to 75 percent of that amount. Prior to the war, U.S. British rentals were around $50 million yearly. *Variety* admitted that boom was predicated on war time spending and American Lend-Lease aid. For 1944, Hollywood's take increased with worldwide revenues at $480 million ($310 million domestically, $170 million foreign). It was "a very good year," noted *Variety*.[71]

Even the situation in Axis centers turned out good for the cartel. As late as September 1941, MGM and Paramount were still distributing in occupied France with some U.S. product running in other Nazi-occupied areas such as Denmark and Hungary until late in 1942. As soon as Germany surrendered in May 1945, Arthur Loew was at work retrieving MGM funds from formerly occupied Europe. Surprisingly the Germans had not confiscated MGM money in Berlin, almost 1 million marks. Similar sums were found intact in Tokyo, Rome, Budapest, Bucharest and other capitals.[72]

Essentially the Soviet Union had been closed to American films since the 1930s. Representatives from Russia's official trading organization met in New York with Hollywood agents in 1942 to possibly arrange a film deal. That possible change in direction was due to the fact that Russia was then an ally, willing to pay for any product in U.S. currency and had "a general aptitude towards meeting American terms." Nothing happened.[73]

Closer to the end of the war, *Variety* saw a battle looming over the world film screens between the U.S., the Soviet Union and Britain. Of course, that did not take place. America and Russia remained virtually closed to each other's films with Russia having no presence in other nations except those within its own sphere. Britain's industry was too busy just trying to survive domestically. In order to win that battle of the screens which never took place, Hollywood was again well assisted by the government. Of the estimated 50,000 film projectors taken abroad by the armed forces (16mm), only 5000 to 6000 were expected to be brought back with the remainder left in foreign countries "to ensure showing of U.S. films." At the same time that the majors wanted to remain free of government supervision, they also wanted to get more aid. "While in some U.S. film quarters there is an inclination to seek stronger government support in furthering film distribution abroad, the objective is to achieve such support without placing U.S. film business too greatly under government control."[74]

As war loomed in the late 1930s, Hollywood worried; when war broke out, Hollywood worried; as war continued Hollywood worried; when the war's end was in sight Hollywood worried and went crying to Uncle Sam for even more aid. Piled up during the war years were many hundreds of films which had never been screened in some countries—all that extra money. However, all that old product would compete against Hollywood's new product being churned out—all that extra worry. Paramount vice-president John W. Hicks also worried about a flood of old product, and new releases, hitting some countries all at once, warning that the industry "must be very careful not to create a buyer's market." Hollywood must not make it "a cinch for the exhibitor." An enlarged and reopened world market was counted on by the majors to cushion any decline in the domestic market "should a temporary unemployment problem develop when American troops are demobilized."[75]

Equally troublesome to the cartel was the fear that "many European nations would have no great surplus of money for the purchase of films after food, clothing, medicinal and other materials are provided for." To remedy that, Hollywood looked to its government to provide currency stabilization in Europe, and more loans. Speaking of the French market, Hollywood film executives delivered themselves of the self-serving opinion that "the reentry of American product into that market is one of the most pleasurably anticipated events." Many film people felt the rehabilitation of Europe should include entertainment relief; "if producers of food, clothing, etc. are paid when supplies are sent in to rehabilitate a country, the same payment should apply to films," explained one executive.[76]

Reporting in the *New York Times*, Thomas Pryor declared in 1943 that the majors were worried about an increase in quotas and other restrictions at war's end along with increased competition from native industries which could be helped by government support. Mentioning of support led Pryor to continue the fiction that such government assistance was nonexistent for the majors. He wrote, "On the other hand, the American film industry is at present without any such official representation abroad and there has been no indication as yet that the government is contemplating such a step. While the industry shrinks from the thought of any governmental meddling in its affairs, foreign department executives nevertheless believe some form of official representation to be desirable."[77]

Former Hollywood executive Harold Hopper, then chief of the Motion Picture Section of the War Production Board, argued that Hollywood had to present a united front at the peace table if it hoped to retake the position it held before the war. Hoping the writing of the peace treaty would provide a means of removing restrictions and embargoes on U.S. movies, Hopper thought if the industry properly presented its case, "a way will be opened for giving it greater access to world markets than ever before."[78]

Francis de Wolf, head of State's telecommunications division (which then included motion pictures), wanted to see peace terms incorporate "the basic American ideals of freedom to listen and freedom to see." He was then working with George Canty to insure American movies got into Europe with the least possible amount of restrictions.[79]

More upbeat on the outlook for U.S. films abroad after the war was Nathan Golden, still Motion Picture unit chief in Commerce's Bureau of Foreign and Domestic Commerce. He described it (in January, 1944) as "very bright indeed. Our backlog of hundreds of American films produced and exhibited in the United States but never shown in markets now closed will give our American industry a signal advantage over our European competitors." On the issue of film quality, he declared that foreigners wanted to see U.S. product because it was the best. Golden had no objection to Hollywood providing a moderate amount of technological help to foreign film industries provided "the intent of the foreign interests is not to create an industry abroad that will subsequently be protected by discriminatory or overly harsh legislation or regulation of a kind that would actually operate to restrict the importation and exhibition of American films." Golden went on, "We all want to see relatively freer foreign trade.... This is particularly true in the motion picture field. In that field, we desire and hope to see all forces shaping themselves in such a way as to promote a greater and ever-greater amount of playing time for the excellent and appealing products of our motion-picture studios." Hollywood's product, stated Golden, "will always remain superior to that of any of its competitors, regardless of where they may be located." Agreeing the cartel members had turned to his Commerce Department over the years for detailed information about the international film market, Golden explained, "They have drawn on the bureau for trade statistics, market surveys, names of selling outlets, exchange conditions, tariffs, local regulations, laws pertaining to commerce, prevailing trade practices, competition, local tastes and similar basic data representing all the elements into foreign trade analysis and promotion. The bureau intends at the close of the war to resume all these services in the fullest possible scope and effectiveness."[80]

Even Latin America worried Hollywood with respect to competition that might emerge. That led to another off-the-wall idea which died almost as quickly as it was put forward: "One major company is considering making the learning of Spanish compulsory for young contract players so they can alternate in English- and Spanish-language pictures," reported the *New York Times*.[81]

Hays biographer Raymond Moley spun more than a little fiction when he observed in 1945, "The American industry has worked entirely with private capital, with no government subsidy." America's film industry "could not have held its foreign markets through the years except for the fact that in every country the people themselves liked American pictures."[82]

During the 1920s Hays had loudly touted the value of U.S. films abroad in selling other American goods. That was toned down when it was seen as generating hostility, and restrictions, abroad. Next Hays touted U.S. films as promoting peace, good will, tolerance, etc. In view of the war it could hardly be used again (American films had dominated the world's screens from the 1920s through the war). Still, other mantras could be found. So Hays, and some in government noted above, picked up and ostentatiously carried the banner of free trade and free expression. Beginning in 1943 Hays and other film executives met from time to time with State officials to discuss the possibility of obtaining government aid to insure a free market abroad after the war. Hays stressed "the importance of freedom of expression everywhere in the world."[83]

In other MPPDA activity, rumor had it in 1944 that Eric Johnston, president of the U.S. Chamber of Commerce, would be offered a post in the Hays Office as a result of a growing consciousness in Washington, engendered by the CIAA, of the "missionary powers of Hollywood pictures." The MPPDA members were also discussing, prior to 1945, the formation of a formal export association as a response to the end of the war. Ostensibly it would deal with government-encouraged film monopolies abroad. Of course the cartel had always acted as one abroad in important matters. They already had such an organization, de facto.[84]

Taking up the "free" banner was Fox movie mogul Darryl Zanuck, who remarked in a 1945 dinner speech, "I ask for a free screen throughout the world, a competitive screen. We will do our part. Protection—yes. We need the active aid of our State Department, as does every export industry. Guidance—yes. We need that, too, so that we do not offend nationals anywhere. But censorship in any form or governmental interference will cripple our efforts to aid in this great task." A reporter covering that speech added the thought that Hollywood "desperately needs government assistance in overcoming foreign barriers to its films." Conveniently ignored was the fact that no country erected barriers against foreign films until their screens had been overwhelmed by U.S. product. None of those restrictions were aggressive first strikes against a tiny and barely present American presence but rather were defensive measures aimed at lessening the amount of money lost by the nation in the film trade and the total destruction of whatever native film industry existed.[85]

President Harry Truman ended Lend Lease in September 1945. Suddenly nations like Britain and Canada had to find dollars for U.S. goods within war-weakened economies. Hollywood was upset, as were other American industries. However, another cash cow would soon emerge which Hollywood and other industries could milk just as easily directly or indirectly: the Marshall Plan.

6. Under the Celluloid Boot: 1945–1952

With the end of the war, the majors moved quickly to reestablish the dominance on film screens they held before the war in any nations where it had been shut down. As the Allied occupying forces broke down impeding structures in countries like Italy and Germany, doing away with state film monopolies, the task became easier. Additionally, native film industries were badly damaged, offering even less competition. Cinemas had also been damaged but the U.S. government fixed many of them up for Hollywood—no charge. Recapturing those markets would have been easier still if only those nations had not been so broke. Wanting to spend what little money they had on items such as food, medicine and shelter, nations were not pleased by the prospect of Hollywood reconnecting its money-sucking pump. That money could be put to far better use in the countries involved. Again the U.S. government came to the rescue with cash money in aid, first with loans and then through the Marshall Plan which helped ease Hollywood's way with the taxpayers' money quickly returned to the private coffers of the major studios. As in the past, the government lent a hand at the negotiating table whenever needed, which was often enough itself to intimidate smaller nations into compliance with Hollywood's will. Countries in what became the Soviet East Bloc would be lost but the cartel fought to keep them from slipping away. The biggest blow suffered by the industry in this period came domestically when in 1948 the U.S. Supreme Court held the majors to be a monopoly operating in restraint of trade under the Sherman Act. They were ordered to divest themselves of their theater ownership with block and blind booking also barred, domestically. In due course the majors sold off their cinemas. Block booking continued to be imposed in nations around the world, except in the few which barred the practice themselves, and is to this day. Those court rulings did virtually nothing to shake the majors' grip in the domestic market; they had no effect on foreign operations. Illustrating the degree of market control exercised by the cartel was the fact that in 1943–1944 the eight majors received over 94 percent of the domestic box office receipts.[1]

Several changes took place within the cartel itself in 1945. One was the appointment of Eric Johnston as head of the MPPDA in September of that year to replace the retiring Will Hays. The former had served four terms as president of the U.S. Chamber of Commerce. Also that year the MPPDA rechristened itself the Motion Picture Association of America (MPAA), the name it still carries.[2]

One of Johnston's first pronouncements was that foreign revenue was "the lifeblood of the American motion picture industry. At least one-third of the cost of negatives for motion pictures produced in this country must be derived from foreign distribution." Pointing out the obstacles U.S. films faced in some lands, Johnston stressed the need for strong government backing to remove obstacles and obtain a free flow of product into foreign countries.[3]

In his first annual report as the cartel's new leader, Johnston declared, "Our government's policy of free exchange of media of expression is ... a powerful asset in the highly competitive situation which confronts the American industry. We expect this policy to be vigorously prosecuted and also implemented in numerous treaties and trade agreements to be negotiated with foreign countries."[4]

In the MPAA's 1947 annual report, Johnston proclaimed, "The American motion picture will carry the ideas of Canton, Ohio, to Canton, China; the point of view of Paris, Maine, to Paris, France." At a series of meetings with Hollywood executives at the various studios, he told them he had established "a close liaison with President Truman, Secretary of State Marshall and himself." Almost every day he was at the MPAA Washington headquarters, he claimed he was in and out of the State Department assuring the executives that the White House was aware "of the importance of the movies in carrying to the world the American message of political democracy and economic free enterprise." While at the Warner lot he suggested showing scenes of sybaritic eating and drinking could stir envy and discontent in the less fortunate nations and were therefore perhaps not constructive. Johnston and several film executives met with President Truman in 1947 to discuss the difficulties of distributing films in some areas as well as the problem of frozen revenues in some countries.[5]

Just a few years after his appointment to head the cartel, Johnston was spinning his own revisionist history of U.S. films abroad. Prior to World War II, he said, product had flowed "almost leisurely" around the world; only after the war did the industry have to get tough and fight restrictions "most vigorously." Nor was income from abroad all that important in the earlier period, he claimed; "Up to the end of World War II the foreign market was regarded by some as a sort of 'gravy' field. The war's end changed all that. The 'gravy' became the life blood of an industry." Just when the industry found it could not depend solely on the domestic market, "it was hit by an array of restrictions." Exactly why foreign income was suddenly crucial whereas before the war it was just an extra was not explained by Johnston. In any event it created a problem: how to keep U.S. films flowing around the world "a project considered of prime importance by the United States government, as well as by the industry itself." How was Hollywood to get paid for its movies "which were never more popular with people everywhere?" Citing the fact that if an industry generated 8–10 percent of its gross sales abroad it was enough to classify it as a big exporter, the MPAA president then declared Hollywood—taking over one-third from abroad—as the world's biggest exporter in terms of percentage of sales abroad. Acknowledging his industry was mostly an entertainment medium, Johnston still saw each American film as a package "of freedom and democracy for the world to unwrap ... because our films are free from any conscious propaganda, people flock to see our pictures and stay away from Russian films." Hollywood was "the world's greatest exporter of ideas—American ideas, of freedom and democracy," with Johnston convinced that American film "is the most vital link remaining between the democratic world and the shattered world behind the Iron Curtain." Presumably most of Johnston's rhetoric was designed to get the federal government even more on Hollywood's side than it already was. He had pushed all the hot buttons—fear of Communism, the specter of a Hollywood helplessly being kicked around by other nations, the idea that the U.S. film industry would face imminent collapse if it lost any more markets abroad, and so on. As well, Johnston may have been establishing a rationale for the organization of the Motion Picture Export Association (MPEA), the formal monopoly established in 1945, to operate outside the U.S. It was to meet the threat posed by all those new restrictions that the MPEA "was established under the Webb-Pomerene Act. This allows American film companies to operate together in countries where individual operation is impossible," explained Johnston. The formation of the MPEA marked the other major change in the structure of the Hollywood cartel.[6]

During the discussions by the majors preparatory to forming the export organization, a few oddball ideas were floated. One was to form a pool of films, choosing only the best ones to send abroad to countries with quotas. All producer trademarks and logos would be stripped from them, leaving an unbranded generic "American film" to ship overseas. The cartel had a committee chaired by N. Peter Rathvon to study the formation of an export association.[7]

With peace discussions and other financial arrangements and trade issue negotiations underway, Hollywood was annoyed because it was not to receive its perceived due of a special place at the bargaining table. The State Department was more than prepared to assist the cartel to maintain its domination but the film industry felt it should be the spearhead of the move towards improved international trade agreements, not just a part. That perceived lukewarm reception led Hollywood to look more intensely into forming its own often-considered export trade association, an idea first considered sometime before the war. Until that time, if one distributor faced discrimination, it could withdraw from that country but there was no guarantee other distributors would follow suit. Although Hollywood had shown strong solidarity in standing as one in all past disputes there was still less than full trust between the cartel members. In view of the cartel's current presence in the courts as a result of the Justice Department's anti-trust action and the opposition from Justice to cartels in general, *Variety* noted, "The film export association would have to be set up so that all relation to that form of operation would be avoided." While the group was touted mainly as an organization to fight trade barriers, a much less publicly presented motive was that the MPEA might be able to regulate the flow of product "so as to avoid glutting the market with U.S. product and thus avert depressing of price levels." That was particularly important in the last half of the 1940s with a huge backlog of films having built up during the war years.[8]

When the MPEA was formed, it had the same eight major studios as members as in the MPAA. Acting as the agent, the MPEA negotiated for all cartel members, initially in 13 nations (Germany, Korea, Japan, Austria, Bulgaria, Czechoslovakia, Hungary, the Netherlands, the Dutch East Indies, Poland, Romania, the Soviet Union and Yugoslavia). No producer was allowed to negotiate independently in any of those countries. Revenues from those areas were pooled and divided among the cartel in proportion to their share of domestic receipts in the preceding year. Describing the MPEA, Johnston called it the film industry's "sole defense against either government monopolies or government-sponsored monopoly set-ups." Then with a straight face he added that the MPEA members "are against cartels ... because free competition is preferred." In an effort to negotiate with those named countries, the MPEA would pool "the best American films which best portray the American way of life." Johnston summarized the new group by saying, "Much as we disbelieve in monopolistic cartels, our only defense for the time being is in dealing as a collective unit. As soon as we are free to deal competitively in these countries, the association will be dissolved." It remains in existence today, although with a lower profile. Johnston was head of the MPEA and the MPAA.[9]

The MPEA was formed under the protection of the Export Trade Act (adopted by Congress in 1918), better known as the Webb-Pomerene (WP) Act after the bill's co-sponsors Senator Pomerene and Congressman Webb. Under that law, U.S. firms were granted exemption from all American anti-trust laws which regulated businesses domestically. Webb-Pomerene allowed U.S. firms to join together to fix prices, and so on, outside of the U.S. Although block booking and price fixing were illegal practices for Hollywood to engage in domestically, the cover of Webb-Pomerene allowed them to engage in them abroad—subject of course, to the laws of the host country. One qualification under Webb-Pomerene was that U.S. export firms were not allowed to use practices abroad which were illegal at home if those practices damaged the trade of a non-member American firm trying to do business in that land. Over the first half century of the Webb-Pomerene law, over 200 organizations registered officially.[10]

One historian, looking back on the formation of the MPEA, remarked, "The Export Association then had a second objective; with the cooperation of the State Department, which saw the movies as a means to inculcate ideology, it would fight to create an open market for American films everywhere." Another source commented the MPEA was referred to as "The Little State Department."[11]

Hollywood always operated abroad as a solid cartel before the MPEA was formed. It was the same eight majors who now called themselves the MPAA and the MPEA instead of just the MPAA. Perhaps it was formalized to secure favor with at least some parts of the government at a time when at least one branch, Justice, was on the attack against it. As well, there was always some distrust, some worry one or more producers would try and take advantage of some situation by breaking ranks; the MPEA could be used more vigorously to control product flow and prices. It was a sort of public bonding ritual in which the majors repledged the "all for one, one for all" mantra. Certainly Hollywood was unnerved by the late prewar experiences in both Germany and Italy where governments shut them out. Hollywood was not forced out of Italy, it chose to walk when Mussolini told them they could distribute on his terms only—no compromise. America's producers imposed those conditions on others; they did not allow themselves to be subjected to them. They could have still made a profit in Italy—not as much as they would have liked—but that rate was set by Italy; that was a principle that Hollywood considered wholly unprincipled. With the MPEA in place it meant a sole Hollywood agent, empowered to act for all, would negotiate in such situations. Dealing with an Italian-style situation caused Hollywood to worry that a foreign government might actively try to orchestrate a breakdown in the ranks by dealing with the majors one at a time. That was less likely with the MPEA in place. The MPEA was most publicly active in the period 1945–1952, for it was then that the East Bloc formed up and eventually shut off most U.S. films. Always an underlying fear motivating much of the cartel's moves was that if U.S. movies were removed from screens, and replaced by those of one or more other nations, then American films would have an even harder time in getting back if the situation changed. Hollywood's bluster that people rushed to see its films because they were the best was never supported by facts. In nations where U.S. movies have disappeared from the screens, the people have turned out in equal numbers to see the replacement product. Nobody ever rioted in the streets because U.S. films had disappeared from the screens—although the reverse has occurred.

Johnston moved into action in a number of ways to bolster Hollywood abroad. One way was to paint an unreal, bleak economic outlet for his industry.

In a 1947 report prepared by the cartel head, he named three terrors confronting the industry: a hard money crisis, social chaos and virulent nationalism. Johnston predicted economic gloom and doom in the future—unless, of course, Hollywood were to get more aid from its government, along with the imposition of "free trade" on the world at large. Johnston used his downbeat scenario to pitch the House foreign trade committee and the International Trade Conference in Geneva that year as part of his plea for his desired solutions. Addressing Britain as an example where agitation was "what amounts to a national crusade in support of British films and against American films," Johnston argued that without American films exhibitors would be in a disastrous position, as would the British treasury, which in 1946 received $40 million. The figure is suspect, but films from any nation would have done the same while more British films would have been even more advantageous—plus having a chance themselves of earning foreign income. Also not mentioned by Johnston was that Britain handed approximately $100 million to the U.S. annually—receipts from the box office repatriated by the majors. Some in the media bought the gloom and doom idea. When Archer Winsten wondered how long Hollywood's domination could last, he thought the question was academic as that domination "has already ended."[12]

On another front the MPAA decided to send a contingent of Hollywood stars and its best films to a 1947 world film festival held in Brussels. The last international festival before Brussels, held in Cannes in the fall of 1946, was given a miss by the U.S. industry with the result that British and Soviet movies won most of the awards. With American product under siege from many quarters, the MPAA decided there was value in winning international awards, especially since U.S. films were often sneered at abroad for being "lowbrow." By sending a group of stars to Brussels, the Americans believed U.S. films could hardly escape the attention of the awards committee.[13]

To counter complaints from State and many other quarters about stereotyping foreigners and generally unacceptable film content, the MPAA set up the International Information Center in Hollywood in 1947 to catch "unfortunate" representations of U.S. or foreign nations before they got past the script stage. A second stage was a "selectivity committee" in New York which supposedly screened every single film to determine whether or not it should go overseas. Disregarding such complaints would be poor commercial policy as well as being unpatriotic, explained the MPAA.[14]

Taking this public relations initiative farther, the MPAA in 1948 began special film screenings abroad which consisted of screening "quality" movies made by its members before elite audiences of government officials, newspaper publishers and so on. Those screenings were "motivated by the observation that many Europeans in government and cultural circles had neither the time nor the disposition to attend movies in public." As a result, noted MPAA international division managing director John McCarthy, "their attitudes toward American pictures were influenced either by their own preconceived notions of Hollywood movies, colored by what others thought of them, or else distorted under a chauvinistic zeal to promote patronage for home-market products." Those people were the leaders of European public opinion who constituted Hollywood's "most relentless critics."[15]

Another tactic to ameliorate such complaints was for Hollywood to bring foreign censorship officials to the U.S. to familiarize them with the workings of the industry's Production Code and other blue-pencil activities by state, municipal and religious organizations within America. Among other treats, those foreign visitors were shown the workings of the Catholic Church's National Legion of Decency. The idea was to convince the visitors that Hollywood's vetting system was so efficient there was no need to look closely at those films abroad. "With their eyes thus opened ... censors generally take a more enlightened attitude on their return to home base," reported *Variety*.[16]

On still another front the MPAA decided to set up a committee for advising foreign producers on how to get the maximum income from the U.S. It was to give them the benefit of advice as to how U.S. firms "milked" the home market—it was not set up to actually promote foreign films domestically. Additional advice was to be offered about how to get the best type of distribution deal; "Percentages for top pictures will be favored over the flat fees now being paid foreign filmmakers for their product." Hollywood had done away with receiving flat prices for its product decades ago, wherever possible. That meant that what few foreign movies did get screened in America were poorly paid. Summing up the reason for forming this committee, Johnston said, "If we want to do business in foreign countries we must make sure that trade is a two-way street." All of these measures were window dressing by the MPAA; no substantive changes took place.[17]

Illustrating the problem of screening foreign product in the U.S. was the experience of the U.K.'s J. Arthur Rank Company, a large producer/distributor/exhibitor, the most important film company in the U.K. outside of the cartel. In 1950 Rank had 150 movies gathering dust on the shelves, never having been screened in America. Rank turned U.S. distribution over to the small, U.S. independent Pentagon Pictures. Pentagon did not even attempt to find first-run outlets but looked to small art houses and neighborhood cinemas. In the past Rank product was distributed in the U.S. by Universal. However, this package was turned down by Universal "as unsuitable for major distribution in the U.S."[18]

Others from Hollywood beat the drum in various ways. Fox president Spyros Skouras spoke of what he called the "sacred duty of our great medium to help enlighten humanity" when he commented, "It is a solemn responsibility of our industry to increase motion picture outlets throughout the free world because it has been shown that no medium can play a greater part than the motion picture in indoctrinating people into the free way of life and instilling in them a compelling desire for freedom and hope for a brighter future. Therefore, we as an industry can play an infinitely important part in the worldwide ideological struggle for the minds of men and confound the Communist propagandists."[19]

MPPA International Division executive Gerald Mayer said of restrictions imposed on Hollywood, "These barriers to our films abroad exist despite the additional fact that American motion pictures have been beneficial to the economics of the countries in which they have been distributed." Regarding the U.K. quota law Mayer exclaimed that "American companies thus stimulate the development of the British industry at their own expense." Understandably Mayer presented no figures to substantiate those claims. And, he added, "No one has ever attempted to calculate—and it probably would be an impossible task—the indirect effect of American motion pictures on the sale of American products."[20]

When last heard from, George Canty was a motion picture expert with the State Department. In 1951 he worked as the MPAA representative in Italy. Canty enthused, "The prestige of American films throughout the world exceeds that of the films of any other country.... Without any doubt whatever all the South American countries esteem Hollywood's pictures beyond those produced anywhere else." He felt that the situation was the same in Europe. "American motion pictures would not be welcomed, and indeed loved, in all these countries, if their influence was not considered constructive," concluded Canty. "How can [foreign audiences] help but be fascinated with the things we have—our homes, schools, factories, the extravagances of our dinner tables, wardrobes, and gadgets." Only in one situation could U.S. movies do damage in a foreign land, thought Canty. "This is in countries where there is a primitive population unable to differentiate between drama and fact. In such countries the responsible authorities should select the motion pictures shown to such populations." In many nations, said Canty, American films "are the only proof that there still is a land where there is government of, by and for the people."[21]

Hardly to be found was a domestic naysayer. One reporter did note that the cartel members left themselves open to the charge that "they are all for one world ... theirs."[22]

Cries for money were delivered incessantly by Hollywood figures. Universal vice-president Al Duff, who had just returned from a European trip in the summer of 1945, stressed, "We need vigorous treatment now on the part of the government if American pictures are to pave the way for other U.S. industries in the foreign field." Arguing that Hollywood deserved as much aid as other industries for which dollar credits were supplied in the rehabilitation of war-ravaged nations, he noted ominously that in one [unspecified] city he visited, four of the seven first-run houses were screening Soviet movies. Duff felt that was the case because methods used by distributors handling

Russian product were "unorthodox," although he did not bother to explain that term.[23]

Even before Duff spoke, Hollywood's call was heeded—at the international level. During the summer of 1944 the United Nations Monetary and Financial Conference was held in New Hampshire at the behest of the U.S. At that Bretton Woods Conference—as it was better known—representatives of 44 nations met to discuss the postwar economic order. From that conference evolved both the International Monetary Fund (IMF) and the International Bank for Reconstruction and Development (IBRD), popularly known as the World Bank. One goal of Bretton Woods was to have nations adopt resolutions that would eliminate restrictions on royalty payments—such as frozen coin—while still allowing countries to bar hot money flight. Nations were then less likely to try to freeze money owed abroad for the purchase of goods than for payments of royalties and rentals, which movie receipts were. Industry reports were prepared for various sectors as to the impact of the Bretton Woods proposals. For motion pictures the report stated, "The film industry is in a position to benefit more than other industries from such monetary proposals, designed chiefly to set up machinery whereby payment can be received for goods sold abroad." Adoption of Bretton Woods proposals would eliminate restrictions on royalty payments and, "by contributing to the maintenance of a high income level abroad, will assure a steadier market for American films."[24]

During 1940s GATT (General Agreement on Tariffs and Trade) negotiations which were held mainly in Geneva, America's aim was to get nations to remove all restrictions on the free circulation of movies such as quantitative import quotas. A compromise attempt was made when the U.S. grudgingly agreed that any country would be allowed to establish a reasonable screen-playing time requirement for native product. Being short of dollars as well as desiring to generate film industries of their own, European nations led by the U.K. strongly opposed and defeated American efforts to impose total unrestricted access to American movies on the world under the cloak of free trade. Virtually the same scene would be played out in 1990s GATT talks; both times film became an exempted cultural item.[25]

While America made loans and extended general economic credit to various war-damaged nations between 1945 and 1948, the program became larger and more efficiently focused under the European Recovery Plan—known as the Marshall Plan for then Secretary of State George Marshall—which ran from 1948 to 1952. Historian Thomas Guback remarked that Marshall Plan aid "was supposed to strengthen faltering economies against risings from the left, American films were seen as propaganda vehicles for strengthening western European minds against pleas from the left. The argument to foreign governments was: If you take our dollars, you can take our films." During the plan's first year, up to $15 million was earmarked to be spent to aid films, magazines, newspapers, and so on, which had money frozen abroad by currency restrictions. Hollywood collected around $10 million of that total. Supposedly the money was for funds frozen after the Marshall Plan began, not retroactively. Attempting to counter critics, *Variety* said, "The Law is not to help Hollywood avoid normal business risks. It applies only to the special problem of frozen funds." While perpetually touting the blessings of the free market and free trade, Hollywood (like all industries) was unwilling to subject itself to market discipline. At the least sign of trouble, the industry went running to the government to be bailed out.[26]

As Paul Jarrico reported in the *New Republic* on U.S. aid to Europe, "A skillful lobbyist named Eric Johnston tried to swing a deal in which one of the conditions of American aid to Europe was relative freedom for Hollywood film exporters. To Johnston it was simply a question of free trade, a concept America has always defended except when protection was more profitable."[27]

Battles took place in many individual nations to reestablish American film hegemony, or to insure that such domination was not lessened. Most of those battles took place in Europe but even Canada voiced objections. Back in 1939 Canada established the government-funded National Film Board (NFB). It trained filmmakers but funded only full-length documentaries or short subjects—the kind of product that would not compete for cinema screens. It was structured that way precisely so as not to antagonize Hollywood, which might have become irked if that institution funded fiction full-length features. At one point it did try to move into the field of feature films but was stopped after U.S. interests raised objections with the Canadian government. Still, a trained documentary or short subject filmmaker might make a move to fiction. However, the NFB was allowed to live. Today the NFB still exists, finally moving into the production of dramatic feature films for theatrical release in 1963–1964, but never in a big way. During Britain's first quota period (1928 to 1938), U.S. producers started a small branch plant making a total of 22 films in Canada over that time. However, all were made to meet the U.K. quota which allowed any product produced in one of its dominions to count as British-made. As well, those films were all cheaply-produced, low-quality quota quickies. Recognizing that as an error and a loophole, the British corrected it in the 1938 quota act which disqualified such product as British for the sake of the quota. Immediately that Canadian film industry disappeared entirely with output back to its usual level—zero.[28]

Canada had a serious war-related dollar shortage of its own by 1947. That year $20 million left Canada to pay for imported films; $17 million of that went to the U.S. cartel, with the remainder going to British and French film concerns. Not one cent was earned from Canadian films abroad—because there were none. Because of the hard currency crisis, Canada's government was considering imposing restrictions on various goods imported from the U.S. to avert an impending dollar devaluation. Such sweeping restrictions were imposed on a wide variety of U.S. goods that year under the Emergency Foreign Exchange

Conservation Act. Initially movies were targeted to be subjected to quotas and the freezing of coin within Canada from foreign films to be channeled into native film production. However, after Hollywood had finished lobbying, films were left out of the act, suffering no restrictions of any kind.[29]

MPEA executive Francis Harmon convinced Canadian Trade and Commerce Minister Clarence D. Howe that a quota on foreign film imports was not in Canada's interests as it might infuriate moviegoers in Canada. Instead, he assured Howe that the MPEA would find a solution to correct the dollar outflow. Within the House of Commons the quota issue was debated at length. When an opposition member asked Howe why he did not want a quota favoring British films, the minister replied, "They are entirely free to come into this market."[30]

That MPEA solution was to successfully sell to the Canadian government a public relations scam called the Canadian Cooperation Project (CPP) which proposed the Hollywood cartel would promise to make short subjects, newsreels and some features in Canada. No specific commitment was given by the MPEA about the number of such movies, the budget size, or where they would be distributed and exhibited, or even if they would be distributed and exhibited. Canadian film historian Manjunath Pendakur wrote, "Most of the promises were never kept. They were never intended to be kept. The MPEA's strategy was to insure that Canada would not follow Great Britain in imposing a film import quota or a duty on the rentals. The CCP took the place of those restrictions." One result of the project was that Canadian places were mentioned sometimes in American movies. One example was *New York Confidential* in which the line "They caught Louis Engleday in Detroit" was changed to "They caught Louis Engleday on his way to Canada."[31]

Presumably those mentions of Canada in U.S. movies were to encourage more north-of-the-border tourism, which would lead to a reversal of the dollar flow. As ludicrous as such an idea was, a representative of Canada was specially appointed to reside in Hollywood to supervise small changes in dialogue and location in American films. Celluloid vacationers spent time in the Canadian Rockies instead of California; lovers eloped to Ottawa rather than Chicago.[32]

Additionally the MPEA organized a propaganda campaign against the NFB for competing unfairly with private sector filmmakers and for harboring subversives (this was during the McCarthy Red-hunting era). Domestically Hollywood cooperated with the U.S. government in its systematic attack on the arts community. That propaganda campaign was successful enough in Canada to spur the Canadian government to attack the NFB as riddled with Reds. An Ottawa newspaper which defended the NFB noted in 1949 that "conclusive evidence has been produced to show how private filmmaking companies in Canada, backed by Hollywood, made [the NFB] the object of a concentrated attack." As a result of those attacks, NFB head Ross McLean was dismissed to be replaced by a man with no film experience.[33]

America's State Department also lent assistance. In a September 7, 1949, letter to Francis Harmon, U.S. Ambassador to Canada Lawrence A. Steinhardt alerted Harmon to dissatisfaction with the CCP in certain government circles. He warned the MPEA that the Canadian government might impose further restrictions on U.S. imports or freeze currency. Two weeks later Harmon arrived in Ottawa where he met with Howe and other government officials to assure them the MPEA intended to expand and continue the CCP into the 1950s. After those meetings an MPEA report on the CCP declared, "As a result of these meetings, we have the assurance of the Canadian government that no adverse action will be taken in the near future against the American Motion Picture Industry…. Although at no time did we commit the Industry to any definite amount of production in Canada, we have indicated that at least three feature pictures will be produced in whole or in part during 1950. This particular part of the Project makes the greatest impression on the Canadian government. The amount of money spent by the American companies is not really as important, it seems, as the fact that they are there on location and are seen actually shooting a film." Perhaps the Canadian government was also looking for a public relations gimmick in the CCP.[34]

Wrote Pendakur, "The CCP was clearly being steered by the American majors to suit their goals, and the Canadian government went along. Consequently, for a total of three possible films to be produced in Canada, the government allowed the MPEA to extract $17 million a year under foreign exchange crisis conditions. The outcome of the CCP, a public relations scheme, was continuation of American control of the Canadian film market. The MPEA silenced its critics effectively with full cooperation of the government." When the currency crisis ended in 1951, the CCP was dropped. During 1952 Secretary of State Lester Pearson (later Prime Minister) wrote a letter to Eric Johnston stating, "It was encouraging to learn of the CCP's success in maintaining interest in Canada and to hear also about some of the long-term benefits which are emerging as a result of the policies pursued by the Motion Picture Association of America through this means." In 1959 the cartel released 305 movies in Canada; Canada produced one film that year. By 1974 the amount of money from film rentals traveling from Canada to the U.S. had risen to $54.3 million annually, bestowing the dubious honor on Canada of being Hollywood's largest foreign market.[35]

Even though Hollywood was busy taming Europe, Latin America was not forgotten entirely. People in Ecuador were said to like action films, jungle movies and comedies if "not too subtle, for the Ecuadorian audience is not a sophisticated one." Of the movies screened there, 75 percent were American, 19 percent Mexican. However, those Mexican features captured about 50 percent of the playing time. Hollywood projected its own deficiencies onto the Ecuadorians and other Latins. In the late 1940s the cartel was still experimenting with dubbed and subtitled films going into Latin America. *Variety* admitted those movies were not always dubbed very well, being conspicuously out of synch. For a time some of the majors considered narration instead of dubbing, allowing the removal of most subtitles. Narration had the advantage of being cheaper than either of the other two methods. In the end the majors stuck primarily with subtitles in Latin America. One disadvantage with subtitles was that illiterate people—a considerable number in some areas—could not read them. It may have been that Ecuadorian and other "unsophisticated" Latins preferred action films precisely because they relied less on dialogue and were thus easier to follow. That may also explain the popularity of Mexican films which, of course, were in Spanish, as well as being closer to being an indigenous product.[36]

Colombia's government banned block booking right after World War II. As a result, the U.S. share of released movies there dropped from 78 percent in 1939 down to 50 percent in 1947. Over half of the nation's cinemas were owned by Cine Colombia, a government monopoly. If Hollywood let that law pass without much of a fight, perhaps it was because the market there was very small or they were busy elsewhere. Lima, Peru, had a total of eight first-run houses in 1948. MGM, Paramount, RKO, Warner and Universal each owned or controlled one; a sixth house screened only Columbia or Universal product. Thus only two venues were left to the competition with UA releasing to those two, along with the rest of the world. That left Fox as the only homeless major in Lima. Two years later that was remedied when Fox built its own house in that city.[37]

In 1949 Hollywood occupied around 73 percent of all Latin American playing time with that market providing 20 percent of the cartel's foreign revenue. Latin journalist Hernane de Sa described Hollywood's portrayal of Latin Americans as having gone through two phases with the first depicting Latin Americans in films as invariably villainous, referred to as "greaser." That was supplanted by the bumbling, goodly peasant. That first phase by Hollywood was one of scorn and insult, moving to condescension in the second phase, a phase which infuriated even more Latins. Once, explained de Sa, an enraged Argentine audience burned down the house after the showing of a Hollywood film depicting Argentineans as a simple, primitive and unspoiled people. Although that was an isolated example, audiences throughout Latin America had smashed up seats, hurled objects at the screen and dropped burning newspapers from the balcony when confronted with Hollywood's portrayal of their land. De Sa hoped that such depiction was a thing of the past.[38]

Faced with currency problems, inflation and other economic problems, Brazil's Central Price Commission moved in to impose restrictions on foreign films. By decree, distributors could receive a maximum of 40 percent of the gross revenue from the box office receipts with the cost of movie ads, taxation and cinema employees' salaries to be deducted from that 40 percent. Additionally the price of cinema admission was lowered and fixed by law at 20¢ to

36¢ U.S., depending on the quality of the house, down from the scale of 40¢ to 50¢. Immediately the majors stopped selling new product in Brazil and started complaining. Other American products such as cars and clothing were allowed to rise in price along with inflation but not films. Movies were often the sole diversion for the people and the government understood the need to keep them readily accessible to the masses as a type of pacification control.[39]

In 1941, 460 films were released in Brazil (383 U.S., 20 U.K., 12 France, 11 Germany and 4 Brazil); in 1945, 347 movies were released there (310 U.S., 9 Argentina, 9 Brazil); and in 1951, 573 films were released (441 U.S., 25 U.K., 23 Italy and 23 Brazil). At the time the restrictions were imposed, Hollywood was extracting close to $6 million a year from Brazil. Cartel members felt that State did not respond quickly enough in Brazil to help them, complaining that "the U.S. State Department is indifferent to the fate of American pix overseas." Hollywood continued to smart over its perceived lack of special treatment from the Marshall Plan allocations. Nonetheless, pressure from Hollywood and State caused the Brazilians to compromise by completely dropping the idea of making any deductions from the distributor's gross as well as fixing the rental rate at an average of 42 percent, allowing higher rates for some cases as long as the average was met. In the recent past rental rates in Brazil had run from 25 to 50 percent with the low end being for really old, really bad B product. What the majors did, as can be seen from the number of releases between 1945 and 1951, was to ship in more product, older movies sold at low rates in order to receive what they felt was their due for current product and still stay within the mandated average. That settled, the majors continued to harass Brazilian authorities to increase the admission price. The fact that so many impoverished nations had low cinema admission prices always galled Hollywood. During the years after World War II they would actively try to change that situation.[40]

Brazil's Vera Cruz Studios was founded in Sao Paulo in 1949 to generate native films with the hope of producing quality films that also had commercial appeal. Unfortunately for the Brazilians, they modeled it on Hollywood's MGM, adopting the studio system rather than an *auteur* one. As one critic noted, Vera Cruz films were "made for the rich by the rich." Because the lavish cost of production of films at Vera Cruz exceeded what could be recovered from the home country, the studio was dependent on foreign income. To reach those international markets, the studio naively left distribution in the hands of Columbia which was, commented a Brazilian film historian, "an organization more interested in promoting its own films than in fostering a vital Brazilian industry." Needless to say, virtually no foreign income was ever earned. Since it could not recover costs in Brazil, only one of the studio's films made a profit. Vera Cruz went bankrupt in 1954.[41]

Brazil attempted to implement an 8-to-1 quota law in 1951—for every eight foreign films exhibited, one Brazilian movie had to be screened. Distributors were joined by exhibitors in opposing the measure, causing Brazil's government to change it to a 16-to-1 quota. When the MPAA considered various restrictions, they always felt a screen quota was the "least undesirable" of possible protectionist measures with restrictions on the number of imports the worst. Even a 16-to-1 quota was unacceptable. Continued opposition by Hollywood and local exhibitor chains caused the measure to die completely. Around the same time, Brazilian film personnel requested unsuccessfully that the government ban block booking, citing the fact the practice had recently been banned in America.[42]

In response to its dollar crisis, Argentina tried to impose certain restrictions on the import of U.S. films, and other goods, early in 1949. That led the majors to announce a boycott. Enormous pressure was applied on Juan Peron and other Argentinean officials by the American ambassador to Argentina Stanton Griffis, who was then also still chairman of the executive committee of Paramount Pictures. As part of the pressure, Griffis had Hollywood films flown to Buenos Aires in diplomatic pouches, then held special screenings at the Embassy residence for Peron and other important Argentineans. After a year-and-a-half boycott with almost no new Hollywood product having entered the country, an agreement was finally signed. However, it was reluctant on the part of the Latins since on the day of the official signing all Argentinean officials involved found themselves needed elsewhere. One reason for the reluctance was the fact the pact permitted unlimited imports of U.S. films. Next the nation's treasury department succeeded in delaying implementation of the pact through various red tape procedures. Then the Argentinean government issued a series of decrees "onerous" to the U.S. such as providing higher rental rates to native films. All the while, prints of old U.S. movies that were in the country before the boycott continued to be rerun. Finally, in July 1951 new product flowed back into Argentina as the dollar crisis eased. The only concession was that the country was able to freeze a percentage of U.S. revenues. Except for that, there were no restrictions on the import of American movies.[43]

One problem in Latin America for the cartel was the situation whereby Hollywood boosted the Mexican industry, as a check on the Argentinean product. Once a native industry got started, just shutting off the aid, as Hollywood had done by war's end, was not sufficient. Such a native industry could then be self-sustaining, earning enough from each film to pay the bills and provide seed money for the next one. Mexico was in that position in the mid–1940s, producing around 70 to 80 films per year. Yet its position was precarious since it had no reserves to fall back on; it literally lived from film to film. Commenting on the situation, *U.S. News & World Report* wrote that while Argentina and France may have complained about competition from Hollywood, it was not true in Mexico. Cooperation between Mexico and the U.S. started in war time when the U.S. wanted Latins to see plenty of pro–Allied films. "It chose Mexico as its agent and sent crews, directors, raw film, cameras, lights, etc." That pushed Mexican production to new heights. "Meanwhile, the Argentine industry, nearly cut off from U.S. film stock, had a hard time getting along." Without explanation, this account noted Mexican feature production had dropped 50 percent since the war. Most of the account was distorted, to say the least. Mexico was chosen to check Argentina. Production had fallen drastically in Mexico as observed, but there was a reason.[44]

More accurate was a 1946 *Business Week* article which noted Mexico would produce less movies in 1946 than in 1945. "The reason is not scarcity of capital but the fact that completed pictures are lying idle, unable to find a market. They represent an investment of about $5 million financed by the semi-governmental investment bank the Banco Cinematografic. Until those pictures start to produce income, the bank will not be able to grant more credits to the particular producers concerned." According to Raul de Anda, chairman of the Mexican film producers association, native films could not get screened because exhibitors could get cheaper films. (From where was unexplained.) Exhibitors argued they were not exhibited because they were poor quality films. That account was closer to reality but still missing something.[45]

During the first six months of 1948, 35 Mexican films were produced but only six were exhibited. American movies held 90 percent of the screen time. Hollywood also flooded the market with a large number of old movies which, of course, were offered to exhibitors at cheap rates. The cartel cut off access to exhibitors with a deluge of old reissues at low rates, plus the old standby control device, block booking. Exhibitors argued they booked the films they thought would earn the most money, although they acknowledged their gross receipts were lower than a year earlier. With very low rental rates it was possible for an exhibitor to make more profit from a lower gross. Even Hollywood was not losing anything since these old reissues had not been planned to be used in the first place. Credit for Mexican producers soon dried up because their films, blocked from screen time, lost money.[46]

Gamely the Mexican government tried to fight back by enacting a law which required exhibitors to screen from 30 to 50 percent native product (depending on class of the house). It was a move praised by Mexican filmmakers and damned by Hollywood. Predictably the majors threatened a boycott if the law was enforced. Also, they called on State to help fight against the law. MGM executive Maurice Silverstein said, with no hint of irony, "No one can find reason for the law. Everybody seems completely satisfied with the present setup." Mexican exhibitors fought the law in court. In August 1951, the Mexican Federal Court issued an injunction forbidding the government from putting the law into effect as unconstitutional. It amounted to a more or less permanent injunction. The law was dead.[47]

In writing about this period, Latin American film historian Gaizka Usabel noted that the majors imposing their movies on Latin Americans "promoted life styles and cultural values that were foreign to the Hispanic filmgoer. Rather than being 'ambassadors' of good will, too often their films acted as promotional vehicles for Hollywood's ideologies, mid–America's beliefs and Fifth Avenue's latest trends." Continuing, Usabel commented that American film executives did not try to improve living conditions; "social and political issues were beyond their scope.... Film distribution was a part of the larger financial interest of American business." Hollywood made the same mistake that Jose Marti pointed out regarding North American politics, thought Usabel, both displayed "Ignorance of the Latin culture, indifference toward its future, and greed for its resources and revenues."[48]

The greatest difficulties for the cartel were the countries rapidly becoming the East Bloc at war's end. State Department officials said American films could provide Western Europe's strongest bulwark against Communism. However, to achieve the best advantage, care had to be taken in film selection with gangster productions as well as the likes of *The Grapes of Wrath* and *Tobacco Road* best left at home. Movies did not need to be anti–Soviet, simply pro–American.[49]

Around mid–1946 the situation in those nations was handled for Hollywood by the MPEA doing all the negotiations in those "problem" countries. Poland and Yugoslavia were reportedly showing old, leftover U.S. films, without permission. No money was paid to the majors for those screenings. In Bulgaria and Romania the MPEA was distributing with complete control of prints, although all revenue was frozen there. Russia bought seven films from the MPEA but paid only a small, flat rate. It was not known what happened to a print after it arrived in that country.[50]

Criticism of Hollywood product intensified in the East Bloc. Polish media attacked the state monopoly Film Polski for the distribution of "worthless" American movies. Singled out for having presented "murder, vulgar brawls and drinking in an attractive light, and even glorifying them" was *My Darling Clementine*.[51]

Early in 1948 Hungary banned the films of six Hollywood stars (Robert Taylor, Robert Montgomery, Gary Cooper, Adolphe Menjou, Allan Jones and George Murphy) because, said a government official, the actors involved "expressed hatred of our 'peoples' democracies'" when testifying in a Congressional investigation of Hollywood." It was a move hailed in the local press as the banning of "American trash." Later that year an editorial in the Hungarian *Szabad Nep* urged an end to the showing of U.S. movies "which make idiots of the people." In a further burst of invective, those films were described as an "international infection, carefully prepared attacks on public intelligence."[52]

When the MPEA sent in a group of 30 films from its members to Romania, a MPEA representative said those movies would probably represent a "100 percent loss" but the films "were intended to secure the Rumanian market."

Competition then came from "cheap" Hungarian product. Admission prices in Romania in 1947 were 3 ½¢ U.S., compared to 30¢ in pre-war times. After testimony in the U.S. before the House Committee investigating Un-American Activities, Romania followed Hungary's example by banning the screening of any movies involving 11 stars including Taylor, Montgomery, Barbara Stanwyck, Ginger Rogers, Greta Garbo and Clark Gable. Presumably the ban was imposed because those actors were deemed to be not pro–Communist. On November 2, 1948, the Romanian film industry was nationalized; the next day the government took over the MPEA Bucharest office, seizing all films found there.[53]

Czechoslovakia set up its own postwar monopoly agency which handled all importing and distributing of movies. Russian films were allotted 50 percent of the screen time. During negotiations between the government and the MPEA, the Czechs offered the cartel 35 percent of the gross receipts minus a tax of 10 percent, or a net of 31.5 percent. However, that was to be split evenly between the Czech monopoly and the distributor, leaving cartel members with 16 percent. Of course, that was unacceptable to the MPEA, which continued to negotiate. At the end of 1947 the Czech monopoly demanded that proceeds from American films be balanced completely by the screening of Czech movies in the U.S. With that demand, the MPEA broke off talks and walked out of the market.[54]

Russia had bought no U.S. product since the summer of 1945 when they purchased a few. Negotiations between the Soviets and the MPEA continued for several years with a deal seemingly concluded late in 1948 whereby Russia would pay an unspecified flat rental rate. A list of 100 films was to be submitted to a Russian review board which would select 20 titles to exhibit. Under the agreement the Russians were to be allowed to delete lines and scenes but could not add material to a film. That deal ultimately did not come off.[55]

A few years later the State Department sent a note to the Russians to return two films to their rightful owners and cease screening them in Russia. According to State, the two 1930s Columbia titles *Mr. Smith Goes to Washington* and *Mr. Deeds Goes to Town* were being shown in mutilated and distorted form to serve Soviet propaganda purposes. Columbia had never authorized those movies to be shown in the Soviet Union. (Russia obtained those films during the war in Germany.) Refusing to return them, Russia described them as "trophies of war." State Department officials were convinced both films were being used to show Russians that Americans were "money-mad" and "corrupt." In *Deeds* Gary Cooper's character played a small town man who came into $1 million. Then he headed to the big city where evildoers tried to get his money and where he was subjected to a court sanity hearing when he tried to give his money away to help poor farmers hurt in the Depression. Cooper won the day by being declared sane and, of course, winning the girl. In the Russian version the film ended with Cooper being taken away from his girl and being committed to an insane asylum. The State Department was unsure as to whether the Germans or the Russians had distorted the film.[56]

Success in the East Bloc by the MPEA was limited to Yugoslavia. After spending ten fruitless days in Moscow late in 1948 trying to sell movies to the Russians, Eric Johnston traveled to Belgrade where he met personally with Marshal Tito. Fancying himself a diplomat, Johnston reported he and Tito talked for hours about world issues "on every possible subject." Not forgetting Hollywood, Johnston signed a deal with Tito whereby Yugoslavia would take 25 Hollywood features in the coming year. MPEA European manager Irving Maas reported the Yugoslavs were "pretty choosy" with the country not yet ready for any movie considered as "definitely anti–Commie."[57]

Sadly the MPEA announced in 1950 that U.S. film screenings behind the Iron Curtain had mostly all dried up, except in Yugoslavia. That sadness was twofold, squeezing out the flag and inflicting a financial loss since "the eastern European territories produced quite a pile of coin for Hollywood in pre-war days and again in 1946 and 1947." By that time the MPEA had submitted two lists of 100 titles each to Moscow, and screened 50 films there for officials. Reportedly the Soviets would pay $50,000 to rent each title. However, Kremlin officials claimed they could not find 20 satisfactory movies.[58]

Nothing puzzled Europeans in this period more than the McCarthy witch hunt for Reds within Hollywood as Congressional committees claiming Hollywood was spreading Communism came to the fore. U.S. film producer Paul Graetz said on his return from Europe that idea was regarded there as "ludicrous" when the Communists themselves were "so vehement in their hatred and distrust of Hollywood pictures." European Communists damned the American film industry regularly as a tool of capitalism. Among Europeans in general, such McCarthyite allegations were regarded as "completely ridiculous."[59]

China's government suddenly increased the customs duty on imported movies in 1948, moving it from $250 to $1,200 per feature. Ostensibly the hike was a means for the government to get more money to fight the Communists. Although Hollywood was indeed virulently anti–Communist, both on and off the screen, that orientation did not extend to agreeing with China's move. The cartel slapped a boycott on China, cutting no more new deals. One year later the Communists had taken power in China. Shanghai's state paper criticized U.S. films as vehicles for spreading "imperialist poison" and for "doping" the minds of Chinese audiences with "sex and legs." Just before the Communist takeover, of the 211 movies shown in Shanghai 142 (67 percent) were American. Soon thereafter China became a closed market.[60]

One market felt to be safe for Hollywood was the Philippines, where Nathan Golden felt the market looked good with little chance of a crackdown because the domestic industry could not meet the demand and because the revenue from U.S. movies, from taxation, was an important source of government income. Golden neglected to mention the huge outflow of money caused by foreign film domination of the screens. Actually the natives were not that happy with the situation. Since about 1946 the city of Manila had been trying unsuccessfully to have a law imposed that exhibitors screen native movies at least 10 percent of the time. It was always resisted by the exhibitors and distributors.[61]

Assessing the cartel's future in Europe after the war, *Business Week* worried at the end of 1945 that some of the European nations had gotten "big ideas" about the propaganda value of pictures to sell "ways of life, policies of governments and the industrial product of nations." With possibly intensified efforts made to increase barriers due to currency shortfalls and national culture concerns, Hollywood had prepared itself by forming the MPEA "and is working hand in hand with the U.S. Department of Commerce and the State Department, each concerned with different but related aspects of the problem of reopening markets for U.S. films." One thing the cartel opposed adamantly was dealing with a national monopoly. Of all the possible moves against U.S. films, noted the account, "the trend toward nationalization and state monopolies is viewed with the greatest alarm, while restrictions imposed by lack of exchange cause the least. U.S. interests are prepared to waive immediate payments in favor of accumulations which can be transferred later, and will even accept some funds in local currencies, if necessary. But state monopolies are another matter."[62]

Fortune magazine agreed early in 1946, stating the most pressing reasons behind restrictions targeting Hollywood product came from fear of a dollar shortage along with the desire for a national cinematic art. To deal with recalcitrant governments, the majors formed the MPEA "which seems to have the full backing of the State Department. In addition to pressing for maximum film exports, the group insists on unrestricted distribution facilities abroad, in direct conflict with the government monopolies."[63]

Variety felt Hollywood's immediate strategy at the beginning of 1946 was to go into those war-closed or disrupted nations to establish a "beach head for eventual reconquest" of those markets. Film executives wanted the restoration of European stability along with the creation of an international "open door." Although the majors used all their clout to get the U.S. government to give loans and aid to Europe, the cartel members stood "irreconcilably opposed to American government interference in their business," even though "they are looking to the U.S. State Department to grease their way into Europe."[64]

When Nathan Golden assessed the situation in 1951, he argued that while the dollar shortage was the most important factor underlying restrictions in the immediate post-war era, it then gave way to activities by nations to establish native film industries. Because of that trend the number of imported U.S. films was limited; as those native industries developed, their movies "are offering more serious competition" to the U.S. Citing in particular Italy, France

and Germany, Golden said movies produced there were increasing in number, improving in quality "and are being exported to other foreign markets,
reducing U.S. films' screen time in those markets." That was highly exaggerated but even a minuscule dent in U.S. screen control could cause Hollywood
to shake in fear, reaching heights of excessive hyperbole. Still, Golden admitted the reason was largely cultural preservation and enrichment; indirectly he
also conceded restrictions could successfully accomplish that.[65]

One example of the close relationship between the film industry and the
government occurred when U.S. Senator J. William Fulbright introduced
Warner president Harry M. Warner at a 1946 dinner by saying the "future of
all the countries of the world may be shaped by the policies set forth by this
man." Some American businesses were then experimenting with minute-long
movie ads, dubbed in foreign languages, to display their products to foreign
countries in an effort to win back lost war markets. That old saying "trade follows the film" could easily become, wrote *Variety*, "everything follows the
film."[66]

Testifying before the House Ways and Means Committee in 1947, Eric
Johnston advocated reciprocal trade agreements, a stimulation of world trade
and especially free trade. The problem as he saw it was the scarcity of dollars
abroad. Other nations could not buy from America if they were short of dollars; they could not get dollars unless Americans bought from them; because
they were war-ravaged, they had little to sell. The solution: give them money
and credits. Johnston stated that in 1946 Hollywood's foreign remittances
totaled $125 million, "almost exactly the total profit of the motion picture
producing companies the same year." He added, "It is foreign trade in short
which permits our industry to function on its present scale. If it had to depend
entirely on the domestic market, it could not possibly maintain the high quality of its products or its high levels of employment, wages and salaries."
Although the cartel often told foreign nations of the economic benefits derived
from U.S. film screen dominance, Johnston was more forthright when he told
the Congressional committee, "Motion picture-goers in Mexico, in Britain,
in France and in Denmark, for example, contribute to the economy of this
country." Smugly he told the committee he would not ask for any barriers in
the U.S. against foreign films; the industry "will take its chances on competition for the world markets."[67]

Begging for dollars in 1948, the MPAA presented facts and figures to State
claiming its costs of operating in some 30 nations abroad were an extra $40
million due to various restrictions (frozen coin was not included in that figure).
These were "expenses." State Department officials agreed to ask Congress for
$10 million to aid the industry, after both sides agreed the first figure was unre-
alistic. President Truman urged Johnston and his MPEA to continue to send
movies into Germany, Japan and East Bloc nations, promising he would look
into the cost situation. Truman expressed "concern at threats that America's

most powerful medium for selling the democratic way of life should be cut off." That was ironic in that Hollywood was then under heavy fire from segments of the government for its Communist tendencies and for being riddled with Reds.[68]

Secretary of State Dean Acheson ordered the problem of America's film industry put on the agenda of a forthcoming international trade conference to take place in Washington, D.C. At a press conference Acheson said he would do everything "within the bounds of propriety" to obtain fair and nondiscriminatory treatment for U.S. movies from foreign governments.[69]

In March 1950, U.S. Senator William Benton, then also Assistant Secretary of State, called for a "Marshall Plan in the field of ideas," explaining that State planned to do everything within its power along political and diplomatic lines "to help break down the artificial barriers to the expansion of private American news agencies, magazines, motion pictures and other media of communications throughout the world.... Freedom of exchange of ideas generally is an integral part of our foreign policy." Benton added, "Nothing equals the motion picture in its capacity for gripping and holding masses of peoples and communicating information and attitudes in vivid, remarkable form.... Their impact can indeed change the face of history."[70]

Still, Hollywood could get upset at the merest perceived slight. In 1946 the Motion Picture Unit in the Commerce Department lost its independent status, being moved into a newly created General Products Division with items such as rubber, typewriters and office furniture. At the same time the State Department transferred film oversight from its Telecommunications Division to a desk in the Commercial Policy Division. These downgrades happened, moaned *Variety*, "despite all that pix has done for the government." While film did get moved around within State and Commerce, more than occasionally it was all cosmetic and had no effect on the amount or type of aid extended to Hollywood. Around the same time as those moves, Benton told the press, "I think there is no industry in this country with a more legitimate right to expect the assistance of the State Department along every legitimate line than the motion picture; that if the power of the government and the influence of the State Department are to be used to help any American industry in its expansion abroad, it should be used to help the motion picture industry."[71]

There was still a certain amount of antagonism between Hollywood and the government over film content. In a 1945 State report called "Memorandum on the Postwar International Information Program of the United States," Arthur Macmahon addressed the responsibility issue by raising two points: avoidance of "more positive forms of offense" and development of an "awareness of other peoples which will compliment them and facilitate friendly relations." Discussing the relationship between the industry and State, "it can be said that there must at least be frequent contact between the industry and the State Department. There is evidence that a closer working relationship is already being established under the president of the Motion Picture Association, Eric Johnston. Several former members of the State Department, including a former Assistant Secretary of State, are now associated with the Motion Picture Association of America."[72]

Members of a House subcommittee on foreign trade attacked Hollywood in 1946 for the quality of movies sent abroad. Chairman Eugene Worley suggested the possibility that the government would regulate film exports if the industry failed to take satisfactory self-regulatory steps. Hollywood argued steps for self-regulation had already been taken in the formation of the MPEA, one of whose duties was to weed out films that did not give a fair picture of American customs and life. MPAA vice-president Francis Harmon expressed confidence the problem would be solved through self-regulation just as growth of domestic censorship was checked by the adoption of the Production Code. Another two or three years would see an end to the "dumping of inferior products," said Harmon.[73]

It was such criticism which prompted the industry to take measures such as establishing the Hollywood Information Center and in general appear to heed its critics. Within two years State was reportedly happy with the industry's response to foreign critics and by their vetting of all movies in two steps by all MPAA members. Criticism of U.S. films had by then "virtually died out in Western Europe" although the East Bloc still damned the product as "capitalist culture." Films first were screened before a MPAA "selectivity committee" which passed on their export suitability. Then the MPEA checked them over before granting final approval. Unstated was the fact that the same people belonged to both groups. The crucial test that a film had to pass "is its ambassadorial role for the U.S."[74]

Hollywood had to at least pay lip service to such criticism from its government since it constantly went begging to Uncle Sam for more money. In 1951 the industry claimed the speed and loss of dollar balances abroad "has come as a shock to the film industry. Only a vast outpouring of economic aid by Washington for overseas aid can save picture companies from taking a severe cut in foreign income for 1952." The pace at which "U.S. has pushed its allies abroad to rearm is seen as the principle cause of the strain on their economies." Foreign income was then close to an all-time high, around 40 to 50 percent of the overall take, and was "sorely needed as compensation for the domestic b.o. slip"—a reference to the initial inroads of television. A worry was that nations such as Britain and France would have to make cuts in such "quasi-luxury" items as movies in order to keep up imports of foodstuffs and other dire necessities. At the time of that call for economic aid, the Marshall Plan had been in place for over two years and was already pouring money into Europe, with some of it recycled back to Hollywood.[75]

Three nations in Northern Europe resisted the cartel's pricing policy at war's end. Prior to the war, distributors in Norway received 30 percent of the box office gross, regardless of the type of film shown. Immediately after the war, the majors insisted on a sliding scale of film rental varying from 30 to 45 percent of the gross, depending on quality of the film. Cinema owners declared they could not afford that much due to high taxation. The majors launched a boycott, sending in no more new films—those on hand in the country continued to be screened. Later in 1946 Hollywood and Norway reached an agreement whereby the distributors would receive rentals of 25 to 40 percent of the gross. When the *New York Times* mentioned the story, they referred to it as a "Norwegian boycott."[76]

Denmark had limited foreign exchange after the war and wished to preserve it for vital imports. With that in mind, the MPEA offered to sell Denmark fewer but better pictures. Under those conditions, MPEA wanted 40 percent of the gross instead of the 30 percent maximum the Danes had imposed. Negotiations continued for a time. When the Danes suggested even more stringent restrictions to limit the dollar outflow, MPEA called such proposals "confiscatory and totally unacceptable." Another almost-boycott was lifted when Denmark agreed to "reconsider" its position. Although Denmark produced few native films, they were always popular. "A Danish picture of middle quality would always get bigger earnings than the biggest U.S. films," admitted *Variety*. Usually a Danish feature did not exceed $45,000 in cost.[77]

More troublesome was Holland. The Dutch trade organization was the Bioscoop Bond which controlled both distribution and exhibition, with the blessing of the government. The Bond attempted to regulate the number of films imported as well as the rental rates for distributors. U.S. majors complained of "monopolistic practices" with the Dutch dictating "the terms they wanted to pay." Hollywood was helpless, the industry whined, because the "distributors, and in turn, the exhibitors, could dictate terms to U.S. distributors." The MPEA was in Holland to deliver this message: "Here are our pictures and here are our terms.... Take it or leave it." When the inevitable boycott was announced by the majors, the *New York Times* called it a "Dutch ban." One film executive said that in prewar times the Bond could get away with its monopolistic dealings by playing one U.S. company against another in order to get the lowest possible rental, a situation presumably rectified by the formation of the MPEA. When most of the majors withdrew from the Netherlands Society of Motion Picture Exhibitors, that organization charged the withdrawal was "another step in a campaign a few American film companies started against the Dutch business because they have not yet succeeded in establishing an economic dictatorship nor in dictating to the Dutch people what films they should see and what prices they should pay."[78]

An agreement was reached wherein the MPEA became a member of the Bond and was allowed to distribute to members of that group, with a maximum rental of 32.5 percent of the gross. Additionally the Netherlands government agreed to remove a restriction which had limited U.S. movies to a maximum playing time of 28 weeks (not applied to films from any other nation). Johnston and the MPEA had worked for months to achieve this victory, considered the first major postwar victory over restrictions on U.S. movies. Aiding in applying pressure was U.S. Ambassador Herman Baruch in the Hague. It was Baruch who phoned Johnston with word of Holland's capitulation.[79]

Spain took action against the majors in 1945 when the government froze rents from distribution of U.S. films after five years of release. Mostly it was smaller cinemas which played product that was old. Government officials hoped the move would force Hollywood to send in more current releases rather than have old pictures circulate for years. Instead Hollywood withdrew all its product from Spain that was five years old or over. It was a spite move, for the majors believed many of those smaller houses would be forced to close. They had no intention of circulating newer material in Spain, explaining that even if they did those small venues could not afford to rent them.[80]

When Spain negotiated with the cartel over the number of new U.S. films to be admitted, their initial suggestions were unacceptable to the cartel, causing them to threaten to cut the Spaniards off from raw film stock for domestic producers—still in short supply in the immediate postwar period. It was an effective "bargaining bludgeon," noted *Business Week*, causing Spain to reluctantly agree to the distribution of 120 American movies the following year. Pressure from the local industry mounted. Combined with a belief that sufficient raw stock could be found in Europe, it emboldened the Spaniards back to the table to decrease the number to 100 films admitted the next year.[81]

Having worked his film magic in Argentina at the end of the 1940s, Stanton Griffis moved on to Spain where he performed similar work for the industry while he served there as U.S. Ambassador from 1951 to 1952. As before he was still on the Paramount board of directors, where he remained until 1966. Griffis was able to convince Spain to admit more U.S. films than they had in the past. Reportedly the Spanish relaxation of rules was connected with American financial aid and the export to Spain of certain foodstuffs and materials.[82]

France had similar problems with old U.S. movies. Early in 1945 authorities there barred American films over two years old. That decree affected about 1400 films which had backlogged since the war began. Hollywood had produced more films than that but 1400 were the number judged exportable. Since 1939 only a small number of U.S. films had been screened in France. The cartel worried such action could spread to other nations as well as being annoyed since the backlog was expected to "produce much soft profit over the coming five years."[83]

Later in 1945 serious negotiations got underway. Under the prewar pact, America got about 150 of the 188 import licenses each year. France proposed a law requiring exhibitors to show native films 7 weeks out of each 13 (55 percent) as well as desiring to limit U.S. imports to about 100 per year. Already active in the negotiations, State immediately reminded France of an old trade pact with the U.S. whereby France guaranteed it would take no steps which would place the American film business at a disadvantage. It was such proposals from France, and other nations, that the cartel would point to as justification for formation of the MPEA. As talks continued, the French suggested they could take a maximum of 80 U.S. films per year as this was the most they could import due to a shortage of dollars. Hollywood responded that "the minimum for profitable operation" was 108. That caused the cartel to call a boycott, sending in no more new product. Once again the *New York Times* termed that a "ban" by the French.[84]

In May 1946, a film pact was signed by Leon Blum for the French government and by James Byres, U.S. Secretary of State. Incredibly, that agreement did away with virtually all restrictions on U.S. film imports. In place of an import quota, a screen quota was established which reserved 4 weeks in each 13-week quarter (31 percent) for the exhibition of native movies. There was no ban on old movies. One commentator noted that in contrast to the British screen quota, which had been generally fixed above its industry's production capacity, the French quota "was retrogressive and fixed far below the actual possibilities of home production." Prior to the war, France's share of its home market was greater than 31 percent. Whenever such quotas were set, they were meant to be a minimum requirement but invariably they also became a maximum. As part of general 1946 economic aid, France's war debt was erased and it received a 30-year $318 million loan as well as getting $650 million in credits from the U.S. Export-Import Bank. Johnston stated that in the three-year period ending in 1939, the majors released an average of 179 features a year there. Union of French Film Producers president Pierre Forjeres condemned the pact since it provided only about half the seven weeks per quarter French producers wanted. Additionally he worried about that big backlog of old movies flooding into France. Details of the pact were released slowly to the public, which caused even more opposition. Even conservative financial journals were appalled at the agreement.[85]

Regarding the pact, *Business Week* called it an improvement on conditions expected just a few months earlier. It showed that Hollywood had figured out ways of doing business "even where the government runs the show," thought the publication, although it noted the pact "was arranged in the shadow of the French negotiations for $1,400,000,000 credit in the U.S."[86]

Predictably the pact was a disaster for the French film industry, leading to crisis and unemployment. France produced about 140 films in 1946, 74 in 1947 and was heading for less than 50 in 1948. Sixty percent of the film industry personnel were idled, half the studios shut down. Said one French filmmaker, "It is not the quality of American films that is hurting the French movie industry. It is the fact that U.S. films are cheaper." French distributors could get U.S. movies for $10,000 while a French movie cost at least 10 times as much to produce. Cinema owners got 50 percent of the box office gross on American movies compared to 40 percent or less on French product. Those American films could be sold for less in France because production costs were covered by screenings in America. Due to the price difference, French distributors and exhibitors gave U.S. product preference over French films.[87]

Writing in the *New Republic*, Paul Jarrico compared governments with respect to film negotiations when he wrote that unlike the British government "which has consistently tried to support the interests of its film workers, the French government has consistently sold its own film industry down the river. The Blum-Byrnes agreement opened wide the frontiers. French producers found themselves fighting not only their American competitors but their government, which had failed them." A coalition of French film workers, producers and creators waged a furious fight against the agreement. For support they went into cinemas, mounted the stage during intermissions and appealed directly to the audience. Even though the audiences had usually turned out to see a U.S. film, "its response to the appeal was invariably warm." On the eve of Bastille Day in 1948, the coalition organized a huge street dance during which most of the French screen stars appeared to urge renegotiation of the pact. One historian noted that by the middle of 1948, "American movies had overrun the country."[88]

Some months before that, French officials tried to pressure the U.S. by threatening to enforce the ban on product over two years old (it never had been enforced, or removed from the books). As well the French passed an order which would have suspended all dubbing. It was rescinded after the MPAA lobbied vigorously through the U.S. embassy. Those defeats angered some left newspapers to the point where they called for a complete boycott of American movies by their readers.[89]

Opposition was so intense that it spilled over into the French Assembly. Talks with the cartel reopened in 1948 and in September a new pact was signed which raised the screen quota from four to five weeks per quarter (38 percent). Of the 186 dubbed movies to be imported yearly, U.S. majors received 110 licenses with 11 going to American independents. The rest of the world was thus limited to a total of 65 imports. Britain received only 18 licenses, which they complained about and got raised to 20 for the following year. Of that struggle, the British Film Producers' Association wrote, "Such experiences are not encouraging and reflect to some extent the poor bargaining powers of sterling against dollars and the powerful effect of Marshall Aid upon the economy of so many countries."[90]

When *Variety* commented upon the new agreement, it referred to the 1946 pact as containing a "very favorable film clause." That pact was for a four-year period. Hollywood wanted to reopen the pact at yearly intervals but only to assess whether the number of films admitted could be raised—if, for example, the dollar shortage had eased. However, the U.S. did not want the entire pact subject to reopening, which would raise the possibility of adding new restrictions. France declined. Hollywood called in State. Within a few days France agreed to do it the American way—only the number clause would be subject to an annual reopening.[91]

Then there were the three Axis powers. Right after the war the Allies broke up the state film monopoly, forcing changes on the Italian film industry which the producers did not want. Quotas were abolished completely with all foreign films admitted on free entry with no restrictions of any kind. Implementation of the new rules were stalled by the Italian government but finally passed into law in October 1945. However, nothing got through as the Treasury Department held up movies on various technicalities. Hollywood then had at least five high-level executives in Rome trying to pressure the government. Finally they asked the State Department to see that the Italian authorities lived up to the law.[92]

During the first three years after the war, Italy became a wholly open market being bombarded with more than 800 foreign films annually. In 1946 850 imports were released, 600 of them American, 65 native-made. By 1948 U.S. imports numbered 668, Italian films were down to 54; U.S. films took 75 percent of all revenue while Italian product captured 13 percent. As one writer noted, the "post–1947 governments accepted the massive influx of American films not simply so as to avoid irritating the majors or in order to appease the State Department but also because the Hollywood style was compatible with regnant conservative ideologies. The Christian Democratic party claimed Hollywood stars as its allies during the crucial 1948 electorial campaign."[93]

During that Italian election, the U.S. intervened in a variety of ways to insure the party of its choice won. The U.S. Information Service made extensive use of documentary and feature films to sell the American way of life. Hollywood's 1939 film *Ninotchka*, which satirized life in Russia, was singled out as a particularly effective feature film. It was shown throughout working-class areas with the Communists making several determined efforts to prevent its exhibition. After the election win by the Christian Democrats, a pro–Communist worker was quoted as saying, "What licked us was Ninotchka."[94]

Early in 1949, a crowd of 5,000 including film industry workers and other labor people attended a Rome rally agitating for government protection of the Italian film industry. Yells of "Down with American films" were heard and carried as slogans on placards. Rally speakers included Vittorio de Sica, producer of *Shoeshine* and Anna Magnani of *Open City* fame. As far as the *New York Times* was concerned, "it was the Communists who ran the show."[95]

In Japan the MPEA arranged in the spring of 1946 for the exhibition of 60 movies approved by the State and War departments. Income earned by the MPEA (then around $200,000 per month) accumulated in Japan as it was frozen. MPEA vice-president Irving Maas reported that American movies were packing in the crowds. In order to combat the theater circuits which before the war had held the cartel down to 15 to 20 percent of the gross, Maas announced the MPEA was "favoring indie exhibs … building up their strength." As a result the majors were getting 50 percent rentals.[96]

Toward the end of 1947, the MPEA notified government officials in Washington and occupation heads in Germany and Japan that they would be forced to stop distribution of U.S. films in those countries unless there were assurances of sufficient dollar revenue to offset actual costs. According to Maas, the MPEA had spent over $900,000 in costs to distribute films in Germany and Japan since the end of the war—at the request of the State and War departments. Said Maas, "We haven't taken a penny out. We have reached a point where we can't afford to put more money into the operation." Technically he was right. However, the money was accumulating and was eventually all unfrozen with no loss to the majors. Maas also overlooked the fact the U.S. government fixed all those damaged cinemas at no cost to the cartel and that they had dismantled all protectionist measures in the Axis nations, giving Hollywood totally free entry—at least for a time. The MPEA wanted government reimbursement for its "losses" in Germany and Japan. In this case the government declined to pay. Maas's withdrawal threat was hollow because U.S. film men were loathe to abandon any territory. They did it in Denmark earlier in 1947 but were already considering returning "even if no coin is forthcoming—the vacuum left by the absence of Hollywood films is immediately jumped into by British, Russian, French and foreign producers.… Once a territory is abandoned, it is a mighty hard job to get back in. Contacts with exhibitors … are lost. U.S. players and pictures are forgotten, as audiences get used to the stars and product of competing nations," reported *Variety*. Even if the situation changed, making it profitable to reenter a nation from which it had withdrawn, the U.S. did so at "a great disadvantage."[97]

In pre-war Japan the U.S. had 16 percent of Japanese film business, all other foreign had 2 percent while Japanese product captured 82 percent of the revenue (Japan produced about 550 films per year, pre-war). By 1948 the U.S. had 42 percent of the business with Japan down to 42 percent, having produced only about 120 movies per year in 1947 and 1948. Commenting on the drop in native business, MPEA executive Charles Mayer stated that if Japanese films were really good, they would "outshine anything we could bring in."[98]

In 1950 the Army's Civil Affairs Division (CAD) still controlled films going into occupied countries like Japan. Grumbling that the CAD censors were too hard on U.S. product, an MPEA spokesman said, "The Army would like to have 52 *Snow White*s a year." CAD also censored locally produced films by the Japanese and Germans to ensure that militaristic and fascistic ideas were not spread and that the Occupation and Allied powers were not being defamed or criticized. However, they did not censor morals in locally made movies because "they have no desire to be responsible for the morals of the Germans or Japanese people."[99]

Reviewing operations in Japan, Charles Mayer said in 1950 that the impact on audiences of U.S. films had "improved tremendously" after the MPEA employed Japanese lecturers to tour schools, colleges and factories. For several years those lecturers had been explaining "the cultural, artistic and entertainment aspects of Yank films." Those talks were invaluable, said Mayer, "since with superimposed titles there was always the chance that the filmgoer would miss the meaning." A prime supporter of American films was the American Movie Cultural Association, founded by some 30 prominent Japanese including legislators, publishers and scientists. With 10,000 members, the group interpreted U.S. films through round table forums, radio broadcasts and special publications.[100]

Before the war, Hollywood sent 300 films yearly to Japan. During the occupation period, 350 foreign films were admitted yearly, 300 of them American. That "quota" was based on the highest number of movies imported during the 1930s. What remained of the local film industry lobbied the Japanese government in 1950 for restrictions on foreign movie imports once the occupiers departed. Hollywood argued a quota would only encourage the production of shoddy movies, ineptitude and so on. One studio executive claimed Japanese producers "fail to apply themselves to making pictures the way we do. Because the studios and the theater chains are owned by the same people, the public is forced to see the junk." Of course the U.S. studios and theater chains were owned by the same people, although divestment was coming.[101]

At war's end the Allied Powers believed that disarming Germany was not enough. They believed eradication of its ideologies of superior nationhood along with the right to make war in order to acquire territory was just as important as curtailing Germany's physical ability to wage war. That led to an intensive propaganda campaign designed to reeducate Germany as well as to impose control over communications media. The first item of business was to deal with the giant German government-controlled company UFI (which included UFA) which produced, distributed and exhibited, controlling the German field. Quickly the Military Government (MG) rendered it neutral by more or less disbanding it. That was a measure Hollywood had lobbied furiously for, with one American film executive remarking, "We would not want to see a monopoly here." Eric Johnston said, "With the monopoly powers of UFA under the Nazis still clearly in mind, MPEA doesn't propose to let this threat to one of its most valuable foreign markets go unchallenged."[102]

Film exhibition in Germany was prohibited completely until July 1945 when 20 houses were allowed to open in the American zone. By mid–September about 50 houses were open, all screening U.S. movies with German subtitles. Prior to July, OWI Overseas Motion Picture Bureau retiring chief Robert Riskin warned Hollywood not to be overly hard in its depiction of Germans on film as they were future customers. Reeducation of Germans could be accomplished in the long run "only if we supplant documentary films with entertainment films," thought Riskin, but he agreed that they should be forced to see documentaries then. By September the MPEA had submitted films to the U.S. War Department, who were officially doing the distribution. Cartel members were to receive percentage rentals varying from 35 to 50 percent of the gross, depending on the category of the movie. However, distribution went more slowly than anyone expected. MPEA firms blamed Army red tape, transportation problems and German taste. One motion picture featured a German submarine deliberately ramming a lifeboat full of Allied sailors. When it was screened it caused mass walkouts of Germans, leading to scenes being cut from the film. It caused the majors to question the "wisdom" of sending such movies into Germany. Also a problem was the low admissions (ranging from 10¢ U.S. to 40¢). MPEA wanted the price raised; the MG did not. One factor which the majors hoped would help attendance was the fact that cinemas were generally better heated than most homes. While the Germans did have some money to buy items such as fuel, it was at times simply unavailable.[103]

In between July 1945 and December 1946, only 43 U.S. films were screened in Germany, as well as 4 other foreign and 11 "politically approved" German films. By May 1947, only 50 U.S. movies had been released in Germany. Late in 1945 General Robert A. McClure had a number of meetings in the U.S. with industry leaders to try and resolve differences so the flow of product could be speeded up. When he returned to Germany he reported the industry had shown a desire to "utilize the military occupation to establish an exclusive position for American films and American distribution machinery." While the MPEA wanted only its members' films released in Germany, the MG wanted to include some product from U.S. independent producers. Additionally the majors wanted to use their frozen marks to economically penetrate the German film industry by buying up houses and studios. That idea was opposed by the MG, which wanted to see the rebuilding of a private industry that would be German-owned and run, not a U.S. subsidiary. Those 11 German films were released by the MG partly as a response to a lack of product from the MPEA and partly as a pressure tactic. Frozen coin could be used in Germany but only in ways approved by the MG. Historian Albert Norman noted that the shortage of Hollywood product was a problem that could have been resolved except for "the inability of the American motion picture industry to cooperate along policy lines laid down by the United States government for the occupation of Germany." Ultimately the MG did allow the majors a distribution monopoly as well as entry into film production, though the latter was little utilized.[104]

Nor did the U.S. films which did screen make much of an impression. Military information control personnel reported that with few exceptions they "had no observable effect in the political and psychological re-education of the Germans and have, on the contrary, reduced American cultural prestige." With little to spend their money on and with a limited choice of entertainment,

Germans attended in large numbers. They did not like what they saw. In a report prepared late in 1946 by the military's Information Control Division Intelligence Office, sharp criticism was leveled at both the artistic quality and type of film being screened in Germany. It declared Hollywood's movies "have been generally unpopular with the Germans," that Germans slammed them for "poor artistic quality" and that those films had actually impeded the democratization of Germany. Also attacked was the fact many of the films screened were cheap old ones, with Germans complaining their country was being used as a "dumping ground" by the cartel. That report also concluded that the drawing power of the movies could be improved "by adequate subtitles and synchronization" although that problem was minor compared to the other issues. Especially disliked were fantasy and trick films such as *Here Comes Mr. Jordan* which "tend to excite ridicule and disgust." State Department officials were concerned about the level of violence in those Hollywood films. They worried that with the economic privation, social disorder and general unrest in ravaged nations such as Germany, films which played up violence "may indoctrinate the more unstable with the idea of taking matters into their own hands." In the face of such a negative report, the *New York Times* found a note of optimism: "Despite criticism, however, Hollywood's pictures appear to rank second in popularity only to German-made films." For all intents and purposes, though, there were only two horses in that race.[105]

At the invitation of the U.S. Army, Father Flanagan, the man behind Nebraska's famed Boys Town, was in Germany and Austria in 1948 studying youth conditions. He died suddenly in Berlin that year but he told the Army in a posthumously released report that a very bad influence being exercised over Austrian youth came from crime, detective and adventure films. "Welfare authorities say they are Hollywood productions," concluded Flanagan.[106]

MPEA representative in Germany Marion F. Jordan remarked that message pictures "which are shown to teach the advantages of democracy to Germans, meet with resistance and have little appeal."[107]

In February 1948, the MPEA officially took over film distribution from the Information Services Division of the MG, establishing seven branches to take care of the British, French and American zones of Germany. Eric Johnston complained about money, saying that Hollywood sent its films into Germany in response to requests from U.S. occupation officials; "The film industry provided the pictures at no profit to itself but rather at an actual loss from out-of-pocket expenses. I don't know of any industry giving away cloth or clothes or steel or anything, but we gave away films, not only gave them away but paid for the means of showing them in dollars out of our own pockets, at an expense of about $500,000 a year." None of that was true as frozen coin continued to mount, but help was at hand for the needy rich.[108]

Washington started the Informational Media Guaranty (IMG) Program in 1948 as part of the Economic Cooperation Administration. That program permitted the converting of certain foreign currencies into dollars at attractive rates, providing the information materials earning the money reflected the best elements of American life. Each approved film was eligible to have an amount equal in earnings to $25,000 from exhibition converted from marks into dollars. Out-of-pocket expenses incurred by distributors were also covered (such as the cost of raw film stock to strike prints, German subtitling, etc.). The major claimed that those costs ran around $12,000 per film (a very inflated figure). From the IMG's beginning in August 1948 until its February 1953 termination in Germany, payments by the IMG to the majors totaled $5.1 million (Hollywood got more money from the IMG for other countries over various time periods). That handout essentially "unfroze" blocked currency in Germany at favorable rates of exchange plus paying the majors whatever they claimed their expenses to have been. A film not approved by the IMG could still be distributed but was not eligible for the payouts. IMG funding depended on amounts Congress appropriated for it year-to-year. Not surprisingly, the advent of the IMG program unleashed a stream of films into Germany. In 1948–1949, 64 U.S. films were released there, the next year it was 145, in 1950–1951 it was 202, and in 1951–1952 the number released was 226. Twenty percent of those movies were made prior to 1940.[109]

By 1950, West Germany's film industry was in poor shape with few movies being produced, no capital and, in any event, little available screen time even if the movies had been made. The market was open. German government officials tried to get the majors to agree to a limit of 150 films imported yearly, all to the majors with no permits to the American independents. Those independents complained about that but, as *Variety* noted if you added a "flock" of independent product to the 150, "it becomes obvious that the German market will be flooded." Dr. Rudolf Vogel, chairman of the West German parliamentary study committee on film problems, commented that movie imports constituted "a serious problem to our economically-ailing film industry."[110]

Then the Germans proposed Hollywood limit itself to importing 100 films yearly. However, the German government had little power in 1950 because the Allied High Commission maintained veto power over West German parliamentary legislative powers. The commission could veto items approved by Parliament if it felt they did not contribute to the reconstruction and rehabilitation of Germany, or if they violated the commission's own law. In June 1950, under a vaguely worded statute on freedom of the media, the commission rejected Parliament's desire to limit U.S. film imports.[111]

Unsure whether the commission would rule the same way in the future and/or of its right to rule at all due to the vagueness of the law, the MPEA visited the State Department in Washington later in 1950 to impress upon State the propaganda value of U.S. films for rebuilding West Germany. The aim of the mission was to win State's approval for the principle of unrestricted access to the German market. Arguing that Germany "is the focal point in the current battle of ideologies" and that it would be "illogical to restrict the powerful message that American pictures could carry to the Western zone of Germany," the MPEA worried that the message was in danger of being hindered through the desire of the West German industry to protect itself against Hollywood. Further, they argued that if State really wanted to assure maximum exposure of the U.S. message, then it had no alternative but to instruct the High Commission to prohibit any further measures to restrict U.S. films. Shortly after, State instructed the High Commission that it preferred to see no quota on the importation of U.S. films. Thus the cartel established its own informal quota by determining the best number of movies to send to Germany, on economic grounds. As a public relations gesture, Hollywood announced it would limit its exports to Germany to 200 films per year, double what the Germans had proposed. That native industry grudgingly agreed to the number, giving the impression that a mutual agreement had been reached. However, this "gentlemen's agreement" contained no penalties for exceeding the number of imports allowed. Nor was it honored; a 1951 report of the U.S. High Commissioner for Germany noted, "Foreign competition continued to plague the German motion picture industry ... since many of the companies did not adhere to their self-imposed quotas."[112]

During the war, restrictions on U.S. films in the U.K. had been dropped, such as Lend-Lease economic aid leading to unfreezing of coin. Some barriers were left on the books such as the quota law but ignored as and when necessary. As soon as the war ended, agitation against American films intensified. In the House of Commons, MP Robert Boothby complained of money being sent out of the country when food was scarce, saying, "If I were compelled to choose between Bogart and bacon, I am bound to say I would choose bacon at the present time." Labor MP H. L. Austin attacked U.S. movies as "slush and shoddy entertainment." While Hollywood was said to understand a dollar shortage in Europe was a basic reason for raising barriers, it "contends it should not be used as a smoke screen for the raising of discriminatory trade barriers."[113]

Philip Carr in the *Spectator* condemned the product as "it is almost always decorated with a meretricious exaltation of mere wealth and tasteless luxury.... It displays no sort of artistically artificial synthesis of life. It is merely a jumble of the sort of inconsequent cheap effects and showy vulgarity.... Is it a healthy thing to leave to a private monopoly in this one country such a powerful instrument in the formation of the character of all the peoples of the world?"[114]

Britain's second quota, to expire in March 1948, stood at 17.5 percent for exhibitors in 1946, when there was much agitation in the U.K. for a higher quota. Moderates wanted a 30 percent screen quota and "extremists" wanted 50 percent. Although Hollywood wanted no quota at all, they realized that was impossible so they fought to keep it as low as possible. At war's end the U.K. market represented perhaps 55 percent of the foreign take. Eric Johnston journeyed to London where he stated that the screen "must be free from repression and it must be free from reprisal. It must be free from propaganda." Countering him was U.K. film magnate Alexander Korda, who stated there were many limitations of that freedom: "Greed is a limitation. Too much effort for the comfortable formula of universal box office; bottlenecks in distribution built by the great organizations are limiting factors" in screen freedom. What Johnston was really talking about was "the freedom of selling Hollywood films abroad." What Hollywood really had in mind was "to keep the screens of the world preponderantly Hollywood's property."[115]

President Truman came through in July 1946 when he approved a $3.75 billion loan to the U.K. That was believed to be a move to permanently lift the threat that the U.K. Parliament might again place currency withdrawal restrictions on U.S. earnings in the U.K. Also important was the hope that approval of the loan might free billions of dollars in the sterling area which could be spent by other nations to buy U.S. movies. Hollywood was happy with the loan as one of its conditions had the U.K. agree to abolish all controls affecting U.S. exports to the U.K. Of course, an internal screen quota favoring native pictures was not considered such a control.[116]

That loan would be exhausted by early in 1948 but the U.K. was in economic troubles before that, reaching the height of a fuel famine in early 1947, plus other economic woes. With little money to pay for imports, more agitation was mounted against U.S. films with "we-want-bacon-not-Bogart" an oft-heard rallying cry. Hollywood was in a cold sweat with film executives believing that tied to the fate of Britain is "the fate of the whole world market without which American industry, above all the film industry, could not survive. If Britain collapses in bankruptcy, forces alien to the U.S. concept of trade would rush into [that] vacuum, spread into Europe and write finis over American trade prospects there."[117]

Cartel members controlled distribution in the U.K., as they had for decades. However, since the first U.K. quota act was passed in 1927, some of the majors moved into cinema ownership in a substantial way. Between that time and 1948, three large chains emerged in the U.K.: Gaumont British, Associated British Pictures (ABC) and Odeon. Fox bought a large block of shares in Gaumont around 1929 or 1930, gaining a seat on the board of directors. ABC became intertwined with First National (shortly before National was swallowed by Warner) around the same time. Half the capital to establish Odeon came directly or indirectly from UA. By late in the 1930s those three circuits held about 25 percent of all U.K. theaters but took in 66 percent of the entire exhibitor gross in the U.K. "A booking by one of the major circuits was indispensable for successful exploitation of a British feature film," said the *Times* of London. As the 1927 quota act outlawed block and blind booking, the newspaper believed "the American participation in the new circuits was no doubt in part a response to this measure." Warners moved on to increase its stake in ABC in the 1940s, perhaps gaining a controlling interest. Of 204 movies made in Britain in 1946, 86 were produced cheaply for cartel members to meet quota requirements.[118]

As 1947 rolled by, the time to renegotiate the 1938 quota law (to expire in 1948) drew closer. The distributors' quota then stood at 17.5 percent. While the British Film Producers' Association (BFPA) was completely in favor of protecting the U.K. film industry from U.S. domination, it argued in a memo to the Board of Trade that the distributors' quota should be abolished completely as it had not worked. In order to meet the quota, U.S. distributors were "bringing native production into disrepute by financing the making of poor quality, cheap and hastily made films." Industrially and financially that was more desirable than importing similar films from America, "but as long as such films could be used by American renters and cinema proprietors to meet their statutory requirements, genuine British producers had less chance of getting their work a decent showing than if the renter's quota had not existed." If those movies were ever shown outside of the U.K., the earnings accrued to the U.S., not the U.K. The BFPA thus wanted no distributor quota but one on exhibitors—one that was strictly enforced, as the 1938 quota had *not* been. It should be enforced, the BFPA insisted, because "there are exhibitors whose cinemas have made good profits and have been free of competition for years. They would experience no difficulty in booking good British pictures and could easily satisfy their quota obligations. But they consistently book cheap American pictures because they are plentiful and can be obtained at low rents."[119]

For 1947 Hollywood extracted about $60 million from the U.K., accounting for about 4 percent of British expenditures on U.S. goods.[120]

Suddenly and unexpectedly the U.K. slapped a 300 percent ad valorem tax on U.S. films in August 1947 which effectively would take 75 percent of U.S. film revenue in Britain (it was 300 percent levied on 25 percent of the total rental receipts). Within 24 hours, the cartel announced a boycott with no new product going in. It would last for seven months although it had no effect whatsoever on screening time or domination. As in all countries, America had a six-month or so backlog of product in the country ready to go; the tax only applied to new product entering after the levy was announced. An irate Johnston exclaimed, "If the British want American pictures they shouldn't expect to get a dollar's worth for a quarter." Most likely the U.K. knew full well such a tax would never stand but hoped it could function as a bargaining chip. Johnston added that "American films are an important part of the total British economy. Five dollars out of every six earned by American films remained in Britain in the form of British taxes, British profits and British wages." Even the *New York Times*, usually credulous with Hollywood numbers, had to balk at that by reporting Hollywood's yearly remittable earnings from the U.K. at about $68 million, "all of which could be regarded as clear profit, since most pictures manage to get back their production costs from showing in the domestic market." U.K. cinemas screened 465 features in 1946 (328 from America, 20 from all other foreign and 117 native productions). To try and remove that tax, the MPEA had its legal firm Sullivan Cromwell lobby the State Department. The lawyer was Allen Dulles.[121]

Although Hollywood was quick to call boycotts in a variety of nations over a long period of time, they were nervous about them. Perhaps that was one of the reasons for keeping a large supply of movies in virtually all nations. Hollywood would have the psychological advantage that native exhibitors and others would nervously watch the pile of films decline while no actual lack of product was experienced. As well, old films in the specific nation could be recycled almost indefinitely, thanks to distribution/exhibition control and block booking. As *Time* noted about the cartel's fear of its own boycott, "A prolonged dearth of U.S. films, they thought, might give the British industry an opportunity to cop the home market for good." Those same cartel members, added the account, "also control almost 80 percent of the first-run outlets" in the U.S. That was the year before the court-ordered divestment.[122]

Addressing the same U.K. tax situation *Variety* remarked it was no secret that movies were a habit and U.S. producers, "no matter whether they get a profit out of England or not, for the time being, won't take a chance for long on the British people losing the habit of seeing American pix or forgetting American stars." An additional worry was that a company might break ranks with the cartel to ship product to the U.K. Speaking on how Hollywood felt about keeping its films before the public in foreign lands in general, *Variety* said evidence could be seen in many areas of Europe where "there is no coin coming out. In fact, it costs the companies money to show their pix, since they have to provide the raw stock for prints. Yet they want to keep their trademarks and their stars on the screen to avoid opening theaters up to product of other countries." Believing that the crisis in each nation would eventually pass, American producers "don't want to have to go in as strangers when that day comes." Undoubtedly the majors would have absorbed losses if necessary, at least to some extent. However, most of the time their own government was all too quick to pay for any "losses."[123]

Even the idea that Hollywood faced collapse if they lost their U.K. income was false. Foreign take was around $125 million in 1946, equal to the industry's reported profit that year. Assuming tax paid on that sum was $45 million (in the U.S.), that left a foreign net of $80 million which (when subtracted from $125 million) still left Hollywood with a $45 million profit in 1946, even if they had not received one cent in foreign income.[124]

In March 1948, the U.K. and the U.S. reached an agreement whereby Hollywood was guaranteed to be allowed to take $17 million a year out of the U.K. in direct remittances plus was given a few extras such as the earnings of British films in the U.S. and Latin America. Given that the U.K. released figures that American remittances were $68 million in 1946, $52 million in

1947 and estimated at $55 million in 1948, Hollywood was said to be mainly satisfied. The remaining money was frozen in the U.K. where it could be used in a variety of ways, including within the local film industry. An editorial in the *Times* of London was satisfied with the arrangement, remarking that films "are in the practical world of today necessary amenities without which workers would not give their best. The new agreement will afford them the relaxation they need on terms that a realistic view of national economy can accept."[125]

Johnston agreed that the cartel was generally satisfied although he added there was some member criticism "because we did not get enough money." Asked which side got the better of the deal, he called the settlement a "victory for the people of the countries involved since it demonstrated a spirit of willingness to work out an agreement."[126]

Less happy was Woodrow Wyatt in the *New Statesman and Nation*, who said the British started to worry when Hollywood celebrated the pact with champagne; "The mystery of the agreement is why we allowed Hollywood to take so much, and why we have given her such advantageous terms in using unremitted sterling to compete in production of films in this country, with the British industry." Wyatt said the real reason for Johnston's victory was that Washington would, in the absence of an agreement, include those $60–$70 million of U.S. movies in the list of commodities allocated to Britain under the Marshall Plan. That threat caused Board of Trade president Harold Wilson to conduct a retreat and reach an agreement. Additionally, with no agreement there was a danger that an increasing number of houses might close, hurting the home market. Critics of the pact worried that allowing U.S. producers a foothold in the home market would allow them to compete with money for personnel, film rights to books, and so on.[127]

Equally unhappy was the *Financial Times* newspaper in which an editorial said, "We couldn't have come off worse in the negotiations if we had been represented by the four Marx brothers." All during the seven-month long boycott, Hollywood continued to suck $5 million a month out of the U.K. This editorial felt what finally made the British give in was the cost to exhibitors because "when the supply of U.S. films began to thin out, many British theaters had to close and others had to shorten their shows."[128]

Later in 1948 the U.K. imposed an exhibition quota mandating 45 percent of first features (A films) and 25 percent of B films must be home-product in each house. Immediately the British Cinematograph Exhibitors' Association lobbied the government that it was too high, asking for a quota of 15 percent maximum. That was up considerably from the old exhibitor quota which had reached 20 percent in 1947 under the old pact. At the time most British film programs featured double bills with the U.S. product usually run as the A feature. A worry was that many B U.K. features would be played first to reach the quota, relegating many U.S. A films to the B position (second) on double bills. It made a difference as the distributor gross from the exhibitor was roughly 45 percent; on double bills the A feature got 30 percent, the B 15 percent. Attacking the quota, Johnston announced that henceforth no U.S. movies would appear on a British screen with a U.K. cofeature. "This is not a revenge measure," he said with a straight face, "nor is it a desire upon our part to charge more for American films. It was forced upon us by this quota regulation which Britain established." Although the pact allowed Hollywood to keep earnings made from U.K. features screened in the U.S., those amounts were meager. In 1945 they were only a few hundred thousand dollars, $1 million in 1946, $4.25 million in 1947 and less than $1 million in 1948.[129]

Times of London editors were less pleased this time, due to American meddling. After the ad valorem tax was imposed and before the 45 percent quota was mandated, "the Americans were prepared to lose money on the sale of films here during the dollar crisis with the object of preserving their market when the crisis has passed." Regarding the quota, the editorial said, "An American trade association cannot claim a right to be consulted when a quota is fixed by the British government.... This country's economic nationalism in films is resented, not primarily for the barrier it presents to the free flow of ideas but because it threatens to narrow the market for American films at a time when other countries also are pursuing restrictive policies." As to the quality of American product, the *Times* sneered, "An occasional artistic impulse may break through but it is quickly suppressed."[130]

During the period 1948–1949, of the 4,182 operating houses close to 1,500 were granted reduced quotas ranging from 40 percent down to 10 percent. When factored with those venues who did meet quotas the average screen presence of U.K. features was 37 percent.[131]

Hollywood was unanimously irate over the new quota, claiming it "sabotaged" the 1948 film pact as well as making it "impossible" for American films to get worthwhile playing time on U.K. screens. The MPEA asked State to make a "vigorous protest against the action. Wilson defended the quota level as necessary and realistic, adding, "We want American films. We don't want them very badly. But we must have them if we are going to keep our cinemas open."[132]

Americans continued to apply pressure to have the British remove or reduce the U.K. quota and the remittance limits. Senator William F. Knowland (R–California) blasted the U.K. in the Senate for discrimination against U.S. films. Then he sent a letter to Secretary of State Dean Acheson asking what steps were being taken to remove those barriers. Five Republican Senators, Knowland, Styles Bridges (New Hampshire), Robert A. Taft (Ohio), Edward Martin (Pennsylvania) and Owen Brewster (Maine), followed with a similar but more general letter to Acheson. Some members of Congress contemplated adding amendments to various foreign aid bills in order to obtain open door policy for American films. *Variety* believed the agitation from Congress, particularly the California delegation, had the groundwork laid by the

MPAA feeding them facts. At a press conference, Acheson supported Hollywood's position by calling for the U.K. government to reconsider the screen quota. Congressman Cecil R. King (D–California) complained of the U.K. restrictions, placing a statement in the *Congressional Record* which said, in part, "The victim of this perfidy today is one of our largest American industries. Its eventual victim may be the whole world recovery program."[133]

Harold Wilson yielded to the pressure when he lowered the quota for A features from 45 percent down to 40 percent in March 1949. He was under pressure from all sides, pulling in opposite directions. Exhibitors and the British Films Council wanted 33 percent. U.K. film producers wanted it left at 45 percent while trade unions in the film industry wanted a 60 percent quota. Of course, the quota reduction was not enough for Hollywood. Johnston issued a statement which said, "Because the quota is so clearly unreasonable and excessive and runs directly counter to the spirit and purposes of trade agreements between Britain and the United States, we feel that the State Department should immediately and vigorously take up the matter again with the British government to relieve this intolerable condition."[134]

One year later in March 1950, the quota for first features was reduced to 30 percent. There was much less opposition to that move as a fatalistic acceptance seemed to have set in. Harold Wilson felt the new figure more accurately reflected the actual number of movies expected to be produced in the coming year.[135]

Negotiations on a new pact to replace the old one-year agreement were then under way. Wilson threatened to allow the majors to remit less than $17 million yearly while Hollywood fought to move the figure up to at least $25 million. In the end, Hollywood was allowed to remit $21 million, effective October 1950, in the new pact. Giving the U.S. the money earned from screenings of U.K. product in America was dropped. When Wilson proposed that remittances be lowered if the quantity of U.S. production in Britain was not equal to that of the past two years, the defeat of that idea was "clearly the result of State Department intervention."[136]

Unhappy with that agreement was Nicholas Davenport in the *New Statesman and Nation*, who complained the "film talks ended in an agreement more favorable to Hollywood than the last." Partly that was because when the old pact expired both sides knew "that the British film-producing industry no longer constituted any threat to Hollywood." *Business Week* gloated, "Competition from Britain—Hollywood's main postwar threat—seems definitely at an end." Arguing that Hollywood needed foreign income because "without foreign revenues, few movie men could break even on their production—much less show up in the black," the magazine also noted that Britain needed American films if it wished to keep its cinemas open. "The same thing is true of practically all nations that have a large investment tied up in theaters."[137]

Chancellor of the Exchequer R. A. Butler blasted the cartel in the House of Commons in 1952, warning that the U.K. wanted a revision in the film pact. He complained that Hollywood was getting 90 percent of its money out every year, one way or another, despite the remittance ceiling.[138]

During this period there were many restrictions placed on American films abroad ranging from maximum amounts allowed to be charged for rentals to frozen coin to taxation to maximums for cinema admission prices. With considerable exaggeration, *Variety* estimated that $100 million in foreign take, 80 percent of the usual $120 million foreign gross, was in jeopardy in one form or another. It was one of the tactics designed to enlist aid from the government. Along with that went the idea that without that foreign income, Hollywood would collapse. At a meeting of film studio executives, one remarked, "That foreign dough is vitally important to us. Let's face it—without that revenue from film rentals abroad, we're out of business, or at least a lot of us are out of jobs. It concerns every one of us." With foreign revenue said to be 45 percent of the total in 1946, the executive added, that income "helped to account for the unprecedented profit margins of the major film companies."[139]

On another occasion Paramount president Barney Balaban argued, "No amount of effort has brought picture budgets down to where domestic income alone would give the companies a profit." Professing to be mystified, he added, "We wish we knew how to do it. Then we wouldn't worry about the foreign market." Loew's International exhibition executive Orville Hicks warned that unless U.S. producers had free access to foreign markets, they would have to make "a substantial increase in admission prices to cinemas." He also noted the importance films played in opening markets for other U.S. products because "the sight in movies of American conveniences creates a demand for radios, washing machines, refrigerators, automobiles and other goods."[140]

When revenue was frozen overseas, Hollywood often found ways to nonetheless get it out of the country in question. In Finland the majors produced Bibles in English, using Finnish labor and materials, then sold them in the U.S. for dollars. The MPAA purchased raw materials in one country, had them manufactured into finished products in a second nation, then sold them in a third country. In Italy the studios bought wine and marble to be sold in America. One company used blocked kroner to build a ship in Sweden, which they then sold in the U.S. How much money was actually frozen at any given time was never clear with stated amounts seemingly tailored for the audience in mind; Johnston reported a high figure to State to obtain aid, while at the same time reporting a much lower figure to U.S. trade unions. *Business Week* claimed that at one time $50 million was frozen abroad while in 1950 it was said to be less than $15 million, $6 million of that in Britain. Around the same time Johnston held a meeting in Hollywood with film industry labor unions who were worried that frozen coin abroad would lead to more movie production overseas which would decrease Hollywood employment (most nations allowed and encouraged frozen coin to be used to produce movies within that country). Johnston calmed the union people by telling them there was actually very little frozen coin anywhere, most having been extracted. Film executives felt Johnston may have exaggerated a little to soothe the unions but generally confirmed his assertion. No publicity had been given to that fact until then because it could have had "undesired effects in Hollywood, where economy is being drilled into the industry, partially on the basis of poor overseas returns, and in Washington." For those reasons no accurate figures were released. Just a few months before the union meeting, Johnston claimed publicly that $40 million was frozen. Insiders declared then that was "much too high then and it is known now that the sum can be no larger than a minor fraction of that."[141]

Despite all of the cartel's whining and complaining, this period was financially very lucrative. Foreign income in 1945 was reported by *Variety* as $190 million, up to $210 million in 1946 when the foreign percentage of total receipts was about 40 percent, compared to a prewar ratio of a fairly steady 35 percent. Those sums of money were gross receipts. Of that $210 million MGM took $38 million, Fox $34 million, Paramount $30 million, Warner $30 million, Universal $23.1 million, RKO $22 million, Columbia $16 million and UA $16 million. In all cases that income excluded the U.S. and Canada except for Universal, which included Canadian receipts in the above total.[142]

For 1946 the Department of Commerce reported that the U.S. film industry netted $138 million from overseas with the eight majors taking $125 million of that amount; Britain contributed $70 million of the total.[143]

Several years later the Commerce Department reported the foreign take for the film industry as follows: 1946 $142 million (revised), 1947 $124 million, 1948 $130 million, 1949 $120 million, 1950 $120 million, 1951 $160 million. In 1951 $88 million came from European nations "aided by the Marshall Plan," $15 million from Canada, $26 million from Latin America and $31 million from all others. Those sums were dollars in New York and frozen coin. Compared to those figures was the take for foreign movies screened in America: 1949 $4 million, 1950 $4 million, 1951 $11 million. And some of *that* money accrued to U.S. distributors.[144]

Commerce Department film executive Nathan Golden noted the health of the industry, despite all the restrictions, when he said, "U.S. film companies have fared better during 1949 than in the previous two years." Barriers were "primarily aimed at the conservation of dollar exchange and assistance to native film industries. U.S. motion picture companies will therefore need every assistance to keep their films on the world's motion picture theater screens." Golden declared that 38 percent of the industry's receipts came from international markets.[145]

Commenting on U.S. world screen domination, a 1950 report prepared for UNESCO declared, "The large number of cheap American films available (initially increased, except in the United Kingdom, by the films which could not be shown during the war), apart from adding to the dollar deficit, is only one of the factors prejudicing the development of national film production industries. These industries, unable to recover their outlay on the films which they produce, are stunted in growth and become unable to meet the demands of the national market. The exhibitors, therefore, are driven to depend for their existence upon foreign, largely American, films." In 1953, when Johnston was testifying before the U.S. Senate Committee on Foreign Relations, he commented on that flood of old films by stating, "Immediately after the cessation of the Second World War, there was a tremendous backlog of pictures that had not been shown in most foreign countries, and these pictures flooded in, even more than the countries could absorb. This is a perfectly natural commercial phenomenon. You can't blame the companies for that."[146]

One source estimated that the cartel had a backlog of 3000 films with which to flood Europe when the war ended. That was in addition to the continuing annual output of some 500 films. Of course, not every film went into every market; it depended on the size of that market and its affluence.[147]

Debate within the U.S. concentrated more on whether American films sent abroad gave a good or bad image of the U.S. and the place of Hollywood in fighting the Red Menace. *Saturday Review of Literature* editor Norman Cousins started a debate in his weekly magazine which dragged on for many months with editorials from Cousins, rebuttals from industry spokesmen and many letters to the periodical from its readers. Cousins argued that U.S. films gave a bad impression to foreigners, for the usual reasons of sex, violence, alcohol, silly plots and so forth, with the result that Russia got a "free ride" since America's low quality product weakened the cause of democracy abroad.[148]

Eric Johnston responded by citing such experts as Generals Douglas MacArthur and George Marshall, who claimed that American films did indeed aid the spread of democracy. Marshall was cited as claiming upon his return from a 1947 mission to China that the movie *State Fair* did more to tell the Chinese about America, "about its heart and soul and about its people than I could possibly have told them in hours of talking." Johnston claimed that he had had many talks with President Truman who regarded films as "ambassadors of good will." Among the several films Johnston mentioned specifically were *The Pride of the Yankees* and *The Babe Ruth Story*. Those illustrate the extreme jingoism within Hollywood and its lack of concern for the culture of anywhere else. Those films would be liked and enjoyed and understood only where baseball formed part of the national culture. It did not do so in most nations. The fact that people starved for amusement and diversion attended such films was a reflection of that situation, as Cousins argued, as well as a testament to Yankee control of distribution, not a manifestation of love for all things American. Also rebutting Cousins along the same lines was producer Samuel Goldwyn, who remarked the American film had built 90 percent of the world's screens, and kept them all going. Cousins was unmoved by rebuttal from either man, accusing them of failure to even acknowledge a problem, let alone suggest a plan of remedial action. "The problem is that a damaging and false conception of America is being created by our films abroad," he concluded. Johnston estimated 110 million Europeans saw U.S. films every week.[149]

A couple years earlier, one source put weekly worldwide film attendance at 235 million; of that number 90 million per week attended in the U.S. That peak American attendance was reached in the years of 1946 and 1947 and before that late in the 1920s. That peak number was regularly approached in the 1930s. Film attendance was the main factor behind a huge surge in numbers going to paid commercial entertainment. Gerald Mayer estimated that in 1890, in the pre-film era, "certainly no more than 20,000,000 Americans paid admission to some form of professional entertainment, per year." Just 30 years later, 90 million Americans went to the movies every week, a 224 times increase. Additionally many Americans attended vaudeville and many other forms of commercial entertainment.[150]

Also in 1950, producer Walter Wanger had another article in a prestigious publication (*Public Opinion Quarterly*) expressing similar chauvinistic ideas to those he had voiced in the past. Claiming Hollywood had worldwide acceptance, that it was the closest thing to a "Marshall Plan for ideas," he raved, "Without doubt, Hollywood is one of the greatest developments of the Twentieth Century.... It is a veritable celluloid Athens." Wanger marveled that U.S. films "have never been nationalistic" because large numbers of foreign experts in the studio kept a watchful eye to insure nothing got through which would offend people abroad." In the 71,740 cinemas then operating in 115 foreign countries, American product comprised 72 percent of all films screened. "We have done a great service in not only selling America but also American products." In the category of extreme exaggeration was Wanger's pronouncement that Hollywood had "no subsidy" for its product. Hoping Hollywood would be recognized as the logical capital of this Marshall Plan for ideas he said, seriously, "Donald Duck as World Diplomat!" All of this after Wanger started off saying we must first disabuse ourselves of the idea "that what is good for the United States is good for all other peoples" (evidently something Wanger could not bring himself to do personally). Nowhere in the mutterings of Wanger, Cousins, etc., was there any acknowledgment of the major problems of U.S. film domination—the economic drain of a nation's dollar-starved treasury and the resultant damage done to any native industry due to a lack of money and U.S. control of distribution and exhibition.[151]

Nathan Golden was at times more realistic in his assessment of the reasons for Hollywood's dominance. But not at the beginning of 1952 when he surveyed the situation. Seventy-four percent of features shown on the world's foreign screens (outside of the Communist nations) were American-made. "U.S. films with their broad appeal to all audiences, continue to be the favorite of moviegoers throughout the world," he enthused. That was so, he thought, because when U.S. film men planned a movie, they usually took into account foreign customs, habits, religious practices and so forth, "producing a film that will please people in all walks of life throughout the world. Largely as a result of this practice, wherever the masses of the people have a free choice in selecting their movies, U.S. films thrive and flourish." Additionally Golden reiterated the fiction that the world market spelled the difference between profit and loss for Hollywood.[152]

When *Variety* looked to the future on a couple of occasions in 1952, they saw a few trouble spots. One was what they felt would be a continuing problem in converting foreign currency to dollars with that caused by U.S. pressure on the entire non–Communist world to build up its defense. That outstripped the ability of economics to stand the strain; "These countries are being forced to choose among guns, butter and pictures." Hope for a remedy to that problem lay in U.S. government aid to those nations, giving them more dollars to spend on goods such as movies, and "the State Department's belated but increasing enthusiasm for showing of U.S. films abroad." A second cloud on the horizon was the fact that native film industries were seen as growing, behind the restrictions as *Variety* acknowledged. Due to that situation, "some American execs now feel that the U.S. industry has been too big-hearted in helping producers abroad through acceptance of subsidy arrangements." Italy then gave the native film industry a direct subsidy, as France would soon follow. It was the domino theory again. England then had the Eady plan whereby a portion of the box office take was skimmed off the top by the government and divided among producers and distributors. However, U.S. companies got their share.[153]

By the end of 1951, the foreign currency problem was in fact rapidly fading away. Frozen coin would soon be no problem. Hollywood successfully had reopened the European markets lost to war and reestablished their old dominance. Once again those nations which were America's main film competitors (Germany, Italy, France and Britain) had war-decimated native film industries, and economies in general. Whatever protective measures which had been adopted were stripped away by the Allied occupying governments; the region was then flooded with the backlog of American films on top of the current crop. Old markets like Latin America, untouched by the war, remained firmly under the boot of Hollywood. What was lost was what became the East Bloc. With the exception of a film or two here and there, the Soviet Union had been closed for many years. Outside of a few cities such as Shanghai, China was never really penetrated by U.S. product; it was too poor. China was lost in the wake of that nation's revolution. If income from overseas dropped during the late 1940s, it was fairly slight and temporary, the result of war-related shortages, lack of money for purchases abroad and various other economic problems. By 1952 those were ending, as the Marshall Plan would end that year. Things looked good for Hollywood. Seemingly they smashed most barriers erected, or got around them one way or another, or at least lessened their effects. Hollywood's greatest danger at the start of the 1950s originated at home—television. It would affect domestic filmgoing before its effects spread internationally. Australia, for example, had no television at all before 1956. Effects from television would lead to a major restructuring of the program delivered to the local screen; consumers would get much less for the same cost. It would be a principal cause in the death of one of the majors. Soon the Big Eight would be reduced to the Big Seven.

7. Hollywood Sells Everywhere: 1952–1979

This period was one of considerable turbulence for the majors. Television was soon available in nearly every home, leading to a rapid decline in cinema attendance. That led Hollywood to turn to gimmicks such as Cinema-Scope and 3-D to try and hold the crowds. Nothing succeeded, so Hollywood ended the studio system of signing creative talent for long periods as well as drastically reducing the number of films produced annually. What made production cutbacks easier was the court-ordered divestment of theaters owned by the majors. In any case, the cinemas could not survive on such a reduced production level. Two choices were possible: obtain foreign product to fill the gaps or drastically alter the software package presented to consumers. No evidence exists that the first option was considered by anyone. Beginning in the 1950s, the standard program package presented to filmgoers—an A feature, a B film, a newsreel and a cartoon—slowly declined. Newsreels went first since they could not compete with television. Cartoons and any other short material disappeared, as did the second feature. After a time, the standard package presented to consumers—still standard today—was in place: one feature film, period. Except for coming attractions, nothing else was presented.

Since beginning filmmakers often start out by producing short material as they learn their craft, that software change afforded an ideal opportunity for each nation to give its beginners a chance for exposure. It didn't happen. Consumers found themselves getting half what they used to receive, for the same price. What saved the U.S. film industry of the 1950s from even more distress as domestic attendance plummeted was foreign business, which did not feel the effects of television until much later. Foreign income held up, as did domestic drive-in business during the 1950s, becoming even more important. Despite the turmoil of this era, which caused significant structural changes in the cartel itself, one constant was a continuation of American film dominance of the screens of the world. One reason was the ongoing distribution/exhibition control exercised by the majors. That also explained why other film material did not surface to fill the screen gaps when Hollywood cut back production.[1]

Australian writer Diane Collins wrote that "until the 1970s many Australians had never seen an Australian movie." During the period 1957 to 1975, noted historian Ina Bertrand, distribution was "dominated by the American subsidiaries of the 'Seven Sisters' of Hollywood ... and, to a slightly lesser extent, by Disney and British EMI." (RKO had by then disappeared). The dominance of that group and its interlocking relationship with both U.S. producers and local exhibitors meant that "the Australian film industry was to all intents and purposes 'vertically integrated' into the American film industry." By 1972, Bertrand continued, "the resistance of the major distribution and exhibition chains to Australian films was almost total." Fox continued to hold a 51 percent share of the large exhibition chain Hoyts while MGM owned a small chain, MGM Theaters.[2]

As *Variety* observed in 1954, "American films have their strongest foreign allies in theater operators who like and want and profit with U.S. features. These foreign exhibitors increasingly cry out against their own governments' efforts to foster native filmmaking by limiting the importation of Yank product via a quota system."[3]

With Hollywood production in steep decline by the 1960s, and the investment in each film increased, the cartel tried to extract even more money from foreign nations by using distributor control in an effort to increase rental rates. Cartel members were regularly members of foreign film trade associations—often it was required by law. Thus U.S. firms were normally members of foreign film groups through their subsidiaries. However, European film companies had no representative in similar U.S. film trade groups. That was indicative of the small amount of business done in the U.S. by foreign movies. Even those European producers who did make it to America had their product distributed by U.S. firms, usually independent companies. In Switzerland during the early 1960s the exhibitor and distributor organizations were locked in a battle for more than three years over rental rates. Among themselves the exhibitors agreed not to accept any movie for which rentals were more than 50 percent. And that rate was to be only for specials or spectaculars. Distributors wanted 60 to 70 percent for such movies. When negotiations stalled, the matter was taken to court by Swiss distributors with U.S. firms paying about half the legal costs.[4]

Later in the 1960s distributors in Germany demanded 70 percent of the gross for blockbuster pictures. Rental rates for an average film were 44.4 percent, up from 41 percent not long before. Once a movie showed potential, its rate shot up to 50 percent or more. In Chile the majors charged 70 percent of the gross for spectaculars and 60 percent on everything else.[5]

Canada was dominated by two U.S.–controlled cinema chains, Famous Players and Odeon. Over the five years 1971 to 1975 Famous paid a total of

$53.4 million to five cartel members (Paramount, Warner, Fox, UA—the latter was then distributing MGM product). Columbia and Universal released their product on the Odeon circuit; Disney released through Paramount Canada. On occasion a major switched affiliation; in 1975 Universal moved from Famous to Odeon while UA moved from Odeon to Famous. Even Columbia felt somewhat trapped; its Canadian president Wayne Case remarked, "Changes cannot be made, even if, for any reason, Columbia wanted to change. Famous is totally booked up with commitments from other major companies and probably couldn't handle the additional business. Everyone is locked into the system without much margin for maneuvering." If cartel member Columbia complained, what chance did a Canadian producer have of gaining access to first-run houses?[6]

Film historian Manjunath Pendakur remarked, "Through their block-booking policy, the leading American producer-distributors controlled almost all of the screen time available in the Canadian first-run market." For 1977 the eight largest film distributors in Canada—all subsidiaries of U.S. firms—took in 77.8 percent of the total film rental income, while the other 75 distributors shared the remaining 22.2 percent. Of the gross receipts the eight majors remitted 67.1 percent of it to America—dollars in New York. No Canadian producer received any royalties from those eight companies. In cities and towns where independent houses operated in competition to the cinemas affiliated with the dominant circuits, the independents did not get any first-run films from the majors. It was a matter of policy not to offer first-run product to independents in the same market where either of the two major circuits operated. Independents operated about 60 percent of all screens in Canada although, because they were smaller on average, the number of seats owned by the independents was much less, probably under 40 percent.[7]

John P. Rocca owned two houses in the Halifax, Nova Scotia, area in the 1970s. Of the 16 venues in Halifax, 11 were controlled by Famous, three by Odeon and two by Rocca. Filing a complaint with the Nova Scotia Amusements Regulation Board in 1975, Rocca charged the major distributors with discrimination in not allocating first-run movies to him, illegal under the Nova Scotia Theater and Amusements Act. "All the major distributors have refused to offer us a single first-run film, good or bad," alleged Rocca, who wanted a three-way proportional split of first-run product. Because the distributors guaranteed a share of product to Famous and Odeon, that is what Rocca sought. Like all other independent houses, Rocca could have booked the majors' product in second-run, third-run, and so on. Having little option, Rocca was forced to turn to independent distributors, reduced to booking mostly sexploitation films. Faced with the complaint from Rocca, Paramount and UA each offered to supply him one first-run movie, but no guarantee beyond that. After the complaint was formally filed, Warner offered "some" first-run product to Rocca, but gave no guarantees.[8]

Distributors argued they refused to supply Rocca because he was new to the exhibition scene, had no track record for his venues and no record of acceptable grosses. However, the 1975 inquiry found they had refused to supply Rocca from the start, precluding the development of a track record. Rocca could not demonstrate an acceptable grossing capacity given the absence of the majors' first-run pictures. Rocca's lawyer could show systematically how a certain historical pattern of product allocation existed in the Halifax region but could not demonstrate that the U.S. distributors were legally bound to give their first-run films to Famous and Odeon, even though those chains were owned by the majors themselves. Thus, Rocca lost the case because he could not prove the guarantee aspects of movie allocation in a black-on-white on paper way. Except for those circumstances, the inquiry head stated, "I would have no hesitation in finding each guilty of unjust discrimination were it not for the following circumstances." Four months after the case was decided, Rocca sold his houses. He had the money to challenge the majors in court—although it didn't help in this case—but many did not.[9]

Another way the majors tried to extract more money was to force admission prices up in countries and areas where Hollywood felt the citizenry simply wasn't paying enough to see an American movie. In 1954 UA foreign operations vice-president Arnold Picker said there was a "crying need" for raising admission prices throughout South America. Often those prices were set and controlled by governments. Top admission price in Lima, Peru, was 21¢ U.S. Picker felt all South American nations had good business conditions and were on a sound economic basis, and therefore he saw no reason why the "poverty level" admission rates should not be raised. Distributors and exhibitors were lobbying various governments to do so.[10]

A couple of years later, MPEA executive Robert J. Corkery complained he was continually fighting to get local governments in Latin America to raise their low admission rates. Overall he commented, "The Latin America market is growing all the time. The birthrate is perhaps the highest in the world. I see the market becoming more valuable to us all the time." Peru finally yielded to pressure, raising admission prices by 100 percent. When that led to rioting by the public, Peruvian authorities reduced the hike to a 50 percent increase. However, that left the majors unhappy.[11]

During the mid-1950s Brazil had admission fixed at 10 cruzeiros (15¢ U.S.) for standard features and 14 cr. for CinemaScope epics. Commerce Department executive Nathan Golden, whose title was then Director, Scientific, Motion Picture and Photographic Products Division, Business and Defense Services Administration, said, "The U.S. film industry has been making a strong effort to secure higher admission prices to Brazilian theaters." It worked because Brazil raised prices to 12 cr. and 18 cr. for the two categories. Unsatisfied with that move, U.S. distributors joined with local Brazilian exhibitors in filing court action against low admission prices, calling them discriminatory and asking for complete liberation from price controls. With the cinema being virtually the only entertainment medium within reach of the masses in impoverished countries, governments sometimes tried to fix admission prices at a level to keep it that way. Films were the only commodity then so regulated in Brazil. Although the controlling regulation said price controls were in place "in order to avoid excess profits," at least part of the reason was the use of theaters in the social control of the masses. Hollywood was actually ahead somewhat in Brazil as that nation was one of the very few countries in Latin America that allowed higher admission prices for Cinema-Scope features.[12]

When Mexico devalued the peso in 1954 from a value of 11.6¢ U.S. down to 8¢ U.S., the majors were irate because the government refused to alter the cinema admission price, keeping it fixed at 4 pesos for first-run films and 3 pesos for reissues. Politicians in Mexico felt cinemas should be kept inexpensive as the "poor man's theater." At the time, before devaluation, Hollywood took in $7 million gross in Mexico annually, remitting $4.5 million to America. Of course, the cartel began immediately to lobby for raised prices. Eight years later the cartel was still agitating for an increase. American distributors complained they were "forced" to sacrifice top films at bargain rates in Mexico or keep those top pictures out of the market entirely. Columbia, for example, refused to release *Bridge on the River Kwai* and *The Guns of Navarone* in Mexico. Cartel persistence paid off in 1962 when Mexico allowed an increase on reissues from 3 to 4 pesos (old films played more regularly in Mexico, and many other places, than they did in the U.S.) along with allowing an increase from 4 to 5 pesos for "Ben-Hur" and from 4 to 8 pesos for the 70mm version of *Spartacus*. Although an increase was allowed on only two first-run pictures, the MPEA was optimistic that a precedent had been set and that other such exceptions would soon be allowed.[13]

Returning to the U.S. from a trip to the Far East in 1959, Eric Johnston cited low admission prices throughout that area as the main problem facing the U.S. film industry. In Indonesia the U.S. received only 1¢ U.S. to 1-3/4¢ per admission. Still, Hollywood extracted $600,000 from Indonesia in the previous year. Johnston also hoped U.S. film companies would build more cinemas in the Far East because there were not enough of them. However, he advised that the building be done with locals so "conflict can be avoided." A few years later Johnston returned from another Far East trip. He was able to announce an increase of almost 50 percent had been put through in Indonesia, after much pressure. Hollywood was then extracting around $1 million annually from Indonesia.[14]

Turkey devalued its currency in 1970 which meant that blocked Hollywood funds in that country worth $500,000 would have been remitted at only $200,000 due to devaluation. MPEA Mid-East director Leo Hochstetter sped to Turkey where he engineered a deal with Turkish officials whereby blocked funds were remitted at the old rate—$500,000. While he was in Turkey, Hochstetter spoke directly to the mayor of Ankara, convincing him to increase cinema admission prices (set in Turkey by local municipalities) to compensate Hollywood for future losses due to devaluation. This led the MPEA to believe that Istanbul would follow and then all Turkish cities would come into line. Ankara's mayor did keep his promise but the increase was not considered large enough by the cartel. "Although this is a step in the right direction, it clearly is inadequate in terms of compensation for the loss incurred by devaluation. It is to be hoped that further adjustments will be made and that other key cities in Turkey will follow suit," explained Hochstetter.[15]

Declining cinema attendance in this period brought changes to the cartel structure. RKO was in financial trouble by the late 1940s. One of its problems was that it produced more B pictures than the other majors. As the second half of the double bill disappeared, RKO was unable to adjust and produce just A features. Howard Hughes took control of the company in 1948, and his erratic leadership added to its woes. RKO went out of the film production business in 1958 although it continued in broadcasting and television production. RKO even briefly returned to produce a few feature films in the late 1980s. Most of the film library of RKO product was sold to media mogul Ted Turner, owner of the Cable News Network (CNN) among other holdings. Walt Disney Productions had its product distributed through RKO but bailed out of the deal in 1953, probably realizing RKO's problems would not be resolved. Instead of going through another major, Disney established its own distribution outlet, Buena Vista. That was a first step toward attaining the status of a major. Understanding that short material—cartoons in Disney's case—would soon be nonexistent on the screens, Disney turned to producing features. By the time this period ended Disney was a fully-fledged member of the cartel. In 1973 MGM ceased distributing its own films, licensing domestic distribution to UA and foreign distribution to CIC (an offshore consortium of Paramount, Universal and MGM). Paramount merged into Gulf + Western in 1966. Decca Records became the controlling shareholder in Universal in 1952. Ten years later MCA Inc. consolidated with Decca Records, making Universal a subsidiary of MCA. During the 1940s and 1950s a syndicate slowly took control of UA, buying shares from the four founding stars or their estates and gaining 100 percent of the stock in 1956. In 1967 UA became a subsidiary of Transamerica Corporation, a service company and a major supplier of life and property insurance. A subsidiary of Canadian company Seven Arts Production Ltd. acquired Warner in 1967, renaming it Warner Bros.-Seven Arts Limited. Excluded from that deal was Warner's pre–1948 film library which had been sold to UA in 1956. Warner/Seven was acquired in 1969 by conglomerate Kinney National Service, Inc. with a name change in 1971 to Warner Communications. The studio reverted to its original name of Warner Bros. Only Columbia and Fox were essentially unchanged in this period. It all marked a trend in which the once stand-alone studios became merged into ever larger companies. That trend would continue in the 1980s and 1990s.[16]

Specific budget details for the MPAA and MPEA have never been publicly released. It was believed that annual levies were assessed against the majors on the basis of their share of the domestic market. That is, an MPAA member which captured 20 percent of the domestic box office in a given year would pay 20 percent of the cartel's budget that year. *Variety* estimated the MPAA budget to be $1.5 to $2 million in 1956 with the only high-salaried person being Eric Johnston with a salary of $100,000 plus expenses, a salary said to be "nominal for a man of his stature." For 1970 the MPAA budget was estimated at $7.9 million annually. The MPEA received its funding directly from the MPAA although, of course, they could hardly be called separate organizations.[17]

After World War II, more Hollywood product was shot in foreign lands than in the past. During the 1950s and 1960s most U.S. overseas financial participation centered in the U.K., Italy and France, in that order. Each had a film subsidy program. While costs were cheaper in Spain, there was little U.S. production there because it had no subsidy plan, until 1965, when interest increased. West Germany had no subsidy plan until 1968. Until then there was little interest although film production costs then were no less in Britain than in Germany. Low labor costs played some role in making Europe attractive for the MPAA members but, noted historian Thomas Guback, "the availability of subsidies and sufficiently large markets dictated the nations in which most of the U.S. investment would be made." Production costs were lower in many parts of the world yet U.S. investment gravitated to a handful of Western European nations—all with subsidized film production. If the MPAA was quick to condemn countries for establishing subsidies for a native movie industry, it was just as quick to take advantage of such programs, reducing funds available to the locals who really needed them.[18]

Typifying the chauvinism of the cartel was the 1953 pronouncement of Fox president Spyros Skouras, who wanted to see Hollywood "encourage and foster new outlets in the form of additional theaters" in various countries. He was appalled that in India, with a population of 500,000,000, there were only 3000 cinemas with less than 700 of them screening U.S. product. With more cinemas in more nations, "it will enable us to diligently discharge the sacred duty of our great medium to help and enlighten humanity." Skouras also expressed thanks he was an American "because of the privilege our country has in helping to serve its neighbors."[19]

One of the oddest assertions came from outside the cartel, but reinforced the chauvinism of the MPAA. Italian producer Dino De Laurentiis, forecasting the future of films in 1962, said they would all be filmed in English regardless of whether they were made in Italy, Germany or France or any other

Western nation. The English language was needed for the vast Anglo market which, said the Italian, "would not accept dubbing." On the other hand, the French, Italians and so on were traditionally accustomed to hearing English voices in the respective translations in titling.[20]

As head of the MPAA and MPEA, Eric Johnston continued to stress certain themes in his public utterances. One was expansion. As early as 1952 he noted that U.S. producers should consider how to exploit new markets rather than rely solely on existing ones for revenue. He believed some markets were yielding as much as they could and that Hollywood would be better off looking to new markets instead of attempting to extract a few extra dollars from exhausted markets. Specifically he recommended U.S. producers look to such markets as Africa and the Far East. A year later he declared Europe was becoming a static market; "We have to fight for it, but we should begin to concentrate more attention on other great markets like South America, Asia, the Middle East and Africa" even though initially "they may be low income areas."[21]

The cartel head also continued to declare that the free distribution of films—meaning no restrictions—was an important contribution to the cause of world peace.[22]

Of course, the real reason for free distribution was money. Stressing the importance of foreign income, Johnston said in 1955, "Without it, there would be no Hollywood." According to him, a large measure of the "acceptability of American films throughout the world" is due to the standards of "decency established by the Production Code." One year later Johnston predicted strong expansion abroad for U.S. films in the next decade. However, he added, "the maintenance of vital foreign markets requires constant vigilance and negotiation with foreign governments in the face of strong local protection and restrictions." Progress abroad by Hollywood was based "on its contributions to the economics of other nations in the free world."[23]

The specious idea that Hollywood could not survive without foreign income along with the idea that countries unfairly placed restrictions on U.S. films without cause were used by Johnston to justify and rationalize the cartel and its monopoly power imposed on other countries. In reality, nations only imposed restrictions after they had been overrun by Hollywood product, leaving their native industry in disarray. Claiming there were at least 20 nations trying to impose restrictions on U.S. product which had never drawn press attention—in addition to those that had—Johnston explained that each would have been burdensome to U.S. producers "unless a firm policy was adopted and all MPEA member companies committed themselves to it." With U.S. product filling about 60 percent of the world's screen time, Johnston boasted that when any country tried to impose restrictions, "I can go to the Finance Minister, not threateningly, but to simply state that our films keep more than half of the theaters open. This means employment and a bolstering factor of the economy of whichever country is involved. And I can tell the Finance Minister of the tax revenue which these theaters yield. But if only two or three American companies were to accept the restrictions on their own, my argument with the Finance Minister would lose its weight. My position would be an impossible one if our ranks are to be broken. We must have uniformity of policy." These candid remarks were given to *Variety* in a private interview.[24]

Nor was his bragging about access to high places overblown. On a trip to Russia he went wearing an "official State Department hat," meeting privately with Soviet leader Nikita Khrushchev. During a visit to Japan he saw both the Emperor and the Prime Minister before getting down to film negotiations with the finance minister. Once in France he went over the head of a high level bureaucrat to deal directly with the minister, getting his way. However, he was later stymied at the working level of the bureaucrat.[25]

As critics continued to snipe at the content of Hollywood product for the usual reasons of sex, drinking, violence and a worry "that American films are handing over victory in the world's ideological struggle to the Kremlin on a celluloid platter," Johnston told them to "lay off Hollywood." Their world success, he declared, was partly because "the freedom of American movies from propaganda gives them an unmatched authority and authenticity ... along with entertainment people abroad get rich dividends of democracy from American films." Then he quoted Stanton Griffis, U.S. ambassador to four different nations since the war: "I have on many occasions accomplished more with good American pictures than with all the formal activities and paraphernalia of official diplomacy. It is my conviction that good American films, both screened privately, as I used them, and in the theaters, are an invaluable adjunct to American foreign policy."[26]

In a 1955 article, Johnston claimed movies helped "foster international understanding. Since movies appealed to the mind and the heart, "Whether this appeal furthers the cause of understanding or contributes to friction depends upon the ideals and the motivations of the producers." Citing the old films *Viva Zapata* and *Down Argentine Way*—which he did not say were roundly condemned and booed off the screens throughout Latin America—Johnston said, "Yet who will say that these pictures have failed to give the world some favorable impression of the 'South American way'?" Noting that films could never be as effective on the scale they could and should attain as long as barriers were placed in the way of international distributions, U.S. producers gave "material support to the efforts of foreign producers to distribute and present their films in the United States," he said, erroneously.[27]

The idea of films leading to sales of other goods was usually not mentioned in the general media; the cartel remained still gun-shy on the issue. However, it was not a forgotten or disbelieved concept. Johnston dealt with it at length in a 1957 address to a meeting of the New York Executives Club. For more general consumption the cartel liked to stress understanding, harmony and so forth as the major reasons for needing U.S. films abroad. In that address Johnston talked of "the Hollywood that is America's traveling salesman to all the world, a salesman of goods and services, of language and culture, of ideas and hopes." It succeeded from its beginnings as "America's master salesman despite itself. It has served in a way that sales executives and advertising executives cannot possibly serve. Hollywood has portrayed the American family using the newest devices from industry but portrayed that family as people, not consumers; people using and enjoying products in their natural settings." It had been so, he thought, from the very first pictures. As Hollywood spread around the globe it "created demand for sewing machines, refrigerators, rumble seats, the pop-up toaster—the list is endless…. It also sold America into mass production, which wasn't on its mind at all." Johnston argued it was those mass demands generated from U.S. films which created the mass manufacturing industry. He remarked, "American mass production … the American assembly line … received its momentum and reached full speed in very large degree from the selling power of the Hollywood film." As for the accusation that pictures had stirred too many demands in too many places, perhaps had even invented materialism, Johnston replied, "To my mind, there is nothing wrong with stirring up demands in the world—and showing that productivity can meet them. If Hollywood does that, aren't we surely on the side of the angels?" To illustrate a second role for films (note the order) as an agent for democracy, Johnston told a perhaps apocryphal story of being in Djakarta, Indonesia, where an MPEA representative lived. Each Saturday night he put up a bed sheet on his front lawn as a screen, inviting the whole countryside to see a U.S. movie. The night Johnston was there the movie was "a rather antique but complicated Western, without subtitles. I doubted that the audience could make head or tail of it. But they cheered and responded in the right places." How that would expand democracy was unclear and unexplained. How could they clap in the right places when they didn't understand it?[28]

In August 1963, Eric Johnston died suddenly in office. During his tenure the MPAA had grown considerably in size and scope. Even as early as 1963 the MPAA/MPEA provided service for the majors who had television films they wished to market abroad. After close to three years of being officially leaderless, Jack Valenti, former White House aide to President Lyndon Johnson, was named president of the MPAA/MPEA in May 1966. Many believed his Washington influence and connections were his most valuable assets. When Johnston died, one film executive explained the search by saying "our selection must be a man of stature who has entry to the White House and respect in international diplomatic channels."[29]

At the beginning of 1967 Valenti noted with pride that every day of the year, some place in the world, a Tarzan film (the series began in 1918) was screening. A year later he took up the cartel mantra by decrying protectionism while praising free trade in general. Acknowledging that Hollywood took then 54 percent of its total gross from abroad he said, "It does not follow that size alone gives Americans any special advantage in the markets of the world, or that our companies are engaged in any way in activities inimical to the interest of others." Worrying about various restrictions applied to U.S. product, he remarked, "The result is to force foreign interests to submit to unnecessary, costly and unfair practices in order to do business at all."[30]

Valenti was able to report in 1977 that only three countries in the world were off-limits completely to U.S. films: Cuba, North Korea and Vietnam. Once relations were established with those nations, Valenti was confident American movies would be there; "We deal with all kinds of political ideologies — democracies, dictatorships, despots, monarchies, left wing, right wing. We do business with everybody. It doesn't make any difference — Muslims, Jewish, Christian, Zoroastrianism, whatever."[31]

During the 1940s U.S. film production averaged 445 movies per year, 373 per year in the 1950s and 163 annually in the 1960s. In 1950 America produced 383 movies, 254 in 1955, 154 in 1960 and 153 in 1965. Not all of these were produced by the majors. Nevertheless the majors controlled 68.83 percent of the domestic market in 1970. On the world scene many nations produced more motion pictures than did America. In 1969 some 4,000 feature films were produced worldwide with Japan leading the way with 494, India 308, Italy 301, Taiwan 246 and the U.S. with 232. The next five leading producers were Korea, with 229, Turkey 224, France 173 and Hong Kong and the Philippines with 169.[32]

Since not every movie went to every country, Hollywood was always bedeviled trying to determine which movies to send to which countries, to maximize revenue. U.K. film distributor Michael Deeley reiterated conventional wisdom when he remarked, "In America there is an educated and relatively sophisticated audience that will listen to talking pictures. The rest of the world wants action." Writing in the *New York Times* in 1978, John Wilson talked about films designed to have international appeal "even at the risks of diminished acceptance in the United States." Characteristics of such films were said to be big stars, limited acting skills required, one-dimensional characters, stars serving as foils for action and "limited witty repartee."[33]

MGM did a long-term study of the problem (it began in the 1940s and lasted into the 1950s). Their idea was to develop a scientific method of selecting movies to go abroad that would supplement the opinions of individuals. Initially they studied the U.S. market, looking at certain areas such as cinemas located in Italian neighborhoods hoping they would be an index for Italy, and so forth. However, that method was abandoned when MGM determined there were no houses in America where box office results differed materially and consistently. Next they compared the overall results of movies in the U.S. with those abroad. Substantial differences were found. They were least pronounced in the British Commonwealth, and yet even there one of every three films did differently at the box office than in the U.S. Thus MGM determined it was not possible to estimate the business a movie would do in any nation based on what it did in America. Finally MGM computed how much business a representative group of movies did during a period of time in each country, establishing a base figure of the yearly gross average for each nation in six different movie categories: action (six subtypes), drama, drawing-room comedies (dialogue-oriented), musicals, mysteries (crime, spy, detective, etc.) and slapstick (physically oriented) comedy. Then when MGM sent a new film to a specific country, its gross was compared to the appropriate category and ranked in one of six classes. If it did 1 to 39 percent of the established average it was rated Very Poor. If it did 200 percent or more of the average gross, it was rated Excellent. In its survey MGM found that musicals ranked first in popularity followed by action, drama, drawing-room comedies, mysteries and slapstick comedies last. Of all of MGM's releases over a four-year period, only one film obtained an Excellent rating in all nations, *The Three Musketeers*. Additionally MGM rated nations into seven groups with nations in group one having tastes closest to Americans, group two a little more removed, etc. Group 1 contained the U.K., Australia, New Zealand and South Africa; group 2, Denmark, Finland, Norway, Sweden; group 3, Austria, Germany and the Netherlands; group 4, Belgium, France, Greece, Italy, Portugal and Spain; group 5, Latin America; group 6, India, the Near East, Egypt, Iraq and Lebanon; group 7, Hong Kong, Indo-China, Indonesia, Japan, Malaya, Siam and the Philippines.[34]

Frozen coin was still an issue for the majors in the 1950s although not as significantly as in the 1940s. It became even less important as time passed. Mostly the majors extracted that blocked money in indirect ways, always open and legal. In Chile the MPEA bought Scotch-type whiskey with blocked pesos, then shipped it to America where it was sold. MGM decided to make its film *Quo Vadis* in Italy to use its blocked lire. When that amount was used up it bought wood pulp in Sweden using frozen kroner, then shipped it to Italy where it was sold for lire which was used for the film. When MGM needed more funds for that movie, rather than import dollars, the MPEA used the blocked lire of other majors to complete the film. Then, of course, accounts were settled between the majors in America. Of these methods Johnston said, "We hope the day will come when restrictions on trade and currencies are at a minimum. But we can't hold our breath until the day arrives. We are just trying to get along in the world as it is."[35]

Into the 1950s, double shooting of U.S. films remained a frequent practice which undermined any idea of a universal film or of Hollywood enforcing its Production Code on a worldwide basis. Those films were shot vividly for export and vapidly for domestic consumption. Sometimes there was just one shoot with cuts made to the U.S. version. Since it was a practice which cast no credit on Hollywood, its existence was categorically denied. Johnston asserted, "No one has ever been able to cite a specific film. As far as I know they go abroad the way they are shown here." *Time* magazine then went on to list four such movies. *Cry Tough* included a bedroom scene between John Saxon and Linda Cristal. The latter wore a slip in the U.S. version, only panties in the foreign release. An unnamed film executive explained they asked for Cristal's cooperation in order "to get a little more mileage out of it in Europe." Actor Jana Davi scampered naked up a hillside in *Gun Fever*—but only in the export version. Patricia Owens did a bump-and-grind sequence in bra and panties for the export version of *Hell to Eternity*. In the U.S. release she was seen only from the neck up or in long shots. Then the American version faded out while in the foreign release actor Jeffrey Hunter unhooked her bra. A bedroom scene between Lee Remick and Yves Montand in *Sanctuary* differed in the domestic and foreign versions.[36]

Profit margins on U.S. films released abroad were extraordinarily high, which has always been the reason Hollywood has fought so hard to control and dominate the world's screens. Little additional cost was involved once a film had been produced in America. As noted throughout this book the dollars remitted to New York, as a percentage of the producer/distributor share of the gross box office take, have ranged from about 40 to 80 percent. Once in New York the only other charge on the money was U.S. corporate income tax. During an early 1950s hassle with Belgium, a compromise was reached which included restricting U.S. studios to remitting a maximum of 50 percent of their gross rental receipts. However, Universal executive Americo Aboaf remarked that the new rule left the situation much as it had been since print costs and all other Belgium operating costs totaled about 50 percent.[37]

An example of chauvinism occurred in the way Hollywood sent musicals abroad. In 1961 *West Side Story* went abroad with a different type on the screen for the musical numbers (italic type versus roman type for dialogue). Lyrics had been frequently cut out of foreign prints because of "dubbing difficulties" or simply left in as English only. *West Side Story* was the first musical to go abroad with subtitles for the musical parts.[38]

Government pressure continued to be applied against the cartel for the perceived inappropriateness of some movies. While film company executives felt there should be no forced selections of American films abroad by U.S. government agencies, they did admit that "the release of certain types of films is undesirable as it tends to counteract the impressions of the U.S. disseminated by American information agencies at a very high cost." However, they argued, "no one denies that the Communists are using Hollywood to distort conditions in this country in the eyes of the foreign audience." But executives did not want to see self-censorship, such as banning the export of, say, Westerns to the Far East (where they were very much criticized) because such action "would result in a serious loss of revenue." Hollywood's much ballyhooed efforts such as its Information Center set up in the late 1940s, the hiring of experts by studios, etc., to "advise" companies on which movies should be sent where, were all long dead by 1953. It was the highly individualistic attitudes of the majors which caused those agencies to quickly die, they said. Yet that individualism was not a bar to forming the MPAA/MPEA cartel.[39]

In 1953 a Senate Foreign Relations subcommittee attacked Hollywood exports, claiming they had complaints and letters that those films depicted either the seamy side of life or the ultra-luxurious penthouse lifestyle, "often destroying the good work done by our official propaganda source"—referring to State's overseas informational and educational programs. Subcommittee chair Senator Bourke Hickenlooper (R–Iowa) condemned specific films including *Devil's Doorway*, *No Way Out*, *711 Ocean Drive*, and *Pinky*. Johnston appeared before the senators to defend the product.[40]

Representative H. Allen Smith (R–California) introduced a resolution in the House in 1959 calling on the industry to refrain from exporting films which "portray immorality or wrong-doing as prevalent and typical" of the U.S. Smith felt the best way to handle the situation was for the industry to police itself. Claiming to be opposed to censorship, he suggested as an alternative, failing self-regulation, that State apply controls over exported product, or at least have the House hold a public investigation of the issue. Representative Glenard Lipscomb (R–California) added that he was not opposed to a Congressional investigation but thought the industry was capable of exerting more effort to screen movies for export. Representative John J. Rooney (D–New York) agreed the House should look into the issue. This time the cartel made no official response to Smith. Disingenuously *Variety* thought the problem lay not so much with the majors as it did with the independents who turned out low-budget quickies just to cash in on the exploitation angle while the majors turned out "responsible" product; audiences could not tell the difference. Independent product had a hard enough time getting screened in America; its presence abroad was very small.[41]

Nathan Golden defended the industry, claiming America made movies for one market—the world. "The producer must, and does, take into account foreign customs, habits and religious practices. The U.S. film industry would not knowingly offend any foreign country or its nationals thus causing unfavorable reaction towards the United States film industry…. United States films are seldom criticized on this score. This is one of the reasons why U.S. films are well received by foreign audiences and generally preferred to pictures from other countries."[42]

One of the more controversial films of the 1950s was *Blackboard Jungle* which was banned in a number of places. Finally it was sent abroad with a foreword added explaining that the conditions in the school depicted in the movie were not typical of conditions prevailing in U.S. schools generally. *New York Times* foreign correspondent C.L. Sulzberger noted of exported movies, "The film industry has come to be a signally important arm of policy for its unconscious propaganda effect upon foreign minds is immense." For Sulzberger the most conspicuous propaganda angle was "the incredibly high standard of living mirrored by our movies is a source of envy and incredulity in many lands."[43]

Praise and damnation alternated from governmental and other political sources. UN Secretary Dag Hammarskjöld praised the product in a 1954 dinner speech delivered in Hollywood to an audience of movie moguls. Asserting that U.S. films helped spread tolerance and understanding among the world's peoples, he said, "The American motion picture has had much to do with the fact that through a large part of the world when somebody has an inclination to bang his neighbor on the head, he stops and thinks twice before doing it.... I have learned that generally the movies oppose intolerance. Without them the peoples of the world would know much less about each other and we would be much farther from our goal of living together peaceably."[44]

Many U.S. information officials in Asia considered "motion pictures and jazz bands" the most potent weapons the U.S. had in its Cold War propaganda campaign in the area." Reportedly children in Indonesia, Cambodia and Burma often dressed like American cowboys, just as they did in America. Even a year after the movie *Shane* played in Bangkok, the title cowboy was still a hero in Thailand. Unexplained was how children in a very poor country could afford to dress like American cowboys; the impression was left that very many did so.[45]

The State Department cautioned the industry's own Production Code Administration in 1955 that an impression was spreading abroad that, judging by U.S. films, "Americans favored force over reason as a means of argument." It was at State's request that *Ninotchka* was widely distributed during Italy's 1948 election for it agreed with reporter Sulzberger that the industry's "unconscious propaganda effect upon foreign minds is immense."[46]

One of the more noted attackers was famed newsman Edward R. Murrow, then the head of the United States Information Agency (USIA). Speaking to an assembly of Hollywood's top echelon in 1961, Murrow asserted that Hollywood movies spread a bleak, exaggerated and undesirable image of American culture to the world at large and created a great handicap for the U.S. Apparently Murrow was concerned over sex in movies. Admitting audiences liked extremes in storytelling, he compared the situation to kids and candy; kids liked candy but what parent would allow kids to eat it to excess? "Self restraint and control make a healthy child. I suggest that the image conveyed abroad of our land is not always a healthy one, and self-restraint may nowadays be a good prescription," he concluded.[47]

Even the Webb-Pomerene (WP) law under which the MPEA formed, very briefly came under fire. The Senate Anti-Trust and Monopoly Subcommittee indicated it might want to look at the WP act to learn if the results from that act matched the law's original intention. (That intent, said Subcommittee head

Senator Philip Hart [D–Michigan], was to give smaller companies a break in export operations against their larger competitors.) How Hart came to see that as the real intent of WP is unclear. Responding to Hart, a MPEA spokesman said if WP were modified to prevent U.S. companies from acting in concert overseas, the American trading position "would be chopped to pieces," with foreign earnings of all U.S. film companies dropping by as much as $100 million a year. Film companies then (in 1965) accounted for 1.5 percent of all U.S. foreign exchange earned annually through commercial channels. Such earnings would be drastically reduced if picture companies were prevented from acting in concert, argued the MPEA, which also reiterated the fiction that the WP was vitally necessary to permit U.S. companies to pool their strength in competing with government monopolies and foreign syndicates. It was only because the MPEA spoke for all the majors that it could successfully negotiate film treaties with those nations where film business was government-protected and subsidized. No investigation of WP took place. What the MPEA did not mention was that Hollywood had acted in concert as a cartel back to the 1920s. Forming and taking the name MPEA was just that—putting a name on a long-standing practice. That cartel with its domination of the film world caused nations to turn to state protection and subsidy in order for native industries to survive or emerge.[48]

As usual, the cartel spent much of its time whining to the government, begging bowl in hand. It was particularly worried in 1953 with cuts in the foreign aid allocated by the U.S. government (the Marshall Plan had ended in 1952). Conceding that the industry's excellent overseas showing over the previous two years "has been due, to a considerable extent, to the foreign aid program," executives complained that many foreign exhibitors wanted to equip themselves with new projection systems. They depended on money for that purpose from their governments' dollar allocations to purchase equipment, and some of those dollars came from U.S. foreign aid.[49]

Appearing before the U.S. Senate Select Committee on Small Business in 1956, a Paramount vice-president told the committee that "if the Hollywood producers ... had to depend upon revenue from the United States and Canadian markets, neither Paramount nor other companies could possibly remain in business." An executive with UA told the same committee that without foreign earnings, "the industry would soon face insolvency and bankruptcy, or would have to change its method of production in such a way that the type and nature of its films would radically change." Data presented to the committee revealed that in 1950, 1951 and 1952 Paramount released 71 films of which 51 failed to recoup their negative costs in the U.S. and Canada. Two things are seriously wrong with such data. Everywhere in the entertainment world (books, music, films, etc.), the firms involved produce many losers, often a greater number than winners. What counts, and what the individual companies rely on, is the total for a given period of time. A record company will accept 90 records out of every 100 losing money if those remaining 10 put the position of the company into an overall profit of acceptable proportions. Secondly, Hollywood is notorious for its creative accounting, as mentioned herein for the 1930s and ahead in the 1980s section. It is possible for every film to "lose" money—through apportioning fixed costs as a percentage of a film's budget and having one arm of a company buy costumes and sell them to a second arm at inflated prices, for example. This prevented anyone from collecting who had a contract for a percentage of the net profit. Thus every film potentially, could show a loss yet the company itself could turn a large profit.[50]

Johnston conferred with Commerce Department officials in 1960, at their request. Listing 17 types of restrictions ranging from import quotas to discriminatory tariffs to special taxes to blocked coin which were arrayed against Hollywood product "everywhere we go," the cartel head appealed for government aid in easing those foreign barriers.[51]

At the same time Johnston sent a memo to Commerce detailing those restrictions which, he said, "we feel they are clearly at odds with the spirit and interest of GATT." He agreed that some of the barriers may have once been necessary and justified by economic circumstances, but said that was no longer true. Hollywood, said Johnston, accepted the principle of screen quotas—as allowed and defined by Article IV of GATT only on condition that there would be no discrimination among imported films competing for screen time remaining beyond the quotas along with the understanding that screen quotas would prevent any other form of trade restriction. Since Johnston said that was not true, he argued that Article IV not be continued in its present form. In a bizarre argument, Johnston declared that a nation which allowed unlimited entry for U.S. films might find itself remitting less money to America than a country which had a fixed, limited quota. Operating within a limited quota, a U.S. film exporter would "naturally" select pictures for his licenses which he felt would be the most successful commercially. "In view of the substantial local cost of distributing a film in most markets, it is quite conceivable that a completely free market would produce less in the way of net remittable earnings than a limited market."[52]

When Jack Valenti met with government officials in 1971, he sounded a familiar theme but made it even graver when he declared that a loss of only 10 to 15 percent of the overseas market—then remitting around $300 million annually—"would cue an industry and Hollywood disaster." Valenti laid out 10 threats (all non-tariff barriers) to Hollywood product abroad:

1. export quotas (in 9 nations)
2. screen-time quotas (19 nations)
3. discriminatory admission taxes (4 nations)
4. film rental control with at best a 50 percent cut to the distributor (12 nations)

5. currency remittance restrictions (15 nations)
6. requirement that prints be struck within the country of exhibition (6 nations)
7. dubbing to be done locally (3 nations) or a specific prohibition against dubbing, with subtitling permitted (4 nations)
8. foreign prohibition against alien distributors (6 nations)
9. high income taxes (6 nations)
10. production subsidies/incentives (20 nations).

Over the previous five years Valenti claimed the cartel's efforts had saved $75 million which otherwise would have been lost to overseas restrictions. Pleading for aid, Valenti stated, "We cannot survive without the foreign market."[53]

One item Valenti secured was a deal by which up to 80 percent of the value of a film's foreign revenue potential could be funded by a loan from the Export-Import Bank. While a regular loan in most respects, it carried a standard Eximbank provision for political and credit risks, enhancing repatriation of foreign revenue earned. Available to many industries, the federal Export-Import Bank provided for a taxpayer bailout of a company operating in a foreign country in the event that a revolution, a drastic currency devaluation, or other catastrophe should prevent the company from repatriating its money. A credit-worthy film producer with a $2 million movie budget could get a loan of $800,000 from Exim (80 percent of the estimated $1 million direct cost allocated to the foreign market—based on foreign revenue being 50 percent of the total). The other $1.2 million would come from a commercial bank loan.[54]

Congressman Barry Goldwater, Jr. (R–California), took up Hollywood's cause in 1972 when he complained that U.S. films were subject to "a barrage of attempts by foreign governments and their trade groups to limit the importation of film and remittance of earnings." In a letter to Secretary of State William Rogers, Goldwater asked the federal government to review the "unbelievable tariff restriction" and develop a plan of action to end the trade barriers. "The elimination of these barriers would greatly aid the ailing motion picture industry and, hopefully, action will be forthcoming," Goldwater wrote. His report to Rogers declared there was a little over $13 million in frozen coin, half of it in India. The other countries blocking money were Pakistan, Egypt, Burma, Algeria and Morocco. That total of six nations contradicted Valenti's statement of one year earlier that 15 countries imposed remittance restrictions. The amount of money blocked was suspect but even if accepted, along with Hollywood's $300 million annual foreign take, the amount frozen was only 4 percent. In any event it was all unfrozen in time. By this time none of the world's richer countries was freezing coin, just the more impoverished ones; it was in those areas that Hollywood was vigorously moving, part of its insatiable expansion.[55]

When the USIA conducted a 1962 survey on Western European attitude to U.S. movies, it claimed to have found a "generally favorable" impression of America from viewing those films. Good impressions of the American standard of living, level of culture and of American women and working men were found but Hollywood's presentation of crime, adolescents and treatment of blacks left a bad taste with Europeans. U.S. movies were ranked as the second favorite in Britain, Italy and West Germany (behind the home product in each case) while in France U.S. product came third, behind French and Italian fare.[56]

Valenti bragged in 1968 that "the motion picture industry is the only U.S. enterprise that negotiates on its own with foreign governments." That was likely true. He could have also added that the State Department often negotiated for it directly, either on its own volition of under the prodding of Hollywood.[57]

One helpful program for Hollywood was the USIA's Informational Media Guaranty program (IMG) which continued until around 1966. As in the past, the program paid Hollywood dollars for any blocked coin in the nations in which the program operated, leaving the government the problem of unblocking the money. It also exchanged local currency into dollars at rates favorable to Hollywood in other "problem" situations. During the annual money allocations in Congress, USIA director George V. Allen appeared before the House Appropriations Subcommittee in 1959 and explained that since the purpose of the USIA was to present a favorable impression of America, the IMG conveyance of dollars was withheld on films not considered worthy examples of American life and character. Allen gave the subcommittee a list of 82 films deemed unworthy for one unnamed nation covered by the IMG (a film unworthy for one nation was usually deemed unworthy for all nations covered under the program). Included in the list were *Baby Doll, Rebel Without a Cause, Sweet Smell of Success, All the King's Men, All Quiet on the Western Front, The Defiant Ones, The Last Hurrah, I Want to Live,* and *A Hatful of Rain*. Hollywood could and did distribute these disapproved films anywhere they wanted; it was just that cited films were not eligible to take advantage of the program's handouts. In 1959 the IMG operated in 12 nations (Burma, Chile, Indonesia, Israel, Pakistan, Poland, Spain, Formosa, Turkey, Vietnam, Yugoslavia and the Philippines. Before the House approved the 1959 appropriations for IMG, Representative H.L. Gross (R–Nebraska) calling the IMG a "lush subsidy," said the MPEA "has been given a pretty good ride on the informational media gravy train" and dismissed Johnston as a "lobbyist." Johnston maintained that, under the program, distributors were providing a Cold War service which would cost incalculable millions more if undertaken by the government. One source estimated that over the life of the IMG, from 1948 to 1966 when it ended, U.S. film companies received around $16 million.[58]

Regarding Europe in general, the cartel fretted about any kind of European film unity which might rise up to challenge the MPAA. The cartel worried about that almost from the time it had formed; it never *stopped* worrying despite the absence of any but the most perfunctory discussion of the idea among Europeans. During a 1955 meeting of the International Federation of Film Producers Association in Washington, D.C., some of the European delegates got together privately to discuss the idea of a European producers union which would attempt to treat the European market as a single unit rather than as a group of many nations. Basically the concept was to give the Europeans the same kind of market U.S. producers enjoyed domestically. After getting wind of the private discussion, an irate Johnston made it clear to the delegates there would be no discussion of any pool in the federation. Two years earlier at the group's Berlin meeting, Johnston declared the U.S. might withdraw from the federation if there was "any such discussion." So much for freedom of speech.[59]

When Germany and France spoke briefly in 1956 about some sort of film reciprocity pact between them as a way to a new film relationship, an anguished *Variety* went over the top with a headline reading "Europe: Hates 'Competition.'" Nothing came of any talks for a union, at any time.[60]

Hollywood was especially prone to coming unhinged over just the thought of any European film union in the 1950s and 1960s as its domestic audience contracted dramatically due to the inroads of television. Attempting to analyze this reaction from the cartel, *Variety* declared, "Partly it is because the Americans are conditioned to distrust 'joint action' and arbitrary 'protective' decisions." While the concept of a cartel might be acceptable to Europeans, the newspaper added, "To Americans it leaves a sour taste partly because on past occasions these very methods have been used in an attempt to squeeze the Yanks out of the market."[61]

Not surprisingly, the formation of the European Common Market (CM)—with six original members in 1960—also terrorized the cartel. Opinion of MPEA executives in 1959 on the issue was "that the real purpose of the Common Market re films was a unified defense against the domination of the U.S. motion picture on the European." One MPEA executive said European film industry people "aren't really interested in liberalizing trade. They're principally interested in building up some kind of defense against U.S. films." Publicly Eric Johnston displayed more than a little ambivalence. At one point he strongly endorsed the principle of the CM, much to Hollywood's surprise. When he was in that mood, he thought the CM would make the member nations richer so they could buy more U.S. goods, including movies. However, he was often in a different frame of mind, as he was in 1960 when he said the CM "represents a new kind of discrimination that must be fought." In that mood he feared that member nations would lower barriers to each others product, thereby disadvantaging Hollywood.[62]

Fear of the CM had receded by 1963 when it had existed for a few years. One unnamed U.S. film executive stationed in Europe argued that any attempt to further limit Hollywood access to the CM nations would damage their native film industries more than it would hurt the cartel. That would happen because U.S. distributors with their worldwide releasing organizations were beginning to distribute more European product, thus bringing in more export revenue for the CM film companies than all the European distribution firms combined. By this time film attendance was declining significantly in Europe, again as a result of television. Prior to that decline, a European producer could finance a film project on the basis of making a number of separate distribution deals on a territorial basis. As the market shrank, so did the money distributors were willing to pay. Banks began to demand more globally encompassing distribution deals before becoming financially involved. As well, this executive believed CM exhibitors would rise *en masse* to defeat any protectionist measures against American films which the CM might try and enact. At that time in Italy, American films took 45.6 percent of the total movie receipts, Italian 41.9 percent, French 2.2 percent; in the French market French movies took 52.2 percent, U.S. 28.8 percent, Italian 5.48 percent. For the total CM, U.S. movies took 36.9 percent of all film revenue while product from France, Italy, Germany, Holland and Belgium (the five then-producing CM nations) together accounted for 49 percent.[63]

Fear of any separate film unity pact had also eased by 1966 with the Americans involved in more co-productions with European producers than in the past. Reasons included cheap labor, availability of government subsidies (from the foreign nations) as well as a still continuous need of product to feed their worldwide distribution organizations. *New York Times* writer Bosley Crowther broke no new ground when he stated "no nation's film industry can prosper to any continuing extent just on the domestic sale of its films. Indeed, if Hollywood had to depend on the sale of its films only in the United States, it would be dead in a year or the nature of its output would be vastly reduced." That was part of his rationale for Europeans to co-produce with the Yanks, with the former benefiting from U.S. backing "since the best—indeed, the only—far-reaching and efficient facilities for distributing films in the world market are controlled by the American companies." It all meant, thought Crowther, a movement toward denationalized movies, the standardization of films. "Without the backing of American money and the offering of American salesmanship, filmmaking in Europe would sink to a disastrously low estate," he concluded.[64]

Also easing fears of film unity in Europe was the cartel's successful embrace of television (domestically and internationally) by selling old films to broadcasters, making films specifically for TV, producing series for television and so on. That was in stark contrast to their initial stance to not deal at all with television, to do what the majors did best—boycott it. Internationally they vigorously sold their old movies to the growing number of TV stations. In 1973 the MPEA announced it had achieved a breakthrough in driving up the prices European stations paid for feature films. First the MPEA imposed a 40 percent increase on the Spanish, then moved to Italy where the price was doubled. For some years Italy's RAI-TV had paid the MPEA $6,000 per film. Effective in 1975 the price became $12,000. MPEA executive Marc Spiegel, who handled the Italian negotiations, admitted the cartel took a hard line before getting an Italian agreement, having "to choke off supply of U.S. product in initial Italo talk stages early last summer."[65]

Norway held firm through the 1940s in allowing film distributors a maximum rental of 30 percent of the box office receipts. Hollywood continued to lobby for higher rates into the 1950s. After what were called "strenuous negotiations" at the government level, the rental was finally increased to 40 percent of the gross in 1953 with the possibility that "special" movies could receive 45 percent. One stipulation by Norway was that American films offered in other markets would be offered in Norway. That meant that a movie rented for, say, 65 percent elsewhere had to be offered in Norway even though it could receive no more than 45 percent. When that pact expired in 1954, the Norway Municipal Cinema Association declared it would not renew under the old terms, refusing to pay 45 percent for special movies. Organization spokesman Kristopher Aamot said, "We'll agree to pay 40 percent for all American films—including the super movies ... We are not prepared to pay 45 percent for the super movies. They are nothing but glary comic strips." Apparently those special movies were not very popular at the Norwegian box office. When Warner and Paramount both refused to ship some special movies to Norway for 40 percent instead of the 45 percent, the Norwegian exhibitors placed a ban on all product from both studios. That ended after a few months when both sides accepted the conditions of the old pact, with 40 and 45 percent categories.[66]

As Hollywood upped their take in Norway to 40 percent, they tried to do the same in Denmark where the maximum rental was fixed at 30 percent. Exhibitors refused to allow any increase in the rate. The MPEA argued the rental structure in Denmark was below that existing in Norway and Sweden, making it difficult to continue to get 40 percent in those markets when the Danes were getting the same movies for 30 percent. Denmark did agree to a compromise which would move the ceiling to 40 percent, on the condition that Hollywood would ship in all its films at that rate, not withholding specials. Hollywood refused, wanting a sliding scale of 25 to 50 percent. American producers preferred to withhold their specials from low-rent markets pending the day they stood to receive what they felt to be adequate rentals. For a moment there was almost a crack in the cartel as three majors (Fox, Warner and Universal) announced they had dropped demands for higher rates for special films from Danish exhibitors. However, the cartel closed ranks with the result that the MPEA imposed a boycott on Denmark in May 1955. Hollywood thought it would last no longer than three months. Ultimately it lasted for three full years with the product gap filled by British, French and Italian fare. Local movies picked up strength; some U.S. independent films were also screened.[67]

Eighteen months into the boycott, the cartel was getting seriously worried. MPAA public relations director Taylor M. Mills claimed the Danish 30 percent rate was "imposed upon them by joint action of the Danish exhibitors." Since the Danes would not compromise, it left "no alternative but to continue in the market at the unfair terms imposed by Danish exhibitors or to withdraw from selling in Denmark." If the Danes had accepted MPEA proposals for higher rental rates, said Mills, "It would have established normal free market conditions in Denmark." A few months later *Variety* admitted the boycott in Denmark, and one in Spain, were lasting longer than expected, wondering if the industry should do more pre-planning instead of just being reactive when unpleasant things happened. "There was a time when such an embargo would have forced native exhibition to capitulate within a matter of weeks. Today, thanks to inter–European trade, it can survive much longer without the American product," worried the publication.[68]

During negotiations, the Danes argued that 40 percent was too much for exhibitors to pay. Hollywood said that should be no problem; raise the admission prices. MPEA representative Fred Gronich went so far as to claim there was no U.S. boycott; "The only blockade now existing is that imposed by Danish exhibitor organizations which are preventing the Danish theaters from freely showing American films to the American public." (Note the Freudian slip by Gronich or the Freudian typo by *Variety*.) The end of the boycott was attributed largely to discussions between the U.S. ambassador to Denmark, the Danish Prime Minister, Finance Minister and the exhibitor association. Under the pact, Danish cinemas were divided into three classes with the first to pay 40 percent rentals (first-run) while the other two classes paid 36 and 30 percent. One feature of the agreement allowed each major to send to Denmark up to two films annually on which the rental rate was "freely negotiable," up to 70 percent.[69]

As the existing film pact with France neared expiry in mid–1952, a French press campaign agitated against the import of U.S. films as an aid to that country's ailing native industry as well as to reduce the drain on France's small supply of dollars. Arriving in Paris to negotiate, Eric Johnston complained that only 121 American movies were allowed in per year, compared to the "free" Italian market which took 280 to 300 yearly—in other words, all that the majors cared to send in. Johnston also groused about the rule that native films had to be screened five weeks out of every 13 and about an import tax based on footage which was about $4,000 per full-length film. "France is the most restricted film market in the world outside of the Iron Curtain countries," complained the cartel head. When the French attempted to lower American imports to 90 a year, the MPAA called in State to negotiate, getting the number back up to 110 films per year, assisted by the cartel which shipped no new product to France for three months.[70]

A few years later France's Economic Council issued a report stating the film industry was in a crisis. It provided some recommendations, all of which would have made entry of American movies more difficult. Although that council was made up of mainstream representatives from government, labor and industry, *Variety* dismissed them as "Reds." The U.S./France 1957–58 film pact continued to allow the MPEA 110 import licenses per year. However, in the second year 40 of those permits were given by the French themselves directly to the MPEA members which the French felt had done the most for the French film industry. In any country where the number of American imports was fixed at a specific number, the cartel always insisted that it and it alone would decide how those licenses should be apportioned among its members. In the case of this pact, a journalist noted the "MPEA fought bitterly against that provision, but finally accepted it for the sake of an overall deal."[71]

When another new pact with the French came into effect in mid–1959, Hollywood did even better being allowed 116 imports in the first year, 125 and 135 for the second and third years and 70 in the first half of year four. More importantly for the cartel was the abolishing of the provision whereby France directly distributed import licenses to U.S. producers. As in the past, the MPEA would do the apportioning. Before that pact expired, the French gave up import quotas completely. In June 1961 the French authorities published a decree lifting the restrictions on the number of foreign films that could be shown in France.[72]

American distributors joined West Germany's central film industry trade organization Spitzenorganisation der Filmwirtshcaft (SPIO) in 1950. Membership was voluntary with cartel members feeling affiliation was important because SPIO's job, noted film historian Thomas Guback, "is to make recommendations to the German government on all things affecting films. The Americans, as members, have a full vote equal to that of any of the German delegates and thus far a right to cast a veto, as all decisions must be unanimous." Membership also enabled Americans to know at all times what German film personnel were thinking and planning "and can head off any recommendations to the Reich government that appear dangerous to American interests. It amounts to a veto before the fact, and the companies are very pleased that they have been able to get into SPIO at all."[73]

During the mid–1950s the West Germans tried to limit U.S. imports to 150 per year; they tried to levy certain taxes on the earnings of American films; they tried to set an age limit on imports to prevent the import of previously unreleased old product in West Germany. All those efforts failed due to pressure from the MPEA and the State Department. When German film producers agitated in 1954–1955 to have the government legislate a screen quota requiring native product to be screened for 35 days every three months, cinema owners managed to block the effort. As for the quality of German films at the time, the *New York Times* sneered, "With meager means, the German film industry tends to produce a routine product consisting of vaudeville acts and sentimental or humorous episodes tied together with the familiar feeble narrative." By 1960 the cartel was so arrogant in its control of the West German market that an MPEA representative told a reporter that while there were continuing efforts to restrain U.S. product, "nonetheless we can be reasonably confident that we can thwart any such moves."[74]

Britain continued to maintain the 30 percent statutory exhibitor quota during the 1950s and 1960s with it being continuously exceeded from 1956 onward. Native industry personnel continued to lobby for tougher rules, but to no avail. Rules on the amount of money allowed to be remitted annually were eased over time; they were never much of a problem to start with, although the cartel protested and pretended otherwise. In 1963 the Federation of British Film Makers urged the U.K. government to increase the screen quota from 30 to 50 percent. As the number of cinemas declined due to falling attendance, fewer movies were needed to fill the quota.[75]

A quota increase didn't happen but would have perhaps not helped anyway. Government assistance to U.K. filmmakers came from the British Film Production Fund (the Eady Fund). Under the legislation, to be a British film the maker of the movie had to be either a British subject or a company incorporated under the laws of any Commonwealth nation and with a majority of its directors being British subjects. (No mention was made of the nationality of the stockholders.) Thus an American company which owned wholly a British subsidiary (and most of the majors did) could produce movies which met the legal criteria for being designated "British," giving them access to the Eady Fund. One estimate for the year ending October 1965 said the Eady Fund paid out $12.4 million in film subsidy money with $10 million (80 percent) going to those U.S. subsidiaries. No official figures were ever released. For the years 1962 to 1966 inclusive, the National Film Finance Commission determined that 57 percent of British features exhibited at the two major chains were financed wholly or partly by U.S. companies. U.S. sources provided almost 75 percent of the production money for British movies in 1965 and 1966. In 1969 the *Times* of London reported the British film industry operated on an annual investment of about £40 million with 90 percent of that contributed by American producers.[76]

During the early 1950s, American film imports to Spain were limited to about 100 annually. Negotiations over a new pact broke down in the summer of 1955 over Spain's demand that for every four foreign films imported the distributor had to distribute one Spanish movie (a 4-to-1 ratio). When the Ministry of Information imposed that measure through the issuance of a ministerial order, the MPEA immediately launched a boycott (in August 1955), sending no more product to Spain. One unnamed Hollywood executive complained that if that demand was met, "there is no doubt that all film producing nations would impose the same condition on the distribution of United States films in their territory." He also argued that such an order placed "the distributors of foreign films at the mercy of Spanish producers." Also opposed to the measure was the Spanish Ministry of Commerce, perhaps because recent general economic negotiations with the U.S. had led Congress to appropriate $50 million in economic aid to Spain that fiscal year.[77]

Likely the MPEA saw the boycott as another short-term successful tactic. But it dragged on. Eighteen months later U.S. Ambassador in Madrid John Davis Lodge personally intervened to arrange a meeting between MPEA representative Charles Baldwin and Spanish Commerce Minister Ullastres. Association of Spanish distributors president Joaquin Agusti said the MPEA refused to meet with his group to discuss differences or the situation. As negotiations dragged on, U.S. independent producers and Spanish distributors tried to strike a deal to replace MPEA features. According to *Variety*, when Baldwin saw his bargaining position weaken he "got on the phone to Washington and New York." Under pressure from the State Department and from Eric Johnston, the independent representative was "ordered to pull in his horns." No deal was made. In March 1958 the cartel ended its embargo, shipping new films to Spain despite the fact no film pact had been agreed upon. Spain's Director General for Cinema Munoz Fontan received a letter from the MPEA explaining the boycott was terminated "as a gesture of friendship and goodwill from the U.S. motion picture industry to further cement Spanish-American relations." Of course, it was done because American films were not missed by the Spanish audiences and the cartel worried it would lose Spain permanently. The reasons in the letter were simply to save face.[78]

Spain imposed more stringent conditions in the early 1960s, using a complicated point system whereby Spain awarded some licenses to specific MPEA members based on points accumulated, in addition to maintaining the 4-to-1 contingency. Once again this infuriated the cartel, which wanted the MPEA to receive the licenses in bulk, in turn passing them on to individual cartel members. Thus no new film pact was signed with the two sides getting along on the basis of a "tenuous understanding" year by year with the majors getting a little over 100 of their features into Spain annually. When Biddle Duke was appointed Ambassador to Spain in the mid–1960s, he was firmly in Hollywood's corner, believing in a long-range program to encourage the widest distribution of U.S. films in Spain. About the film industry Duke said, "No other investment by U.S. industry or commerce will guarantee a net inflow of gold or cash in as short a period of time as the U.S. film industry. Oil is a strong contender in this respect but the average company's outlay for continued research and pre-exploitation is so tremendous it leaves the U.S. film companies well out in front."[79]

Spain did yield although it took a few years. In 1971 the government abolished the 4-to-1 contingency and the "baremo" point system replacing them with a system based on granting distributors import licenses on the basis of the box office earnings of Spanish films in Spain. At the time, total foreign films imported into Spain were limited to 120 annually, mostly American. The new system was set to such a low standard (one import license for each 6 million pesetas—$87,000—in box office earnings. Spain's box office totaled 2 billion pesetas annually.) that, based on the 1970 box office take, up to 300 foreign imports would be allowed entry.[80]

Basically Hollywood made little headway in the Communist world. The Soviet Union continued in the 1950s to allow unauthorized screenings of American films, with the prints having apparently been seized in Germany during the war. America continued to ask for their return, the exact number of titles being unclear but likely well over 10. Russia continued to refuse to return them, claiming them as "trophies of war." Reported to be popular were four Tarzan titles which made their way around the country, exhibited at villages and on farms. Russian newspaper *Pravda* criticized the state-run film distributor for allowing peasants to watch "trashy" stuff like Tarzan and old cowboy films. According to the paper, when those films were screened in rural areas, "by the continuous screaming and shooting, chickens are awakened from their sleep and panic is caused among the livestock in the barns and villages at night."[81]

When correspondent Harrison Salisbury returned from Moscow in 1954, he urged Hollywood to sell Russia its films. Until then the MPEA had declined, citing a fear of Russia editing its product and a "guideline" from State not to do so. Salisbury commented, "The mere fact that we can make films without propaganda content is in our favor and always a matter of comment. There is no question that in Russia, as everywhere else, American pictures are the best and most forceful medium for selling the U.S." The MPEA reiterated it would not sell or negotiate until it got a "go" from State.[82]

Around the same time, both Secretary of State John Foster Dulles and U.S. Ambassador to the USSR Charles Bohlen were making it known they would like to see American films made available to Russia. Hollywood used State as an excuse for their reluctance while more cogent reasons included the cartel's fear any movies shown in the Soviet Union would be considered propaganda, thus hurting the grosses of those movies all over the world. Additionally the cartel worried that exporting product to Russia might antagonize red-hating groups at home.[83]

Nothing much happened for several years until the U.S. and the USSR signed a cultural exchange agreement in January 1958. Then U.S. representative to the UN Henry Cabot Lodge challenged the Russians to take "a step for peace" by accepting Hollywood movies. According to Lodge, those films could make important contributions toward creating "a community of independent nations which understand each other and respect each other regardless of all the differences in their ways of life … The motion picture industry can do things which are beyond the power of a free government." Negotiations did get underway that year with the MPEA submitting a list of 164 titles to the Russians, a list okayed by the United States Information Agency. Later in 1958 the Russians picked a group of 10 U.S. movies to screen while the U.S. took 7 USSR features. American films chosen were *Marty, Oklahoma, Roman Holiday, The Old Man and the Sea, Lili, The Great Caruso, Rhapsody, Beneath the Twelve Mile Reef, 7th Voyage of Sinbad,* and *Man of a Thousand Faces.* Russia paid a flat rental of $67,000 per title which allowed the Soviet Union to screen each movie as much as it wanted for five years. Dubbing, subtitling and changes of any kind made to a film had to be approved by the other nation. On November 1, 1959, the first of the group (*Marty*) was screened in Moscow, dubbed by Russian actors.[84]

Still, little trade took place. Ten years later, in 1969, the Russians had bought a total of 44 U.S. films. Russia's press complained that State blocked the sale of Hollywood product to Russia which showed the seamier side of life, mentioning specifically *The Incident, The Chase* and *Seven Days in May.* Deputy Assistant Secretary of State Robert J. McCloskey confirmed his department "advised" distributors not to release the three cited titles in Russia but emphasized distributors asked for a State review of movies on a voluntary nonbinding basis. He could cite no instance in which his department's recommendation had been rejected.[85]

Before agreement was reached with the Soviet Union, Eric Johnston made a personal trip to the Kremlin in 1956 to try and sell movies. Prior to departing from the U.S., Johnston conferred with President Eisenhower. In Russia Johnston and three accompanying MPEA executives got as high up as to meet and negotiate with Premier Nikolai Bulganin. After leaving Moscow, the MPEA head journeyed to Czechoslovakia, Hungary and Poland but had little success in selling Hollywood product. Czechoslovakia did buy ten U.S. films in 1958 for a total flat rental of $125,000. Hungary took an average of eight to ten U.S. films per year through the 1960s, paying a flat rate of $1,500 to $3,000 per title which gave them screening rights for five years. All the Communist nations refused to pay a percentage rental which, of course, infuriated the cartel. Hollywood refused to sell Hungary (and presumably all other East Bloc lands) any films which they perceived put America in a bad light such as *Pinky, Elmer Gantry, Advise and Consent* and *Dr. Strangelove.* Hungary screened 170 features in 1965 with ticket prices averaging 15¢. The same year Romania imported about 100 films, 20 of them American, with admission ranging from 10¢ to 20¢ for first-run down to 5¢ for subsequent run. Romania paid from $2,000 per title up to near $7,000 for a blockbuster movie.[86]

Greater success was achieved by the cartel in Yugoslavia which, in 1956, screened 190 movies, 113 of them from Hollywood. For several years America exported close to 120 movies annually to Yugoslavia. In the late 1950s, however, the number was reduced to around 60 after President Tito spoke out against the showing of too many "trashy films." Vice-president Aleksandar Rankovic added, "It is necessary to approach more decisively ... the showing of many bad and ideologically alien films." Commenting on the IMG program, the *New York Times* reported that those movies were shown in Yugoslavia under "what amounts to a subsidy from the United States Government through the so-called International Media Guarantee Program. Yugoslav exhibitors pay their screening fees in dinars and the United States Information Agency reimburses the Hollywood producers in dollars."[87]

China was even more tightly closed to U.S. films with only an occasional title going in and even then it was screened just for an elite audience, not for the general population. Not that the cartel tried too hard to break into that market. That was explained by Jack Valenti when he returned from a trip to China in 1979. He was not enthused about China as a film market because "the kind of price the Chinese want to offer for films, at this point, I think I can say, does not measure up to what our people believe is the intrinsic market place value of those films."[88]

Beginning in the 1950s, the cartel paid more attention to the Pacific Rim and Far Eastern nations. It was a response to Hollywood's never-ending drive to expand, a declining audience at home and to saturated foreign markets. During a five-week trip to the region in 1959, Eric Johnston remarked that the principal problems hindering the expansion of Hollywood there were low admission prices, which limited profits, and the need for increased cinema construction. On that junket Johnston met with government and film officials in Indonesia, Japan, Thailand, Hong Kong, Malaya, Singapore and Taiwan. For 1958 the U.S. majors earned $12 to $15 million from Japan but only $600,000 from Indonesia where, said Johnston, "American profits are curtailed by 'fixed' admission prices."[89]

In 1952 MPEA vice-president Irving Maas visited Tokyo and announced that "powerful forces" were at work there to try to further restrict the import of American movies to Japan. Maas said his statement might be called "pretty strong language" but he had to be honest. As evidence Maas cited pressure exerted against Hollywood product in letters attacking the "cultural" value of the features published in the letters columns of Japanese newspapers. Conspiracy theory reared its head because those letters appeared "with a regularity and a quantity which is no natural phenomenon, and are undoubtedly part of a planned campaign." Such criticism was inappropriate thought Maas since the cartel "wanted only to continue to contribute to the prosperity of the Japanese film industry and to the Japanese public."[90]

Those criticisms continued for years with Maas lashing out at anti–U.S. film attacks in Japan in 1958. By then the movies were even being attacked in the Japanese legislature, the Diet. Japan then allowed 185 film imports per year with 101 of those permits going to the cartel members. That year Japan demanded the right to make its own allocation of those 101 permits directly to Hollywood producers. Surprisingly, the MPEA agreed, "but at the same time achieved a tacit understanding that it would have the right to re-allocate the permits later." Likely the majors agreed to the move so the Japanese government could publicly appear to seem to have at least taken some step against American screen domination.[91]

Native production in Japan began to make a comeback. While American films took 40 percent of the box office in 1955, that was down to 30 percent in 1957 and 21 percent in 1959. Mainly it was due to the Toho exhibition chain being the only foreign film distributor outside Tokyo and the biggest of only two (Tokyu being the other) in Tokyo. Shochiku was the only other exhibitor chain then in Japan but it no longer distributed foreign films. Japan was then in the process of reconstructing a strong, vertically integrated native industry, as they had prior to the war. It was the only way to fight Hollywood. Facing that declining market share, one U.S. major's Japanese representative complained, "It's a squeeze. Everybody's ganging up on the American companies. We can't defend ourselves." Still, the money Hollywood took out of Japan increased. In 1964 the cartel reached a new high when it grossed $22.5 million in Japan. Of that amount, $11 million was remitted to America. Additionally the MPEA generated $7 to $8 million in Japan in 1963 from sales of films to television. Even though America's share of Japan's market was down, and total Japanese film attendance was also down significantly, admission prices had risen dramatically.[92]

Singapore's government imposed a new tax on foreign film rentals in 1959 after a study by acting Finance Minister Dr. Toh Chin Chye found that foreign producers reaped large profits without paying local taxation. Through transfer pricing, local distributors (almost all were subsidiaries of American producers) showed on their books greater amounts paid to overseas producers than in reality, lowering profits of those local distributors, on which taxes were assessed. In the face of that move, *Variety* dismissed it all "as another step by the Red-controlled regime to make it tough for foreign interests, especially American, since their pix dominate the market here."[93]

When General Ne Win and the military took control of Burma in 1962, the MPEA announced that was a hopeful development in that it might stabilize the nation's rapidly deteriorating economy and curb a "strong leftist trend" from the civilian government of the ousted U Nu. However, it was a mixed blessing, for General Win had led a previous military government which lasted until 1960, before yielding to U Nu. Win had tried during that administration to force U.S. companies to relinquish their distribution offices and turn them over to independent Burmese businessmen. That issue remained a "sore point" with the cartel. General Win drafted an order to effect that change; it was put into effect by U Nu. Under U Nu, as a result of MPEA pressure which included a boycott of 18 months, a compromise was reached whereby Burmese employees of the American branches were able to qualify as import agents. In other words, Hollywood's distribution was totally unchanged while the Burmese government was allowed a face-saving measure. Hollywood worried whether or not General Win's new regime would go along with that compromise. It did.[94]

Thailand's prime minister in the early 1970s was M.R. Kukrit Pramaj, who had had a part opposite Marlon Brando in the film *The Ugly American*. When he was out of politics, he never forgot his connection to Hollywood. Throughout the 1970s and 1980s, in his popular newspaper column he consistently promoted the import demands of the MPEA. During the mid–1970s, 85 percent of Thai screen time was in the hands of foreign distributors, mainly American, with an estimated $25 million a year sent out of Thailand by foreign distributors (from theatrical receipts and from film sales to television). Gross box office receipts were $81.8 million. Of all the foreign exchange paid out in a year for movies, 62.5 percent went to the eight majors (the seven plus Disney), all of whom had set up offices in Bangkok in the 1950s. As a result of that situation, in December 1976, the Thai government increased the tax per meter of imported film by 1,400 percent. That tax cut imports by one-third (including Chinese movies—the second largest exporting nation). However, within one year the Chinese had recaptured their position by sending in negative prints (paying the tax once only) and striking the necessary number of positive prints in Thailand. Local film production was also stimulated, moving from 80 to 140 features per year within a few years. Although many foreign producers learned to live with the Thai tax, Hollywood resorted to its usual tactic by boycotting the market completely; it lasted several years. MPEA lobbyists regularly lobbied changing Thai governments to drop the tax. In 1980 it was reduced by half, down to 75¢ per meter (around 3000 meters in an average-length film). Still the MPEA boycotted until May 1981, when the cartel lifted the embargo. Apparently the cartel felt that the tax would never be reduced again or removed and they would have to live with it. When the tax was first imposed, the Thai exhibitors sided with Hollywood in agitating for repeal of the tax.[95]

Early in the 1950s, Eric Johnston contemplated the MPEA putting into practice a global public relations campaign designed to answer criticism of American films, strengthen their prestige and widen the appeal of Hollywood product. That did not happen. A major target at the time was India, where the U.S. got only a fraction of the potential. Generally recognized was that U.S. films faced a handicap in India "which can be overcome only via an educational campaign, since the problem isn't so much one of attendance as it is one of native preference for local product." Fox executive Murray Silverstone was incensed when a native production in India, *Aan*, blown up from a 16mm negative, outgrossed "all U.S. imports combined." America then took only about three percent of India's audience, with most of that in just four cities. Silverstone blamed a global pride in native films, particularly in Asia, as a grave danger to his cartel's dominance, noting "This wave of insularity is hurting us all over. It causes native product to do fantastic business." Several years later, in 1960, India raised the import duty on film from 5.7¢ per foot to 13.7¢ upon the expiration of the U.S./India film pact. As usual the majors called a boycott. India's government reduced the tax to 5.7¢ within a couple months. Vague promises by the cartel to help give Indian film more exposure in the U.S. helped sway India's government to sign a new three-year film pact with the tax at the old level. Hollywood sent close to 200 films yearly to India, grossing about $1 million on them. The *New York Times* mentioned that Indian films had never been successful in America; "They are often two-and-a-half hours long."[96]

When that pact expired in 1963, the Indian government raised the tax again to 13.7¢. Again the majors launched a boycott. Reporter Thomas Brady explained the majors "have long opposed any taxes on films at the source, preferring taxes on ticket sales that make consumers aware of the burden." Arguing for assistance from State in the battle with India, the majors pointed to the "propaganda value of movies." Hollywood was remitting then about $400,000 annually from its $1 million gross. Usually only two prints of each title were sent to India. Both were English-language only, with no dubbing or subtitling done. Even the complete loss of the Indian market would not have been a serious loss for the cartel due to the small amount of money involved; however, they fought the tax measure rather than ignoring the nation because the industry considered "setting an example for other countries more important." In this case, capitalist solidarity cracked with the majors returning one by one over the coming months to the Indian market, paying the tax, which added perhaps $800 to the cost of a film. They returned "because the distributors who, in some cases, have leased theaters in major cities, need new celluloid to keep their screens lit." Indian producers had long complained that U.S. interests controlled the best houses in the big cities. Although the number of such houses was small, they were crucial in that they were the most important venues financially. Native producers wanted their government to give them more screen time in those key venues.[97]

In the summer of 1971, Indian criticism flared up again when India Foreign Trade Minister I.N. Mishra complained in Parliament that the MPEA had not kept the terms of its contract to popularize Indian films in America. He also announced that the government-owned State Trading Corporation would hereafter import movies for India, favoring nations that imported and popularized Indian films. Until then, distribution was all done in the private sector. Responding to the criticism, the MPEA said it could not force U.S. houses to screen films it didn't want; "for the American film companies to do that would be in violation of our anti-trust laws." Additionally the MPEA complained "there's no monetary profit to be made" in the Indian market. About 90 percent of foreign films screened there came from the U.S. although foreign films took much less than half of all box office receipts. Regarding the potentially smaller number of U.S. films to go into India, one U.S. reporter remarked, "It will be a boon, for the American imports to date have been generally a mediocre lot." Indian film executive A.M. Tariq said, "We must end the stranglehold of Hollywood on India." In keeping with MPEA philosophy of not dealing with a cartel (the Indian distribution agency), Hollywood sent no more new product in until 1975 when a new pact was signed allowing around 120 U.S. films in per year, without using the government agency. For 1975 India imported 139 foreign films, 103 from the U.S., 15 from France, 15 from the U.K., 2 from Italy and 1 each from Yugoslavia, Japan, Indonesia and Canada.[98]

Over those years, India had continued to block varying proportions of money which the cartel was allowed to remit. In 1978 the Kinematograph Renters' Society, which represented the major American firms, in looking for ways to use the blocked rupees, offered the government an interest-free loan of 10 million rupees to the Film Finance Corporation on the condition the money be used to stimulate the building of new Indian cinemas. Repayment of the loan would not begin for five years; it would then be converted and remitted. It was an offer the government accepted. Hollywood long had agitated for more venues in any and all nations the cartel felt were underserved. The more theaters, the more the opportunity to screen Hollywood product.[99]

Another problem country for the cartel was Indonesia. In response to 1953 criticism of the impact of U.S. movies on the Indonesian populace, MPEA executive Irving Maas said that among the gravest problems confronting the nation in its newly-won independence as it struggled with economic and political crises "are those concerning public morale and unrest." Critics were overlooking "the fact that the teeming millions of heavily populated Indonesia depend almost solely on motion pictures for diversion from the toil and worries of their daily existence." Films which did not attract the people "solve neither the economic nor the morale problems involved. This is why 'action' films are popular in Indonesia and why pictures on serious social themes often play to empty theaters." Maas added that American films did a "magnificent" job in "stimulating and raising the hopes of Indonesians for a better future."[100]

As far as Hollywood was concerned, Indonesia was one of the toughest censoring countries in the world. Film censor board chair Maria Santoso commented, "In the Westerns, the white men do terrible things to the Indians. In Asia, today, this message, particularly if fanned by hostile elements, isn't lost."[101]

During a trip to the U.S. in 1956, Indonesia President Sukarno paid a visit to Hollywood where he praised American movies "as being amongst the greatest of all revolutionary forces." Implicit themes he found in those movies were "democracy, equality of opportunity [and] national self-esteem." By showing ordinary people with refrigerators and automobiles, he said the film producers had "helped to build up the sense of deprivation on man's birthright."

Millions of people, therefore, would never again be content to lack those items and had acquired an irresistible determination to have them; "That is why I say you are revolutionaries and that is why I salute you." Sukarno stressed that the have-nots of the world were not jealous of the material wealth displayed on the screen, merely envious. "This is important, because jealousy can be the forerunner of bitterness, envy is the forerunner of emulation."[102]

Back home a few years later, Sukarno called for society to fight against the evils of liberalism so that Indonesians could live according to national ideology. Leaders of the nation's Communist Party took that as a mandate to whip up anti–American sentiment. One activity was a boycott put into effect against Hollywood movies by a group called Papfais (Action Committee for the Boycott of Imperialist American films). Attempts by Indonesia to nationalize foreign films distributors were beaten back by MPEA lobbying and pressure. Agitation increased, however, on other fronts. In 1964 Indonesian airport workers refused to handle American films scheduled for Indonesian houses as a protest, part of a boycott of Hollywood product to protest the presence of units of the U.S. Seventh Fleet in the Indian Ocean. Riots took place outside the offices of film distributors with the result that the majors refused to send any more new films into the nation. It would be two years before regular shipments were resumed. During that period, old films still in the country were being exhibited, not at theaters, but at weekend screenings in the Hotel Indonesia ballroom for elites who arrived in limousines. Since there was no payment to Hollywood for those screenings, the MPEA complained about them to the government. It did no good because it was the government's Ministry of Information which arranged those screenings. Then Indonesia had a change of government, agitation against Hollywood died down and things got back to normal—for Hollywood.[103]

One market largely ignored by the cartel prior to 1950 was sub–Saharan Africa, except for South Africa. For a population of some 30 million, West Africa had less than 100 cinemas in 1953, most of them being open-air. Journalist Stephen Watts reported at that time a tale that a venue in Sierre Leone had shown *King Kong* three nights a week and *The Mark of Zorro* three nights a week, continuously for five years. On the seventh night of the week the pair were run as a double bill. "The two films named are perfect examples of what the African likes," claimed Watts—action. According to him, practically everybody spoke English but he did admit "they are quickly out of their vocabulary depth." He also acknowledged that one of the biggest film hits in the area was a documentary about West African life. *The Boy Kumasenu* was shot in the Gold Coast by a U.K. director. That movie almost didn't get distributed at all and then "only for a ridiculously low flat rate" before becoming a hit.[104]

During 1959, MPEA representatives made an inspection tour of the West African market. Cartel members then extracted only about $125,000 in total. By 1966 they had increased it to almost $500,000. Eric Johnston personally toured the African market the following year. There were then moves in Guinea by the government to nationalize film distribution as a government function. One Hollywood executive noted, "In such a situation, doesn't it make sense to have someone like Johnston go right to the top man and talk the matter over?" Speaking of another African nation, unnamed, the same executive said, "Typical of the kind of 'protectionist' and/or unrealistic thinking in many of these areas ... was that to be found in one newly independent African country ... which has decided to build its own film industry by placing prohibitive taxes on all foreign distributors.... The Johnston tour is designed to check this sort of situation, if possible, before it starts." Many of the African nations were gaining independence in this period. Hollywood wanted to insure it would be welcomed with open arms, and no barriers.[105]

French West and Equatorial Africa with 20 million people had 100 theaters (35mm) in 1960 while Kenya, Uganda and Tanganyika had 60 in total, for 20.8 million people. Nigeria had just 40 houses for its population of 34 million. On his tour Johnston met with heads of government to stress the need of maintaining trade freedom. Independence often led to rising nationalism. (In colonial times, what little business the cartel did in the region was carried on mainly through the majors' foreign branches located in the various colonizing countries [the U.K., France, and so forth].) American film industry personnel worried the situation in Africa could become chaotic for them unless they could convince local government heads of the "economic importance of trade as unrestrictive as possible." Johnston was also eager to gain assurances that Hollywood film prints would get free passage from one African nation to another—no border duties, taxes, etc. Because the African market was small, Hollywood did not make prints for each country but sent a print to one country, then shipped it to a second land, and so on. Additionally Johnston urged the Africans to build more cinemas, although how that was to be accomplished was not clear. Said an MPEA spokesman, "At this stage of the game, these things have to be handled at the top level. We have to make them aware of the U.S. film industry, and of the fact that we are interested in the future of their countries." Africa was not much of a market for Hollywood in 1960, but the cartel was looking to the future.[106]

In 1961 the majors set up a new company, the American Motion Picture Export Company (Africa)—AMPEC—to "coordinate" the West African markets of Liberia, Nigeria, Gambia, Ghana and Sierre Leone. Technically AMPEC was separate from the MPAA and the MPEA but of course it was not; all staff were from the existing cartel. AMPEC was also registered under Webb-Pomerene, allowing it to operate as a complete monopoly in that region. The first office opened in Lagos, Nigeria, in 1962. Soon thereafter CinemaScope equipment arrived and was installed in a few venues. Since one objective was to stimulate new cinema construction, three new ones were being built in Lagos, two to be air-conditioned. The cartel was aiming to provide modern up-to-date venues "which will attract the patronage of Lagos' 20,000 Europeans and 30,000 middle-class Nigerians who have eschewed going to the open air hardbench 'theaters' previously available." The majors were able to encourage such construction by offering investors "a guaranteed supply of good films under long-term contracts." That was one way of describing block booking.[107]

The venture was not as profitable as expected, with a number of problems surfacing. One requirement was to "re-educate native exhibs to modern biz practices." Major among those practices was the payment by exhibitors of a minimum guarantee against a percentage of the gross. Until then the little business done had been on a flat rate basis. Also many in Africa criticized AMPEC for its "monopolistic" aspects since all but two of the majors dealt exclusively through it. Attempting to rebut that attack, the cartel claimed the exhibitors welcomed having only one supplier to dicker with. So balky did Nigerian exhibitors become that the cartel had to impose a short-term boycott for the purpose of adjusting rental terms. When it ended, U.S. films commanded higher rates.[108]

In a 1962 UNESCO report discussing the informational needs of the African continent, one section said, "Governments should take all possible measures to assure the expansion of national film production. They might consider levying an import tax on foreign films commercially distributed in their countries." Hollywood worked for an opposite result. Given the small amount of money extracted from the region, one historian wrote, "It has been suggested that propaganda considerations of the American government were part of the motives behind the American film companies' movement into this area."[109]

When the government-controlled Kenya Film Corporation (KFC) proposed putting all foreign film distribution under the KFC, the MPEA said no, shut down two U.S.–owned cinemas in Nairobi and, of course, initiated a boycott. After eight months of stalemate, an agreement was reached whereby the MPEA recognized KFC as a distribution organization which would be operated with U.S. "advice."[110]

Ethiopia's filmgoers were drawn from the affluent educated minority with admission averaging 75¢ in 1971 when the majority of people had monthly incomes ranging from $12 to $40 for white collar workers and $80 to $120 for government employees. Spectators had to know another language since no films were dubbed or subtitled into Amharic, the official language. Cinemas were ramshackle, sound quality was poor and the films were old and third-rate. Ethiopia's government was dissatisfied because "a large percentage of Ethiopia's national income is paid in foreign exchange for films," said Board of Film Review head Tadesse Abebe. He and others urged the government to take over film importing and distribution as they believed natives would do a better job of film selecting. Fox had an office then in Addis Ababa headed by Bob Zyon, who had initial success with exhibitors but less and less as exhibitors rebelled against his escalating rental demands. Zyon was then involved in a vitriolic newspaper debate with the venue owners. Zyon described the situation as "impossible" and in the pages of local papers accused the exhibitors of monopolistic practices and of cheating the public by refusing to import his more expensive offerings settling instead for "low-cost" movies from nations such as India, Egypt and Italy. Exhibitors called Zyon an exploiter and a monopolist. Cinema owner Robert Djerrahian termed Zyon "a nonsensical money-collector threatening to break down the growth of our cinema business." A different owner got his U.S. movies from Beirut. Although he received a list of titles to select from, he never got to see the movies beforehand nor, he admitted, did he know much about them. American films arriving from Beirut came with French and Arabic subtitles. This owner made his own Italian titles on a little screen under the big screen as many Ethiopians understood Italian (Italy had once occupied Ethiopia).[111]

Sometimes the cartel fought over the most trivial amounts. In the North African country of Tunisia the government instituted a tax of 25 millimes (6¢) a meter on imported films ($180 for an average-length feature) in October, 1960. Immediately the majors launched a boycott with no new product shipped in for many months. MPAA executive Griffith Johnson visited Tunisia but could not eliminate the tariff. He declared that it was too high. Admitting the tax would not eliminate profit, the *New York Times* defended the necessity of the fight because "behind the Tunisian fight is the remainder of the African market and the precedent set by the Tunisian tax." Tunisia had a total of 60 theaters. To fill the gap, the nation bought 15 Czech and 5 Soviet features—all of which paid the tax. That purchase, said the *Times*, was "an almost perfect illustration of the built-in advantage that Communist countries have over free-enterprise countries in the cultural and economic competition in the under-developed world." An agreement was reached between the two sides early in 1961 whereby the majors would pay the tax until July 1, 1961, when it would drop to 20 mil for 6 months and go down in 5 mil steps periodically until it was entirely eliminated at the end of 1964. Initially Tunisia had imposed the tax to finance cinemas in remote areas and to develop a Tunisian film industry for newsreels and educational material.[112]

As early as 1948 Arab nations began to embargo the films of certain actors because they were deemed to be pro–Zionist. That year Egypt put a stop on the movies of Danny Kaye and Mickey Rooney on the grounds those men contributed money to Zionism. Such bannings continued in the Arab world in the 1950s and early 1960s. Jordan banned all Danny Kaye movies in 1956 and the films of Elizabeth Taylor, as did the United Arab Republic with respect to Taylor. As well the UAR banned the works of Eartha Kitt and Edward G. Robinson because "they have shown pronounced Israeli sympathies and have helped collect donations for Israel. From time to time the Arab League's central office in Damascus made film boycott recommendations which the ten member nations (Libya, Tunisia, Morocco, Iraq, Jordan, Saudi Arabia, Syria,

Lebanon, Yemen and Egypt) adopted or not. The ban on Robinson was lifted in 1959 while a ban was imposed on Susan Hayward films in 1958, then lifted the next year. In 1963 Taylor and Kaye were still on the blacklist throughout the Arab world along with Joanne Woodward, Juliette Greco, Frank Sinatra and Paul Newman.[113]

Egypt went even further in June 1967 when officials banned all screenings of U.S. films. Long unhappy with the violence and sex in American movies along with the glorification of wealth and luxury in so many Hollywood features, Egypt used that month's Arab-Israeli war and the resulting severance of diplomatic relations with the U.S. as the catalyst for imposing the ban. Said one cinema manager, "Stopping American films would really have started a riot. But with the war and the downgrading of the United States' status in the public mind, the censor had gained the upper hand." Within a year Egypt had concluded a film pact with the MPEA allowing the cartel to regain its dominance of 80 percent of Egyptian screen time. About 150 Hollywood features entered each year, earning the cartel about $1.782 million. One motivation for the deal was that the MPEA lent the Egyptian government $51,500 for the renovation of two government-owned cinemas. It was an interest-free loan. A few months later Egypt lifted a ban of several years standing on Tarzan films. They were banned when it was decided at least some of them reflected a colonialist outlook—mastery of the jungle by a high-born white Englishman."[114]

Over a five-year period up to 1974 Iran raised the price of its exported oil by some 400 percent. Normally that would have nothing to do with the motion picture trade but it did in this case because Paramount was then owned by Gulf + Western Industries. Company chairman Charles G. Bluhdorn was annoyed because Iran had not raised the prices paid for U.S. movies for 10 years. Iranian admission prices ranged from 58¢ to 73¢, set by government decree. A further irritation to Bluhdorn came when he learned Paramount's blockbuster feature *The Godfather* did not screen at higher, special admission rates in Iran, as it did in many other areas. With fixed admission rates there was a lower return on film rentals. Bluhdorn felt an equitable settlement would be an increase in film receipts to the cartel of 400 percent—in line with oil increases—through higher admission prices, or through government subsidy if Iran insisted on maintaining low admission rates. Bluhdorn demanded cartel head Jack Valenti work harder to effect a settlement in Iran, saying, "Paramount will no longer accept a double standard in foreign trade." Valenti went to work, stating, "These admissions are below those charged in comparable areas of the Middle East, Mediterranean and African markets." America then sent about 100 to 125 movies into Iran yearly, extracting about $2.5 million. An agreement was almost reached to increase rentals to U.S. exporters by about 40 percent through an increase in admission prices plus a reduction in taxes on admissions. However, when local authorities, who received those admission tax receipts, heard of the proposal they rebelled. That deal fell through. Even before those negotiations were completed, an impatient Bluh-dorn ordered Paramount to impose a boycott on Iran, which it did in Sep-tember 1974, halting all film shipments to Iran. Paramount argued its actions would not be seen as arbitrary since the "concentrated price action of Iran and its partners in the [oil] exporters' group would violate United States antitrust laws if it took place among American companies." It marked a crack in the cartel solidarity as no other Hollywood producer, nor the MPEA adopted the boycott. Bluhdorn was so angry with the situation and his perception that Valenti had not been forceful enough in negotiations that he threatened to withdraw Paramount from the MPAA.[115]

When negotiations with Iran finally collapsed in spring 1975, five other majors joined Paramount in its boycott—Warner, Fox, UA, MGM and Uni-versal—although Columbia did not. The MPEA did not call a boycott itself but rather merely announced the names of the participating producers. In a communication to Iran's arts and culture minister, Valenti complained about the low admission prices: "In these times it seems to us to be unfair for the U.S. motion picture industry, in effect, to subsidize the Iranian moviegoer." Later that year, 1975, Iran issued a decree placing the distribution of foreign films in Iran exclusively in the hands of native companies. It was a move to crack the cartel since there was a time limit involved. In order to qualify, Warner, Columbia, UA and Fox returned to Iran in 1976 to jointly form the Film Importers Association, a "native" firm. Paramount remained out. Not that it mattered much. A couple of years later the Iranian government, then under the Ayatollah Khomeini, banned all karate and kung fu movies as well as all "imperialistic" films. A few months after that Iran banned all U.S. films. Sub-sequent to that the MPEA announced a boycott on film shipments to Iran. It was an odd, too-late gesture with Valenti admitting the gesture at that point was academic only.[116]

Back in the Western Hemisphere, agitation against Hollywood's domi-nation continued. Canada's native filmmakers formed separate organizations of film producers in both Francophone and Anglophone areas of Canada to lobby for national policies to break the American monopoly. They advocated measures such as film quotas, taxes on the earnings of U.S. majors with the proceeds to be used to finance Canadian feature film production, and for laws giving them access to screen time. In response the federal government had a report prepared by economist Jack Firestone, who suggested the possibility the majors might earmark 10 percent of their earnings to be invested in Canadian production. Naturally, the MPAA dismissed such a proposal out-of-hand. One reason given, which also contained a not-so-subtle threat, was that "it would establish Canadian Government interferences with U.S. private enterprise interests which have hitherto operated without such interferences in Canada and it could bring retaliatory action from the U.S. Government affecting Cana-dian business in the United States." Not wanting to challenge the cartel, that matter died. However, in 1967 Canada's federal government created the Canadian Film Development Corporation (CFDC) which provided funds from general tax revenue to develop the native film industry, yet it did not attack the stranglehold that the majors had on Canadian distribution and exhibition. Officially the CFDC's position was to rely on "moral suasion" to get U.S. distributors to distribute Canadian movies within Canada. The government had decided against screen quotas because, said Secretary of State Judy LaMarsh in the House of Commons, "Canadian films must make it on their own merits. But in rejecting quotas we are counting on film distributors and cinema chains to give more than ordinary support to the aims of this program." The number of Canadian films made did increase but few films actually got screened. Canada's share of Canadian screen time between 1966 and 1972 inclusive varied from a low of .02 percent to a high of almost 1 percent. Of those movies produced through CFDC assistance, observed film writer Manjunath Pendakur, "only a very small proportion ... ever reached Canadian screens (the majors' monopoly of distribution and exhibition saw to that)."[117]

By 1973, pressure for quotas in Canada had increased. The CFDC was almost out of money; it had succeeded in getting Canadian films made but not shown (U.S. distributors had not cooperated). Agitation from the film community for quotas and/or a tax continued. Secretary of State Hugh Faulkner decided to investigate those two options. Since the provinces had jurisdiction over the construction, operation and licensing of cinemas, as well as doing their own movie censoring, Faulkner surveyed them. He found some support for quotas but none for a ticket tax, even if only a small amount. That lack of enthusiasm combined with lobbying from Hollywood caused him to back away from both ideas. The cartel and Canadian house owners wrote letters to members of parliament protesting any such proposals to support native film production. What emerged was a deal negotiated in 1974, signed in 1975, between Faulkner and Canada's only two major exhibition chains (both U.S.–owned, Famous Players and Odeon). Under that deal each house in the chains agreed to run one Canadian film for one week in each 13-week quarter. It was purely voluntary. Also voluntary was a commitment by Famous to invest $1.2 million and Odeon to invest $500,000 in Canadian films over the coming year. That agreement was the third such pact negotiated since 1966 by three different secretaries of state. Although the government could clearly see the need for intervention, it always chose instead to negotiate with the MPAA's Canadian arm, now called the Canadian Motion Picture Distributors Association (CMPDA). That agreement, and its predecessors, had no effect in increasing the distribution of Canadian movies in Canadian cinemas.[118]

Next to tackle the situation was Jason Roberts, who was appointed new Secretary of State in 1976. He related he was negotiating with the MPEA to persuade them with "moral suasion or fiscal measures" to provide for an equitable distribution of Canadian movies in the Canadian market. During an address to a broadcasting committee Roberts explained, "A continuing concern to me is the degree to which the revenues generated at the box office in Canada are drained out of Canada and contribute very little to the financing of Canadian productions.... I have discussed these concerns with both the CMPDA and its parent MPAA. I have also brought home to them that the present imbalance of rentals and returns on investment for Canadian productions cannot endure.... I intend to assess over the next 12 months their practical response to the problem I have described and to judge to what degree they have met our concerns." In response to that criticism Hollywood strengthened its lobby by hiring a management consulting firm with good connections in various government departments. Valenti and CMPDA members met with Roberts and gave a vague promise to help Canadian producers get their films screened in Canada by prospective U.S. distributors. It was all smoke and mirrors; nothing happened.[119]

Unsatisfied with the lack of response, Roberts proposed in 1978 to his Cabinet colleagues a 10 percent tax on U.S. distributors' annual gross rental revenue from non–Canadian films in Canada with a rebate conditional on their distribution of Canadian product at home and outside Canada. He said Canada's film industry was "struggling to cope with foreign domination and to compete with a heavy volume of imported products laid down in Canada at prices which the Canadian filmmaker had difficulty matching.... The major foreign-owned distributors have not so far invested in Canadian pictures. Nor have their parent houses in the U.S. decided to leave some funds in Canada and invest them in whatever parts of the Canadian film industry seem most promising to them." That proposed fiscal measure was strongly opposed by Finance Minister Jean Chretien (currently Prime Minister of Canada). Chretien was reportedly under pressure from the MPEA lobby and the U.S. State Department. A junior State Department official called on Canada's Washington embassy to make it clear to Canada that the U.S. government would not like it if the tax was imposed. At the same time the CMPDA spelled out the threat of U.S. retaliation in a brief submitted to the Department of Finance; "The U.S. is likely to regard any significantly discriminatory taxation of the industry by this country as being regarded in the international community as a precedent. There would appear to us, therefore, to be a real risk of a serious U.S. reaction that would not necessarily be limited to the taxation of film royalties, indeed, the field of taxation." When he first presented his tax proposal, Roberts warned Chretien and the Finance ministry of the probable reaction by saying, "The foreign distributors will rise up violently against the fiscal measures and will use their influence in Washington. The American government will probably threaten to take measures of reprisal, notably to exclude Canadian films from the American market." Of course the latter was a silly threat as Canadian movies could barely crack their home market, let alone a foreign one. Nonetheless Roberts could not get Cabinet support for his tax proposal, so it died. He was left with no leverage except moral suasion. Valenti expressed sympathy with Roberts' concerns, but again, nothing happened except talent drain. Director Norman Jewison left Canada in the 1960s to make films in Hollywood; there were no opportunities for him in Canada.[120]

As Canadian writer Manjunath Pendakur observed, "The U.S. film industry has preserved its domination of the Canadian feature film market with the assistance of the U.S. State Department which helped it take advantage of Canada's economic and political dependence."[121]

Latin America remained firmly under Hollywood domination in this period. Around 1960 America controlled 70 percent of screen time, despite high-level anti–American sentiment in general in the region. Hollywood controlled a minimum of 50 percent of the screen time in every country except Mexico where it held 40 percent. Major studios and exhibition chains were state-owned in Mexico. Some other foreign films that were available in Latin America were distributed there by the cartel members, but not in the U.S. Hollywood then extracted $9 million annually from Brazil, $8 million from Mexico. While many U.S. government officials worried about the spread of Fidelism in Latin America, Hollywood executives did not; they worried about the spread of television. All Latin American markets were totally free except for Argentina which allowed the majors to import a maximum of 200 movies per year, more than they actually used. Reporter Vincent Canby noted, "Latin American tastes are remarkably similar to those of citizens of Des Moines or Brooklyn."[122]

Shortly after Fidel Castro took power in Cuba, the U.S. placed a sweeping embargo on all shipments of goods to Cuba. Excluded from that embargo were motion pictures, presumably because they were regarded as effective propaganda weapons. Hollywood grossed about $3 million annually in billings from Cuba. Just a couple months later Cuba seized all the assets of Hollywood in Cuba, calling U.S. films "obnoxious, childish, and poison for the minds of young people." Film executives felt Castro had erred in denying Cubans access to American movies because "the Cubans liked American product and got it cheap. It fit in with the bread-and-circuses idea long followed by dictators as a means of keeping the populace content."[123]

When the MPEA disputed Mexico's right to a government-controlled exhibition monopoly, MPEA executive Robert Corkery called Latin America a speculative market of tremendous potential but "we'll never participate in its development if we allow national agencies to handle our films."[123]

Brazil gradually increased the number of quota days devoted to the screening of native films. Every increase was vigorously fought by exhibitors and distributors. Brazilian film production did increase due to the quota increases. During economic difficulties in 1976, Brazil proposed higher taxes be levied on U.S. firms (in all industries). In response Jack Valenti traveled to Brazil and met with finance minister Mario Henrique Simonsen. Officially he was there to participate in a "Week of American Cinema"; however, the real reason was to argue against increased taxes. Valenti told the MPAA that the proposal "would have cost us several million dollars per year, with the possibility of sterner measures later." The proposal had been prompted by Brazil's rapidly enlarging trade deficit due to lower demand for its main products such as coffee and sugar. In 1975 Latin America produced $80 million annually for Hollywood—15 percent of total U.S. foreign film receipts—with Brazil and Mexico each contributing about 20 percent of the $80 million. In his private talks Valenti got Brazil to withdraw the tax proposal for the film industry. In return Hollywood gave nothing except a promise to alert the U.S. Congress to Brazil's huge trade deficit problems. The finance minister said to Valenti, "You have powerful friends in the Congress who listen to you with respect."[125]

Argentina's government ordered cinemas in 1963 to screen one native film for every six foreign ones exhibited. Under that measure, cinemas were only required to show local films rated "first class." As well the government covered them for any financial loss resulting from the screening of those movies. Nevertheless cinema owners staged a two-day protest during which they closed their houses. Argentina promised to reconsider the measure, withdrawing it "temporarily." A year later, when Argentinean film producers agitated unsuccessfully to reduce U.S. film imports from 200 to 100 per year, MPEA executive Robert Corkery found it difficult to understand why Argentinean exhibitors "have allowed the local producers to push for the reduction."[126]

When Argentina imposed an additional tax on film imports in 1969, the majors launched another boycott, extending to the foreign, mostly European films they distributed in the area. *Variety* called this boycott "a lethal blow for film biz here." Yet film attendance, already in decline from the effects of television, showed no effect. For the first 43 weeks of 1967 to 1969, tickets sold amounted to 9 million in 1967, 8 million in 1968, 7.5 million in 1969. However, yielding to the pressure, the Argentina government authorized film imports on a "temporary" basis (with no new taxes) while the matter was studied further. Hollywood lifted the boycott. Argentina then rearranged existing film taxes, promising Hollywood they would be no higher in total. Film observers felt those rearranged taxes would actually be "much less than before." Another boycott of six months duration was lifted by the majors in 1976 after Argentina allowed an increase in ticket prices. With economic chaos in Argentina came currency devaluation. With currency devaluation came lower revenue for Hollywood. A partial solution was an increase in admission prices.[127]

In Chile on several occasions in the 1960s, one of the majors withdrew all its material from a theater chain because it had made playing time available to an independent distributor. With the election of Salvador Allende to lead Chile came a series of restrictions on foreign films including admission price controls, quotas and so on, all under the oversight of state-run Chile Films. As of July 1971, the majors launched a boycott of Chile. Eighteen months later *Variety* reported the void had been filled by product from other nations with the absence of U.S. product creating no stir or protest from the populace. Journalist Hans Ehrmann commented on the problems involved in replacing U.S. films with other product. With American films publicized in advance in the media, it created an appetite in audiences who had heard, seen and read about some movie. That constant interplay between "news" items on films successful in America and not available in Chile did create some pressure on Chile Films. "This conditioning is an invisible power U.S. films have abroad and, at times of stress, is a particularly useful ally as audiences do not take easily to substitutes." It was difficult to find alternate fare and difficult to get the audience to accept it. Such conditions were carefully developed over the years by the majors' business practices and control of exhibition. When the Allende regime was ousted by a military dictatorship in 1974, the majors lifted their boycott and soon recaptured 67 percent of the Chilean market, the same amount they held prior to Allende. Chile Films was rapidly phased out. Film schools and libraries established under Allende were closed; subsidies to native producers were halted. Between 1975 and 1978 no Chilean films were produced. During the military government's first year, the price of a movie ticket went up 800 percent and unemployment tripled; cinema attendance dropped from a high of 75 million in 1967 to 11.5 million in 1982.[128]

When Chile instituted a new tax measure on films in 1975, an MPEA representative went to Chile to argue against it. New and very rigid censorship rules had upset most members of the Chilean film community but the MPEA was not concerned about them, said *Variety*. They were worried only by "those aspects that affect distribution and exhibitor revenue, while the freedom of expression angle leaves them unconcerned."[129]

Domestically Hollywood had a record year in 1946 when the box office receipts totaled $1,692 million. Then came seven straight years of decline to $1,252 million in 1953. One of the reasons the percentage of the world gross attributable to foreign sources increased was the decline in domestic attendance from television at an earlier time and to a greater extent than in foreign lands. For the years 1946 and 1947 foreign remittances were $142 million (a record high) and $124 million respectively (dollars in New York). For 1952 gross foreign rentals were $250 million with net receipts—dollars in New York—of $140 million, 42 percent of Hollywood's total income. The "dollars in New York" figure was less the costs of striking prints, advertising, distribution costs and all other expenses—it was all profit, subject only to U.S. corporate taxes. It was pure profit under the assumption that the entire negative cost of the film was written off against domestic revenue. That was an assumption under which all other nations had to work. For 1953 the foreign take was $170 million net with an estimated 200 million per week attending American films abroad. Britain contributed the most money with Canada second (remitting $20 million) and Germany third ($10 million). *Business Week* gloated that "the U.S. industry is the only film production industry in the world that does not live by a government subsidy in some shape or form. This is largely because Hollywood dominates the world's screens, getting about 70% of the total playing time." Only India was said to be immune to Hollywood, contributing less than $1 million annually to its coffers. According to a 1953 Department of Commerce report, U.S. films took up 74 percent of the world's screen time with American percentage of screen time in Europe being 63 percent, South America 64 percent, Mexico and Central America 76 percent, Caribbean 84 percent, Far East 48 percent, Middle East 57 percent, South Pacific 65 percent, Africa 63 percent, Atlantic Islands 73 percent, Canada 75 percent, U.S. 90 percent.[130]

For the years 1953 and 1954, Commerce reported U.S. films earned $170 and $200 million respectively, each a record year. Sixty-eight percent of world screen time was taken up by U.S. product in 1954, down from 71 percent in 1951. Some 42 percent of the industry's total came from foreign sources in 1954. Paramount producer Don Harman predicted foreign films would continue to run a poor second to Hollywood product: "Italian, French and other products still don't represent any threat to Hollywood and I can't see the time when they will." American film companies spent around $6 million annually in foreign nations in 1953 to advertise their pictures, about 3 percent of their take. For 1954 the amount spent on foreign advertising (excluding Canada) was $8.5 million which included salaries, ads, trade shows, etc. Of that amount, $1.75 million was spent in the U.K., $2 million in the rest of Western Europe and $1 million in Japan.[131]

Eric Johnston reported that Hollywood's gross foreign take for 1955 and 1956 was $212 million and $217 million respectively. Thirty million dollars in 1956 was contributed by Canada. After deducting expenses from the 1956 gross, Johnston put the 1956 dollars in New York figure at "about $170,000,000." Fifty percent of the total income then came from abroad. In 1958 cartel members grossed $590 million worldwide, about $300 million outside the U.S., reported Johnston. For the same year the Department of Commerce said dollars in New York from foreign sources were $215 million—the same as in 1957, amounting to 45 percent of total revenue.[132]

Worldwide cinemas had increased from 79,000 in 1949 with a capacity of 42.7 million up to 154,900 in 1960 with a capacity of 73.8 million. Domestically there were 18,200 cinemas in the U.S. in 1948, 17,600 in 1961. For 1961 the film industry grossed $557 million worldwide, compared to $626 million in 1955 (it was an upturn from a low point in between). Domestic take was $267 million in 1961, $326 million in 1955 while foreign receipts were $278 million in 1961, $290 million in 1955. Currency devaluation was a major reason for the foreign decline. Fifty percent of the foreign billing came from six nations: the

U.K., Canada, France, Italy, Germany and Japan. Seven countries (Brazil, Mexico, Spain, South Africa, Argentina, Belgium and Australia) comprised another 25 percent. Fifteen other nations brought in another 15 percent with the remaining 10 percent coming from 77 other countries. According to the MPAA, in 1962 U.S. film companies took $275 million domestically (including Canada), $310 million foreign (54.6 percent) with American movies controlling 60 percent of screen time in the free world. The Department of Commerce reported dollars in New York from foreign sources for 1962 and 1963 at $210 million and $220 million respectively. The U.K. contributed $35 million to Hollywood in 1963, Italy $29 million, Germany $27 million, France $25 million, Japan $20 million, Australia, New Zealand and other Asia $58 million, Latin America and the Caribbean $47 million.[133]

Foreign take continued to increase with the 1970 figure being $359 million. Nineteen nations provided 77.16 percent of that amount: U.K. 10.42 percent, Italy 9.30, Canada 7.94, France 6.92, Japan 5.76, Germany 5.16, Brazil 4.86, Australia 4.81, Spain 4.49, Mexico 3.42, South Africa 3.36, Sweden 1.88, Argentina 1.73, Belgium 1.32, Venezuela 1.29, Switzerland 1.24, Philippines 1.19, Colombia 1.04, and the Netherlands 1.03 percent. Receipts from overseas totaled $415.4 million in 1973; part of that increase came from a U.S. dollar devaluation of 8.75 percent in 1971.[134]

Worldwide theatrical film billings for the U.S. majors hit a new peak in 1974 of $1,047,418,375, up nearly 28 percent from the $819,376,624 in 1973 with new peaks reached domestically and internationally. Domestic billings were $545,867,286 in 1974 (up from $390,493,622 in 1973) while foreign billings were $501,551,089 (up from 1973's $428,883,002—the previous foreign high). Foreign receipts were 48 percent of the total. For 1976, worldwide theatrical film rental billings were $1,147,000,000 (down from the record high of $1,232,000,000 in 1975). Foreign billings (including Canada) were $570 million against $577 million domestically.[135]

Needless to say, foreign films did not do very well in America, despite Johnston's 1954 pronouncement that his organization "believes in assisting" filmmakers of other nations in obtaining wider distribution of their movies in the U.S. At the time the U.S. Treasury Department applied a 30 percent withholding tax on the gross earnings of foreign movies. One sore point with foreign producers was a belief that their product had harsher censorship applied against it under the Production Code than did domestic films. The cartel still did not like its home control to be publicized; "The U.S. distribs don't like to see the domestic earning power of their films publicized for the simple reason that this implants in the mind of foreign observers the—erroneous—idea that most films get their money back from the American theaters." That is, other nations might attempt to impose more taxes.[136]

Complaints were raised in the U.K. Parliament in 1956 about the difficulties in getting U.K. movies exhibited in America. *Variety* said no discrimination existed but added, "No one denies, however, that the average American is more interested in, and better able to identify with characters in a film dealing with the U.S." Regarding the acceptability of British films in the U.S., a Theater Owners of America survey declared, "The aim of British producers should be to reach the patrons of the regular houses, and to make pictures more in keeping with Hollywood's approach. They must find out what the American public wants." One specific complaint was that the U.K. film *Richard III* was not getting U.K. bookings. However, countered *Variety*, it had been booked on NBC-TV and was being released at the same time at one New York City cinema. Then it was being roadshown because past American experience had not shown "that a classic such as this is served best via large exposure on the chains." Distributor UA did well, said the publication, with *Henry V* although it never received "mass bookings" but was "nursed along," benefiting from a "tailor-made ad-pub campaign." Since the majors had been forced to sell off their cinema holdings, pointed out *Variety*, the "film magnates no longer can 'force' a picture to play the circuits. The choice is now up to the exhibitors"— meaning at one time they could and did. Overall the publication dismissed European complaints about lack of U.S. access as "a stubbornly fixated ignorance of conditions in the motion picture markets of North America." When Theater Owners of America chairman E.D. Martin returned from Europe that same year, he remarked that although he saw many "beautifully made" movies, "they won't benefit us here." Stressing he had nothing against foreign films, he was certain U.S. audiences would find it "difficult to appreciate the quality and artistic value of the pictures."[137]

German film producer Wolf Schwarz, considered pro–American as he was against quotas and any government intervention in industry, remarked that German audiences accepted dubbed films "but the American firms won't do anything with dubbed pictures. It practically amounts to a boycott." Noting the U.S. producers took $15 million a year out of Germany, he wondered "why we shouldn't get back at least 6,000,000 marks ($1,500,000) from the U.S.?" Things actually got worse for Germany. In 1957–1958 Germany remitted $18 million to the cartel, with America holding 30 percent of the screen time, while in the same year German movies remitted $208,000 from America. For 1956 foreign films grossed around $7.1 million in America (excluding Mexico's gross of $3 million from Spanish-language-only movies shown in America in ethnic cinemas). Expenses had to be deducted from that $7 million—some of the money accrued to U.S. distributors who distributed some of those films. None of the foreign producers did their own distributing in the U.S. Of that total, Italy garnered $2.3 million (from 52 movies), France $2.2 million (from 38), the U.K. $1.7 million (from 50), Germany $282,000 (from 74), Japan $247,000 (from 6), Russia $194,000 (from 31), Sweden $80,000 (from 3) and Greece $16,000 (from 12). Some of that money also came from ethnic screenings in the original language only.[138]

Italian director Sergio Leone started his career as a bit player in Vittorio de Sica's *The Bicycle Thief* in 1947. Years later he directed the famous spaghetti-western trilogy which turned Clint Eastwood into a superstar. The first was *A Fistful of Dollars*, a 1964 Italian/German/Spanish coproduction made on a $200,000 budget. The producers decided it would have a better chance of success if it was billed as an American western rather than an Italian one. Credits were Americanized on the screen so Leone became Bob Robertson, actor Gian Maria Volonte became John Welles and so on. *Dollars* opened in Naples in an English-language version with Italian subtitles. It was a big hit in Italy, the rest of Europe, South America and Japan, as were all three in the series. After filming the second film *For a Few Dollars More* in 1965, Eastwood, while in Rome, appeared in a cameo role in De Sica's *Le Streghe* (The Witches)—a compilation work with sections by five directors. All three films in the trilogy (*The Good, the Bad and the Ugly* [1967] was the third) were big hits over much of the world. Eastwood was a big star everywhere except home in America. Still, the trilogy was not exhibited in the U.S. Finally UA bought the rights to all three as a single package for release in America. The delay was put down to skepticism on the part of the majors as to the potential of the films. By the time UA bought the rights to the trilogy, they had Eastwood under contract to make a U.S. western for them. As for *The Witches*, it "was never shown outside Europe, mostly because United Artists bought it in order to suppress it once they had Eastwood on their books." When Eastwood left Hollywood for Europe in successive summers to shoot the films, there was a feeling, commented Eastwood's biographer, that "an American actor making an Italian move was sort of taking a step backward."[139]

At the start of this 1952–1979 period, Hollywood was highly resistant to television, viewing it as a rival draining away attendance from the silver screen. The cartel refused to deal with television, withholding its old films. Within a few years the attitude changed as, one by one, they made their films available. Long before this period ended, Hollywood had embraced television, producing made-for-TV movies, series and so forth, in addition to selling it their theatrical features. In some countries, observers naively thought television might aid their native film industry—it would provide an outlet for those films, a chance to make some money which they couldn't make as they were shut out of their local exhibition circuits. They had not counted on Hollywood dominating foreign TV screens with U.S. films and series. As Australian historian John Tulloch noted in 1982, "Australian exhibitors in the 1920s (and Australian television companies today) have been able to get films and TV programs at costs far below equivalent Australia-produced material." In 1980 just 2 percent of all feature films shown on Brazilian TV were Brazilian. Of the movies aired, 1,325 were American, U.K. 161, Italy 152 and Brazil 32. As cinema audiences declined worldwide, TV revenue became more important.

Television in Brazil did not provide the native film industry with additional income to compensate for the decline of theatrical revenues. Hollywood films had already covered their costs and thus could be sold cheaper to TV than could the Brazilian product.[140]

Valenti remarked in 1978 that foreign film revenue was indispensable to the continuing production of films for theaters "and for the financing of prime American TV programs. It is not profit. It is the return of needed production capital." Sales of U.S. TV programs were then estimated to exceed $200 million from 120 markets outside the U.S. The MPEA then had a Television Program Export Committee. During the 1970s foreign TV sales moved from 20 percent to 24 percent of the world gross. Valenti didn't see a 50–50 domestic/foreign split in world TV income (films were close to that then) anytime in the future because TV was subsidized in many nations, owned by the government in some and seen as an instrument of national policy in others, while cinema exhibitors were motivated by "economic necessity."[141]

Some cartel members went so far as to form their own mini-cartel, a monopoly within a monopoly. In the 1970s Paramount, Universal and MGM formed Cinema International Corporation (CIC) as their offshore distribution company. One move they made in 1976 occurred in South Africa where CIC-Warner (the latter joined here but otherwise was not a CIC member) acquired full ownership of the MGM theater circuit of 19 houses and one drive-in. It screened its own product in its own theaters and enjoyed a "healthy relationship" with South Africa's largest exhibition chain, Ster-Kinekor. Every important film in South Africa then played in up to 45 houses at the time of release whereas prior to 1976 a 20-print release was thought to be excessive. That was one way for Hollywood to continue its dominance as the number of films it produced and distributed declined—book each film into more houses. Booking 100 films into 40 houses each gave the same domination as booking 200 films into 20 theaters each.[142]

The formation of the CIC did not mean the MPAA/MPEA was any less important or active. *Variety* summarized some of the MPEA's recent successes in 1978, comparing the cartel to the Marines, fighting for America from the Halls of Montezuma to the shore of Tripoli. MPEA efforts in Singapore defeated a proposed extra film tax; in New Zealand the MPEA got "relief" from a tax problem; in Mexico the MPEA resolved an unspecified "problem." A government proposal for a film tax in Canada was beaten when the MPEA joined with the Canadian Motion Picture Distributors Association to defeat it. Left unsaid was that the MPEA and the CMPDA were essentially the same group. The cartel had joined with itself. Lastly the Indonesian government insisted that film trade be carried out through a government-sponsored consortium which annoyed the cartel because it was "in effect a monopoly, the only importing distrib in town. MPEA says it doesn't do business with monopolies, thus no trade," said *Variety*. The usual boycott was followed by the usual government capitulation. A deal was struck in which the MPEA was allowed to deal with a number of private importers.[143]

One complaint Hollywood had in 1980 was the increasing costs of marketing a film overseas through posters, radio, TV ads and so forth. Overseas media buyers were upset to find a lack of demographics such as available in the U.S. Because France did not permit film companies to advertise on TV, Fox arranged to have a 15-minute documentary on *The Empire Strikes Back* aired on French TV. That film's opening was tied to a series of consecutive showings of the documentary. A favored tactic was to open a movie in a country where overheads were lowest. That way the producer could test the reaction to see if it was worthwhile buying ads in more expensive nations.[144]

Ahead for the majors lay the video cassette revolution. That was no threat to Hollywood nor was it regarded as such. In fact, the video revolution could not have happened without the cartel making its movies available in that format. Hollywood would become even richer. Video cassettes were first available about 1977 but there was no market to speak of until the 1980s.

8. Hollywood Dreams of Hollyworld: 1980–1995

Restructuring of the cartel continued in the 1980s and 1990s. Columbia was purchased in 1982 by Coca-Cola. Under its aegis the studio was one of three firms (Home Box Office and CBS were the others) to join forces to finance a new production company, Tri-Star Pictures. While it was technically separate, Tri-Star used Columbia's distribution system. Formed during a 1987 restructuring by Coca-Cola was its entertainment sector Columbia Pictures Entertainment (CPE), which consisted of two producing arms (Columbia Pictures and Tri-Star Pictures), two television arms (Columbia Pictures Television [producers of prime time network series and distribution of syndicated programs] and Merv Griffin Enterprises [first-run syndication]) and Loews Theatre Management Corporation, a theater circuit with about 635 screens in 180 locations. In 1989 Sony Corporation of Japan bought CPE. As part of the complex deal, Sony gave Time Warner the right to distribute Columbia's film and made-for-TV movies on cable. Tristar dropped the hyphen from its name in 1990. Gulf + Western changed its name to Paramount Communications in 1989. In 1983 Disney created the production subsidiary Touchstone Pictures, designed to make more adult-oriented movies without tarnishing the company's image. Another division, Hollywood Pictures, was started in 1993. Illustrative of the tendency of the cartel to swallow up any competition was the case of the independent distributor Miramax Films, which was perhaps Hollywood's largest such independent in the early 1990s. Miramax was bought by Disney in 1993, which continued to run it as a separate company. Warner was acquired by Time, Inc. in 1989 with the new entity called Time Warner. Other subsidiaries included cable networks Cinemax, HBO, home video outlet HBO Video as well as theater interests through holding companies in Mann Theatres, Festival Theatres in California and Translux Theatres in the East. Transamerica sold UA to MGM in 1981 with the entity being named MGM/UA in 1983. Turner Broadcasting System (CNN, Superstations TBS and TNT, among other holdings) purchased

MGM/UA in 1986 then sold everything to Tracinda Corporation with the exception of the MGM film library which Turner retained (adding to the previously purchased RKO library). MGM/UA continued to produce and distribute films. Pathé Communications Corporation acquired MGM/UA in 1990 with Italian financier Giancarlo Parretti rechristening the entity MGM-Pathé. When Parretti defaulted on a $1 billion note in 1992, ownership passed into the hands of the note holder, French banking concern Credit Lyonnais. Following that move, the company was renamed Metro-Goldwyn-Mayer Inc. (once again, MGM). French authorities have given the bank until 1997 to sell MGM. To that end the bank has divided the company into two parts, the producing/distributing arm and the cinema arm, which owned 500 screens in the U.K. and Ireland, 70 screens in the Netherlands plus a half interest in a company that owned nine cinemas in Denmark. Among the many firms interested in the theaters were Sony and Warner.[1]

Fox merged with a company owned by financier Marvin Davis in 1981. Four years later Davis sold the company to media baron Rupert Murdoch, who exercised control through his Australian company, News Corporation. Also in 1985 Fox Inc. was formed with three main operating divisions, 20th Century–Fox Film Corporation, Fox Television Stations Inc. and Fox Broadcasting Co. The film producing unit's name was shortened to Fox Film Corporation. Murdoch is currently trying to establish his television station holdings into America's recognized fourth network (joining CBS, NBC and ABC). MCA Inc. (owner of Universal) was purchased in 1990 by the Matsushita Electrical Industrial Company of Japan. That move meant that two of the seven majors were owned by Japanese companies (also one by Australians, one by the French). It made sense from a capitalist perspective of rationalization as both Japanese companies were heavily involved in producing TV hardware, receiving sets and VCRs. All the majors were moving increasingly into control of the television and video markets in all the areas of producing/distributing/exhibiting. However, something went wrong in this case, resulting in Matsushita selling 80 percent of its MCA stake in 1995 to the Canadian conglomerate Seagram Co., best known as a producer of alcoholic beverages and Tropicana orange juice. Generally, insiders felt the purchase was the result of Seagram president Edgar Bronfman, Jr. (who had inherited his position and power from his father), being overly star-struck. He was a known long-time Hollywood groupie with his earlier hostile takeover bid for Time Warner having been blocked by that firm. Seagram had no holdings in the media/entertainment area. Sony was said to be less than satisfied with the performance of Columbia, causing a major change in executives in 1995. Nonetheless Sony announced it was still committed to be a fully integrated electronics and entertainment company, "powerfully positioned for the future." Sony retiring president Norio Ohga pointed to such outlets as the company satellite service which still had "many, many empty channels that can be filled with programs."[2]

Cartel members expanded in all directions. One of the most startling statistics was that theatrical attendance was responsible for 80 percent of the domestic receipts of a feature film in 1980—the rest came principally from television. By 1993 it was only 25 percent with television and home video accounting for the other 75 percent. It was not that film revenue was falling but that television income was increasing faster and home video surged out of nowhere. Similar changes were occurring all over the world. Film attendance was static or decreasing in many parts of the world although revenues held steady or increased as admission prices rose at a faster rate than attendance levels fell. Within the U.S. the total number of commercial TV stations (VHF and UHF) totaled 515 in 1960, 734 in 1980 and 1,093 in 1990, plus cable stations. Despite the decline of theatrical income as a percentage of a film's total income, that theater release became even more crucial as the more successful a film was in theatrical release the more the producer could charge for it in television sales and the more money it generated in video sales. In 1979 there were around 700 video retail outlets and in 1990 there were 60,000; half were specialty stores while the other half carried videos as an extra product line. A blockbuster film which grossed over $100 million theatrically sold more than nine copies per video retailer while movies which took in less than $5 million at cinemas sold less than two copies per retailer. For 1989 the top seven home video suppliers were the seven majors who controlled 65.2 percent of the market and some $2.2 million in domestic revenues. Warner had a 14.3 percent share, Buena Vista (Disney) 13.1 percent, Paramount 9.2 percent, CBS/Fox 8.1 percent, MCA 6.7 percent, MGM/UA 6.7 percent and RCA/Columbia 6.4 percent. By 1994 the majors had tightened their grip on the domestic home video market, holding down 82.7 percent of the market: Buena Vista 19.3 percent, Columbia/Tristar 17.3 percent, Warner 14.5 percent, MCA/Universal 10.6 percent, Paramount 8.8 percent, Fox 8.6 percent and MGM/UA 3.6 percent. (Those two sets of figures are not strictly comparable as the second set surveyed only titles with initial sales of 50,000 copies or more.) Similar changes happened overseas as the number of TV stations expanded rapidly (often as governments turned more of the system over to private capital), satellite and pay TV services appeared and home video arrived. During the first 11 months of 1994, U.S. producers had revenues of $4 billion from domestic home video—and $3 billion in foreign home video income for the same period. Foreign theatrical rentals for the majors for all of 1994 totaled $2 billion. Some studios claimed they could estimate with a fine degree of accuracy the video sales of a given title. For example, if a film grossed $100 million worldwide in theatrical rentals it was predicted the video should yield $32 to $40 million. For a theatrical release that generated business of $20 to $40 million, video returns were expected to yield $12 to $15 million. However, it was generally agreed nobody knew whether a film would be a huge hit or a bomb; no one could predict accurately with the box office being mostly a crapshoot.[3]

Domestically Warner bought Liberty, New York–based Cablevision Industries with 1.3 million subscribers in 1995. It was the second large cable acquisition by Time Warner in two weeks, giving it a total of 11.5 million domestic subscribers in America and moved it from second largest cable operator in the U.S. to a tie with industry leader Tele-Communications Inc. Cablevision Industries (which had been the seventh largest operator) claimed it was too small to compete.[4]

Overseas in 1994 the MPEA urged all satellite-carried Malaysian and Indonesian channels to encrypt and thus protect copyright. Both countries were then doing so, coinciding with the launch of five pay TV channels, CNN International, HBO Asia, ESPN, the Discovery Channel and Turner's combined TNT/Cartoon Network. Perhaps encouraging the Indonesians to comply was the fact that each station was partnered with a division of the Bimantra Citra conglomerate—owned by one of the sons of Indonesia's President Suharto.[5]

Australia launched its first-ever satellite pay TV service in 1995. Two rival companies competed for customers. One consortium called Foxtel was headed by Rupert Murdoch's News Corporation. Among its partners were Fox, Paramount, Universal and Sony. Rival Optus Vision's partners included Warner, Disney and MGM/UA.[6]

In America Murdoch was attempting to buy TV stations in enough big markets to become a real fourth network and charge the high advertising rates that the Big Three did due to their huge audience base. Murdoch spent a great deal of money to buy the rights to televise NFL professional games, outbidding CBS, but couldn't charge enough in ad rates because he didn't have enough stations in his Fox network in major markets. He was losing money broadcasting football. Of course, there was no way of creating new stations as all VHF frequencies (the most lucrative ones, channels 2–13) had long been allocated. Fox had to buy existing stations. Many public broadcasting stations were located on the VHF band—allocated before the UHF band was in general use. A major critic of PBS was Republican House Speaker Newt Gingrich, along with other Republicans. If Congress cut public broadcasting funds, forcing those stations off the air, the government could reissue those licenses. Not long after Gingrich was offered a controversial book deal with Harper-Collins which was to pay him a $4.5 million advance, Murdoch asked for and got closed door meetings with top Republicans, including Gingrich. While no official report of those meetings was released, rumor had it that turning public broadcasting channels over to private broadcasters was a topic of discussion. HarperCollins was owned by Murdoch's News Corporation. Because of the public controversy over the book deal, Gingrich backed away from it.[7]

Publicity and promotion remained a major method by which the majors maintained their domination. When *Superman II* arrived in Japan in 1981, it did so after newspapers and TV all over the country had promoted the film for months in a massive advertising campaign. A typical blockbuster then had $1.75 million spent on it in publicity in Japan. Whereas in the U.S. promotion ads began about one month before a film's release, in Japan the campaign began six months and even a year before the release date. Although most movies got separate ad campaigns in different lands, the majors tried to standardize and use one campaign in as many countries as possible. Fox executive John Simenon reported that in Europe a uniform campaign was run for *Alien*, explaining, "we spread the word of *Alien*'s enormous success in America—slightly inflating that, in fact ... Now in that campaign there was total standardization. Only one country went with its own artwork. With other films, on the other hand, the strategy can vary enormously country by country." European campaigns in the early 1980s were geared more to posters while U.S. promotion relied heavily on television. The difference was because in Europe, TV ads for films were much more expensive, and not even legal in France.[8]

France, Italy, Germany and Spain were the only countries that received most of their foreign films in a dubbed version; everybody else usually got a subtitled release. Around 1992 the cost of dubbing an average movie was $32,000 in Spain, $42,000 in France, $48,000 in Germany and $55,000 in Italy. On the other hand, the costs of generating a subtitled version ranged from $2,000 to $6,000 per film. Some changes were necessary when movies were shipped abroad. Polish jokes, which meant nothing in France, were turned into Belgian jokes—which did mean something. Even though the majors bragged they turned out an international product, films that were uniquely American were exported anyway. A film that depended heavily on word play like *My Cousin Vinny* died in Europe while something like *Wayne's World* with its impossible-to-translate phrases such as "I think I'm about to hurl" was also shipped abroad. That films such as those did any business at all was testament not to foreigners' love of U.S. product or its "quality" but the majors' control of distribution/exhibition along with a huge advertising blitz plus free plugs under the guise of "news/information" on such outlets as CNN, etc., then available everywhere.[9]

One observer noted that in the late 1980s he found Rambo posters all over Asia, even in rural parts, publicizing *First Blood*. Disney release *Cocktail* was an example of a movie that "had everything you want for a film to do well overseas. It was a very glossy picture, with a popular star, a good soundtrack, and it was filmed in exotic locations." Note the absence of concepts such as plot, character, story line, etc. Of course, by then movies were not produced, they were packaged. *Police Academy 4* grossed $13 million domestic but over $26 million foreign while *Animal House* made $70 million in the U.S., but only $9 million overseas. More and more the majors tried to use American marketing tactics abroad. Before Universal released *The Secret of My Success* abroad it held foreign screenings to get audience reaction—long a common practice in the U.S.[10]

Typically a major film opened in foreign countries months after its U.S. release. In the 1990s that time span regularly shortened to a few weeks. One reason was to get the jump on pirates who got hold of a copy in America, made duplicates and had it in foreign video markets before its theatrical release. A second reason was to take advantage of a more homogenized ad campaign along with, as journalist Richard Gold reported, TV "information" programs picked up on cable and from satellites around the world. Foreign audiences were plugged into what was hot on American marquees. With the explosion of European TV services such as CNN International and MTV Europe, the American boom in entertainment information media had spread abroad, closing the gap between domestic and foreign marketing. Said Fox executive Joel Coler, "Now when an American film makes a lot of money it becomes a selling tool in other parts of the world." While TV ads were expensive in Japan, all five of the networks offered programs that spotlighted films plus viewers had access to CNN's *Showbiz Today* series. All of this exposure was free to the cartel but amounted to advertisements. When Buena Vista flogged *Dick Tracy* overseas it used the American trailers. Company executive Kevin Hyson acknowledged European audiences were not likely familiar with the source cartoon character but said, "We don't believe that's a concern for us in the marketing of the picture." MCA/Universal film division chairman Tom Pollock predicted in 1990 that big companies would ultimately drive out the small ones as screens proliferated, new and unregulated private TV burgeoned and marketing costs soared. When Columbia released *Kramer vs. Kramer* overseas in 1982 it spent $2.5 million on advertising with that film becoming the studio's biggest foreign grosser to that time. Not quite 10 years later, when Columbia spent $9 million abroad for ads for *Look Who's Talking*, it became the studio's second highest foreign grosser. More media spaces was obtained with the $2.5 million.[11]

One advantage in having foreign release lag domestic release by several months was that it allowed an ad campaign to be altered if it failed in America. An example was *Last Action Hero* which bombed in the U.S. For overseas the ad campaign focused on making star Arnold Schwarzenegger look tougher. Blatant Americanisms were sometimes removed from ads. *Addams Family Values* stressed a play in the domestic ad campaign on "family values." However, it was not used overseas because that term, said a studio spokesman, did not have "the same conservative connotation outside the U.S." Columbia vice-president Duncan Clark said there was a fundamental difference in the approach and philosophy of ad campaigns in the U.S. and abroad; "In the U.S. TV drives nearly every film. We don't have the luxury of using TV in some markets, either because the law forbids it or it's uneconomic." Posters were used extensively overseas, with radio heavily relied on in Germany and the U.K.; both were little used domestically.[12]

As to marketing a film in the U.S., Columbia overseas distribution chief

J. Edward Shugrue noted, "In the U.S. it's simple. You line up 1,600 theaters, buy several million dollars' worth of national TV, plus a bunch of cooperative newspaper advertising—you press a button, and boom, you're out there." Shugrue admitted it was harder overseas but United Cinemas executive Millard Ochs was more optimistic as he looked "forward to the day when pictures will roll out in perfect sync around the world on 3,500 screens."[13]

The peak of Hollywood publicity and hype was reached in 1993 with the MCA/Universal release of Steven Spielberg's *Jurassic Park*. No film had ever had so much money spent on it or so many commercial tie-ins. With Kenner Products as its worldwide toy licensee, McDonald's as its lead promotional partner and a roster of hundreds of licensees and marketing partners in locales as diverse as Norway and New Zealand, the film went on to become the highest grosser in history, no longer just a movie, enthused *Advertising Age*, but a "global brand." Its box office take (domestic and foreign) was well over $900 million within a year or so of release, over $500 million of that earned overseas. It was no accident, said reporter Marcy Magiera, but "the culmination of a carefully crafted marketing and merchandising plan set in motion in late 1991 for the movie." *Park* opened in almost all English-speaking nations within a month of its U.S. release date. Kenner signed on as worldwide toy licensee in 1992, followed by McDonald's signing a promotional deal for the U.S. and a handful of other countries. Sega of America and Nintendo software marketer Ocean of America also signed on early, giving *Park* what MCA/Universal marketing executive Elizabeth Gelfand called the three must-have categories for film promotion: "toys, fast-food and video games." Other partners included Kmart Corporation in Canada, Weetabix in France, Pepsi in Scandinavia, Coca-Cola in Latin America and Nisson Foods in Japan. Of course, MCA's then-owner Matsushita promoted the movie in its 24,000 Panasonic consumer electronic stores in Japan. During 1992 MCA invited 40 to 50 key promotional partners to a licensing strategy meeting wherein everybody exchanged ideas. "McDonald's got up there and shared with the lunch box guy and the pajama guy their vision for what *Jurassic Park* was going to be," recalled Gelfand. That winning spirit caused the group to call itself the "Dinosaur Dream Team." Spielberg and the film's cast all appeared at the American International Toy Fair in New York to insure retailers would devote shelf space to a bewildering array of *Park* licensed products. Key to unifying products, promotions and the film became the yellow, red and black *Park* dinosaur skeleton logo which appeared on every licensed product or promotional item to be marketed, regardless of language. Ultimately 500 licensees flogged over 5000 products with sales of licensed merchandise passing $1 billion nine months after the film's release. *Park* had an advertising budget estimated at $15 to $20 million while an additional sum estimated at $60 million was spent in ads by the various film partners—McDonald's spent an estimated $25 million of the total in media support for its promotions. When MCA released *The Flintstones* in 1994, McDonald's had a cross-promotional tie in 38 nations. *Park* was credited with breaking down the geographic boundaries to entertainment promotions.[14]

Cinema ownership abroad was intensified with the cartel reaching levels never attained in the past. In America theaters were all huge venues from the 1920s onward with even fairly small cities having one or more 2,000-seaters. A small theater in that era held maybe 800 to 1000 people. It was a way of control by the cartel as it froze out potential competitors who didn't have the money to build a palace. Audiences got used to the huge, plush venues, which became an integral part of a night at the movies. By the 1950s and 1960s they were all dinosaurs, in light of the huge audience decline. They were erased to be replaced by the multiplex of several auditoriums with the largest one perhaps having 400 seats, the smallest maybe 150 to 200. If any potential independent exhibitor thought he might then be able to enter the exhibition arena because he could afford a 200-seat venue, he soon learned otherwise. Those multiplexes were just like the palaces of the earlier era since each one had 2,000 seats or more—they just had more than one screen. As well those multiplexes were usually built in conjunction with a mall, away from the abandoned downtowns, the site of the old palaces. Similar changes occurred overseas, only some years later. While multiplexes began domestically at the end of the 1970s, they did not arrive in Europe in a serious way until 1990 or thereabouts. The majors also had been convinced from their earliest days that the entire world—outside America—did not have nearly enough cinemas. They set out to remedy the situation. Additionally the majors got back into domestic cinema ownership in a big way.

Commenting on the situation was Universal's chairman Thomas P. Pollock, who said in early 1990, "We all see Europe as a major growth area in film and television. The privatization of television means new outlets that will have to be fed. The multiplexing of Europe will enable us to release twice as many movies. In partnership with Paramount and United Artists Theatres, we own or are building more than 300 screens in the United Kingdom. We hope we can do the same in Germany, Spain and other countries." Warner then owned about 100 houses in the U.K. and several multiplexes in Germany and Denmark. Sky Channel had five 24-hour-a-day, satellite-delivered pay-TV channels that needed programs. Rupert Murdoch owned Sky Channel.[15]

Germany's Ruhr Valley got its first new theaters in decades when two multiplexes opened in 1991, one built by Warner, the other by United Cinemas International (UCI)—a joint venture of Paramount and Universal. Both Warner and United were planning multiplexes in Spain and Italy in the near future while United also had its eye on sites in Moscow where poor TV programming and crowded living conditions had kept the cinema a favorite escape. Muscovites attended the movies twice as often as Americans but paid less than one-tenth as much for a ticket. Yankees attended 4.5 times per capita, per year, twice as often as Europeans. All of these new European moviehouses were air-conditioned with U.S.–style concession stands. Many houses in Europe had little or nothing in the way of concessions—even in 1991, 40 percent of Italian venues had no air-conditioning. Of these new venues, *Forbes* writer John Marcom, Jr., remarked, "The underlying implication: These new theaters can only be good for U.S.–made movies, which already command anywhere between 50 percent and 80 percent of the money spent at the box office in many countries.... The U.S. movie business dominates the world entertainment scene.... These days, Hollywood dreams of Hollyworld."[16]

Warner joined with Japanese supermarket chain Nichii Co. to build in Japan up to as many as 30 multiplexes with six to twelve screens each, mostly in Nichii shopping centers. The first two opened in 1993; one had 1,970 seats with seven screens, the other had eight screens with 2,073 total seats. Japan had one film screen for every 65,000 people while in the U.S. it was one screen for every 11,000 people. With one of the highest ticket prices in the world—$12.50 U.S. and rising due to the decline of the dollar against the yen—Japan was a particularly inviting market. Japanese ticket sales fell from 164 million in 1980 to 125 million in 1992 with the number of theaters dropping from 2,364 to 1,744 over the same period. Local exhibitors and distributors were reluctant to construct new venues because of the cost. Said Shochiku's Takeo Hisamatsu, "Our biggest problem is the high cost of foreign films. If foreign distributors could reduce the prices they charge us we could afford to open new cinemas." It was easier still when locals put up the money but let Hollywood control the venue. A consortium announced in 1994 that it had raised $60 million to build a chain of 60 screens throughout China. United Cinemas International owned just 5 percent; however, UCI was to manage the cinemas. Underlying the drive to build cinemas was that while foreign income was close to domestic income, the U.S. had only 5 percent or so of the world's population. A lot of that contrast shrank when the number of domestic screens was compared with the number overseas. One unnamed studio executive remarked, "Let's face facts. The U.S. market is pretty much operating at capacity, while overseas continues to evolve like a sprawling adventure saga. It's exciting and challenging and, best of all, rewarding."[17]

Warner (with local partners) was building multiplexes in the Netherlands in 1995 while United Artists (with local partners) had an agreement to build multiplexes in India. The rise of the multiplex was blamed in Hong Kong for a decline in attendance (from 44.8 million tickets sold in 1989 down to 29.1 million sold in 1994). Ticket prices had doubled over that time and were most expensive at the multiplexes. Warner opened its first Spanish multiplex in 1995. At that time MGM's venue-holding in the U.K. made it the largest exhibitor there with 20 percent of all U.K. screens. They were very profitable. When those MGM venues were put up for sale it was reported they made profits of $30 million on sales of $180 million. European producers were wary of the trend, seeing it as skewing the market even more towards big-budget U.S. blockbusters.[18]

Domestically the Cineplex Odeon cinema chain (MCA was the controlling shareholder) announced it would merge with the sixth largest movie chain in the U.S., Dallas-based Cinemark USA. That merger would give the new entity 2,839 screens in North America, 600 more screens than the then-largest domestic chain, owned by United Artists. However, a couple months later Cinemark walked away from the deal without reporting a reason. Rumor had it that Cinemark felt it would be overwhelmed by Seagram because since the deal was first announced Seagram announced its takeover of MCA. Seagram's Edgar Bronfman already had a piece of Toronto-based Cineplex through the Charles R. Bronfman Trust—a piece to be enlarged by the latter merger.[19]

Cineplex Odeon announced in June 1995 that it planned to build bigger cinemas with cushier seats, fancier foods and video games in the lobby. First venue in the ambitious plan was to be a 16-screen 5000-seat complex to open in 1998 in Universal City, Florida, next to Universal Studio's theme park. While other giant multiplexes were planned for North America, company president Allan Karp admitted that "long-term growth lies outside North America." Cineplex even coined a new term for its proposed giant venues— megaplexes.[20]

UA prepared for a major cinema expansion by obtaining a large bank loan in 1995. Then holding 2,300 screens domestically, it was America's largest cinema chain. *Variety* called it "an aggressive expansion program which parallels similar efforts being made domestically and internationally by other major U.S. exhibitors."[21]

Distribution networks became even more intertwined. Paramount, Universal and MGM's combined offshore distribution entity CIC continued under a new name, United International Pictures (UIP). In France, Buena Vista International signed a joint distribution deal in 1992 with France's Gaumont. Three years later Fox signed a similar deal for distribution and co-production with French major UGC. All Fox product would be distributed in France while "selected" UGC films would be distributed worldwide. Iceland's Sam Film was a local distributor company with a 50 percent share of the market. Sam distributed Disney, Fox and Warner, among others. Heavily criticized for handling so much American product, Sam president Arni Samuelsson replied, "American films are the most popular, so we've tended to show them the most." Icelandic Film Fund spokeswoman Anna Maria Karlsdottir declared the equation was not that simple. "It's not just a question of box office. Hollywood films get far more coverage from the local press than local Icelandic or even European product." Of the 203 films released in Iceland in 1993, 164 were U.S. product.[22]

In mid–1995 Hollywood's majors were reported to be increasingly aggressive about cherry-picking the best independent films for release in the most lucrative foreign territories. What they offered was a worldwide distribution network but also the reality that a pick-up would never get the same attention as a major's own production. Independent distributors had a smaller range (necessitating using several to cover large areas of the globe) but offered more attention to a title along with having a better knowledge of local markets. Also unappreciated by independent producers was the majors' penchant for cross-collateralizing their multi-territory acquisitions—that is, profits in one country were written off against a loss in another, reducing the producer's chance of receiving a profit. An even bigger worry was that this trend was another move by the majors to squeeze out independent film distributors, attaining even greater control for themselves.[23]

Block booking remained an important tool of control for the majors. German exhibitors alleged in the early 1980s that U.S. distributors charged them excessively high rentals for hit movies, demanded rental money far in advance and imposed block booking. UIP was granted an antitrust waiver in 1989 by the European Community (E.C.) allowing the three studios to distribute films in Europe through their single organization. When the E.C. was considering whether UIP should or should not receive an extension to that waiver (it did), European Commissioner Joao do Deus Pinheiro charged the company impeded competition by, for example, forcing houses to block book lesser movies in order to exhibit Universal's *Jurassic Park*. Miramax International imposed block booking on the local distributors it dealt with, closing two such deals in 1995, one for 10 films with Italy's Cecchi Godi and one for five films with Japan's Shochiku. Using newspeak, *Variety* commented, "Such bulk acquisitions are unusual in Japan" while also noting that "such multifilm deals make it harder to cherry-pick from the company's varied production slate."[24]

Poaching of talent continued. UA vice-president William Stewart said in 1981, "American cinema is still the major factor in all world markets. It's the same with foreign directors—they come over here. We must be doing something right." The *Times* of London published a lament for eight U.K. directors who had gone to Hollywood to make films due to the moribund state of the British industry. It was a continuation of a trend stretching back decades, from Alfred Hitchcock in the 1930s to John Schlesinger and Peter Yates in the 1960s to the group who left in the 1980s, which included Michael Apted, Stephen Frears, Roland Joffe, Alan Parker and Ridley Scott. "Yet the machine is inescapable, just like American culture in general. After all, most British directors, past and present, picked up their enthusiasm for popular filmmaking from rip-roaring, escapist Hollywood," concluded the paper. Todd Gitlin saw that the importing of foreigners to make films did not represent Hollywood's openness to foreign styles but "the capacity to buy film workers into submission."[25]

By driving the cost of a film higher and higher, Hollywood made it impossible for anyone to compete on that level. Toward the end of the 1980s the negative cost for an average film from one of the majors stood at around $20 million. Added to that were $10 million or so for advertising and distribution costs. The subsidy paid by the average ticket buyer was from the rest of the world to the U.S., allowing those big-budget movies and keeping ticket prices relatively cheap domestically. In 1981 the average ticket price in Brazil was $1.00 U.S. which represented 1 percent of the average monthly wage; in the U.S. it was 0.4 percent of the average monthly wage. During 1994 MPAA members produced 115 films with an average negative cost of $34.3 million plus $16.1 million for advertising, distribution and print costs—a total of $50.4 million per movie.[26]

Kenyan writer Ngugi wa Thiong'o explained what it was like in 1981 for a person in Kenya who went to a film: "He will be sitting in cinemas owned by foreigners (20th Century–Fox, for instance) to see American offerings on the screen. These offerings range from the moderately good like *Coming Home* which was slightly critical of American imperialist adventurism in Indo-China, to the mass-produced, mindless trash like *The Omen* and *Magic* where change, the possibilities of change, are seen in doomsday and the end of human civilization. The message is clear: Any change from the American-dominated present is the end of civilization. Agents of change are devils. The heroes (all American, of course) are those fighting against the villains from Hades or outer space who threaten the present world stability guaranteed by American dollars and guns."[27]

Equally annoyed, but more resigned and cynical about U.S. domination was a writer in *The Australian Weekend Magazine*, June 22, 1985, edition. At issue at the time was whether to allow U.S. nuclear naval units into Australia; "What's the point of saying no to America's nuclear ships when we've said yes, a thousand times yes, to the Trojan horse of American culture, dragging it throughout city gates into our very loungerooms. MGM is mightier than the CIA. Paramount more powerful than the Pentagon. Warner Bros. wields more influence than the White House.... For it has changed the way we see the world.... Day by day, hour by hour, word by word, as idiom yields to idiom, our very identity is being modified and molded.... We are, all of us, little by little, becoming ventriloquial dolls for another society. We are losing our authenticity, our originality, and becoming echoes."[28]

Despite the monopoly control exercised by U.S. product over the world's screens, or perhaps because of it, many observers continued to hype the official party line. *U.S. News & World Report* recruited University of Southern California professor Art Murphy, who said the domination continued because they concentrated on good stories and action: "Escapist and adventure pictures are the most popular in America. They are the most popular in foreign countries, too. American filmmakers always have one eye on the world market." In an internal memo Disney studio chief Jeffrey Katzenberg claimed the clear formula for global success was "a good story, well executed." That was what counted, "not stars, not special effects, not casts of thousands, not megabudgets, not hype." During the 1989–1990 season, American movies took 71 percent of the Italian box office, home product captured about 25 percent—one of the smallest shares of the domestic market by Italian films since the end of World War II. Fox official in Italy Sandro Pierotti said, "The fact is, Italians haven't made pictures up to American standards of entertainment for a long time." Agreeing was UIP Italian chief Mario Pesucci, who added, "The success of American product here ... derives from the public's decreased interest in Italian films." Record and film producer David Geffen remarked, without irony, "No other country can match U.S. stars. No one can recreate a Michael Jackson or a Sylvester Stallone." This is true. But who would want to? Closer to the mark was *New York Times* reporter Geraldine Fabrikant who observed that the growing market for U.S. movies abroad "is encouraging American studios to pay close attention to foreign moviegoers," but then turned around to add, "Still, the truth is that American studios usually think first and last about the United States markets." Schwarzenegger and Stallone vehicles translated well abroad as they rarely depended on subtleties—"a grunt is a grunt."[29]

Within the MPAA, the cartel philosophy remained unchanged, chanting the mantras of free trade and global understanding to be achieved through the dissemination of Hollywood product. Jack Valenti remained cartel head with a contract extending through the end of 1996. Barring his sudden departure, that would take the MPAA to the eve of its 75th anniversary, with just three leaders in all that time. In a newspaper article under his own byline, Valenti pointed out the U.S. film and television industry returned over $1 billion annually in surplus balance of payments to America. Hollywood product was universally popular "because we create a special magic that citizens in other lands find bewitching. The stories that we tell on film or tape are sought after because we tell stories better than most." Praising free trade while railing against restrictions and piracy, Valenti concluded, "If we demonstrate, without hesitation, that our country will insist on fair trading principles, 'competitive marketplace' will become more than a phrase; it will be a reality." Additionally he noted, without elaboration, that U.S. film and television production costs were the highest in the world. Probably it was noted as a boast, certainly not to suggest that those high costs played a role in the domination, a role greater than that of storytelling ability.[30]

Canada's small, private TV network Can-West Global announced in 1995 that its 1995–1996 schedule would feature more American comedies, dramas, TV movies, etc., because they were "less expensive" than Canadian product. Expensive product whose cost was amortized at home could be offered in foreign lands at cheaper prices than local product. As a result, profits increased, allowing for the greater control money bought. Those foreign profits allowed Hollywood to continue producing and hyping high cost product.[31]

Soon thereafter Valenti reiterated his commitment to free trade in the industry and to helping create stronger local film industries abroad. "This cannot be achieved with government intervention," he warned.[32]

Columbia chairman David Puttnam announced in November 1986 that South African exhibitors had been put on notice that Columbia would not book any more films into theaters remaining segregated after May 1, 1987. There was then much agitation in America for U.S. firms in general to disinvest there. Puttnam declared his stand was similar to that of other MPAA-member companies. No one was more surprised by that idea than Valenti, who quickly announced he had no knowledge of any studio making such a move—it was not a policy of the MPAA/MPEA. He went on to defend the MPAA's ongoing, although never formally announced, policy of placing no restrictions on the showing of U.S. movies and TV product in South Africa. Unlike other areas of investment such as auto or construction steel manufacture, the exhibiting of Hollywood product advanced the cause of apartheid opposition because it exposed the population to the example of a multiracial society. "If we withdraw them the only people who would be hurt would be the black majority. The affluent (white) South Africans have VCRs, and pirates would move in quickly and they would have all their movies to see, but the blacks would be denied," explained Valenti.[33]

During a 1989 round-table discussion with five MPEA vice-presidents, Gerald Adler said his group had to live with quotas "until they become so onerous and discriminatory that we simply have to confer with that country's government, as well as enlist our own, to remedy unacceptable situations ... It isn't the proliferation of American films that knocks out the foreign-produced movies. It's the fact that the foreign-produced films haven't come up in enough force, strength and acceptability to be a significant factor in the local markets." Adler took pains to stress that the cartel deplored the falling off of local production. Norman Alterman added that "local citizens call the shots on what films they want or don't want." He did admit there were difficulties in obtaining money to make movies in foreign lands.[34]

As the 1990s began, Hollywood was not particularly worried about any future quotas from the E.C. as it believed Europe would not be able to supply the programming required to meet the explosion in television-cable-satellite outlets. The hardware was outrunning the software. In any event, as the cartel admitted, quotas had historically been ignored as often as they were honored, for various reasons such as a lack of product. "As the decade ended, the major companies dominated the foreign market as never before.... American films are the overwhelming force in the world market and there is no sign of them being challenged."[35]

As always the cartel was at the front of the line, feeding voraciously at the public trough. When Congress was debating in 1980 whether or not to preserve the Webb-Pomerene (WP) law, Valenti defended the act in a U.S. Chamber of Commerce–sponsored speech before a convention of export trading companies by saying, "Without the embrace of Webb-Pomerene the U.S. film and television industry would have been seriously, perhaps fatally, crippled in its efforts to win the admiration and the patronage of foreign audiences.... Without Webb-Pomerene the American film industry would be an invalid.... Without this congressional authority we would stand no chance at all to survive." Valenti explained his industry daily faced a panoply of obstructions designed to shrink the U.S. share of the world film and television market; "The American film industry is peculiarly vulnerable to unfavorable action by foreign governments and by combinations of foreign private interests, by industry cartels, and by an avalanche of non-tariff trade barriers that are both endless and ingenious." Any idea that a nation could develop a flourishing native film industry by containing American movies was false, declared the cartel head. Because of those restrictions and rampant anti–Americanism, without the canopy of Webb-Pomerene "we would be powerless to counter these restrictions ... Moreover, in the vast majority of foreign nations with which we deal, film and television material is viewed as a major cultural element, burdening us still further with a national zeal for protectionism." Regarding the tendency in some (mainly third-world) nations for the government to attempt to organize state-run film distribution, "Only by a resolute stand on our part have we been able to beat back the spread of this trend, by refusing to deal with such a monopoly." According to Valenti, the MPEA then provided around 47 percent of all the export trade earnings reported by the 36 WP associations then in existence. As to why the U.S. dominated the world film and TV market, Valenti said there were two reasons, "the creative and seemingly unduplicatable genius of American filmmakers and television producers" and "the worldwide organization of the Motion Picture Export Association whose mission it is to preserve the freedom of the American film industry to compete fairly in the world entertainment marketplace." Summing up, he asked the Chamber of Commerce to help lobby against opponents of WP who "nourish the persistent belief that what we are doing abroad to enlarge American markets has some evil effects on the domestic market." Valenti pleaded: "Enforce the antitrust laws but don't harass American export marketers." WP remained in place.[36]

Led by CBS chairman Thomas Wyman, a group of film and TV executives submitted a report to the U.S. Trade Representative. Chief among the problems detailed in their report was copyright infringement—piracy. Second among the problems was the "failure of the U.S. government to voice effectively its objections to trade barriers that are imposed by foreign governments under the guise of political or cultural concerns."[37]

Addressing the Council of Foreign Relations in 1985, Valenti again attacked foreign nations for placing restrictions on American movies, calling them unfair trade practices and "a matter of survival for the U.S. film industry." To him it was a one-way street because countries erected barriers believing they can "with impunity, choke off the entry of films and TV material while they enjoy with profit and freedom the ample market of the U.S.A." Complaining about the crises of the moment imperiling the industry, Valenti demanded more government action to obtain "market access to foreign countries on a scale equal to the hospitality which their goods and their businessmen find in our country."[38]

A year later Valenti was somewhat pacified, explaining without specific details that appropriate agencies of the U.S. government were acting as intervenors in stepping up efforts to knock down barriers to films. "We're doing various things in the political arena with our government," he declared. As well, the MPEA held meetings with "various" foreign ministers to ease restrictions.[39]

With listening posts in 60 nations, the MPAA then had 300 employees overseas; "We operate a small State Department," enthused Valenti. Those people monitored legislation and barriers, alerting headquarters in Washington "where campaigns are mounted to get the barriers lifted, usually with the support of the real State Department and the Office of the United States Trade Representative." Over the two decades Valenti had then headed the cartel, he said more and more of his time was devoted to "foreign policy." By his own count he had personally led 80 negotiations with foreign governments. "The most ingenious people in the world," he exclaimed, "are those who sit in those foreign chanceries and figure out ways to inflict curbs on the American motion picture industry." Particularly annoying the cartel at the moment were India, Indonesia, Spain, Korea and Canada where "barriers stand guard against us.... These countries are mostly our allies and friends, but who, under the banner of 'cultural sovereignty' resolutely erect unscalable trade walls." At no time was Canada unscalable. Then, as always, Hollywood had 80 to 90 percent of screen time. Canadian Embassy spokesperson Pamela Chappell complained that Hollywood "wants the whole pie." Despite all the barriers, Valenti admitted U.S. movies were screened in over 100 nations. They were, he said, "America's secret weapon—the supreme visual force in the world, dominating screens in theaters and in living rooms.... "People like what we create better than what others create." With the U.S. trade deficit then around $150 billion annually, Valenti was quick to point out the motion picture industry brought in a surplus of $1 billion yearly, with 40 percent of its revenue coming from overseas.[40]

As early as 1990 Valenti urged the U.S. government to stand firm in opposing any proposed exclusion of audiovisual industries from the Uruguay round of the GATT talks then underway in Geneva. Bowing to E.C. demands to exclude film, TV and home video programs from the final GATT accord would give America's trading partners "the power to pull the trigger to kill fair trade." Such an exclusion, predicted the cartel head, would lead to the collapse of the U.S. film/entertainment industry, a "unique American asset."

Europe was after such an exclusionary GATT accord to achieve the E.C.'s "baronial objective" which was to "manacle" U.S. product from entry into world markets, hiding their intent "under the guise" of protecting national culture. Valenti then praised U.S. Trade Representative and chief GATT negotiator Carla Hills, commending her work in allowing Hollywood product to move "freely and unhobbled around the world." It would be three more years before the GATT talks came to a head over the audiovisual issue.[41]

House Speaker Newt Gingrich (R–Georgia) reportedly won over a group of Hollywood executives during a 90-minute closed-door meeting in 1995 between himself, other politicians and executives from all MPAA companies. He pledged to tear down international trade barriers on Hollywood's behalf, declaring the industry had "not been adequately represented by the U.S. government in negotiations." Valenti stated Gingrich's comments drew a "cheerful response. It was exactly what they wanted to hear." According to Valenti, the Speaker was "prepared to use the weight of the House of Representatives to open up markets rather than close them." He warned that Congress "could easily pass" retaliatory trade legislation against nations not open to Hollywood.[42]

Markets in the Far East remained less than satisfactory for the cartel. Complaining about access there in general, MPEA Far East vice-president A. Stephen Clug grumbled there are "certainly markets that should yield a lot more [to American companies] than they do now. We're not asking for any privileges. We're asking for the right to compete fairly in the same countries that are afforded that same welcome in the U.S." Piracy was rampant in many of these areas. The major disadvantage of the video cassette revolution was that pirates could sell directly to consumers. (Films had been pirated to some extent since the beginning of the industry; however, the pirate needed a theater or venue of some sort to screen his illicit copy.) One bright spot in the region was Australasia wherein the cartel had 70 percent of New Zealand's film business with U.S. independents taking another 20 percent. Seventy percent of Australia's box office went to cartel members. As a journalist commented, "U.S. pics dominate the Aussie box office.... [With] a moviegoing audience brought up on U.S. fare, that's not about to change."[43]

Principal trouble spot for the majors in the Far East was South Korea where the majors managed to send in just 14 films in 1984 compared to 70 in Japan, 80 in Singapore, 80 in Malaysia and 65 in Taiwan. A screen quota in Korea required all cinemas to screen at least 40 percent local product; the same quota held for movies and for programming on TV. Korean law also prohibited American film companies from establishing offices in Korea. What little product the majors placed in Korea had to go through local, Korean-owned distribution firms. Said Clug, "We want the right to open our own offices there, we want an elimination on the ceiling on film royalties." When negotiations failed, the MPEA filed an unfair trade complaint with the Office of the

U.S. Trade Representative urging the federal government to take action against South Korea to counter its policies limiting the distribution of U.S. films. That complaint charged the Korean barriers caused "serious injury" to the U.S. movie, TV and home video industries. "We are free traders," said Valenti. "But we do insist that the golden rule be followed. That is, we want to be treated in Korea with the same hospitality and freedom that Korean businessmen have in this country. We ask no more. We ask no less." Valenti warned that Hollywood was prepared to take similar action against other nations which took similar action. Back in 1971 Korea imported 52 U.S. movies.[44]

After negotiations with the Korean Ambassador in Washington, that trade complaint was dropped. Time passed with more discussion taking place. From those talks came a 1987 pact with Korea allowing the majors to open offices in Korea and distribute directly. Hollywood looked forward eagerly to Korea becoming their second largest Asian market (after Japan), expecting to extract anywhere from $25 to $40 million annually. However, this was another example of an "agreement" which was signed by the one side only under pressure of some type because the Koreans immediately, and successfully for a time, turned around and jammed the deal. The government's censoring agency, the Korean Performance Ethics Committee, ruled it would not allow any company to have more than one film on its censorship list at one time. Since approval of a film took two to three months, a quota of four to six imports per year per company had in effect been imposed. Actually it was even harder on the majors than it first appeared since there, as in many nations, UIP (handling the three majors) functioned as a single entity. Effectively UIP was limited to four to six imports in total for all three of its component producers. Fox was the only other major who by then had established an office in Seoul.[45]

Stonewalled and angry, the MPEA filed another unfair trade complaint, in 1988, with the U.S. Trade Representative, charging Korea was not complying with the film pact. One of the complaints Korean distributors had, in the years leading up to the fight, according to film historian John Lent, was that "importers are saddled with package deals of U.S. distributors, which include mediocre titles of a flop status as conditions for obtaining desirable films"—block booking. As 1988 negotiations continued, and pressure was applied, UIP opened *Fatal Attraction* in September 1988 in Seoul, marking the debut of a U.S. producer as a direct distributor. That set off a violent response from Koreans which included threats, intimidation, vandalism in which screens were sprayed with paint plus the unleashing of snakes in theaters. Thirty houses in Seoul were closed for a day. Several dozen local filmmakers were arrested in Seoul when they stormed one cinema (of eight screening the release) harassing ticket buyers and spray painting the screen with slogans such as "Drive Out Yankee Movies." In November 1988 a settlement was reached, worked out by the Korean government and the U.S. Trade Representative; the Korean government agreed to make "good faith" to open their market. There would be no restrictions on the number of U.S. imports or the number of prints in circulation nor would there be any screen quotas for native product.[46]

When UIP opened *The Living Daylights* in Korea in February 1989, there were only minor demonstrations. By then the cartel was hoping to extract $80 million annually from the country. The MPEA was also complaining about discriminatory advertising rates charged the majors. Daily newspapers did not refuse to accept ads for *Daylights* but tried to charge UIP 50 percent more than the usual rates. (They later asked for a reduced rate, but it was still 30 percent more.) Refusing to pay, UIP limited its ad campaign to two papers, one owned by the Reverend Moon, the other "a leftist organ." Next to open was *Rain Man* which drew more protests with snakes left in theaters along with harassment of cinema owners. Promising to stay the course, UIP president Michael Williams-Jones pointed out the Korean public should realize it was getting access to movies like *Rain Man* much earlier than in the past under the old system. Helping out an harassed cinema owner, UIP itself filed a criminal complaint against one Il Mok Lee, alleged to have threatened to burn down a theater. "Business interference" was the charge. By the end of 1989, *Variety* reported enthusiastically that all film restrictions by then had been dropped. Disney executive Kevin Hyson noted that was remarkable as only a few years earlier Korea did only flat-rate deals. Under the old system Korean distributors, in exchange for importing one foreign film, were required to underwrite up to four local productions. With the new deal allowing direct distribution, those native distributors wouldn't be importing much. It had the potential to kill the local industry. For 1991 Korean box office receipts went over $200 million with over 80 percent of that going to foreign films, mainly American.[47]

South Korea was one of many countries where piracy was a problem. With a strong VCR potential as well as an increasing number of TV channels, both commercial and satellite (another reason the majors wanted to distribute directly), the cartel tried to reduce piracy by enlisting local filmmakers to press for stricter copyright enforcement; in return the studios offered the local film industry financial backing for new theaters. Unsurprisingly, such "generosity" was ignored by the Koreans. In Japan the majors constantly prodded the government to clamp down on piracy. When the MPAA decided the moves by the Japanese government were not successful, the cartel assigned film executives in Japan to seek out and investigate illegal copies of films and videos. Moaning that 66 nations lacked adequate protection for "intellectual property"—which included films, video cassettes, TV shows and products based on film characters—Valenti wailed, "The most precious possession we have is copyright."[48]

Grumbling about the small number of cinemas in Japan, one-sixth as many as in the U.S. on a per capita basis, a *Forbes* writer complained, "It is not at all easy for foreign filmmakers to get their product into the relatively small number of theaters that do exist." Two integrated Japanese firms (Toho and Shochiku) continued to produce/distribute/exhibit while a third company, Toei, worked with Shochiku to release foreign films. If independent houses wanted access to Toho or Shochiku, said *Forbes*, "they must agree to run everything the company picks; it's similar to the kind of block booking outlawed in the U.S. decades ago." Unsaid by *Forbes* was that the U.S. continued to block book all over the world. Just a couple of years later the cartel would in fact block book on Shochiku. Japan had largely escaped the practice from Hollywood due to the strength and integration of its own film industry. Through most of the 1980s Japanese films were able to maintain a market share of about 50 percent at home. Comparable figures for home product in Britain, Germany and France were, respectively, under 20 percent, under 20 percent and 35 percent. Japanese movies' share of the home market was down to 40 percent in 1990—which *Forbes* tried to argue showed monopoly control did not work. However, Japanese share of the domestic market, even at 40 percent, was higher than for the major European producers. The cartel extracted $236 million from Japan in rentals in 1990.[49]

Things got worse for Japan. In 1993 the majors took just over 60 percent of the market, amassing film rentals of $350 million while Japanese movies took $220 million. That marked the first time U.S. films took in more money than did the home product and the first time Hollywood cracked the 60 percent barrier. Because 1993 was the year of *Jurassic Park*, it was unclear if such results would hold over time, although the U.S. share for the first half of 1994 remained slightly over 60 percent, with *Park* gone. Majors then operating in Japan were Warner, Buena Vista International, Fox, Sony Pictures Entertainment, (Columbia, Tristar and Orion) and UIP (Paramount, Universal, MGM/UA).[50]

The majors moved back into Thailand with new product in 1981 after a 4½-year boycott, originally instituted when the import duty on film was sharply increased. Throughout the embargo period all the majors continued to operate—at a reduced level—with reissues. That practice could sometimes be even more profitable for the majors, forcing old, already-screened product back into cinemas. Although the Thais had not altered the tax, the cartel declared it was returning to the Thai market to test "profitability (in the light of the existing tax)." A more salient reason was rampant piracy. Hollywood did not give up in harassing the Thais about that tax. It took 12 years but the efforts finally bore fruit, 16 or 17 years from the start of the boycott, when late in 1993 the Thais cut the tax on imported film from 30 Baht ($1.20) per meter to 10 Baht (40¢). For an average-length movie that meant a new tax of around $1,200. As well the Thais planned to reduce the tariff to five Baht per meter in the near future.[51]

Under a new four-year pact signed with India in 1980, the MPEA was allowed to import 100 films each year, down from 150 under the old accord. The signers of the new agreement were Jack Valenti and members of the Indian cabinet. On the surface it appeared to be a loss for the cartel; however, the MPEA termed the deal "very significant" in that it exempted the U.S. film industry from many strict regulations governing foreign ownership in India. For other commodity areas India's insistence on a specified degree of local ownership in any American subsidiary had already led firms like IBM and Coca-Cola to withdraw from the Indian market. Included in the language of the new pact was the "theoretical" demand that U.S. majors channel their product through local "liaison offices"—i.e., state-controlled film distribution. In practice the cartel continued to operate through their own fully-owned Indian offices. The language in the pact implying Hollywood had to use some type of centralized state film distribution was merely rhetoric, inserted to pacify hard-liners. Had that part of the accord been put into effect the MPEA would have launched an embargo. "It's a matter of firm principle that we're not going to do business in any country where American films are singled out for socialized treatment if the nation's own basic economy isn't socialistic," MPEA vice-president Joseph Bellfort said of all film pacts.[52]

Distribution remained out of state hands in India but the cartel did have to deal with the quasi-governmental National Film Development Corporation (NFDC), the agency that determined the number of films allowed imported. By the late 1980s the MPEA complained about being allowed to import only 100 films per year—India's motion picture industry produced 773 features in 1988. Observed *Variety*, "Apparently because the Indian film industry is so remarkably prolific, demand for foreign films is not high and the NFDC can set whatever terms it likes on outsiders."[53]

In 1993 it was reported that India relaxed trade barriers which had restricted American movies "to a tiny number of screens and measly grosses in a market of 907 million people." Indian films took 95 percent of the box office receipts. Traditionally even Hollywood blockbusters sent in no more than 30 prints for all of India. Happy with the eased restrictions, the MPEA admitted they had made little progress in persuading India's government to crack down on piracy. Hollywood planned to crack the market open with *Jurassic Park* in 1994. During the week of that film's American release in June 1993, there was a rumor it played on a Bombay cable TV channel. Whether it did or did not remained unclear, but when the MPEA heard the rumor of the planned screening of *Park* it contacted Bombay's police chief urging him to put a stop to it. When *Park* opened in India in April 1994, 82 Hindi-dubbed prints plus 30 copies of the original English-only print were sent in. It became the most successful Western film in Indian history. The same thing happened in Pakistan where 25 prints of *Park* (21 dubbed in Urdu) were shipped. Dubbing in either nation was rare with usually only the English-language print going in—no subtitles either. Only in the early 1990s did India allow the dubbing of foreign films. Dubbing costs in India were around $35,000 per film. Pakistani producers unsuccessfully lobbied the National Assembly to block the release of *Park*. Then they threatened to withdraw their films from any exhibitor who dared to play the Urdu version of the film. It had no effect.[54]

Turkey's film production fell from 186 features in 1987 to 25 in 1992; the number of cinemas in the 3 main cities fell 20 percent over that time; admission prices increased 20-fold, from 1,500 Turkish lire to 30,000 ($3.20). Film production fell, reported *Variety* with unusual candor, because it was "squeezed by a combination of fewer screens, Yank distribs' hegemony and escalating costs." American films from cartel members took 74 percent of the Turkish market in 1993 on 68 releases. U.S. independents released a further 66 titles, all other nations released 12 titles in total while Turkey produced just 6 titles that year. The problem was, thought the distributors, Turkey needed more cinemas.[55]

One country where the cartel did have to deal with a state-controlled monopoly was in the Soviet Union. Over the decades from the end of World War II little product entered the Soviet Union, but what did always came in on a flat-rate rental. State-run film agency Goskino took the films, distributed them nationally and kept all the receipts. When Valenti met with Soviet film minister Alexander Kamshalov in Moscow in 1987, he urged Russia to buy more Hollywood product but insisted flat-rate deals made no sense for a great power. He also complained there had been no increase in the going rate for cartel product over the past five years. As to why America dominated the international film arena, Valenti explained to Kamshalov there were two reasons: Hollywood did not make movies for an insular society but films which engaged audiences. Secondly, they spent enormous sums of money and labor in global marketing. That last point was particularly irksome for the cartel head in view of what the Soviet Union paid then, which was "chicken feed," said Valenti. Things brightened in October 1988 when Valenti announced he had signed pacts with the Soviets giving U.S. films "unprecedented" access to the Russian film market. Under the agreement, U.S. distributors could negotiate a percentage rental, could lease cinemas and were assured of stricter Soviet controls over piracy.[56]

Disadvantages quickly outweighed the advantages. The changes allowing that new accord reflected many other changes in the nation, leading to the disintegration of the Soviet Union. Hollywood could indeed negotiate big percentage rentals but the Russians had no money to buy. Worse yet, piracy was pervasive, apparently by the state itself. A frustrated cartel announced in June 1991 it banned all future sales of U.S. movies to the Soviet Union. In a letter to Soviet Deputy Foreign Minister Vladimir Petrovsky, Valenti stated the boycott was instituted due to widespread piracy and would remain in effect until the country adopted and enforced adequate copyright protection laws. The illegal copying "seems to be beyond any perimeters. There doesn't seem to be anything done about it." With the majors having extracted only $767,000 from Russia in 1990, the boycott was mainly symbolic. According to Valenti, Petrovsky's own government was involved in piracy; Valenti alleged that Goskino ran video salons for profit where pirated U.S. cassettes were shown; that a state-owned Moscow cinema screened a pirated copy of *Rain Man* to paying customers; that state-run television aired unlicensed copies of the movies *Predator* and *Commando*.[57]

At the end of 1992, that boycott by the MPEA was lifted on the republics of Russia and the Ukraine, because they were poised to introduce copyright measures. MPEA officials were then working "closely" with Russian authorities on framing the copyright law. Once it was on the books, the MPEA was prepared to send "high-level teams" to Moscow and Kiev to help develop anti-piracy programs. "The MPEA has been a catalyst for similar programs in other parts of Eastern Europe," observed a journalist. [58]

Nevertheless piracy was still rampant in early 1994. The majors soldiered on, but in a very narrow circumscribed way. When *Tombstone* was released in Moscow it was screened at the American House of Cinema which was just six months old and located within an American hotel. With U.S.-style admission costs of $5–$7 per ticket, the film was targeted mainly at Moscow's expatriate population. Many precautions were taken to discourage piracy. The print of *Tombstone* was escorted through customs, hand-delivered to the cinema and locked in a safe between shows. During screenings, checks were made in the auditorium for video cameras because taping during a film screening had become a crude but common method of piracy.[59]

China was another "problem" country for Hollywood. Again not much product entered the country and what did was bought only for a flat rate. During an MPAA visit and tour during 1980, cartel members showed a few films in 20 cities, hoping to sell more. Ministry of Culture film bureau head Chen Po explained in 1981 that China would like to buy more American films but they were too expensive. Chen always vetoed any percentage rental proposal; he only bought for a flat rate. Although China had some foreign currency, Chen said it wished to use most of it for items such as industrial machinery with the consequence that what was spent on entertainment had to be used wisely. Thus China imported films from other nations such as Japan and Hong Kong, on much better terms. Their films were inexpensive and popular.[60]

Paramount and Universal signed a 1986 deal with China Film Corporation of Beijing to distribute in China. Terms were not disclosed but film executive Charles Paul admitted, "We asked for a percentage of the box office gross. They refused." However, he added, "The payment would be related to the popularity of the film, though not precisely a percentage of the box office." The initial financial value of the agreement was secondary, claimed Paul: "The primary impact will be cultural and strategic." He was trying to put a better face on what was just another flat-rate deal. Hollywood was beginning to get a little desperate given the huge size of the Chinese market. It was then a poor market but its future potential was enormous. Hollywood wanted to get more of its product on Chinese screens at almost any price to develop the habit, to establish a presence. Although there was little Hollywood product exhibited in China, the population had not exactly taken to street demonstrations to demand more.[61]

China had a contingency system whereby the government allowed in one imported feature for each three native-produced movies. For 1992 that meant 50 foreign imports in total, 12 to 15 of them from Hollywood, at a reported rental of $30,000 to $50,000 each. The cartel continued to complain the sales system was "not based on revenue sharing." Revenge of a sort was taken in that, under those rental conditions, the MPEA released to China only movies that were at least four to five years old. Negotiations continued off and on as they had for years. Finally, in 1994, China Film announced it was prepared to buy foreign films on a percentage basis, planning to keep 60 percent with 40 percent to the producer/distributor, close to the going rate. Hollywood hailed the move as a "major step forward." One studio executive estimated his studio would collect $3 to $5 million annually under the new arrangement. Since China only imposed fines—no jail sentences—on copyright law violators, the MPEA was lobbying the Chinese government to toughen and enforce those laws. Late in that year Warner opened *The Fugitive*, marking the first time in 40-odd years that a recent U.S. film was shown in Chinese cinemas in general release. Warner took a smaller than usual percentage to be that first major. U.S. motion picture executives saw that breakthrough as an important opening to the world's biggest potential entertainment audience.[62]

Initially the collapse of the East Bloc Communist system was greeted with great hope and enthusiasm by the cartel. In 1989 Hungary began to buy on a percentage basis, the first time in over 40 years. UIP quickly entered the market with a spokesman saying on the fall of Communism, "It introduced the idea of percentages." So much U.S. product was flooding in, a backlog was said to be building as not enough screens existed to exhibit it all. It was a worry. Disney vice-president Kevin Hyson declared the political upheaval in Eastern Europe would be a boon to the cartel with an expected big growth in revenue from the area as more films went in, all on percentage deals. Under the old system almost everything went in on flat-rate sales with all of those rates regarded as being too low by the majors.[63]

Some of the enthusiasm had waned by 1991 when the MPEA warned Eastern Europe "not to get greedy." The cartel announced, with no specific details, that it was instituting a box office checking system in its Eastern European markets starting with Poland and Hungary. According to MPEA executive Frank Tonini, some theaters in Poland were singled out as the most blatant perpetrators of underreporting. "If three cinemas are playing the same film, two say they have 90 percent capacity and the third reports 30 percent, something is wrong," he said. Warsaw admission prices were 10,000 zlotys (about $1). One alleged scam in the city was for an exhibitor to say he sold discounted tickets to seniors, cultural groups and others for one zloty.[64]

Even more enthusiasm was gone by 1993. Warner director of European sales Gary Hodes said of Eastern Europe, "The bottom line is not as lucrative as we had originally hoped." Falling cinema attendance from harsh economic conditions and widespread piracy were the chief culprits. Videocassettes were in shops within weeks of a film's release in nearby countries, regularly appearing before the film was booked into theaters. Cinema attendance in Poland dropped from 20 million in 1991 to 11 million in 1992. In response the majors tried to release their product faster, subtitled rather than with the more costly dubbing. A resigned Hodes added, "We have revised our expectations and abandoned hopes of turning those markets into another Austria, Switzerland or Norway."[65]

One example of how difficult it was for a country to make a film and recover its costs at home could be seen in Czechoslovakia in 1994, but it could apply to many lands. Admission prices were then about $1 with the exhibitors keeping half. With the cost of a Czech film averaging $1 million, 2 million tickets had to be sold to recoup costs. However the necessary 20 percent of Czechoslovakia's 10 million people did not attend the cinema. Which illustrated the need for subsidies.[66]

Canada adopted a cultural policy in the late 1970s and early 1980s of providing tax incentives to channel private capital into film production. It was a policy which led to co-productions with Americans turning out Hollywood-type product. Because of that policy, Canada produced such gems as *Porky's* and *Meatballs.* Summing up the feeling of national expropriation and international orientation of the Canadian film industry that many film unions felt, Quebec's Syndicate National du Cinema president Maurice Leblanc said, "Co-productions are nothing but shit. All the energy we've wasted, all the money we've spent, it's always been on co-productions. It's always there that we've had problems: lower salaries, for instance. It's like Mexico or Spain used to be: They come over here to film the natives." When Canada's Minister of Communications Francis Fox pointed to international pressure on creative people he said, "Canadian producers and other key creators in film feel constrained to mold their productions into U.S. facsimiles because they are given to believe that unless they do this, the majors will not consider distributing them in Canada or anywhere else. This is appalling." In the governmental Canadian Film Development Commission's 1981–1982 annual report was the following statement: "Motion pictures are the most pervasive and powerful means of expression in our time. For any independent nation which wishes to nurture its people, or convey to others a distinctive identity, the development of an indigenous, authentic motion picture is indispensable." Yet at the time about 97 percent of Canada's screen time was taken by foreign films—the vast majority being American product. One government report estimated that of the nearly $1 billion in annual revenue from the film and video markets, 90 percent of it was controlled by the U.S. majors.[67]

During investigation of the film industry in the early 1980s, the federal Combines Investigation Branch accused the six majors distributing in Canada through subsidiaries with failing to supply "commercially valuable pictures" to Canada's third largest exhibition chain, the locally owned Cineplex, then with 17 multiplexes in 11 cities. Alleged by the Combines Branch was that the U.S. distributors "have maintained long-standing arrangements whereby they supply motion pictures to the two largest exhibition chains (the U.S.–owned Famous Players and Canadian Odeon) to the exclusion of Cineplex and others." Said Cineplex president Garth Drabinsky in 1982, "It is absolutely crucial to break up the relationship among Famous Players and Odeon and the major distributors.... Market dominance in Canada by the distributors has been present since 1920." Those charges were never followed up by any court action against the cartel. Francis Fox's Task Force on Film Distribution recommended in 1983 the breaking up of the U.S. control of distribution and exhibition, declaring, "This situation is economically unhealthy for everyone— except the two chains." Although agreeing that Canadian film producers and exhibitors were hurt by an industry structure dominated by foreign oligopolies in collusion with the major exhibitors, the task force offered no concrete suggestions as to how to break up the monopoly. Nothing was done.[68]

The old voluntary agreement from the mid–1970s whereby the two cinema chains agreed to voluntarily run one Canadian film for one week in each 13 weeks was still theoretically in effect in 1984 when Cineplex bought the Odeon chain. Of course that agreement had been ignored by everyone. Nonetheless one of Drabinsky's first acts as head of the new Cineplex Odeon entity was to terminate that agreement, arguing the policy was designed to pressure foreign chains but since he was Canadian it did not apply. The same Drabinsky who had appealed to his federal government for state intervention to assist Cineplex only a couple of years previously completed his reversal in 1986 when the feds again made some weak noises about doing something for Canada's film industry. Those proposals were labeled by Cineplex as "unethical" and "alarming." What was true in Canada, and elsewhere, was that native capital sought state intervention when pitted against foreign capital. However, when it was in their interest to join with foreign capital, native capital invoked the myth of the free market. After an alliance, native capital would then oppose any state intervention within the alliance. A capitalist, foreign, native or international, would always act like a capitalist. Cineplex continued to expand, even passing Famous to become Canada's largest chain. Then it became American again in the 1980s when it was merged into MCA, then Japanese in 1990 when Matsushita bought MCA; then Canadian again in 1995 when Seagram purchased MCA.[69]

Provincially Quebec tangled with the majors in the 1980s. With a platform of Quebec independence, the Parti Quebecois (PQ) came to power in 1981. To the PQ the domination of Quebec screens by the U.S. cartel as well as the lengthy delays in releasing French versions of movies were all evidence of the domination of Anglo culture in North America. A commission was formed to study the Quebec film situation. Its report became the basis for a bill stipulating that any company involved in commercial distribution had to be 80 percent Canadian-owned—as mandated by federal law with respect to broadcast station ownership. The idea was to give a percentage of the market to local firms, generating a cash flow that would in turn aid in financing local production. "To consider only the laws of the market, and, in addition, to promote that option, would mean to turn over Quebec's cinema industry to the American majors, bound hand and foot. This would be tantamount to assassinating Quebec's entire cinema industry." Of course the MPEA attacked the bill ferociously. They worried that if passed it might become a model for a Canada-wide measure. At hearings on the bill, the MPEA claimed it would eliminate its members from the Quebec market; that its members had operated in Quebec for almost 60 years and thus those "acquired rights" must be preserved. Under such pressure, PQ compromised by agreeing to allow existing companies to obtain a special license to distribute any film they produced or held worldwide rights to. Additionally a portion of the gross distribution income (not to exceed 10 percent) was by law to be invested in Quebec film. That compromise bill was enacted in June 1983.[70]

Prior to passage of the bill, the U.S. Embassy in Ottawa issued a terse communiqué to the PQ calling the proposals "restrictive" and "protectionist." The MPEA's Canadian arm, the Canadian Motion Picture Distributors Association (CMPDA), described the bill as "unacceptable," warning its passage would result in Quebeckers being "deprived of seeing American films." At the time of the bill's passage, according to Quebec cultural affairs minister Clement Richard, the majors controlled 97 percent of the film market in Anglo-Canada, along with 41 percent of the screen time, and 56 percent of the box office receipts in Quebec. Quebec Premier René Levesque admitted that "pressure" sent his government back several times to redraft the legislation but the only accommodation that the majors would accept was "total surrender." An initial provision of the bill requiring a film to be dubbed in French within Quebec was dropped.[71]

Although the bill was passed into law, it would not be enforced until enabling regulations were also passed. The majors continued to apply pressure with Jack Valenti making a personal call on the Quebec cabinet. His demand to meet personally with Levesque was refused by the Premier. President Ronald Reagan raised objections about the law to Prime Minister Brian Mulroney. Virtually all of the Quebec and Canadian film personnel groups supported the PQ and the bill. However, by then the PQ was on shaky political ground with an election looming; they put the whole mess on hold. In December 1985 the Liberal Party swept the PQ out of office. That new regime hired Francis Fox (no longer in federal politics) to negotiate a film settlement with Valenti. He did so, striking a deal which essentially was the old status quo. The majors were allowed to conduct business as usual. One unhappy official within the Quebec government wondered, "Was Francis Fox working for Jack Valenti?"[72]

Quebec made more modest demands later in the 1980s in an effort to get French-language versions of U.S. films closer to the original English-language release date for the rest of North America. To that end Quebec passed a decree requiring a French-dubbed version be delivered within 60 days of the original release, later toughened to 45 days. What Quebec was attempting to achieve was day-and-date release with the original. American control of Quebec screens rose from 74 percent to at least 80 percent in early 1993. Surprisingly that law proved to be a bonanza for the majors and a disaster for some Canadian distributors. Warner executive Barry Reardon admitted that getting the French version to Quebec screens faster was "absolutely, positively" part of the reason for the increased screen control. The increased number of U.S. hits made it even harder to place independent product. Unintentionally that decree had aided the cartel, perhaps because the earlier French release played more on the surrounding media hype emanating from Anglo-America. When releases were many months later, much of the impact of that original publicity was long forgotten.[73]

Undeterred by the carnage in Quebec, the federal government of Canada tried again. In 1985 another task force inquiry was held which recommended control of distribution by Canadian companies through appropriate legislative and regulatory measures. It did not recommend elimination of foreign control of the Canadian market by the U.S. cartel but merely suggested shifting some control over to Canadian-owned distributors, thereby giving them a portion of the distribution revenues. That report became the basis for Flora MacDonald, who became Minister of Communications in July 1986, to propose a new distribution bill. One catalyst was the debacle in Quebec; the second was Paramount's raid on Canadian-owned independent distributor Norstar which had a subdistribution agreement with Atlantic Releasing of New York under which it marketed independently produced U.S. and foreign movies in Canada—about two titles per month. After some two years of that relationship, Paramount bought out the subdistribution from Atlantic, thereby cutting off Norstar's supply and destroying the company. It was a raid to eliminate competition, as slight as it was. Commented Norstar president Daniel Weinzweig, "We hope that it sends a clear signal loud and clear to Ottawa and Mr. Mulroney in particular, who seems to think the Americans can do no wrong."[74]

MacDonald announced in February 1987 that the government would introduce a licensing system for the importation of films. Foreign distributors could import only those movies into Canada for which they held world distribution rights; pick-ups by the majors would have to be made available to Canadian distributors. If, say, Paramount produced a film, then it obviously held world rights but if Paramount picked up a film from an outside producer who negotiated a license with Paramount, then Paramount may have held world rights, or for a lesser area. About one-third of films handled by cartel members at that time were reported here to be pick-ups. Film historian Manjunath Pendakur reported that in 1986 the majors controlled $150 million in rentals or about 97 percent of the total revenue from the market—$322 million in gross box office receipts. As well the U.S. majors controlled an estimated 60 percent of the $170 million home video market and $70 million of ancillary markets (broadcast TV, pay TV and syndication). MacDonald's proposals were minor in impact. The National Association of Canadian Film and Video Distributors estimated the proposed legislation would shift about 7 percent of those revenues to Canadian-owned distributors.[75]

Predictably the cartel reacted with outrage. Within days Valenti was petitioning the Canadian government for an audience. Prodded by Prime Minister Mulroney's office, MacDonald met Valenti in an atmosphere reported as "cool." He suggested a few alternatives, principally a tax at the box office to generate revenues for domestic production. MacDonald was not enthusiastic. Also strongly against the bill was Cineplex Odeon and its president Drabinsky. When he returned home, Valenti intensified his lobbying in high places. Hollywood trotted out the old argument that such a bill (if enacted) would encourage other trading partners to follow Canada's example, as well as reducing revenue. At least twice Valenti met President Reagan to discuss the matter. Then at a general economic summit meeting in April 1987 with Mulroney, Reagan brought up the matter, publicly denouncing the legislation. Apparently Mulroney assured Reagan that the bill would in no way reduce Hollywood's freedom to do business in Canada. The two nations were then in the process of negotiating a general economic union, the Free Trade Agreement (FTA). At Valenti's urging the U.S. House of Representatives and the Senate sent a letter signed by 54 members to Mulroney expressing their "strongest objections" to the bill. Calling such measures protectionist the letter declared, "So, while the successful negotiations of a comprehensive free trade agreement will be difficult, its implementation by the Congress would be entirely inconsistent with the existence of the restrictive MacDonald Policy." Senator Pete Wilson (R–California) worried that if such a law was implemented, "it would play into the hands of those countries throughout the world which oppose expanded trade in services and investment—areas in which we are very competitive internationally." European distributors, from whom Canadian independent distributors bought films, were not helpful to the Canadian firms as they were reluctant to sell Canadian territory rights separately from U.S. rights.

They feared losing potential sales to the U.S. market through the majors. Reportedly they too were under pressure from Valenti. Canada's proposed bill stalled; it was not tabled; it quickly died.[76]

During that battle Flora MacDonald admitted, "No fewer than seven Ministers since World War II have attempted ... to reach a negotiated agreement which would assure a Canadian presence on Canadian screens. None has succeeded." Chalk up number eight.[77]

Late in 1987 the two nations signed the FTA although it would not go into effect until the beginning of 1989 as it had to be ratified by the legislature in each country. MacDonald's bill was then dead but Hollywood was not sure of that. Under FTA the audio-visual segment had been left off the table— the agreement was designed to reduce and eliminate tariffs, restrictions and so on between the nations opening each up totally and equally to the other. Hollywood, in its lobbying efforts, prepared a Congressional brief titled "U.S. Film Industry's TRADE CRISIS in Canada." Early in 1988, 41 California members of Congress sent a message to the House Ways and Means Committee demanding "safeguards from future barriers Canada may impose on the distribution of U.S. films, home videos and television programs." Their letter quoted liberally from the MPAA brief. All the while, of course, Hollywood controlled some 97 percent of Anglo-Canadian screens and 80 percent in Franco-Canada. Complaining the Canadians refused to go forward with the FTA unless audio-visual material was kept out, the MPAA declared, "As of this moment, we are at an impasse, with our member companies held hostage to the impasse. We have tried. God knows we have tried, to placate the Canadians. We have more than met them halfway." Because of the domino effect, the crisis was not limited to Canada, said the brief. "It is a matter of survival ... If Canada gets away with its handcuffing of the U.S. industry, there will be an epidemic of such barriers ... We dominate world screens, in the cinema and in the home, all over the globe. Therefore we are vulnerable to anti–American sentiment and a target for producers and distributors who are envious of our success with their own people. It is important to remember that the folks making decisions favoring U.S. movies over Canadian movies in Canada are not Americans. It is the Canadian people who have made these choices." Cultural sovereignty, said the brief, was a "fiction." Using vastly inflated figures, the MPAA claimed if MacDonald's bill went through, cartel members would lose $50 million a year from its Canadian revenue and "the U.S. movie industry would suffer a massive economic hemorrhage."[78]

Valenti did finally get the White House to append special language to the FTA designed to make any new cultural policy initiatives in Canada next to impossible to implement. It said that any attempt by government to take action to impede the production, distribution, sale or exhibition of film, video recordings or television programs would provoke U.S. trade retaliation. Aim of the retaliation was to balance the commercial effects of such action and to discourage others. In other words, a new attempt to introduce a MacDonald-type bill would be even more difficult. When Valenti delivered a speech in Toronto to an audience of Canadian elites, one of the nation's best-known print commentators, Allan Fotheringham, slammed the event. "Only in Canada would we offer a platform to a bully from another nation to tell us how to run our country and our economy and our life.... Jack Valenti is a short, white-haired bully, one of the most powerful lobbyists in the United States, representing one of the richest lobbies in the United States ... the highest-paid hit man in the famed elysian fields of Washington flakdom."[79]

When the FTA was signed, Canada's national magazine *Macleans* observed that "American companies now control virtually all movie distribution rights in Canada." In the U.S. *Variety* predicted the FTA "will give U.S. interests continued domination over Canada's cultural industries."[80]

Within a few years FTA was superseded by NAFTA (North American Free Trade Agreement), an economic free trade pact between Canada, the U.S. and Mexico. Still upset that Hollywood had been left out of the FTA, Valenti vowed it would not happen in the NAFTA talks. Essentially he wanted all Canadian content quotas and protection stripped away. One man opposed was Canadian Gordon Ritchie, a former ambassador and architect of the FTA agreement, who said, "It's not a question of access; it's a question of total dominance here. Jack Valenti and that crowd have incredible access to the Canadian market." U.S. television product represented then 70 percent of English-language Canadian TV; U.S. movies held 97 percent of Anglo-Canadian screen time, 78 percent in Franco-Canada. Self-described as a "committed free-trader," Ritchie added, "We already allowed a great deal of erosion of Canadian culture. So what we're saying now is that we've allowed you to go that far and no further. Period. Absolutely, totally non-negotiable. What we're talking about is protecting the last 3 percent to 30 percent."[81]

According to *Variety*, the MPAA, backed by President Bush and State, was indeed "eager to get unlimited access to Canada's film and home video distribution business under the agreement." Without comment and apparently noting no contradiction, the publication went on in 1991 to state that U.S. companies, chiefly the majors, then controlled about 93 percent of Canada's annual film and home video distribution revenues, 90 percent of recording revenues, 50 percent of Canada's leading cinema chains and reaped around $C350 million per year from TV program sales.[82]

Canada held firm with U.S. Trade Representative Carla Hills reluctantly letting Canada exempt its "cultural industries" from the NAFTA pact finalized in 1992. Valenti was outraged, urging Congress to flex its muscles and order U.S. negotiators to reopen talks. Canada's exemption provision was described by Valenti as "ominous and threatening" and he warned it could become a "soiling precedent" spreading perhaps to Europe. Because of the exclusion granted on cultural industries, Valenti whined it gave "the U.S. creative community

nothing with respect to Canada." Neither the FTA nor NAFTA was a victory
for Canada in film distribution and exhibition. Rather, it continued the status quo; it meant a continuation of almost total U.S. dominance. What was
protected were items such as content rules for TV programming, foreign ownership of broadcast outlets, a protection for Canadian print outlets against the
so-called Canadian editions of U.S. periodicals (designed of course to destroy
the Canadian counterpart) and so forth.[83]

Although Hills permitted the cultural exemption for Canada, it was not
given to Mexico in the NAFTA accord. Mexico was also required to begin
strictly protecting intellectual property which, the majors hoped, could trigger a U.S. video boom in Mexico. There was then reportedly much piracy.
Another NAFTA clause "allows" Mexican cinema owners to reduce from 50
percent to 30 percent the percentage of screen time devoted to Mexican product. Valenti hailed the passage of NAFTA through the Congress—at least the
part related to Mexico.[84]

Canada's Heritage Minister (charged with film oversight) Michel Dupuy
announced in January 1995 that he was pondering ways to get more Canadian
films in cinemas, remarking, "I would like to see more screen time for Canadian films.... I think we have to strengthen our distribution sector. And I hope
that our American friends will understand our problems." When asked about
the long history of failure to change that situation, Dupuy replied, "I intend
to be realistic about this," but insisted bolstering the film, TV and video industries would be a priority for his department in 1995. Back in the late 1970s
when John Roberts tried to take action against the domination, the chief stumbling block was fellow cabinet minister Jean Chretien, then Finance Minister. When Dupuy made his announcement, Chretien was Canada's Prime
Minister. Nothing more has been heard from Dupuy.[85]

Within Europe as a whole the cartel worried in 1989 about the European
Community's (E.C.) plans for the future and the possibility the E.C. would
set limits on the number of U.S. programs in the European marketplace. Fueling that fear was the fact that that same year the E.C. issued a directive that
called on TV stations to reserve a majority of air time for European-made
product, where practicable. Most nations interpreted that as 50 percent—
France defined it as 60 percent. Valenti said he was saddened by that quota
system which, he said, "is totally useless, worthless and needn't have been
done." Singled out as the quota agitators were the U.K., Spain, Italy and especially France while "eight other countries don't want them, don't need them,
but they imposed on them." Taking hyperbole to a greater level, Valenti howled,
"Quotas are like the beginning of a cancer. Quotas are odious.... A quota is
not going to solve the basic problem. Never in the history of cinema and television is there a known example in the world where a quota has done that."[86]

One reason for Europe to try and take a united step to attempt to
strengthen its film industry was the fact that, as a journalist noted in 1990,

"the majors are increasingly dominating the marketplace in Europe as they are in the U.S." Some independent producers (New World, Cannon and others) which supplied independent distributors had collapsed while others had signed distribution deals with the majors (Carolco with Columbia, Imagine Films with UIP and Orion Pictures with Columbia).[87]

At a panel on the state of European filmmaking, sponsored by the European Film Academy at the 1992 Cannes, France, film festival, director Wim Wenders called for strict quota regulations against the U.S. majors. He called for tough sanctions, arguing U.S. films had become an "addiction" of European audiences and withdrawal was necessary. Understanding that most U.S. product contained a good deal of violence, one of his proposals called for a ban on movies containing a certain amount of violence; "If we draw the line at showing this or that it could help to block American distribution," explained Wenders. Close to 80 percent of European-produced films were never exhibited outside their country of origin. Another panelist was German director Hark Bohm, who lashed out at American screen domination: "If only one monopolistic group offers product, you can't begin to talk about a market." Wenders agreed the U.S. had a state of utter domination, adding, "If there's no free market, why do we pretend we must follow the rules of a free market?... It's not going to help American moviemaking if theirs is the only moviemaking left."[88]

Just two weeks later Valenti claimed in a speech that America was in a "World War of Trade" in which the E.C. was bent on erecting barriers to the entry of U.S. films and TV programs; "There is among the leaders of the E.C. an awful squinting toward 'fortress Europe.'" According to the cartel head, U.S. film and TV industries created an annual $3.5 billion trade surplus for the domestic economy, a trade asset under attack by a "new trade religion" in which the "high priests ... threaten us and coerce us to bend to their long-term objectives." E.C. TV programming quotas that reserved time for European-origin programming "inhospitably consign the American creative film and TV program to a new form of purgatory.... Our clamors to enter [go] unheeded and unheard." Urging the U.S. government to resist quotas, Valenti warned if those quotas were not resisted, "one of America's most valuable trade assets will have been fatally wounded."[89]

In the early 1980s when European TV aired 100,000 hours of programming, 22 percent was of U.S. origin. By 1992 400,000 hours aired annually, 35 percent being U.S. product. Satellite TV service boosted Yankee product considerably. Servicing the U.K. was the six-channel BSkyB which relied heavily on imported shows (especially U.S. films) for its three movie channels. The four-fold increase in just ten years in hours of TV programming aired was the reason the MPEA was fighting just as hard for TV access as for film screen control. Valenti could be heard muttering, "We have to be able to move freely around the world and let audiences decide if they want to see our product."[90]

Switzerland deregulated the film business significantly in 1993, allowing distributors to import an unlimited number of movies, allowing foreigners to own theaters, etc. One restriction was that a distributor could not gross more than 25 percent of the market. Due to the number of majors it was a restriction that would have absolutely no effect. Privately-owned TV stations were on the way. The American share of the Swiss film market was 49.7 percent in 1991, 55.5 percent in 1992. With the new rules, it could only increase. During 1993, half of all movies screened in Germany were American. That half took 88 percent of the box office receipts.[91]

Supposedly fed up from repeated anti–American and especially anti-multinational articles in Spain's largest circulation daily *El País*, all the U.S. majors stopped all advertising of U.S. movies in the newspaper on the same day, May 1, 1988. The cartel claimed the action was not a joint embargo but rather each major had come to that action on its own, a coincidence. Some of the barbs from the paper which rankled Hollywood included "any European film is better than an American one" and "the coarse fare of present-day American high-budget films, which live off cinema without contributing anything to cinema." Perhaps just as important was that the majors were annoyed at *El País* for its "virtual absence of coverage of the film sector in general." U.S. movies took 75.73 percent of Spanish box office revenues in 1993 while Spanish films took 8.52 percent.[92]

As a result of a 1983 investigation of the film industry in the U.K., the Monopolies and Mergers Commission (MMC) declared film distribution and exhibition in Britain to be a monopoly. Two distribution entities, Columbia-EMI-Warner and United International Pictures had about 50 percent of the market while two cinema chains, EMI Cinemas and Rank Leisure, took around 60 percent of the exhibition market. While the MMC report declared the only remedy was a reduction in control, it added "this would not be practical." Eight years later the MMC announced it would conduct another film investigation in view of the charge that the Hollywood majors were squeezing out independent companies. Small cinema owners were being denied access to product. After a ten-month investigation the MMC declared a monopoly did exist in the supply of film for U.K. exhibition. However, it recommended only two minor changes: The first was an end to the practice of alignment whereby a distributor had a "habitual exclusive" arrangement with a particular cinema chain (block booking by another name). The second was a reduction in the period distributors could require films to be screened to two weeks for a first-run film; distributors sometimes demanded an exhibitor guarantee a run of four weeks or even six weeks for blockbusters.[93]

Britain's exhibitor quota had stood at 30 percent reserved for home product for decades, until it was reduced to 15 percent in 1981. Hollywood's share of the UK's 1990 box office gross of £240 million was estimated to be 80 percent. In 1993 U.S. movies took about 93 percent of the British box office.

France, in 1992, held the U.S. share down to 58 percent of the box office. Regarding the $150 million in yearly subsidy from France to its film industry, the *Times* of London commented, "It seems to work effectively." According to the *Times*, the U.S. held around 85 percent of the world's film market; 90 percent of European films never appeared outside of their home country; in fact, 60 percent of them never reached a cinema at all. Sardonically the newspaper remarked that if the European film industry died completely, Hollywood would have no more talent to steal.[94]

France was indeed the European country that put up the greatest fight to U.S. domination in this period. Film director Bertrand Tavernier remarked in 1980 that U.S. domination not only threatened national film industries in some countries but had virtually "wiped out" the British film industry. All through its domination America bought virtually no foreign films.[95]

French Minister of Culture Jack Lang complained in 1981 that Hollywood had too big a slice of France's film business, that U.S. cinema "is based on a powerful worldwide distribution network" and that the MPEA "puts pressure on European countries in order to thwart their policies for the development of their own film industries. And the subsidiaries of the American companies, strongly implanted in France, with accomplices in France, occupy an overly important place in the production and distribution of films. They impose productions that are not always the best, far from the best." Lang went on to call for a "crusade" against U.S. entertainment which he condemned as "a financial and cultural imperialism that no longer or rarely grabs territory but grabs consciousness, ways of thinking, ways of living." His most famous attack occurred at a 1982 UNESCO conference in Mexico where in a speech Lang attacked U.S. "cultural imperialism," speaking of large nations who "have no other morality than that of profit, who seek to impose a uniform culture on the whole world and to dictate their laws to free and independent countries."[96]

Until 1986, French films always outgrossed U.S. movies in France. However, by 1989 American films took 55 percent of the French box office with 34 percent going to home product (an all-time high and low, respectively). Hollywood didn't publicly boast of its ascendancy though, due to the stringent government quotas placed on non–French TV programs. France had a rule that 60 percent of TV programming had to be European-made, and 40 percent had to be French-made. Although the government had no plans to impose similar quotas on cinemas, the majors took no chances because (said a journalist), "Some Americans fear a backlash from an industry that has been unduly embarrassed by its own weakness in the face of the American juggernaut." Yet the U.S. attendance in France was not really expanding; everything else was contracting. During 1983–1984 UIP took 265 million francs when the U.S. share was 35 percent and tickets sold totaled 180 million. In fiscal 1988–1989 UIP took 264 million francs when the U.S. share was 55 percent and tickets were 120 million.[97]

While in Deauville, France, in September 1993, Valenti tried to argue that American films were not taking over because French attendance at American films had essentially held steady, slipping from 70 million in 1982 to 68 million in 1992. However, Valenti did not mention that over that same period attendance at French-made films dropped from 93 million to 40 million.[98]

That same month the French film industry took its case to the European Parliament in Strasbourg, demanding protection from the domination of Hollywood. Included in the delegation were Communications Minister Alain Carignon as well as actors Gerard Depardieu and Isabelle Huppert. Cinema cannot "be treated like a product," said Carignon. With the nations of the world then in the midst of negotiating freer trade in the GATT accord, Depardieu remarked, "Culture should be the exception in world trade…. If cinema is included in GATT, we cannot fight on equal terms against American power." Said director Claude Berri, "If the GATT deal goes through as proposed, European culture is finished." If audio-visual industries were included in GATT, it would mean an end of all forms of direct and indirect protection. Europe would have to revoke its rule that 50 percent of TV programming be made in Europe. France would have to cancel subsidies and other indirect financial assistance given the French motion picture industry. Despite the inroads by Hollywood product, French cinema was surviving "while the movie industries of, say, Italy and Germany are close to extinction." When a new, more right-wing government came to power in France, Lang was replaced as culture minister by Jacques Toubon in 1993. Hollywood hoped he would be more pro–American than Lang but he proved to be no less nationalistic. Toubon complained to the press that *Jurassic Park*—then on its way to France—was to be screened in 25 percent of the 1,800 houses in cities and large towns. "What's left for the others? I'm opposed to this occupation of screens by a single genre of cinema," he explained. Toubon added that Valenti told him President Bill Clinton would not sign a GATT that excluded audio-visual trade.[99]

The Uruguay round of GATT negotiations, which began in that nation in 1986, were into the last stage of the final leg of discussion in Brussels and Geneva, late in 1993. Failure of the world's nations (most were involved) to reach an agreement by a self-imposed deadline of December 1993 would have meant scrapping the entire round. Just two issues held up an agreement at the end; one was agricultural products, the second was audio-visual industries. Usually GATT talks never made it off the business pages of newspapers. This time, however, because of the wrangle over audio-visual product, GATT negotiations made front page headlines across the globe.

Late in 1992, 112 European directors and producers gathered in France for a film forum where they urged European GATT negotiators to hold the line for TV quotas and keep audio visual out of GATT. Noting that U.S. anti-trust laws prevented UIP from operating within its own borders, the filmmakers argued it was strange Europe should allow UIP to operate freely. Europe's imports of U.S. films, video and TV programs in 1992 were worth $3.7 billion, up from $2.3 billion five years earlier. On the other hand the E.C.'s exports to the U.S. for the same items in 1992 were only $300 million. When the French objected to the one-sided nature of the trade, President George Bush's chief GATT negotiator Carla Hills told them "Make films as good as your cheeses and you will sell them!" The *Economist* magazine, however, noted that American films arrived in Europe at cut-rate prices and that "audience ratings show that French viewers usually prefer French films to comparable American ones, but they cost ten times as much." European calculations had it that in 1991 American movies took 81 percent of the screen time and 54 percent of all dramas and comedies aired on television. The *Economist* argued the broadcast quota was surely doomed as the Europeans could not meet it currently and would have no chance in the future when there were tens or even hundreds more channels. With regard to French film subsidies, the *Economist* argued those subsidies had not prevented the quality of French films from declining; "Arguably, many of the best European films have come from unsubsidized Hollywood—through directors such as Paul Verhoeven, Ridley Scott, Alan Parker and Jean-Jacques Arnaud." Apparently the magazine did not wish to see the talent-poaching connection—those directors were all trained in subsidized institutions in their home nations, then poached to churn profits for Hollywood. During that time, of course, they could not produce for their home nation. Indeed, Hollywood received, and had *always* received huge indirect subsidies from its own government with untold help from State and Commerce. Moviegoers the world over subsidized Hollywood every time they attended—by adding to Hollywood's profits and power, which were used in turn to crush local competition, gain control of local exhibition, build multiplexes, poach talent and generate even more hype for the next blockbuster, which sold more tickets, etc. Every foreign ticket sold kept the price paid by U.S. cinemagoers down to a reasonable level. In 1994 U.S. films took 60 percent of the French box office; French movies took just 28 percent. Again those figures were an all-time high and low, respectively.[100]

By September 1993 with *Jurassic Park* stomping all over Europe, Toubon condemned the film's distributor UIP for abusing its "dominant position" in Europe to "prevent competition.... Culture is about diversity and pluralism.... GATT rules are not compatible with the existence of an autonomous cultural system." Toubon said, *Jurassic Park* was not a film: "It is only an assembly of special effects." Not all E.C. nations were avid to exclude audio visuals from GATT, at least in the beginning. What tended to move them in that direction was the coming of *Jurassic Park* which took up so many screens at the same time, and the hysterical and erroneous diatribes emanating from Valenti. Toubon was also strongly supported by film personnel including the European director group ARP which included Claude Berri, Volker Schlondorf, Roman Polanski and Bertrand Tavernier. The ARP continued to lobby, unsuccessfully, to the European Commission to ban the agreement which allowed distributor UIP and U.S.–controlled cinema chain UCI to exist and operate.[101]

As the impasse over audio visual lasted into December 1993, one European official commented, "Not only in France, but throughout the community, there is a feeling that we must have some protection for the European entertainment industry or it will simply disappear." The U.S. chief GATT negotiator was then President Clinton appointee Mickey Kantor, formerly a lawyer in Hollywood for the entertainment industry. Kantor remained firm on trying to get all subsidies abolished, at one point arguing that part of the box office tax levied by France—which was used to subsidize home production— be given to Hollywood as most of the films screened in France were theirs. "We are willing to try and deal with broadcast quotas and to work on the question of subsidies but we are not willing to sell out the rights of hard-working individuals to collect their royalties. American producers and actors are not getting their full royalties," explained Kantor, who implied Clinton had drawn a line in the sand on the issue. In an op ed. piece in the *New York Times*, William Safire stated that Hollywood "deserves" an end to subsidies for unprofitable French films, that "the French public prefers the American product." California Republican Governor Pete Wilson told Clinton "We must walk away from a bad GATT agreement." Valenti continued to whine to anybody and everybody, "All we want is access to a market and fairness."[102]

At the prodding of Valenti, directors Martin Scorsese and Steven Spielberg came out publicly against protectionism. Former head of both Universal and Columbia Frank Price declared, "This is simple protectionism, it's arrogant, as anti–American as you can get." From the other side European directors Pedro Almodavar (Spain), Bernardo Bertolucci (Italy), Wim Wenders (Germany) and Stephen Frears (U.K.) issued a public letter saying, "We are only desperately defending the tiny margin of freedom left to us. We are trying to protect European cinema against its complete annihilation." There was in France then an 11 percent tax on cinema admissions. According to the MPAA, the U.S. film, television and home video industry accounted for $18 billion in annual worldwide income. Approximately $8 billion of that—over 40 percent—came from foreign markets with Europe contributing around $4 billion of that.[103]

Most European negotiators, initially listless on the issue, rallied to France's side. One thing that particularly incensed them was Valenti's oft-repeated remark that the foreign films didn't sell in the U.S. because Americans would not go to see dubbed or subtitled films—yet, of course, that is what Europeans had to do. Said Valenti's French counterpart Daniel Toscan de Plantier, president of Unifrance, "There is invisible protectionism in the United States. Films circulate throughout the world, but not in the United States." President of France Francois Mitterand joined in to say that what was at stake was the right of every country to create its own images: "A society which abandons the means of depicting itself would soon be an enslaved society."[104]

The U.S. began to crack. Desperately Kantor tried to make compromises. He asked that some of France's box office tax be given to U.S. producers (ostensibly to be spent by U.S. producers in European production), that the TV quota not apply to prime time hours, that only half of all new stations generated by coming cable services be subject to quotas, that when video on demand came into being it not be subject to quotas. All were flatly rejected by European negotiators. The E.C. chief negotiator was the U.K.'s Leon Brittan, who observed, "The United States already has 80 percent of the European movie market, and that market is growing. This is not an American industry fighting for survival. The European Community wants to have the capacity to support its own culture, and that seems to me to be reasonable." A GATT deal was struck just hours before the deadline. Audio-visual product was left out of GATT completely, allowing each nation to set its own cultural policies. Calling the deal "blatant protectionism," Valenti fumed, "I am disturbed by the refusal of the European community to negotiate seriously." Jack Lang hailed the result as "a victory for art and artists over the commercialization of culture." French director Jean-Jacques Beinex (of the cult hit *Diva*) cautioned, "We came close to catastrophe, so we shouldn't rejoice too much. We removed the threat that European culture would be completely eliminated.... I wouldn't exist if there were no subsidies.[105]

Alain Carignon hailed the GATT exemption as a "great and beautiful victory for Europe and for French culture." Kantor had already dropped the affair down the memory hole for he said of the Europeans, "They didn't win. In fact, the French people lost. They are going to be denied the right to their freedom of choice." Vaguely he threatened Europe with unspecified retaliatory trade measures. One outraged observer was Shawn Tully, who wrote in *Fortune*, "In a maneuver worthy of Inspector Clouseau, the French are shooting themselves in the film canister. Rampant protectionism fostered the U.S. takeover of Europe's entertainment business in the first place." Of course, the reverse was true. Only when Europe found itself overrun did it try and protect its industry. Given the U.S. had about 75 percent of the European box office, the protectionism was singularly unsuccessful. However, the protection and subsidies kept it from complete eradication. The GATT was neither a victory nor a defeat; it was a last-minute defensive stop. Certainly it was necessary but it continued the status quo which, of course, was U.S. dominance, creeping ever upward. Summarizing the GATT pact *Variety* declared, "If the U.S. had lost the series, it was the MPAA's Jack Valenti who had struck out." By choosing a hard-line approach, "Valenti managed to rally previously apathetic Europeans behind the French position."[106]

A more somber assessment came from French producer Marin Karmitz: "The real battle at the moment is over who is going to be allowed to control the world's images, and so sell a certain lifestyle, a certain culture, certain products and certain ideas. With the globalization of satellite and cable systems, that is what is at stake." Marauding across the globe, Hollywood intended to standardize the world's taste at the level of *Jurassic Park* and Sylvester Stallone's *Cliffhanger.* Remarked French philosopher and writer Regis Debray, "An American monoculture would inflict a sad future on the world, one in which the planet is converted to a global supermarket where people have to chose between the local ayatollah and Coca-Cola."[107]

One year later, late in 1994, Valenti was in Europe where he announced a cash grant to a Spanish media business school because a renaissance of European film was "a prime objective of all of us." Also at that time the MPEA was renamed the Motion Picture Association which gave it an acronym, MPA, very close to that of the MPAA. Officially the name change was to emphasize the global nature of the film industry and the links between MPAA members and European film industry as a whole. How a name change did that was unstated. Perhaps the word "export" had taken on unfavorable connotations in too many minds. It was part of a feeble peacemaking effort by Valenti, as was the cash grant. But his real reason for being in Europe was to lobby the foreigners again. In Brussels the E.C. was considering whether or not to revise the 1989 "Television Without Frontiers" directive which set the TV quotas at a European-made majority "where practicable," a vague definition. Someone must have reined Valenti in back home before they unleashed him on Europe again for when he appeared in Brussels he did not let loose with his customary harangue, but simply urged the E.C. to exercise restraint in drafting any new directive, telling them that imposing quotas would only damage the European industry in the end. There were times when Valenti was one of Hollywood's more formidable enemies.[108]

During an early 1995 meeting of E.C. culture ministers there was reportedly little support for stricter quotas; a few nations favored it, a few opposed, some had other ideas. By March the E.C. was prepared to debate the TV quota directive as it was, to discuss whether or not to delete the "where applicable" phrase which had been used by many of the E.C. nations as a loophole. With the phrase gone, the directive would be toughened. Additionally a welter of other proposals were to be considered, opening the possibility of months and years of European discussion of the matter. On one point the E.C. ministers were unanimous: to double the money given to the film and television industry over the coming five years to $495 million, most for distribution, training and development.[109]

The foreign share of the cartel's total income was as high as 50 percent in 1973, then dropped to 40.7 percent in 1978, 46 percent in 1979 and 44 percent in 1980. For 1980 Hollywood's majors received rentals of $2.1 billion of which foreign receipts totaled $910 million. A 1985 survey by the European Parliament showed the U.S. held 70 percent of the Greek market, 80 percent in the Netherlands and 92 percent in Britain. American films took 70 percent of Italy's business in 1990 and in Spain that year Hollywood outgrossed home product by $253 million to $29.4 million. Two years later, in 1992, American films took 77 percent of Spain's theatrical business with $363 million from the box office while collaring 85 percent of the home video market, for $320 million.[110]

By 1990 the U.S. film industry's revenues from foreign theatrical release had risen to $1.94 billion. At the same time its overseas television revenues were $2.33 billion, home video revenues stood at $2.39 billion and its foreign pay–TV revenues were $320 million. CNN was then accessible in 136 nations and territories, up from two in 1982.[111]

Worldwide theatrical film rentals in 1989 for the U.S. majors was almost $3.13 billion (up 28 percent from the prior record of $2.43 billion set in 1988). That take consisted of $1.78 billion domestically (up 26 percent from $1.41 billion in 1988) and $1.35 billion foreign (up 32 percent from $1.02 billion in 1988). Just a decade earlier, theatrical rentals accounted for 80 percent of a movie's total receipts; in 1989 it was down to 30 percent. Over the decade of the 1980s, revenue from all media at least quadrupled from $2.5 billion to $10 billion. "And the principle driving force of this media and revenue expansion is the flow of feature films from theaters into what is essentially 'subsequent run.'" The top five export markets contributed 53.1 percent of the total foreign take in 1989; 77.3 percent from the top 10 markets and 85.2 percent from the top 15 markets. The five biggest markets were Japan 15 percent, $201.6 million; Canada 11.3 percent, $152.5 million; France 9.5 percent, $127.6 million; West Germany 8.7 percent, $117.5 million; U.K./Ireland 8.6 percent, $115.3 million.[112]

In the first six months of 1994 the majors took $870 million in foreign rentals, $511 million from Europe, $261 million from the Far East and Australasia, $82 million from Latin America. Warner took $198.2 million (22 percent), Universal $165.9 million (19 percent), Columbia/TriStar $145.4 million (17 percent), Disney $144.7 million (17 percent), Fox $120.3 million (14 percent), Paramount $73.6 million (8 percent), MGM/UA $4.9 million (1 percent). Illustrating how insignificant income from pick-ups could be was that UIP took $16.5 million (2 percent) of its combined gross from that source. For the full year of 1994 the majors grossed $4.07 billion from theatrical release with domestic sources contributing $2.03 billion versus $2.04 billion from foreign locales. When Canada was included with the U.S., the domestic/foreign split was $2.16 billion/$1.91 billion.[113]

For 1994, *Variety* estimated that the worldwide box office gross receipts were $8.34 billion—domestically it was $5.39 billion on 1.29 billion tickets sold—with American films accounting for 90 percent of that total. Buena Vista took an estimated $1.66 billion worldwide, Warner had $1.39 billion, Universal grossed $1.31 billion, Paramount took over $1 billion—no estimates were made for Columbia/Tristar, Fox and MGM/UA, however, a second article listed the foreign box office grosses for those three (domestic receipts would have to be added) at $768 million, $481 million and $55 million respectively. Some of that money would go back to independent producers, domestic and foreign, from pick-ups distributed by the majors. Still, the above figures totaled $6.66 billion of the $8.34 billion total (80 percent) with domestic grosses absent for three majors. Noting that Europeans were becoming more "thin-skinned" about the survival of their cultural heritage, the majors were assuming an extremely low profile with respect to their domination, observed *Variety*. The paper which also commented that while moviegoing was on the rise in industrialized nations, "the position held by national film industries is eroding as U.S. pix gain ground."[114]

Hollywood had complained for decades that without foreign income they would not survive. Domestically the cartel claimed it did not do well. Merrill Lynch analyst Harold Vogel said in 1989 that only one film in twenty turned a profit at the box office with maybe three or four out of ten being profitable when all ancillary sources such as TV sales, home video, etc., were included. That was true only if one accepted Hollywood's creative accounting. Already mentioned herein was the example from the 1930s of padded expenses, which continues to this day. *Forrest Gump* had a worldwide box office gross of $480.9 million at the close of 1994, much higher now. Winston Groom sold the rights to his book to Paramount for $350,000 plus a percentage of the net profit. When he got his statement in 1995, Paramount informed him he got no more money; *Gump* had run a loss.[115]

Writer/humorist Art Buchwald took a film idea to Paramount in 1983 with the studio signing a deal to turn it into a film. Buchwald was to receive $65,000 plus 1.5 percent of the net with his partner Alain Bernheim to get $200,000 plus 17.5 percent of the net profit, to produce the film. Nothing happened for years with Buchwald assuming Paramount had changed its mind and scrapped the idea, not unusual in Hollywood. Then he saw the 1988 release *Coming to America* with the story credited to the movie's star Eddie Murphy. Buchwald recognized it as his idea. The two men sued and won a decision which ruled they were entitled to the money due them from their original contract. A second phase of the trial was held to determine how much profit the film had made. *Coming to America* was one of the ten top-grossing films of 1988, taking $275 million worldwide at the box office. Through December 23, 1989, Paramount declared it had received $125.3 million as producer/distributor. Expenses were: distribution fee $42.3 million, distribution costs $36.2 million, other costs $58.5 million (including $39.5 million of development, production and post-production costs; overhead charges of $8 million; $10 million to Eddie Murphy, $1 million for director John Landis) and interest costs of $6.4 million. Thus expenses totaled $143.4 million, leaving the film with a loss to that date of $18.1 million. Negative cost was the $58.5 million. The $8 million

added on (16 percent) was a way of charging off the cost of plant and personnel not involved directly in the film's production such as maintenance personnel, clerical staff and so on. Commented Richard Stevenson in the *New
York Times*, "Charging such a fee is standard industry practice, although industry executives say it usually amounts to far more than a film's fair share of maintaining a studio's lot." Note also that Paramount charged a distribution fee of
$42.3 to itself and distribution costs of $36.2 million (including $15.7 mil-
lion advertising in the U.S. and $8.3 million in foreign advertising). Para-
mount should have charged only one off. The $42.3 million was paid to Para-
mount the distributor which should have then called it income, deducting the
$36.2 million. Or, if Paramount was not pretending it was two separate com-
panies, then Paramount should have deducted only the $36.2 million from its
books, not the $42.3 million in addition. The $6.4 million in interest cost was
Paramount charging itself to use its own money.[116]

Paramount lawyer Charles Diamond said, "The net profit definition in
our Art Buchwald contract is essentially the same as every contract, not only
with Paramount Pictures but the entire motion picture industry. The books
and records will show the accounting we have provided is honest, straight-
forward and accurate." There was nothing improper about it; everyone in Hollywood had used the same accounting methods for decades, declared the
lawyer. Judge Harvey Schneider called the standard Hollywood accounting
procedures fundamentally flawed. He dismissed Paramount's figures as mere
"sleight-of-hand" accounting, accusing Paramount of "charging overhead on
overhead" and other questionable practices. Schneider decided to determine
the amount due by another route, ultimately awarding Buchwald $150,000 and
Berheim $750,000. Diamond complained, "We are astonished by the unprece-
dented decision to strike down a clearly defined agreement negotiated by well-
represented parties in good faith. It flies in the face of the free market system
for a judge to take this prerogative on himself." While the film ostensibly lost
money, as Stevenson wrote, "the studio and the film's star and director profited
handsomely." Buchwald's legal bills were about $2.5 million with Paramount
spending an estimated $2 to $3 million in legal fees. When it was all over in
1992, after a four-year legal battle, Paramount issued a statement reading, in
part, "This is a victory for Paramount and clearly a loss for Buchwald and Bern-
heim."[117]

Foreign films in America continued to fare dismally. In 1991 films from
other countries (including English-language ones) took less than 2 percent of
the U.S. box office gross. Their best year was in 1973 when they reportedly
took around 9 percent. For 1993 the foreign take was again less than 2 percent. At the end of 1993 the highest grossing foreign films of all time in the
U.S. were *I Am Curious Yellow* (1968) with $22.5 million, *La Dolce Vita* (1961)
with $19.5 million and *Like Water for Chocolate* (1993) with $19.5 million.
While the latter film was likely to become the all-time leader since it was still

in first-run release, it had sold only one-fifth as many tickets, to that date, as did *La Dolce Vita*. The higher earnings were due to higher admission prices. Total domestic box office receipts in 1992 were $4.9 billion with foreign-language films grossing just $22 million of that. English-language foreign imports grossed $44 million that year (arms-length films only, excluding such releases as *Lawnmower Man* nominally a U.K. product but filmed in the U.S. with American financial involvement). Thus the total and true import gross amounted to $66 million of the $4.9 billion domestic gross, just 1.3 percent, which (said *Variety*) was "a typical result over the past decade."[118]

9. Monoculture

Sometime before his death in 1924, Vladimir I. Lenin commented that "capitalism's world-historical tendency to break down national barriers, obliterate national distinctions and to assimilate nations is a tendency which manifests itself more and more powerfully with every passing decade...." Although he was not talking about the motion picture industry, or the U.S. specifically, Lenin's remarks are appropriate in describing what America has done and is doing to the world's film industry.[1]

When European writer and contributor to *The Nation* Daniel Singer observed in 1994 that Rambo was splashed all over Asia, that recent American soaps, sitcoms and movies dominated the TV screens of Western Europe while older (and cheaper) U.S. material did the same in Eastern Europe, he warned, "If this trend is allowed to continue, we will be sentenced to a sinister uniformity of heroes and models, metaphors and dreams. Mastery of the image may well become both the instrument and the symbol of leadership in the new world order."[2]

Hollywood likes to claim that the world is dominated by American films because the world selects them and loves U.S. movies best of all, but as Alexander Cockburn wrote, "It has actually been force-fed to the world through the careful engineering of taste, ruthless commercial clout, arm-twisting by the U.S. Departments of Commerce and State, threats of reverse trade embargoes and other such heavy artillery." Hollywood's cartel has worked through a combination of economic and political pressure rationalized mainly in terms of free trade—but also as a Cold War weapon—driven all the while by the insatiable greed of the producing studios for more and more profits.[3]

People in foreign countries did not exercise free choice in selecting U.S. films over local productions since those local movies were normally foreclosed by unfair trade practices used by the U.S. producers. Through at least the 1970s most Australians had never even seen an Australian movie; most Canadians had never seen a Canadian film. As Canadian film historian Manjunath Pendakur wrote, "Audiences can only be formed for films that are effectively available to them. The free-choice argument is no more than the myth of consumer sovereignty which masks the demand created by film-distributing companies through massive advertising and promotion. Furthermore, the free-choice argument assumes free and open competition between American and Canadian film production and distribution companies for theatrical markets."[4]

With its huge domestic base and quick-to-develop cartel, Hollywood's handful of major studios went on to dominate in fully integrated fashion, producing, distributing and exhibiting at home and abroad. The star system, publicity machinery and huge, plush cinemas were put into place and extended with the large profits flowing to the cartel. It was a business strategy suited to a wealthy cartel, forced into cinemas around the world, which produced more profits and led to greater control. Nations fought back but with little effect. One tactic was for a country to impose restrictive measures (indirect government supports) through such things as screen quotas, import limits and high tariffs. Support measures were direct government aid through film subsidies, easier bank loans, and so forth. Comprehensive steps involved a government simultaneously using both restrictive and supportive tactics. Yet there always seemed to be a snag. When a screen quota was imposed, the exhibitor often turned to a pool of cheaper foreign movies, declining to show any more local movies once he met the quota. Thus the screen quota which was meant to be a minimum often became at the same time a maximum quota. When imports were limited to a certain number per year, extended runs by those films severely curtailed local access. And extended runs could be imposed on local exhibitors through contracts as well as through the practice of block booking wherein an exhibitor was compelled to take a certain number of films from a studio in order to book the single film he was really interested in. Although illegal in America for close to 40 years, the Hollywood cartel members imposed it on nations around the world, and had since 1915.

U.S. mass culture is the most prolific disseminator of images in history. If films are viewed as a medium of expression, then the context for judging its purpose changes from one of profit to one of communications. In broad terms film is a conveyor of a society's values and beliefs. It is a medium through which artists, allied with their culture and their own perceptions, can provide the public with views of life and its problems. It carries images of people and society—all carry ideas and have the power to impart them to the viewers. This is especially so when there are no other images and ideas of other cultures with which to compare them. Often the ideas may be in direct conflict with those of the importing nations.

Hollywood myth is that an individual can change society and can even change the world. Complex reality is simplified. U.S. films cannibalize history and present it through a prism that simply entertains Americans but does not move them to action. Reclaiming and reinterpreting history should be a high priority for decolonized nations. Films can play a vital role in that process but if those films are made to profit from the U.S. market they can hardly serve such a purpose. The state is responsible for the maintenance and perpetuation of national heritage and culture; the authority of the state gives it the mission to preserve and encourage art and culture for it is the only institution representative of its people and their traditions.

State support has been necessary everywhere because of Hollywood's domination of the local markets. Foreign control is in the interests of certain national groups (such as large exhibitor chains) who benefit financially from cooperation with foreign producers and distributors. Hollywood integrates its consumers from the top down; producing a product for mass consumption, then creating a demand for it. There is no common demand from the bottom up, forcing the cartel to produce certain types of movies. The U.S. industry is not subject to public demand, rather the public is the subject of calculation and manipulation by the industry. Film, and all cultural material, are of course, also commodities but to Hollywood they are only commodities with no cultural or artistic facets, no different from ball bearings. Movies such as *Jurassic Park* are programmed for release around the world even before the first script stage. Originality was and is the enemy of this instrumental efficiency, unless co-opted. Thus individuality is reduced to formula. What parades as progress in Hollywood, as the ever new, remains a cloak for an unchanging sameness of the product.

Daniel Singer saw no solution but a radical transformation of society, but "we are not even moving in that direction." He saw the immediate future as gloomy with the expansion of cable, the spread of satellites and Europe's continued deregulation, concluding, "We are actually going the other way."[5]

Meanwhile the cartel got bigger and bigger. A 1994 merger saw media company Viacom Inc. acquire Paramount Communications along with home video concern Blockbuster Entertainment. Among the holdings of this new colossus were 12 TV stations, 14 radio outlets, cable networks MTV, Showtime, the Movie Channel and 1.1 million cable subscribers. Additionally the entity held 1,927 movie screens, 3,500 home video stores, 3,790 films in the Paramount library plus such TV shows (in reruns) as *I Love Lucy* and *Cheers*. One year later, in July 1995, the Walt Disney Co. announced it was buying Capital Cities/ABC, giving Disney one of the Big Three U.S. TV networks, cable stations ESPN, A&E and Lifetime, along with eight TV stations, 21 radio stations plus various other holdings. Both CEOs, Disney's Michael Eisner and Cap Cities' Thomas Murphy, said the key to the merger was the opportunity it provided for Disney to expand overseas. "I could see how I could protect [Disney] for five or six more years being done. But I don't know how I could protect it for another 20 years without some partner to compete in Europe, to get into India and China, to keep access for our children's programs," explained Eisner.[6]

Coming soon to the cinemas, the TV screens and the home video outlets of the world: Hollywood monoculture.

Appendix: Statistics of the United States Film Industry Abroad

U.S. Film Exports and Imports

(Positive and negative exposed film, in feet. Unless otherwise noted, source is *Variety*, August 18, 1926, p. 46.)

	Exports	*Imports*
1913	32,000,000*	16,000,000 **
1917	158,751,786†	
1918	146,342,191§	2,267,975
1919	153,237,260	2,910,284
1920	175,233,307	6,233,463
1921	140,878,345	10,131,884
1922	133,790,618	9,025,646
1923	148,434,916	9,338,623
1924	178,447,606	6,730,691
1925	235,585,794	6,920,993
Total	1,245,496,233	53,559,559

Exports of 1913 and 1925 Compared‡

(In millions of feet unless otherwise indicated)

1913		*1925*		
U.K.	16.7	U.K.	36.0	
other Europe	0.3	France	14.0	(1913: 275,000 feet)
Far East	4.5	Germany	6.5	(1913: 25,000 feet)
Latin America	1.5	Italy	3.0	(1913: 8,000 feet)
		other Europe	26.0	
		Far East	54.0	

*_Variety_, February 17, 1926, p. 35.

†_New York Times_, July 9, 1917, p. 7.

§William W. Sniffen, "World Markets for American Manufacturers," _Scientific American_ 118 (June 8, 1918): 526.

**C.J. North, "Our Foreign Trade in Motion Pictures," _Annals of the American Academy of Political and Social Science_ 128 (Nov. 1926): 108.

‡North, 102.

Percentage of Screen Time Held by U.S. Product

	1930	1951
Argentina	90	35
Australia	—	75
Austria	50	45
Belgium	70	75
Bermuda	90	90
Bolivia	—	65
Brazil	—	70
Britain	75	70
Bulgaria	15	—
Ceylon	85	38
Chile	90	70
China	83	—
Colombia	90	60
Costa Rica	90	85
Cuba	95	70
Czechoslovakia	43	—
Denmark	58	75
Dominican Republic	90	70
Ecuador	80	75
Egypt	70	50
Estonia	75	—
Finland	60	70
France	48	50
Germany	32	40
Greece	50	70
Guatemala	90	70
Haiti	95	70
Holland	75	70
Honduras	90	75
Hungary	60	—

	1930	*1951*
India	80	40
Italy	65	65
Jamaica	90	90
Japan	22	40
Mexico	98	60
New Zealand	88	80
Nicaragua	—	75
Norway	—	55
Panama	100	75
Paraguay	95	60
Peru	90	45
Philippines	95	70
Poland	75	—
Portugal	80	65
Romania	50	—
South Africa	80	70
Spain	85	40
Sweden	75	60
Switzerland	50	50
Syria	75	60
Turkey	80	70
Uruguay	95	50
Venezuela	85	65
Yugoslavia	65	40

Sources: **1930**: Kristin Thompson, *Exporting Entertainment: America in the World Film Market 1907–1934* (London: BFI, 1985), pp. 219–222. **1951**: *International Motion Picture and Television Almanac 1953–54* (New York: Quigley, 1953), pp. 7–9.

Percentage of Screen Time Held by U.S. Product Abroad

Australia	1992:70
Canada	1986:97
Franco-Canada	1992:80
France	1962:28.8
	1985:47
	1989:55
	1993:60
Germany	1978–1980:40–50
	1993:88

Greece	1985:70
India	1970:2
Italy	1990:71
Japan	1993:60
Mexico and Central America	1952:76
Netherlands	1985:80
New Zealand	1992:70
Spain	1993:79
U.K.	1992:80
	1993:93
Europe	1992:85
	1928:60.6
	1985:50
	1992:70
	1993:80
South America	1992:95
	1952:64
	1955:70
Latin America	1915:15
	1936:85
	1939:70
	1949:73
	1960:70
World	1925:75
	1937:70
	1938:65
	1948:72
	1952:74
	1962:60
	1992:62
	1993:85

Sources: **Australia:** *Variety,* June 7, 1993, p. 1. **Canada:** Manjunath Penda-kur, *Canadian Dreams and American Control* (Toronto: Garamond, 1990), p. 266. **Franco-Canada:** *Variety,* Feb. 8, 1993, p. 42. **France:** *Variety,* May 15, 1963, p. 1; *Variety,* Sept. 10, 1986, p. 5; *Variety,* March 21, 1990, p. 38; *Washington Post,* Dec. 15, 1993, p. B2. **Germany:** *Variety,* May 13, 1981, p. 206; *Variety,* Oct. 10, 1994, p. 47. **Greece:** *New York Times,* Sept. 22, 1985, sec. 2, p. 27. **India:** *New York Times,* Aug. 30, 1971, p. 34. **Italy:** *Variety,* Nov. 26, 1990, p. 45. **Japan:** *Variety,* Sept. 19, 1994, p. 59. **Mexico and Central America:** *Variety,* June 17, 1953, p. 3. **Netherlands:** *New York Times,* Sept. 22, 1985, s. 2, p. 27. **New**

Zealand: *Variety,* June 7, 1993, p. 1. **Spain:** *Variety,* Sept. 26, 1994, p. 42. **United Kingdom:** *Variety,* June 7, 1993, p. 1; *Times* (London), Dec. 16, 1993, p. 31.
 Europe: Gaizka S. Usabel, *The High Noon of American Films in Latin America* (Ann Arbor, Mich.: UMI, 1982), p. xv; *Variety,* April 3, 1929, p. 2; *Variety,* Sept. 10, 1986, p. 5; *Variety,* Dec. 20, 1993, p. 27; *New York Times,* Jan. 2, 1994, sec. 2, p. 1. **Latin America:** Kristin Thompson, *Exporting Entertainment: America in the World Film Market 1907–1934* (London: BFI, 1985), p. 81; "Latin Uproar," *Time* 37 (Feb. 10, 1941): 69; "Latin Uproar," 69; Hernane Tavares, "Hollywood Needs Latin America," *Americas* 1 (October 1949): 2; *Variety,* Nov. 8, 1961, p. 3. **South America:** Usabel, p. xv; *Variety,* June 17, 1953, p. 3; *International Motion Picture and Television Almanac 1957* (New York: Quigley, 1958), p. 14A.
 World: C. J. North, "Our Foreign Trade in Motion Pictures," *Annals of the American Academy of Political and Social Science* 128 (Nov. 1926): 101; *Variety,* April 6, 1938, p. 19; *Variety,* March 15, 1939, p. 14; Walter F. Wanger, "Donald Duck and Diplomacy," *Public Opinion Quarterly* 14, no. 3 (Fall 1950): 445; *Variety,* June 17, 1953, p. 3; *Variety,* Nov. 6, 1963, p. 1; *Variety,* June 28, 1993, p. 11; *Times* (London), Dec. 16, 1993, p. 31.

Theatrical Film Receipts

(Figures are expressed in millions of dollars. Canadian figures are definitely included in domestic for 1962 and definitely excluded for 1941, probably included for other years. Gross refers to producer/distributor share of box office receipts. "$ in NY" is money Hollywood has left after all expenses except U.S. corporate taxes.)

	Domestic	Foreign
1926		75
1941	252	140–160
1943		175–200
1944	310	160–170
1945		190
1946		210 gross
		142 $ in NY
1947		124 $ in NY
1948		130 $ in NY
1949		120 $ in NY
1950		120 $ in NY
1951		160 $ in NY
1952	250	140 $ in NY
1955	326	290 gross
1956		217 gross
		170 $ in NY

	Domestic		Foreign
1958	290		300 gross
			215 $ in NY
1960			330 gross
1961	267		278 gross
			210 $ in NY
1962	275		310 gross

	Domestic	Foreign	Total
1963	239.4	293.0	532.4
1964	263.2	319.9	583.1
1965	287.2	343.5	630.7
1966	319.5	361.5	680.9
1967	355.9	357.8	713.7
1968	372.3	339.0	711.3
1969	317.4	348.4	665.8
1970	381.3	360.4	741.7
1971	336.7	347.5	684.2
1972	426.4	388.8	815.2
1973	390.5	415.5	806.0
1974	545.9	501.5	1,047.4
1976	577.0	570.0	1,147.0
1980	1,190.0	910.0	2,100.0
1983	1,297.4	838.8	2,136.2
1984	1,313.2	654.1	1,967.2
1985	1,109.1	619.9	1,729.0
1986	1,165.1	798.3	1,963.4
1987	1,244.5	935.1	2,179.6
1988	1,413.6	1,020.3	2,433.9
1989	1,780.0	1,350.0	3,130.0
1990*	1,829.0	1,649.5	3,478.5
1991	1,840.0	1,430.0	3,270.0
1992	2,000.0	1,440.0	3,440.0
1994	2,039.5	2,040.0	4,079.5

Sources: Figures for the following years are taken from *Variety*, issue dates and page numbers as noted: **1926:** August 17, 1927, p. 8. **1941:** Sept. 2, 1942, p. 5. **1943:** Oct. 25, 1944, p. 1. **1944:** Jan. 3, 1945, p. 3. **1945:** Feb. 5, 1947, p. 5. **1946:** Feb. 5, 1947, p. 5; Dec. 3, 1952, p. 3. **1947–1951:** Dec. 3, 1952, p. 3. **1952:**

*In 1990 all U.S. film companies not MPAA members grossed $254.2 million in foreign income. Thus, of the $1,903.7 million in total foreign income, the majors took 86 percent.

June 3, 1953, p. 1. **1955:** Sept. 12, 1962, p. 3. **1956:** April 10, 1957, p. 1. **1958** (except $ in NY): May 27, 1959, p. 7. **1960:** Sept. 6, 1961, p. 7. **1961:** Sept. 12, 1962, p. 3; April 29, 1964, p. 33. **1962:** Nov. 6, 1963, p. 1. **1963–1973:** May 15, 1974, p. 34. **1974:** June 25, 1975, p. 30. **1976:** Aug. 24, 1977, p. 1. **1983–1988:** June 14, 1989, p. 11. **1989:** June 13, 1990, p. 7. **1990:** June 17, 1991, p. 10. **1991–1992:** June 28, 1993, p. 11. **1994:** May 1, 1995, p. 32. Figure for $ in NY for **1958** is taken from the *New York Times*, Feb. 4, 1959, p. 27. Figure for **1980** is taken from Michael Dempsey, "Selling American Films Overseas," *American Film* 7 (Nov. 1981): 58.

World Gross Film Receipts for Major Studios, From All Sources
(Including theatrical release, home video, pay–TV, free TV)

1980: $2.5 billion—of which $2.1 billion (84%) from theatrical release
1989: $10 billion
1992: $14-15 billion—of which $3.44 billion (25%) from theatrical release
1993: $18 billion—of which $8 billion from foreign sources, $4 billion of that from Western Europe

Sources: **1980, 1989**: *Variety*, June 13, 1990, p. 7. **1992, 1993**: *Variety*, December 20, 1993, p. 27.

Top 15 Markets
(Gross receipts for the majors, in millions of dollars)

1963		1973	
U.K.	32.7	Italy	43.1
Italy	28.9	Canada	39.5
West Germany	25.4	West Germany	32.2
France	22.8	U.K.	31.9
Japan	18.8	France	31.6
Canada	16.8	Japan	31.3
Spain	13.3	Australia	29.9
Australia	10.7	South Africa	16.2
Mexico	7.5	Brazil	16.0
Brazil	7.2	Spain	15.5
South Africa	6.7	Mexico	12.3
Argentina	5.5	Sweden	7.2
Belgium	5.0	Switzerland	5.9
Venezuela	4.3	Venezuela	5.4
Sweden	4.2	Argentina	5.0

1990		*1992*	
Japan	236.7	Japan	165.1
West Germany	175.2	Germany	162.3
France	164.2	France	141.0
Canada	148.3	Canada	130.4
U.K./Ireland	144.4	U.K./Ireland	127.4
Italy	117.0	Spain	122.5
Spain	110.4	Australia	67.4
Australia	70.4	Italy	65.2
Brazil	48.4	South Korea	39.6
Sweden	39.8	Mexico	36.9
South Korea	34.9	Sweden	31.8
Switzerland	27.5	Belgium	26.1
Taiwan	26.9	Switzerland	24.3
Belgium	26.4	Argentina	24.2
Netherlands	24.8	Brazil	23.1

Sources: **1963, 1973**: *Variety*, May 29, 1974, p. 20. **1990**: *Variety*, June 17, 1991, p. 10. **1992**: *Variety*, June 28, 1993, p. 11.

Notes

Chapter 1

1. Victoria de Grazia. "Mass Culture and Sovereignty: The American Challenge to European Cinemas, 1920–1960." *Journal of Modern History.* 61:63 March, 1989.

2. Erik Barnouw and S. Krishnaswamy. *Indian Film.* 2nd ed. New York: Oxford, 1980, p. 10; Thelma Gutsche. *The History and Social Significance of Motion Pictures in South Africa 1895–1940.* Cape Town: Howard Timmins, 1972, p. 108.

3. Randal Johnson. *The Film Industry in Brazil: Culture and the State.* Pittsburgh: University of Pittsburgh Press, 1987, pp. 24–25, 32.

4. Gaiza S. Usabel. *The High Noon of American Films in Latin America.* Ann Arbor: UMI, 1982, pp. xv, 3.

5. Ina Bertrand and William D. Routt. "The Big Bad Combine" in Albert Moran, ed. *The Australian Screen.* Melbourne: Penguin, 1989, pp. 5, 9.

6. "American Pictures the Best." *Variety.* 14:11 March 20, 1909; Diane Collins. *Hollywood Down Under.* North Ryde, NSW: Angus & Robertson, 1987, p. 46.

7. "Gaumont in Canada." *Variety.* 16:12 October 23, 1909.

8. Manjunath Pendakur. *Canadian Dreams and American Control.* Toronto: Garamond, 1990, p. 49.

9. Ibid., p. 132.

10. Kristin Thompson. *Exporting Entertainment: America in the World Film Market 1907–1934.* London: BFI, 1985, pp. 2–5; John A. Lent. *The Asian Film Industry.* London: Christopher Helm, 1990, p. 150.

11. Kristin Thompson, op. cit., p. 39.

12. Ibid., p. 41.

13. "Movie-itis in Central America." *Literary Digest.* 49:590 September 26, 1914.

14. Kristin Thompson, op. cit., p. 45.

15. Ibid., pp. 29, 31, 35, 37.

16. "Better Films in Europe." *New York Times.* September 11, 1913, p. 4; "Pictures in China." *Variety.* 31:8 July 25, 1913.

17. "Chinese Film Market." *Variety.* 43:27 August 11, 1916.

18. "Americans to Oppose Pathé in English Picture Market." *Variety.* 30:15 March 7, 1913.

19. Raymond Moley. *The Hays Office.* Indianapolis: Bobbs-Merrill, 1945, p. 169.

20. Kristin Thompson, op. cit., pp. 3, 12–13, 17.

21. Ephraim Katz. *The Macmillan International Film Encyclopedia.* new ed. New York: HarperCollins, 1994, p. 799.

22. Thelma Gutsche, op. cit., p. 139.

23. Raymond Moley, op. cit., pp. 20–21.

24. Ibid., pp. 30–31.

25. Ian Jarvie. *Hollywood's Overseas Campaign: The North Atlantic Movie Trade, 1920–1950.* Cambridge: Cambridge University Press, 1992, p. 276.

26. Barry Monush, ed. *International Motion Picture Almanac 1994.* 65th ed. New York: Quigley, 1994, pp. 514–519; Leslie Halliwell. *Halliwell's Filmgoer's and Video Viewer's Companion.* 7th ed. London: Grafton, 1988, p. 592.

27. Barry Monush, op. cit., pp. 512–513.

28. Aubrey Solomon. *Twentieth Century–Fox: A Corporate and Financial History.* Metuchen, New Jersey: Scarecrow, 1988, pp. 4–5.

29. Kristin Thompson, op. cit., pp. 72–73, 81.

30. Gaizka S. Usabel, op. cit., p. xv; "South American Trade." *Variety.* 42:26 May 26, 1916; "Chance Seen to Clean Up Big Picture Profits Now in Mexico." *Variety.* 56:64 November 21, 1919.

31. Kristin Thompson, op. cit., p. 50; "Bright Outlook for Features." *Variety.* 36:23 October 10, 1914; "Movies Prosper in Europe." *New York Times.* December 15, 1914, p. 13.

32. Ina Bertrand, op. cit., p. 14.

33. Kristin Thompson, op. cit., pp. 55, 77.

34. "U.S. Replacing Italian Films." *Variety.* 54:97 March 28, 1919.

35. Randal Johnson, op. cit., p. 37.

36. "Movies in Japan." *New York Times Magazine.* November 26, 1916, sec. 5, p. 3; "Film in South America." *Variety.* 41:24 February 18, 1916.

37. "Foreign Film Buyers Pool Their American Purchases." *Variety.* 44:32 September 22, 1916.

38. Kristin Thompson, op. cit., p. 83; "English Open Market Doomed as Film Makers Deal Direct." *Variety.* 40:17 September 10, 1915.

39. "Britons Criticise Films." *New York Times.* December 27, 1916, sec. 3, p. 9.

40. "English Complain Against Americans' Lack of Interest." *Variety.* 39:4 July 30, 1915.

41. Kristin Thompson, op. cit., pp. 86, 89.

42. Manjunath Pendakur, op. cit., p. 45; Kristin Thompson, op. cit., pp. 93–94.

43. Kristin Thompson, op. cit., pp. 93, 95–96.

44. Ibid., pp. 97–99.

45. William W. Sniffen. "World Markets for American Manufacturers." *Scientific American.* 118:526 June 8, 1918.

46. Samuel Goldwyn. "Our Movies Speak for U.S." *Saturday Review of Literature.* 33:11 April 1, 1950.

47. Kristin Thompson, op. cit., p. 93.

48. William W. Sniffen, op. cit.

49. "France and Pictures." *Variety.* 53:183 December 27, 1918.

50. Kristin Thompson, op. cit., pp. 101–103.

51. Ibid., p. 104.

52. "Foreign Sales Outlook Poor." *Variety.* 60:38 November 12, 1920; "Foreign Market Dead." *Variety.* 61:30 December 24, 1920; Randall Johnson. op. cit., p. 36; Thelma Gutsche, op. cit., p. 141.

53. "The Superiority of American to European Films as Explained by a French Critic." *Current Opinion.* 63:250–251 October, 1917.

54. "Films for Germany." *Variety.* 53:41 January 3, 1919; "Germans Bar American Films." *Variety.* 56:66 October 10, 1919.

55. "Canadian Legislation May Cut U.S. Film Importation." *Variety.* 53:57 January 31, 1919.

56. "Danger of Foreign Films." *Variety.* 52:54 October 4, 1918.

57. "British Cinema Exhibitors to Fight American Invasion." *Variety.* 55:78 August 15, 1919; "Distribution in England." *Variety.* 56:64 September 26, 1919.

58. "U.S. Film Enterprise in Britain." *Times* (London). June 25, 1919, p. 9; "Protest Film Invasion." *New York Times.* July 16, 1919, p. 13; "Drastic Film Boycott Proposed." *Times* (London). July 16, 1919, p. 10.

59. "The Movie Crisis." *New York Times.* July 19, 1919, p. 8.

Chapter 2

1. Raymond Moley. *The Hays Office.* Indianapolis: Bobbs-Merrill, 1945, pp. 32, 47–48, 172; Ian Jarvie. *Hollywood's Overseas Campaign: The North Atlantic Movie Trade, 1920–1950.* Cambridge: Cambridge University Press, 1992, p. 295.

2. Raymond Moley, op. cit., p. 5; Dan E. Moldea. *Dark Victory.* New York: Viking, 1986, pp. 25–26.

3. "U.S. Films in World Accord." *Variety.* 86:5 February 9, 1927; Liz-Anne Bawden, ed. *The Oxford Companion to Film.* New York: Oxford, 1976, p. 480; Raymond Moley, op. cit., pp. 53, 55–59, 70, 82–83.

4. Ian Jarvie, op. cit., p. 295.

5. Roger Shaw. "American Movies Abroad." *Review of Reviews.* 78:80 July, 1928.

6. Diane Collins. *Hollywood Down Under.* North Ryde, NSW: Angus & Robertson, 1987, p. 13; Ina Bertrand, ed. *Cinema in Australia: A Documentary History.* Kensington, NSW: New South Wales University Press, 1989, p. 71; John Tulloch. *Australian Cinema: Industry, Narrative and Meaning.* Sydney: George Allen & Unwin, 1982, pp. 58, 60.

7. Manjunath Pendakur. *Canadian Dreams and American Control.* Toronto: Garamond Press, 1990, pp. 80–81.

8. Ian Jarvie, op. cit., pp. 32–33; Manjunath Pendakur. op. cit., pp. 81–82.

9. Diane Collins, op. cit., p. 65.

10. Ibid., pp. 149, 151, 158–159.

11. Ibid., pp. 161–162.

12. Ibid., p. 163.

13. Ibid., pp. 146–149.

14. Erik Barnouw and S. Krishnaswamy. *Indian Film.* 2nd ed. New York: Oxford, 1980, p. 50.

15. Ibid., pp. 40–41; Charles Higham. *Warner Brothers.* New York: Scribner's 1975, pp. 40–42, 80.

16. O. R. Geyer. "Winning Foreign Film Markets." *Scientific American.* 125:132 August 20, 1921.

17. Manjunath Pendakur, op. cit., pp. 58–59; Ian Jarvie, op. cit., pp 25, 33; "Canada's Offense at Our Movies." *Literary Digest.* 86:27 August 16, 1925.

18. Kristin Thompson. *Exporting Entertainment: America in the World Film Market 1907–1934.* London: BFI, 1985, p. 126.

19. "Foreign Governments Opposing U.S. Films Obliging Americans to Buy or Build Abroad." *Variety.* 88:15 September 7, 1927.

20. "Around the World with Paramount." *Variety.* 96:6, 66 August 7, 1929.

21. C. J. North. "Our Silent Ambassadors." *The Independent.* 116:690 June 12, 1926.

22. Thelma Gutsche. *The History and Social Significance of Motion Pictures in South Africa 1895–1940*. Cape Town: Howard Timmins, 1972, pp. 118–119, 191–194.

23. Erik Barnouw, op. cit., p. 47.

24. Manjunath Pendakur, op. cit., pp. 76–77.

25. "Booking of Films." *Times* (London). April 29, 1921, p. 7; "Loew Advises British to Learn Movie Game." *New York Times*. June 17, 1926, p. 21.

26. "Hits American Films New Zealand Sees." *New York Times*. October 13, 1926, p. 23.

27. "American Movies Popular in Chile." *New York Times*. August 6, 1922, p. 18.

28. "The Movie Business in Buenos Aires." *Bulletin of the Pan American Union*. 58:286 March, 1924.

29. Erik Barnouw, op. cit., p. 42.

30. Ina Bertrand and William D. Routt. "The Big Bad Combine" in Albert Moran and Tom O'Regan, eds. *The Australian Screen*. Melbourne: Penguin, 1989, p. 14.

31. Erik Barnouw, op. cit., p. 46; George Mooser. "Japan and the Near East." *Variety*. 72:19 September 6, 1923; "Motion Pictures for China." *New York Times*. June 20, 1920, sec. 2, p. 11.

32. "Government Is Interested in Export Raw Pictures." *Variety*. 63:38 July 22, 1921; "How Our Films Misrepresent America Abroad." *Literary Digest*. 71:28 November 26, 1921.

33. "Sexy Films for Abroad." *Variety*. 84:1, 75 August 18, 1926; Charles Merz. "When the Movies Go Abroad." *Harper's Monthly Magazine*. 152:163 January, 1926.

34. "Germany Puts Ban on American Movies." *New York Times*. December 12, 1920, sec. 2, p. 1.

35. Kristin Thompson, op. cit., p. 106.

36. "Nat'l Ass'n Would Have U.S. Fight Foreign Film Embargo." *Variety*. 61:47 February 18, 1921.

37. "All Hollywood Now Lining Up Against German Made Films." *Variety*. 62:1–2 May 20, 1921.

38. "600 American Films Annually Are Suitable for German's Use." *Variety*. 77:26 December 24, 1924; "American Films in German Houses Are Liked and Disliked." *Variety*. 76:26 September 17, 1924; "German Producers Want Imported Pictures Limited." *Variety*. 76:22 September 3, 1924.

39. "Would Bar All Our Films." *New York Times*. September 13, 1924, p. 26; "Hays Will Speak to Film Men of Foreign Sales Departments." *Variety*. 77:26 December 17, 1924.

40. Courtney Ryley Cooper. "Films Across the Sea." *Saturday Evening Post*. 198:27 June 5, 1926.

41. Kristin Thompson, op. cit., pp. 106–107.

42. "German View of Our Films." *Literary Digest*. 90:22 July 17, 1926.

43. Lincoln Eyre. "American Has Grip on German Movies." *New York Times*. November 11, 1925, p. 25.

44. "Germany Restricts Use of Our Films." *New York Times*. December 27, 1925, sec. 8, p. 3.

45. Kristin Thompson, op. cit., pp. 108–111; "American Film Men Make German Deal." *New York Times*. December 31, 1925, p. 10.

46. "Europe Awaiting Outcome of British Film Quota Bill." *Variety*. 87:13 June 15, 1927.

47. "German Owners Attack U.S. Films." *Variety*. 84:9 September 15, 1926.

48. Ibid., "Film Quota in Germany." *Literary Digest*. 94:29 August 27, 1927.

49. "German 2-for-1 Plan Now Possible." *Variety*. 87:4, 15 July 20, 1927; "Germany

Abolishes Contingent 1-1; Cuts Down Foreign Film Importations." *Variety.* 89:9 November 30, 1927; "German Film Rules in Effect Next July." *Variety.* 93:6 December 19, 1928.

50. "Germany Movement Foreseen." *Variety.* 93:6 December 26, 1928.

51. "German Restrictions for Club on American Pictures." *Variety.* 94:6 January 23, 1929.

52. "French Movie Plan Worries Americans." *New York Times.* December 13, 1927, p. 7; "Film Ratio Decree Planned by France." *New York Times.* January 28, 1928, p. 1; John Carter. "Hollywood Has a Foreign War." *New York Times.* March 4, 1928, sec. 10, p. 13.

53. "Paris Movie Houses Threaten to Close." *New York Times.* February 2, 1928, p. 17; "French Defer Curb on American Films." *New York Times.* March 29, 1928, p. 24; "French Film Rules as Sales Forcing Device." *Variety.* 90:5 March 21, 1928.

54. "French Defer Curb on American Films." *New York Times.* March 29, 1928, p. 24; "Need Action to Protect U.S. Films in France." *Variety.* 90:5 March 7, 1928.

55. Raymond Moley, op. cit., p. 174; "Europe Needs Advice." *Variety.* 90:3 March 7, 1928.

56. "French Defer Curb on American Films." *New York Times.* April 5, 1928, p. 10.

57. "Reprisal Talked of Against French If Herriott's Severe." *Variety.* 90:10 April 4, 1928.

58. "France Recedes—Or Else." *Variety.* 91:3 April 25, 1928; "France Abandons 4-to-1 Film Quota." *New York Times.* May 4, 1928, p. 6.

59. "France Abandons 4-to-1 Films Quota." *New York Times.* May 4, 1928, pp. 1, 6; "Americans Accept French Film Plan." *New York Times.* May 5, 1928, p. 4; "The Film-Flam War." *The Independent.* 120:468 May 19, 1928.

60. Ian Jarvie, op. cit., p. 321.

61. "French Film Peace Desired by Poncet." *New York Times.* April 21, 1929, p. 4.

62. "Sapene Utters Downright Boycott Threat Against American Trade." *Variety.* 94:2, 60 March 27, 1929.

63. "French Exhibs Raise Protest Against More Quota Barriers." *Variety.* 94:2 March 13, 1929; "Our Film Men Plan French Quota Fight." *New York Times.* March 28, 1929, p. 31; "French Film Men Cling to Quota." *New York Times.* April 18, 1929, p. 9.

64. "Americans Protest French Film Quota." *New York Times.* April 12, 1929, p. 29.

65. "French Quota Smashed by Washington." *Variety.* 95:2 May 8, 1929; Carlisle MacDonald. "French Again Seek 3-to-1 Film Quota." *New York Times.* May 18, 1929, p. 6; Carlisle MacDonald. "French Recommend New 4-to-1 Film Quota." *New York Times.* May 28, 1929, p. 7; "Americans Reject French Film Quota." *New York Times.* June 6, 1929, p. 8.

66. "Hints at Reprisals on French Exports." *New York Times.* June 8, 1929, p. 4; "Sapene Centre Entire French Situation." *Variety.* 95:6 June 5, 1929; "French Quota Reaches Floor of Senate." *Variety.* 95:9 June 12, 1929; "Washington's Stand on French Quota Row Staggers Americans." *Variety.* 95:9 June 12, 1929.

67. "1,000 Lose Film Jobs in French Quota Fight." *New York Times.* June 15, 1929, p. 18; Carlisle MacDonald. "French Link Films to Our Trade Rise." *New York Times.* September 10, 1929, p. 11.

68. Carlisle MacDonald. "French Fix Accord With U.S. on Films." *New York Times.* September 20, 1929, p. 7; "French Rush to Take on U.S. Films under Latest Quota." *Variety.* 96:5 September 25, 1929.

69. Ian Jarvie, op. cit., p. 332.

70. Gaizka S. Usabel, op. cit., p. 79; "French Loathe Our Films But British Enjoy Them." *New York Times.* July 5, 1925, sec. 7, p. 3.

71. Reginald Wright Kauffman. "War in the Film World." *North American Review.* 229:351–353 March, 1930; "Down With American Films." *Review of Reviews.* 81:116–117 April, 1930.

72. "Shun Tax on Our Films." *New York Times.* July 5, 1923, p. 14; "British Movie Makers Score American Films." *New York Times.* September 9, 1923, p. 20.

73. "England Would Stop Invasion of American-Made Pictures." *Variety.* 72:24 September 13, 1923; "Hays Will Speak to Film Men of Foreign Sales Departments." *Variety.* 77:26 December 17, 1924.

74. "British Film Field." *Variety.* 88:12 September 7, 1927.

75. "Shall Britons be Slaves to Our Films?" *Literary Digest.* 85:35 June 6, 1925; "More British Movie Agony." *Literary Digest.* 85:27 June 20, 1925.

76. "Our Films in England." *New York Times.* May 16, 1925, p. 16; "Their Novelties Need No Protection." *New York Times.* August 5, 1926, p. 20.

77. "British Films." *Times* (London). June 23, 1925, p. 17.

78. "The Film World." *Times* (London). August 25, 1925, p. 8; "British Films." *Times* (London). December 15, 1925, p. 17; "The Film World." *Times* (London). July 13, 1926, p. 12; "French Loathe Our Films But British Enjoy Them." *New York Times.* July 5, 1925, sec. 7, p. 3.

79. "Seek to Save British Films." *New York Times.* December 29, 1925, p. 5.

80. "British Merger for Quota." *Variety.* 86:5, 21 March 30, 1927; "British Quota Bill Under Inspection in Washington But No Action Likely." *Variety.* 87:3 April 20, 1927.

81. "British Film Field." *Variety.* 88:12 September, 1927.

82. Victoria de Grazia. "Mass Culture and Sovereignty: The American Challenge to European Cinemas 1920–1960." *Journal of Modern History.* 61:51 March, 1989.

83. Ian Jarvie, op. cit., pp. 115, 318.

84. Roger Shaw. "American Movies Abroad." *Review of Reviews.* 78:78 July, 1928; John Carter. "Hollywood Has a Foreign War." *New York Times.* March 4, 1928, sec. 10, p. 13; Frank Tilley. "Will U.S. Put Down Whip and 'Play Ball' on British Quota?" *Variety.* 90:13 February 8, 1928.

85. Manjunath Pendakur, op. cit., p. 85; John MacCormac. "London Film Notes." *New York Times.* December 9, 1928, sec. 10, p. 7; Raymond Moley, op. cit., pp. 178–179.

86. "Polish Gov't Confounded." *Variety.* 84:3 September 1, 1926; "Warsaw Resents Foreign Meddling." *Variety.* 85:4 December 8, 1926; "Poland's Mixed Dilemma." *Variety.* 85:5, 10 January 5, 1927.

87. "Film Boycott on Hungary." *New York Times.* March 6, 1926, p. 13; "American Films Taken Out of Hungary." *Variety.* 82:30 March 31, 1926; "Austria Rearranges American Film Quota." *New York Times.* January 26, 1927, p. 16; "American Films Hit Again." *New York Times.* July 3, 1929, p. 19; "Hays Protests Film Ban." *New York Times.* February 24, 1929, p. 2.

88. Kristin Thompson, op. cit., p. 104.

89. "Austria's 10 to 1 Only Raising Import Licenses." *Variety.* 85:10 January 12, 1927; "Austria's 10 for 1." *Variety.* 85:4 December 8, 1926; "Austria Rearranges American Film Quota." *New York Times.* January 26, 1927, p. 16.

90. "Czecho-Slovakia Declaring Its Own Film Quota System." *Variety.* 93:6 October 17, 1928.

91. "Italy's Picture Quota Bill to Promote Native Industry." *Variety.* 87:1, 51 April 27, 1927.

92. "Italy's Personality Made Conditions for U.S. Films May Mean None at All." *Variety.* 93:6 December 26, 1928.

93. Helen Ormsbee. "Europe's Film Quotas." *New York Times.* February 19, 1928, sec. 8, p. 3.

94. "Survival of Fittest in Films Abroad." *Variety*. 86:4 April 27, 1927; "Foreign Resentment Is Hot Against U.S. Films." *Variety*. 82:24 April 14, 1926.

95. "How to Handle Europe for American Films." *Variety*. 93:4 November 21, 1928; "Europe's Solid Front." *Variety*. 92:6 September 12, 1926; "Hollywood, Unlimited." *New York Times*. December 21, 1927, p. 24.

96. "German and Italian Trusts Merge to Fight our Films." *Variety*. 59:39 June 25, 1920; "For Movie Locarno Against Our Films." *New York Times*. October 9, 1926, p. 6.

97. "Deplores Barriers Against Our Movies." *New York Times*. August 4, 1927, p. 25; Ian Jarvie, op. cit., p. 325.

98. Diane Collins, op. cit., pp. 13, 51; John Tulloch, op. cit., pp. 36, 67.

99. John Tulloch, op. cit., pp. 27, 32, 35; Diane Collins, op. cit., p. 64.

100. "Australian Film Importers Protest Against Taxation." *Variety*. 64:62 September 2, 1921.

101. "Australian Hostility to Our Films." *Literary Digest*. 78:20 September 29, 1923.

102. "Australia's 25% Tax on U.S. films." *Variety*. 81:30 February 3, 1926.

103. "Australia Prefers Our Films." *Literary Digest*. 94:27–28 September 10, 1927; Ina Bertrand, ed., op. cit., p. 75.

104. "Australia and Britain Work to Cut Down American Films in Australia." *Variety*. 91:6 July 4, 1928.

105. "Movie Influence Assailed." *New York Times*. September 19, 1929, p. 11.

106. Diane Collins, op., cit., p. 184; John A. Lent. *The Asian Film Industry*. London: Christopher Helm, 1990, pp. 186–187.

107. "Charge Films Mar Prestige of British." *New York Times*. April 20, 1926, p. 25; "How Our Films Misrepresent America Abroad." *Literary Digest*. 71:28–29 November 26, 1921; "Our Films Not Corrupting the East." *Literary Digest*. 101:28 June 1, 1929.

108. "Our Films Disillusioning the East." *Literary Digest*. 90:26 August 7, 1926.

109. Diane Collins, op. cit., pp. 181–183.

110. "How Our Films Misrepresent America Abroad." *Literary Digest*. 71:28–29 November 26, 1921.

111. "Hits American Films New Zealand Sees." *New York Times*. October 13, 1926, p. 23; R. Le Clerc Phillips. "French Flirts and English Fops." *New York Times*. December 11, 1927, sec. 9, p. 7.

112. "Yankee Films That Disagree with John Bull." *Literary Digest*. 64:62–63 February 21, 1920.

113. "American Films Menace Decent British Homes." *Variety*. 79:1, 3 July 1, 1925; Charles Merz. "When the Movies Go Abroad." *Harper's Monthly Magazine*. 152:159, 160 January, 1926.

114. "Canada's Offense at Our Movies." *Literary Digest*. 86:27 August 15, 1925.

115. "British India Attacking U.S. Films." *Variety*. 86:5 January 19, 1927; "Our films Not Corrupting the East." *Literary Digest*. 101:28 June 1, 1929.

116. "Baden-Powell Draws the Line at Rotten American Films." *Literary Digest*. *New York Times*. October 20, 1929, sec. 2, p. 2.

117. Gaizka S. Usabel. *The High Noon of American Films in Latin America*. Ann Arbor: UMI, 1982, pp. xv, 8, 12.

118. "Say Movies Lead Stage to Decency." *New York Times*. April 3, 1927, p. 14.

119. Gaizka S. Usabel, op. cit., pp. 36, 58.

120. Muriel Baily. "Moving Pictures in Pan America." *Bulletin of the Pan American Union*. 50:606 June, 1920; "Diplomats from Countries South Guests of the Picture Industry." *Variety*. 71:18 June 21, 1923.

121. "American and German Films Competing in South America." *Variety*. 72:21 September 27, 1923.

122. "Favorable Exchange Costing U.S. South American Market." *Variety*. 62:46 May 6, 1921; "Americans Best." *Variety*. 70:19 May 3, 1923.

123. Randal Johnson. *The Film Industry in Brazil: Culture and the State*. Pittsburgh: University of Pittsburgh Press, 1987, p. 39.

124. Tim Barnard. "Popular Cinema and Populist Politics." in Tim Barnard, ed. *Argentine Cinema*. Toronto: Nightwood, 1986, pp. 18, 23–24.

125. "Mexico's Ban on Mexican Movie Villains." *New York Times*. February 11, 1922, p. 15; "Mexico Will Not Lift Ban Against Pathé and Vitagraph." *Variety*. 76:22 November 5, 1924; "Mexico Barring Film Makers Showing Mexicans as Villains." *Variety*. 87:1 June 15, 1927; "Mexico Bars Our Films." *New York Times*. August 26, 1927, p. 15; "Spain bars all M-G Films." *Variety*. 89:5 October 26, 1927.

126. Erik Barnouw, op. cit., pp. 38, 46, 48, 56–58; "India Sends Protest on American Films." *New York Times*. November 15, 1926, p. 4; "India-Made Native Picture Driving Out American Films." *Variety*. 80:25 October 21, 1925.

127. Michael Spencer. "U.S.-Canada Film Relations 1920–1986." *Cinema Canada*. n. 131:12 June, 1986.

128. "Canadian Women Rap Imported U.S. Films." *Variety*. 83:7 July 7, 1926.

129. "British Film Field." *Variety*. 88:12 September 7, 1927.

130. "Hollywood's Stranglehold on Canada, Say Canadians." *Variety*. 89:9 December 28, 1927.

131. Manjunath Pendakur, op. cit., pp. 84–85.

132. Ibid., p. 132.

133. Kristin Thompson, op. cit., pp. 121–122.

134. Ibid., p. 123.

135. "Favorable Exchange Costing U.S. South American Market." *Variety*. 62:46 May 6, 1921.

136. Hardie Merkin. "Our Foreign Trade." *Variety*. 77:24 December 31, 1924.

137. Edward G. Lowry. "Trade Follows the Film." *Saturday Evening Post*. 198:12 November 7, 1925.

138. Ibid., p. 13.

139. Courtney Ryler Cooper, op. cit., p. 26.

140. Edward G. Lowry, op. cit., pp. 151, 154, 158.

141. Charles Merz. "When the Movies Go Abroad." *Harper's Monthly Magazine*. 152:161–163 January, 1926.

142. "Uncle Sam and the Movies." *Congressional Digest*. 7:298 November, 1928.

143. Kristin Thompson, op. cit., p. 123, Charles Merz. op. cit., p. 162; "Hays Raps Critics of Film Industry." *New York Times*. April 20, 1928, p. 6; Ian Jarvie, op. cit., p. 16; "Hollywood, Unlimited." *New York Times*. December 21, 1927, p. 24.

144. Ian Jarvie, op. cit., pp. 16, 305, 309.

145. "Spain's Low Admissions and American Films." *Variety*. 72:22 November 1, 1923; "American-Made Films Leaders in Italy." *Variety*. 73:18 December 27, 1923; "American Films Lead World." *Variety*. 75:1, 43 May 23, 1924; Hardie Meakin. "Our Foreign Trade." *Variety*. 77:24 December 31, 1924.

146. Kristin Thompson, op. cit., p. 117; Ian Jarvie, op. cit., p. 311.

147. "U.S. Gov't Officially Notices Pictures." *Variety*. 82:27 March 3, 1926.

148. "American and British Films Coming to Grips." *Literary Digest*. 90:23 August 28, 1926.

149. Kristin Thompson, op. cit., pp. 117–118.

150. "Uncle Sam and the Movies." *Congressional Digest*. 7:299 November, 1928.

151. Ian Jarvie, op. cit., pp. 313, 323.

152. Fred Eastman. "Ambassadors of Ill Will." *Christian Century*. 47:146 January 29, 1980.

153. "To Aid Film Business." *New York Times.* July 7, 1929, p. 12.

154. Ian Jarvie, op. cit., p. 314.

155. Victoria de Grazia, op. cit., p. 59.

156. C. J. North. "Our Foreign Trade in Motion Pictures." *Annals of the American Academy of Political Science and Social Science.* 128:101–102 Nov. 1926; "Tax Gross of All Imported Film as Foreign Situation Remedy." *Variety.* 84:46 August 18, 1926.

157. Gaizka S. Usabel. *The High Noon of American Films in Latin America.* Ann Arbor; UMI, 1982, p. xv; Muriel Baily. "Moving Pictures in Pan America. *Bulletin of the Pan American Union.* 50:610 June, 1920; Maurice Ventura. "Foreign Pictures in Egypt." *Variety.* 77:23 November 19, 1924; "$75,000,000 Export Estimated for American Film Producers." *Variety.* 79:43 May 20, 1925.

158. Ian Jarvie, op. cit., p. 315.

159. C. J. North. "Our Foreign…," op. cit., pp. 101–104.

160. Ibid., pp. 104–108.

161. C. J. North. "Our Silent Ambassadors." *The Independent.* 116:689–690 June 12, 1926.

162. "Latin-American Countries Lead Rest of World." *Variety.* 84:5 August 4, 1926.

163. Roger Shaw. "American Movies Abroad." *Review of Reviews.* 78:77 July, 1928.

164. "555 First-Line Features." *Variety.* 91:4 May 30, 1928; "From 400 to 500 Foreign Pictures." *Variety.* 91:10 May 23, 1928.

165. '28 Foreign Screens were 60.6% American." *Variety.* 94:2 April 3, 1929.

166. "Tax Gross of All Imported Film as Foreign Situation Remedy." *Variety.* 84:46 August 18, 1926; "Foreign Film Imports Drop $14,664 on Year." *Variety.* 84:15 August 11, 1926; Edward G. Lowry, op. cit., p. 158; C. J. North. "Our Foreign…," op. cit., p. 108.

167. "Australia Prefers Our Films." *Literary Digest.* 94:27–28 September 10, 1927; "American grip on films." *New York Times.* October 17, 1926, sec. 8, p. 7.

168. "$71,000,000 from Foreign Sales." *Variety.* 88:8 August 17, 1927; "$75,000,000 Export Estimated for American Film Producers." *Variety.* 79:43 May 20, 1925; C. J. North. "Our Foreign…," op. cit., p. 101; C. J. North. "Our Silent…," op. cit., p. 690.

169. Charles Merz, op. cit., p. 164.

170. Courtney Ryley Cooper, op. cit., p. 222; "Europe May Recall Actors." *Variety.* 91:3 May 23, 1928.

171. Victoria de Grazia, op. cit., p. 57; "Foreign Trade Draws News Attention." *Variety.* 82:35 February 17, 1926; John Tulloch, op. cit., p. 35.

172. "Predecessors of American Films." *New York Times.* July 1, 1926, p. 22; "Goldwyn Hits Film Quotas." *New York Times.* March 4, 1928, sec. 9, p. 5; John MacCormac. "London Film Notes." *New York Times.* December 9, 1928, sec. 10, p. 7; "Europe May Recall Actors." *Variety.* 91:3 May 23, 1928; "Government Is Interested in Export Raw Pictures." *Variety.* 63:38.

173. Courtney Ryley Cooper, op. cit., p. 221.

174. C. J. North. "Our Silent…," op. cit., p. 690.

175. Raymond Moley, op. cit., p. 170.

1176. Charles Merz, op. cit., pp. 159–160.

177. C. J. North. "Our Foreign…," op. cit., p. 100.

178. Kristin Thompson, op. cit., p. 114.

179. Ruth Vasey. "Foreign Parts: Hollywood's Global Distribution and the Representation of Ethnicity." *American Quarterly.* v. 44, no. 4:619 December, 1992.

180. "Tax Gross of All Imported Film as Foreign Situation Remedy." *Variety*. 84:46 August 18, 1926.

181. Kristin Thompson, op. cit., pp. 123–124; Ian Jarvie, op. cit., p. 310.

182. Ian Jarvie, op. cit., p. 326.

183. Kristin Thompson, op. cit., p. 147.

184. Victoria de Grazia, op. cit., p. 58.

Chapter 3

1. "America's Film Monopoly." *Living Age*. 341:373 December, 1931.

2. Ina Bertrand, ed. *Cinema in Australia: A Documentary History*. Kensington, NSW.: New South Wales University Press, 1989, p. 49; John Tulloch. *Australian Cinema: Industry, Narrative and Meaning*. Sydney: George Allen & Unwin, 1982, p. 17.

3. "U.S. Leaving Foreign Tongue Markets to Locals and Indies." *Variety*. 93:4, 16, November 21, 1928; Kristin Thompson. *Exporting Entertainment: America in the World Film Market 1907–1934*. London: BFI, 1985, p. 91.

4. "Mexican Protest Against English Talker Dialog." *Variety*. 95:9 June 12, 1929; Gaizka S. Usabel. *The High Noon of American Film in Latin America*. Ann Arbor: UMI, 1982, pp. 84–85; "Doubles Tax on Talkies in English." *New York Times*. June 4, 1930, p. 33.

5. "Mexican Movies." *Time*. 36:91 December 16, 1940.

6. Randal Johnson. *The Film Industry in Brazil: Culture and the State*. Pittsburgh: University of Pittsburgh Press, 1987, pp. 44–45; "Talkies in English Opposed in Brazil." *New York Times*. November 18, 1929, p. 7; Gaizka S. Usabel, op. cit., p. 83

7. "Talkies Under Fire in Argentina Press." *New York Times*. April 28, 1930, p. 5; "Talkies Assailed Anew in Argentina." *New York Times*. April 29, 1930, p. 30.

8. Gaizka S. Usabel, op. cit., p. 83.

9. "Faked Spanish Dialog Gets Razzed in S.A." *Variety*. 97:3 November 27, 1929.

10. "Threaten to Ban Talkies." *New York Times*. April 29, 1930, p. 30; "Would Boycott Our Films." *New York Times*. January 21, 1931, p. 10; "Deny Inciting Film Riots." New York Times. October 1, 1930, p. 12.

11. C. Hooper Trask. "Our Talkies in Germany." *New York Times*. June 15, 1930, sec. 8, p. 3; "Germans See End of U.S. Film Over There." *Variety*. 97:5 October 16, 1929; Kristin Thompson, op. cit., p. 159.

12. "Italy Making It Plenty Tough for U.S. films." *Variety*. 98:7 February 19, 1930; "Italian Film Trade Combines in Petitioning." *Variety*. 100:7 July 16, 1930; "Mussolini O.K.'s 10% Foreign Dialog." *Variety*. 100:7 November 12, 1930.

13. Kristin Thompson, op. cit., p. 159; "French Razzes English Shorts." *Variety*. 95:2 June 12, 1929; "France's Anti-U.S. Spasm." *Variety*. 97:5 November 6, 1929; "French Restriction of Eng. Dialog in Talkers Foretells Possible World-wide Trend." *Variety*. 100:7 August 6, 1930.

14. "Duke Alba Befriends American Pictures." *Variety*. 98:4 February 12, 1930.

15. "Jap Censors Worry over America's Slang." *Variety*. 98:4 March 5, 1930.

16. Gaizka S. Usabel, op. cit., p. 83; Thelma Gutsche. *The History and Social Significance of Motion Pictures in South Africa 1895–1940*. Cape Town: Howard Timmins, 1972, p. 223.

17. Carlisle MacDonald. "Demand Looming for Native Talkies." *New York Times*. December 16, 1929, p. 5.

18. "Talkies for Europe Baffle Americans." *New York Times*. December 28, 1929, p. 4.

19. Kristin Thompson, op. cit., p. 160.

20. John McCabe. *Babe: The Life of Oliver Hardy*. London: Robson, 1990, p. 99.

21. William A. Johnston. "The World War of Talking Pictures." *Saturday Evening Post*. 203:31+ July 19, 1930.

22. "Talkies in Foreign Languages Keep American Films on Top." *Business Week*. February 25, 1931, p. 22; Maurice L. Ahern. "The World Gets an Earful." *Commonweal*. 11:333–335 January 22, 1930.

23. Victoria de Grazia. "Mass Culture and Sovereignty: The American Challenge to European Cinemas, 1920–1960." *Journal of Modern History*. 61:69, 71 March, 1989.

24. John MacCormac. "Austrians Boycott our Sound Films." *New York Times*. May 11, 1930, sec. 2, p. 1.

25. "Sound Killing Quotas." *Variety*. 97:7, 68 June 4, 1930.

26. "Producers Optimistic Again That the 40% Foreign Revenue Will Return to Former Status." *Variety*. 100:7, 58 August 13, 1930; "Americans Redoubling Drive on World Markets." *Variety*. 98:5 January 29, 1930.

27. Ruth Vasey. "Foreign Parts: Hollywood's Global Distribution and the Representation of Ethnicity." *American Quarterly*. v. 44, no. 4:622 December, 1992.

28. Kristin Thompson, op. cit., p. 148.

Chapter 4

1. John McCabe. *Babe: The Life of Oliver Hardy*. London: Robson, 1990, p. 123.

2. Gaizka S. Usabel. *The High Noon of American Films in Latin America*. Ann Arbor: UMI, 1982, p. 165.

3. Diane Collins. *Hollywood Down Under*. North Ryde, NSW.: Angus & Robertson, 1987, p. 73; "The Americanization of Amusement." *Saturday Review*. 151:521–522 April 11, 1931; Charles Higham. *Warner Brothers*. New York: Scribner's, 1975, p. 75.

4. Ian Jarvie. *Hollywood's Overseas Campaign: The North Atlantic Movie Trade, 1920–1950*. Cambridge: Cambridge University Press, 1992, p. 330.

5. "America's Film Monopoly." *Living Age*. 341:373–374 December, 1931.

6. Diane Collins, op. cit., p. 73.

7. "World Blanketing Scheme." *Variety*. 100:11 November 26, 1930.

8. "Hays Taking on the World." *Variety*. 100:7, 47 October 8, 1930.

9. James Tooker Ford. "Motion Pictures and Foreign Missions." *Missionary Review of the World*. 54:611 August, 1931.

10. Samuel King Gam. "Missionaries and Motion Pictures." *Missionary Review of the World*. 59:86 February, 1936.

11. Frederic Siedenburg. "Motion Pictures Abroad." *Commonweal*. 12:381, 383 August 13, 1930.

12. "American Films too Filthy for Turkey." *Literary Digest*. 108:21 January 10, 1931.

13. Wilbur Burton. "Chinese Reactions to the Cinema." *Asia*. 34:597, 599 October, 1934.

14. "An Author in Search of a Gun." *New York Times*. January 27, 1935, sec. 8, p. 4.

15. "Fight Film Censorship." *New York Times*. July 12, 1936, p. 19; "To Halt Films to Cuba." *New York Times*. July 17, 1936, p. 20.

16. "Argentina Scores Movies." *New York Times*. August 3, 1931, p. 15.

17. "Metro Wins the Battle of *Ah, Wilderness*." *New York Times*. January 19, 1936, sec. 9, p. 5.

18. "Censors Working Overtime." *Variety*. 129:13 February 9, 1938.

19. "American Movies Abroad." *New York Times*. April 13, 1932, p. 18.

20. "Pix Aim to Please 'Em All." *Variety*. 127:1, 34 July 28, 1937.

21. Anthony Bower. "Films." *The Nation*. 152:153 February 15, 1941.

22. Dorothy B. Jones. "Hollywood's International Relations." *Quarterly of Film, Radio & Television*. 11:368 Summer, 1957.

23. Ruth Vasey. "Foreign Parts: Hollywood's Global Distribution and the Representation of Ethnicity." *American Quarterly*. v. 44, no. 4:623, 631–632 December, 1992.

24. Ivan T. Sanderson. "Foreigners See Our Films." *Atlantic Monthly*. 168:238–240 August, 194.

25. Meyer Levin. "Glory Poison for the Screen." *Reader's Digest*. 29:101–102 December, 1936.

26. "Bombs Over Cuban Theaters." *New York Times*. November 4, 1934, sec. 9, p. 4; Raymond Moley. *The Hays Office*. Indianapolis: Bobbs-Merrill, 1945, p. 174.

27. "Too Much Gab for Foreigners." *Variety*. 128:15 November 10, 1937.

28. "Dialog Behind the 8-Ball." *Variety*. 129:13 March 9, 1938.

29. "World Wide for Hays Code." *Variety*. 102:5, April 15, 1931.

30. "H'wood's World Good-Will." *Variety*. 114:5, 59 May 8, 1934.

31. "Hays Clamps Down on Hypoing Films for Foreign Spots." *Variety*. 115:5 August 14, 1934.

32. Ruth Vasey, op. cit., p. 629.

33. Thelma Gutsche. *The History and Social Significance of Motion Pictures in South Africa 1895–1940*. Cape Town: Howard Timmins, 1972, pp. 232–237, 255–258.

34. Gaizka S. Usabel, op. cit., p. 125.

35. John Tulloch. *Australian Cinema: Industry, Narrative and Meaning*. Sydney: George Allen & Unwin, 1982, pp. 23, 67; Ina Bertrand. *Cinema in Australia: A Documentary History*. Kensington, NSW.: New South Wales University Press, 1989, p. 126; Diane Collins, op. cit., p. 17.

36. Randal Johnson. *The Film Industry in Brazil: Culture and the State*. Pittsburgh: University of Pittsburgh Press, 1987, pp. 34, 50.

37. "Threaten American Films." *New York Times*. March 26, 1930, p. 12; "Charge We Dominate Danish Film Industry." *New York Times*. February 27, 1931, p. 18.

38. Manjunath Pendakur. *Canadian Dreams and American Control*. Toronto: Garamond Press, 1990, p. 90; Ian Jarvie, op. cit., pp. 34–35.

39. Ian Jarvie, op. cit., p. 36.

40. "Films, Radio, Reading Disturbing Canadians." *New York Times*. August 2, 1931, sec. 3, p. 6; Manjunath Pendakur, op. cit., p. 91.

41. Frederic Siedenburg. "Motion Pictures Abroad." *Commonweal*. 12:383 August 13, 1930; "Kent's Testimony on Foreign Loss." *New York Times*. April 7, 1939, p. 25.

42. Diane Collins, op. cit., pp. 167–172.

43. Mary Pickford. "Ambassadors." *Saturday Evening Post*. 203:6–7 August 23, 1930.

44. Ruth Vasey, op. cit., p. 625.

45. "Envoys Warn Producers." *Variety*. 101:7, 43 December 17, 1930.

46. "U.S. Cuts Down Film Exports." *Variety*. 111:19 July 25, 1933; Ian Jarvie, op. cit., p. 341.

47. "Film Export Unit Set Up in Capital." *New York Times.* July 1, 1937, p. 33.

48. "U.S. May Force No Quota." *Variety.* 113:11, 18 February 6, 1934; "Roosevelt Views Movies' Problems." *New York Times.* October 29, 1937, p. 14.

49. "Revolt in the West." *New York Times.* November 24, 1935, sec. 9, p. 4.

50. "Rasputin's Foreign Difficulties Bring Protests." *Variety.* 114:13 May 1, 1934.

51. "Foreign Picture Money Embargo on in Australia." *Variety.* 98:5 March 5, 1930; "Foreign Countries' Ban on Exporting Money Can Turn into Embargo on U.S. Films." *Variety.* 104:15 October 20, 1931; "Money Embargo Remedy." *Variety.* 105:11 December 22, 1931.

52. "U.S. Filmers Nix Foreign Nations' Bid for a Goods Barter System." *Variety.* 133:6 January 18, 1939.

53. Gaizka S. Usabel, op. cit., p. 82.

54. "Mexico Told to Reduce Film Tax." *Variety.* 104:15 October 20, 1931; "International Resume." *Variety.* 108:3, 27 September 13, 1932; "Defeat of Mex Anti-Import Bill Promises Break for U.S. Film Biz." *Variety.* 129:13 March 9, 1938.

55. "Brazil's Film Tax." *New York Times.* December 20, 1931, sec. 8, p. 4.

56. Randal Johnson, op. cit., p. 50.

57. "First Brazil Film Survey Shows $8,000,000 Annual Biz." *Variety.* 121:22 February 26, 1936.

58. "Tax Increased 15 Times." *Variety.* 101:13, 45 March 4, 1931; "No Gesture from Government with Argentine Theaters on Eve of Closing Over Tax." *Variety.* 102:13 April 8, 1931; "International Resume." *Variety.* 108:3, 27 September 13, 1932.

59. "Latin Uproar." *Time.* 37:69–70 February 10, 1941; Douglas W. Churchill. "Hollywood's Footlights Club." *New York Times.* June 20, 1937, sec. 10, p. 3.

60. George Gercke. "Pan-American Pictures." *New York Times.* December 18, 1938, sec. 9, p. 6.

61. Gaizka S. Usabel, op. cit., p. 161; "Latin Uproar." *Time.* 27:69–70 February 10, 1941; Douglas W. Churchill. "Hollywood Snags the Good Neighbor Policy." *New York Times.* November 10, 1940, sec. 9. p. 5.

62. "New Script Quest Points to Pix Biz Going the South American Way." *Variety.* 136:5 October 25, 1939.

63. Robert E. Sherwood. "Sailing into Summer—and Return." *New York Times.* March 19, 1939, sec. 11, p. 2.

64. "U.S. Pic Industry Sees Exploitation of Latin America Market as Out of Proportion With its Potential Value." *Variety.* 134:11 April 26, 1939.

65. "Japs Ganging Up on U.S." *Variety.* 125:13, 50 February 17, 1937; "Distributors Panicked over Japanese Ban on Foreign Films." *Variety.* 128:13 October 13, 1937.

66. "Double Featuring, Prod Shortage Worry Japan." *Variety.* 114:13 May 8, 1934.

67. "Hollywood Found Molding Near East." *New York Times.* May 8, 1935, p. 21.

68. Wilbur Burton. "Chinese Reactions to the Cinema." *Asia.* 34:594 October, 1934; "78% Pix Shown in China from the U.S." *Variety.* 118:14 April 3, 1935.

69. Wilbur Burton, op. cit., p. 594; "Chinese Filmers Inspire Trick Law That May Force U.S. Out of Market." *Variety.* 111:19 July 25, 1933; "China's Gov't Film Commissioner Scans Industry in U.S. and Europe." *Variety.* 127:16 June 16, 1937.

70. "Anzac Film Probe Continues." *Variety.* 114:12 April 3, 1934.

71. Ina Bertrand, op. cit., p. 126; "There's a Quota in Australia But 'What Quota?' Asks Pic Biz." *Variety.* 124:14 November 4, 1936.

72. "American Films Hit in New South Wales." *New York Times.* March 31, 1937, p. 29; "Storm Over Australia." *Variety.* 125:13 April 7, 1937.

73. Ina Bertrand, op. cit., pp. 126, 152–153; "U.S. Distribs to Ignore NSW Quota." *Variety.* 130:13 April 6, 1938.

74. Michael Spencer. "U.S.-Canada Film Relations 1920–1986." *Cinema Canada*. n. 131:12 June, 1986; Ian Jarvie, op. cit., p. 82.

75. Joseph Shaplen. "Dominions Prevent Curb on Our Films." *New York Times*. August 19, 1932, p. 4.

76. Manjunath Pendakur, op. cit., pp. 85–87.

77. "Americans Combat Yugoslav Film Curbs." *New York Times*. March 7, 1932, p. 13; "Close Yugoslav Offices." *New York Times*. May 16, 1932, p. 19.

78. "Yugoslavs Invite Americans Back to Spur Trade." *Variety*. 108:11 December 6, 1932; "Desperate Exhibs Speed End of Yugoslav Quota." *Variety*. 109:13 March 7, 1933.

79. "Films of U.S. for Czechs." *New York Times*. January 20, 1935, sec. 2, p. 7; "New Czech Import Law Still Has Yank Filmites Dizzy." *Variety*. 116:21, 58 November 27, 1934.

80. "Battle on to Make Belgium Change Mind on Dubbing." *Variety*. 117:21 February 27, 1935.

81. "U.S. Producers Study Shutdown of All Europe as Quota Protest." *Variety*. 106:11 May 31, 1932; "U.S. Movie Exports Set Record." *Business Week*. June 26, 1937, pp. 50–51.

82. "U.S. Films Out of Germany." *Variety*. 100:3, 37 July 23, 1930; "New German Quota Law Bars Jews." *Variety*. 111:11, 31 July 4, 1933; "Kontingents No Good." *Variety*. 109:15, 52 January 31, 1933; Raymond Moley, op. cit., p. 172; Claire Trask. "Berlin Communique." *New York Times*. August 4, 1935, sec. 9, p. 2.

83. Charles Higham. *Merchant of Dreams: Louis B. Mayer, MGM and the Secret Hollywood*. New York: Donald I. Fine, 1993, pp. 271, 275, 287.

84. Ibid., p. 292.

85. Ibid., pp. 287–288.

86. Ibid., pp. 293, 300.

87. Victoria de Grazia. "Mass Culture and Sovereignty: The American Challenge to European Cinemas, 1920–1960." *Journal of Modern History*. 61:65, 67 March, 1989. Arnaldo Cortesi. "Italian Film Edict Hits Our Industry." *New York Times*. October 15, 1933, sec. 4, p. 3.

88. "Il Duce Relents." *Variety*. 121:13 January 22, 1936.

89. "U.S. Pix Stay Out of Italy." *Variety*. 124:21 October 21, 1936.

90. Charles Higham, op. cit., p. 264; Raymond Moley, op. cit., p. 175;"Curbs on Our Films Dropped by Italy." *New York Times*. November 26, 1936, p. 38; "Films' Victory in Italy." *Variety*. 125:5 December 30, 1936.

91. Raymond Moley, op. cit., p. 175; Charles Higham, op. cit., p. 264.

92. Charles Higham, op. cit., pp. 264–265, 270–271.

93. Victoria de Grazia, op. cit., pp. 75–76; "Hays Officially Reports on U.S. Film Companies' Washup of Italian Biz." *Variety*. 133:15 February 8, 1939; Raymond Moley, op. cit., p. 176.

94. Carlisle MacDonald. "France Likely to End Curbs on Our Films." *New York Times*. June 24, 1931, p. 1.

95. "France Shuts Out Foreigners." *Variety*. 106:7 May 24, 1932; "New Ban in France on American Films." *New York Times*. July 29, 1932, p. 18; "Say France Closes Door to Our Films." *New York Times*. July 30, 1932, p. 16.

96. "French Quota Not So Bad." *Variety*. 111:19, 54 July 25, 1933; "French Theaters Demand Our Films." *New York Times*. July 25, 1933, p. 8; "Overloading France on U.S. Film Spurs Native Embargo Agitators." *Variety*. 111:21 July 11, 1933; "Ban on Our Films Is Asked in Paris." *New York Times*. May 19, 1934, p. 6.

97. "French Blow at U.S. Films." *Variety*. 114:13 May 22, 1934.

98. "U.S. Gov't to the Rescue." *Variety*. 114:15, 27 May 29, 1934.

99. "French Deputies Join Exhibs in Battle Against U.S. Quota." *Variety*. 115:21 June 29, 1934.

100. "Deval Pans American Films, and Press Kids Him for It." *Variety*. 117:17 December 18, 1934; Georges Clarriere. "The Western Peril." *Sight & Sound*. v. 3, no. 12:153–155 Winter 1934–1935.

101. "Halt Anti–U.S. Film Law." *Variety*. 118:15, 61 April 10, 1935; "Extension of French Film Quota Law for 1 Year a Break for U.S. Pix." *Variety*. 118:13 June 5, 1935.

102. "Washington Expected to Enter Fight Against New French Law." *Variety*. 120:17 October 16, 1935; "Hays Sends French Rep." *Variety*. 120:19, 69 October 30, 1935.

103. "French Move Seen to Rule U.S. films." *New York Times*. October 17, 1935, p. 19.

104. "Uphold American Movies." *New York Times*. April 29, 1937, p. 17.

105. "French Movie Bill Limits Film Length." *New York Times*. March 18, 1939, p. 9; "French Lift Quotas on Some Alien Films." *New York Times*. August 11, 1939, p. 17.

106. Reginald Wright Kauffman. "War in the Film Market." *North American Review*. 229:353 March, 1930.

107. Basil Wright. "British Films and Quota." *Spectator*. 159:54 July 9, 1937.

108. "Films in Committee." *Times* (London). December 7, 1937, p. 17; Thomas M. Pryor. "Complications Abroad." *New York Times*. October 17, 1937, sec. 11, p. 4.

109. "British Open Fight Against Our Films." *New York Times*. November 14, 1931, p. 15; "British Now Have 2 Way Squawk on Quota." *Variety*. 98:4 February 19, 1930.

110. Ian Jarvie, op. cit., pp. 332, 341; Basil Wright, op. cit., p. 54.

111. "British Exhibs in Panic; Can't Get More Than Half Enough Local Pix to Fill Quota." *Variety*. 123:34 August 26, 1936; "CEA, KRS Join Hands in London to Lobby for 10–15% Quota." *Variety*. 122:13 June 3, 1936; "Control of British Cinemas." *Times* (London). October 15, 1936, p. 12.

112. "British Film Act Report." *Variety*. 124:11 December 9, 1936; "First Aid for Films." *Times* (London). June 24, 1937, p. 17; "The Films Bill." *Times* (London). December 29, 1937, p. 11; "Beware of America." *Variety*. 128:15 September 22, 1937.

113. Ian Jarvie, op. cit., p. 163.

114. "New Quota Law Will Boost Cost of U.S. Biz in England 40%–50%." *Variety*. 130:13 April 6, 1938; Basil Wright, op. cit., p. 55.

115. "Film Quotas Eased in New British Act." *New York Times*. April 3, 1938, sec. 2, p. 2.

116. "U.S. No Help on Pix Quota." *Variety*. 127:23 June 30, 1937; Charles Higham, op. cit., p. 262; Raymond Moley, op. cit., p. 180.

117. Alexander Cockburn. "In Bed with America." *American Film*. 16:43 November/December, 1991.

118. "Kontingents No Good." *Variety*. 109:15, 52 January 31, 1933; "U.S. Still Leads Abroad." *Variety*. 109:13, 54 March 7, 1933.

119. Aubrey Solomon. *Twentieth Century–Fox: A Corporate and Financial History*. Metuchen, NJ: Scarecrow, 1988, pp. 28, 31, 67.

120. Ruth Vasey, op. cit., p. 622.

121. "Uncle Sam Takes Inventory of Picture Distribution Situations in Various Foreign Countries." *Variety*. 126:13 June 2, 1937.

122. Thomas M. Pryor. "More on Foreign Quotas." *New York Times*. October 24, 1937, sec. 11, p. 6; Thomas M. Pryor. "Complications Abroad." *New York Times*. October 17, 1937, sec. 11, p. 4; "Yank Cos.' Low Net in Aussie." *Variety*. 132:13 October 19, 1938.

123. "U.S. Execs Think Foreign Lands Will Feel Film Shortage This Winter." *Variety*. 103:7, 91 September 8, 1931.

124. "While 70% of World's Screens Still Serviced by U.S." *Variety*. 130:5, 19 April 6, 1938.

125. "Foreign Market Dipped in 1938." *Variety*. 134:14, 54 March 15, 1939.

126. "U.S. Beats Foreign Snags." *Variety*. 130:15 June 8, 1938.

127. Walter Wanger. "120,000 American Ambassadors." *Foreign Affairs*. 18:45, 50–51, 53–54, 59 October, 1939.

128. Douglas Churchill. "Films Ban Abroad Hurt Hollywood." *New York Times*. January 8, 1939, sec. 4, p. 7.

Chapter 5.

1. "Gang Up on Uncle Sam." *Variety*. 115:29, 73 June 19, 1934.

2. John A. Kouwenhoven. "The Movies Better Be Good!" *Harper's Monthly Magazine*. 190:535 May, 1945; "Foreign Coin Curb Held Biggest Bugaboo for Yank Pictures." *Variety*. 134:11 June 7, 1939.

3. Mike Wear. "Foreign Film Outlook." *Variety*. 136:7 September 13, 1939; "Films' 8–9% Foreign Loss." *Variety*. 136:1, 18 October 4, 1939.

4. "U.S. Economists Also See Ultimate Worldwide Boon to American Pix Biz." *Variety*. 136:19 October 4, 1939.

5. "Nazi Expansion Seen as Curb on U.S. Films." *New York Times*. April 9, 1939, p. 33.

6. "Invasion of Finland, Good Market, New Blow to U.S. Films." *Variety*. 136:12 December 6, 1939; Thomas M. Pryor. "Film News of the Week." *New York Times*. May 19, 1940.

7. "France's Capitulation Means Complete Blackout of Europe for U.S. Pix." *Variety*. 139:12 June 19, 1940.

8. "War Loss Assayed by Concerns Here." *New York Times*. December 9, 1941, p. 44.

9. Ian Jarvie. *Hollywood's Overseas Campaign: The North Atlantic Movie Trade, 1920–1950*. Cambridge: Cambridge University Press, 1992, p. 90.

10. "Foreign Censorial Vagaries Add to U.S. Films' Already Complicated Distrib Problems in Other Lands." *Variety*. 136:13 October 25, 1939; "Metro Dubbing All Pix into Spanish for Latin America." *Variety*. 155:8 July 12, 1944.

11. Douglas W. Churchill. "Matters of More or Less Moment in Hollywood." *New York Times*. June 30, 1940, sec. 9, p. 3.

12. Ezra Goodman. "Hollywood Belligerent." *Nation*. 155:213 September 12, 1942; Bosley Crowther. "Howdy, Neighbors." *New York Times*. February 14, 1943, sec. 2, p. 3.

13. Tim Barnard. "Popular Cinema and Populist Politics." in Tim Barnard, ed. *Argentine Cinema*. Toronto: Nightwood, 1986, p. 37; Gaizka S. Usabel. *The High Noon of American Films in Latin America*. Ann Arbor: UMI, 1982, pp. 158, 163.

14. "So. America, 'Land of Fulfillment,' Was Big Snag to U.S. Pic Cos. in '40." *Variety*. 141:73 January 8, 1941.

15. "U.S. Film Stars the Best Good Will Ambassadors, Say Latin Americans." *Variety*. 141:1, 21 February 19, 1941.

16. "Mickey Mouse is Rated Among Better U.S. Envoys of Goodwill." *Variety*. 142:13 May 28, 1941.

17. "Goodwill a Hot Potato." *Variety*. 142:3, 15 June 4, 1941.

18. Ray Josephs. "H'wood's Pan-Am Bad Will." *Variety*. 143:3, 34 June 25, 1941.

19. "Pix Tricks Mix Latins." *Variety*. 144:1, 20 October 8, 1941.

20. "U.S. Pix Biz Up an Average of 16% Over a Year Ago in Latin America." *Variety*. 144:18 October 29, 1941.

21. "Fear Latin Film Threat." *Variety*. 147:23 August 26, 1942.

22. "Argentine Court Dismisses Exhib Suit." *Variety*. 148:16 November 18, 1942.

23. Thomas M. Pryor. "U.S. Films Favored in the Americas." *New York Times*. December 6, 1945, p. 31.

24. Tim Barnard, op. cit., pp. 32–33.

25. Ibid., pp. 35–36, 38.

26. Gaizka S. Usabel, op. cit., pp. 172, 177, 181.

27. Randal Johnson. *The Film Industry in Brazil: Culture and the State*. Pittsburgh: University of Pittsburgh Press, 1987, p. 61; Florence Horn. "Formidavel, Fabulosissimo." *Harper's Monthly Magazine*. 184:60–62 December, 1941.

28. Florence Horn, op. cit., p. 59.

29. "Ex-Showman Joe Kennedy Does Straight for American Film Biz on British Quota and Coin." *Variety*. 136:3, 20 October 25, 1939; "Britain in Accord on American Films." *New York Times*. November 23, 1939, p. 39; "Unfreezing Foreign Coin." *Variety*. 138:7, 12 April 10, 1940.

30. "Hopkins to Pry Film Coin." *Variety*. 143:5, 16 July 30, 1941; "British Coin Tilts '41 Net." *Variety*. 144:5, 18 November, 1941.

31. "British Quota Showdown." *Variety*. 144:15 December 3, 1941.

32. "Hays in Washington to Ask Gov't Aid on British Unfreezing of U.S. Coin." *Variety*. 147:5, 22 July 8, 1942.

33. "No More Brit Coin Freeze." *Variety*. 150:5 May 5, 1943.

34. "Films Across the Sea." *New Statesman & Nation*. 27:167–168 March 11, 1944; J. L. Hodson. "Hollywood Argument." *Spectator*. 172:471 May 26, 1944.

35. "England's Chronic Complaint." *Variety*. 153:3 March 1, 1944.

36. "British Deplore Glut of U.S. Films." *New York Times*. December 21, 1944, p. 16.

37. Ina Bertrand, ed. *Cinema in Australia: A Documentary History*. Kensington, NSW.: New South Wales University Press, 1989, p. 188; Eric Gorrick. "War Doesn't Discourage Australian Film-Going." *Variety*. 141:73 January 18, 1941.

38. "Shanghai Supports U.S. Film." *Variety*. 141:73 January 8, 1941.

39. "ANZAC and Far East Represent 18% of U.S. Foreign Film Income." *Variety*. 145:3, 55 December 10, 1941.

40. "Vichy Blackout on U.S. Pix Fails to Stir Yanks." *Variety*. 147:16 August 19, 1942; "U.S. Films Barred from Vichy's Areas." *New York Times*. August 6, 1942, p. 7.

41. Thomas M. Pryor. "Survey of American Films Abroad." *New York Times*. January 11, 1942, sec. 9, p. 4.

42. "American Films Played to Tatters in Nazi Controlled Countries." *Variety*. 142:13 June 4, 1941.

43. Herbert L. Matthews. "Anti–U.S. Actions in Italy Increase." *New York Times*. April 5, 1941, p. 5.

44. Thomas M. Pryor. "Sundry Matters About Films and People." *New York Times*. February 15, 1942, sec. 8, p. 5; Dorothy B. Jones. "Hollywood's International Relations." *Quarterly of Film, Radio & Television*. 11:369 Summer, 1957; "Movies Must Submit Scenarios to the OWI." *New York Times*. December 19, 1942, p. 1.

45. "Foreign Sales Dept. Heads Oppose OWI Handling of U.S. Prints Abroad." *Variety*. 150:7 May 26, 1943.

46. Fred Stanley. "Diplomatic Hollywood." *New York Times*. October 7, 1945, sec. 2, p. 1.

47. "A.E.F. Daily Decries Movie Flag-Waving." *New York Times*. April 13, 1943, p. 1.

48. "Films About Americans." *Asia and the Americas*." 42:658–659 November, 1942.

49. Paul K. Lee. "Influence of Films Abroad." *New York Times*. March 28, 1943, sec. 2, p. 3.

50. Herman A. Lowe. "Washington Discovers Hollywood." *American Mercury*. 60:410–412 April, 1945.

51. Ian Jarvie, op. cit., p. 376.

52. Ibid., pp. 379–381.

53. "State Dept. to Break Down Barriers Slowing U.S. Films Selling Abroad." *Variety*. 155:3, 55 June 28, 1944; Mori Krushen. "D.C. Aid to Film Biz Abroad." *Variety*. 155:3, 11 September 6, 1944.

54. Nathan D. Golden. "What Prospect for the Road Ahead in Foreign Film Markets?" *Variety*. 157:112, 132 January 3, 1945.

55. Herman A. Lowe, op. cit., p. 407.

56. "Rush U.S. Films to No. Africa." *Variety*. 148:16 November 18, 1942.

57. Thomas M. Pryor. "Censorship or Advice." *New York Times*. December 13, 1942, sec. 8, p. 3.

58. Ibid., Thomas M. Pryor. "Films Go Abroad Again." *New York Times*. January 2, 1944, sec. 2, p. 3.

59. "Adapt U.S Pix for World." *Variety*. 149:3, 47 February 24, 1943.

60. Gaizka S. Usabel, op. cit., pp. 187–188.

61. "OWI Seizes Fascist Pix." *Variety*. 151:3, 56 September 15, 1943.

62. Thomas M. Pryor. "By Way of Report." *New York Times*. August 13, 1944, sec. 2, p. 3.

63. Thomas M. Pryor. "Looking for Encouragement." *New York Times*. April 22, 1945, sec. 2, p. 3.

64. Ibid.

65. Samuel Goldwyn. "Our Movies Speak for U.S." *Saturday Review of Literature*. 33:11 April 1, 1950.

66. Nathan D. Golden. "Prospects for Post-War Foreign Pix Biz Looms Strong." *Variety*. 153:44 January 5, 1944; Mori Krushen. "Europe as Top Foreign Market." *Variety*. 157:3, 18 January 10, 1945; John A. Kouwenhoven, op. cit., p. 537.

67. Victoria de Grazia. "Mass Culture and Sovereignty: The American Challenge to European Cinemas 1920–1960." *Journal of Modern History*. 61:81 March, 1989.

68. "U.S. Firms' Total World Revenue Has Dropped 20% Due to War." *Variety*. 138:12 June 5, 1940.

69. "Rely on Domestic Sales." *Variety*. 143:5 August 20, 1941.

70. "U.S. Picture-Goers Contribute 64% of the World Wide Revenue." *Variety*. 147:5 September 2, 1942.

71. "Lend-Lease Cut May Hit Pix." *Variety*. 156:3, 12 October 11, 1944; "Films' $480,000,000 a Year." *Variety*. 157:3, 158 January 3, 1945.

72. Charles Higham. *Merchant of Dreams: Louis B. Mayer, MGM and the Secret Hollywood*. New York: Donald I. Fine, 1993, p. 348.

73. "U.S. Film Companies, Soviet Negotiate Product Deal." *Variety*. 145:16 February 18, 1942.

74. "10-Yr. Foreign Pix War Looms." *Variety*. 156:1, 55 October 25, 1944.

75. "U.S. Pix Heads Ogle Europe." *Variety*. 150:5, 8 June 9, 1943; "Hicks Warns of Post-War Dangers in Creating Foreign Buyer's Market." *Variety*. 154:25, 36 March 15, 1944.

76. "Post-War U.S. Pix Biz in Europe Will Hinge on Int'l Currency Stability." *Variety*. 151:5, 28 July 14, 1943.

77. Thomas M. Pryor. "Competition Ahead." *New York Times*. October 10, 1943, sec. 2, p. 3.

78. "Urges Steps to Get Lost Film Markets." *New York Times*. January 2, 1944, p. 37.

79. "Free World Via Pix, Radio." *Variety*. 154:1, 26 March 29, 1944.

80. Nathan D. Golden. "Prospects for Post-War Foreign Pix Biz Looms Strong." *Variety*. 153:44 January 5, 1944.

81. Fred Stanley. "Hollywood Ponders." *New York Times*. July 16, 1944, sec. 2, p. 1.

82. Raymond Moley. *The Hays Office*. Indianapolis: Bobbs-Merrill, 1945, p. 185.

83. "Free World Market for Films Discussed." *New York Times*. January 14, 1944, p. 15.

84. Fred Stanley. "Hollywood Ponders," op. cit., Raymond Moley, op. cit., p. 221.

85. John A. Kouwenhoven, op. cit., pp. 538, 540.

Chapter 6

1. Erik Barnouw and S. Krishnaswamy. *Indian Film*. 2nd ed. New York: Oxford, 1980, p. 154.

2. "Eric Johnston New head of MPPDA." *Variety*. 160:3, 12 September 19, 1945.

3. "Films Plan Campaign." *New York Times*. June 4, 1946, p. 19; "Johnston Stresses Strong Gov't Aid to Combat Foreign Snags to U.S. Pix." *Variety*. 162:21 March 27, 1946.

4. Tino Balio. *United Artists: The Company Built by the Stars*. Madison, Wisc.: University of Wisconsin Press, 1976, p. 220.

5. "Movie Man's Burden." *New Republic*. 117:37–38 July 21, 1947; "Say Curtain Bars Films." *New York Times*. April 8, 1947, p. 34.

6. Eric Johnston. "Projecting the American Idea Around the World Makes U.S. Pix a Very Worthwhile Export Biz." *Variety*. 177:7 January 5, 1950.

7. "Plan Pix Pool for Abroad." *Variety*. 158:3, 19 May 23, 1945.

8. Mori Krushen. "Hedge vs. 'Peace Table' spot." *Variety*. 158:5, 20 March 14, 1945.

9. "United Action in Foreign Market Only Out, Sez Johnston." *Variety*. 162:13 April 10, 1946; "Movies Begin to Fight Foreign Monopolies." *New York Times*. April 5, 1946, p. 21.

10. Jack Valenti. "Webb-Pomerene." *Vital Speeches*. 47:26 October 15, 1980; Thomas H. Guback. *The International Film Industry: Western Europe and America Since 1945*. Bloomington: Indiana University Press, 1969, p. 91.

11. Tino Balio, op. cit., p. 220; Thomas H. Guback, op. cit., p. 92.

12. "U.S. Films in Global Crisis." *Variety*. 166:1, 26 April 30, 1947; Archer Winston. "Movies." *United Nations World*. 1:59 February, 1947.

13. "Film Stars as Envoys Abroad." *Variety*. 166:5, 20 April 2, 1947.

14. "Self-Policing Pays Off Abroad." *Variety*. 167:3, 20 June 25, 1947.

15. "Leaders in Europe Warm to U.S. Films." *New York Times*. August 24, 1949, p. 29.

16. "Easing of Censorship Abroad." *Variety*. 184:5, 16 November 28, 1951.

17. "MPAA's Advice Bureau for Foreign Prods. Backs 'Two-Way' Street Idea." *Variety*. 176:3, 19 November 9, 1949.

18. "More Grief for Movie Exports." *Business Week*. July 15, 1950, pp. 108–110.

19. Manjunath Pendakur. *Canadian Dreams and American Control*. Toronto: Garamond, 1990, p. 38.

20. Gerald M. Mayer. "American Motion Pictures in World Trade." *Annals of the American Academy of Political and Social Science*. 254:32–33 November, 1947.

21. George R. Canty. "American Films Abroad." *Films in Review*. 2:12–13, 30 May, 1951.

22. Archer Winston, op. cit., p. 60.

23. "U's Al Daff Gives Close-up of U.S. Pix Int'l Future." *Variety*. 159:18 August 1, 1945.

24. "Pix Gain Most in Bretton Woods Plan." *Variety*. 159:9, 15 June 13, 1945.

25. Ian Jarvie. *Hollywood's Overseas Campaign: The North Atlantic Movie Trade, 1920–1950*. Cambridge: Cambridge University Press, 1992, p. 252; Nathan D. Golden. "Trade Agreements Help U.S. Companies to Overcome Many Foreign Pic Curbs." *Variety*. 181:193 January 3, 1951.

26. Thomas H. Guback, op. cit., p. 23; "$8,000,000 Boost in Foreign Take Seen Via ERP, New D.C. Bill." *Variety*. 170:3, 23 April 7, 1948.

27. Paul Jarrico. "They Are Not So Innocent Abroad." *New Republic*. 120:17 January 31, 1949.

28. Manjunath Pendakur, op. cit., p. 134; Anthony Smith. *The Geopolitics of Information*. London: Faber & Faber, 1980, p. 53.

29. Manjunath Pendakur, op. cit., pp. 134–135.

30. Ibid., pp. 135–136.

31. Ibid., pp. 136–137.

32. Anthony Smith, op. cit., p. 52.

33. Manjunath Pendakur, op. cit., pp. 137–138.

34. Ibid., pp. 138–139.

35. Ibid., pp. 140–141.

36. "Ecuador Goes for U.S. Action Films But Mex Gets Half Play Time with 19% Pix." *Variety*. 168:15 December 3, 1947.

37. Gaizka S. Usabel. *The High Noon of American Films in Latin America*. Ann Arbor: UMI, 1982, pp. 216–217, 228–229.

38. Hernane Tavares de Sa. "Hollywood Needs Latin America." *Americas*. 1:2–3 October, 1949.

39. "New Issue in Brazil: Movie-Ticket Prices." *U.S. News & World Report*. 25:61 November 26, 1948; "New Brazilian Restrictions Again Accent That Our State Dept. Seems Blind to Film Industry's Problems." *Variety*. 172:6 October 6, 1948; "Compromise on Brazil's Foreign Film Edict Saves $6,000,000 Yank Market." *Variety*. 172:11 October 27, 1948.

40. Randal Johnson. *The Film Industry in Brazil: Culture and the State*. Pittsburgh: University of Pittsburgh Press, 1987, p. 61; "Brazil Gets No U.S. Films." *New York Times*. February 4, 1949, p. 31.

41. Randal Johnson, op. cit., pp. 62–63.

42. Ibid., pp. 69–70, 76.

43. "Movie Man Griffis Plans Private Shows for Peron." *New York Times*. December 15, 1949, p. 21; "Argentines Again Give Runaround to Yanks in Attempt to Effect Pact." *Variety*. 180:4, 20 September 27, 1950; "Argentina Gets U.S. Cars, Films." *New York Times*. August 3, 1951, p. 4.

44. "Hollywood Discovers New Fields in Mexico." *U.S. New & World Report*. 24:65–66 June 11, 1948.

45. "Films Go Begging." *Business Week*. July 27, 1946, p. 106.

46. "Blame Ills of Mexico's Film Biz on Few Playdates for Native Product." *Variety*. 172:13 September 15, 1948.

47. "New 50% Playing Time Law for Mex Pix Causes Withdrawal Threats." *Variety*. 183:16 August 22, 1951; "Mexican Court Acts on Law on Film Times." *New York Times*. August 29, 1951, p. 19.

48. Gaizka S. Usabel, op. cit., pp. 254–255.

49. "See Pix as Best Anti–Red Brake." *Variety*. 162:3, 63 May 29, 1946.

50. "U.S. Pix Behind Iron Curtain." *Variety*. 163:3, 28 August 21, 1946.

51. Sydney Gruson. "Poles Say Rumors Cause Food Lack." *New York Times*. September 17, 1948, p. 8.

52. "Hungary Bars Films with Six U.S. Actors." *New York Times*. January 17, 1948, p. 10; "U.S. Movies Feared by Reds in Hungary." *New York Times*. December 7, 1948, p. 43.

53. "Rumania Gets U.S. Films." *New York Times*. January 20, 1947, p. 19; "Five of 11 U.S. Stars Are Banned by Rumania." *New York Times*. October 28, 1947, p. 14; "Rumania Seizes U.S. Film Office." *New York Times*. November 4, 1948, p. 38.

54. "American Films Reach Accords with Holland, Czecho, Denmark." *Variety*. 164:13 September 18, 1946; "Czech Film Monopoly Freezes U.S. Pix." *Variety*. 160:23 September 26, 1945; "Jap Theaters Pack 'Em in with Yank Pix." *Variety*. 169:12 December 31, 1947.

55. "Russians Would Like U.S. Pix But Insist on 'Auditioning' Them First." *Variety*. 165:21 March 5, 1947; "Russia to See U.S. Films." *New York Times*. October 26, 1948, p. 13.

56. "U.S. Asks Return of 2 Motion Picture Films." *New York Times*. January 23, 1951, p. 8.

57. "Eric Johnston Sells Films to Yugoslavia." *New York Times*. October 5, 1948, p. 3; "Yank Pix Prospects Good in Tito-land, Maas Finds." *Variety*. 176:13 November 23, 1949.

58. "H'wood Pix in Virtual Blackout Behind Iron Curtain." *Variety*. 178:1, 26 April 12, 1950.

59. "Europeans See H'wood as Capitalistic Hence Puzzled by U.S. Commie Probe." Variety. 167:2 June 18, 1947.

60. "Stop Film Flow to China." *Variety*. 172:15 September 8, 1948; "China Increases Film Tax." *New York Times*. September 8, 1948, p. 36; Henry R.Lieberman. "American Films Attacked in China." *New York Times*. September 25, 1949, sec. 2. p. 5.

61. "U.S. Pix Market in Philippines Bullish." *Variety*. 169:15 February 4, 1948; "Filipino Senate sets 10% Local Pix Must." *Variety*. 175:20 July 27, 1949.

62. "U.S. Films Face Fight Abroad." *Business Week*. December 29, 1945, pp. 109–110.

63. "Battle of the Screen." *Fortune*. 33:200 March, 1946.

64. "U.S. Film Industry's Strategy Now Is to Establish Beachheads in Europe." *Variety*. 161:4 February 27, 1946.

65. Nathan D. Golden. "Trade Agreements Help U.S. Companies to Overcome Many Foreign Pic Curbs." *Variety*. 181:193 January 3, 1951.

66. "Everything Follows the Films." *Variety*. 161:3, 38 January 9, 1946.

67. "Calls Trade Boom Vital." *New York Times*. May 2, 1947, p. 33; "U.S. Films' $125,000,000 Foreign Take About Equals Biz's Total Profit." *Variety*. 166:11 May 7, 1947.

68. "Govt Coin for Pix Aid O'seas?" *Variety*. 169:15 February 11, 1948; "Truman Studies Aid to U.S. Pictures in Foreign Markets Not Paying Off." *Variety*. 169:1, 53 February 4, 1948.

69. "Acheson Orders Foreign Problems of Yanks Included in D.C. Int'l Talks." *Variety.* 174:16 April 20, 1949.

70. Manjunath Pendakur, op. cit., p. 36; Thomas H. Guback, op. cit., p. 125.

71. "D.C. Kicking Pictures Around." *Variety.* 162:3, 24 March 27, 1946.

72. Harry L. Hansen. "Hollywood and International Understanding." *Harvard Business Review.* v. 25, no. 1:28–29, 43 Autumn, 1946.

73. "Film Head Pledges Reform in Exports." *New York Times.* December 21, 1946, p. 13.

74. "Hollywood Pix Get Extra O.O. to Assist State Dept. Cause Abroad." *Variety.* 170:1, 18 May 12, 1948.

75. "Pix Eye D.C. Aid for Aid Abroad." *Variety.* 184:3, 48 November 14, 1951.

76. "Norwegian Boycott of U.S. Films May End." *New York Times.* February 28, 1946; p. 19; "U.S. Film Producers Reach Norway Pact." *New York Times.* April 11, 1946, p. 33.

77. "U.S. Films Face Fight Abroad." *Business Week.* December 29, 1945, p. 110; "Film Leaders Reject Proposal by Danes." *New York Times.* October 2, 1947, p. 30; "U.S. Films in Huge Demand in Denmark." *Variety.* 159:18 August 29, 1945.

78. "U.S. Film Studios Break Dutch Ban." *New York Times.* March 23, 1946, p. 8; "Film Export Assn's Stand in Holland Will Be Key to Other Foreign Marts." *Variety.* 160:15 November 7, 1945; "Dutch Society of Pix Exhibs Feels U.S. Export Assn. Setup, Squawks." *Variety.* 161:13 February 20, 1946.

79. "American Films Reach Accords with Holland, Czecho, Denmark." *Variety.* 164:13 September 18, 1946; "Netherlands Lifts Bans on U.S. Films." *New York Times.* August 6, 1947, p. 28.

80. "Withdraw U.S. Films in Spain." *Variety.* 158:7, 18 May 9, 1945.

81. "U.S. Films Face Fight Abroad." *Business Week.* December 29, 1945, p. 110.

82. Thomas H. Guback, op. cit., p. 222.

83. "Europe May Bar 800 U.S. films." *Variety.* 158:1, 10 March 21, 1945.

84. Mike Wear. "U.S. Warns France of Trade Pact After Try to Cut Yankee Imports Down." *Variety.* 159:18 August 1, 1945; "U.S. Films Face Fight Abroad." *Business Week.* December 29, 1945, p. 110; "Film Head Criticizes French on U.S. Ban." *New York Times.* February 27, 1946, p. 21.

85. Thomas H. Guback, op. cit., p. 21; Alexander Cockburn. "In bed with America." *American Film.* 16:43 November/December, 1991; "France to Get 124 Films." *New York Times.* June 14, 1946, p. 16; "French Hit Film Accord." *New York Times.* June 16, 1946, sec. 2, p. 3.

86. "Film Comeback." *Business Week.* July 6, 1946, pp. 24, 26.

87. "French Earn More from U.S. Movies." *U.S. News & World Report.* 24:65 April 2, 1948.

88. Paul Jarrico. "They Are Not So Innocent Abroad." *New Republic.* 120:17–18 January 31, 1949; Victoria de Grazia. "Mass Culture and Sovereignty: The American Challenge to European Cinemas, 1920–1960." *Journal of Modern History.* 61:82 March, 1989.

89. "U.S. Films Suffer as French Left Wages Anti–American Warfare." *Variety.* 168:16 November 5, 1947.

90. Thomas H. Guback, op. cit., pp. 22–23.

91. "State Dept's Influence in French Film Accord." *Variety.* 171:5, 22 August 25, 1948.

92. "Italian Producers Seen Back of Delay in Getting U.S. Pix into Italy." *Variety.* 161:15 February 27, 1946.

93. Victoria de Grazia, op. cit., pp. 82–83; Alexander Cockburn, op. cit., p. 43.

94. William Blum. *The CIA: A Forgotten History.* London: Zed, 1986, p. 27.

95. "Rome Rally Scores U.S." *New York Times.* February 21, 1949, p. 20.

96. "Film Comeback." *Business Week.* July 6, 1946, p. 26; "Jap Theaters Pack 'Em In with Yank Pix." *Variety.* 169:12 December 31, 1947.

97. "MPEA Threatens Film Withdrawal." *New York Times.* December 30, 1947, p. 18; "Unlikely U.S. Filmers Will Withdraw from Germany, Japan Despite Costs." *Variety.* 169:5, 12 December 31, 1947.

98. "MPEA Firms' Frozen Yen May Thaw in Japan." *Variety.* 172:25 September 29, 1948.

99. "Sex in Jap, German Local-Made Pix Too Much Competish for U.S. Product." *Variety.* 173:3, 12 February 2, 1949.

100. "Better U.S. Distrib Setup in Japan Near But Coin Still Partly Frozen." *Variety.* 178:15 March 22, 1950.

101. Ray Falk. "Tokyo to Limit American Pictures." *New York Times.* May 13, 1950, sec. 2, p. 5.

102. Thomas H. Guback, op. cit., pp. 128–129, 135.

103. Ibid., p. 129; "Riskin Says Voluntary Export Film Censorship Being Studied by U.S." *Variety.* 158:10 May 30, 1945; "80 U.S. Films Set to Go into Germany." *Variety.* 160:1, 32 September 26, 1945; "U.S. Film Distribution in Germany Snafued; Krauts 'Choosey' on Pix." *Variety.* 161:1, 22 December 19, 1945.

104. Thomas H. Guback, op. cit., pp. 129–131.

105. Dana Adams Schmidt. "Our Movies Leave Germans Hostile." *New York Times.* July 23, 1946, p. 21; "German Markets." *New York Times.* November 24, 1946, sec. 2, p. 5; "Gov't Storm on U.S. Pix Abroad." *Variety.* 164:1, 64 November 24, 1946.

106. "Crime in Austria Laid to U.S. Films." *New York Times.* August 22, 1948, p. 26.

107. "Germany's Pix Biz Off 40% in Six Months." *Variety.* 175:18 August 10, 1949.

108. Thomas H. Guback, op. cit., pp. 128–129, 131.

109. Ibid., pp. 132–134.

110. "German Market Viewed as Possibly 2d to Britain Eventually for Americans." *Variety.* 177:5, 54 February 1, 1950; "Limit Set on U.S. Films." *New York Times.* October 6, 1950, p. 22.

111. Thomas H. Guback, op. cit., pp. 103–104.

112. Ibid., p. 105.

113. Sydney Gruson. "Britain Would Cut Cost of U.S. Film." *New York Times.* November 17, 1945, p. 14; Thomas M. Pryor. "U.S. Films Facing Restraints Abroad." *New York Times.* December 4, 1945, p. 33.

114. Philip Carr. "One Hollywood." *The Spectator.* 175:507 November 30, 1945.

115. Charles E. Egan. "U.S. Leaders Fight British Quota." *New York Times.* November 14, 1946, p. 39; Alexander Korda. "Is the Screen Really Free." *New York Times.* December 1, 1946, sec. 2, p. 5.

116. "Loan's O.K. Big Break for Pix." *Variety.* 163:3, 20 July 17, 1946.

117. "Brit Crisis Fateful to U.S. Pix." *Variety.* 165:3, 24 March 5, 1947.

118. "The British Film Industry." *Times* (London). January 21, 1948, p. 5.

119. Norman MacKenzie. "Films and Quotas." *New Statesman and Nation.* 33:451–452 June 2, 1947.

120. Thomas H. Guback, op. cit., p. 18.

121. "Foreign Trade." *Time.* 50:81 August 18, 1947; "Film 'Big 8' Bans Movies for Britain." *New York Times.* August 9, 1947, pp. 1, 5; Ian Jarvie, op. cit., p. 229.

122. "Foreign Trade." *Time.* 50:81 August 18, 1947.

123. "Americans Wary of British Losing the Hollywood Habit." *Variety.* 167:1, 46 August 20, 1947.

124. "$75,000,000 U.S. Net Can Still Be Gotten Without British Market" *Variety*. 167:1, 34 August 13, 1947.

125. "Did London 'Out-Trade' H'wood?" *Variety*. 170:1, 9 March 17, 1948; "Dollars and Films." *Times* (London). March 12, 1948, p. 5.

126. "MPEA Approves Johnston's Agreement." *New York Times*. March 19, 1948, p. 29.

127. Woodrow Wyatt. "Champagne for Hollywood." *New Statesman & Nation*. 35:231 March 20, 1948.

128. "Bacon and Bogart, too." *Fortune*. 37:122 June, 1948.

129. "Exhibitors and the Film Quota." *Times* (London). July 20, 1948, p. 3; "War with Britain." *Newsweek*. 32:66 September 13, 1948; Charles E. Egan. "Sale of U.S. Films Limited in Britain." *New York Times*. September 1, 1948, p. 20; "British Must Choose Between World Mart or Local Protection—Johnston." *Variety*. 171:6 September 1, 1948.

130. "Policy for Films." *Times* (London). September 7, 1948, p. 5.

131. Thomas H. Guback, op. cit., p. 34.

132. "British Increase Own Screen Times." *New York Times*. June 15, 1948, p. 32; "U.S. Film Leaders Ask Quota Protest." *New York Times*. June 18, 1948, p. 19.

133. "D.C. Politicos' Assault vs. Brit Film Quota Mounts." *Variety*. 174:3, 18 March 31, 1949; "Acheson Backs U.S. Films." *New York Times*. April 21, 1949, p. 29; "Acheson Orders Foreign Problems of Yanks Included in D.C. Int'l Talks." *Variety*. 174:16 April 20, 1949.

134. "Britain Shaves Quota by Scant 5%." *Variety*. 174:3, 4 March 23, 1949; "Two Film Groups Join in New Quota Protest." *New York Times*. June 4, 1949, p. 8.

135. "British Cut Film Quota." *New York Times*. March 11, 1950, p. 9; "Gloom in Commons on 30% quota." *Variety*. 178:13, 18 April 5, 1950.

136. "Britain, U.S. Set Up Film Bonus Plan." *New York Times*. August 3, 1950, p. 19; "State Dept. Help Ends Incentive Plan, Insures Yanks $17,000,000 Minimum." *Variety*. 179:3, 30 July 26, 1950.

137. Nicholas Davenport. "Hollywood and Mr. Wilson." *New Statesman & Nation*. 40:197–198 August 19, 1950; "Hollywood's Exports Pay Off." *Business Week*. April 29, 1950, p. 113.

138. "Brit Film Biz Moves to Prevent Harsh Govt. Action vs. Yank Pix." *Variety*. 185:13 February 20, 1952.

139. "$100,000,000 of Films' Normal O'seas Take Hit by Foreign Market Snafu." *Variety*. 168:6 November 12, 1947; "Hollywood." *New Republic*. 116:42 March 31, 1947.

140. "H'wood Has Yet to Make Pix Profitably for Domestic B.O. Only—Balaban." *Variety*. 172:3, 36 September 29, 1948; "Says Sales Abroad Cut Film Prices Here." *New York Times*. April 22, 1947, p. 32.

141. "Hollywood's Exports Pay Off." *Business Week*. April 29, 1950, pp. 113–114.

142. "Yanks' $210,000,000 Abroad." *Variety*. 165:5, 20 February 5, 1947.

143. "$138,000,000 Net for All Firms in '46 Foreign Coin." *Variety*. 169:12 December 31, 1947.

144. "While Eyeing Foreign Earnings Record, Distribs Face Upped Curbs Abroad." *Variety*. 188:3, 15 December 3, 1952.

145. Nathan D. Golden. "1950 Foreign Outlook Pessimistic for U.S. Film Companies." *Variety*. 177:175 January 4, 1950.

146. Thomas H. Guback, op. cit., pp. 16–17.

147. Paul Jarrico. "They Are Not So Innocent Abroad." *New Republic*. 120:17 January 31, 1949.

148. Norman Cousins. "The Free Ride." *Saturday Review of Literature*. 33:24–25

January 21, 1950; Norman Cousins. "The Free Ride, Part II." *Saturday Review of Literature.* 33:20–21 January 28, 1950; Norman Cousins. "The Free Ride, Part III." *Saturday Review of Literature.* 33:22–23 February 4, 1950.

149. Eric Johnston. "Messengers from a Free Country." *Saturday Review of Literature.* 33:9–13, 28 March 4, 1950; Norman Cousins. "Let's Look at the Message." *Saturday Review of Literature.* 33:12–13, 28 March 4, 1950; Samuel Goldwyn. "Our Movies Speak for U.S." *Saturday Review of Literature.* 33:10–12 April 1, 1950; Norman Cousins. "Our Films Speak for Hollywood." *Saturday Review of Literature.* 33:12–13, 34 April 1, 1950.

150. Gerald M. Mayer, op. cit., p. 31.

151. Walter F. Wanger. "Donald Duck and Diplomacy." *Public Opinion Quarterly.* v. 14, no. 3:443–446 Fall 1950.

152. Nathan D. Golden. "Optimism Prevails in Int'l Market for U.S. Pix After Encouraging '51." *Variety.* 185:193 January 2, 1952.

153. "See Record '51 Foreign Income." *Variety.* 185:5, 15 January 16, 1952; "'52 Peak on Foreign Income." *Variety.* 188:3, 22 September 17, 1952.

Chapter 7

1. Erik Barnouw and S. Krishnaswamy. *Indian Film.* 2d ed. New York: Oxford, 1980, pp. 137, 154.

2. Diane Collins. *Hollywood Down Under.* North Ryde, NSW.: Angus & Robertson, 1987, p. 1; Ina Bertrand, ed. *Cinema in Australia: A Documentary History.* Kensington, NSW.: New South Wales University Press, 1989, pp. 243, 259.

3. "Exhibitors in Foreign Lands Seen U.S. Distrib' Main Ally." *Variety.* 194:7, 18 April 28, 1954.

4. Thomas H. Guback. *The International Film Industry: Western Europe and America Since 1945.* Bloomington: Indiana University Press, 1969, pp. 108, 113.

5. "UFA Exec Suggests Doubling of Admission Scale in Germany." *Variety.* 243:19 July 6, 1966; "New Price Freeze on Film Rentals in Chile." *Variety.* 247:15 July 26, 1967.

6. Manjunath Pendakur. *Canadian Dreams and American Control.* Toronto: Garamond, Press, 1990, pp. 116–119.

7. Ibid., pp. 120, 122.

8. Ibid., pp. 123, 125.

9. Ibid., pp. 125–127.

10. "Picker Finds Admissions Too Low in Latin America." *Variety.* 194:4 March 31, 1954.

11. "Boxoffice Controlled, Not Births, So Latin Lands' Market Value Grows." *Variety.* 204:4, 20 November 21, 1956.

12. Nathan D. Golden. "Exporting U.S. Film Glamour." *Variety* 205:5, 204 January 9, 1957; "Yanks, Brazil Exhibs United to Fight Admissions Kept Low." *Variety.* 206:3 April 10, 1957.

13. "Decry Mexico's 32¢ Top Admish." *Variety.* 194:7, 20 May 5, 1954; "Mexico's Long Frozen 32¢ Boxoffice Top Finally Thawed." *Variety.* 225:7, 15 January 24, 1962.

14. "Low Admissions a Discouragement." *Variety.* 214:3 March 18, 1959; "Spell Backward Nations Backwards." *Variety.* 229:15 December 19, 1962.

15. "MPEA Unblocks 500G in Turkey." *Variety.* 260:5 September 16, 1970; "Turks to Remit MPEA Companies at Old 9-to-1 Rate." *Variety.* 261:3 December 16, 1970.

16. Barry Monush, ed. *International Motion Picture Almanac 1994, 65th ed.* New York: Quigley, 1994, pp. 488, 512–518.

17. "Okay Johnston Offices' Joint Budget; Global Fence-Mending Looming Bigger." *Variety.* 201:3 February 29, 1956; "Foresee MPAA Budget Trim." *Variety.* 258:3 May 4, 1970.

18. Thomas H. Guback, op. cit., p. 166.

19. Spyros P. Skouras. "Skouras Sees Greater Global Markets for U.S. Films." *Variety.* 189:15 January 7, 1953.

20. Gene Arnell. "Talk English, Not Subsidy." *Variety.* 226:3 February 28, 1962.

21. Thomas H. Guback, op. cit., p. 98.

22. "Film Gains Surveyed." *New York Times.* March 5, 1954, p. 15.

23. Thomas M. Pryor. "Hollywood Stand." *New York Times.* May 29, 1955, sec. 2, p. 5; "Good Movie Year Seen." *New York Times.* April 24, 1956, p. 26.

24. "Un-united Americans Sure to Lose." *Variety.* 204:11 October 10, 1956.

25. "Unique Status of Eric Johnston." *Variety.* 212:4 November 5, 1958.

26. Eric Johnston. "H'wood Still Best U.S. Ambassador Despite Some Contrary Opinions." *Variety.* 189:5, 65 January 7, 1953.

27. Eric Johnston. "Mirrors of Society." *Americas.* 7:3–6 July, 1955.

28. Eric Johnston. "Hollywood: America's Traveling Salesman." *Vital Speeches.* 23:572–574 July 1, 1957.

29. "Eric Johnston, MPAA Prez Who Sold Hollywood Around the Globe, Dies at 66." *Variety.* 232:4, 22 August 23, 1963; "MPAA Setup Post–Johnston." *Variety.* 232:3 October 23, 1963; Ronald Gold. "Ex-LBJ Aide's Film Vision." *Variety.* 243:1, 52 June 1, 1966; Thomas H. Guback, op. cit., p. 141.

30. Jack Valenti. "Spirit of '76." *Variety.* 245:10 January 4, 1967; Jack Valenti. "Protectionism NG for Pix Biz." *Variety.* 249:7, 28 January 3, 1968.

31. Will Tusher. "U.S. Pix 32% Up on 1976." *Variety.* 286:1, 126 April 6, 1977.

32. Cobbett Steinburg. *Film Facts.* New York: Facts on File, 1980, p. 43; "Nine MPAA Members Control Over 68% of Domestic Pic Market." *Variety.* 262:35 May 12, 1971; "Japan (494), India (308), Italy (301), U.S. (300), Taiwan (246) Most Active." *Variety.* 262:37 May 12, 1971.

33. Aljean Harmetz. "If a Movie Goes in America, Will Rest of World Buy It?" *New York Times.* August 1, 1977, p. 19; John M. Wilson. "The Global Film: Will It Play in Uruguay." *New York Times.* November 26, 1978, sec. 2, pp. 1, 26.

34. Ronald Carroll. "Which Films Should Go Abroad?" *Films in Review.* 3:443–448 November, 1952.

35. Ben Pearse. "How the Movies Get Their Money out of Europe." *Saturday Evening Post.* 227:43 November 27, 1954.

36. "Sexports." *Time.* 76:61, 63 September 19, 1960.

37. "Aboaf Sees Situation in Belgium Easing for U.S." *Variety.* 186:5, 16 April 16, 1952.

38. "Subtitle Plot, Lyrics in Italics." *Variety.* 223:4 August 9, 1961.

39. "Nix 'Selective' Export Process." *Variety.* 189:3, 18 January 14, 1953.

40. "Johnston Defends Pix Going O'seas Before Senate Foreign Relations Unit." *Variety.* 190:5, 61 March 11, 1953.

41. "Ask Resolution vs. Film Exports Damaging U.S. Prestige Abroad." *Variety.* 215:1, 13 August 19, 1959.

42. Nathan D. Golden. "Exporting U.S. Film Glamour." *Variety.* 205:5, 204 January 9, 1957.

43. "Export *Blackboard Jungle.*" *Variety.* 198:7, 22 April 20, 1955.

44. Thomas M. Pryor. "U.S. Films Hailed by Hammarskjold." *New York Times.* May 15, 1954, p. 12.

45. Robert Alden. "Hands of U.S. Tied in Asia 'Cold War.'" *New York Times.* June 11, 1956, p. 11.

46. C.L. Sulzberger. "Foreign Affairs." *New York Times.* April 13, 1955, p. 28.

47. "Murrow Dubs U.S. Film Product 'Funhouse Mirrors' as Seen O'seas." *Variety.* 224:1, 78 November 8, 1961.

48. "Threaten O'seas Film Front." *Variety.* 237:5 February 10, 1965.

49. "Fear Govt's Foreign Aid Slash Will Cut into U.S. Pix Remittances." *Variety.* 191:3, 16 August 5, 1953.

50. Thomas H. Guback, op. cit., p. 11.

51. "Movies Seek U.S. Help." *New York Times.* March 20, 1960, p. 40.

52. "Johnston's Sarcastic Admiration for Foreign Ingenuity." *Variety.* 218:5, 20 March 2, 1960.

53. A.D. Murphy. "Valenti's Inventory of Alien Threats to U.S. Films." *Variety.* 262:5 April 28, 1971.

54. A.D. Murphy. "Export-Import Bank Film Aid." *Variety.* 264:3, 23 October 13, 1971.

55. "Overseas Choke U.S. Films & TV." *Variety.* 267:1, 60 May 31, 1972.

56. "European Reaction to U.S. Films." *Variety.* 233:2, 54 January 1, 1964.

57. Alexander Cockburn. "In Bed with America." *American Film.* 16:43 November/December, 1991.

58. "Name Films Not Fit for O'seas." *Variety.* 214:5 May 27, 1959; "U.S. Lists Movies It Limits Abroad." *New York Times.* May 24, 1959, p. 46; "Congressman Jibes Media Guaranty." *Variety.* 215:17 June 3, 1959; Thomas H. Guback, op. cit., p. 134.

59. "Cartel-Conditioned Europeans Favor Pix Pool But Yanks Dead Against It." *Variety.* 200:1 November 16, 1955.

60. "Europe: Hates 'Competition.'" *Variety.* 203:5, July 11, 1956.

61. "Cartel Ideas of Europeans Big Fear Phobia with Yankee Film Leaders." *Variety.* 214:5 May 27, 1959.

62. Thomas H. Guback, op. cit., pp. 97–99; "Johnston's Sarcastic Admiration for Foreign Ingenuity." *Variety.* 218:20 March 2, 1960.

63. "Common Market Needs U.S. Pox." *Variety.* 230:1, 86 May 15, 1963.

64. Bosley Crowther. "The Multinational Film." *New York Times.* July 5, 1966, p. 41.

65. "U.S. Distribs Crack Freeze on Film Prices by Europe TV." *Variety.* 273:1, 40 December 26, 1973.

66. Thomas H.Guback, op. cit., p. 114; "Norway Film Group to Cancel U.S. Pact." *New York Times.* August 1, 1954, p. 77; "Balk at Norway Monopoly." *Variety.* 197:11 January 26, 1955.

67. Thomas H. Guback, op. cit., pp. 115–116; "Balk at Norway Monopoly." *Variety.* 197:11 January 26, 1955; "Studios Drop Danish Demands." *New York Times.* January 22, 1955, p. 9.

68. "Danes Forced Yanks' Withdrawal." *Variety.* 204:4 October 31, 1956; "More Foresight, Less Grab and Run." *Variety.* 205:10 February 13, 1957.

69. Fred Hift. "Can Yank Films Crack Danes' Boycott." *Variety.* 207:5, 28 June 12, 1957; Thomas H. Guback, op. cit., pp. 115–116.

70. "Johnston Decries French Film Bars." *New York Times.* May 13, 1952, p. 19; "Film Deadlock Broken." *New York Times.* November 15, 1952, p. 15; "French Decree Slashing U.S. Imports Seen Bid for Subsidy of Gallic Prod." *Variety.* 187:4, 21 July 23, 1952.

71. "Reds Prod Paris on U.S. Pix." *Variety.* 205:7, 18 December 26, 1956; "Johnston Boost for Common Market in Europe Puzzles Some Yanks." *Variety.* 210:7, 16 April 16, 1958.

72. Vincent Canby. "Spain, Please See French Text." *Variety*. 219:11, 15 August 10, 1960; "France Lifts Foreign Film Curb." *New York Times*. June 15, 1961, p. 51.

73. Thomas H. Guback, op. cit., p. 177.

74. Ibid., pp. 105, 117; Albion Ross. "Bonn Film Group Asks Import Curb." *New York Times*. January 2, 1955, p. 63.

75. "British Film Makers Will Ask Govt. to Intervene in Industry Crisis." *Variety*. 232:23 November 6, 1963.

76. Thomas H. Guback, op. cit., pp. 167, 170–171; "Discussions Due on U.S. Films Cutback." *Times* (London). December 27, 1969, p. 9.

77. "Spain Renews Film Pact." *New York Times*. November 23, 1953, p. 32; Camille M. Cianfara. "U.S. Film Exports to Spain Halted." *New York Times*. August 21, 1955, p. 95.

78. Hank Werba. "More Flashes from Spanish Front." *Variety*. 206:5 March 27, 1957; "Rain in Spain Falls Mainly on the Plain." *Variety*. 206:11 April 17, 1957; "U.S. Distribs End Boycott of Spain." *Variety*. 210:1, 18 April 2, 1958.

79. "Spain Starves U.S. on Licenses." *Variety*. 223:11 August 2, 1961; Vincent Canby. "Spain's Quota Pains Yanks." *Variety*. 236:3 October 21, 1964; Hank Werba. "Pro-Pix U.S. Envoy to Spain." *Variety*. 239:13 July 21, 1965.

80. Peter Besas. "Spain Abolishes Film Quota." *Variety*. 262:5, 22 March 10, 1971.

81. "Soviet Rebuffs U.S. on Return of 5 Films." *New York Times*. September 22, 1952, p. 19; "Pravda Scolds at Tarzan Films." *New York Times*. December 28, 1953, p. 2.

82. Fred Hift. "Sell Russia Our Pix, Urges Salisbury." *Variety*. 196:4 September 22, 1954.

84. "Lodge Prescribes Films for Soviet." *New York Times*. April 14, 1958, p. 18; Bosley Crowther. "Films for Export." *New York Times*. April 20, 1958, sec. 2, p. 1; Max Frankel. "U.S., Soviet Agree to Film Exchange." *New York Times*. October 10, 1958, p. 36; "4 More U.S. Movies Chosen for Soviet." *New York Times*. March 20, 1959, p. 3; Max Frankel. "U.S. Movie Series Opens in Moscow." *New York Times*. November 11, 1959, p. 40.

85. James F. Clarity. "Russians' Charge on Films Denied." *New York Times*. May 8, 1969, p. 2.

86. Charles E. Egan. "U.S. Will Offer Films to Soviets." *New York Times*. October 5, 1956, p. 21; "Satellites Agree to Buy U.S. Films." *New York Times*. October 26, 1956, p. 33; "Czechs Make Deal for Ten U.S. Films." *New York Times*. November 29, 1958, p. 18; Hans Hoehn. "Hungarians Ban All Westerns." *Variety*. 244:28 September 14, 1966; "Rumania Yens More Yank Films." *Variety*. 243:17 July 13, 1966.

87. "Belgrade to Cut U.S. Film Imports." *New York Times*. December 8, 1957, p. 157.

88. "Culture Joins Cash Resistance to U.S. Films in Red China." *Variety*. 295:2, 94 June 27, 1979.

89. "Movie Problems Found in Far East." *New York Times*. March 14, 1959, p. 26.

90. "Powerful Forces Aiming to Restrict U.S. Pix in Japan Denounced by Maas." *Variety*. 189:5, 17 December 10, 1952.

91. "Maas Blasts Anti-U.S. Films Drive." *Variety*. 210:8 April 30, 1958; "The Japanese 'Obstacle Race' MPEA Battles New Restrictions." *Variety*. 212:7, 16 September 3, 1958.

92. "Sovereign Japan Kicks Pix." *Variety*. 219:11, 12 July 20, 1960; "Japan Okay, Rest of Far East Not." *Variety*. 235:3, 29 July 29, 1964.

93. "New Duty on Foreign Films Playing Singapore." *Variety*. 216:11 October 28, 1959.

94. "Burma Coup Might Be Helpful." *Variety*. 226:7 March 7, 1962.

95. John A. Lent. *The Asian Film Industry*. London: Christopher Helm, 1990, pp. 201, 216–217, 219.

96. "Global Goodwill Plan Set." *Variety.* 192:5, 14 September 16, 1953; "India Cuts Duty on Foreign Films." *New York Times.* July 16, 1960, p. 10; "Love Our Own Pix Endangers U.S. Foreign Sales, Sez Silverstone." *Variety.* 193:7, 18 February 3, 1954.

97. Thomas F. Brady. "Indian Film Tariff Stirs a Boycott." *New York Times.* August 26, 1963, p. 21; Thomas F. Brady. "On Indian Film." *New York Times.* December 1, 1963, sec. 2, p. 7.

98. "Breach of Contract on U.S. Film Import Charged in India." *New York Times.* July 16, 1971, p. 16; "India Barely Worthwhile for U.S. Films." *Variety.* 263:23 July 21, 1971; Sydney H. Schanberg. "New Delhi: Pillage in the Eyes of Gods." *New York Times.* August 30, 1971, p. 34; "India to Admit 150 U.S. films." *Variety.* 277:3 December 4, 1974; "U.S. Leading Exporter of Films to India in 1975." *Variety.* 284:38 September 29, 1976.

99. Erik Barnouw, op. cit., p. 288.

100. "American Films Defended." *New York Times.* March 5, 1953, p. 26.

101. "Blame Naive Natives and Red Hecklers." *Variety.* 208:5 October 2, 1957.

102. Thomas M. Pryor. "Sukarno Praises Role of U.S. Films." *New York Times.* June 2, 1956, p. 13; Erik Barnouw, op. cit., p. 167.

103. John A. Lent, op. cit., p. 202; "Spell Backward Nations Backwards." *Variety.* 229:15 December 19, 1962; "Indonesian Bar U.S. Films." *New York Times.* May 11, 1964, p. 11; "Indonesians View U.S. Films Again." *New York Times.* June 19, 1966, p. 10; "Indonesian Exhib Again." *Variety.* 243:5 June 22, 1966.

104. Stephen Watts. "On the African Movie Menus." *New York Times.* April 26, 1953, sec. 2, p. 4.

105. Thomas H. Guback, op. cit., pp. 98–99.

106. Vincent Canby. "Africa: New Map, New Marts." *Variety.* 219:3, 13 August 24, 1960.

107. Thomas H. Guback, op. cit., p. 100; "MPEA's Nigeria Pool Starting." *Variety.* 225:5 December 20, 1961; "Box Office Buzzes Overseas." *Business Week.* November 7, 1964, pp. 64, 68.

108. Vincent Canby. "Slow U.S. Start in W. Africa." *Variety.* 227:5 July 11, 1962; Thomas H. Guback, op. cit., p. 100.

109. Thomas H. Guback, op. cit., pp. 100–101.

110. "MPEA Recognizes Kenya Film Corp." *Variety.* 252:5 September 18, 1968.

111. Herrick Warren. "Ethiopia: Films for a Few." *Variety.* 262:169–170 May 12, 1971.

112. "Tunisian Film Tax is Aiding Red Bloc." *New York Times.* February 5, 1961, p. 83; "West and Tunisians Agree on Film Tax." *New York Times.* April 8, 1961, p. 13.

113. "Egypt Bans Rooney and Kaye." *New York Times.* June 20, 1948, p. 52; "Jordan Bans All Kaye films." *New York Times.* October 1, 1956, p. 21; "Miss Taylor Banned in Jordan." *New York Times.* April 28, 1959, p. 41; "Arabs Ban More U.S. films." *New York Times.* January 22, 1960, p. 17; "Pan-Arab Boycotts of H'wood Stars." *Variety.* 217:1, 62 December 23, 1959; "Arabs Ban 2 Actresses' Films." *New York Times.* July 17, 1963, p. 20.

114. "Egypt Bans U.S. films." *New York Times.* June 18, 1967, p. 18; "American Films Barred by U.A.R." *New York Times.* September 17, 1967, p. 121; Thomas F. Brady. "Egypt continues U.S. Film Imports." *New York Times.* May 31, 1968, p. 22; Eric Pace. "Cairo Is Willing to Let Tarzan Films Return." *New York Times.* November 24, 1968, p. 115.

115. Ernest Holsendolph. "Paramount Halts Films Exports to Iran Over Oil Prices. *New York Times.* September 26, 1974, p. 24; "6 Companies to Halt Film Shipments to Iran." *New York Times.* March 28, 1975, p. 10; "Par Out of Iran on B.O. Curb." *Variety.* 276:4 October 2, 1974.

116. "6 Distribs (Not Columbia, AA) Embargo Their Prints in Chagrin That Iran Keeps Low Admissions." *Variety*. 278:3, 42 April 2, 1975; "Yank Cos. Fly Iranian Flag." *Variety*. 283:69, 91 May 19, 1976; "Iran's Islamic Regime Kicks Out Bruce Lee & Imperialistic Films." *Variety*. 295:2, 102 July 18, 1979; "Ban on Pix to Iran an Economic Issue, Not Politics: Valenti." *Variety*. 297:1, 55 December 26, 1979.

117. Manjunath Pendakur, op. cit., pp. 22, 31; Michael Spencer. "U.S.–Canada Film Relations 1920–1986." *Cinema Canada*. n. 131:13–14 June, 1986.

118. Manjunath Pendakur, op. cit., pp. 160, 163; Michael Spencer, op. cit., pp. 14–15.

119. Manjunath Pendakur, op. cit., p. 164.

120. Ibid., p. 167; Michael Spencer, op. cit., pp. 15–16.

121. Manjunath Pendakur, op. cit., p. 168.

122. Vincent Canby. "Yanks' Latin Markets Okay." Variety. 224:3, 76 November 8, 1961; Randal Johnson. *The Film Industry in Brazil: Culture and the State*. Pittsburgh; University of Pittsburgh Press, 1987, p. 7.

123. Vincent Canby. "Our Men in Havana—Stay." *Variety*. 220:5 October 26, 1960; "Cuba Confiscates, Caramba!" *Variety*. 122:5 May 24, 1961.

124. "Mexico: Get Lost, Uncle Sam." *Variety*. 233:1, 54 December 11, 1963.

125. Randal Johnson, op. cit., pp. 123, 179; "Brazil Eases Up on Tax, Take-Out." *Variety*. 282:1, 126 May 19, 1976.

126. "Argentine Theaters Protest Curb on Foreign Movies." *New York Times*. June 24, 1963, p. 21; "Argentina Producers Behind Quota Slash of U.S. Pictures." *Variety*. 237:5 January 27, 1965.

127. "Buenos Aires Exhibs Reel as Lack of Yank Product Puts B.O. in Dive." *Variety*. 257:35 November 19, 1969; "U.S. Distribs Resume Pix Exports." *Variety*. 257:35 December 10, 1969; "U.S. Film Famine Ends in Argentina." *Variety*. 281:6 January 14, 1976.

128. Hans Ehrmann. "Remittance Blues in Chile." *Variety*. 264:21 September 22, 1971; Hans Ehrmann. "Chile Won't Pay, U.S. Won't Play." *Variety*. 269:88 January 3, 1973; Hans Ehrmann. "Chile: We Want Good, Healthy Films Like *The Godfather*." *Variety*. 274:54 May 8, 1974; Alexander Cockburn. "In Bed with America." *American Film*. 16:50 November/December 1991.

129. "Alterman visits Chile for MPEA." *Variety*. 279:37 July 30, 1975.

130. Thomas M. Pryor. "Hollywood Global Review." *New York Times*. October 31, 1954, sec. 2, p. 5; "$150,000,000 O'seas Film Take." *Variety*. 190:1, 13 June 3, 1953; "Hollywood Focus Is Overseas." *Business Week*. October 9, 1954, p. 158; "U.S. Pix on World Scale." *Variety*. 191:3 June 17, 1953.

131. "Seating Capacity at Movies Rise." *New York Times*. February 25, 1955, p. 19; "Despite Critics, Don Hartman Sees H'wood Unmenaced Around the World." *Variety*. 194:5, 15 May 5, 1954; "Films' Overseas Advertising." *Variety*. 192:3, 6 November 18, 1953; Hy Hollinger. "$8,500,000 for O'seas Ads." *Variety*. 197:5, 54 February 23, 1955.

132. "U.S. Films Still Gaining Ground." *Variety*. 206:1, 78 April 10, 1957; "Films May Help Save Crazy World." *Variety*. 214:7 May 27, 1959; "U.S. Films Sell Abroad. *New York Times*. February 4, 1959, p. 27.

133. "Johnston's Upbeat Horizons." *Variety*. 228:3, 15 September 12, 1962; "54.6% of U.S. Sales Now Overseas." *Variety*. 232:1 November 6, 1963; Mike Mosettig. "Take-Out of $$ Eased Globally." *Variety*. 234:33 April 29, 1964; "Box Office Buzzes Overseas." *Business Week*. November 7, 1964, p. 68.

134. Gene Arnell. "Devaluation: Film Biz Boon." *Variety*. 265:1, 70 December 22, 1971; "Britain, Italy, Canada, France, Japan 40% of U.S. Films' Foreign Market." *Variety*. 264:4 October 20, 1971; "How U.S. Majors Perform Overseas." *Variety*. 275:1, 34 May 15, 1974.

135. A.D. Murphy. "Yanks 1974 Global Film Take Up 28%." *Variety*. 279:3, 30 June 25, 1975; A.D. Murphy. "O'seas Inflation Clips U.S. Films." *Variety*. 288:1, 16 August 24, 1977.

136. Thomas M. Pryor. "Johnston Expects New Movie Gains." *New York Times*. October 8, 1954, p. 27; John D. Morris. "Excise Tax Study Seeks Inequities." *New York Times*. October 7, 1955, p. 12; "Europe's a Code for a Code." *Variety*. 196:1, 16 October 6, 1954; "American Film Comeback Induces Envy in Foreign Industries." *Variety*. 197:3 December 8, 1954.

137. "Yanks See Quota Cry, Other Angles." *Variety*. 201:16 February 15, 1956; "Careless Errata Weaken British Side of Case." *Variety*. 201:16 February 15, 1956; "Europe Needy—For U.S. Facts." *Variety*. 201:7 February 22, 1956; "Beautifully Made But Too Few European Films Right for U.S." *Variety*. 203:5 July 11, 1956.

138. Fred Hift. "Pro–U.S. and It's Tough." *Variety*. 203:5, 22 July 11, 1956; Hazel Guild. "Love U.S. Films: Germany." *Variety*. 213:25, 60 January 7, 1959; Fred Hift. "Foreign Films 'Arrive' in U.S." *Variety*. 205:1, 62 January 30, 1957.

139. Minty Clinch. *Clint Eastwood*. London: Hodder & Stoughton, 1994, pp. 35, 42, 45–46, 48.

140. John Tulloch. *Australian Cinema: Industry, Narrative and Meaning*. Sydney: George Allen & Unwin, 1982, p. 16; Randal Johnson, op. cit., p. 175.

141. Jack Valenti. "Valenti Values Film-TV Coin in O'seas Mart." *Variety*. 289:5, 64 January 4, 1978.

142. Hank Werba. "Turks Desperate for Yank Pic Products." *Variety*. 285:30 December 29, 1976; "Films That Do Poorly Elsewhere Often Large S. African Grossers." *Variety*. 296:26 October 17, 1979.

143. "Like the Marines, MPEA Fights for U.S. Industry from Halls of Montezuma to Shores of Tripoli." *Variety*. 291:7, 42 June 21, 1978.

144. Geri Fabricant. "O'seas Marketing Costs Soar." *Variety*. 299:12, 330 May 7, 1980.

Chapter 8

1. Barry Monash, ed. *International Motion Picture Almanac 1994*, 60th ed. New York: Quigley, 1994, pp. 511–516; Adam Dawtrey. "Carlton Won't Nab MGM Cinemas." *Variety*. 358:127–128 April 3–9, 1995.

2. Barry Monash, op. cit., pp. 516–518; "Showbiz Lures Bronfman." *Times-Colonist* (Victoria, BC). April 11, 1995, p. B8; Owen Robinson. "Power Shift at Sony Corp." *Variety*. 358:15, 22 March 27–April 2, 1995.

3. Barry Monash, op. cit., p. 21; *International Television & Video Almanac*. 36th ed. New York: Quigley, 1991, pp. 20A, 603, 608, 610; "Video Champs." *Variety*. 358:12 February 27–March 5, 1995; Don Groves. "Veni, Video, Vici." *Variety*. 358:1, 46 April 3–9, 1995.

4. "Time Warner Buys Another Cable Firm." *Times-Colonist* (Victoria, BC) February 8, 1995, p. C11.

5. Don Groves. "Sat Channels Scramble to Protect Signal." *Variety*. 355:29 June 20, 1994.

6. Don Groves. "Field Pared to Pair." *Variety*. 358:44 March 13–19, 1995.

7. Russell Sadler. "Murdoch, PBS, and Congress." *Z Magazine*. 8:12–13 April, 1995.

8. "What Makes a Film Fly in Japan." *Business Week*. June 29, 1981, p. 97; Harlan Kennedy. "Fox's Man in London." *American Film*. 7:60–61 November, 1981.

9. "Yank Pix Mine B.O. Gold as Euro Dubbers Get in Synch." *Variety*. 348:1, 72 August 10, 1992.

10. Stuart Emmrich. "Foreign Intrigue." *American Film*. 14:40–41, 54 September 1989; Geraldine Fabrikant. "Box Office Abroad." *New York Times*. September 28, 1987, pp. DI, D8.

11. Richard Gold. "U.S. Pix Tighten Global Grip." *Variety*. 340:1, 96 August 22, 1990.

12. Don Groves. "Distribs Voting to Revise Pic Campaigns O'seas." *Variety*. 352:5, 8 September 13, 1993.

13. John Marcom, Jr. "Dream Factory to the World." *Forbes*. 147:101 April 29, 1991.

14. Marcy Magiera. "Promotional Marketer of the Year." *Advertising Age*. 65:S1, S8 March 21, 1994.

15. Aljean Harmetz. "Hollywood Starts an Invasion of Europe's Booming Product." *New York Times*. January 11, 1990, pp. C19–C20.

16. John Marcom, Jr., op. cit., pp. 98, 101.

17. Garth Alexander. "Opposition Bristles as Warners Plexes Japan." *Variety*. 350:36–37 April 19, 1993; Don Groves. "Modern Multiplexes to Make China Smile." *Variety*. 354:12 April 4, 1994; Leonard Klady. "Exceptions Are the Rule in Foreign B.O." *Variety*. 357:7, 12 November 14, 1994.

18. Adam Dawtrey. "Carlton Won't Nab MGM Cinemas." *Variety*. 358:128 April 3–9 1995; "UA Theaters to Build in India." *Variety*. 358:14 February 20–26, 1995; Fionnuala Halligan. "Cantonese Take Out." *Variety*. 357:93 January 16–22, 1995; "Carlton Bids for MGM Cinemas." *Variety*. 358:44 March 13–19 1995; Adam Dawtrey. "Euros Go on Screen-Building Spree." *Variety*. 358:1, 15 February 6–12, 1995.

19. "Cineplex, Cinemark Create Largest Chain." *Times-Colonist* (Victoria, BC). March 3, 1995, p. D2; "Cineplex, Cinemark Agree Not to Merge." *Times-Colonist* (Victoria, BC). May 13, 1995, p. C15.

20. "Cineplex Odeon Plans Megaplexes." *Times-Colonist* (Victoria, BC). June 10, 1995, p. B8.

21. Martin Peers. "UA Theaters Ready to Pump $350 Million into Worldwide Expansion Program." *Variety*. 359:18 May 29–June 4, 1995.

22. Gale Eisenstodt. "A Cozy Japanese Near Monopoly." *Forbes*. 148:55 September 30, 1991; Michael Williams. "Fox, UGC Ink Distrib'n Co-Prod Deal." *Variety*. 357:20 January 16–22, 1995; "Distribber Freezes Out Its Competish." *Variety*. 357:40 March 20–26, 1995.

23. Adam Dawtrey. "H'wood: Tomorrow the World." *Variety*. 359:1, 242 May 15–21, 1995.

24. Hazel Gould. "Theaters & Studios Owe Much to Success of U.S. Theatricals in Germany." *Variety*. 303:206 May 13, 1981; Richard W. Stevenson. "Europeans Threaten Big U.S. Film Distributor." *New York Times*. February 23, 1994, p. D3; Adam Dawtrey. "Miramax Intl. Takes a World View." *Variety*. 358:24 March 6–12, 1995.

25. Michael Dempsey. "Selling American Films Overseas." *American Film*. 7:58 November, 1981; "Britain's Best Has All Gone West." *Times* (London). July 16, 1991, p. 13; Todd Gitlin. "World Leaders: Mickey, et al." *New York Times*. May 3, 1992, sec. 2, pp. 1, 30.

26. Aubrey Solomon. *Twentieth Century–Fox: A Corporate and Financial History*. Metuchen, NJ: Scarecrow, 1988, p. xiii; Randal Johnson. *The Film Industry in Brazil: Culture and the State*. Pittsburgh: University of Pittsburgh Press, 1987, p. 179; Leonard Klady. "H'wood: Land of the Rising Sum." *Variety*. 358:14 March 13–19, 1995.

27. Ngugi wa Thiong'o. "Kenyan Culture: The National Struggle for Survival."

in Jorg Becker, ed. *Communication and Domination: Essays to Honor Herbert I. Schiller.* Norwood, NJ: Ablex, 1986, p. 114.

28. Manjunath Pendakur. *Canadian Dreams and American Control.* Toronto: Garamond, 1990, pp. 16–17.

29. "Where U.S. Still Rules: Movies, Television." *U.S. News & World Report.* 99:28 July 15, 1985; John Marcom, Jr. op. cit., p. 101; Deborah Young. "Dominance at Italo B.O. Could Bring Backlash." *Variety.* 341:45, 75 November 26, 1990; Geraldine Fabrikant. "When World Raves, Studios Jump." *New York Times.* March 7, 1990, pp. D1, D8; Ronald Grover. "The World Is Hollywood's Oyster." *Business Week.* January 14, 1991, p. 97.

30. Jack Valenti. "Fair Trade for Film Trade." *Los Angeles Times.* January 19, 1986, sec. 5, p. 5.

31. "Canadian Shows Rate Low at Global." *Times-Colonist* (Victoria, BC). June 17, 1995, p. F2.

32. Jay Stuart. "Korea and Taiwan Looking Up, But Canada Still Irksome, Says Valenti." *Variety.* 327:38 May 13, 1987.

33. Will Tusher. "Col Pledges to Pull Pix from Segregated S. African Theaters." *Variety.* 325:1, 94 November 19, 1986.

34. "The International Movie Marketplace." *Variety.* 334:35, 47 February 22, 1989.

35. Hy Hollinger. "U.S. Pix Biz Sees Good Things Overseas in '90s." *Variety.* 338:24 February 21, 1990.

36. Jack Valenti. "Webb-Pomerene." *Vital Speeches.* 47:26–28 October 15, 1980; "Yank Pic Industry an Invalid Sans Webb-Pomerene: Valenti." *Variety.* 300:7 October 1, 1980.

37. Jack Loftus. "TV & Film Execs Say Copyright Barriers Impede Foreign Trade." *Variety.* 316:3, 164 October 10, 1984.

38. "Valenti Blasts U.S. Trade Policy." *Variety.* 321:4, 33 December 11, 1985.

39. "Valenti Notes Progress Fighting Trade Barriers." *Variety.* 322:7, 24 March 12, 1986.

40. Clyde H. Farnsworth. "Jack Valenti's State Department." *New York Times.* December 18, 1985, p. B12.

41. Morrie Gelman. "Valenti Spurs Pols to Keep U.S. Showbiz in GATT Gab." *Variety.* 341:12 November 12, 1990.

42. Dennis Wharton. "Gingrich Vows to Promote U.S. Film Interests." *Variety.* 358:20 March 20–26, 1995.

43. Frank Segars. "American Majors in Asia Fight Poor Boxoffice & Trade Barriers." *Variety.* 320:337, 413 October 16, 1985; Mark Lewis. "Mysterious East B.O. Feast." *Variety.* 351:1, 63 June 7, 1993.

44. Frank Segars, op. cit.; Penny Pagano. "Studios Ask U.S. to Fight Trade Curbs." *Los Angeles Times.* September 11, 1985, sec. 6, p. 4.

45. John A. Lent. *The Asian Film Industry.* London: Christopher Helm, 1990, pp. 122–123.

46. Ibid., pp. 122, 130, 143–144; Frank Segars. "Wheel of Misfortune Persists for Yank Distribs in Far East." *Variety.* 335:335–336 Cannes '89 Special Issue; Steve Pond. "Thaw in the Russian Market." *Washington Post.* October 7, 1988, p. B7.

47. Frank Segars. "Wheel...," op. cit.; Frank Segars. "South Korean Opposition to UIP Entry Remains Strong Despite Denials." *Variety.* 335:1, 3 June 28, 1989; Garth Alexander. "U.S. Majors Tops in Korea." *Variety.* 346:53, 182 April 6, 1992; Joseph McBride. "U.S. Distrib'n Boon Seen as Road-Blocs Crumble." *Variety.* 337:21 December 13, 1989.

48. Andrea Adelson. "Entertainment Industry Adds Anti-Piracy Tricks." *New York Times*. November 21, 1988, p. D8.

49. Gale Eisenstodt. "A Cozy Japanese Near Monopoly." *Forbes*. 148:52, 54 September 30, 1991.

50. Karen Regelman. "U.S. Majors on Top in Japan." *Variety*. 354:30 April 11, 1994; Karen Regelman. "Industry Stages Silent Revolution." *Variety*. 356:59, 62 September 19, 1994.

51. Paul Calnio. "Yank Majors Ease Thai Boycott." *Variety*. 303:47–48 June 3, 1981; "Thais Give Imported Pix a Tax Break." *Variety*. 354:58 April 11, 1994.

52. Stephen Klain. "India's New Film Pact with U.S. Majors." *Variety*. 301:41, 46 November 5, 1980.

53. "India's Policy on Film Imports Hurting Us, Say U.S. Majors." *Variety*. 335:348 Cannes '89 Special Issue.

54. Don Groves. "'Park' Bow Taps Indian Distrib Doors." *Variety*. 354:13, 34 April 11, 1994; Don Groves. "Dino Dub Rubs Coin in India, Pakistan." *Variety*. 354:27–28 April 25, 1994.

55. Vivienne Heston. "Can TV Rescue Battered Filmbiz?" *Variety*. 350:59 April 12, 1993; Jennifer Clark. "Distribs Cheer Growing Market." *Variety*. 354: T5–T6 April 11, 1994.

56. Harold Myers. "Valenti Urges Soviets to Buy More U.S. Pix, Widen Audience." *Variety*. 327:5, 23 July 22, 1987; Steve Pond. "Thaw in the Russian Market." *Washington Post*. October 7, 1988.

57. Will Tusher. "MPAA Bans the Sale of U.S. Pictures to USSR." *Variety*. 343:8 June 10, 1991; Keith Bradsher. "Hollywood Bars Films to Protest Soviet Piracy." *New York Times*. June 12, 1991, pp. C13, C16.

58. Don Groves. "Majors to End Embargo on CIS." *Variety*. 349:47, 90 December 7, 1992.

59. Tom Birchenough. "Western Distribs Move Cautiously into Russia." *Variety*. 354:22 February 14, 1994.

60. Hank Werba. "China's Economy Slows U.S. Pic Inroads." *Variety*. 304:5, 30 October 28, 1981.

61. Geraldine Fabrikant. "Hollywood Returns to China." *New York Times*. February 7, 1986, pp. D1, D4.

62. Mark Lewis. "Mysterious East No B.O. Feast." *Variety*. 351:1, 63 June 7, 1993; Don Groves. "China Deals for Yank Pix." *Variety*. 354:1, 18 March 21, 1994; Rone Tempest. "Fugitive Movies Wows 'Em in China." *Times-Colonist* (Victoria, BC). December 2, 1994, p. D5.

63. Hy Hollinger. "Hungary Hungry for H'wood." *Variety*. 337:11, 14 November 22, 1989; Joseph McBride. "U.S. Distrib'n Boon Seen as Road-Blocs Crumble." *Variety*. 337:7, 21 December 13, 1989.

64. Don Groves. "MPEA Warns E. Europe Not to Get Greedy." *Variety*. 342:54 March 25, 1991.

65. Don Groves. "Too Quiet on the Eastern Front." *Variety*. 349:1, 95 January 18, 1993.

66. Jeremy Battis. "Czech Pix Seek Western Bounce." *Variety*. 354:33 April 4, 1994.

67. Manjunath Pendakur, op. cit., pp. 29, 192–193, 213.

68. "Canada Bares Teeth at U.S. Distribution." *Variety*. 309:7, 20 December 29, 1982; Antonia Zerbisias. "Canadian Study Urges U.S. Pullback." *Variety*. 310:7, 187 March 16, 1983; Manjunath Pendakur, op. cit., pp. 252–253.

69. Michael Spencer. "U.S.–Canada Film Relations 1920–1986." *Cinema Canada*. n. 131:15 June, 1986; Manjunath Pendakur, op. cit., pp. 23–25.

70. Manjunath Pendakur, op. cit., pp. 259–260.

71. Antonia Zerbisias. "U.S. Gov't Protests Quebec Distrib Ban." *Variety*. 311:5, 38 June 22, 1983.

72. Manjunath Pendakur, op. cit., pp. 262–264.

73. Suzan Ayscough. "Yank Majors Parlez Quebec Pics Into Cash." *Variety*. 350:42–43 February 8, 1993.

74. Manjunath Pendakur, op. cit., pp. 264–265.

75. Ibid., pp. 264–266; "The Domino Game." *Cinema Canada*. n. 152:21 May, 1988.

76. Manjunath Pendakur, op. cit., pp. 271–272, 275.

77. Ibid., pp. 20–21.

78. "The Domino Game," op. cit., pp. 19–21.

79. "Obituary for a Culture." *Cinema Canada*. n. 157:4 November, 1988; Allan Fotheringham. "No Flying Buns for a Bully Boy." *Macleans*. 102:116 October 30, 1989.

80. Ian Austen. "Arguments with Muscle." *Macleans*. 101:24 March 28, 1988; Sid Adilman. "U.S. Interests to Be Served in Canada Pact." *Variety*. 328:1, 101 October 7, 1987.

81. Suzan Ayscough. "Clash of Cultures: Canadians vs. MPAA." *Variety*. 344:35, 42 August 19, 1991.

82. Sid Adilman. "Canada, MPAA Lock Horns Over Free Trade." *Variety*. 343:35 June 17, 1991.

83. Dennis Wharton. "MPAA Blasts Free-Trade Agreement." *Variety*. 348:3, 5 September 14, 1992.

84. Dennis Wharton. "MPAA Hails NAFTA Win." *Variety*. 353:18 November 29, 1993.

85. Jim Bronskill. "Dupuy Wants Spotlight on Canadian Movies." *Times-Colonist* (Victoria, BC). January 26, 1995, Look sec., p. 5.

86. Jim Robbins. "E.C. Quotas a Cancer, Says Worried MPAA Prexy." *Variety*. 337:2 October 18, 1989.

87. Claudia Eller. "Yank Majors Fatten Up on European Film Business." *Variety*. 339:1, 99 May 16, 1990.

88. Rebecca Lieb. "Wenders Wants Curbs on U.S. Pix in Europe." *Variety*. 347:5 May 18, 1992.

89. "Valenti Sees World War of Trade." *Variety*. 347:23 June 1, 1992.

90. Terry Ilott. "Yanks Still Fill Europe's Bill." *Variety*. 349:1, 90 December 7, 1992.

91. Bruno Loher. "Steady Foreign Influx Alters Show Biz Scene." *Variety*. 351:31 August 9, 1993; David Molner. "Movie Director." *Variety*. 356:47–48 October 10, 1994.

92. "U.S. Distribs Yank Ads from Spain's Daily Blatt El País." *Variety*. 331:5, 32 June 1, 1988; "U.S. Movies Again Reign in Spain." *Variety*. 354:58 April 11, 1994.

93. Christopher Warman. "Distribution of Cinema Films Criticized by Monopolies Commission." *Times* (London). May 12, 1983, p. 3; Adam Dawtrey. "U.K. Looks Into Cinema Squeeze." *Variety*. 352:69–70 October 11, 1993; Adam Dawtrey. "U.S. Distribs in U.K. Cleared." *Variety*. 356:24 October 10, 1994.

94. "British Film Quota Halved." *Times* (London). July 1, 1981, p. 2; Don Groves. "U.S. Majors Take 80% of the Pic Pie." *Variety*. 342:58 January 21, 1991; David Robinson. "A Case of Hollywood or Bust." *Times* (London). December 16, 1993, p. 31.

95. "Tavernier Cries Domination." *Variety*. 301:7, 24 November 19, 1980.

96. "French Socialists Not Anti–U.S. Pix, but—." *Variety*. 304:3, 49 September 9, 1981; "Where U.S. Still Rules: Movies, Television." *U.S. News & World Report*. 99:28 July 15, 1985; "Taking Cultural Exception." *Economist*. 328:61 September 25, 1993.

97. Bruce Alderman. "Yank Majors Cleaning Up at French Wickets." *Variety*. 338:38, 54 March 21, 1990.

98. John Rockwell. "For Unholy Hollywood's Devotees, a Pariah Film Festival in France." *New York Times*. September 9, 1993, p. C13.

99. Alan Riding. "French Film Industry Circles the Wagons." *New York Times*. September 18, 1993, pp. 11, 14.

100. Michael Williams. "Gauls Called Over GATT Proposals." *Variety*. 349:33 October 26, 1992; "Taking Cultural Exception." *Economist*. 328:61 September 25, 1993; "Cola v Zola." *Economist*. 329:81 October 16, 1993; "Squeeze in France." *Variety*. 358:5 March 13–19, 1995.

101. Adam Dawtrey. "GATT Gets France's Goat." *Variety*. 352:31–32 September 27, 1993; Michael Williams. "French Still Gun for GATT Exemptions." *Variety*. 353:28 November 15, 1993.

102. Roger Cohen. "Once Dull, GATT Enters Realm of Pop Culture." *New York Times*. December 7, 1993, pp. D1, D6; Roger Cohen. "Culture Dispute with Paris Now Snags World Accord." *New York Times*. December 8, 1993, pp. A1, D2; William Safire. "Hold That GATT." *New York Times*. December 9, 1993, p. A31.

103. Bernard Weinrub. "Directors Battle Over GATT's Final Cut and Print." *New York Times*. December 12, 1993, sec. 1. p. 24.

104. Roger Cohen. "Film Issue Snags Trade Talks." New York Times. December 13, 1993, pp. A1, D5; Karl E. Meyer. "High Noon at Uruguay Gulch." *New York Times*. December 13, 1993, p. A16.

105. Roger Cohen. "With Time Waning, Europeans Reject U.S. Movie Compromise." *New York Times*. December 14, 1993, pp. A1, D6; Keith Bradsher. "U.S. and Europe Clear the Way." *New York Times*. December 15, 1993, pp. A1, D18; Roger Cohen. "A Realignment Made Reluctantly." *New York Times*. December 15, 1993, p. D19; Sharon Waxman. "GATT-astrophe Averted." *Washington Post*. December 15, 1993, p. B2.

106. Matthew Fraser. "A Question of Culture." *Macleans*. 106:50–51 December 27, 1993; Shawn Tully. "Bad Box Office." *Fortune*. 129:24 January 24, 1994; Michael Williams. "GATT Spat Wake-up on Yank Market Muscle." *Variety*. 353:45, 49 December 27, 1993.

107. Roger Cohen. "Aux Armes! France Rallies to Battle Sly and T. Rex." *New York Times*. January 2, 1994, sec. 2, pp. 1, 22.

108. Andy Stern. "Valenti Continues Euro Peace Efforts." *Variety*. 357:22 November 7, 1994.

109. Andy Stern. "French Fried in Quota Quibble." *Variety*. 358:173–174 February 20–26, 1995; Michael Williams. "Quotas Find Brussels Muscle." *Variety*. 358:39, 42 March 27–April 2, 1995.

110. Will Tusher. "Majors O'seas Gross 30–35% of Total." *Variety*. 306:5, 52 March 31, 1982; Michael Dempsey. "Selling American Films Overseas." *American Film*. 7:58 November, 1981; Richard Grenier. "When It Comes to Movies, the World Looks to America." *New York Times*. September 22, 1985, sec. 2, p. 27; Peter Biskind. "McMovies." *Sight & Sound*. 1:8 July, 1991; Peter Besas. "TV and Film Brace for Big Rebound." *Variety*. 352:51, 60 October 4, 1993.

111. "And a Boffo U.S. Box Office Abroad Rakes in Billions." *Business Week*. September 21, 1992, p. 22.

112. A.D. Murphy. "Globe Gobbling Up U.S. Pix in Record Doses." *Variety*. 339:7, 10 June 13, 1990.

113. Don Groves. "O'seas Exhibs Lack of Christmas Spirit." *Variety*. 356:11, 27 October 10, 1994; Don Groves. "Summer Forecast: Fare Hot!" *Variety*. 359:32–33 May 1–7, 1995.

114. Leonard Klady. "Earth to H'wood: You Win." *Variety*. 358:1, 63 February 13–19, 1995; Leonard Klady. "H'Wood: Land of the Rising Sum." *Variety*. 358:14 March 13–19, 1995; Don Groves. "The Mouse That Roars Is Foreign B.O. King." *Variety*. 357:11, 22 January 16–22, 1995.

115. Stuart Emmrich. "Foreign Intrigue." *American Film*. 14:53 September, 1989.

116. Richard W. Stevenson. "The Magic of Hollywood Math." *New York Times*. April 13, 1990, pp. D1–D2.

117. Ibid.; Larry Rohter. "Buchwald Gets Damages in Film Suit Dispute." *New York Times*. December 22, 1990, pp. 17, 22; Bernard Weinraub. "Art Buchwald Awarded $150,000 in Suit Over Film." *New York Times*. March 17, 1992, p. 13.

118. Lewis Beale. "Finding a Niche for Foreign Films." *Washington Post*. January 5, 1992, pp. G1, G10; Roger Cohen. "Aux Armes! France Rallies to Battle Sly and T. Rex." *New York Times*. January 2, 1994, sec. 2, p. 22; "Hot Numbers." *Variety*. 353:8 January 3, 1994; Lawrence Coh. "'Mediterraneo': '92's Most Moneyed Import." *Variety*. 349:5, 63 January 11, 1993.

Chapter 9

1. V.I. Lenin. *Critical Remarks on the National Question. The Rights of Nations to Self-Determination*. Moscow: Progress, 1951, p. 16.

2. Daniel Singer. "GATT & the Shape of Our Dreams." *The Nation*. 258:55 January 17, 1994.

3. Alexander Cockburn. "In Bed with America." *American Film*. 16:42 November/December, 1991.

4. Manjunath Pendakur. *Canadian Dreams and American Control*. Toronto: Garamond, 1990, p. 32.

5. Daniel Singer, op. cit., p. 56.

6. "Paramount's Last Chapter—Not Quite." *U.S. News & World Report*. 116:12 February 28, 1994; Kevin Maney. "Merger Mania Spreads to Disney World." *USA Today*. August 1, 1995, pp. 1B–2B; David Lieberman. "Disney Intent on Big Role in World Market. " *USA Today*. August 1, 1995, pp. 1A–2A.

Bibliography

"Aboaf Sees Situation in Belgium Easing for U.S." *Variety*. 186:5, 16 April 16, 1952.

"Acheson Backs U.S. Films." *New York Times*. April 21, 1949, p. 29.

"Acheson Orders Foreign Problems of Yanks Included in D.C. Int'l Talks." *Variety*. 174:16 April 20, 1949.

"Adapt U.S. Pix for World." *Variety*. 149:3, 47 February 24, 1943.

Adelson, Andrea. "Entertainment Industry Adds Anti-Piracy Tricks." *New York Times*. November 21, 1988, p. D8.

Adilman, Sid. "Canada MPAA Lock Horns Over Free Trade." *Variety*. 343:35 June 17, 1991.

_____. "U.S. Interests to Be Served in Canada Pact." *Variety*. 328:1, 101 October 7, 1987.

"A.E.F. Daily Decries Movie Flag-Waving." *New York Times*. April 13, 1943, p. 1.

Alden, Robert. "Hands of U.S. Tied in Asia 'Cold War.'" *New York Times*. June 11, 1956, p. 11.

Alderman, Bruce. "Yank Majors Cleaning Up at French Markets." *Variety*. 338:38, 54 March 21, 1990.

Alexander, Garth. "Opposition Bristles as Warners Plexes Japan." *Variety*. 350:36–37 April 19, 1993.

_____. "U.S. Majors Tops in Korea." *Variety*. 346:53, 182 April 6, 1992.

"All Hollywood Now Lining Up Against German-Made Films." *Variety*. 62:1–2 May 20, 1921.

"Alterman Visits Chile for MPEA." *Variety*. 279:37 July 30, 1975.

"American and British Films Coming to Grips." *Literary Digest*. 90:23 August 28, 1926.

"American and German Films Competing in South America." *Variety*. 72:21 September 27, 1923.

"American Film Comeback Induces Envy in French Industries." *Variety*. 197:3, 20 December 8, 1954.

"American Film Men Make German Deal." *New York Times*. December 31, 1925, p. 10.

"American Films Barred by U.A.R." *New York Times*. September 17, 1967, p. 121.

"American Films Defended." *New York Times*. March 5, 1953, p. 26.

"American Films Hit Again." *New York Times*. July 3, 1929, p. 19.

"American Films Hit in New South Wales." *New York Times*. March 31, 1937, p. 29.

"American Films in German Houses Are Liked and Disliked." *Variety*. 76:26 September 17, 1924.

"American Films Lead World." *Variety*. 75:1, 43 May 28, 1924.

"American Films Menace Decent British Homes." *Variety*. 79:1, 3 July 1, 1925.

329

"American Films Played to Tatters in Nazi-Controlled Countries." *Variety*. 142:13 June 4, 1941.
"American Films Reach Accords with Holland, Czecho, Denmark." *Variety*. 164:13 September 18, 1946.
"American Films Taken Out of Hungary." *Variety*. 82:30 March 31, 1926.
"American Films Too Filthy for Turkey." *Literary Digest*. 108:21 January 10, 1931.
"American Grip on Films." *New York Times*. October 17, 1926, sec. 8, p. 7.
"American-Made Films Leaders in Italy." *Variety*. 73:18 December 27, 1923.
"American Movies Abroad." *New York Times*. April 13, 1932, p. 18.
"American Movies Popular in Chile." *New York Times*. August 6, 1922, p. 18.
"American Pictures the Best." *Variety*. 14:11 March 20, 1909.
"The Americanization of Amusement." *Saturday Review*. 151:521–522 April 11, 1931.
"Americans Accept French Film Plan." *New York Times*. May 5, 1928, p. 4.
"Americans Best." *Variety*. 70:19 May 3, 1923.
"Americans Combat Yugoslav Film Curbs." *New York Times*. March 7, 1932, p. 13.
"Americans Protest French Film Quota." *New York Times*. April 12, 1929, p. 29.
"Americans Redoubling Drive on World Markets." *Variety*. 98:5 January 29, 1930.
"Americans Reject French Film Quota." *New York Times*. June 6, 1929, p. 8.
"Americans to Oppose Pathé in English Picture Market." *Variety*. 30:15 March 7, 1913.
"Americans Wary of British Losing the Hollywood Habit." *Variety*. 167:1, 46 August 20, 1947.
"America's Film Monopoly." *Living Age*. 341:373–374 December, 1931.
"An Author in Search of a Gun." *New York Times*. January 27, 1935, sec. 8, p. 4.
"And a Boffo U.S. Box Office Abroad Rakes in Billions." *Business Week*. September 21, 1992, p. 22.
"ANZAC and Far East Represent 18% of U.S. Foreign Film Income." *Variety*. 145:3, 55 December 10, 1941.
"ANZAC Film Probe Continues." *Variety*. 114:12 April 3, 1934.
"Arabs Ban More U.S. Films." *New York Times*. January 22, 1960, p. 17.
"Arabs Ban 2 Actresses' Films." *New York Times*. July 17, 1963, p. 20.
"Argentina Gets U.S. Cars, Films." *New York Times*. August 3, 1951, p. 4.
"Argentina Producers Behind Quota Slash of U.S. Pictures." *Variety*. 237:5 January 27, 1965.
"Argentina Scores Movies." *New York Times*. August 3, 1931, p. 15.
"Argentine Court Dismisses Exhib Suit." *Variety*. 148:16 November 18, 1942.
"Argentine Theaters Protest Curb on Foreign Movies." *New York Times*. June 24, 1963, p. 21.
"Argentines Again Give Runaround to Yanks in Attempt to Effect Pact." *Variety*. 180:4, 20 September 27, 1950.
Arnell, Gene. "Devaluation: Film Biz Boon." *Variety*. 265:1, 70 December 22, 1971.
_____. "Talk English, Not Subsidy." *Variety*. 226:3 February 28, 1962.
"Around the World with Paramount." *Variety*. 96:6, 66 August 7, 1929.
"Ask Resolution vs. Film Exports Damaging U.S. Prestige Abroad." *Variety*. 215:1, 13 August 19, 1959.
Austen, Ian. "Arguments with Muscle." *Macleans*. 101:24 March 28, 1988.
"Australia and Britain Work to Cut Down American Films in Australia." *Variety*. 91:6 July 4, 1928.
"Australia Prefers Our Films." *Literary Digest*. 94:27–28 September 10, 1927.
"Australian Film Importers Protest Against Taxation." *Variety*. 64:62 September 2, 1921.
"Australian Hostility to Our Films." *Literary Digest*. 78:20 September 29, 1923.
"Australia's 25% Tax on U.S. Films." *Variety*. 81:30 February 3, 1926.

"Austria Rearranges American Film Quota." *New York Times.* January 26, 1927, p. 16.
"Austria Wants Pictures Made Over There." *Variety.* 87:5 June 29, 1927.
"Austria's 10 for 1." *Variety.* 85:4 December 8, 1926.
"Austria's 10 to 1 Only Raising Import Licenses." *Variety.* 85:10 January 12, 1927.
Ayscough, Suzan. "Clash of Cultures: Canadians vs. MPAA." *Variety.* 344:35, 42 August 19, 1991.
_____. "Yank Majors Parlez Quebec Pics into Cash." *Variety.* 350:42–43 1993.
"Bacon and Bogart, Too." *Fortune.* 37:122 June, 1948.
"Baden-Powell Draws the Line at Rotten American Films." *New York Times.* October 20, 1929, sec. 2, p. 2.
Bailey, Muriel. "Moving Pictures in Pan America." *Bulletin of the Pan American Union.* 50:606–623 June, 1920.
Balio, Tino. *United Artists: The Company Built by the Stars.* Madison, Wisc.: University of Wisconsin Press, 1976.
"Balk at Norway Monopoly." *Variety.* 197:11 January 26, 1955.
"Ban on Our Films Is Asked in Paris." *New York Times.* May 19, 1934, p. 6.
"Ban on Pix to Iran an Economic Issue, Not Politics: Valenti." *Variety.* 297:1 December 26, 1979.
Barnard, Tim., ed. *Argentine Cinema.* Toronto: Nightwood, 1986.
Barnouw, Erik, and S. Krishnaswamy. *Indian Film.* 2d ed. New York: Oxford, 1980.
Battis, Jeremy. "Czech Pix Seek Western Bounce." *Variety.* 354:33 April 4, 1994.
"Battle of the Screen." *Fortune.* 33:200 March, 1946.
"Battle on to Make Belgium Change Mind on Dubbing." *Variety.* 117:21 February 27, 1935.
Bawden, Liz-Anne., ed. *The Oxford Companion to Film.* New York: Oxford, 1976.
Beale, Lewis. "Finding a Niche for Foreign Films." *Washington Post.* January 5, 1992, pp. G1, G10.
"Beautifully Made But Too Few European Films Right for U.S." *Variety.* 203:5 July 11, 1956.
"Belgrade to Cut U.S. Film Imports." *New York Times.* December 8, 1957, p. 157.
Bertrand, Ina. ed., "The Big Bad Combine" in Albert Moran and Tom O'Regan. eds. *The Australian Screen,* Melbourne: Penguin, 1989.
_____. *Cinema in Australia: A Documentary History.* Kensington, NSW.: New South Wales University Press, 1989.
Besas, Peter. "Spain Abolishes Film Quota." *Variety.* 262:5, 22 March 10, 1971.
_____. "TV and Film Brace for Big Rebound." *Variety.* 352:51, 60 October 4, 1993.
"Better Films in Europe." *New York Times.* September 11, 1913, p. 4.
"Better U.S. Distrib Setup in Japan Near but Coin Still Partly Frozen." *Variety.* 178:15 March 22, 1950.
"Beware of America." *Variety.* 128:15 September 22, 1937.
Birchenough, Tom. "Western Distribs Move Cautiously into Russia." *Variety.* 354:22 February 14, 1994.
Biskind, Peter. "McMovies." *Sight & Sound.* 1:8 July, 1991.
"Blame Ills of Mexico's Film Biz on Few Playdates for Native Product." *Variety.* 172:13 September 15, 1948.
"Blame Naive Natives and Red Hecklers." *Variety.* 208:5 October 2, 1957.
Blum, William. *The CIA: A Forgotten History.* London: Zed, 1986.
"Bombs over Cuban Theaters." *New York Times.* November 4, 1934, sec. 9, p. 4.
"Booking of Films." *Times* (London). April 29, 1921, p. 7.
Bower, Anthony. "Films." *The Nation.* 152:153 February 15, 1941.
"Box Office Buzzes Overseas." *Business Week.* November 7, 1964, pp. 64, 68–69.

"Boxoffice Controlled, Not Births, So Latin Lands' Market Value Grows." *Variety*. 204:4, 20 November 21, 1956.

Bradsher, Keith. "Hollywood Bars Films to Protest Soviet Piracy." *New York Times*. June 12, 1991, pp. C13, C16.

_____. "U.S. and Europe Clear the Way." *New York Times*. December 15, 1993, pp. A1, D18.

Brady, Thomas F. "Egypt Continues U.S. Film Imports." *New York Times*. May 31, 1968, p. 22.

_____. "India Film Tariff Stirs a Boycott." *New York Times*. August 26, 1963, p. 21.

_____. "On Indian Film." *New York Times*. December 1, 1963, sec. 2, p. 7.

"Brazil Eases Up on Tax, Take-out." *Variety*. 283:1, 126 May 19, 1976.

"Brazil Gets No U.S. films." *New York Times*. February 4, 1949, p. 31.

"Brazil's Film Tax." *New York Times*. December 20, 1931, sec. 8, p. 4.

"Breach of Contract on U.S. Film Import Charged in India." *New York Times*. July 16, 1971, p. 16.

"Bright Outlook for Features." *Variety*. 36:23 October 10, 1914.

"Brit Crisis Fateful to U.S. Pix." *Variety*. 165:3, 24 March 5, 1947.

"Brit Film Biz Moves to Prevent Harsh Govt Action vs. Yank Pix." *Variety*. 185:13 February 20, 1952.

"Britain in Accord on American Films." *New York Times*. November 23, 1939, p. 39.

"Britain, Italy, Canada, France, Japan 40% of U.S. Films' Foreign Market." *Variety*. 264:4 October 20, 1971.

"Britain Shaves Quota by Scant 5%." *Variety*. 174:3, 4 March 23, 1949.

"Britain, U.S. Set Up Film Bonus Plan." *New York Times*. August 3, 1950, p. 19.

"Britain's Best Has All Gone West." *Times* (London). July 16, 1991, p. 13.

"British Cinema Exhibitors to Fight American Invasion." *Variety*. 55:78 August 15, 1919.

"British Coin Tilts '41 Net." *Variety*. 144:5, 18 November 19, 1941.

"British Cut Film Quota." *New York Times*. March 11, 1950, p. 9.

"British Deplore Glut of U.S. Films." *New York Times*. December 21, 1944, p. 16.

"British Exibs in Panic; Can't Get More Than Half Enough Local Pix to Fill Quota." *Variety*. 123:34 August 26, 1936.

"British Film Act Report." *Variety*. 124:11, 13 December 9, 1936.

"British Film Field." *Variety*. 88:12 September 7, 1927.

"The British Film Industry." *Times* (London). January 21, 1948, p. 5.

"British Film Makers Will Ask Govt. to Intervene in Industry Crisis." *Variety*. 232:23 November 6, 1963.

"British Film Quota Halved." *Times* (London). July 1, 1981, p. 2.

"British Films." *Times* (London). June 23, 1925, p. 17.

"British Films." *Times* (London). December 15, 1925, p. 17.

"British Increase Own Screen Time." *New York Times*. June 15, 1948, p. 32.

"British India Attacking U.S. Films." *Variety*. 86:5 January 19, 1927.

"British Merger for Quota." *Variety*. 86:5, 21 March 30, 1927.

"British Movie Makers Score American Films." *New York Times*. September 9, 1923, p. 20.

"British Must Choose Between World Mart or Local Protection—Johnston." *Variety*. 171:6 September 1, 1948.

"British Now Have 2 Way Squawk on Quota." *Variety*. 98:4 February 19, 1930.

"British Open Fight Against Our Films." *New York Times*. November 14, 1931, p. 15.

"British Quota Bill Under Inspection in Washington But No Action Likely." *Variety*. 87:3 April 20, 1927.

"British Quota Showdown." *Variety*. 144:15 December 3, 1941.

"Britons Criticize Films." *New York Times*. December 27, 1916, sec. 3, p. 9.

Bronskill, Jim. "Dupuy Wants Spotlight on Canadian Movies." *Times-Colonist* (Victoria, BC). January 26, 1995, Look sec., p. 5.

"Buenos Aires Exhibs Reel as Lack of Yank Product Puts B.O. in Dive." *Variety*. 257:27 November 19, 1969.

"Burma Coup Might Be Helpful." *Variety*. 226:7 March 7, 1962.

Burton, Wilbur. "Chinese Reactions to the Cinema." *Asia*. 34:594–600 October, 1934.

"Calls Trade Boom Vital." *New York Times*. May 2, 1947, p. 33.

Calnio, Paul. "Yank Majors Ease Thai Boycott." *Variety*. 303:47–48 June 3, 1981.

"Canada Bares Teeth at U.S. Distribution." *Variety*. 309:7, 20 December 29, 1982.

"Canada's Offense at Our Movies." *Literary Digest*. 86:27 August 15, 1925.

"Canadian Legislation May Cut U.S. Film Importations." *Variety*. 53:57 January 31, 1919.

"Canadian Shows Rate Low at Global." *Times-Colonist* (Victoria, BC). June 17, 1995, p. F2.

"Canadian Women Rap Imported U.S. Films." *Variety*. 83:7 July 7, 1926.

Canby, Vincent. "Africa: New Map, New Marts." *Variety*. 219:3, 13 August 24, 1960.

_____. "Our Men in Havana—Stay." *Variety*. 220:5 October 26, 1960.

_____. "Slow U.S. Start in W. Africa." *Variety*. 227:5 July 11, 1962.

_____. "Spain, Please See French Text." *Variety*. 219:11, 15 August 10, 1960.

_____. "Spain's Quota Pains Yanks." *Variety*. 236:3 October 21, 1964.

_____. "Yanks' Latin Markets Okay." *Variety*. 224:3, 76 November 8, 1961.

Canty, George R. "American Films Abroad." *Films in Review*. 2:12–13, 30 May, 1951.

"Careless Errata Weaken British Side of Case." *Variety*. 201:16 February 15, 1956.

"Carlton Bids for MGM Cinemas." *Variety*. 358:44 March 13–19, 1995.

Carr, Philip. "One Hollywood." *The Spectator*. 175:507 November 30, 1945.

Carroll, Ronald. "Which Films Should Go Abroad?" *Films in Review*. 3:443–449 November, 1952.

"Cartel-Conditioned Europeans Favor Pix Pool But Yanks Dead Against It." *Variety*. 200:1 November 16, 1955.

"Cartel Ideas of Europeans Big Fear Phobia with Yankee Leaders." *Variety*. 214:5 May 27, 1959.

Carter, John. "Hollywood Has a Foreign War." *New York Times*. March 4, 1928, sec. 10, p. 13.

"CEA, KRS Join Hands in London to Lobby for 10–15% Quota." *Variety*. 122:13 June 3, 1936.

"Censors Working Overtime." *Variety*. 129:13 February 9, 1938.

"Chance Seen to Clean Up Big Picture Profits Now in Mexico." *Variety*. 56:64 November 21, 1919.

"Charge Films Mar Prestige of British." *New York Times*. April 20, 1926, p. 25.

"Charge We Dominate Danish Film Industry." *New York Times*. February 27, 1931, p. 18.

"China Increases Film Tax." *New York Times*. September 8, 1948, p. 36.

"China's Gov't Film Commissioner Scans Industry in U.S. and Europe." *Variety*. 127:16 June 16, 1937.

"Chinese Film Market." *Variety* 43:27 August 11, 1916.

"Chinese Filmers Inspire Trick Law That May Force U.S. Out of Market." *Variety*. 111:19 July 25, 1933.

Churchill, Douglas W. "Films Ban Abroad Hurt Hollywood." *New York Times*. January 8, 1939, sec. 4, p. 7.

_____. "Hollywood Snags the Good Neighbor Policy." *New York Times.* November 10, 1940, sec. 9, p. 5.

_____. "Hollywood's Footlights Club." *New York Times.* June 20, 1937, sec. 10, p. 3.

_____. "Matters of More or Less Moment in Hollywood." *New York Times.* June 30, 1940, sec. 9, p. 3.

Cianfra, Camille M. "U.S. Film Exports to Spain Halted." *New York Times.* August 21, 1955, p. 95.

"Cineplex, Cinemark Agree Not to Merge." *Times-Colonist* (Victoria, BC). May 13, 1995, p. C15.

"Cineplex, Cinemark Create Largest Chain." *Times-Colonist* (Victoria, BC). March 31, 1995, p. D2.

"Cineplex Odeon Plans Megaplexes." *Times-Colonist* (Victoria, BC). June 10, 1995, p. B8.

Clarity, James F. "Russians' Charge on Films Denied." *New York Times.* May 8, 1969, p. 2.

Clark, Jennifer, "Distribs Cheer Growing Market." *Variety.* 354:T5-6 April 11, 1994.

Clarriere, Georges. "The Western Peril." *Sight & Sound.* v. 13, n. 12:153–156 Winter 1934–1935.

Clinch, Minty. *Clint Eastwood.* London: Hodder & Stoughton, 1994.

"Close Yugoslav Offices." *New York Times.* May 16, 1932, p. 19.

Cockburn, Alexander. "In Bed with America." *American Film.* 16:40–43, 50–51 November/December, 1991.

Cohen, Roger, "A Realignment Made Reluctantly." *New York Times.* December 15, 1993, p. D19.

_____. "Aux Armes! France Rallies to Battle Sly and T. Rex." *New York Times.* January 2, 1994, sec. 2, pp. 1, 22.

_____. "Culture Dispute with Paris Now Snags World Accord." *New York Times.* December 8, 1993, pp. A1, D2.

_____. "Film Issue Snags Trade Talks." *New York Times.* December 13, 1993, pp. A1, D5.

_____. "Once Dull GATT Enters Realm of Pop Culture." *New York Times.* December 7, 1993, pp. D1, D6.

_____. "With Time Waning, Europeans Reject U.S. Movie Compromise." *New York Times.* December 14, 1993, pp. A1, D6.

Cohn, Lawrence. "Mediterraneo': '92's Most Moneyed Import." *Variety.* 349:5, 63 January 11, 1993.

"Cola v Zola." *Economist.* 329:78, 81 October 16, 1993.

Collins, Diane. *Hollywood Down Under.* North Ryde, NSW: Angus & Robertson, 1987.

"Common Market Needs U.S. Pix." *Variety.* 230:1, 86 May 15, 1963.

"Compromise on Brazil's Foreign Film Edict Saves $6,000,000 Yank Market." *Variety.* 172:11 October 27, 1948.

"Congressman Jibes Media Guaranty." *Variety.* 215:17 June 3, 1959.

"Control of British Cinemas." *Times* (London). October 15, 1936, p. 12.

Cooper, Ryley. "Films Across the Sea." *Saturday Evening Post.* 198:26–27+ June 5, 1926.

Cortesi, Arnaldo. "Italian Film Edict Hits Our Industry." *New York Times.* October 15, 1933, sec. 4, p. 3.

Cousins, Norman. "The Free Ride." *Saturday Review of Literature.* 33:24–25 January 21, 1950.

_____. "The Free Ride, Part II." *Saturday Review of Literature.* 33:20–21 January 28, 1950.

_____. "The Free Ride, Part III." *Saturday Review of Literature.* 33:22–23 February 4, 1950.

_____. "Let's Look at the Message." *Saturday Review of Literature*. 33:12–13, 28 March 4, 1950.

_____. "Our Films Speak for Hollywood." *Saturday Review of Literature*. 33:12–13, 34 April 1, 1950.

"Crime in Austria Laid to U.S. Films." *New York Times*. August 23, 1948, p. 26.

Crowther, Bosley. "Films for Export." *New York Times*. April 20, 1958, sec. 2, p. 1.

_____. "Howdy Neighbors." *New York Times*. February 14, 1943, sec. 2, p. 3.

_____. "The Multinational Film." *New York Times*. July 5, 1966, p. 41.

"Cuba Confiscates Caramba!" *Variety*. 122:5 May 24, 1961.

"Culture Joins Cash Resistance to U.S. Films in Red China." *Variety*. 295:2, 94 June 27, 1979.

"Curb on Our Films Dropped by Italy." *New York Times*. November 26, 1936, p. 38.

"Czech Film Monopoly Freezes U.S. Pix." *Variety*. 160:23 September 26, 1945.

"Czecho-Slovakia Declaring its Own Film Quota System." *Variety*. 93:6 October 17, 1928.

"Czechs Make Deal for Ten U.S. Films." *New York Times*. November 29, 1958, p. 18.

"Danes Forced Yanks' Withdrawal." *Variety*. 204:4 October 31, 1956.

"Danger of Foreign Films." *Variety*. 52:54 October 4, 1918.

Davenport, Nicholas. "Hollywood and Mr. Wilson." *New Statesman & Nation*. 40:197–198 August 19, 1950.

Dawtrey, Adam. "Carlton Won't Nab MGM Cinemas." *Variety*. 358:127–128 April 3–9, 1995.

_____. "Euros Go on Screen-Building Spree." *Variety*. 358:1, 15 February 6–12, 1995.

_____. "GATT Gets France's Goat." *Variety*. 352:31–32 September 27, 1993.

_____. "H'wood: Tomorrow the World." *Variety*. 359:1, 242 May 15–21, 1995.

_____. "Miramax Intl. Takes a World View." *Variety*. 358:24 March 6–12, 1995.

_____. "U.K. Looks Into Cinema Squeeze." *Variety*. 352:69–70 October 11, 1993.

_____. "U.S. Distribs in U.K. Cleared." *Variety*. 356:24 October 10, 1994.

"D.C. Kicking Pictures Abroad." *Variety*. 162:3, 24 March 27, 1946.

"D.C. Politicos' Assault vs. Brit Film Quota Mounts." *Variety*. 174:3, 18 March 30, 1949.

"Decry Mexico's 32¢ Top Admish." *Variety*. 194:7, 20 May 5, 1954.

"Defeat of Mex Anti-Import Bill Promises Break for U.S. Film Biz." *Variety*. 129:13 March 9, 1938.

de Grazia, Victoria. "Mass Culture and Sovereignty: The American Challenge to European Cinemas 1920–1960." *Journal of Modern History*. 61:53–87 March , 1989.

Dempsey, Michael. "Selling American Films Overseas." *American Film*. 7:58–62 November, 1981.

"Deny Inciting Film Riots." *New York Times*. October 1, 1930, p. 12.

"Deplores Barriers Against Our Movies." *New York Times*. August 4, 1927, p. 25.

"Desperate Exhibs Speed End of Jugoslav Quota." *Variety*. 109:13 March 7, 1933.

"Despite Critics, Don Hartman Sees H'wood Unmenaced Around the World." *Variety*. 194:5, 15 May 5, 1954.

"Deval Pans American Films. and Press Kids Him for It." *Variety*. 117:17 December 18, 1934.

"Dialog Behind the 8-Ball." *Variety*. 129:13 March 9, 1938.

"Did London 'Out-Trade' H'wood?" *Variety*. 170:1, 9 March 17, 1948.

"Diplomats from Countries South Guests of the Picture Industry." *Variety*. 71:18 June 21, 1923.

"Discussions Due on U.S. Films Cutback." *Times* (London). December 27, 1969, p. 9.

"Distribber Freezes Out Its Competish." *Variety*. 358:40 March 20–26, 1995.

"Distribution in England." *Variety.* 56:64 September 26, 1919.

"Distributors Panicked Over Japanese Ban on Foreign Films." *Variety.* 128:13 October 13, 1937.

"Dollars and Films." *Times* (London). March 12, 1948, p. 5.

"The Domino Game." *Cinema Canada.* n. 152:19–21 May, 1988.

"Double Featuring, Prod Shortage Worry Japan." *Variety.* 114:13 May 8, 1934.

"Doubles Tax on Talkies in English." *New York Times.* June 4, 1930, p. 33.

"Down with American Films." *Review of Reviews.* 81:116–117 April, 1930.

"Drastic Film Boycott Proposed." *Times* (London). July 16, 1919, p. 10.

"Duke Alba Befriends American Pictures." *Variety.* 98:4 February 12, 1930.

"Dulles Favors Films for Russia." *Variety.* 197:1, 55 December 29, 1954.

"Dutch Society of Pix Exhibs Feels U.S. Export Assn. Setup, Squawks." *Variety.* 161:13 February 20, 1946.

"Easing of Censorship Abroad." *Variety.* 184:5, 16 November 28, 1951.

"Ecuador Goes for U.S. Action Films But Mex Gets Half Play Time With 19% Pix." *Variety.* 168:15 December 3, 1947.

Egan, Charles E. "Sale of U.S. Films Limited in Britain." *New York Times.* September 1, 1948, p. 20.

_____. "U.S. Leaders Fight British Film Quota." *New York Times.* November 14, 1946, p. 39.

_____. "U.S. Will Offer Films to Soviet." *New York Times.* October 5, 1956, p. 21.

"Egypt Bans Rooney and Kaye." *New York Times.* June 20, 1948, p. 52.

"Egypt Bans U.S. Films." *New York Times.* June 18, 1967, p. 18.

Ehrmann, Hans. "Chile: We Want Good Healthy Films Like *The Godfather.*" *Variety.* 274:54 May 8, 1974.

_____. "Chile Won't Pay, U.S. Won't Play." *Variety.* 269:88 January 3, 1973.

_____. "Remittance Blues in Chile." *Variety.* 264:21 September 22, 1971.

"$8,000,000 Boost in Foreign Take Seen Via ERP, New D.C. Bill." *Variety.* 170:3, 23 April 7, 1948.

"80 U.S. Films Set to Go Into Germany." *Variety.* 160:1, 32 September 26, 1945.

Eisenstodt, Gale. "A Cozy Japanese Near Monopoly." *Forbes.* 148:52, 54–55 September 30, 1991.

Eller, Claudia. "Yank Majors Fatten Up on European Film Business." *Variety.* 339:1, 99 May 16, 1990.

Emmrich, Stuart. "Foreign Intrigue." *American Film.* 14:38–41+ September, 1989.

"England Would Stop Invasion of American-Made Pictures." *Variety.* 72:24 September 13, 1923.

"England's Chronic Complaint." *Variety.* 153:3 March 1, 1944.

"English Complain Against Americans' Lack of Interest." *Variety.* 39:4 July 30, 1915.

"English Open Market Doomed as Film Makers Deal Direct." *Variety.* 40:17 September 10, 1915.

"Envoys Warn Producers." *Variety.* 101:7, 43 December 17, 1930.

"Eric Johnston, MPAA Prez Who Sold Hollywood Around the Globe, Died at 66." *Variety.* 232:4, 22 August 28, 1963.

"Eric Johnston New Head of MPPDA." *Variety,* 160:3, 12 September 19, 1945.

"Eric Johnston Sells Films to Yugoslavia." *New York Times.* October 5, 1948, p. 3.

"Europe Awaiting Outcome of British Film Quota Bill." *Variety.* 87:13 June 15, 1927.

"Europe: Hates 'Competition.'" *Variety.* 203:5 July 11, 1956.

"Europe May Bar 800 U.S. Films." *Variety.* 158:1, 10 March 21, 1945.

"Europe May Recall Actors." *Variety.* 91:3 May 23, 1928.

"Europe Needs Advice." *Variety.* 90:3 March 7, 1928.

"Europe Needy—For U.S. Facts." *Variety.* 201:7 February 22, 1956.
"European Reaction to U.S. Films." *Variety.* 233:2, 54 January 1, 1964
"Europeans Like U.S. Movies." *New York Times.* March 31, 1964, p. 30.
"Europeans See H'wood as Capitalistic Hence Puzzled by U.S. Commie Probe." *Variety.* 167:2 June 18, 1947.
"Europe's a Code for a Code." *Variety.* 196:1, 16 October 6, 1954.
"Europe's Solid Front." *Variety.* 92:6 September 12, 1928.
"Everything Follows the Films." *Variety.* 161:3, 38 January 9, 1946.
"Exhibitors and the Film Quota." *Times* (London). July 20, 1948, p. 3.
"Exhibitors in Foreign Lands Seen U.S. Distribs' Main Ally." *Variety.* 194:7, 18 April 28, 1954.
"Export *Blackboard Jungle.*" *Variety.* 198:7, 22 April 20, 1955.
"Ex-Showman Joe Kennedy Does Straight for American Film Biz on British Quota and Coin." *Variety.* 136:3, 20 October 25, 1939.
"Extension of French Film Quota Law for 1 Year a Break for U.S. Pix." *Variety.* 118:13 June 5, 1935.
Eyre, Lincoln. "America Has Grip on German Movies." *New York Times.* November 11, 1925, p. 25.
Fabrikant, Geraldine. "Box Office Abroad." *New York Times.* September 28, 1987, pp. D1, D8.
_____. "Hollywood Returns to China." *New York Times.* February 7, 1986, pp. D1, D4.
_____. "When World Raves, Studios Jump." *New York Times.* March 7, 1990, pp. D1, D8.
Fabricant, Geri. "O'seas Marketing Costs Soar." *Variety.* 299:12, 330 May 7, 1980.
"Faked Spanish Dialog Gets Razzed in S.A." *Variety.* 97:3 November 27, 1929.
Falk, Ray. "Tokyo to Limit American Pictures." *New York Times.* May 13, 1950, sec. 2, p. 5.
Farnsworth, Clyde H. "Jack Valenti's State Department." *New York Times.* December 18, 1985, p. B12.
"Favorable Exchange Costing U.S. South American Market." *Variety.* 62:46 May 6, 1921.
"Fear Govt's Foreign Aid Slash Will Cut Into U.S. Pix Remittances." *Variety.* 191:3, 16 August 5, 1953.
"Fear Latin Film Threat." *Variety.* 147:23 August 26, 1942.
"54.6% of U.S. Sales Now Overseas." *Variety.* 232:1 November 6, 1963.
"'52 of Foreign Income." *Variety.* 188:3, 22 September 17, 1952.
"Fight Film Censorship." *New York Times.* July 12, 1936, p. 19.
"Filipino Senate Sets 10% Local Pix Must." *Variety.* 175:20 July 27, 1949.
"Film 'Big 8' Bans Movies for Britain." *New York Times.* August 9, 1947, pp. 1, 5.
"Film Boycott on Hungary." *New York Times.* March 6, 1926, p. 13.
"Film Comeback." *Business Week.* July 6, 1946, pp. 24, 26.
"Film Deadlock Broken." *New York Times.* November 15, 1952, p. 15.
"Film Export Assn's Stand in Holland Will be Key to Other Foreign Marts." *Variety.* 160:15 November 7, 1945.
"Film Export Unit Set Up in Capital." *New York Times.* July 1, 1937, p. 33.
"The Film-Flam War." *The Independent.* 120:468 May 19, 1928.
"Film Gains Surveyed." *New York Times.* March 5, 1954, p. 15.
"Film Head Criticizes French on U.S. Ban." *New York Times.* February 27, 1946, p. 21.
"Film Head Pledges Reform in Exports." *New York Times.* December 21, 1946, p. 13.
"Film in South America." *Variety.* 41:24 February 18, 1916.
"Film Leaders Reject Proposal by Danes." *New York Times.* October 2, 1947, p. 30.

"Film Quota in Germany." *Literary Digest*. 94:29 August 27, 1927.

"Film Quotas Eased in New British Act." *New York Times*. April 3, 1938, sec. 2, p. 2.

"Film Stars as Envoys Abroad." *Variety*. 166:5, 20 April 2, 1947.

"The Film World." *Times* (London). August 25, 1925, p. 8.

"The Film World." *Times* (London). July 13, 1926, p. 12.

"Films About Americans." *Asia and the Americas*. 42:658–659 November, 1942.

"Films Across the Sea." *New Statesman & Nation*. 27:167–168 March 11, 1944.

"The Films Bill." *Times* (London). December 29, 1937, p. 11.

"Films' 8–9% Foreign Loss." *Variety*. 136:1, 18 October 4, 1939.

"Films for Germany." *Variety*. 53:41 January 3, 1919.

"Films' $480,000,000 a Year." *Variety*. 157:3, 158 January 3, 1945.

"Films Go Begging." *Business Week*. July 27, 1946, p. 106.

"Films in Committee." *Times* (London). December 7, 1937, p. 17.

"Films May Help Save Crazy World." *Variety*. 214:7 May 27, 1959.

"Films of U.S. for Czechs." *New York Times*. January 20, 1935, sec. 2, p. 7.

"Films' Overseas Advertising." *Variety*. 192:3, 6 November 18, 1953.

"Films Plan Campaign." *New York Times*. June 4, 1946, p. 19.

"Films, Radio, Reading Disturbing Canadians." *New York Times*. August 21, 1931, sec. 3, p. 6.

"Films That Do Poorly Elsewhere Often Large S. African Grossers." *Variety*. 296:26 October 17, 1979.

"Films' Victory in Italy." *Variety*. 125:5 December 30, 1936.

"First Aid for Films." Times (London). June 24, 1937, p. 17.

"First Brazil Film Survey Shows $8,000,000 Annual Biz." *Variety*. 121:22 February 26, 1936.

"555 First-Line Features." *Variety*. 91:4 May 30, 1928.

"Five of 11 U.S. Stars are Banned by Rumania." *New York Times*. October 28, 1947, p. 14.

"For Movie Locarno Against Our Films." *New York Times*. October 9, 1926, p. 6.

Ford, James Tooker. "Motion Pictures and Foreign Missions." *Missionary Review of the World*." 54:611–612 August, 1931.

"Foreign Censorial Vagaries Add to U.S. Films' Already Complicated Distrib Problems in Other Lands." *Variety*. 136:13 October 25, 1939.

"Foreign Coin Curb Held Biggest Bugaboo for Yank Picture Films." *Variety*. 134:11 June 7, 1939.

"Foreign Countries' Ban on Exporting Money Can Turn Into Embargo on U.S. Films." *Variety*. 104:15 October 20, 1931.

"Foreign Film Buyers Pool Their American Purchases." *Variety*. 44:32 September 22, 1916.

"Foreign Film Imports Drop $14,664 on Year." *Variety*. 84:15 August 11, 1926.

"Foreign Governments Opposing U.S. Films Obliging Americans to Buy or Build Abroad." *Variety*. 88:15 September 7, 1927.

"Foreign Market Dead." *Variety*. 61:30 December 24, 1920.

"Foreign Market Dipped in 1938." *Variety*. 134:14, 54 March 15, 1939.

"Foreign Picture Money Embargo On in Australia." *Variety*. 98:5 March 5, 1930.

"Foreign Resentment Is Hot Against U.S. Films." *Variety*. 82:24 April 14, 1926.

"Foreign Sales Dept. Heads Oppose OWI Handling of U.S. Prints Abroad." *Variety*. 150:7 May 26, 1943.

"Foreign Sales Outlook Poor." *Variety*. 60:38 November 12, 1920.

"Foreign Trade." *Time*. 50:81 August 18, 1947.

"Foreign Trade Draws News Attention." *Variety*. 82:35 February 17, 1926.

"Foresee MPAA Budget Trim." *Variety*. 258:3 May 4, 1970.

Fotheringham, Allan. "No Flying Buns for a Bully Boy." *Macleans*. 102:116 October 30, 1989.
"4 More U.S. Movies Chosen for Soviet." *New York Times*. March 20, 1959, p. 3.
"France Abandons 4-to-1 Film Quota." *New York Times*. May 4, 1928, pp. 1, 6.
"France and Pictures." *Variety*. 53:183 December 27, 1918.
"France Lifts Foreign Film Curb." *New York Times*. June 15, 1961, p. 51.
"France Recedes—or Else." *Variety*. 91:3 April 25, 1928.
"France Shuts Out Foreigns." *Variety*. 106:7 May 24, 1932.
"France to Get 124 Films." *New York Times*. June 14, 1946, p. 16.
"France's Anti–U.S. Spasm." *Variety*. 97:5 November 6, 1929.
"France's Capitulation Means Complete Blackout of Europe for U.S. Pix." *Variety*. 139:12 June 19, 1940.
Frankel, Max. "U.S. Movie Series Opens in Moscow." *New York Times*. November 11, 1959, p. 40.
_____. "U.S., Soviet Agree to Film Exchange." *New York Times*. October 10, 1958, p.36.
Fraser, Matthew. "A Question of Culture." *Macleans*. 106:50–51 December 27, 1993.
"Free World Market for Films Discussed." *New York Times*. January 14, 1944, p. 15.
"Free World vis Pix, Radio." *Variety*. 154:1, 26 March 29, 1944.
"French Blow at U.S. Films." *Variety*. 114:13 May 22, 1934.
"French Decree Slashing U.S. Imports Seen Bid for Subsidy of Gallic Prod." *Variety*. 187:4, 21 July 23, 1952.
"French Defer Curb on American Films." *New York Times*. March 29, 1928, p. 24.
"French Defer Curb on American Films." *New York Times*. April 5, 1928, p. 10.
"French Deputies Join Exhibs in Battle Against U.S. Quota." *Variety*. 115:21 June 29, 1934.
"French Earn More From U.S. Movies." *U.S. New & World Report*. 24:65 April 2, 1948.
"French Exhibs Raise Protest Against More Quota Barriers." *Variety*. 94:2 March 13, 1929.
"French Film Men Cling to Quota." *New York Times*. April 18, 1929, p. 9.
"French Film Peace Desired by Poncet." *New York Times*. April 21, 1929, p. 4.
"French Film Rules as Sales Forcing Device." *Variety*. 90:5 March 21, 1928.
"French Hit Film Accord." *New York Times*. June 16, 1946, sec. 2, p. 3.
"French Lift Quotas on Some Alien Films." *New York Times*. August 11, 1939, p. 17.
"French Loathe Our Films but British Enjoy Them." *New York Times*. July 5, 1925, sec. 7, p. 3.
"French Move Seen to Rule U.S. Films." *New York Times*. October 17, 1935, p. 19.
"French Movie Bill Limits Film Length." *New York Times*. March 18, 1939, p. 9.
"French Movie Plan Worries Americans." *New York Times*. December 13, 1927, p. 7.
"French Quota Not So Bad." *Variety*. 111:19, 54 July 25, 1933.
"French Quota Reaches Floor of Senate." *Variety*. 95:9 June 12, 1929.
"French Quota Smashed by Washington." *Variety*. 95:2 May 8, 1929.
"French Razzes English Shorts." *Variety*. 95:2 June 12, 1929.
"French Restriction of Eng. Dialog in Talkers Foretells Possible Worldwide Trend." *Variety*. 100:7 August 6, 1930.
"French Rush to Take on U.S. Films Under Latest Quota." *Variety*. 96:5 September 25, 1929.
"French Socialists Not Anti–U.S. Pix, But—." *Variety*. 304:3, 49 September 9, 1981.
"French Theaters Demand Our Films." *New York Times*. July 25, 1933, p. 8.
"From 400 to 500 Foreign Pictures." *Variety*. 91:10 May 23, 1928.
Gam, Samuel King. "Missionaries and Motion Pictures." *Missionary Review of the World*. 59:86 February, 1936.

"Gang Up on Uncle Sam." *Variety.* 115:29, 73 June 19, 1934.

"Gaumont in Canada." *Variety.* 16:12 October 23, 1909.

Gelman, Morrie. "Valenti Spurs Pols to Keep U.S. Showbiz in GATT Gab." *Variety.* 341:12 November 12, 1990.

Gercke, George. "Pan-American Pictures." *New York Times.* December 18, 1938, sec. 9, p. 6.

"German and Italian Trusts Merge to Fight our Films." *Variety.* 59:39 June 25, 1920.

"German Film Rules in Effect Next July." *Variety.* 93:6 December 19, 1928.

"German Market Viewed as Possibly 2d to Britain Eventually for Americans." *Variety.* 177:5, 54 February 1, 1950.

"German Markets." *New York Times.* November 24, 1946, sec. 2, p. 5.

"German Owners Attack U.S. Films." *Variety.* 84:9 September 15, 1926.

"German Producers Want Imported Pictures Limited." *Variety.* 76:22 September 3, 1924.

"German Restrictions for Club on American Pictures." *Variety.* 94:6 January 23, 1929.

"German 2-for-1 Plan Now Possible." *Variety.* 87:4, 15 July 20, 1927.

"German View of Our Films." *Literary Digest.* 90:22 July 17, 1926.

"Germans Bar American Films." *Variety.* 56:66 October 10, 1919.

"Germans See End of U.S. Film Over There." *Variety.* 97:5 October 16, 1929.

"Germany Abolishes Contingent 1-1; Cuts Down Foreign Film Importations." *Variety.* 89:9 November 30, 1927.

"Germany Movement Foreseen." *Variety.* 93:6 December 26, 1928.

"Germany Puts Ban on American Movies." *New York Times.* December 12, 1920, sec. 2, p. 1.

"Germany Restricts Use of Our Films." *New York Times.* December 27, 1925, sec. 8, p. 3.

"Germany's Pix Biz Off 40% in Six Months." *Variety.* 175:18 August 10, 1949.

Geyer, O.R. "Winning Foreign Film Markets." *Scientific American.* 125:132, 140 August 20, 1921.

Gitlin, Todd. "World Leaders: Mickey, et al." *New York Times.* May 3, 1922, sec. 2, pp. 1, 30.

"Global Goodwill Plan Set." *Variety.* 192:5, 14 September 16, 1953.

"Gloom in Commons on 30% Quota." *Variety.* 178:13, 18 April 5, 1950.

Gold, Richard. "U.S. Pix Tighten Global Grip." *Variety.* 340:1, 96 August 22, 1990.

_____. "Ex–LBJ Aide's Film Vision." *Variety.* 243:1, 52 June 1, 1966.

Golden, Nathan D. "Exporting U.S. Film Glamour." *Variety.* 205:5, 204 January 9, 1957.

_____. "1950 Foreign Outlook Pessimistic for U.S. Film Companies." *Variety.* 177:175 January 4, 1950.

_____. "Optimism Prevails in Int'l Market for U.S. Pix After Encouraging '51." *Variety.* 185:193 January 2, 1952.

_____. "Prospects for Post-War Foreign Pix Biz Looms Strong." *Variety.* 153:44 January 5, 1944.

_____. "Trade Agreements Help U.S. Companies to Overcome Many Foreign Pic Curbs." *Variety.* 181:193 January 3, 1951.

_____. "What Prospects for the Road Ahead in Foreign Film Markets?" *Variety.* 157:112, 132 January 3, 1945.

Goldwyn, Samuel. "Our Movies Speak for U.S." *Saturday Review of Literature.* 33:10–12 April 1, 1950.

"Goldwyn Hits Film Quotas." *New York Times.* March 4, 1928, sec. 9, p. 5.

"Good Movie Year Seen." *New York Times.* April 24, 1956, p. 26.

Goodman, Ezra. "Hollywood Belligerent." *The Nation.* 155:213–214 September 12, 1942.

"Goodwill a Hot Potato." *Variety*. 142:3, 15 June 4, 1941.

Gorrick, Eric. "War Doesn't Discourage Australian Film-Going." *Variety*. 141:73 January 8, 1941.

Gould, Hazel. "Theaters & Studios Owe Much to Success of U.S. Theatricals in Germany." *Variety*. 303:206 May 13, 1981.

"Government Is Interested in Export Raw Pictures." *Variety*. 63:38 July 22, 1921.

"Govt Coin for Pix Aid O'seas?" *Variety*. 169:15 February 11, 1948.

"Gov't Storm on U.S. Pix Abroad." *Variety*. 164:1, 64 November 20, 1946.

Grenier, Richard. "When It Comes to Movies, The World Looks to America." *New York Times*. September 22, 1985, sec. 2, p. 27.

Grover, Ronald. "The World Is Hollywood's Oyster." *Business Week*. January 14, 1991, p. 97.

Groves, Don. "China Deals for Yank Pix." *Variety*. 354:1, 18 March 21, 1994.

_____. "Dino Dub Rubs Coin in India, Pakistan." *Variety*. 354:27–28 April 25, 1994.

_____. "Distribs Voting to Revise Pic Campaigns O'seas." *Variety*. 352:5, 8 September 13, 1993.

_____. "Field Pared to Pair." *Variety*. 358:44 March 13–19, 1995.

_____. "Majors to End Embargo on CIS." *Variety*. 349:47, 90 December 7, 1992.

_____. "Modern Multiplexes to Make China Smile." *Variety*. 354:12 April 4, 1994.

_____. "MPEA Warns E. Europe Not to Get Greedy." *Variety*. 342:54 March 25, 1991.

_____. "O'seas Exhibs Lack of Christmas Spirit." *Variety*. 356:11, 27 October 10, 1994.

_____. "*Park* Bow Taps Indian Distrib Doors." *Variety*. 304:13, 34 April 11, 1994.

_____. "Sat Channels Scramble to Protect Signal." *Variety*. 355:29 June 20, 1994.

_____. "Summer Forecast: Fare Hot." *Variety*. 359:32–33 May 1–7, 1995.

_____. "The Mouse That Roars Is Foreign B.O. King." *Variety*. 357:11, 22 January 16–22, 1995.

_____. "Too Quiet on the Eastern Front." *Variety*. 349:1, 95 January 18, 1993.

_____. "U.S. Majors Take 80% of the Pic Pie." *Variety*. 342:58 January 21, 1991.

_____. "Veni, Video, Vici." *Variety*. 358:1, 46 April 3–9, 1995.

Gruson, Sydney. "Britain Would Cut Cost of U.S. Film." *New York Times*. November 17, 1945, p. 14.

_____. "Poles Say Rumors Cause Food Lack." *New York Times*. September 17, 1948, p. 8.

Guback, Thomas H. *The International Film Industry: Western Europe and America Since 1945*. Bloomington: Indiana University Press, 1969.

Guild, Hazel. "Love U.S. Films: Germany." *Variety*. 213:25, 60 January, 1959.

Gutsche, Thelma. *The History and Social Significance of Motion Pictures in South Africa 1895–1940*. Cape Town: Howard Timmins, 1972.

Halligan, Fionnuala. "Cantonese Take Out." *Variety*. 357:92–93 January 16–22, 1995.

"Halt Anti–U.S. Film Law." *Variety*. 118:15, 61 April 10, 1935.

Hansen, Harry L. "Hollywood International Understanding." *Harvard Business Review*. v. 25, no. 1:28–45 Autumn, 1946.

Harmetz, Aljean. "Hollywood Starts an Invasion of Europe's Booming Market." *New York Times*. January 11, 1990, pp. C19, C24.

_____. "If a Movie Goes in America, Will Rest of World Buy It?" *New York Times*. August 1, 1977, p. 19.

"Hays Clamps Down on Hypoing Films for Foreign Spots." *Variety*. 115:5 August 14, 1934.

"Hays in Washington to Ask Gov't Aid on British Unfreezing of U.S. Coin." *Variety*. 147:5, 22 July 8, 1942.

"Hays Officially Reports on U.S. Film Companies' Washup of Italian Biz." *Variety*. 133:15 February 8, 1939.

"Hays Protests Film Ban." *New York Times*. February 24, 1929, p. 2.
"Hays Raps Critics of Film Industry." *New York Times*. April 20, 1928, p. 6.
"Hays Sends French Rep." *Variety*. 120:19, 69 October 30, 1935.
"Hays Taking In the World." *Variety* 100:7, 47 October 8, 1930.
"Hays Will Speak to Film Men of Foreign Sales Departments." *Variety*. 77:26 December 17, 1924.
Heston, Vivienne. "Can TV Rescue Battered Filmbiz?" *Variety*. 350:59 April 12, 1993.
"Hicks Warns of Post-War Dangers in Creating Foreign Buyer's Market." *Variety*. 154:25, 36 March 15, 1944.
Hift, Fred. "Can Yank Films Crack Danes' Boycott." *Variety*. 207:5, 28 June 12, 1957.
_____. "Foreign Films 'Arrive' in U.S." *Variety*. 205:1, 62 January 30, 1957.
_____. "Pro–U.S. and It's Tough." *Variety*. 203:5, 22 July 11, 1956.
_____. "Sell Russia Our Pix, Urges Salisbury." *Variety*. 196:4 September 22, 1954.
Higham, Charles. *Merchant of Dreams: Louis B. Mayer, MGM and the Secret Hollywood*. New York: Donald I. Fine, 1993.
_____. *Warner Bros*. New York: Scribner's, 1975.
"Hints at Reprisals on French Exports." *New York Times*. June 8, 1929, p. 4.
"Hits American Films New Zealand Sees." *New York Times*. October 13, 1926, p. 23.
Hodson, J.L. "Hollywood Argument." *Spectator*. 172:471 May 26, 1944.
Hoehn, Hans. "Hungarians Ban All Westerns." *Variety*. 244:28 September 14, 1966.
Hollinger, Hy. "$8,500,000 for O'seas Ads." *Variety*. 197:5, 54 February 23, 1955.
_____. "Hungary Hungry for H'wood." *Variety*. 337:11, 14 November 22, 1989.
_____. "U.S. Pix Biz Sees Good Things Overseas in '90s." *Variety* 338:24 February 21, 1990.
"Hollywood." *New Republic*. 116:42–43 March 31, 1947.
"Hollywood Discovers New Fields in Mexico." *U.S. News & World Report*. 24:65–66 June 11, 1948.
"Hollywood Focus is Overseas." *Business Week*. October 9, 1954, pp. 158–160.
"Hollywood Found Molding New East." *New York Times*. May 8, 1935, p. 21.
"Hollywood Pix Get Extra O.O. to Assist State Dept. Cause Abroad." *Variety*. 170:1, 18 May 12, 1948.
"Hollywood, Unlimited." *New York Times*. December 21, 1927, p. 24.
"Hollywood's Exports Pay Off." *Business Week*. April 29, 1950, pp. 113–114.
"Hollywood's Foreign Film Sales: 1963–1973." *Variety*. 275:20 May 29, 1974.
"Hollywood's Stranglehold on Canada, Say Canadians." *Variety*. 89:9 December 28, 1927.
Holsendolph, Ernest. "Paramount Halts Film Exports to Iran Over Oil Prices." *New York Times*. September 26, 1974, p. 24.
"Hopkins to Pry Film Coin." *Variety*. 143:5, 16 July 30, 1941.
Horn, Florence. "Formidavel, Fabulosissimo." *Harper's Monthly Magazine*. 184:59–64 December, 1941.
"Hot Numbers." *Variety*. 353:8 January 3, 1994.
"How Majors Perform O'seas." *Variety*. 275:34 May 15, 1974.
"How Our Films Misrepresent America Abroad." *Literary Digest*. 71:28–29 November 26, 1921.
"How to Handle Europe for American Films." *Variety*. 93:4 November 21, 1928.
"How U.S. Majors Perform Overseas." *Variety*. 275:1, 34 May 15, 1974.
"Hungary Bars Films with Six U.S. Actors." *New York Times*. January 17, 1948, p. 10.
"H'wood Has Yet to Make Pix Profitably for Domestic B.O. Only—Balaban." *Variety*. 172:3, 36 September 29, 1948.
"H'wood Pix in Virtual Blackout Behind Iron Curtain." *Variety*. 178:1, 26 April 12, 1950.

"H'wood's World Goodwill." *Variety*. 114:5, 59 May 8, 1934.

"Il Duce Relents." *Variety*. 121:13 January 22, 1936.

Ilott, Terry. "Yanks Still Fill Europe's Bill." *Variety*. 349:1, 90 December 7, 1992.

"India Barely Worthwhile for U.S. Films." *Variety*. 263:23 July 21, 1971.

"India Cuts Duty on Foreign Films." *New York Times*. July 16, 1960, p. 10.

"India Sends Protest on American Films." *New York Times*. November 15, 1926, p. 4.

"India to Admit 150 U.S. Films." *Variety*. 277:3 December 4, 1974.

"India's Policy on Film Imports Hurting U.S., Say U.S. Majors." *Variety*. 335:348 Cannes '89 Special Issue.

"India-Made Nature Pictures Driving Out American Films." *Variety*. 80:25 October 21, 1925.

"Indonesian Exhib Pirates Pic." *Variety*. 243:5 June 22, 1966.

"Indonesians Bar U.S. Films." *New York Times*. May 11, 1964, p. 11.

"Indonesians View U.S. Films Again." *New York Times*. June 19, 1966, p. 10.

"The International Movie Marketplace." *Variety*. 334:35, 47 February 22, 1989.

"International Resume." *Variety*. 108:3, 27 September 13, 1932.

International Television & Video Almanac. 36th ed. New York: Quigley, 1991.

"Invasion of Finland, Good Market, New Blow for U.S. Films." *Variety*. 136:12 December 6, 1939.

"Iran's Islamic Regime Kicks Out Bruce Lee & Imperialistic Films." *Variety*. 295:2, 102 July 18, 1979.

"Italian Film Trade Combines in Petitioning Home Government to Allow in More Foreign Film." *Variety*. 100:7 July 16, 1930.

"Italian Producers Seen Back of Delay in Getting U.S. Pix into Italy." *Variety*. 161:15 February 27, 1946.

"Italy Making It Plenty Tough for U.S. Films." *Variety*. 98:7 February 19, 1930.

"Italy's Personality Made Conditions for U.S. Films May Mean None at All." *Variety*. 93:6 December 26, 1928.

"Italy's Picture Quota Bill to Promote Native Industry." *Variety*. 87:1, 51 April 27, 1927.

"Jap Censors Worry Over America's Slang." *Variety*. 98:4 March 5, 1930.

"Jap Theaters Pack 'Em In with Yank Pix." *Variety*. 169:12 December 31, 1947.

"Japan (494), India (308), Italy (301), U.S. (300), Taiwan (246) most active." *Variety*. 262:37 May 12, 1971.

"Japan Okay, Rest of Far East Not." *Variety*. 235:3, 29 July 29, 1964.

"The Japanese 'Obstacle Race' MPEA Battles New Restrictions,." *Variety*. 212:7, 16 September 3, 1958.

"Japs Ganging Up on U.S." *Variety*. 125:13, 50 February 17, 1937.

Jarrico, Paul. "They Are Not So Innocent Abroad." *New Republic*. 120:17–19 January 31, 1949.

Jarvie, Ian. *Hollywood's Overseas Campaign: The North Atlantic Movie Trade, 1920–1950*. Cambridge: Cambridge University Press, 1992.

Johnson, Randal. *The Film Industry in Brazil: Culture and the State*. Pittsburgh: University of Pittsburgh Press, 1987.

Johnston, Eric. "Hollywood: America's Traveling Salesman." *Vital Speeches*. 23:572–574 July 1, 1957.

_____. "H'wood Still Best U.S. Ambassador Despite Some Contrary Opinions." *Variety*. 189:5, 65 January 7, 1953.

_____. "Messengers from a Free Country." *Saturday Review of Literature*. 33:9–13, 28 March 4, 1950.

_____. "Mirrors of Society." *Americas*. 7:3–6 July, 1955.

_____. "Projecting the American Idea Around the World Makes U.S. Pix a Very Worthwhile Export Biz." *Variety*. 177:7 January 5, 1950.

Johnston, William A. "The World War of Talking Pictures." *Saturday Evening Post*. 203:31+ July 19, 1930.

"Johnston Boost for Common Market in Europe Puzzles Some Yanks." *Variety*. 210:7, 16 April 16, 1958.

"Johnston Decries French Film Bars." *New York Times*. May 13, 1952, p. 19.

"Johnston Defends Pix Going O'seas Before Senate Foreign Relations Unit." *Variety*. 190:5, 61 March 11, 1953.

"Johnston Stresses Strong Gov't Aid to Combat Foreign Snags to U.S. Pix." *Variety*. 162:21 March 27, 1946.

"Johnston Tips That Yank Producers Thawed Out Most Foreign Frozen Coin." *Variety*. 177:4, 16 February 22, 1950.

"Johnston's Sarcastic Admiration for Foreign Ingenuity." *Variety*. 218:5, 20 March 2, 1960.

"Johnston's Upbeat Horizons." *Variety*. 228:3, 15 September 12, 1962.

Jones, Dorothy B. "Hollywood's International Relations." *Quarterly of Film, Radio & Television*. 11:362–374 Summer, 1957.

"Jordan Bans All Kaye Films." *New York Times*. October 1, 1956, p. 31.

Josephs, Ray. "H'wood's Pan-Am Bad Will." *Variety*. 143:3, 34 June 25, 1941.

Katz, Ephraim. *The Macmillan International Film Encyclopedia*. new ed. New York: HarperCollins, 1994.

Kauffman, Reginald Wright. "War in the Film World." *North American Review*. 229:351–356 March, 1930.

Kennedy, Harlan. "Fox's Man in London." *American Film*. 7:60–61 November, 1981.

"Kent's Testimony on Foreign Loss." *New York Times*. April 7, 1939, p. 25.

Klady, Leonard. "Earth to H'wood: You Win." *Variety*. 358:1, 63 February 13–19, 1995.

_____. "Exceptions Are the Rule in Foreign B.O." *Variety*. 357:7, 12 November 14, 1994.

_____. "H'wood: Land of the Rising Sum." *Variety*. 358:14 March 13–19 1995.

Klain, Stephen. "India's New Film Pact with U.S. Majors." *Variety*. 301:41, 46 November 5, 1980.

"Kontingents No Good." *Variety*. 109:15, 52 January 31, 1933.

Korda, Alexander. "Is the Screen Really Free?" *New York Times*. December 1, 1946, sec. 2, p. 5.

Kouwenhoven, John A. "The Movies Better Be Good!" *Harper's Monthly Magazine*. 190:534–540 May, 1945.

Krushen, Mori. "D.C. Aid to Film Biz Abroad." *Variety*. 155:3, 11 September 6, 1944.

_____. "Europe as Top Foreign Market." *Variety*. 157:3, 18 January 10, 1945.

_____. "Hedge vs. 'Peace Table' Spot." *Variety*. 158:5, 20 March 14, 1945.

"Latin-American Countries Lead Rest of World." *Variety*. 84:5 August 4, 1926.

"Latin Uproar." *Time*. 37:69–70 February 10, 1941.

"Leaders in Europe Warm to U.S. Films." *New York Times*. August 24, 1949, p. 29.

Lee, Paul K. "Influence of Films Abroad." *New York Times*. March 28, 1943, sec. 2, p. 3.

"Lend-Lease Cut May Hit Pix." *Variety*. 156:3, 12 October 11, 1944.

Lenin, V.I. *Critical Remarks on the National Question. The Rights of Nations to Self-Determination*. Moscow: Progress, 1951.

Lent, John A. *The Asian Film Industry*. London: Christopher Helm, 1990.

Levin, Meyer. "Glory Poison for the Screen." *Reader's Digest*. 29:101–102 December, 1936.

Lewis, Mark. "Mysterious East No B.O. Feast." *Variety*. 351:1, 63 June 7, 1993.

Lieb, Rebecca. "Wenders Wants Curbs on U.S. Pix in Europe." *Variety*. 347:5 May 18, 1992.

Lieberman, Henry R. "American Films Attacked in China." *New York Times.* September 25, 1949, sec. 2, p. 5.

"Like the Marines, MPEA Fights for U.S. Industry from Halls of Montezuma to Shores of Tripoli." *Variety.* 291:7, 42 June 21, 1978.

"Limit Set on U.S. Films." *New York Times.* October 6, 1950, p. 22.

"Loan's O.K. Big Break for Pix." *Variety.* 163:3, 20 July 17, 1946.

"Lodge Prescribes Films for Soviet." *New York Times.* April 14, 1958, p. 18.

"Loew Advises British to Learn Movie Game." *New York Times.* June 17, 1926, p. 21.

Loftus, Jack. "TV & Film Execs Say Copyright Barriers Impede Foreign Trade." *Variety.* 316:3, 164 October 10, 1984.

Loher, Bruno. "Steady Foreign Influx Alters Showbiz Scene." *Variety.* 351:31 August 9, 1993.

"Low Admissions a Discouragement." *Variety.* 214:3 March 18, 1959.

Lowe, Herman A. "Washington Discovers Hollywood." *American Mercury.* 60:407–414 April, 1945.

Lowry, Edward G. "Trade Follows the Film." *Saturday Evening Post.* 198:12–13+ November 7, 1925.

"Maas Blasts Anti–U.S. Films Drive." *Variety.* 210:8 April 30, 1958.

McBride, Joseph. "U.S. Distrib'n Boon Seen as Road-Blocs Crumble." *Variety.* 337:7, 21 December 13, 1989.

McCabe, John. *Babe: The Life of Oliver Hardy.* London: Robson, 1990.

MacCormac, John. "Austrians Boycott Our Sound Films." *New York Times.* May 11, 1930, sec. 2, p. 1.

_____. "London Film Notes." *New York Times.* December 9, 1928, sec. 10, p. 7.

MacDonald, Carlisle. "Demand Looming for Native Talkers." *New York Times.* December 16, 1929, p. 5.

_____. "France Likely to End Curbs on Our Films." *New York Times.* June 24, 1931, p. 1.

_____. "French Again Seek 3-to-1 Film Quota." *New York Times.* May 18, 1929, p. 6.

_____. "French Fix Accord with U.S. on Films." *New York Times.* September 20, 1929, p. 7.

_____. "French Link Films to Our Trade Rise." *New York Times.* September 10, 1929, p. 11.

_____. "French Recommend New 4-1 Film Quota." *New York Times.* May 28, 1929, p. 7.

MacKenzie, Norman. "Films and Quotas." *New Statesman & Nation.* 33:451–452 June 2, 1947.

Magiera, Marcy. "Promotional Marketer of the Year." *Advertising Age.* 65:S1, S8 March 21, 1994.

Marcom, John, Jr. "Dream Factory to the World." *Forbes.* 147:98, 100–101 April 29, 1991.

Matthews, Herbert L. "Anti–U.S. Actions in Italy Increase." *New York Times.* April 5, 1941, p. 5.

Mayer, Gerald M. "American Motion Pictures in World Trade." *Annals of the American Academy of Political and Social Science.* 254:31–36 November, 1947.

Meakin, Hardie. "Our Foreign Trade." *Variety.* 77:24 December 31, 1924.

Merz, Charles. "When the Movies Go Abroad." *Harper's Monthly Magazine.* 152:159–165 January, 1926.

"Metro Dubbing All Pix into Spanish for Latin America." *Variety.* 155:8 July 12, 1944.

"Metro Wins the Battle of *Ah, Wilderness.*" *New York Times.* January 19, 1936, sec. 9, p. 5.

"Mexican Court Acts on Law on Film Time." *New York Times.* August 29, 1951, p. 19.

"Mexican Movies." *Time.* 36:91–92 December 16, 1940.

"Mexican Protest Against English Talker Dialog." *Variety.* 95:9 June 12, 1929.

"Mexico Barring Film Makers Showing Mexicans as Villains." *Variety.* 87:1 June 15, 1927.

"Mexico Bars Our Films." *New York Times.* August 26, 1927, p. 15.

"Mexico: Get Lost, Uncle Sam." *Variety.* 233:1, 54 December 11, 1963.

"Mexico Told to Reduce Film Tax." *Variety.* 104:15 October 20, 1931.

"Mexico Will Not Lift Ban Against Pathé and Vitagraph." *Variety.* 76:22 November 5, 1924.

"Mexico's Ban on Mexican Movie Villains." *New York Times.* February 11, 1922, p. 15.

"Mexico's Long-Frozen 32¢ Boxoffice Top Finally Thawed." *Variety.* 225:7, 15 January 24, 1962.

Meyer, Karl E. "High Noon at Uruguay Gulch." *New York Times.* December 13, 1993, p. A16.

"Miss Taylor Banned in Jordan." *New York Times.* April 28, 1959, p. 41.

"Mickey Mouse Is Rated Among Better U.S. Envoys of Goodwill." *Variety.* 142:13 May 28, 1941.

Moldea, Dan E. *Dark Victory.* New York: Viking, 1986.

Moley, Raymond. *The Hays Office.* Indianapolis: Bobbs-Merrill, 1945.

Molner, David. "Movie Direction." *Variety.* 356:47–48 October 10, 1994.

"Money Embargo Remedy." *Variety.* 105:11 December 22, 1931.

Monush, Barry. ed. *International Motion Picture Almanac 1994,* 65th ed. New York: Quigley, 1994.

Moosher, George. "Japan and the Near East." *Variety.* 72:19 September 6, 1923.

"More British Movie Agony." *Literary Digest.* 85:27 June 20, 1925.

"More Foresight, Less Grab and Run." *Variety.* 205:10 February 13, 1957.

"More Grief for Movie Exports." *Business Week.* July 15, 1950, pp. 108–110.

Morris, John D. "Excise Tax Study Seeks Inequities." *New York Times.* October 7, 1955, p. 12.

Mosettig, Mike. "Take-out of $$ Eased Globally." *Variety.* 234:33 April 29, 1964.

"Motion Pictures for China." *New York Times.* June 20, 1920, sec. 2, p. 11.

"The Movie Business in Buenos Aires." *Bulletin of the Pan American Union.* 58:285–287 March, 1924.

"The Movie Crisis." *New York Times.* July 19, 1919, p. 8.

"Movie Influence Assailed." *New York Times.* September 19, 1929, p. 11.

"Movie-itis in Central America." *Literary Digest.* 49:590 September 26, 1914.

"Movie Man Griffis Plans Private Shows for Peron." *New York Times.* December 15, 1949, p. 21.

"Movie Man's Burden." *New Republic.* 117:37–38 July 21, 1947.

"Movie Problems Found in Far East." *New York Times.* March 14, 1959, p. 26.

"Movies Begin to Fight Foreign Monopolies." *New York Times.* April 5, 1946, p. 21.

"Movies in Japan." *New York Times* Magazine. November 26, 1916, p. 3.

"Movies Must Submit Scenarios to the OWI." *New York Times.* December 19, 1942, p. 1.

"Movies Prosper in Europe." *New York Times.* December 15, 1914, p. 13.

"Movies Seek U.S. Help." *New York Times.* March 20, 1960, p. 40.

"MPAA Setup Post-Johnston." *Variety.* 232:3 October 23, 1963.

"MPAA's Advice Bureau for Foreign Prods. Backs 'Two-Way Street' Idea." *Variety.* 176:3, 19 November 9, 1949.

"MPEA Approves Johnston's Agreement." *New York Times.* March 19, 1948, p. 29.

"MPEA Firms' Frozen Yen May Thaw in Japan." *Variety.* 172:25 September 29, 1948.

"MPEA Recognizes Kenya Film Corporation." *Variety*. 252:5 September 18, 1968.
"MPEA Threatens Withdrawal." *New York Times*. December 30, 1947, p. 18.
"MPEA Unblocks 500G in Turkey." *Variety*. 260:5 September 16, 1970.
"MPEA's Nigeria Pool Starting." *Variety*. 225:5 December 20, 1961.
Murphy, A.D. "Export-Import Bank Film Aid." *Variety*. 264:3, 23 October 13, 1971.
_____. "Film Universe Expanding: Record Rentals for U.S." *Variety*. 335:11 June 14, 1989.
_____. "Globe Gobbling Up U.S. Pix in Record Doses." *Variety*. 339:7, 10 June 13, 1990.
_____. "O'seas Inflation Clips U.S. Films." *Variety*. 288:1, 16 August 24, 1977.
_____. "Valenti's Inventory of Alien Threats to U.S. Films." *Variety*. 262:5 April 28, 1971.
_____. "Yanks 1974 Global Film Take Up 28%." *Variety*. 279:3, 30 June 25, 1975.
"Murrow Dubs U.S. Film Product. 'Funhouse Mirrors' as Seen O'seas." *Variety*. 224:1, 78 November 8, 1961.
"Mussolini O.K.'s 10% Foreign Dialog." *Variety*. 100:7 November 12, 1930.
Myers, Harold. "Valenti Urges Soviets to Buy More U.S. Pix, Widen Audience." *Variety*. 327:5, 23 July 22, 1987.
"Name Films Not Fit for O'seas." *Variety*. 214:5 May 27, 1959.
"Nat'l Ass'n Would Have U.S. Fight Foreign Film Embargo." *Variety*. 61:47 February 18, 1921.
"Nazi Expansion Seen as Curb on U.S. Films." *New York Times*. April 9, 1939, p. 33.
"Need Action to Protect U.S. Films in France." *Variety*. 90:5 March 7, 1928.
"Netherlands Lifts Bans on U.S. Films." *New York Times*. August 6, 1947, p. 28.
"New Ban in France on American Films." *New York Times*. July 29, 1932, p. 18.
"New Brazilian Restrictions Again Accent That Our State Dept. Seems Blind to Film Industry's Problems." *Variety*. 172:6 October 6, 1948.
"New Czech Import Law Still Has Yank Filmites Dizzy." *Variety*. 116:21, 58 November 27, 1934.
"New Duty on Foreign Films Playing Singapore." *Variety*. 216:11 October 28, 1959.
"New 50% Playing Time Law for Mex Pix Causes U.S. Withdrawal Threats." *Variety*. 183:16 August 22, 1951.
"New German Quota Law Bars Jews." *Variety*. 111:11, 31 July 4, 1933.
"New Issue in Brazil: Movie-Ticket Prices." *U.S. News & World Report*. 25:61 November 26, 1948.
"New Price Freeze of Film Rentals in Chile." *Variety*. 247:15 July 26, 1967.
"New Quota Law Will Boost Cost of U.S. Biz in England 40%–50%." *Variety*. 130:13 April 6, 1938.
"New Script Quest Points to Pix Biz Going the South American Way." *Variety*. 136:5 October 25, 1939.
"Nine MPAA Members Control Over 68% Domestic Pic Market." *Variety*. 262:35 May 12, 1971.
"Nix 'Selective' Export Process." *Variety*. 189:3, 18 January 14, 1953.
"No Gesture from Government with Argentine Theaters on Eve of Closing Over Tax." *Variety*. 102:13 April 8, 1931.
"No More Brit Coin Freeze." *Variety*. 150:5 May 5, 1943.
North, C.J. "Our Foreign Trade in Motion Pictures." *Annals of the American Academy of Political and Social Science*. 128:100–108 November, 1926.
_____. "Our Silent Ambassadors." The Independent. 116:689:690 June 12, 1926.
"Norway Film Group to Cancel U.S. Pact." *New York Times*. August 1, 1954, p. 77.
"Norwegian Boycott of U.S. Films May End." *New York Times*. February 28, 1946, p. 19.
"Okay Johnston Offices' Joint Budget; Global Fence-Mending Looming Bigger." *Variety*. 201:3 February 29, 1956.

"$150,000,000 O'seas Film Take." *Variety*. 190:1, 13 June 3, 1953.

"$138,000,000 Net for All Firms in '46 Coin." *Variety*. 169:12 December 31, 1947.

"$100,000,000 of Films' Normal O'seas Take Hit by Foreign Market Snafu." *Variety*. 168:6 November 12, 1947.

"1,000 Lose Film Jobs in French Quota Fight." *New York Times*. June 15, 1929, p. 18.

Ormsbee, Helen. "Europe's Film Quotas." *New York Times*. February 19, 1928, sec. 8, p. 3.

"Our Film Men Plan French Quota Fight." *New York Times*. March 28, 1929, p. 31.

"Our Films Disillusioning the East." *Literary Digest*. 90:26 August 7, 1926.

"Our Films in England." *New York Times*. May 16, 1925, p. 16.

"Our Films Not Corrupting the East." *Literary Digest*. 101:28 June 1, 1929.

"Overloading France on U.S. Film Spurs Native Embargo Agitators." *Variety*. 111:21 July 11, 1933.

"Overseas Choke U.S. Films & TV." *Variety*. 267:1, 60 May 31, 1972.

"OWI Seizes Fascist Pix." *Variety*. 151:3, 56 September 15, 1943.

Pace, Eric. "Cairo Is Willing to Let Tarzan Films Return." *New York Times*. November 24, 1968, p. 115.

Pagano, Penny. "Studios Ask U.S. to Fight Trade Curbs." *Los Angeles Times*. September 11, 1985, sec. 6, p. 4.

"Pan-Arab Boycotts of H'wood Stars." *Variety*. 217:1, 62 December 23, 1959.

"Par Out of Iran on B.O. Curb." *Variety*. 276:4 October 2, 1974.

"Paris Movie Houses Threaten to Close." *New York Times*. February 2, 1928, p. 17.

Pearse, Ben. "How the Movies Get Their Money Out of Europe." *Saturday Evening Post*. 227:43+ November 27, 1954.

Peers, Martin. "UA Theaters Ready to Pump $350 Million into Worldwide Expansion Program." *Variety*. 359:18 May 29–June 4, 1995.

Pendakur, Manjunath. *Canadian Dreams and American Control*. Toronto: Garamond, 1990.

Phillips, R. Le Clerc. "French Flirts and English Fops." *New York Times*. December 11, 1927, sec. 9, p. 7.

"Picker Finds Admissions Too Low in Latin Lands." *Variety*. 194:4 March 31, 1954.

Pickford, Mary. "Ambassadors." *Saturday Evening Post*. 203:6–7+ August 23, 1930.

"Pictures in China." *Variety*. 31:8 July 25, 1913.

"Pix Aim to Please 'Em All." *Variety*. 127:1, 34 July 28, 1937.

"Pix Eye D.C. Aid for Aid Abroad." *Variety*. 184:3, 48 November 14, 1951.

"Pix Gain Most in Bretton Woods Plan." *Variety*. 159:9, 15 June 13, 1945.

"Pix Tricks Mix Latins." *Variety*. 144:1, 20 October 8, 1941.

"Plan Pix Pool for Abroad." *Variety*. 158:3, 19 May 23, 1945.

"Poland's Mixed Dilemma." *Variety*. 85:5, 10 January 5, 1927.

"Policy for Films." *Times* (London). September 7, 1948, p. 5.

"Polish Gov't Confounded." *Variety*. 84:3 September 1, 1926.

Pond, Steve. "Thaw in the Russian Market." *Washington Post*. October 7, 1988, p. B7.

"Post-War U.S. Pix Biz in Europe Will Hinge on Int'l Currency Stability." *Variety*. 151:5, 28 July 14, 1943.

"Powerful Forces Aiming to Restrict U.S. Pix in Japan Denounced by Maas." *Variety*. 189:5, 17 December 10, 1952.

"Pravda Scolds at Tarzan Films." *New York Times*. December 28, 1953, p. 2.

"Predecessors of American Films." *New York Times*. July 1, 1926, p. 22.

"Producers Optimistic Again That the 40% Foreign Revenue Will Return to Former Status." *Variety*. 100:7, 58 August 13, 1930.

"Protest Film Invasion." *New York Times*. July 16, 1919, p. 13

Pryor, Thomas M. "By Way of Report." *New York Times*. August 13, 1944, sec. 2, p. 3.
_____. "Censorship or Advice." *New York Times*. December 13, 1942, sec. 8, p. 3.
_____. "Competition Ahead." *New York Times*. October 10, 1943, sec. 2, p. 3.
_____. "Complications Abroad." *New York Times*. October 17, 1937, sec. 11, p. 4.
_____. "Film News of the Week." *New York Times*. May 19, 1940, sec. 9, p. 4.
_____. "Films Go Abroad Again." *New York Times*. January 2, 1944, sec. 2, p. 3.
_____. "Hollywood Global Review." *New York Times*. October 31, 1954, sec. 2, p. 5.
_____. "Hollywood Stand." *New York Times*. May 29, 1955, sec. 2, p. 5.
_____. "Johnston Expects New Movie Gains." *New York Times*. October 8, 1954, p. 27.
_____. "Looking for Encouragement." *New York Times*. April 22, 1945, sec. 2, p. 3.
_____. "More on Foreign Quotas." *New York Times*. October 24, 1937, sec. 11, p. 6.
_____. "Sukarno Praises Role of U.S. Films." *New York Times*. June 2, 1956, p. 13.
_____. "Sundry Matters About Films and People." *New York Times*. February 15, 1942, sec. 8, p. 5.
_____. "Survey of American Films Abroad. *New York Times*. January 11, 1942, sec. 9, p. 4.
_____. "U.S. Films Facing Restraints Abroad." *New York Times*. December 4, 1945, p. 33.
_____. "U.S. Films Favored in the Americas." *New York Times*. December 6, 1945, p. 31.
_____. "U.S. Films Hailed by Hammarskjold." *New York Times*. May 15, 1954, p. 12.
"Rain in Spain Falls Mainly on the Plain." *Variety*. 206:11 April 17, 1957.
"Rasputin's Foreign Difficulties Bring Protests." *Variety*. 114:13 May 1, 1934.
"Reds Prod Paris on U.S. Pix." *Variety*. 205:7, 18 December 26, 1956.
Regelman, Karen. "Industry Stages Silent Revolution." *Variety*. 356:59, 62 September 19, 1994.
_____. "U.S. Majors on Top in Japan." *Variety*. 354:30 April 11, 1994.
"Rely on Domestic Sales." *Variety*. 143:5 August 20, 1941.
"Reprisal Talked of Against French If Herriott's Severe." *Variety*. 90:10 April 4, 1928.
"Revolt in the West." *New York Times*. November 24, 1935, sec. 9, p. 4.
Riding, Alan. "French Film Industry Circles the Wagons." *New York Times*. September 18, 1993, pp. 11, 14.
"Riskin Says Voluntary Export Film Censorship Being Studied by U.S." *Variety*. 158:10 May 30, 1945.
Robbins, Jim. "E.C. Quotas a Cancer, Says Worried MPAA Prexy." *Variety*. 337:2 October 18, 1989.
Robinson, David. "A Case of Hollywood or Bust." *Times* (London). December 16, 1993, p. 31.
Robinson, Gwen. "Power Shift at Sony Corporation." *Variety*. 358:15, 22 March 27– April 2, 1995.
Rockwell, John. "For Unholy Hollywood's Devotees, a Pariah Film Festival in France." *New York Times*. September 9, 1993, p. C13.
Rohter, Larry. "Buchwald Gets Damages in Film Suit Dispute." *New York Times*. December 22, 1990, pp. 17, 22.
"Rome Rally Scores U.S." *New York Times*. February 21, 1949, p. 20.
"Roosevelt Views Movies' Problems." *New York Times*. October 29, 1937, p. 14.
Ross, Albion. "Bonn Film Group Asks Import Curb." *New York Times*. January 2, 1955, p. 63.
"Rumania Gets U.S. Films." *New York Times*. January 20, 1947, p. 19.
"Rumania Seizes U.S. Film Office." *New York Times*. November 4, 1948, p. 38.
"Rumania Yens More Yank Films." *Variety*. 243:17 July 13, 1966.
"Rush U.S. Films to No. Africa." *Variety*. 148:16 November 18, 1942.
"Russia to See U.S. Films." *New York Times*. October 26, 1948, p. 13.

"Russians Would Like U.S. Pix but Insist on 'Auditioning' Them First." *Variety.* 165:21 March 5, 1947.

Sadler, Russell. "Murdoch, PBS, and Congress." *Z Magazine.* 8:12–13 April, 1995.

Safire, William. "Hold That GATT." *New York Times.* December 9, 1993, p. A31.

Sanderson, Ivan T. "Foreigners See Our Films." *Atlantic Monthly.* 168:238–240 August, 1941.

"Sapene Centre Entire French Situation." *Variety.* 95:6 June 5, 1929.

"Sapene Utters Downright Boycott Threat Against American Trade." *Variety.* 94:2, 60 March 27, 1929.

"Satellites Agree to Buy U.S. Films." *New York Times.* October 26, 1956, p. 33.

"Say Curtain Bars Films." *New York Times.* April 8, 1947, p. 34.

"Say France Closes Door to Our Films." *New York Times.* July 30, 1932, p. 16.

"Say Movies Lead Stage to Decency." *New York Times.* April 3, 1927, p. 14.

"Says Sales Abroad Cut Film Prices Here." *New York Times.* April 22, 1947, p. 32.

Schanberg, Sydney H. "New Delhi: Pillage in the Eyes of God." *New York Times.* August 30, 1971, p. 34.

Schmidt, Dana Adams. "Our Movies Leave Germans Hostile." *New York Times.* July 23, 1946, p. 21.

"Seating Capacity at Movies Rises." *New York Times.* February 25, 1955, p. 19.

"See Pix as Best Anti-Red Brake." *Variety.* 162:3, 63 May 29, 1946.

"See Record '51 Foreign Income." *Variety.* 185:5, 15 January 16, 1952.

"Seeing America Abroad." *New York Times.* July 9, 1917, p. 7.

"Seek to Save British Films." *New York Times.* December 29, 1925, p.5.

Segars, Frank. "American Majors in Asia Fight Poor Boxoffice & Trade Barriers." *Variety.* 320:337, 413 October 16, 1985.

_____. "South Korean Opposition to UIP Entry Remains Strong Despite Denials." *Variety.* 335:1, 3 June 28, 1989.

_____. "Wheel of Misfortune Persists for Yank Distribs in Far East." *Variety.* 335:335–336 Cannes '89 Special Issue.

"Self-Policing Pays Off Abroad." *Variety.* 167:3, 20 June 25, 1947.

"78% Pix Shown in China from the U.S." *Variety.* 118:14 April 3, 1935.

"$75,000,000 Export Estimated for American Film Producers." *Variety.* 79:43 May 20, 1925.

"$75,000,000 U.S. Net Can Still Be Gotten Without British Market." *Variety.* 167:1, 34 August 13, 1947.

"$71,000,000 from Foreign Sales." *Variety.* 88:8 August 17, 1927.

"Sex in Jap, German Local-Made Pix Too Much Competish for U.S. Product." *Variety.* 173:3, 12 February 2, 1949.

"Sexports." *Time.* 76:61, 63 September 19, 1960.

"Sexy Films for Abroad." *Variety.* 84:1, 75 August 18, 1926.

"Shall Britons Be Slaves to Our Films?" *Literary Digest.* 85:35 June 6, 1925.

"Shanghai Supports U.S. Film." *Variety.* 141:73 January 8, 1941.

Shaplen, Joseph. "Dominions Prevent Curb on Our Films." *New York Times.* August 19, 1932, p. 4.

Shaw, Roger. "American Movies Abroad." *Review of Reviews.* 78:77–80 July, 1928.

Sherwood, Robert E. "Sailing Into Summer—and Return." *New York Times.* March 19, 1939, sec. 11, p. 2.

"Showbiz Lures Bronfman." *Times-Colonist* (Victoria, BC). April 11, 1995, p. B8.

"Shun Tax on Our Films." *New York Times.* July 5, 1923, p. 14.

Siedenburg, Frederic. "Motion Pictures Abroad." *Commonweal.* 12:381–383 August 13, 1930.

Singer, Daniel. "GATT & the Shape of Our Dreams." *The Nation*. 258:54–56 January 17, 1994.

"6 Companies to Halt Film Shipments to Iran." *New York Times*. March 28, 1975, p. 10.

"6 Distribs (Not Columbia, AA) Embargo Their Prints in Chagrin That Iran Keeps Low Admissions." *Variety*. 278:3, 42 April 2, 1975.

"600 American Films Annually Are Suitable for Germany's Use." *Variety*. 77:26 December 24, 1924.

Skouras, Spyros P. "Skouras Sees Greater Global Markets for U.S. Films." *Variety*. 189:15 January 7, 1953.

Smith, Anthony. *The Geopolitics of Information*. London: Faber & Faber, 1980.

Sniffen, William W. "World Markets for American Manufacturers." *Scientific American*. 118:526 June 8, 1918.

Solomon, Aubrey. *Twentieth Century–Fox: A Corporate and Financial History*. Metuchen, NJ: Scarecrow, 1988.

"Sound Killing Quotas." *Variety*. 99:7, 68 June 4, 1930.

"So. America, 'Land of Unfulfillment,' Was Big Snag to U.S. Pic Cos. in '40." *Variety*. 141:73 January 8, 1941.

"South American Trade." *Variety*. 42:26 May 26, 1916.

"Sovereign Japan Kicks Pix." *Variety*. 219:11–12 July 20, 1960.

"Soviet Rebuffs U.S. on Return of 5 Films." *New York Times*. September 22, 1952, p. 19.

"Spain Bars All M-G Films." *Variety*. 89:5 October 26, 1927.

"Spain Renews Film Pact." *New York Times*. November 23, 1953, p. 32.

"Spain Starves U.S. on Licenses." *Variety*. 223:11 August 2, 1961.

"Spain's Low Admissions and American Films." *Variety*. 72:22 November 1, 1923.

"Spell Backward Nations Backwards." *Variety*. 229:15 December 19, 1962.

Spencer, Michael. "U.S.–Canada Film Relations 1920–1986." *Cinema Canada*. n. 131:10–17 June, 1986.

"Squeeze in France." *Variety*. 358:5 March 13–19, 1995.

Stanley, Fred. "Diplomatic Hollywood." *New York Times*. October 7, 1945, sec. 2, p. 1.

_____. "Hollywood Ponders." *New York Times*. July 16, 1944, sec. 2, p. 1.

"State Dept. Help Ends Incentive Plan, Insures Yanks $17,000,000 Minimum." *Variety*. 179:3, 30 July 26, 1950.

"State Dept. to Break Down Barriers Slowing U.S. Film Selling Abroad." *Variety*. 155:3, 55 June 28, 1944.

"State Dept's Influence in French Film Accord." *Variety*. 171:5, 22 August 25, 1948.

Stern, Andy. "French Fried in Quota Quibble." *Variety*. 358:173–174 February 20–26, 1995.

_____. "Valenti Continues Euro Peace Effort." *Variety*. 357:22 November 7, 1994.

Stevenson, Richard W. "Europeans Threaten Big U.S. Film Distributor." *New York Times*. February 23, 1994, p. D3.

_____. "The Magic of Hollywood Math." *New York Times*. April 13, 1990, pp. 1–2.

"Stop Film Flow to China." *Variety*. 172:15 September 8, 1948.

"Storm Over Australia." *Variety*. 125:13 April 7, 1937.

"Studios Drop Danish Demands." *New York Times*. January 22, 1955, p. 9.

"Subtitle Plot, Lyrics in Italics." *Variety*. 223:4 August 9, 1961.

Sulzberger, C.L. "Foreign Affairs." *New York Times*. April 13, 1955, p. 28.

"The Superiority of American to European Films as Explained by a French Critic." *Current Opinion*. 63:250–251 October, 1917.

"Survival of Fittest in Films Abroad." *Variety*. 86:4 April 13, 1927.

"Taking Cultural Exception." *Economist*. 328:61 September 25, 1993.

"Talkies Assailed Anew in Argentina." *New York Times*. April 29, 1930, p. 30.

"Talkies for Europe Baffle Americans." *New York Times*. December 28, 1929, p. 4.

"Talkies in English Opposed in Brazil." *New York Times*. November 18, 1929, p. 7.

"Talkies in Foreign Languages Keep American Films on Top." *Business Week*. February 25, 1931, p. 22.

"Talkies Under Fire in Argentine Press." *New York Times*. April 28, 1930, p. 5.

Tavares, Hernane. "Hollywood Needs Latin America." *Americas*. 1:2–7+ October, 1949.

"Tavernier Cries Domination." *Variety*. 301:7, 24 November 19, 1980.

"Tax Gross of All Imported Films as Foreign Situation Remedy." *Variety*. 84:46 August 18, 1926.

"Tax Increased 15 Times." *Variety*. 101:13, 45 March 4, 1931.

Tempest, Rone. "Fugitive Movie Wows 'Em in China." *Times-Colonist* (Victoria, BC). December 2, 1994, p. D5.

"10-Yr. Foreign Pix War Looms." *Variety*. 156:1, 55 October 25, 1944.

"Thais Give Imported Pix a Tax Break." *Variety*. 354:58 April 11, 1994.

"Their Novelties Need No Protection." *New York Times*. August 5, 1926, p. 20.

"There's a Quota in Australia But 'What Quota?' Asks Pic Biz." *Variety*. 124:14 November 4, 1936.

Thiong'o Ngugi Wa. "Kenyan Culture: The National Struggle for Survival" in Jorg Becker, ed. *Communication and Domination: Essays to Honor Herbert I. Schiller*. Norwood, NJ: Ablex, 1986.

Thompson, Kristin. *Exporting Entertainment: America in the World Film Market 1907–1934*. London: BFI, 1985.

"Threaten American Films." *New York Times*. March 26, 1930, p. 12.

"Threaten O'seas Film Front." *Variety*. 237:5 February 10, 1965.

"Threaten to Ban Talkies." *New York Times*. April 29, 1930, p. 30.

Tilley, Frank. "Will U.S. Put Down Whip and 'Play Ball' on British Quota?" *Variety*. 90:13 February 8, 1928.

"Time Warner Buys Another Cable Firm." *Times-Colonist* (Victoria, BC). February 8, 1995, p. C11.

"To Aid Film Business." *New York Times*. July 7, 1929, p. 12.

"To Halt Films to Cuba." *New York Times*. July 17, 1936, p. 20.

"Too Much Gab for Foreigners." *Variety*. 128:15 November 10, 1937.

Trask, C. Hooper. "Our Talkies in German." *New York Times*. June 15, 1930, sec. 8, p. 3.

Trask, Claire. "Berlin Communique." *New York Times*. August 4, 1935, sec. 9, p. 2.

"Truman Studies Aid to U.S. Pictures in Foreign Markets Not Paying Off." *Variety*. 169:1, 53 February 4, 1948.

Tulloch, John. *Australian Cinema: Industry, Narrative and Meaning*. Sydney: Allen & Unwin, 1982.

Tully, Shawn. "Bad Box Office." *Fortune*. 129;24 January 24, 1994.

"Tunisian Film Tax Is Aiding Red Bloc." *New York Times*. February 5, 1961, p. 83.

"Turks to Remit MPEA Companies at Old 9-to-1 Rate." *Variety*. 261:3 December 16, 1970.

Tusher, Will. "Col Pledges to Pull Pix from Segregated S. African Theaters." *Variety*. 325:1, 94 November 19, 1986.

_____. "Majors O'seas Gross 30–35% of Total?" *Variety*. 306:5, 52 March 31, 1982.

_____. "MPAA Bans the Sale of U.S. Pictures to USSR." *Variety*. 343:8 June 10, 1991.

_____. "U.S. Pix 32% Up on 1976." *Variety*. 286:1, 126 April 6, 1977.

"28 Foreign Screens Were 60.6% American." *Variety*. 94:2 April 3, 1929.

"Two Film Groups Join in New Quota Protest." *New York Times*. June 4, 1949, p. 8.

"U's Al Daff Gives Close-Up of U.S. Pix Int'l Future." *Variety*. 159:18 August 1, 1945.

"UA Theaters to Build in India." *Variety*. 358:14 February 20–26, 1995.

"UFA Exec Suggests Doubling of Admission Scale in Germany." *Variety*. 243:19 July 6, 1966.

"Uncle Sam and the Movies." *Congressional Record*. 7:291–317 November, 1928.

"Uncle Sam Takes Inventory of Picture Distribution Situations in Various Foreign Countries." *Variety*. 126:13 June 2, 1937.

"Unfreezing Foreign Coin." *Variety*. 138:7, 12 April 10, 1940.

"Unique Status of Eric Johnston." *Variety*. 212:4 November 5, 1958.

"United Action in Foreign Market Only Out, Sez Johnston." *Variety*. 162:13 April 10, 1946.

"Unlikely U.S. Filmers Will Withdraw from Germany, Japan Despite Costs." *Variety*. 169:5, 12 December 31, 1947.

"Un–United Americans Sure to Lose." *Variety*. 204:11 October 10, 1956.

"Uphold American Movies." *New York Times*. April 29, 1937, p. 17.

"Urges Steps to Get Lost Film Markets." *New York Times*. January 2, 1944, p. 37.

"U.S. Asks Return of 2 Motion Picture Films." *New York Times*. January 23, 1951, p. 8.

"U.S. Beats Foreign Snags." *Variety*. 130:15 June 8, 1938.

"U.S. Cuts Down Film Experts." *Variety*. 111:19 July 25, 1933.

"U.S. Distribs Crack Freeze on Film Prices by Europe TV." *Variety*. 273:1, 40 December 26, 1973.

"U.S. Distribs End Boycott of Spain." *Variety*. 210:1, April 2, 1958.

"U.S. Distribs Resume Pix Exports." *Variety*. 257:35 December 10, 1969.

"U.S. Distribs to Ignore NSW Quota." *Variety*. 130:13 April 6, 1938.

"U.S. Distribs Yank Ads from Spain's Daily Blatt El País." *Variety*. 331:5, 32 June 1, 1988.

"U.S. Economists Also See Ultimate Worldwide Boon to American Pix Biz." *Variety*. 136:19 October 4, 1939.

"U.S. Execs Think Foreign Lands Will Feel Film Shortage This Winter." *Variety*. 103:7, 91 September 8, 1931.

"U.S. Film Companies, Soviet Negotiate Product Deal." *Variety*. 145:16 February 18, 1942.

"U.S. Film Distribution in Germany Snafued; Krauts 'Choosey' on Pix." *Variety*. 161:1, 22 December 19, 1945.

"U.S. Film Enterprise in Britain." Times (London). June 25, 1919, p. 9.

"U.S. Film Famine Ends Argentine." *Variety*. 281:6 January 14, 1976.

"U.S. Film Industry's Strategy Now Is to Establish Beachheads in Europe." *Variety*. 161:4 February 27, 1946.

"U.S. Film Leaders Ask Quota Protest." *New York Times*. June 18, 1948, p. 19.

"U.S. Film Producers Reach Norway Pact." *New York Times*. April 11, 1946, p. 33.

"U.S. Film Stars the Best Good Will Ambassadors, Say Latin Americans." *Variety*. 141:1, 21 February 19, 1941.

"U.S. Film Studios Break Dutch Ban." *New York Times*. March 23, 1946, p. 8.

"U.S Filmers Nix Foreign Nations' Bid for a Goods Barter System." *Variety*. 133:6 January 18, 1939.

"U.S. Films Barred from Vichy's Areas." *New York Times*. August 6, 1942, p. 7.

"U.S. Films Face Fight Abroad." *Business Week*. December 29, 1945, pp. 109–110.

"U.S. Films in Global Crisis." *Variety*. 166:1, 26 April 30, 1947.

"U.S. Films in Huge Demand in Denmark." *Variety*. 159:18 August 29, 1945.

"U.S. Films in World Accord." *Variety*. 86:5 February 9, 1927.

"U.S. Films' $125,000,000 Foreign Take About Equals Biz's Total Profit." *Variety*. 166:11 May 7, 1947.

"U.S. Films Out of Germany." *Variety*. 100:3, 37, July 23, 1930.

"U.S. Films Sell Abroad." *New York Times*. February 4, 1959, p. 27.

"U.S. Films Still Gaining Abroad." *Variety*. 206:1, 78 April 10, 1957.

"U.S. Films Suffer as French Left Wages Anti-American Warfare." *Variety*. 168:16 November 5, 1947.

"U.S. Firms' Total World Revenue Has Dropped 20% Due to War." *Variety*. 138:12 June 5, 1940.

"U.S. Gov't Officially Notices Pictures." *Variety*. 82:27 March 3, 1926.

"U.S. Gov't to the Rescue." *Variety*. 114:15, 27 May 29, 1934.

"U.S. Leading Exporter of Films to India in 1975." *Variety*. 284:38 September 29, 1976.

"U.S. Leaving Foreign Tongue Markets to Locals and Indies." *Variety*. 93:4, 16 November 21, 1928.

"U.S. Lists Movies It Limits Abroad." *New York Times*. May 24, 1959, p. 46.

"U.S. May Force No Quota." *Variety*. 113:11, 18 February 6, 1934.

"U.S. Movie Exports Set Record." *Business Week*. June 26, 1937, pp. 50–51.

"U.S. Movies Again Reign in Spain." *Variety*. 353:58 April 11, 1994.

"U.S. Movies Feared by Reds in Hungary." *New York Times*. December 7, 1948, p. 43.

"U.S. No Help on Pix Quota." *Variety*. 127:23 June 30, 1937.

"U.S. Pic Industry Sees Exploitation of Latin American Market as Out of Proportion with Its Potential Value." *Variety*. 134:11 April 26, 1939.

"U.S. Picture-Goers Contribute 64% of the Worldwide Revenue." *Variety*. 147:5 September 2, 1942.

"U.S. Pix Behind Iron Curtain." *Variety*. 163:3, 28 August 21, 1946.

"U.S. Pix Biz Up an Average of 16% Over a Year Ago in Latin America." *Variety*. 144:18 October 29, 1941.

"U. S. Pix Heads Ogle Europe." *Variety*. 150:5, 8 June 9, 1943.

"U.S. Pix Market in Philippines Bullish." *Variety*. 169:15 February 4, 1948.

"U.S. Pix on World Scale." *Variety*. 191:3 June 17, 1953.

"U.S. Pix Stay Out of Italy." *Variety*. 124:21 October 21, 1936.

"U.S. Producers Study Shutdown of All Europe as Quota Protests." *Variety*. 196:11 May 31, 1932.

"U.S. Replacing Italian Films." *Variety*. 54:97 March 28, 1919.

"U.S. Still Leads Abroad." *Variety*. 109:13, 54 March 7, 1933.

Usabel, Gaizka S. *The High Noon of American Films in Latin America*. Ann Arbor: UMI, 1982.

Valenti, Jack. "Fair Trade for the Film Trade." *Los Angeles Times*. January 19, 1986, sec. 5, p. 5.

_____. "Protectionism Ng for Pix Biz." *Variety*. 249:7, 28 January 3, 1968.

_____ "Spirit of '76." *Variety*. 245:10 January 4, 1967.

_____. "Valenti Values Film-TV Coin in O'seas Mart." *Variety*. 289:5, 64 January 4, 1978.

_____. "Webb-Pomerene." Vital Speeches. 47:26–28 October 15, 1980.

"Valenti Blasts U.S. Trade Policy." *Variety*. 321:4, 33 December 11, 1985.

"Valenti Notes Progress Fighting Trade Barriers." *Variety*. 322:7, 24 March 12, 1986.

"Valenti Sees World War of Trade." *Variety*. 347:23 June 1, 1992.

Vasey, Ruth. "Foreign Parts: Hollywood's Global Distribution and the Representation of Ethnicity." *American Quarterly*. v. 44, n. 4:617–642 December, 1992.

Ventura, Maurice. "Foreign Pictures in Egypt." *Variety*. 77:23 November 19, 1924.

"Vichy Blackout on U.S. Pix Fails to Stir Yanks." *Variety*. 147:16 August 19, 1942.

"Video Champs." *Variety*. 358:12 February 27–March 5, 1995.

Wanger, Walter F. "Donald Duck and Diplomacy." *Public Opinion Quarterly*. v. 14, n. 3:443–452 Fall, 1950.

_____. "120, 000 American Ambassadors." *Foreign Affairs*. 18:45–59 October, 1939.

"War Loss Assayed by Concerns Here." *New York Times*. December 9, 1941, p. 44.

"War with Britain." *Newsweek*. 32:66 September 13, 1948.

Warman, Christopher. "Distribution of Cinema Films Criticized by Monopolies Commission." *Times* (London). May 12, 1983, p. 3.

Warren, Herrick. "Ethiopia: Films for a Few." *Variety*. 262:169–170 May 12, 1971.

"Warsaw Resents Foreign Meddling." *Variety*. 85:4 December 8, 1926.

"Washington Expected to Enter Against New French Law." *Variety*. 120:17 October 26, 1935.

"Washington's Stand on French Quota Row Staggers Americans." *Variety*. 95:9 June 12, 1929.

Watts, Stephen. "On the African Movie Menus." *New York Times*. April 26, 1953, sec. 2, p. 4.

Waxman, Sharon. "GATT-Astrophe Averted." *Washington Post*. December 15, 1993, p. B2.

Wear, Mike. "Foreign Film Outlook." *Variety*. 136:7 September 13, 1939.

_____. "U.S. Warns France of Trade Pact After Try to Cut Yankee Imports Down." *Variety*. 159:18 August 1, 1945.

Weinraub, Bernard. "Art Buchwald Awarded $150,000 in Suit Over Film." *New York Times*. March 17, 1992, p. C13.

_____. "Directors Battle Over GATT's Final Cut and Print." *New York Times*. December 12, 1993, sec. 1, p. 24.

Werba, Hank. "China's Economy Slows U.S. Pic Inroads." *Variety*. 304:5, 30, October 28, 1981.

_____. "More Flashes from Spanish Front." *Variety*. 206:5 March 27, 1957.

_____. "Pro-Pix U.S. Envoy to Spain." *Variety*. 239:13 July 21, 1965.

"West and Tunisians Agree on Film Tax." *New York Times*. April 8, 1961, p. 13.

Wharton, Dennis. "Gingrich Vows to Promote U.S. Film Interests." *Variety*. 358:20 March 20–26, 1995.

_____. "MPAA Blasts Free-Trade Agreement." *Variety*. 348:3, 5 September 14, 1992.

_____. "MPAA Hails NAFTA Win." *Variety*. 353:18 November 29, 1993.

"What Makes a Film Fly in Japan." *Business Week*. June 29, 1981, p. 97.

"Where U.S. Still Rules: Movies, Television." *U.S. News & World Report*. 99:28 July 15, 1985.

"While Eyeing Foreign Earnings Record, Distribs Face Upped Curbs Abroad." *Variety*. 188:3, 15 December 3, 1952.

"While 70% of World's Screens Still Serviced by U.S." *Variety*. 130:5, 19 April 6, 1938.

Williams, Michael. "Fox UGC Ink Distrib'n Co-Prod Deal." *Variety*. 357:20 January 16–22, 1995.

_____. "French Still Gun for GATT Exemptions." *Variety*. 353:28 November 15, 1993.

_____. "Gauls Galled Over GATT Proposals." *Variety*. 349:33 October 26, 1992.

_____. "Quotas Find Brussels Muscle." *Variety*. 358:39, 42 March 27–April 2, 1995.

Wilson, John M. "The Global Film: Will It Play in Uruguay." *New York Times*. November 26, 1978, sec. 2, pp. 1, 26.

Winston, Archer. "Movies." *United Nations World*. 1:59–60 February, 1947.

"Withdraw U.S. Films in Spain." *Variety*. 158:7, 18 May 9, 1945.

"World Blanketing Scheme." *Variety*. 100:11 November 26, 1930.

"World Wide for Hays Code." *Variety*. 102:5 April 15, 1931.

"Would Bar All Our Films." *New York Times*. September 13, 1924, p. 26.

"Would Boycott Our Films." *New York Times*. January 21, 1931, p. 10.

Wright, Basil. "British Films and Quota." *Spectator*. 159:54–55 July 9, 1937.

Wyatt, Woodrow. "Champagne for Hollywood." *New Statesman & Nation*. 35:231 March 20, 1948.

"Yank Cos. Fly Iranian Flag." *Variety.* 283:69, 91 May 19, 1976.

"Yank Cos.' Low Net in Aussie." *Variety.* 132:13 October 19, 1938.

"Yank Films Big 1974." *Variety.* 279:30 June 25, 1975.

"Yank Pic Industry an Invalid Sans Webb-Pomerene." *Variety.* 300:7 October 1, 1980.

"Yank Pix Mine B.O. Gold as Euro Dubbers Get in Synch." *Variety.* 348:1, 72 August 10, 1992.

"Yank Pix Prospects Good in Tito-Land, Maas Finds." *Variety.* 176:13 November 23, 1949.

"Yankee Films That Disagree with John Bull." *Literary Digest.* 64:62–64 February 21, 1920.

"Yanks, Brazil Exhibs Unite to Fight Admissions Kept Low." *Variety.* 206:3 April 10, 1957.

"Yanks See Quota Cry, Other Angles." *Variety.* 201:16 February 15, 1956.

"Yanks' $210,000,000 Abroad." *Variety.* 165:5, 20 February 5, 1947.

Young, Deborah. "Dominance at Italo B.O. Could Bring Backlash." *Variety.* 341:45, 75 November 26, 1990.

"Yugoslavs Invite Americans Back to Spur Trade." *Variety.* 108:11 December 6, 1932.

Zerbisias, Antonia. "Canadian Study Urges U.S. Pullback." *Variety.* 310:7, 187 March 6, 1983.

_____. "U.S. Gov't Protests Quebec Distrib Ban." *Variety.* 311:5, 38 June 22, 1983.

Index

357

DATE DUE

36916684.